ROCK
CHRONICLES

ROCK
CHRONICLES
SECOND EDITION

Every Legend, Every Line-up, Every Look

General Editor **David Roberts**   Foreword by **Alice Cooper**

FIREFLY BOOKS

A FIREFLY BOOK

Published by Firefly Books Ltd. 2015

First printing

Publisher Cataloging-in-Publication Data (U.S.)

Roberts, David, 1954– .
      Rock chronicles : every legend, every line-up, every look
/David Roberts, general editor ; foreword by Alice Cooper.
2nd edition.
[576] pages : photographs (some color) ; cm.
Includes index.
ISBN-13: 978-1-77085-614-1 (pbk.)
1. Rock groups – History. 2. Rock music – History and
criticism. I. Cooper, Alice. II. Title.
781.6609 dc23 ML3534.R6347 2015

**Library and Archives Canada Cataloguing in
Publication**

Rock chronicles : every legend, every line-up, every look /
general editor, David Roberts ; foreword by Alice Cooper.
2nd ed.
Includes bibliographical references and index.
ISBN 978-1-77085-614-1 (pbk.)
        1. Rock music—Encyclopedias. 2. Rock groups—
History. I. Roberts, David, 1954–, editor
ML3534.R552 2015   781.6609   C2015-902323-8

Published in the United States by
Firefly Books (U.S.) Inc.
P.O. Box 1338, Ellicott Station
Buffalo, New York 14205

Published in Canada by
Firefly Books Ltd.
50 Staples Avenue, Unit1
Richmond Hill, Ontario L4B 0A7

Color separation by Colourscan Print Co Pte Ltd, Singapore

Printed in China by Midas Printing International Ltd

This book was designed and produced by
Quintessence Editions Ltd.
The Old Brewery
6 Blundell Street
London N7 9BH

Update Editor: Elspeth Beidas
Update Designers: Isabel Eeles, Adam
   Hutchinson
Project Editor: Simon Ward
Editors: Bruno MacDonald, Olivia
   McLearon, Frank Ritter
Editorial Assistants: Sara Di-Girolamo,
   Olivia Young
Designers: Alison Hau, Tom Howey
Design Assistant: Isabel Eeles
Production Manager: Anna Pauletti
Editorial Director: Ruth Patrick
Publisher: Mark Fletcher

contents

foreword by alice cooper

Rock 'n' roll is over a half a century old. The British Invasion is forty years old. If you're around seventy right now, you were probably a Beatles or Rolling Stones fan. Why does this music keep going on? Most of the bands from the fifties and sixties are still touring and making records. Is there something magical about this music, or is it just a refusal to grow old? I'm starting to think it's a psychochemical reaction. Rock 'n' roll is all about attitude and image. It's mostly blues-based, and it's akin to an ongoing rebellion against the safe, conservative, acceptable music that our parents and grandparents wanted us to appreciate.

Since most of these artists refuse to die or simply fade away, here's a book about what they did then, what they're doing now, and what they might do later. And even though I have a lady's name, the old adage "it ain't over till the fat lady sings" will never ever apply to me, since I'll never be fat and I'll never quit singing. Long live rock 'n' roll—rock 'n' roll is NOT DEAD. You might want to take your own pulse. If it's too loud, maybe you're dead.

Alice Cooper

introduction by david roberts

Rock Chronicles is a new way of telling the story of this powerful and enduring genre. More than 250 of rock's finest, spanning seven decades, get an in-depth examination, presented in a unique and revealing display that starts and ends with archetypal purveyors of classic rock: AC/DC and ZZ Top. Along the way, you'll be introduced to the personnel who created subgenres, from glam to grunge and psychedelia to punk.

A new kind of rock encyclopedia for the twenty-first century, the book features elements that give a visual overview of each act's long and winding career. A team of experts has compiled the essential biographies found at the core of each act's entry—together with the birth and, sadly, ever increasing death dates of the cast of many hundreds of rock stars.

So far, so traditional. But this is where the similarity to other rock encyclopedias ends. *Rock Chronicles* boasts at-a-glance graphic timelines of the comings and goings of group members set against the albums they made and the labels that signed them. These cleverly designed infographics will help you to pinpoint the key moments in rock history: when line-ups changed, breakthrough albums were released, record deals were brokered and singers departed. Want to know who played drums on Pearl Jam's debut album? Find out how many copies *OK Computer* has sold worldwide? Remind yourself what The Kinks' bassist looked like or when Frank Zappa was inducted into the Rock and Roll Hall of Fame? You'll find all the answers to these and an unimaginable stack of other questions in the fact-packed pages of a very different kind of book.

Delving into *Rock Chronicles,* you will undoubtedly, like me, learn all sorts of trivia. Not facts that you would necessarily look up, but good-to-know, intriguing stuff like the simple story behind how Canadian stars Nickelback got their name and the bizarre fact that French progressive rockers Magma have invented their own lyrical language.

Away from these intriguing diversions, let's answer the big questions most of you will consider when using a rock encyclopedia. First, just how did we make the selection as to which acts are included? Not without a huge amount of thought, debate and argument is the unsurprising answer. The issue of what constitutes a rock act at all, as opposed to a pop outfit, is enough for starters, before determining who fits the bill.

At the heart of most decision-making was the symbol which very firmly dominates the front cover of this book: the electric guitar. Synths made a half-hearted attempt to usurp the guitar in the seventies and eighties, but the definition of a classic rock band is built around the six-strings of Chuck Berry through to present day Kings of Leon.

So, having established a very basic definition, who of the thousands of potential bands to choose and who to lose? Your list and mine will be different, I'm sure, but there's no exact science in deciding who makes the final cut. Highest record sales and best chart statistics just won't do. That way leads to the omission of so much music that is commercially lacking but creatively inspirational. So, fear not, Captain Beefheart and His Magic Band, the Buzzcocks and Pavement all have their place. That said, all the British, Irish and North American rock heavyweights you'd expect to see are included, plus significant acts from across Europe, China, Japan, South America and Australasia.

To get the most out of the book, start by checking out the visual guide to *Rock Chronicles* overpage. Here you can get acquainted with the timelines that run throughout the book and the symbols and graphic devices used to reveal the vast amount of information at your fingertips.

Each timeline covers the period each act has been active, punctuated by core members (and, in the case of solo acts like Bowie, Elvis, and Neil Young, significant others), together with a full chronological rundown of studio albums. All compilations and soundtracks, and most live albums, have been excluded to keep discographies to manageable proportions, but exceptions have been made where the entries would be simply incomplete without them. Fear not, fans of the MC5, Dave Matthews, and Jane's Addiction: those live debut albums are in here. And in a few selected cases—notably Tangerine Dream and Frank Zappa—we have cherry-picked highlights of their huge back catalogs, including live albums (which fans of those acts regard as equally canonical).

All types of album—studio, live, and compilation—qualify for the big four sellers at the top of each double-page spread. A great deal of research has gone into establishing the most accurate estimate for each release. Record sales are often prone to much exaggeration but our figures are based on a combination of expert advice and record industry certifications for platinum, gold and silver sales or shipments. These certifications are given per disc, not per album release—so in the case of George Harrison's terrific triple album, *All Things Must Pass,* the often reported sales total of more than ten million is, in fact, 3.5 million.

The all-important rock stars highlighted in the biographies and on the timelines are pictured on each page for easy identification. For a selection of the more visually exciting and most enduring bands, there are picture features that show the visual changes undergone throughout the decades of fashion changing, hard rocking, touring and general debauchery associated with the "hope I die before I get old" brigade. These are color-coded to key albums, also pictured on those spreads.

Every decade since the seventies has seen predictions of the death of rock. Although the twenty-first century has seen a slow-down in the production line and recorded products have a looser grip on us than they once did, rock is still a massive draw for the buoyant live performance sector. It's also pop music's most fascinating genre to read about—so immerse yourself in the astonishing wealth of fact that is *Rock Chronicles.*

how to use this book

Color coded musical styles

Years active

Grammy-winning band

Name of band

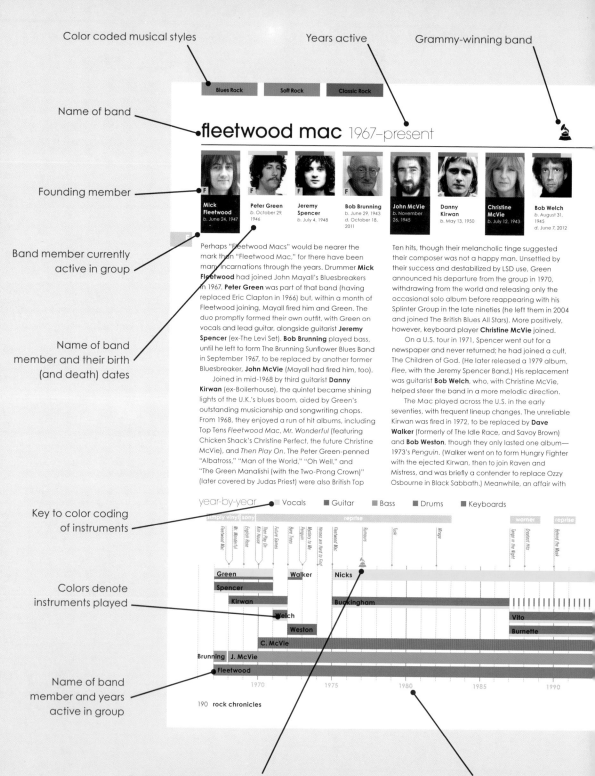

Blues Rock | Soft Rock | Classic Rock

fleetwood mac 1967–present

Founding member

Band member currently active in group

Name of band member and their birth (and death) dates

Mick Fleetwood b. June 24, 1947

Peter Green b. October 29, 1946

Jeremy Spencer b. July 4, 1948

Bob Brunning b. June 29, 1943 d. October 18, 2011

John McVie b. November 26, 1945

Danny Kirwan b. May 13, 1950

Christine McVie b. July 12, 1943

Bob Welch b. August 31, 1945 d. June 7, 2012

Perhaps "Fleetwood Macs" would be nearer the mark than "Fleetwood Mac," for there have been many incarnations through the years. Drummer **Mick Fleetwood** had joined John Mayall's Bluesbreakers in 1967. **Peter Green** was part of that band (having replaced Eric Clapton in 1966) but, within a month of Fleetwood joining, Mayall fired him and Green. The duo promptly formed their own outfit, with Green on vocals and lead guitar, alongside guitarist **Jeremy Spencer** (ex-The Levi Set). **Bob Brunning** played bass, until he left to form The Brunning Sunflower Blues Band in September 1967, to be replaced by another former Bluesbreaker, **John McVie** (Mayall had fired him, too).

Joined in mid-1968 by third guitarist **Danny Kirwan** (ex-Boilerhouse), the quintet became shining lights of the U.K.'s blues boom, aided by Green's outstanding musicianship and songwriting chops. From 1968, they enjoyed a run of hit albums, including Top Tens *Fleetwood Mac*, *Mr. Wonderful* (featuring Chicken Shack's Christine Perfect, the future Christine McVie), and *Then Play On*. The Peter Green-penned "Albatross," "Man of the World," "Oh Well," and "The Green Manalishi (with the Two-Prong Crown)" (later covered by Judas Priest) were also British Top

Ten hits, though their melancholic tinge suggested their composer was not a happy man. Unsettled by their success and destabilized by LSD use, Green announced his departure from the group in 1970, withdrawing from the world and releasing only the occasional solo album before reappearing with his Splinter Group in the late nineties (he left them in 2004 and joined The British Blues All Stars). More positively, however, keyboard player **Christine McVie** joined.

On a U.S. tour in 1971, Spencer went out for a newspaper and never returned; he had joined a cult, The Children of God. (He later released a 1979 album, *Flee*, with the Jeremy Spencer Band.) His replacement was guitarist **Bob Welch**, who, with Christine McVie, helped steer the band in a more melodic direction.

The Mac played across the U.S. in the early seventies, with frequent lineup changes. The unreliable Kirwan was fired in 1972, to be replaced by **Dave Walker** (formerly of The Idle Race, and Savoy Brown) and **Bob Weston**, though they only lasted one album—1973's *Penguin*. (Walker went on to form Hungry Fighter with the ejected Kirwan, then to join Raven and Mistress, and was briefly a contender to replace Ozzy Osbourne in Black Sabbath.) Meanwhile, an affair with

Key to color coding of instruments

Colors denote instruments played

Name of band member and years active in group

year-by-year · ■ Vocals · ■ Guitar · ■ Bass · ■ Drums · ■ Keyboards

Green | Walker | Nicks
Spencer
Kirwan | Buckingham
Welch
Weston
C. McVie
Brunning | J. McVie
Fleetwood

Vito
Burnette

1970 | 1975 | 1980 | 1985 | 1990

190 rock chronicles

Grammy-winning album or rock album of the year

Year

Global sales of top-selling albums

| 35.2M | 8.9M | 11.3M | 16.1M |
| Rumours (1977) | Fleetwood Mac (1978) | Tango in the Night (1987) | Greatest Hits (1988) |

Colors denote instruments played

Dave Walker
b. January 25, 1945

Bob Weston
b. Nov 1, 1947
d. January 3, 2012

Lindsey Buckingham
b. October 3, 1949

Stevie Nicks
b. May 26, 1948

Rick Vito
b. October 13, 1949

Billy Burnette
b. May 8, 1953

Bekka Bramlett
b. April 19, 1968

Dave Mason
b. May 10, 1946

Alphabetical index

Fleetwood's wife Jenny saw Weston fired in September 1973. Then, toward the end of 1974, Welch departed to form Paris and embark on a successful solo career.

With Fleetwood and the McVies now settled in California, the drummer's interest was piqued by a tape of an album by **Lindsey Buckingham** and **Stevie Nicks**. The duo were invited to join the band, creating the band's tenth and most successful incarnation.

After a slow climb, the West Coast-flavored *Fleetwood Mac* made No. 1 in the U.S. in 1976. By the next year, the relationships between Fleetwood and his wife, the McVies, and Nicks and Buckingham were collapsing. "A complete disaster zone…" Fleetwood told writer Craig Rosen. "Emotional hell laced with musical pleasure." Despite (and even inspired by) their friction and cocaine habits, 1977's melodic *Rumours* became one of rock's all-time best-sellers.

Eager to avoid making *Rumours Pt II*, Buckingham pushed for an experimental approach for *Tusk* (1979). The title track and "Sara" were both hits, but the band returned to less controversial waters for *Mirage* (1982).

With Nicks having launched a platinum-selling solo career with 1981's *Bella Donna*, the Mac went their separate ways for three years. They re-formed in late 1985 to create *Tango in the Night* (1987), which proved another huge hit. However, plans for a tour broke down and Buckingham quit, to be replaced by guitarist **Rick Vito** and vocalist **Billy Burnette** (who had played with Fleetwood in the latter's band The Zoo).

The six-strong lineup cut 1990's *Behind the Mask*, but Nicks and McVie quit at the end of the year. The full return of the Mac came in 1993, at the request of President Bill Clinton: Buckingham, Nicks, Fleetwood, and the McVies performed *Rumours*' "Don't Stop" at his inauguration party. However, it proved a one-off—instead, Fleetwood and the McVies recruited vocalist **Bekka Bramlett** and former Traffic guitarist **Dave Mason** for 1995's disappointing *Time*.

The famous five re-grouped again for 1997's live *The Dance* (1997). Coupling originals with old hits, it returned them to the multi-platinum status of old, and preceded a spectacularly successful reunion tour.

Christine McVie departed again in 2003, but the remaining four produced that year's *Say You Will* (despite renewed tension between Buckingham and Nicks) and mounted a tour in 2009. In 2013, just a year after Fleetwood said, "I don't believe Fleetwood Mac will ever tour again," they hit the road once more. **RD**

Bold type for first mention of each band member

Contributor's initials

Record label

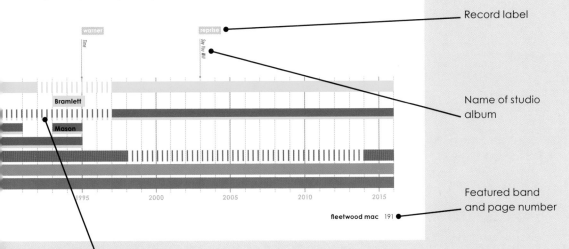

warner

Time

reprise

Say You Will

Bramlett

Mason

1995   2000   2005   2010   2015

Name of studio album

Featured band and page number

fleetwood mac 191

Broken lines indicate time away from group

A

ac/dc 1973–present

Angus Young
b. March 31, 1955

Malcolm Young
b. January 6, 1953

Larry Van Kriedt
b. 1954

Colin Burgess
b. November 16, 1946

Bon Scott
b. July 9, 1946
d. February 19, 1980

Phil Rudd
b. May 19, 1954

"When everybody else was getting into cleverness and synthesizing…" Keith Richards reminisced of late 1970s AC/DC, "these cats [were] laying it out." It's a fitting compliment for a band who, along with the Stones, did much to bring Chuck Berry's formula of addictive riffs and witty wordplay to the masses.

Malcolm and **Angus Young** had been inspired by the success of their elder brother George, who, as part of The Easybeats, had been the first Australian beat group to have a U.K. Top Ten hit. The early days of AC/DC saw a shifting lineup hone their chops on the pub circuit, Angus Young turning heads both with his nimble lead guitar skills and his characteristic school uniform stage attire, which he still wears today.

A key moment in their progress came with the replacement of original singer Dave Evans by Ronald **"Bon" Scott**, a friend of brother George. At the end of 1974, the new lineup recorded *High Voltage*. Success at home came quickly, with AC/DC establishing a reputation for noisy good-time rock 'n' roll with laddish lyrics ("She's Got Balls"). The following year, *T.N.T.* featured the band's first popular anthem, "It's A Long Way to the Top (If You Wanna Rock 'n' Roll)"—which would become a signature tune for Bon Scott. As 1975 drew to a close, they were Australia's top rock act.

The first throes of world domination came in 1976, when the band signed an international deal with the Atlantic label. Spending much of the year touring Europe, they gained valuable experience supporting the likes of Black Sabbath, Kiss, Blue Öyster Cult, and Aerosmith. To coincide with the tour, an "international" version of *High Voltage* was released, compiling tracks from the first two Australian albums.

AC/DC hit their stride with 1976's *Dirty Deeds Done Dirt Cheap*. Like *High Voltage*, this would be issued as an international edition (which hit No. 3 in the U.S. in 1981), although both versions include its three classics: the anthemic title track, the kinetic "Problem Child," and the atypically reflective "Ride On." (Scott later sang "Ride On," just days before he died, with French rockers Trust, who also covered "Problem Child.")

For the remainder of the 1970s, AC/DC continued their upward global trajectory, moving toward rock's top table with *Let There Be Rock* (1977) and Keith Richards's favorite, *Powerage* (1978). Then, in 1979, the group's sound was overhauled by producer Mutt Lange: the harsh edge of earlier recordings was refined, while retaining the all-important energy of their live sound. The resulting *Highway to Hell* (1979) saw AC/DC in the U.S. Top Twenty for the first time.

year-by-year   ▩ Vocals   ■ Guitar   ▩ Bass   ■ Drums

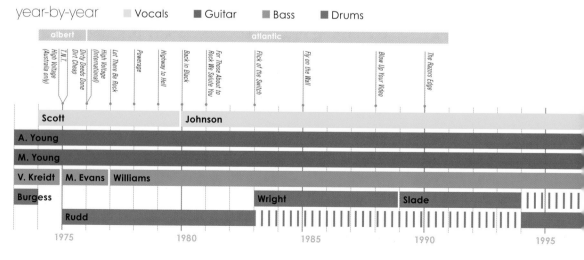

10M	15M	36M	8M
Dirty Deeds Done Dirt Cheap (1976)	*Highway to Hell* (1979)	*Back in Black* (1980)	*For Those About to Rock We Salute You* (1981)

A

Cliff Williams
b. May 12, 1959

Brian Johnson
b. October 5, 1947

Simon Wright
b. June 19, 1963

Chris Slade
b. October 30, 1946

Mark Evans
b. March 2, 1956

Stevie Young
b. November 12, 1956

A new decade kicked off with AC/DC poised to conquer the globe. But on February 19, 1980, after a night of heavy drinking at a London club, Bon Scott was found dead in an associate's car, his passing officially listed as "acute alcohol poisoning." Rejecting their initial instinct to break up, Angus Young recalled that Scott himself had talked about the singer from Geordie, an English band who'd enjoyed a brief flurry of success the previous decade. **Brian Johnson** was invited to audition: within days he was in the studio.

These were inauspicious beginnings for an album expected to turn AC/DC into superstars. But *Back in Black* (1980) proved they were anything but a band in crisis. Fears that fans might reject a new front-man proved spectacularly unfounded, as they unleashed a benchmark classic in heavy rock. Topping the U.K. and Australian charts, *Back in Black* was certified platinum within three months of release and went on to spend 131 weeks on the *Billboard* chart. Over the next three decades it would sell more than twenty-two million copies in the U.S. alone, helping to make it one of the top ten best-selling albums of all time.

With the demise of Led Zeppelin, AC/DC had become the world's most successful hard rock act. *For Those About to Rock We Salute You* (1981) gave

them their first U.S. No. 1, *Who Made Who* (1986) mixed songs old and new, *Blow Up Your Video* (1988) reunited the band with original producers Vanda and Young, and *The Razors Edge* (1990) bore a new classic, "Thunderstruck." Even lesser regarded albums like 1983's *Flick of the Switch* and 1985's *Fly on the Wall* maintained AC/DC's unbroken run of U.S. platinum-sellers. (Along the way, drum duties passed from **Phil Rudd** to **Simon Wright** and **Chris Slade**.)

In latter years, the gaps between albums have widened: 2008's *Black Ice* (by which time Rudd had rejoined) was the group's first new studio album in eight years. The band's return was greeted with open arms and wallets: the album debuted at No. 1 in twenty-nine different countries. The hugely successful stadium tour that followed confirmed that AC/DC were back in business. They capitalized on a new generation's exposure to their brand of pile-driving rock with a soundtrack for the blockbuster movie *Iron Man 2* (a "greatest hits" in all but name).

In 2014, Malcolm Young left the band with the announcement that he was suffering from dementia. Rudd's membership also came under question that year, following his arrest in New Zealand shortly before the release of *Rock or Bust* in November. **TB**

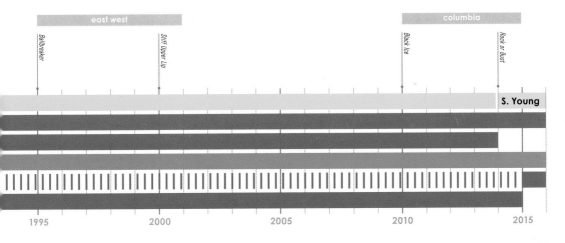

east west columbia

Ballbreaker   Stiff Upper Lip   Black Ice   Rock or Bust

S. Young

1995   2000   2005   2010   2015

High Voltage
(1975)

T.N.T. (1975)

Dirty Deeds Done Dirt Cheap (1976)

Let There Be Rock (1977)

Powerage (1978)

Highway to Hell (1979)

Back in Black (1980)

Blow Up Your Video (1988)

The Razors Edge (1990)

Black Ice (2008)

Very early AC/DC—the school uniform would stay longer than the platform boots.

Bon Scott (left) and **Angus Young** (right) in Hollywood in 1977.

Angus Young and **Scott** explode onstage in the mid-seventies.

Angus Young meets the fans at the Oakland Coliseum in California, 1978.

The band gets mean 'n' moody at Shepperton Studios, London, in 1976.

Studio shot of AC/DC in 1979: **Malcolm Young, Scott, Cliff Williams, Angus Young** and **Phil Rudd.**

Simon Wright in Australia in 1988, on his last tour with the band.

Simon Wright in Australia in 1988, on his last tour with the band.

Bon Scott, Malcolm Young, Angus Young, Phil Rudd, and **Cliff Williams** in a good mood at Shepperton in 1976.

Malcolm Young in Sydney, Australia, on the *Razors Edge* tour.

Brian Johnson giving it his all in 1980.

Johnson (left) and **Angus Young** rock Washington, D.C., on the 2008 *Black Ice* tour.

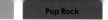
A

bryan adams 1977–present

Bryan Adams
b. November 5, 1959

Mickey Curry
b. June 10, 1956

Tommy Mandel
b. June 2, 1949

Keith Scott
b. July 20, 1954

Dave Taylor
b. February 20, 1953

Phil Thornalley
b. January 5, 1960

Bryan Adams has conquered the world, re-written record books, and transcended musical genres during a solo career that has spanned more than a quarter of a century. But this superstar is also blessed with a "guy-next-door" image that would endear him to your drinking mates *and* your rock-shy grandmother.

The Canadian vocalist, songwriter, guitarist, photographer, and philanthropist was born to British parents in Kingston, Ontario in 1959. His CV is bulging with records, awards, nominations, and accolades, including seventeen Juno (Canadian music) awards, a Grammy for a movie hit, two Ivor Novello awards, a star on the Hollywood Walk of Fame, and much-deserved recognition for his contributions to music and charity. He has been awarded the Order of British Columbia and been made a Companion of the Order of Canada—the country's highest honor for lifetime achievement. So far, so good, for the artist who has sold more than 65 million records worldwide.

Adams bought his first guitar with money made from scrubbing dishes. Rehearsals in his mother's Vancouver basement led to an audition with glam rockers Sweeney Todd, for whom he provided

vocals on *If Wishes Were Horses* (1977). However, the album's closing track, "Say Hello, Say Goodbye," was indicative of the temporary appointment. By 1978, an eighteen-year-old Adams had forged an alliance with songwriter and drummer Jim Vallance that survives to this day. Together, the pair knocked out numerous demos and the track that would become Adams' first single, "Let Me Take You Dancing." However, despite placing tracks on Kiss's *Creatures of the Night* (1982), commercial success would initially prove elusive.

Fast forward to 1984. Following his first venture into the Canadian and U.S. Top Tens with *Cuts Like a Knife* (1983), Adams made his bow on the world stage with *Reckless*, an album that would go on to sell more than five million copies in the U.S. and spend 115 weeks on the U.K. chart. *Reckless* featured six hits, including arm-waving classics like "Run to You," "Heaven," and "Summer of '69," the latter described by Adams as a song about "making love in the summertime."

In the early nineties, with arena rock on the wane and grunge in full, angsty swing, Adams took aim at the mass market with mid-tempo ballads, hitting the bullseye with a cut co-penned by Pink Floyd and

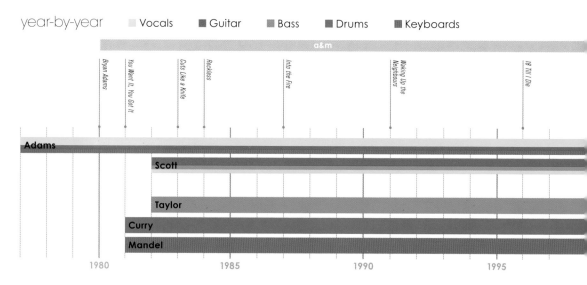

year-by-year   ▨ Vocals   ■ Guitar   ■ Bass   ■ Drums   ■ Keyboards

11.3M	10.8M	15.4M	4.7M
Reckless (1984)	*Waking Up the* *Neighbours* (1991)	*So Far So Good* (1993)	*18 Till I Die* (1996)

A

Gary Breit
b. October, 1960

Norm Fisher
b. October 22, 1963

David Bowie orchestrator Michael Kamen and super-producer Mutt Lange (who made Adams's *Waking Up the Neighbours* and Def Leppard's *Adrenalize* sound like the work of the same act). Clocking in at 6 minutes 34 seconds, "(Everything I Do) I Do it for You," from the soundtrack to the movie blockbuster *Robin Hood: Prince of Thieves*, amassed seven weeks at No. 1 in the U.S. and an unprecedented sixteen consecutive weeks at the top in the U.K., wiping Slim Whitman's thirty-six-year-old "Rose Marie" from the record books.

Chart longevity aside, the track's enduring legacy was to force a change to regulations that had restricted airplay in Adams' homeland for songs lacking sufficient Canadian content. "Everything…" flouted the rules for its recording location (the U.K.) and producer (Zambian-born Lange). Wading into the political debate, Adams declared: "Who wants to have an international record and then be called un-Canadian? It's a disgrace." The resultant publicity prompted a rethink and the rules were amended to allow collaborations with non-Canadians.

With "Everything…" threatening to eclipse his entire eighties output, and no doubt invigorated by his run-in with the Canadian government, Adams returned to the studio and successfully removed the metaphorical millstone from around his neck with moments of heart-wrenching beauty ("Please Forgive Me") and barefaced cheek ("The Only Thing that Looks Good on Me is You"). He also courted more box-office blockbusters: "All for Love" from *The Three Musketeers*, featuring Rod Stewart and Sting, and "Here I Am" from *Spirit—Stallion of the Cimarron*.

In more recent times, Adams has proved an astute judge of musical trends, cashing in on the success of the Spice Girls by hooking up with "Sporty Spice" Melanie C for "When You're Gone" and joining British dance maestro Chicane (aka Nick Bracegirdle) for the U.K. chart-topper "Don't Give Up."

Away from the recording studio, the Bryan Adams Foundation—an educational charity working with young people worldwide—heads a long list of worthy causes supported by the singer. He is an award-winning photographer, his face has graced Canadian postage stamps, and, in 2011, he became a father when his Personal Assistant, Alicia Grimaldi, gave birth to the splendidly named Mirabella Bunny. **MW**

▓ Other percussion

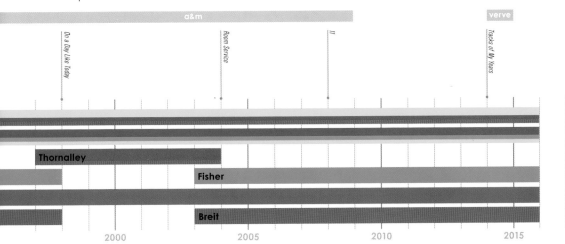

aerosmith 1970–present

Steven Tyler
b. March 26, 1948

Joe Perry
b. September 10, 1950

Ray Tabano
b. December 23, 1946

Tom Hamilton
b. December 31, 1951

Joey Kramer
b. June 21, 1950

Brad Whitford
b. February 23, 1952

"Oh gawd, Aerosmith," moaned Mick Jagger in 1977. "They're just rubbish." A generation disagreed. "There was," recalled Guns N' Roses guitarist Slash, "nothing cooler than Aerosmith coming out of America."

Boston's bad boys convened in 1970. Frustrated at being stuck behind drums in previous groups, **Steven Tyler** insisted on fronting a union with guitarist **Joe Perry**, bassist **Tom Hamilton**, and drummer David "Pudge" Scott. The latter was usurped by **Joey Kramer**, who named the band "Aerosmith," a word he dreamt up at school. **Ray Tabano** came on board as second guitarist, but was replaced in 1971 by **Brad Whitford**.

Aerosmith was released in 1973 to, as Perry noted, "no fanfare." Nonetheless, it heralded their rock-R&B fusion, featuring sax player David Woodford, whose resume would stretch from The Shirelles to P. Diddy. (Woodford toured with Aerosmith and featured on vintage cuts added to 1978's explosive Live! Bootleg.)

Get Your Wings (1974) maintained the brass, courtesy of jazz stars Michael and Randy Brecker (who also graced Bruce Springsteen's Born to Run) and Elephant's Memory alumnus Stan Bronstein. Keyboards were by producer Ray Colcord, the A&R

man who persuaded Columbia to sign the group. Colcord subsequently joined Lou Reed's band, while Jack Douglas took over Aerosmith's production.

Relentless touring fueled the success of Toys in the Attic (1975), featuring pianist Scott Cushnie, late of The Hawks (the group that became The Band). In 1976, Rocks—featuring banjo by Paul Prestopino—and a reissue of 1973's "Dream On" were U.S. Top Ten hits.

Momentum carried Draw the Line (1977) but—having cut five tracks for a follow-up—Perry quit the fatigued band. Night in the Ruts (1979) was completed with guitarists Richie Supa and **Jimmy Crespo**.

Crippled by drugs and debt, Aerosmith entered limbo. Columbia plugged the gap with the eventually multi-million-selling Greatest Hits (1980). Whitford quit and was replaced by **Rick Dufay**, but 1982's Rock in a Hard Place—featuring Paul Harris (formerly of Stephen Stills' Manassas) and John Turi (of Cyndi Lauper's pre-fame band Blue Angel)—halted neither their commercial decline nor their narcotic dysfunction.

A reunion of the vintage lineup was inevitable. However, 1985's Done with Mirrors fared even worse than Rock in a Hard Place. Producer Rick Rubin threw

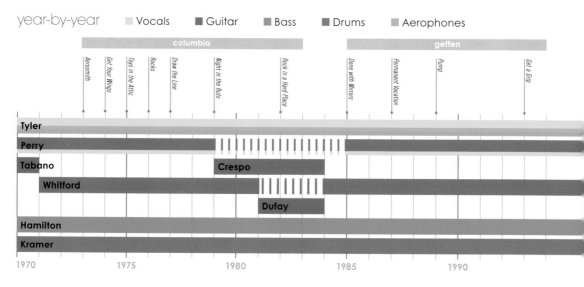

year-by-year   Vocals   Guitar   Bass   Drums   Aerophones

| **11M**
Toys in the Attic
(1975) | **13.9M**
Aerosmith's
Greatest Hits
(1980) | **11.1M**
Pump
(1989) | **13.5M**
Get a Grip
(1993) |

A

Jimmy Crespo
b. July 5, 1954

Rick Dufay
b. February 19, 1952

them a lifeline, recruiting Tyler and Perry to guest on Run-DMC's 1986 cover of Aerosmith's hit "Walk This Way." Although its video featured members of metal group Smashed Gladys deputizing for Whitford, Hamilton, and Kramer, the front-men's appearance catapulted Aerosmith back into the limelight.

Purged of their addictions, the band rose from the flames with the smashes *Permanent Vacation* (1987) and *Pump* (1989), featuring a brass section led by new producer Bruce Fairbairn. Thom Gimbel, later to join Foreigner, handled sax and keyboards on tour.

Now even bigger than in their seventies heyday, they scored their first U.S. No.1 hits with *Get a Grip* (1993) and *Nine Lives* (1997). The former featured Don Henley and Lenny Kravitz; the latter arrangements by David Campbell (father of Beck, and a conductor who worked with Kiss and Metallica, and on Bono and The Edge's *Spider-Man* musical). In between, *Big Ones* (1994) became their second multi-million-selling hits set and Russ Irwin—late of Curt Smith's post-Tears for Fears group, Mayfield—joined as tour keyboardist.

The resurrection was crowned by their first No. 1 single, "I Don't Want to Miss a Thing," from the 1998 movie *Armageddon* (starring Tyler's daughter Liv). However, 2001's *Just Push Play* boasted hi-tech production at odds with their sleazy sound, despite the presence of soul horn legends Tower of Power, and was outsold by *O, Yeah! Ultimate Aerosmith Hits* (2002).

Aerosmith returned to their R&B roots with the covers album *Honkin' on Bobo* (2004). Produced by the returning Jack Douglas, it featured vocalist Tracy Bonham, Chuck Berry's pianist Johnnie Johnson, and soul label Stax's brass section The Memphis Horns.

Ongoing touring yielded the live *Rockin' the Joint* (2005), but a health problem-plagued 2009 outing to promote the *Guitar Hero: Aerosmith* game saw them grind to a halt. With Tyler relapsed into painkiller addiction, Perry announced Aerosmith were seeking a new singer (an invitation Lenny Kravitz declined).

After protracted wrangling—during which Jimmy Page tried to recruit Tyler for a revived Led Zeppelin—the band hit the road once more in 2010. Attempts to complete another album were interrupted by Tyler becoming an *American Idol* judge, but, as Kramer remarked in 2011, "The only thing that's going to stop us is if someone out-and-out dies." **BM**

▓ Other percussion

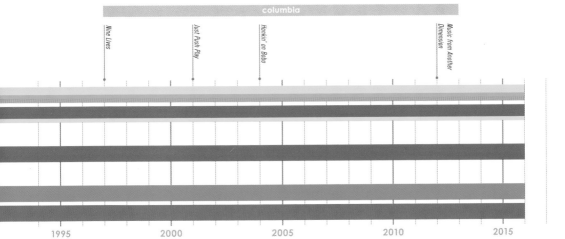

Aerosmith (1973)

Get Your Wings (1974)

Toys in the Attic (1975)

Rocks (1976)

Draw the Line (1977)

Rock in a Hard Place (1982)

Permanent Vacation (1987)

Get a Grip (1993)

Nine Lives (1997)

Just Push Play (2001)

Tom Hamilton (left) and Steven Tyler (right) backstage in 1973.

An exuberant Tyler performing onstage in 1975.

Studio shot of Aerosmith circa 1974: **Joe Perry, Brad Whitford, Tyler** (front), **Hamilton** (back) and **Joey Kramer.**

Tyler cools down after performing at Washington RFK stadium, on May 30, 1976.

Kramer (drums) and Tyler (front) performing live in 1984.

Tyler and Perry—a.k.a. "The Toxic Twins"—live in Germany in August 1977.

Whitford and Hamilton in Minnesota in 1987.

Tyler and Hamilton rehearsing at the 1993 MTV Music Awards.

Tyler rocking out onstage in August 1997.

One of rock's greatest pairings, Perry (left) and Tyler (right) on the *Just Push Play* tour in 2001.

a-ha 1982–2010

Morten Harket
b. September 14, 1959

Magne Furuholmen
b. November 1, 1962

Pål Waaktaar
b. September 6, 1961

Formed in 1982 by singer **Morten Harket**, guitarist and principal songwriter **Pål Waaktaar**, and keyboard player **Magne Furuholmen**, Norwegian pop outfit a-ha became a major success of the eighties. Their timing was good: as they tasted initial success in 1985, teen-appeal rivals Duran Duran were fading and Wham! were anticipating George Michael's departure. The stage was set for a band with good looks and indelible hooks to swoop in and clean up.

The first song they worked on was the future smash "Take on Me," originally called "The Juicy Fruit Song" and later "Lesson One." It didn't come easy: a version recorded with producer Tony Mansfield had little impact but a-ha persevered through re-recordings until an Alan Tarney-helmed take hit paydirt.

The clincher was a groundbreaking video mixing live action with animated sketches. This captured MTV viewers' imagination and propelled the catchy "Take on Me"—with Harket's trademark falsetto and Furuholmen's deathless synth riff—to No. 2 in the U.K. and No. 1 in the U.S. Hunting High and Low (1985) consolidated the breakthrough, making No. 2 in the U.K. and No. 15 in the Billboard 200.

In the U.K., even greater singles success was to follow with "The Sun Always Shines on T.V." It grabbed the No. 1 slot, which had eluded "Take on Me," at the start of 1986. The trio were quick to follow up with Scoundrel Days (1986), a muscular record that was even more accomplished than their debut and

again racked up multi-million worldwide sales. Their stock remained high as Waaktaar penned the theme for the 1987 James Bond movie The Living Daylights with stalwart composer John Barry. The track was the third of an eventual eight No. 1 singles in their native Norway, and a hit around the world (except the U.S., where their profile slumped after 1986's "Cry Wolf").

The downbeat side to a-ha, always present in their more glacial tracks, was drawn out fully on Stay on These Roads (1988). This attitude would be equally prominent on East of the Sun, West of the Moon (1990) and its lead single, a cover of The Everly Brothers' "Crying in the Rain"—another opportunity for Harket to stretch his lovelorn croon.

Memorial Beach (1993) was the final album of a-ha's first phase and reputedly difficult to record. An ensuing hiatus—filled by Harket's attempt at solo fame and Furuholmen and Waaktaar's dabblings in other groups—was broken by the return to form Minor Earth Major Sky (2000). a-ha had slipped nicely into maturity, still unashamedly pop but careworn with it. Lifelines (2002) and Analogue (2005) continued the thread, the latter featuring Graham Nash of Crosby, Stills & Nash on backing vocals, and springing a surprise U.K. Top Ten hit, "Analogue (All I Want)."

After Foot of the Mountain (2009), a-ha chose to call it a day, packing things up neatly with a farewell tour in 2010. Impressive global ticket sales proved how well they had endured. **MaH**

year-by-year ■ Vocals ■ Guitar ■ Keyboards

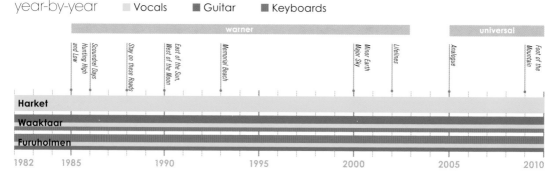

alice in chains 1987–present

A

Jerry Cantrell
b. March 18, 1966

Layne Staley
b. August 22, 1967
d. April 5, 2002

Sean Kinney
b. May 27, 1966

Mike Starr
b. April 4, 1966
d. March 8, 2011

Mike Inez
b. May 14, 1966

William DuVall
b. September 6, 1967

"Pretty music that makes you want to die" was drummer **Sean Kinney**'s verdict on Alice in Chains, whose famous fans range from Metallica to Elton John.

Kinney, singer **Layne Staley**, guitarist **Jerry Cantrell**, and bassist **Mike Starr** convened in 1987. They drew on Black Sabbath-type influences common to Seattle contemporaries Soundgarden and Nirvana, blended with an Eagles-esque flair for melody. Other distinctive elements on their 1990 debut *Facelift* included Cantrell's talkbox on their breakthrough "Man in the Box" and Kinney's piano on "Sea of Sorrow."

A year of touring pushed *Facelift* to gold sales. Then Alice fashioned 1992's acoustic EP *Sap*, featuring Heart's Ann Wilson, Mudhoney's Mark Arm, and Soundgarden's Chris Cornell. With "Man in the Box" a hit, Soundgarden touring with Guns N' Roses, Pearl Jam ascending *Billboard*'s chart and all three acts appearing in Cameron Crowe's *Singles*, "grunge" had arrived. *Dirt* (1992) duly crashed the U.S. chart at No. 6, sharing the Top Ten with the *Singles* soundtrack (featuring Alice's "Would?," a tribute to Andrew Wood of Pearl Jam precursors Mother Love Bone). On the ensuing tour, Starr was fired for drug-fueled apathy and replaced by ex-Ozzy Osbourne bassist **Mike Inez**. *Dirt* itself, featuring Tom Araya of Alice's touring buddies Slayer on the Sabbath pastiche "Iron Gland," sold over four million, while Slash loved it so much that he enlisted Inez for his GN'R sideline Slash's Snakepit.

The bleak *Jar of Flies* (1994) became the first "shortform album" to debut atop *Billboard*'s chart. (Guests included viola player April Acevez, wife of Soundgarden's Matt Cameron.) However, Alice vanished for much of 1994–95, Staley being unwilling—and, given his heroin addiction, unable—to tour. Instead, the singer focused on *Above* (1995) by Mad Season, a short-lived "supergroup" with Barrett Martin (Screaming Trees) and Mike McCready (Pearl Jam).

The defiant *Alice in Chains* (1995) was the band's second U.S. No. 1. However, after *MTV Unplugged* (featuring Heart's Scott Olson) and shows with Kiss in 1996, Alice effectively ceased to be. Staley's fatal overdose in 2002 ended further speculation.

Cantrell, Kinney, and Inez reunited as Alice in Chains in 2005. Early shows featured guests such as Tool's Maynard James Keenan, Ann Wilson, GN'R's Duff McKagan, Pantera's Phil Anselmo, Queensrÿche's Chris DeGarmo, and Puddle of Mudd's Wes Scantlin. However, by the time the group hit the festival circuit, **William DuVall**—latterly of Comes with the Fall and Cantrell's solo live band—was their front-man. With him, *Black Gives Way to Blue* (2009) ranked alongside the best of Alice's back catalog. More remarkably still, its title track featured former Prince associate Lisa Coleman and Elton John. "A dream for me," marveled Cantrell. "To be able to collaborate and make music with the people that inspired *you* to make music." **BM**

year-by-year   ▪ Vocals   ▪ Guitar   ▪ Bass   ▪ Drums

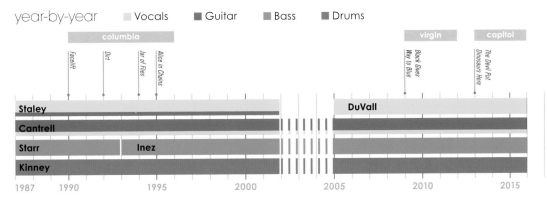

A the allman brothers band 1969–2014

Duane Allman
b. Nov 20, 1946
d. October 29, 1971

Gregg Allman
b. December 8, 1947

Dickey Betts
b. December 12, 1943

Berry Oakley
b. April 4, 1948
d. November 11, 1972

Butch Trucks
b. May 11, 1947

Jai Johanny "Jaimoe" Johanson
b. July 8, 1944

Chuck Leavell
b. April 28, 1952

Lamar Williams
b. April 14, 1949

With a heady mixture of hard rock, country, jazz, and blues on trademark intertwining guitars, The Allman Brothers Band set the standard for Southern rock.

The group was formed in Jacksonville, Florida, in 1969 by brothers **Duane** and **Gregg Allman** (guitar and keyboards respectively) with **Dickey Betts** (guitar), **Berry Oakley** (bass), and both **Jai Johanny "Jaimoe" Johanson** and **Butch Trucks** on drums. Although they quickly established a great live reputation in the South, their debut album, *The Allman Brothers Band*, was only a moderate success. Nevertheless, tracks such as "Whipping Post," "Black Hearted Woman," and "Dreams," all written by Gregg, would become classics. Meanwhile, the group relocated to Macon, Georgia, with which they were to be indelibly linked.

Idlewild South followed in 1970—with "Midnight Rider" by Gregg and "In Memory of Elizabeth Reed" by Betts among its highlights—and found a better commercial reception. But, perhaps unsurprisingly for a group who made their name with stupendous performances, it was a recording of two March 1971 concerts, *At Fillmore East*, that catapulted them to the forefront. In particular, versions of "Whipping Post," "In Memory of Elizabeth Reed," "You Don't Love Me,"

and the comparatively succinct "Statesboro Blues" epitomized what the group could accomplish in the field of sophisticated improvisation. The Allman Brothers Band had truly arrived.

However, double tragedy soon struck. First, Duane was killed in a motorcycle accident in Macon in October 1971. The group had already begun *Eat a Peach* (1972), on which live numbers (such as the epic "Mountain Jam") would flesh out the studio tracks, several recorded after his death. But it proved impossible to replace his unrivaled tone and gloriously free style. "It's really hard for me to believe that what we accomplished with Duane happened in two years —beginning to end," Trucks told *Mojo*. (Apart from the group's early recordings, Allman also made a huge contribution to Eric Clapton's Derek and the Dominos hit album, *Layla and Other Assorted Love Songs*.)

The Allmans had barely recovered from the shock when Oakley died in a bike crash, a year later, barely three streets from the scene of Duane's demise. **Chuck Leavell** (keyboards) had already been added to the roster to free Gregg for more guitar duties; **Lamar Williams** replaced Oakley to finish the recording of *Brothers and Sisters* (1973). The album topped the

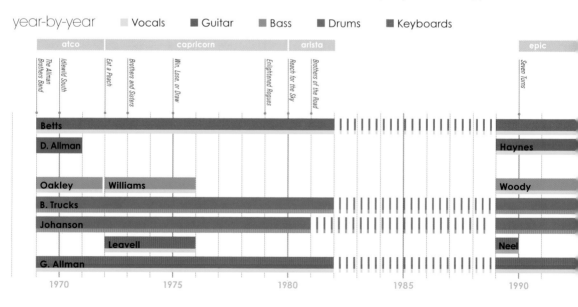

year-by-year ▪ Vocals ▪ Guitar ▪ Bass ▪ Drums ▪ Keyboards

3M	2.5M	2M	2.8M
At Fillmore East (1971)	**Eat a Peach** (1972)	**Brothers and Sisters** (1973)	**A Decade of Hits** (1991)

A

Warren Haynes
b. April 6, 1960

Allen Woody
b. October 3, 1955
d. Aug 26, 2000

Johnny Neel
b. June 11, 1954

Marc Quiñones
b. 1963 or 1964

Oteil Burbridge
b. August 24, 1964

Derek Trucks
b. June 8, 1979

Jimmy Herring
b. January 22, 1962

charts while the single "Ramblin' Man" moseyed to No. 2 in the United States. The mellifluous instrumental "Jessica" was also a stand-out (both written by Betts).

While still a huge live draw, the surviving band members were wracked by drink, drugs, and friction. *Win, Lose, or Draw* (1975) was, by their high standards, uneven. Gregg, in a stormy marriage with Cher, was arrested on drugs charges in 1976 and controversially blamed his minder. The other members vowed not to work with him again and the group effectively split, though they reformed in 1978 to record *Enlightened Rogues* (1979). Guitarist Dan Toler and bassist David Goldflies came in, the latter replacing Williams, who had formed Sea Level with Chuck Leavell (Leavell later became a longstanding associate Rolling Stone).

Having replaced Johanson with David "Frankie" Toler, the group recorded *Reach for the Sky* (1980) and, with Mike Lawler on keyboards, its follow-up *Brothers of the Road* (1981)—but, disappointed by the reception to the latter, decided once more to split. By 1982, the Allman Brothers Band seemed to have run its course, apart from a few impromptu jam sessions and benefit shows arranged by promoter Bill Graham. "I went into a big slump for years," Gregg confessed.

So it stayed until 1989 when the surviving founders, with Johanson restored, reunited for a revival, boosted by guitarist **Warren Haynes**, keyboard player **Johnny Neel**, and bassist **Allen Woody**. Three new albums earned critical plaudits, while they were inducted into the Rock and Roll Hall of Fame (1995) and even won a belated Grammy in 1996 for "Jessica."

Apart from the arrival of **Marc Quiñones** in 1991, the departure of Neel and the replacements of Woody by **Oteil Burbridge** and Haynes by Jack Pearson (soon followed by **Derek Trucks**, Butch's nephew), the nineties were relatively serene—but the harmony could not last. After a rift with Gregg, Betts left the group for "personal and professional reasons" and, having been replaced first by **Jimmy Herring**, then by the returning Haynes, took the others to court. Meanwhile, Allen Woody was found dead.

Fortunately, the modern age has proved kinder. With a stable lineup and a 2003 studio album, *Hittin' the Note* ("The best record we ever made," Trucks maintains), they continue to be an exciting live draw. Meanwhile, Gregg Allman's smash solo album *Low Country Blues* (2011) earned a Grammy nomination for Best Blues Album. **MiH**

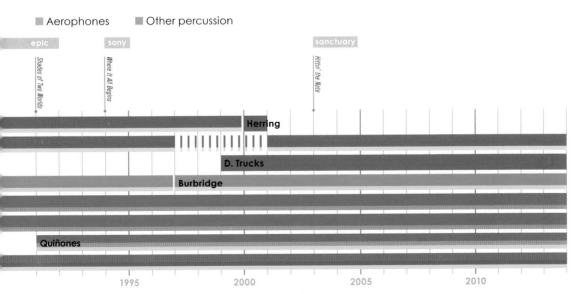

■ Aerophones ▦ Other percussion

epic   sony   sanctuary

Shades of Two Worlds   *Where It All Begins*   *Hittin' the Note*

Herring

D. Trucks

Burbridge

Quiñones

1995   2000   2005   2010

A

the animals 1962–1969

Eric Burdon
b. May 11, 1941

Hilton Valentine
b. May 21, 1943

Alan Price
b. April 9, 1942

Chas Chandler
b. Dec 18, 1938
d. July 17, 1996

John Steel
b. February 4, 1941

Danny McCulloch
b. July 18, 1945
d. January 29, 2015

The grittiest of Britain's "beat boom" bands, The Animals were formed in Newcastle in 1962. Appearing first as the Alan Price Rhythm and Blues Combo, the original lineup consisted of **Alan Price** (keyboards), **Hilton Valentine** (guitar), Bryan **"Chas" Chandler** (bass), and **John Steel** (drums). The group were soon joined by sultry, scowling vocalist **Eric Burdon**, and their uninhibited, energetic performances earned them a local reputation as "animals"—a name they quickly chose to adopt.

Like The Beatles, they were attracted to the money that could be earned performing to lively around-the-clock audiences in Hamburg, Germany. Starting in May 1963, they undertook a two-month fixture at the city's Star Club, where the Fab Four had recorded thirty songs the previous December. They themselves recorded an EP for fans, and this led to offers of work in London.

However, it took a meeting with Yardbirds' manager Georgio Gomelsky to convince The Animals that a move to London was necessary to secure a record deal. Now delivering impressively tight, fiery versions of American blues staples by the likes of Jimmy Reed, John Lee Hooker, and Nina Simone, the group were ready to up their game. Traveling south to the capital, The Animals quickly established themselves as one of the hottest R&B bands on the

London scene. Central to The Animals' sound were the growl of gravel-voiced Burdon and the nimble fingers of Price, who was one of the very few skilled organists working in popular music at that time.

Signing to EMI's Columbia label, The Animals enjoyed immediate Top Twenty success with "Baby Let Me Take You Home," a rocking take on a traditional folk song, "Baby Let Me Follow You Down," that had recently been revived by Bob Dylan. With Valentine's unaccompanied, arpeggiated guitar intro and Price's Vox Continental organ dominating the sound, this debut recipe was repeated to sensational effect on the group's follow-up single (and another old folk tune)—"The House of the Rising Sun." With Burdon giving one of the defining, instantly recognizable vocal performances of the period, this brooding pop masterpiece topped the charts on both sides of the Atlantic, despite EMI arguing that its four-and-a-half-minute duration was too long to attract radio play.

Hits continued in much the same manner over a two-year period, with beat classics "Don't Let Me Be Misunderstood" and "We Gotta Get Out of This Place" (both 1965) reaching the Top Twenty in both the U.S. and the U.K. In common with most of their material, those hits were covers, this time of songs by Nina Simone and Sam Cooke respectively. Another 1965 hit was a cover of bluesman John Lee Hooker's

year-by-year   ▨ Vocals   ■ Guitar   ■ Bass   ■ Drums   ■ Keyboards   ▨ Strings

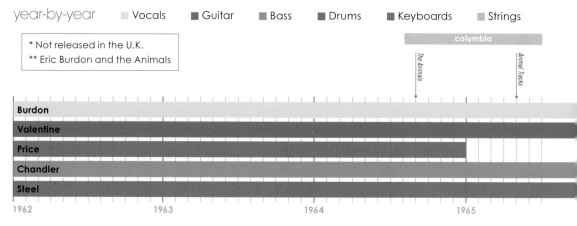

* Not released in the U.K.
** Eric Burdon and the Animals

columbia

The Animals

Animal Tracks

Burdon

Valentine

Price

Chandler

Steel

1962   1963   1964   1965

John Weider
b. April 21, 1947

Barry Jenkins
b. December 22, 1944

"Boom Boom," which rose to No. 43 on the U.S. chart. Yet notwithstanding these triumphs, internal pressures began to emerge. Increasingly at odds with the group's musical direction, and with a fear of flying that threatened to jeopardize their U.S. campaign, Price left the band (he would enjoy enormous success of his own over the two decades that followed). He was replaced by Mick Gallagher (later Hammond organ player with Ian Dury and the Blockheads), then Dave Rowberry (whose audition was reportedly helped by the fact that he looked quite like Price).

At the beginning of 1966, Steel announced his intention to leave the band and go into business in Newcastle. Among names reported in the press for his replacement were The Who's Keith Moon, but the position went to **Barry Jenkins** of English pop group The Nashville Teens. Jenkins played on the 1966 hits "Don't Bring Me Down," a Gerry Goffin/Carole King song that made the Top Twenty in the U.S. and the U.K., and "See See Rider," a Gertrude "Ma" Rainey blues song that, released only in the U.S., reached No. 10 and gave The Animals one of their biggest hits. (It was later a staple of Elvis Presley's performances.)

Despite all this apparent success, the writing was on the wall for The Animals. The group had management problems and their finances were in a desperate state. Another sore point within the group was Burdon's enthusiasm for LSD and the counterculture, while the others were content to sup their beer. With Burdon having begun his own chart career and Chandler quitting to manage Jimi Hendrix (to be replaced by **Danny McCulloch**), The Animals fell apart in late 1966.

Relocating to California, Burdon created a second version of The Animals. This time around, the driving blues of their classic singles was usurped by the prevailing psychedelic sound of the time. Billed as Eric Burdon and the Animals, the new band enjoyed hits such as the anti-Vietnam War song "San Franciscan Nights," including a bizarre and lengthy spoken-word introduction paying tribute to the "beautiful people of San Francisco." The period's stand-out track, "When I Was Young," showcased the electric violin of guitarist **John Weider** (later to be bassist with Brit group Family).

Following a period of shifting personnel (including guitarist Vic Briggs, keyboardist Zoot Money, and future Police man Andy Summers), Burdon disbanded this edition of the Animals in 1969. The final straw was thought to have been a traumatic Japanese tour that, unknown to the band, was being run by Yakuza—organized crime syndicates. It terminated with The Animals abandoning their equipment and fleeing the country for their lives. Burdon went on to join the funk band War before resuming a modest solo career. **TB**

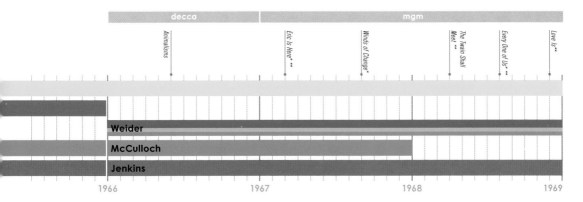

anthrax 1981–present

Scott Ian
b. December 31, 1963

Dan Lilker
b. October 18, 1964

Greg D'Angelo
b. December 24, 1963

Neil Turbin
b. December 24, 1963

Matt Fallon
b. September 30, 1965

Joey Belladona
b. October 13, 1960

John Bush
b. August 24, 1963

Dan Nelson
b. June 21, 1976

"It'd be great to make a lot of money, appear on *American Bandstand* and *The Johnny Carson Show,* have my picture in *16 Magazine* and all that," Anthrax singer **Joey Belladonna** admitted to *Kerrang!* magazine in 1985. "But I can't see it happening!"

History has proved him right, but Anthrax are firmly established alongside Metallica, Megadeth, and Slayer as one of the "Big Four" bands of thrash: the super-speedy metal variant that energized the genre in the same way as punk did to rock in the seventies. To the *de rigeur* howling vocals and histrionic solos, Anthrax added humor and hip-hop—the first distinguishing them from virtually every major thrash act, and the second predating the nü-metal likes of Korn, Limp Bizkit, Linkin Park, and Slipknot.

Two drummers (Dave Weiss and **Greg D'Angelo**), two bassists (Kenny Kushner and Paul Khan), two guitarists (Greg Walls and Bob Berry), and three singers (John Connelly, Jason Rosenfeld, and Tommy Wise) passed through the ranks after **Scott Ian** and **Danny Lilker** conceived Anthrax in 1981. By the time of their 1984 debut, *Fistful of Metal*, the lineup had settled on guitarist Ian, bassist Lilker, drummer **Charlie Benante**, guitarist **Dan Spitz**, and singer **Neil Turbin**.

Falling short of the standards set by Metallica

and Slayer's debut albums the previous year, *Fistful* marked the swansong of both Turbin and Lilker. The former found himself largely written out of Anthrax's history, despite having written lyrics for classics like "Armed and Dangerous." The latter formed Nuclear Assault with early Anthrax singer John Connelly, and resurfaced alongside Ian and Benante—and front-man Chuck Billy—in their hardcore side-project Stormtroopers of Death (whose classic, albeit highly unpleasant, *Speak English or Die* was issued in 1985).

After a short stay by singer **Matt Fallon** (later to spend an equally forgotten period in Skid Row), 1985's splendid *Spreading the Disease* introduced Anthrax's new singer Joey Belladonna and, on bass, Benante's nephew **Frank Bello**. The album crept into the lower reaches of the U.S. chart while the band toured with W.A.S.P. and Black Sabbath. A triumphant outing with former Megaforce label-mates Metallica included, in September 1986, one of the loudest shows ever held at London's hallowed Hammersmith Odeon. Five months later, Anthrax returned to headline at the same venue, a performance eventually issued on 2007's *Caught in a Mosh: BBC Live in Concert.*

Among the Living (1987) made them the thrash band it was okay to like. Their skate shorts, comic

year-by-year   ▨ Vocals   ▪ Guitar   ▪ Bass   ▪ Drums

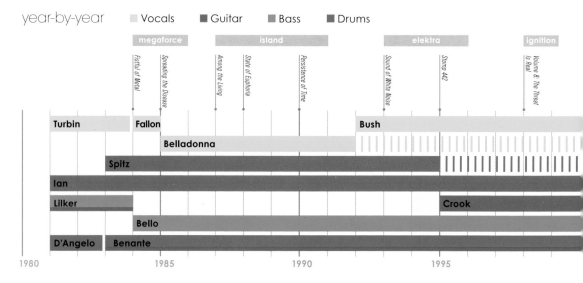

1M
Among the Living
(1987)

1M
Persistence of Time
(1990)

1M
Attack of the Killer B's
(1991)

1M
Sound of White Noise
(1993)

Dan Spitz
b. January 28, 1963

Paul Crook
b. February 12, 1966

Rob Caggiano
b. November 7, 1976

Frank Bello
b. July 9, 1965

Charlie Benante
b. November 27, 1962

Jonathan Donais
b. April 5, year unknown

book references (such as the Judge Dredd-inspired "I Am the Law"), and tongue-in-cheek anthems like "Caught In A Mosh" appealed to folks who didn't buy into metal's *sturm und drang*—and those who did. The former delighted in the mock hip-hop of 1987's *I'm the Man* EP, the latter sent 1988's *State of Euphoria* into the Top Thirty on both sides of the Atlantic.

Persistence of Time (1990) proved another smash, although the lyrics had turned more serious. A cover of new-waver Joe Jackson's "Got the Time" proved their ongoing willingness to defy expectations, though even that was eclipsed by a 1991 hook-up with rap's greatest act, Public Enemy. A reconstructed version of PE's "Bring the Noise"—the original of which included a name check for Anthrax—was the starting gun for a pioneering co-headlining tour by the two groups.

Disenchanted, Belladonna left for a low-key solo career, and was replaced by singer **John Bush**, from metallers Armored Saint. With him, Anthrax scaled new musical and chart peaks with the excellent *Sound of White Noise* (1993), which included orchestration by *Twin Peaks* composer Angelo Badalamenti.

Unfortunately, a debilitating series of personnel upheavals meant they never made good on this second wave of success. Spitz quit, leaving six-string

duties on *Stomp 442* (1995) and *Volume 8: The Threat is Real* (1998) to his guitar tech **Paul Crook**, drummer Charlie Benante, and Pantera's Dimebag Darrell. By 2003, Boiler Room's **Rob Caggiano** had displaced Crook, but not even a return to musical form—plus cameos by Dimebag and The Who's Roger Daltrey—could save *We've Come for You All* from achieving Anthrax's worst chart placings in two decades.

A reunion of the Ian-Benante-Spitz-Belladonna-Bello lineup held up long enough for a 2005 tour, but fans campaigned for Bush's return. They fleetingly got their wish in 2009, before **Dan Nelson** stepped into thrash's least stable shoes. (Nelson resurfaced in 2012 alongside bassist Rudy Sarzo, latterly of Blue Öyster Cult, in a band called Tred.)

After yet another brief Bush revival in early 2010, a Belladonna-fronted lineup, with Ian, Benante, Bello, and Caggiano, embarked on that year's "Big Four" festival tour with their old compadres Metallica, Slayer, and Megadeth. Remarkably, this incarnation of the band stuck together long enough to record *Worship Music* (2011), which garnered enthusiastic reviews and sufficient sales to land it just outside the U.S. Top Ten. They were still at it in 2012, playing the U.S. Mayhem festival alongside Slipknot, Slayer and Motörhead. **BM**

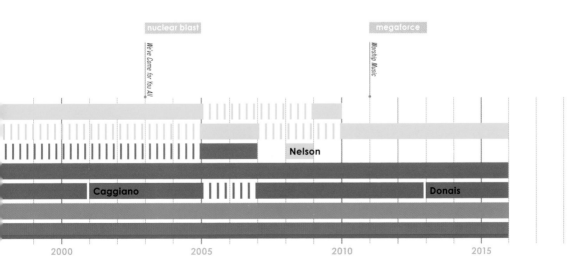

A arcade fire 2001–present

Win Butler
b. April 14, 1980

Régine Chassagne
b. August 18, 1977

Myles Broscoe
b. December 31, 1969

Brendan Reed
b. March 21, 1978

Richard Reed Parry
b. October 4, 1977

Will Butler
b. October 6, 1982

"They're fantastic," said David Bowie of Arcade Fire in 2005. "I discovered them a year ago. Coldplay's Chris Martin has been saying he's discovered them first, but I did. So there. Na na na na na!" It is not hard to see why this multi-instrumental alternative band with theatrical overtones has won admirers from Bowie and Martin to U2 (who took the band on tour and used "Wake Up" as their intro music), Dave Grohl (who, having listened to "Keep the Car Running" on a daily basis, performed it with his Foo Fighters), Bruce Springsteen (who brought them onstage for rapturously received versions of songs by them and him), and even Kanye West (who tweeted "Arcade fire!!!!!!!!!! I feel like we all won when something like this happens!" when *The Suburbs* became the first "indie" release to win a Grammy for Album of the Year).

In the grand art rock tradition, Arcade Fire has achieved the winning combination of critical acclaim and a devoted fan base, while maintaining an enigmatic air, avoiding being over-exposed, and producing challenging yet rewarding music.

Originally called The Arcade Fire, the group began performing together as the trio of **Win Butler**, Josh Deu, and Tim Kyle (now in Wild Light) in Boston in 2001. On moving to Montreal, Win Butler met **Régine Chassagne**, with whom he began writing songs and, before long, forming a romantic attachment.

Kyle left, but the group expanded, adding **Myles Broscoe** on bass, Dane Mills on drums and guitar, and **Brendan Reed** on drums and vocals. Broscoe left before they had finished recording their self-titled and self-distributed debut EP (2003), and **Richard Reed Perry** joined soon afterwards.

During a show to celebrate the release of that EP, Reed quit live on stage after an argument with Butler. Mills swiftly followed, so **Tim Kingsbury** and **Will Butler** (Win's younger brother) joined to form a new lineup (Deu also left in 2003, but still works with them occasionally). Before the year was out, their impressive live form saw them signed to Merge Records.

Its title coined after several band members lost relatives during the recording, their debut album

year-by-year

■ Vocals ■ Guitar ■ Bass ■ Drums ■ Keyboards

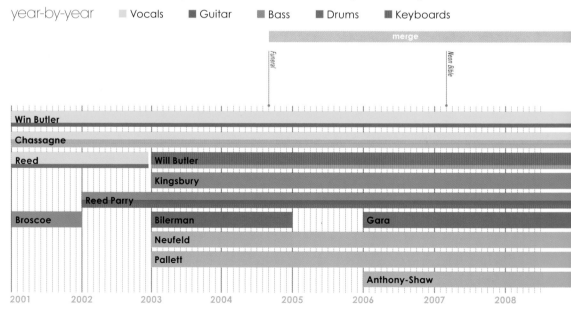

Tim Kingsbury
b. Unkown

Howard Bilerman
b. September 25, 1970

Sarah Neufeld
b. August 27, 1979

Jeremy Gara
b. July 6, 1978

Owen Pallett
b. September 7, 1979

Marika Anthony-Shaw
b. Unknown

Funeral appeared in 2004. New additions to the expanding lineup included **Sarah Neufeld** on violin/strings and **Howard Bilerman** on drums. A success in Canada, the conceptual collection became a slow-burning sensation in the U.K.—where four of its singles hit the Top Forty—and the U.S. In 2005, U2's infatuation began: drummer Larry Mullen Jr. said they were the only band he wished he'd been in, and singer Bono sighed, "I wouldn't want any other group to support us ever again." And when the *Fashion Rocks* TV show requested Bowie's participation, "I told them I'd do it only if they got Arcade Fire to perform." (They duly performed his "Five Years" and their "Wake Up.")

Recording sessions in a deserted church led to the epic *Neon Bible* (2007)—influenced by Dylan, Springsteen, and Elvis, but featuring a pipe organ, military choir, and full orchestra. Another lineup change—**Jeremy Gara** replaced Bilerman on drums—proved no obstacle to Arcade Fire's commercial ascent: buoyed by the hit "Keep the Car Running," *Neon Bible* debuted at No. 1 in Canada and

Ireland, and No. 2 in the U.S. and U.K. Win Butler and Chassagne's guest appearance at a Springsteen show in Canada sealed their extraordinary year.

In the aftermath, Arcade Fire participated in free concerts in support of U.S. presidential candidate Barack Obama. In January 2009, at the new president's request, they joined Jay-Z as the musical guests at the Obama Campaign Staff Ball.

The Suburbs duly topped international charts on its release in 2010. Influenced by the Butler brothers' upbringing in Houston, the album was described by Win as "a mix of Depeche Mode and Neil Young." Its singles ranged from the pounding "Ready to Start," through the Velvet Underground-esque "City with No Children," to a collaboration with David Byrne of Talking Heads, "Speaking in Tongues." The gorgeous "Sprawl II" even introduced an element once lacking in the Arcade Fire experience: a dance routine.

Now able to command stadium-sized audiences, the group capitalized on their success with the release of *Reflektor* in 2013. **OM**

■ Aerophones   ■ Strings   ■ Other percussion

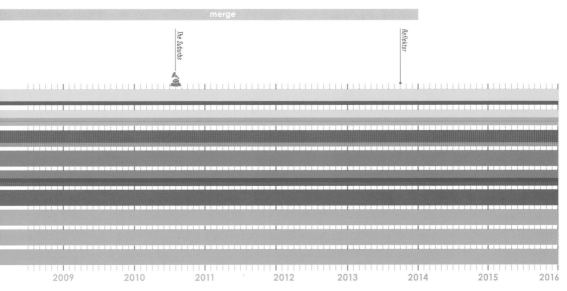

arctic monkeys 2002–present

Alex Turner
b. January 6, 1986

Jamie Cook
b. July 8, 1985

Matt Helders
b. May 7, 1986

Nick O'Malley
b. July 5, 1985

Andy Nicholson
b. Unknown

Glyn Jones
b. Unknown

In 2005, Arctic Monkeys, a young quartet from Sheffield, England, had a spectacular leap to fame when they came from nowhere to score U.K. No. 1 hits with their first two singles, "I Bet You Look Good on the Dancefloor" and "When the Sun Goes Down."

The debut album, *Whatever People Say I Am, That's What I'm Not*, wasn't an obvious blockbuster. It was indie rock released at a time when many were predicting that genre's demise, topped with wry, witty lyrics sung in a distinctively northern English accent. Yet *Whatever People Say...* became the fastest-selling debut album in British history upon its release in January 2006. It also achieved phenomenal international success, topping the Australian and Irish charts, reaching the U.S. *Billboard* Top Twenty and becoming a Top Ten hit all over western Europe.

The story began in 2002, when five friends formed a band. The first Arctic Monkeys lineup consisted of singer **Glyn Jones**, guitarists **Alex Turner** and **Jamie Cook**, drummer **Matt Helders**, and bassist **Andy Nicholson**. Jones soon dropped out, apparently lacking the necessary dedication, and main songwriter Turner took over as frontman. By the following year they were regularly gigging around Sheffield and recording demos.

The Monkeys' masterstroke was to give away CDs of said demos at their live shows. Fans uploaded their songs onto the Internet and news spread not so much by word-of-mouth, as by click-of-mouse—the band's songs went viral. By 2005 a frantic bidding war raged between record companies eager to sign them. Arctic Monkeys rejected offers from major labels and signed to Laurence Bell's indie label Domino.

Their subsequent leap to fame was too much for Nicholson, who took a temporary break "due to exhaustion." He was replaced by **Nick O'Malley** on their first U.S. tour; he would soon become a permanent member after the tour when Nicholson officially left the group. *Favourite Worst Nightmare*, released in April 2007, was another (U.K.) platinum hit, with many declaring it to be even better than their critically lauded debut.

Turner next took a brief break from the group to team up with Miles Kane (then the frontman of The Rascals), to form The Last Shadow Puppets. The duo recorded *The Age of the Understatement* (2008), a collection of dramatic, string-laden sixties-styled songs that gave Turner his third U.K. No. 1 album.

Arctic Monkeys reconvened for *Humbug* (2009)—co-produced by Josh Homme—which featured a denser, darker tone than its predecessors. *Suck It and See* (2011) combined their earlier melodicism with *Humbug*'s heavier sound to great effect and near-universal acclaim. The success of these albums continued with *AM* (2013), which gave Arctic Monkeys their fifth consecutive U.K. chart-topper. **DJ**

year-by-year   ■ Vocals   ■ Guitar   ■ Bass   ■ Drums

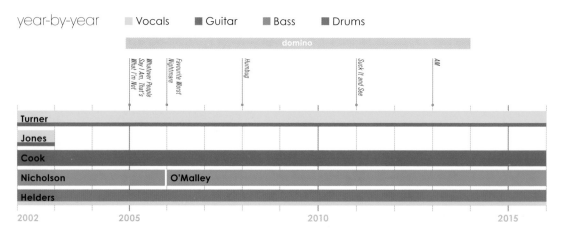

domino

Whatever People Say I Am, That's What I'm Not

Favourite Worst Nightmare

Humbug

Suck It and See

AM

Turner

Jones

Cook

Nicholson   O'Malley

Helders

2002   2005   2010   2015

asia 1981–present

John Wetton
b. June 12, 1949

Carl Palmer
b. March 20, 1950

Geoff Downes
b. August 25, 1952

Steve Howe
b. April 8, 1947

Greg Lake
b. November 10, 1947

Scott Gorham
b. March 17, 1951

John Payne
b. 1958

Steve Lukather
b. October 21, 1957

Asia was big, but it could have been much bigger if it had had fewer personnel changes and avoided excessive reliance on founder-member **John Wetton**, who left and rejoined the supergroup several times. The group grew out of a progressive rock background and were formed in 1981 by Wetton (ex-King Crimson), **Carl Palmer** (from Emerson, Lake and Palmer), **Geoff Downes**, and **Steve Howe** (both from Yes). Their self-titled debut album, released in March 1982, got heavy airplay on MTV and sold ten million copies worldwide, with two singles from it—"Only Time Will Tell" and "Heat of the Moment"—making the U.S. Top Forty. The latter became, with another track from this album, "Sole Survivor," one of the anthemic show-stoppers of their live act.

Asia were off to a flying start with their debut topping the *Billboard* album chart for nine weeks but it was on stage that they really made their mark as one of the prototype arena bands. Their second album, *Alpha*, went platinum, but some fans objected to the spotlighting of Wetton's vocals at the expense of the other band members. Then suddenly the *Alpha* tour was suspended in September 1983. By the time the group next played live—at the "Asia in Asia" Tokyo gig in December—Wetton had been replaced by Palmer's friend from ELP, **Greg Lake**.

Asia's material—rock with a hard core but an MOR casing—did not suit Lake. He quit in early 1984

and Wetton rejoined the group. Then Howe left and was replaced by Mandy Meyer from Krokus. These changes undermined their identity; sales of their third album, *Astra*, were so disappointing that Polydor canceled the planned tour.

Shortly after, the group split. In 1987, Wetton and Downes re-formed Asia with guitarist **Scott Gorham** (ex-Thin Lizzy) and drummer Michael Sturgis (ex-a-ha) but despite this they failed to land a recording deal. They had better luck with their 1989 lineup, which featured John Young on keyboards, and first Alan Darby, then Holger Larish on guitar. A successful European tour prompted the release of *Then & Now* (1990), a best-of compilation with four new tracks featuring Toto guitarist **Steve Lukather**.

In 1991, Wetton left again and was succeeded by **John Payne**, who, together with another new recruit, Al Pitrelli, joined Downes, Howe, and Palmer on *Aqua*. Yet the players remained as fluid as the album title and a myriad of lineup changes in the nineties included Palmer leaving for an ELP reunion.

In 2006, Wetton, Palmer, Downes, and Howe got back together as The Four Original Members of Asia. The following year saw the emergence of Asia Featuring John Payne. The former played only Asia material in which Payne had not been involved; the latter performed songs from the entire history of the band as the complex Asia timeline rumbled on. **GL**

year-by-year   ■ Vocals   ■ Guitar   ■ Drums   ■ Keyboards

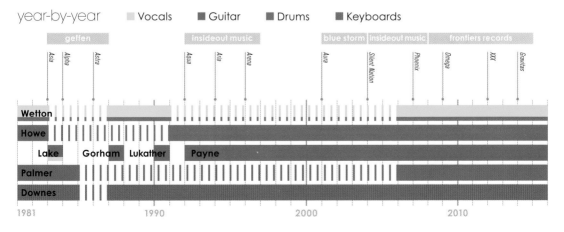

b-2 1988–present

Igor "Lyova" Bortnik
b. 2 September 1972

Aleksandr "Shura" Uman
b. 3 February 1970

Victoria Bilogan
b. Unknown

Grigori Gaberman
b. July 29, 1977

Andrey Zvonkov
b. 1 December 1973

Maxim Andrusschenko
b. 15 October 1978

Boris Lifshitz
b. 9 July 1981

Yanik Nikolenko
b. 25 February 1973

One of Russia's most important rock bands of the past two decades, B-2 have only been releasing albums since the late nineties, although their history stretches back a further one-and-a-half decades.

The story begins in 1985 in Minsk, Belarus, then a republic of the Soviet Union. **Aleksandr "Shura" Uman** and **Igor "Lyova" Bortnik**, two Jewish teenagers with ambitions to be actors, formed the new wave band Bratya Po Oruzhiyu ("Brothers in Arms"). Three years later they adopted the name Bereg Istini ("Shore of Truth"), soon abbreviated to B-2. With it came a new style of music: a kind of eastern-tinged classic rock.

In 1991, Uman and Bortnik moved to Israel. A year later, they won a "battle of the bands," enabling them to make their first professional recordings. Bortnik remained in Israel, serving in the army, while Uman moved on to Australia. In separate continents, the duo collaborated via mail and the Internet, while Uman formed the post-punky Chiron. In 1998, Bortnik joined his colleague's band but, within a year, they opted to concentrate on B-2.

In Australia the duo recorded tracks for what was intended as their debut album, *Byespolaya e Grustnaya Lubov* ("Sexless and Sad Love"); "Serdze" was a hit on Moscow radio. B-2 moved to Russia in

1999 but, with the country in financial crisis, they were unable to secure a release for the album.

Expanding to a full band, B-2 had a breakthrough a year later thanks to Aleksei Balabanov's film *Brat 2*. The soundtrack album was a hit, as was B-2's "Polkovnik." On the back of this success they were able to record their award-winning self-titled album in 2000. *Meow Kiss Me* was an even greater success, as B-2's videos were in heavy rotation on MTV Russia.

Success continued with albums from *Inomarki* ("Foreign Cars", 2004) to *Spirit* (2011), all of which achieved gold sales status. Among their more popular songs is "Bowie," which suggestively twins a reference to the Vladimir Nabokov novel *Lolita* with the simple inquiry, "Do you like David Bowie?"

B-2 often collaborate with other Russian rock acts like Splean, ChayF, Nochniye Snaiperi, and Zemfira. In 2005, with lyricist Mikhail Karasev (Uman's uncle), they produced *Nechetny Voin* ("Strange Warrior"), a CD featuring many of Russia's top pop and rock artists. A second volume emerged two years later.

B-2 continue to enjoy a following in Eastern Europe: the *Spirit* stadium tour continued well into 2012. Unfortunately, however, singing in their native tongue has prevented serious success in the West. **TB**

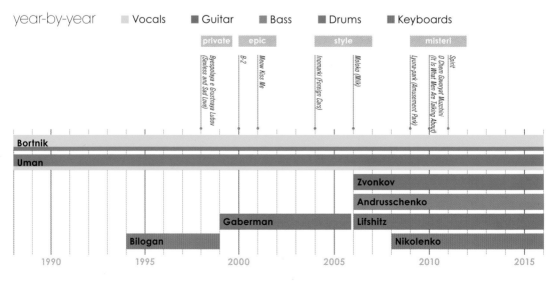

year-by-year ■ Vocals ■ Guitar ■ Bass ■ Drums ■ Keyboards

the b-52's 1976–present

Cindy Wilson
b. February 28, 1957

Ricky Wilson
b. Mar 19, 1953
d. October 12, 1985

Keith Strickland
b. October 26, 1953

Kate Pierson
b. April 27, 1948

Fred Schneider
b. July 1, 1951

Julee Cruise
b. December 1, 1956

Sterling Campbell
b. May 3, 1964

"The women looked like they were from outer space," enthused Dave Grohl of The B-52's, "and everything was linked in: the sleeves, the sound, the clothes, the iconography, the logo… When you're a kid, that's what you're after—a real unified feel to a band."

Fueled by cocktails, siblings **Cindy** and **Ricky Wilson**, **Keith Strickland**, **Fred Schneider**, and **Kate Pierson** decided to form a band on the way home from a meal in their Athens, Georgia hometown. It was a suitably idiosyncratic start for a group who named themselves after southern lingo for the beehive hairdos adopted by Pierson and Cindy Wilson. The quintet made their live debut in Athens on Valentine's Day, 1977, then headed to New York to seek fame.

A self-financed single, featuring "Rock Lobster," snared deals with Warner and Island, and even inspired John Lennon's return to the studio. "It sounds just like Yoko's music," he told *Rolling Stone*, "so I said to meself, 'It's time to get out the old axe and wake the wife up!'" After two gold sets—*The B-52's* and *Wild Planet*—the band pioneered the remix album with 1981's *Party Mix!*. Then, seeking to expand their sound, they worked with Talking Heads' David Byrne. The sessions collapsed in disagreements, but the abortive results were issued as the mini-album *Mesopotamia*.

After 1983's *Whammy!*, the band's profile dipped, but the most serious blow was the death of Wilson, caused by complications from AIDS, in 1985. With the guitarist having co-written the band's music with Strickland, it seemed unlikely they could continue. Yet they bounced back with the hits "Love Shack" and "Roam" from 1989's *Cosmic Thing,* produced by Nile Rodgers and Don Was. Meanwhile, Pierson guested on R.E.M.'s *Out of Time* and Iggy Pop's "Candy."

Despite Cindy Wilson opting out to start a family, 1992's *Good Stuff* and 1994's "(Meet) The Flintstones" maintained the momentum. Live, Wilson was replaced by Strickland's old schoolmate Kim Basinger for one show, then for a tour by "Falling" singer **Julee Cruise**. In the ensuing hiatus, Schneider issued 1996's *Just Fred,* his second solo album (after 1984's *Fred Schneider and the Shake Society,* featuring Pierson and Ricky Wilson alongside Patti Labelle). But with Cindy back in the fold, the band returned to the road and issued the retrospectives *Time Capsule—Songs for a Future Generation* (1998) and *Nude on the Moon* (2002).

Funplex (2008), their first studio album in sixteen years, hit U.S. No. 11, while *With the Wild Crowd! Live in Athens, GA* (2011) proved The B-52's—now featuring Strickland on guitar and former Duran Duran/Soul Asylum/David Bowie drummer **Sterling Campbell**—to be as vibrant as ever. Of the party band that has championed causes from AIDS research to animal rights, Schneider remarked: "We're out there to entertain people, but it's great to get people thinking and dancing at the same time." **BM**

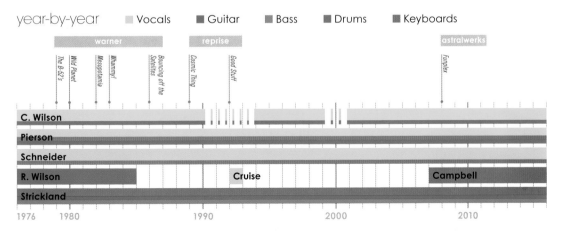

year-by-year ■ Vocals ■ Guitar ■ Bass ■ Drums ■ Keyboards

warner | reprise | astralwerks

The B-52's | Wild Planet | Mesopotamia | Whammy! | Bouncing off the Satellites | Cosmic Thing | Good Stuff | Funplex

C. Wilson
Pierson
Schneider
R. Wilson — Cruise — Campbell
Strickland

1976 1980 1990 2000 2010

bachman-turner overdrive 1973–present

Randy Bachman
b. September 27, 1943

Chad Allan
b. March 29, 1943

Robbie Bachman
b. February 18, 1953

C.F. "Fred" Turner
b. October 16, 1943

Tim Bachman
b. August 1, 1951

Blair Thornton
b. July 23, 1950

This Canadian band did much to keep alive the hard rock tradition during a period when most of the leading groups were soft-centered like Yes or glam like *Ziggy Stardust*-vintage David Bowie. While Bachman-Turner Overdrive's detractors point to their lack of musical ambition, their many fans liken them at their best to mid-period Led Zeppelin.

They were formed by two refugees from The Guess Who—lead guitarist **Randy Bachman** and singer **Chad Allan**—who called in Bachman's kid brother, **Robbie Bachman**, on drums and bassist **C.F. "Fred" Turner** to form Brave Belt, and cut a couple of albums for Reprise. (Turner had been recommended to Randy by compatriot rock star Neil Young.)

Thereafter, they bid farewell to Allan and enlisted another Bachman brother, **Tim Bachman**. Record companies, however, did not flock to their door. "I received about twenty-five or twenty-six refusals," Randy Bachman told *Billboard* book author Craig Rosen. Bachman funded their first album and paid the band's wages with his Guess Who royalties, which ran out just before Mercury finally snapped them up.

BTO's self-titled 1973 debut album was a slow-burner. It took six months to chart in the U.S. (but was eventually certified gold), and the single "Let It Ride"

took a year to reach the U.S. No. 23 spot. But by then *Bachman-Turner Overdrive II* had consolidated their growing reputation. However, Tim Bachman left to become a producer and the band replaced him with guitarist **Blair Thornton**, whose licks and looks helped 1974's *Not Fragile* achieve platinum sales, a *Billboard* No. 1 and the band's only U.K. hit LP (No. 12). Its title was a nod to Yes's breakthrough 1971 album *Fragile*—which, Randy Bachman told Rosen, "was very delicate and symphonic and kind of classical in a way. Ours was the exact opposite. It was just blunt, 'hit them over the head with a guitar and drum beat' kind of thing. But it wasn't a slam against Yes."

This was followed by two hits—"Takin' Care of Business" (U.S. No. 12) and their best-known track, "You Ain't Seen Nothin' Yet" (U.S. No. 1/U.K. No. 2). Although they never repeated this success, *Four Wheel Drive* (1975) went platinum and they had six more U.S. Top Forty singles before the end of 1976.

A year later the band's fortunes took a dip. "My Wheels Won't Turn," was a single from *Freeways*, the band's sixth studio album, which failed to chart. Turner, who took lead vocals on only two of the album's eight tracks, felt that he had been sidelined and refused to appear full-face on the cover.

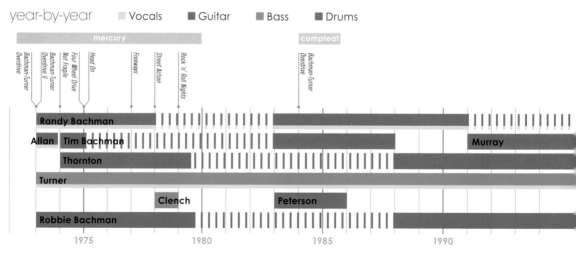

2M	2.2M	1.5M	3.2M
Bachman-Turner Overdrive II (1973)	*Not Fragile* (1974)	*Four Wheel Drive* (1975)	*Best of BTO (So Far)* (1990)

B

Jim Clench
b. May 1, 1949

Garry Peterson
b. May 26, 1945

Randy Murray
b. Unknown

In 1978 Randy Bachman left the band, saying that he and his fellow members just "ran out of common interests." Now without its founder, the group was creatively exhausted, but it soldiered on with **Jim Clench** (ex-April Wine) under the name BTO (Randy retained and zealously guarded rights to the full original moniker). The new-look BTO's first album, *Street Action*, was a disappointment; their second, *Rock 'n' Roll Nights*, a disaster (no more than a quarter of a million sales worldwide); after the promotional tour for the latter, the band split.

The members then did their own things until 1983, when Randy Bachman—who had meanwhile performed in Ironhorse and written some songs with Carl Wilson of The Beach Boys—re-formed the group with brother Tim, Fred Turner, and **Garry Peterson** (the drummer from The Guess Who). When they toured to promote their new album—to which, confusingly, they gave the same title as their first—their drum tech, Billy Chapman, joined them on stage playing keyboards.

In 1986 Bachman-Turner Overdrive opened for Van Halen on the *5150* Tour with the same lineup bar Turner, who, it was said, had been unavailable when the organizers tried to contact him. At the end of the run, Randy Bachman split again but Tim kept

the band going in cut-down form until 1988, when the *Not Fragile* lineup (Randy, Fred, Blair, Robbie) reconvened once more. Only one recording from this incarnation of the group survives—a cover of "Wooly Bully" (originally a 1965 hit for Sam the Sham and The Pharaohs) that was used on the soundtrack of the 1989 Sandy Wilson movie *American Boyfriends*. Then Randy again went his own way and was replaced by **Randy Murray**. This was the dawn of BTO's longest period of stability—the members stayed together from 1991 until the end of 2004. Then, it was announced, they would take a break from touring.

What had been planned as an intermission turned into a hiatus and, when their management company was disbanded, it looked like the end of a very long road. Not quite: In January 2009, Tim Bachman played at a Randy Bachman show and, in December of the same year, the latter got back together with Fred Turner in Winnipeg, Manitoba, Canada. This reunion led to a full-blown tour of North America and Europe in 2010, with the pair backed by Randy's band (Marc LaFrance, Mick Dalla-Vee, and Brent Howard). All was not well in the world, however, as Rob Bachman and Blair Thornton threatened legal action over this group's adoption of the name Bachman & Turner. **GL**

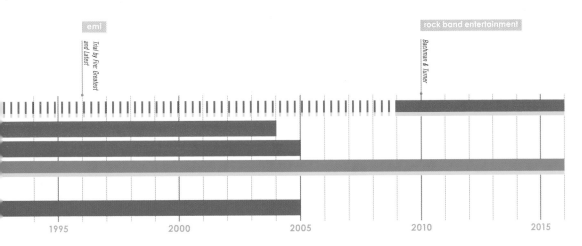

bad company 1973–present

Paul Rodgers
b. December 17, 1949

Mick Ralphs
b. March 31, 1944

Simon Kirke
b. July 28, 1949

Boz Burrell
b. August 1, 1946
d. September 21, 2006

Brian Howe
b. July 22, 1953

Steve Price
b. Unknown

Larry Oakes
b. Unknown

Gregg Dechert
b. May, 13, 1952

A swaggering supergroup formed in 1973 upon the final demise of Free, Bad Company had instant and meteoric success. The chemistry between Free's **Paul Rodgers** (vocals) and **Simon Kirke** (drums), Mott the Hoople's **Mick Ralphs** (guitar) and King Crimson's **Boz Burrell** (bass) was obviously right, and the group soon established a formidable live reputation.

They also proved they were able to reproduce their live punch on record. *Bad Company*, the first album, came out in 1974 and sold extremely well in both the United States (where it went to No. 1) and the United Kingdom. Studded with terrific riffs like "Ready for Love" (which also featured on Mott the Hoople's *All the Young Dudes*) and "Can't Get Enough" as well as the title track, the group had a fuller sound, with bolder brushstrokes, than Free's relatively lean (yet effective) palette. The follow-up *Straight Shooter* (1975)—blessed with more great songs such as "Feel Like Makin' Love," the elegiac "Shooting Star," and "Good Lovin' Gone Bad"—also quickly went gold.

Paul Kossoff, the guitarist from Free who struggled with heroin addiction, formed Back Street Crawler after that group's demise. Free bandmates Rodgers and Kirke invited him to tour with Bad Company in

1976, but it proved an ill omen. Kossoff died before the tour started and, despite *Run with the Pack*, their third album in three years, going platinum in the United States, some of the group's impetus was lost. *Burnin' Sky* (1977) sold gold but made less chart impact, its songs being arguably somewhat formulaic. *Desolation Angels* (1979), aided by the hit "Rock 'n' Roll Fantasy," was a return to form and commercial favor, but more problems were to beset the group.

Peter Grant, Led Zeppelin's legendary manager, had been guiding Bad Company's fortunes and his business acumen made a vital contribution to their triumphs. But Grant was badly affected by the death of Zeppelin's drummer, John Bonham, in 1980 and rather lost interest in managing anyone. The group released the under-performing *Rough Diamonds* in 1982, but were growing disillusioned (punch-ups were not unknown) and decided to call it a day.

Rodgers, his taste for supergroups unsated, set up The Firm with Jimmy Page, who had escaped the Zeppelin wreckage, future AC/DC drummer Chris Slade, and future Blue Murder bassist Tony Franklin. Ralphs entered into a brief partnership of equivalent stature, touring with David Gilmour of Pink Floyd.

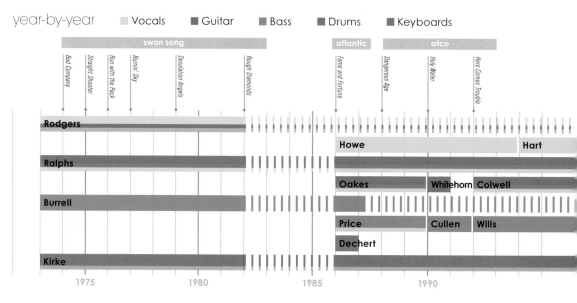

year-by-year ▨ Vocals ▪ Guitar ▪ Bass ▪ Drums ▪ Keyboards

5M	4.2M	3M	3M
Bad Company (1974)	**Run with the Pack** (1976)	**Desolation Angels** (1979)	**10 from 6** (1985)

B

Paul Cullen
b. Unknown

Geoff Whitehorn
b. August 29, 1951

Dave "Bucket" Colwell
b. Unknown

Rick Wills
b. December 5, 1947

Robert Hart
b. November 1, 1958

Jaz Lochrie
b. Unknown

Lynn Sorensen
b. Unknown

Howard Leese
b. June 13, 1951

That is how it stayed for four years until Ralphs and Kirke reformed the group with **Brian Howe** (who had sung with Ted Nugent), **Steve Price** (bass), and **Greg Dechert** (keyboards). With Foreigner's Mick Jones as executive producer and Burrell fleetingly returning (he quit before the ensuing tour), they issued *Fame and Fortune* (1986) to no commercial interest. But with **Larry Oakes** on guitar, the Howe-dominated *Dangerous Age* (1988) returned them to gold sales.

However, problems were mounting once again. There were tensions in the group between Howe and just about everyone else and the recording of *Holy Water* (1990) was fraught with difficulty, although it turned out to be commercially very successful. Ralphs was unable to join the subsequent tour owing to personal problems and was replaced by **Geoff Whitehorn** from Back Street Crawler, then **Dave "Bucket" Colwell**. Meanwhile **Paul Cullen** came in on bass, to be followed by former Roxy Music/Foreigner man **Rick Wills**. The group's *Here Comes Trouble* (1992), another Stateside success, appeared aptly titled.

Howe quit in 1994 to be succeeded by future Manfred Mann's Earth Band singer **Robert Hart** for *Company of Strangers* (1995) and *Stories Told & Untold*

(1996), the latter a mix of new songs and re-recorded favorites, with guests including Alison Krauss, Bon Jovi's Richie Sambora, and the Eagles' Timothy B. Schmidt. But their commercial fortunes once more declined.

In a dramatic turn of events, the group's founders reunited as Bad Company in 1998. Once again, it could not last: Burrell left again the following year and Ralphs had to give up in 2000. Wills (soon succeeded by **Jaz Lochrie**) and Colwell resumed their places but Bad Company dissolved again in 2002. Rodgers returned to his solo career, which included a high-profile stint with Queen from 2004 to 2009.

Bad Company reformed yet again in 2008. With Burrell having died from a heart attack in 2006, Rodgers' solo touring bandmate **Lynn Sorensen** came in on bass, while Heart's **Howard Leese** joined on guitar and keyboards. In Burrell's memory, Rodgers sang his fine composition "Gone, Gone, Gone" (from *Desolation Angels*). An extensive tour in 2010 showed they had lost none of their old pizzazz.

Bad Company's future is uncertain, but it would be wise not to count them out just yet. The group surfed the 1970's hard rock wave with aplomb and wear a rugged, timeless crown today. **MiH**

■ Aerophones   ■ Other percussion

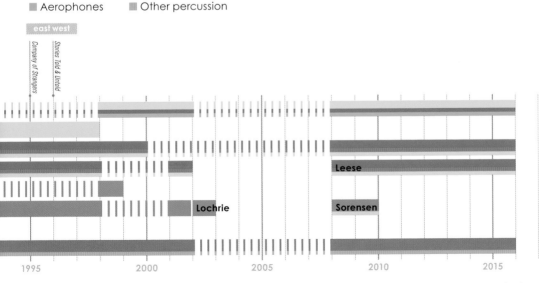

east west

Company of Strangers

Stories Told & Untold

Leese

Lochrie

Sorensen

1995   2000   2005   2010   2015

bad company 43

the band 1964–1999

Rick Danko
b. December 29, 1942
d. December 10, 1999

Levon Helm
b. May 26, 1940
d. April 19, 2012

Garth Hudson
b. August 2, 1937

Richard Manuel
b. April 3, 1943
d. March 4, 1986

Robbie Robertson
b. July 5, 1943

Jim Weider
b. 1951

The Band began life in the early sixties as The Hawks, backing Canadian hellraiser Ronnie Hawkins. **Robbie Robertson** (guitar), **Richard Manuel** (piano), **Rick Danko** (bass), **Garth Hudson** (organ), and **Levon Helm** (drums) would enjoy a successful recording and performing career of their own, but their big break came in 1965 when they hooked up with Bob Dylan.

Having "plugged in" at that year's Newport Folk Festival and declared himself a rock 'n' roller, Dylan needed a band for a world tour. The relationship proved beneficial to both parties. Said Robertson, "I learned from Bob that it's okay to break those traditional rules of what songs are supposed to be."

After a motorcycle accident, Dylan moved to Woodstock, New York, in 1967 and put The Band on a retainer as he recuperated. *The Basement Tapes*, a widely circulated bootleg (officially released eight years later) documented the time. They made their own music, too: namely 1968's electric folk masterpiece *Music from Big Pink*. Part of their strength was an ability to switch instruments: Helm doubled on mandolin, Hudson and Manuel on saxophone, while Manuel, Danko, and Helm were all distinctive vocalists.

The album was named after their communal Woodstock house and featured three songs written or co-written by Dylan ("This Wheel's on Fire," "Tears of Rage," and "I Shall Be Released"). Another track, "The Weight," was featured in the cult classic movie *Easy Rider* and remains their best-known song. "After *Sgt. Pepper,* it's the most influential record in the history of rock 'n' roll," declared Pink Floyd's Roger Waters. "It affected Pink Floyd deeply… Sonically, the way the record's constructed, I think *Music from Big Pink* is fundamental to everything that happened after it."

Robertson penned evocative classics like "The Night They Drove Old Dixie Down" for 1969's *The Band,* while 1970's *Stage Fright* contained some of his best writing. He assumed characters like the Confederate Virgil Cane in "…Dixie…" because he felt "embarrassed by the self-indulgence of 'me me me… here's a little song about me.'"

Cahoots (1971) was the first album to be cut at Woodstock's Bearsville Studios and featured horns arranged by Allen Toussaint. Woodstock neighbor Van Morrison also guested on "4% Pantomime." The Band finished 1971 with a residency at New York's

year-by-year ■ Vocals ■ Guitar ■ Bass ■ Drums ■ Keyboards

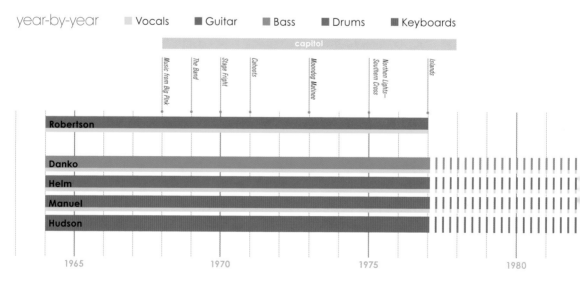

1.4M	2.6M	1.4M	1.3M
Music from Big Pink (1968)	The Band (1969)	Stage Fright (1970)	The Best of the Band (1976)

B

Blondie Chaplin
b. July 7, 1951

Fred Carter Jr
b. December 31, 1933
d. July 17, 2010

Stan Szelest
b. February 11, 1943
d. January 20, 1991

Randy Ciarlante
b. unknown

Richard Bell
b. March 5, 1946
d. June 15, 2007

Academy of Music, augmented by a horn section: recordings from it were issued as *Rock of Ages* (1972), which became their highest-charting U.S. album.

After *Moondog Matinee* (1973)—a set of oldies whose title was taken from a radio show by rock 'n' roll DJ Alan Freed—The Band backed Bob Dylan on his *Planet Waves* album. Much of 1974 would be taken up touring with Dylan, playing their own set as well as his, and appearing on his live *Before the Flood*.

Yet 1976 would bring not only their penultimate album, *Northern Lights Southern Cross*, but also The Band's retirement from live performance. A historic farewell show at San Francisco's Winterland venue on Thanksgiving Day saw them joined by special guests including Dylan, Eric Clapton, Neil Diamond, Ronnie Hawkins, Dr. John, Joni Mitchell, Ringo Starr, Muddy Waters, and Neil Young. The four hours of performance were immortalized on film courtesy of Robertson's former roommate, filmmaker Martin Scorsese. A triple vinyl album (*The Last Waltz*) of highlights appeared alongside the movie, containing many extra songs. However, Helm believed the film concentrated too much on Robertson, whose

decision had prompted the disbandment. This would be the last time the five graced a stage together—*Islands* appeared in 1977 to fulfill their contract.

The Band re-formed without Robertson in the eighties, but their ranks were tragically depleted when Manuel, whose life had been plagued by addictions, hanged himself after a 1986 show. He was replaced by **Stan Szelest**, then by **Richard Bell**. Other additions included **Fred Carter Jr** and **Blondie Chaplin**, while drummer **Randy Ciarlante** came on board in 1990. (That year, The Band appeared with Roger Waters at a re-staging of *The Wall* in Berlin.) Hard-living Danko died in 1999, while Robertson entered the soundtrack realm. In 1994, the year The Band entered the Rock and Roll Hall of Fame, he returned to his roots with the TV soundtrack *Music for the Native Americans*.

The Band are credited with helping to create the Americana genre that would be successfully mined by Ryan Adams, Gillian Welch, and the like. Their second album was belatedly declared platinum in 1991—suggesting that, while they were never big sellers, many important musicians in America and beyond were among those lending them an ear. **MHe**

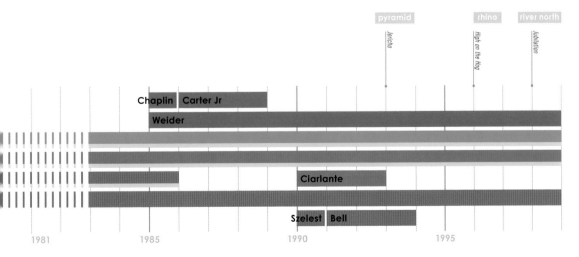

pyramid — rhino — river north

Jericho — High on the Hog — Jubilation

Chaplin | Carter Jr
Weider
Ciarlante
Szelest | Bell

1981 — 1985 — 1990 — 1995

bauhaus 1978–2008

Daniel Ash
b. July 31, 1957

David J
b. April 24, 1957

Kevin Haskins
b. July 19, 1960

Peter Murphy
b. July 11, 1957

"British bands sound the way they do because Britain is overcast and gray and there are lots of churches with gargoyles. That's where Bauhaus come from." So said Perry Farrell of Jane's Addiction, just one of many U.S. groups to cite Bauhaus as an influence.

Little did Walter Gropius know when he founded Staatliches Bauhaus—more commonly known as just Bauhaus—in Weimar, Germany in 1919, that the art school's legend would one day be carried forward by theatrical rockers from Northampton, England.

He also probably didn't suspect that the school's name would later be whispered with reverence by generations of disenfranchised young teens as they shopped at malls for dark eyeliner and vampire gear. Or that if you were making "alternative" music in the late eighties/early nineties in the U.S., Bauhaus were probably a big influence. Nirvana, The Smashing Pumpkins, Soundgarden, and the aforementioned Jane's Addiction are just some of the groups who have cited Bauhaus as inspiring their sound. Chalk all three up as unexpected bonuses in the legacy of the man most responsible for creating the influential Bauhaus Movement in art and architecture.

The members were certainly aware of the school's significance—and relished all the implications that came with borrowing such a lofty title. It was, after all, a more striking moniker than The Craze—the name of

an early group that guitarist **Daniel Ash** and the sibling rhythm section of bassist **David J** and drummer **Kevin Haskins** were in prior to uniting with Ash's school chum **Peter Murphy** in 1978 to form Bauhaus 1919.

The new group honored Gropius's school in more than just name: they also, from the start, showed a commitment to creating a signature style that differed greatly from anything else at the time. Bauhaus 1919 came at the perfect moment, with young Brits hungry for an alternative to what was left of the country's punk scene, as well as to the flash of new wave.

Yet nobody could have expected Bauhaus, who dropped "1919" from their name in 1979, to live up to their potential as quickly as they did with "Bela Lugosi's Dead." That debut single from 1979 was about as far from the norm as possible: a darkly appealing nine-minute tribute to the horror movie icon best known for playing Dracula in Universal Pictures' fabled series. The song, unsurprisingly, failed to dent the charts, but provided notice of a new sound emerging from England's post-punk scene. Bauhaus, and their remarkable debut single, would serve as the definition of what is now known as gothic rock, characterized by dark soundscapes, menacing vocals, and bleak lyrics.

"Bela Lugosi's Dead," the genre's anthem, garnered some radio play and was attractive enough to land Bauhaus a deal with 4AD, on which they

year-by-year ■ Vocals ■ Guitar ■ Bass ■ Drums

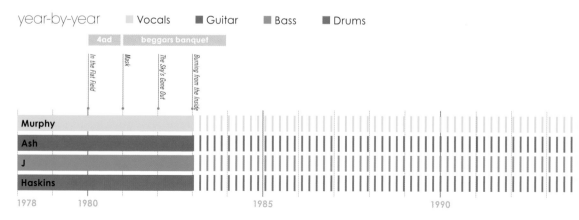

4ad | beggars banquet

In the Flat Field | Mask | The Sky's Gone Out | Burning from the Inside

Murphy
Ash
J
Haskins

1978   1980   1985   1990

200,000
Mask
(1981)

250,000
The Sky's
Gone Out
(1982)

200,000
Burning from the
Inside
(1983)

150,000
1979–1983
(1985)

B

would issue three more commercially unsuccessful singles. The quartet's full-length debut, 1980's *In the Flat Field*, confused critics, who didn't understand what the moaning was all about, but gave Bauhaus their first mini-hit, peaking at No. 72 on the U.K. album chart. More significantly, it stirred a cult-like following, among whom *In the Flat Field* was a badge of honor.

The cult expanded once Bauhaus moved to 4AD's parent label, Beggars Banquet, and released *Mask* (1981). Elevated by its Top Thirty success in the U.K., the group were poised for a commercial breakthrough in 1982. That year brought the quartet their greatest taste of mainstream success, thanks to a hit cover of David Bowie's "Ziggy Stardust" (a non-album track, recorded at a BBC session), a raised middle finger to critics who dismissed them as Bowie clones. The same year also brought them their highest-charting record, *The Sky's Gone Out*, which peaked at No. 4 in the U.K.

Along the way, Bauhaus fans went beyond just listening to a song about Bela Lugosi: they began dressing like him, showing up to gigs in capes and other corpse-chic apparel. Bauhaus's role as posterboys for goth was secured when they featured in the 1983 Tony Scott vampire flick *The Hunger* (starring Bowie), performing, of course, "Bela Lugosi."

The wheels began to fall off around the time they ventured into the studio to record 1983's *Burning from the Inside*—mainly without Murphy, who was too ill with pneumonia to contribute to either writing or recording. Absurd as it now sounds, Bauhaus were attempting to cut an album with hardly any input from their singer. The result, not coincidentally, was less thrilling than the first three albums, but momentum helped carry *Burning…* to No. 13 on the U.K. chart. However, Bauhaus never recovered from those recording sessions, disbanding as the album hit stores.

The Haskins boys and Ash formed Love and Rockets, whose U.S. commercial success—notably 1989's hit "So Alive"—eclipsed their previous band's sales. Meanwhile, Murphy built a low-key solo career, becoming known as the face of a Maxell cassette tape advertisement. In 1984, disbelief greeted his union with Japan's Mick Karn in Dali's Car, often regarded as the most pretentious group of all time.

All the while, however, the group's legacy grew and young goths dreamed of getting the chance to see Bauhaus in concert. The group gave the fans what they wanted with the "Resurrection Tour" in 1988 and a fully fledged reunion in 2005, which lasted three years and included a tour with Bauhaus devotees Nine Inch Nails and an allegedly final album, *Go Away White* (2008). "We come together, burn up, and we leave Bauhaus with fires burning…" said Murphy. "But it's not viable as a band anymore." **JiH**

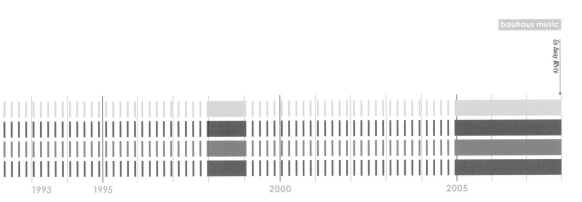

the beach boys 1961–present

B

Brian Wilson
b. June 20, 1942

Carl Wilson
b. December 21, 1946
d. February 7, 1998

Dennis Wilson
b. December 4, 1944
d. December 28, 1983

Mike Love
b. March 15, 1941

Al Jardine
b. September 3, 1942

David Marks
b. August 22, 1948

If there was a U.S. equivalent of The Beatles during the sixties, it was The Beach Boys. They notched up sixteen U.S. Top Thirty singles, plus ten hit albums, with their infectious surf-orientated pop, and—unlike their Brit peers—they are still going over half a century later.

Brothers **Brian**, **Carl**, and **Dennis Wilson**, cousin **Mike Love**, and school pal **Al Jardine** formed The Pendletones (named after the surfing shirts they wore on stage) in L.A. in 1961. Within months they were The Beach Boys and had cut "Surfin'" as their first single.

By the close of 1962 they had signed to Capitol Records and released *Surfin' Safari*, which reached No. 32 in the U.S. chart. They lost Jardine for a year (replaced by **David Marks**), but hit the U.S. top spot with "Help Me Rhonda" and "I Get Around."

In the U.K., "I Get Around"—the group's first U.S. million-seller—became their first Top Ten entry and led to a further nineteen hits during the decade, including the chart-topping "Good Vibrations" and "Do It Again." However, despite their success, Brian Wilson opted out of live work in 1964 to focus on writing

and producing and was briefly replaced by **Glen Campbell**, then permanently by **Bruce Johnston**.

The result of Brian's studio efforts was *Pet Sounds* (1966), which saw him hailed as "a pop genius" by Eric Clapton and was seen, by producer George Martin, as the inspiration for The Beatles' album *Sgt. Pepper's Lonely Hearts Club Band* (this was fitting, as the Fab Four's *Rubber Soul* had helped to inspire *Pet Sounds*).

With Brian collaborating with creative spark Van Dyke Parks and rarely performing live, a stream of greatest hits albums eclipsed The Beach Boys' studio albums in the seventies. However, releases on their new Brother label showed a change of direction with the rock-orientated *Surf's Up* (1971) and *Holland* (1973), boasting environmental and political themes on tracks such as "Student Demonstration Time."

Sandwiched between these two was *Carl and the Passions/So Tough*, which saw Johnston depart (until 1978). Bassist **Blondie Chaplin** and drummer **Ricky Fataar**—Dennis had put his hand through a window— were recruited to a lineup that still, mostly, lacked

year-by-year ▪ Vocals ▪ Guitar ▪ Bass ▪ Drums ▪ Keyboards

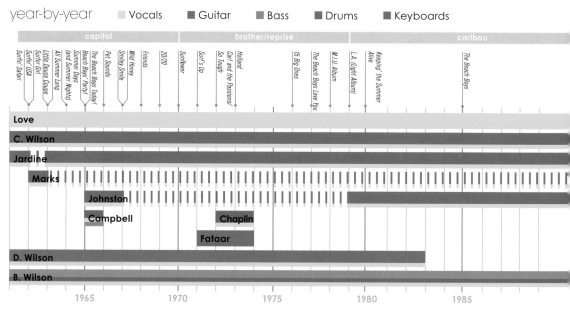

3M	1.9M	1.8M	1M
Best of the Beach Boys (1966)	*Pet Sounds* (1966)	*Endless Summer* (1974)	*20 Golden Greats* (1976)

B

Bruce Johnston
b. June 17, 1944

Blondie Chaplin
b. July 7, 1951

Ricky Fataar
b. September 5, 1952

Glen Campbell
b. April 22, 1936

Brian Wilson. Such was their overhaul at the time that Chaplin took lead vocals on *Holland*'s standout, "Sail on Sailor." The surfing look was also over: the bearded Beach Boys looked more like the Grateful Dead or The Band. (In 1979, Bruce Johnston and a trio of session singers provided the Beach Boys sound on Pink Floyd's *The Wall*. The group had been up for it but declined when they learned they had to sing about worms.)

The first signs of a Beach Boys dissolution came in 1981 when Carl Wilson left (albeit for eighteen months) and brother Brian was fired (although he returned in 1989). Then Dennis—the only actual surfer—drowned while swimming off the Californian coast in 1983.

With Brian Wilson busy on his debut solo album, the Beach Boys avoided the singles charts during the bulk of the eighties until they teamed up with rap act The Fat Boys on "Wipe Out." This was followed by "Kokomo," featured in the movie *Cocktail,* which became their first U.S. No. 1 in twenty-two years.

Legal disputes involving song copyrights and former band manager Stephen Love, brother of Mike,

ran well into the nineties. The group continued to use Terry Melcher as producer on the unsuccessful 1992 *Summer in Paradise,* an album which also saw Jardine suspended from the group.

Carl remained the only Wilson to perform with the band—alongside Love and Johnston—until he died of cancer in 1998, while Brian and Jardine developed their own new groups. The new millennium saw the release of yet more compilations alongside Brian's 2004 version of the long lost album *Smile* (started and abandoned in 1967). While Carl, Dennis, and Love all issued solo albums with little commercial success, Brian's track record as a solo artist spans over twenty years and includes nine U.S. and U.K. chart albums.

In 2006, on the fortieth anniversary of *Pet Sounds*, the surviving Beach Boys—Brian Wilson, Love, Jardine, Johnston, and Marks—assembled for a celebration at Capitol Records in LA. In 2011, they celebrated their fiftieth anniversary with *The Smile Sessions*, a collection of the original recordings made forty-four years previously, and tour and recording plans. **BS**

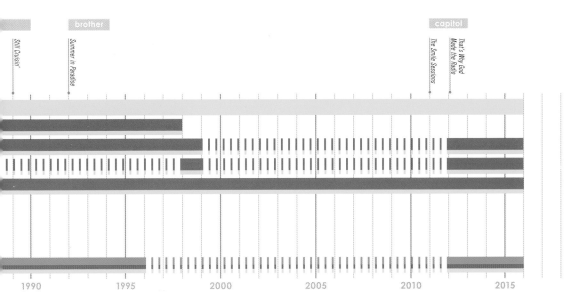

Surfin' Safari (1962)

All Summer Long (1964)

Pet Sounds (1966)

Sunflower (1970)

Surf's Up (1971)

Holland (1973)

Love You (1977)

Keepin' the Summer Alive (1980)

Summer in Paradise (1992)

The Smile Sessions (2011)

Clockwise from top left: **Mike Love, Brian Wilson, Carl Wilson, David Marks,** and **Dennis Wilson**—The Beach Boys circa 1962.

The Beach Boys perform "Wendy" on *The Ed Sullivan Show* in New York in 1964.

Left to right: **Bruce Johnston, Al Jardine, Dennis Wilson, Carl Wilson,** and **Love** during a tour of the U.K. in 1966.

The Beach Boys did a passable imitation of The Band or The Grateful Dead in the seventies: **Ricky Fataar, Blondie Chaplin, Jardine, Love,** and **Carl Wilson.**

Carl Wilson performs onstage in Amsterdam, the Netherlands, in 1971.

Love, Jardine, Dennis Wilson, and Carl Wilson in 1973.

Dennis Wilson in the studio in 1977.

Jardine, Ed Carter, Love, and Carl Wilson at Wembley Arena, London, in 1980.

Love and Johnston appear with John Stamos in the U.S. sitcom Full House in May 1992.

Brian Wilson performs Smile in 2005, six years before The Beach Boys' version finally saw the light.

the beatles 1960–1970

John Lennon
b. October 9, 1940
d. December 8, 1980

Paul McCartney
b. June 18, 1942

George Harrison
b. February 25, 1943
d. November 29, 2001

Ringo Starr
b. July 7, 1940

Pete Best
b. November 24, 1941

Stuart Sutcliffe
b. June 23, 1940
d. April 10, 1962

"When it comes down to pop," mused Nirvana's Dave Grohl in 1991, "there's only one word—the 'B' word. The Beatles." Added bassist Krist Novoselic: "They started it, they did it best, they ended it."

"They" started as teenagers in The Quarry Men Skiffle Group, led by **John Lennon** and named after a line from his Quarry Bank High School song. **Paul McCartney** joined in 1957; McCartney's younger friend **George Harrison** joined in 1958, and by 1960 they were a five-piece rock 'n' roll group called The Silver Beetles, with **Pete Best** on drums and Lennon's best friend **Stuart Sutcliffe** on bass.

Marathon sets in the clubs of Hamburg morphed the quintet—now The Beatles—into no-frills rockers loved by the German art-school crowd. Back in their home town Liverpool (minus Sutcliffe, who died in Hamburg), a residency at The Cavern club attracted record store owner Brian Epstein. He offered to manage them and, in 1962, secured a contract with Parlophone (EMI's comedy subsidiary). Shortly afterwards, Best was out and **Ringo Starr** was in.

Debut single "Love Me Do" made No. 17 in the U.K. and "Please Please Me" made No. 2. The *Please Please Me* album (1963), recorded in one ten-hour session and closing with Lennon's raw reading of "Twist and Shout," shot to the top. *With The Beatles* (1963) followed it, giving the band fifty-one straight weeks atop the U.K. albums chart. Cue Beatlemania.

The Beatles' career was a series of fresh peaks topped with breathless regularity. "I Want To Hold Your Hand" became their first U.S. No. 1 on February 1, 1964. Eight days later, an unprecedented 73 million viewers watched their Stateside debut on *The Ed Sullivan Show*. By April 4, they held four out of the Top Five on the *Billboard* Hot 100. The same year, their big-screen debut *A Hard Day's Night*—funny, inventive, its soundtrack penned solely by Lennon and McCartney—rewrote the book for pop movies. Follow-up movie *Help!* (1965) boasted the Dylan-esque "You've Got to Hide Your Love Away," the thrilling title tune, and McCartney's much-covered "Yesterday."

Seeking out new horizons, The Beatles discovered marijuana (in 1964, courtesy of Bob Dylan) and LSD, and embraced world music via George Harrison's burgeoning love of Indian music. *Rubber Soul* (1965) and *Revolver* (1966) brimmed over with invention and songcraft; *Revolver* in particular saw them test the studio's capabilities—witness the psychedelic "Tomorrow Never Knows." The astonishing double A-side "Strawberry Fields Forever"/"Penny Lane"

year-by-year   ■ Vocals   ■ Guitar   ■ Bass   ■ Drums   ■ Keyboards

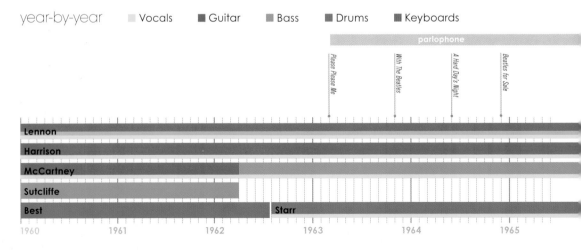

28.5M	32M	13.5M	30.3M
Abbey Road (1969)	Sgt. Pepper's Lonely Hearts Club Band (1967)	Beatles 1967–70 (1973)	1 (2000)

B

followed in 1967 (the songs, later included on the U.S. release of *Magical Mystery Tour*, were kept off the No. 1 spot in the U.K. by Engelbert Humperdinck).

The group's snowballing innovations peaked with *Sgt. Pepper's Lonely Hearts Club Band* (1967), iconic in every way, from its Peter Blake-inspired sleeve to the kaleidoscopic range of music within—notably the dreamlike "Lucy in the Sky with Diamonds" and epic closer "A Day in the Life." Lennon's "All You Need Is Love" captured the zeitgeist of the Summer of Love.

Following Epstein's untimely death in mid-1967, McCartney strove to maintain momentum with the (poorly received) TV movie *Magical Mystery Tour* (1967)—the accompanying double E.P. was much better. Under Harrison's influence, they sought inspiration from Indian guru Maharishi Mahesh Yogi, studying with him in Rishikesh, where they wrote a host of new songs. The resulting double album, *The Beatles* (1968; a.k.a. "The White Album") was sprawling and contained more instant classics ("Back in the U.S.S.R.," "Dear Prudence," "Blackbird," "While My Guitar Gently Weeps"). The same year they released the seven-minute-plus "Hey Jude" ("Revolution" was its rousing B-side). The psychedelic cartoon *Yellow Submarine* (1968) involved precious little new Beatles music, though Lennon's raucous "Hey Bulldog" and Harrison's acid epic "It's All Too Much" impressed.

A bored Starr had quit during "The White Album." A disillusioned Harrison did the same during the depressing sessions for *Let it Be* (1970)—which nonetheless yielded the rousing rocker "Get Back," Lennon's pretty "Across the Universe," and the reflective title track. Recorded after that album, but released before it, *Abbey Road* (1969) was a superior swansong, boasting Lennon's "Come Together," two of Harrison's best songs ("Here Comes the Sun" and the divine "Something"), and a scintillating side two medley masterminded by McCartney.

With the decade they had encapsulated now behind them, The Beatles broke up in a miasma of bad blood. The legend lives on, though, reinvigorated by projects such as 1995's *Anthology* series—for which the "Threatles" reconvened, adding music to two Lennon demos: "Free as a Bird" (U.K. No. 2/U.S. No. 6) and "Real Love" (U.K. No. 4/U.S. No. 11). The singles compilation *1* (2000) remains the fastest-selling album ever (3.6 million copies sold on its first day). And, within a year of their back catalog appearing on iTunes in November 2010, more than ten million tracks, and around 1.8 million albums, had been downloaded. **RD**

■ Aerophones

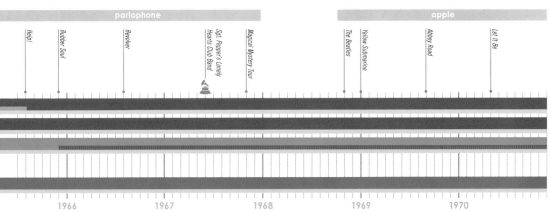

the beatles 53

Please Please Me
(1963)

With The Beatles
(1963)

A Hard Day's Night
(1964)

Help! (1965)

Rubber Soul (1965)

Revolver (1966)

**Sgt. Pepper's
Lonely Hearts
Club Band** (1967)

The Beatles (1968)

Abbey Road
(1969)

Let It Be (1970)

Beatlemania is born. **Paul McCartney**, **George Harrison**, **Ringo Starr**, and **John Lennon** performing at the London Palladium in front of 2,000 screaming fans in October 1963.

Performing together in 1963—**George**, **Paul**, **John**, with **Ringo** in the background.

The Beatles outside Buckingham Palace, after receiving their MBEs from the Queen.

Harrison during the filming of 1964's *A Hard Day's Night*.

Starr strikes a Winston Churchill-style pose outside 10 Downing Street, London, in 1965.

Their last live public concert, on the rooftop of Apple, London, 1969.

McCartney, **Harrison**, **Starr**, and **Lennon** at Abbey Road studios in April 1966.

Harrison, **Starr**, **McCartney**, and **Lennon** before the global TV broadcast of *Our World*.

The Beatles and their partners in Rishikesh, 1968. Left to right from **Starr**: Maureen Starkey, Jane Asher, **McCartney**, Maharishi Mahesh Yogi, **Harrison**, Pattie Boyd, Cynthia Lennon, and **Lennon**, who is talking to Mike Love of The Beach Boys.

Lennon toward the end of the band's extraordinary career.

Bee Gees 1st
(1967)

Horizontal
(1968)

Main Course
(1975)

**Children of the
World** (1976)

**Saturday Night
Fever** (1977)

**Sgt. Pepper's
Lonely Hearts Club
Band** (1978)

**Spirits Having
Flown** (1979)

Staying Alive
(1983)

One (1989)

Still Waters (1997)

Left to right **Barry Gibb, Colin Petersen, Robin Gibb, Maurice Gibb,** and **Vince Melouney:** the less celebrated five-man incarnation of the Bee Gees.

The five-man lineup outside a TV studio in Hamburg, Germany, in 1968.

In New York's Central Park in 1975, just weeks before "Jive Talkin'."

On New York City's Long Island Expressway—and on the road to superstardom.

Barry Gibb in 1977—one of the era's most successful songwriters.

Posing with Peter Frampton (right) in costumes for the ill-conceived and ill-fated 1978 movie version of The Beatles' *Sgt. Pepper's Lonely Hearts Club Band.*

At a UNICEF charity show at the United Nations General Assembly, New York, in 1979.

Robin in 1983, the year of the *Saturday Night Fever* sequel *Staying Alive.*

Maurice, **Robin** and **Barry** relax before a tour in March 1989.

Back on top, collecting International Artist trophies at the American Music Awards in 1997.

chuck berry 1955–present

Chuck Berry
b. October 18, 1926

Johnnie Johnson
b. July 8, 1924
d. April 13, 2005

Willie Dixon
b. July 1, 1915
d. January 29, 1992

Fred Below
b. September 16, 1926
d. August 14, 1988

Lafayette Leake
b. June 1, 1919
d. August 14, 1990

Otis Spann
b. March 21, 1930
d. April 24, 1970

One of the most influential figures from the early days of rock 'n' roll, **Chuck Berry** produced an endless succession of period classics: driving electric rhythm and blues combined with pioneering lyrics that neatly summed up teenage life in fifties America.

Charles Edward Anderson "Chuck" Berry arrived on the music scene relatively late in life. Although he had taught himself a few chords as a high school student, he did not take music seriously until his mid-twenties. Berry's principal influence had been bluesman T-Bone Walker, who was not only a guitarist of rare finesse but also something of a showman.

Moving to Chicago, the hub of the electric blues scene, Berry served his apprenticeship with the **Johnnie Johnson** Trio—their work together continuing until Johnnie's death in 2005. (He also worked with influential blues musician **Willie Dixon**, drummer **Fred Below,** and pianists **Otis Spann** and **Lafayette Leake**.)

A chance meeting with bluesman Muddy Waters put him in contact with Leonard Chess, owner of the famous blues label, Chess Records. Having initially followed a straight blues path, Chess was particularly impressed with Berry's own up-tempo material. A first single at the end of 1955, "Maybellene," was Berry's take on an old country song, "Ida Red." It sold more than a million copies and became the first R&B record to make a big impact with white audiences.

Between 1956 and 1959, Berry enjoyed a succession of million-selling hits, including "Roll Over Beethoven," "Rock and Roll Music," "Sweet Little Sixteen," "Memphis, Tennessee," and "Johnny B. Goode." These tunes would become part of the standard repertoire for the first generation of white beat groups, such as The Beatles and The Rolling Stones: indeed, the latter's Keith Richards would use Berry's guitar playing as a template—an economic style that combined elements of rhythm and lead.

Berry was also vital in the evolution of the pop lyric. His songs were full-blooded mini-soaps at a time when most popular songs of the time skirted around "real" issues. In fact, Berry put the case for the American teenage lifestyle of the fifties better than just about anyone—mildly ironic, given that he was in his thirties when he wrote his classic hits.

By 1959, Berry was one of the most popular figures on the American music scene. However, his career crashed to a halt in December 1959 when he was arrested after an allegation that he had slept with a fourteen-year-old waitress and transported her across state lines. After a series of trials and appeals, in which

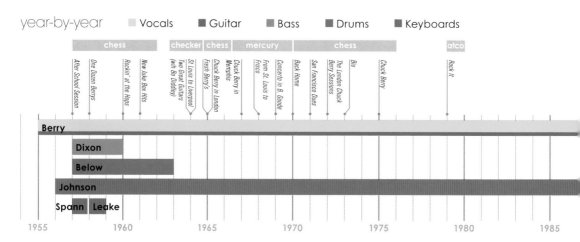

year-by-year　■ Vocals　■ Guitar　■ Bass　■ Drums　■ Keyboards

| 1M | 250,000 | 250,000 | 250,000 |
| Chuck Berry on Stage (1963) | Chuck Berry's Greatest Hits (1964) | The London Chuck Berry Sessions (1972) | Bio (1973) |

B

his claims of a racially prejudiced jury were aired and upheld, Berry served eighteen months in prison.

Following his release in October 1963, Berry tried to rebuild his career. His cause was aided by the "British Invasion" bands (both The Beatles and The Rolling Stones covered his songs) and by new young American groups, such as The Beach Boys, who acknowledged him as an important influence.

He continued to have hits with "Nadine," "No Particular Place to Go," and "You Never Can Tell"—the latter finding a new audience in the nineties following its memorable use in Quentin Tarantino's movie *Pulp Fiction*. In spite of Berry's controversial fall from grace, he still fared better during the sixties than most others from rock 'n' roll's first wave.

He remained a major concert draw throughout the decade, the appealing raw edge of his music being captured in 1967's *Live at the Fillmore Auditorium*, where he was backed by an early incarnation of The Steve Miller Band. In this instance, he was fortunate to have such a group at his disposal. Berry, always conscious of the business side of his work, rarely employed musicians of his own, and was often found playing with unrehearsed local pickup bands of varying (and often sub-standard) quality.

Returning to the Chess label in 1972, having spent most of the sixties with Mercury, Berry enjoyed his biggest and most unexpected chart success. The novelty singalong ditty "My Ding-a-ling" was recorded live in Coventry, England (where his backing group were members of the Average White Band) and this became his first single to top the charts—a feat it achieved on both sides of the Atlantic. The song, based on a series of phallic *double entendres* that, even then, anyone over the age of twelve would have found embarrassing, was about as far away from classic Chuck Berry as anyone could imagine.

Berry has produced no new material of any great worth since the sixties, but even now—well past the age of eighty—he continues to perform in concert. In spite of his indisputable importance in the history and development of rock music, Berry himself seems to have been ambivalent toward such accolades, viewing himself more as a working entertainer than one of *the* great "artists" of the post-war era—a case that many would argue in his favor. Primarily a singles artist, Berry rarely produced memorable studio albums; the casual listener is certainly better served by the many chart compilations that cover the first decade of his recording career. **TB**

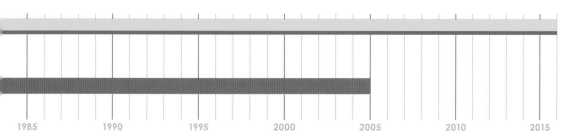

the black crowes 1989–present

Chris Robinson
b. December 20, 1966

Rich Robinson
b. May 24, 1969

Steve Gorman
b. August 17, 1965

Johnny Colt
b. May 1, 1966

Jeff Cease
b. June 24, 1967

Ed Harsch
b. May 27, 1967

Marc Ford
b. April 13, 1966

Sven Pipien
b. May 30, 1967

Like The Kinks two decades before them, The Black Crowes have thrived despite—or possibly because of—a volatile fraternal relationship at the group's core. Two-and-a-half years separate singer **Chris Robinson** and guitarist **Rich Robinson**, but their close bond and songwriting chemistry have led to a series of good-time sleazy rock records and an enviable knack for bouncing back.

Emerging in Atlanta, Georgia, in 1989 from the remains of earlier band Mr. Crowe's Garden, The Black Crowes wasted little time getting their act together. Their signature style—more or less unchanged over twenty years in the business—was in place from the start, aping a louche blues-rock preserved in aspic in the early seventies. Obvious touchstones were *Exile on Main St*-era Rolling Stones, The Allman Brothers, and The Faces. The Black Crowes dressed to match, as if an entire generation of musical and sartorial fashion changes simply didn't happen. For all the throwbacks, in an age of hair metal and production excess the Crowes' approach to rock was almost radical.

As they shook off their old identity, The Black Crowes were signed to Def American by George Drakoulias. With Drakoulias also in the production seat, and joined by guitarist **Jeff Cease**, bassist **Johnny Colt**, and drummer **Steve Gorman**, the brothers wrote all of their debut album *Shake Your Money Maker* (1990), save the cover of Otis Redding's "Hard to Handle." The album was a commercial success—making the *Billboard* Top Five and picking up Top Thirty hits with "Hard to Handle" and "She Talks to Angels"—and enjoyed a fair ride from the critics, but they would soon perfect their whisky-soaked swagger.

The Southern Harmony and Musical Companion (1992) would come to be seen as their masterpiece. Cease had been fired, to be replaced by guitarist **Marc Ford**, but the recalibrated Crowes sounded meatier, funkier, and, crucially, equipped with better songs. Drakoulias was again at the controls and the album—brimming with classics like "Remedy," "Hotel Illness," and "Thorn In My Pride"—strode to the top of the *Billboard* chart and to No. 2 in the U.K.

Amorica (1994) endured a more fraught birth: an entire album, provisionally titled *Tall*, was scrapped before the group settled on a harder but more varied sound. Remembered by many for its pubic hair cover, *Amorica* made the U.K. Top Ten and narrowly missed the same back home. Its promotion saw the

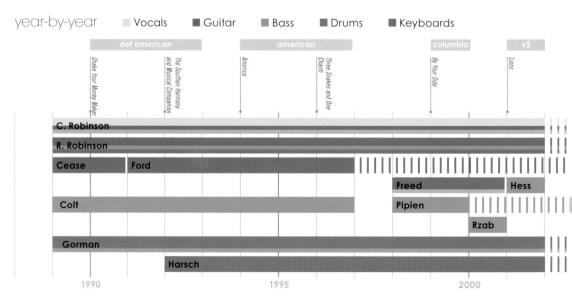

year-by-year ▢ Vocals ■ Guitar ▢ Bass ■ Drums ■ Keyboards

def american · american · columbia · v2

Shake Your Money Maker · *The Southern Harmony and Musical Companion* · *Amorica* · *Three Snakes and One Charm* · *By Your Side* · *Lions*

C. Robinson
R. Robinson
Cease — Ford
Freed — Hess
Colt
Pipien
Rzab
Gorman
Harsch

1990 · 1995 · 2000

6.9M	2.8M	1M	1M
Shake Your Money Maker (1990)	*The Southern Harmony and Musical Companion* (1992)	*Amorica* (1994)	*Live at the Greek* (2000)

Adam MacDougall *b.* August 1974

Luther Dickinson *b.* January 18, 1973

Audley Freed *b.* Unknown

Greg Rzab *b.* 1959

Andy Hess *b.* December 4, 1966

Bill Dobrow *b.* Unknown

Paul Stacey *b.* Unknown

Rob Clores *b.* Unknown

Crowes supporting the Grateful Dead in the U.S., Chris Robinson's insistence on performing barefoot on a rug fitting in nicely with their hippie-rock elders.

Three Snakes and One Charm (1996) saw the Crowes' rougher surfaces dulled and prefaced upheaval: Ford was fired and long-term bassist Colt left. Another album—*Band*—was shelved before the Crowes got back to bluesy basics with *By Your Side* (1999), an effort received as a return to core rock-soul values but only a vague success in commercial terms.

To the delight of fans, the Crowes mounted a two-night engagement in L.A. with Led Zeppelin's Jimmy Page. The resulting cocktail of Zep and blues classics was issued as 2000's *Live at the Greek*. Meanwhile, Chris Robinson carved an unexpected niche in the celebrity spotlight with his marriage to Hollywood star Kate Hudson. The trappings of fame did not prevent one more album—the adventurous *Lions* (2001)—but the group soon bowed to the inevitable with that most modern of splits, the "hiatus."

As it turned out, they had every intention of coming right back—in 2005—once again with the hardy kernel of the Robinson brothers and drummer Gorman, along with bassist **Sven Pipien** and the returning Ford. *Warpaint* (2008), now with keyboard player **Adam MacDougall** and versatile guitarist **Luther Dickinson** on board, enjoyed an unusual publicity boost when *Maxim* magazine gave it a sniffy review, apparently without even hearing it. The consequent uproar saw it become the Crowes' first U.S. Top Ten album since *The Southern Harmony*—but credit is also due to the songs, which were as rich as anything the band had released since that chart-topper.

A looser feel permeated the double album *Before the Frost... Until the Freeze* (2009), recorded in front of an audience as the group continued to explore their abilities. They experimented with release tactics, too, pushing *Before the Frost...* into stores and offering its partner *Until the Freeze* as an online download, but forward motion was then put on hold. *Croweology* (2010) was a mainly acoustic root around the back catalog—an opportunity to show how far the Crowes had come from enthusiastic revivalists to established keepers of the loon-panted, blues-rock flame. As they prepared for another break, Chris Robinson told fans: "With a smile so wide you can count my teeth, and with a heart so full of love that it is spilling over the rim, I offer a humble and simple thank you." **MJH**

■ Aerophones ■ Other percussion ■ Strings

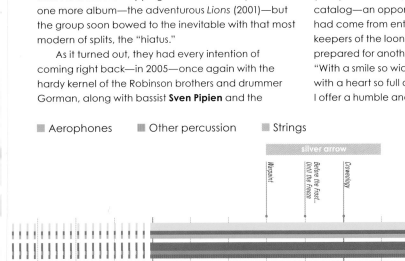

silver arrow

Warpaint

Before the Frost... Until the Freeze

Croweology

Dickinson

Stacey

Dobrow Clores

MacDougall

2005   2010   2015

the black crowes 65

Black Sabbath
(1970)

Paranoid (1970)

Master of Reality
(1971)

**Sabbath Bloody
Sabbath** (1973)

Sabotage (1975)

Heaven and Hell
(1980)

Mob Rules (1981)

Born Again (1983)

Headless Cross
(1989)

Dehumanizer
(1992)

Ozzy Osbourne in 1969, the year Black Sabbath made their debut.

Bill Ward, **Osbourne** (with back to camera), **Geezer Butler**, and **Tony Iommi** conjure an early masterpiece.

Doubtless fueled by "Sweet Leaf," **Butler**, **Iommi**, and **Osbourne** storm Amsterdam in 1971.

Flower power: **Ward** at London's Alexandra Palace in 1973.

Nearing the end of a golden era that shaped an entire genre, **Butler**, **Iommi**, **Osbourne**, and **Ward** rock Copenhagen in October 1975.

Rockin' but sadly far from stylish, **Dio** and **Iommi** at London's Hammersmith Odeon in 1981.

With new singer **Ronnie James Dio** in Paris, where they recorded part of *Heaven and Hell*.

Butler, singer **Ian Gillan**, and **Iommi** with part of 1983's infamous "Stonehenge" stage set.

Mob Rules drummer **Vinnie Appice, Dio,** and **Iommi** reunite in '92.

Iommi—the only member to appear on every album—live in 1989.

The *Dehumanizer* lineup that would become Heaven & Hell.

Bon Jovi (1984)

7800° Fahrenheit (1985)

Slippery When Wet (1986)

New Jersey (1988)

Keep the Faith (1992)

These Days (1995)

Crush (2000)

Bounce (2002)

Lost Highway (2007)

The Circle (2009)

Left to right: **David Bryan**, **Alec John Such**, **Jon Bon Jovi**, **Tico Torres**, and **Richie Sambora** in their poodle-permed glory.

On tour in 1985 for the band's sophomore album *7800° Fahrenheit*.

Tempting fate in Germany as *Slippery…* shoots up the charts.

Rocking Rotterdam near the start of the New Jersey Syndicate Tour in November 1987.

Sambora shows California's Oakland Arena how it's done in 1993.

Bon Jovi poses in Germany, where Crush topped the chart.

Sambora and Bon Jovi, a musical relationship that sustained the band for nearly thirty multi-platinum, stadium-packing years.

Sambora, Bryan, and Bon Jovi at the 2007 Bambi Awards.

Providing halftime entertainment at a Thanksgiving Day football game at Ford Field in Detroit, November 2002.

Still annoyingly handsome at forty-eight, Bon Jovi plays San José.

boston 1976–present

Tom Scholz
b. March 10, 1947

Brad Delp
b. June 12, 1951
d. March 9, 2007

Barry Goudreau
b. November 29, 1951

Fran Sheehan
b. March 26, 1949

Sib Hashian
b. August 17, 1949

Jim Masdea
b. Unknown

David Sikes
b. April 25, 1975

Doug Huffman
b. November 23, 1953

Boston exploded onto the hard rock scene with a self-titled album that remained the highest-selling debut in music history until the advent of Whitney Houston's in 1986. The group pioneered a clean metal sound of layered guitars that was to prove highly influential—a legacy of **Tom Scholz**'s crystalline production and his technical expertise.

The group were formed in Boston, Massachusetts, in 1976 as a vehicle for the songs of Scholz (guitars, keyboards); an accomplished engineer, he had worked on them in his home studio. **Brad Delp** (guitars and lead vocals) and **Barry Goudreau** (guitars) had played with him in groups around the city in the past. **Fran Sheehan** (bass) and **Sib Hashian** (drums) were brought in to bolster the recording and make up a touring band. Their monicker echoed a vogue for places as band names, hence the similarly critically reviled America, Chicago, Kansas, and, later, Asia.

Boston (1976) hit No. 3 on the *Billboard* album chart and went on to sell over seventeen million in the U.S. alone, a phenomenal achievement. It also reached No. 11 in the United Kingdom. The record was packed with memorable songs, not least the opening "More Than a Feeling," which became a No.

5 U.S. hit and enduring classic."Peace of Mind," "Rock & Roll Band," and "Foreplay/Long Time" kept up the tremendously high standard—one that the group would find almost impossible to surpass.

Don't Look Back (1978) stuck with a winning sonic formula, although lyrically it was more introspective, the pressures of sudden fame biting deep. The title track was another hit (U.S. No. 4) and the album raced to No. 1. Songs such as the epic "A Man I'll Never Be," "Don't Be Afraid," and the more up-tempo "Party" were worthy additions to the Boston repertoire. However, the perfectionist Scholz felt the record company had rushed out the album. "The second side is only fifteen minutes long," he complained to writer Craig Rosen. "I would have liked another six months to work on a fifth song on that side."

That was only one of many disagreements. Amid lawsuits and counter-suits, the record company demanded damages for non-delivery of material, while Scholz demanded withheld royalties. It was a wearying business but Scholz—who claimed, credibly, that his perfectionism was a strong contributory factor in Boston's incredible success—eventually emerged the winner and Boston moved to the MCA label.

year-by-year ☐ Vocals ■ Guitar ■ Bass ■ Drums ■ Keyboards

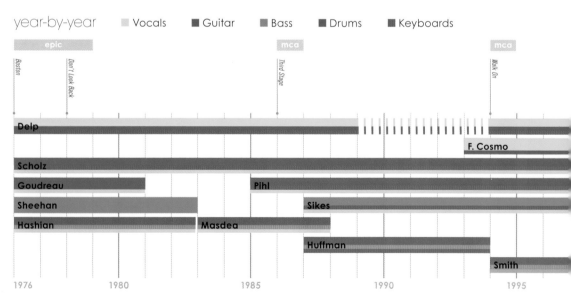

27.8M	11.3M	8.4M	3.5M
Boston (1976)	*Don't Look Back* (1978)	*Third Stage* (1986)	*Greatest Hits* (1997)

Fran Cosmo
b. September 3,

Curly Smith
b. January 31, 1952

Anthony Cosmo
b. Unknown

Michael Sweet
b. July 4, 1963

Gary Pihl
b. November 21, 1950

Kimberley Dahme
b. April 22

Jeff Neal
b. Unknown

Tommy DeCarlo
b. April 23, 1965

Amid a consequent shortfall in live activity (Scholz preferred studio work anyway), Goudreau left in 1981, while Sheehan and Hashian departed in 1983. The latter was replaced by drummer **Jim Masdea**, who had played on many of the original tracks on the first album, with Scholz playing bass. Ex-Sammy Hagar sidekick **Gary Pihl** (guitars, keyboards) joined in 1985.

There was an eight-year gap until *Third Stage* (1986), but it nevertheless became their second U.S. chart-topper. The opening "Amanda" hit No. 1 too, while other fine songs included "We're Ready," "Cool the Engines," and "I Think I Like It." Although the writing did not show quite the development that might have been expected after such a hiatus, Scholz told Craig Rosen that he "did feel much better about the sound quality on *Third Stage*, compared to the first two albums. I felt that I finally learned how to make a record sound the way I wanted it to."

David Sikes (bass) and **Doug Huffman** (drums) joined in 1987, while Delp left in 1989 to join Goudreau in RTZ. No one could accuse Boston of rushing things—it was *another* eight years before *Walk On* (1994) emerged. This time, the album "only" reached No. 7 in the U.S., but went platinum in just three months. "I

Need Your Love" was a minor hit. By that time, **Curly Smith** (drums) and **Fran Cosmo** (vocals) were on board and Delp returned to take part in the tour that followed. A 1997 hits set kept the fires simmering.

Naturally, eight years elapsed before *Corporate America* (2002), with **Anthony Cosmo** (guitar, vocals) and **Kimberley Dahme** (bass). The album reached No. 42 in the U.S. On drums, Anthony Citrinite and Tom Hambridge joined briefly around that time: **Jeff Neal** stayed longer and is still in the lineup (though Smith has deputized for him on tour). Both Cosmos left after a 2004 tour, and tragedy struck when Brad Delp committed suicide in 2007. The group played a benefit show in his honor, uniting all surviving members.

Michael Sweet (vocals, guitar) and **Tommy DeCarlo** (vocals, keyboards) joined, although Sweet left to focus on Christian metal band, Stryper. And a new album? "Progressing at an agonizingly slow rate," Scholz admitted in 2010, "like that would be news— but it is progressing. While I wouldn't want to give away too much about the album, it will contain both the very recognizable Boston sound plus some surprises I think everyone will appreciate—as long as you like big band swing and rap... just kidding!" **MiH**

■ Aerophones   ■ Other percussion

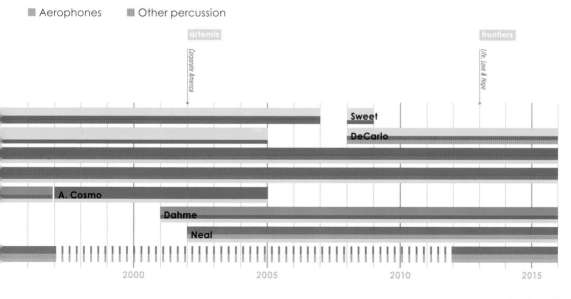

david bowie 1964–present

David Bowie
b. January 8, 1947

Mick Ronson
b. May 26, 1946
d. April 29, 1993

**"Woody"
Woodmansey**
b. ca. 1951

Trevor Bolder
b. June 9, 1950
d. May 21, 2013

Carlos Alomar
b. January 9, 1951

Mike Garson
b. July 29, 1945

Ziggy played guitar... and so did David Jones—but, early efforts at mime aside, Bowie was never a one-man act. However, singles with the King Bees, Lower Third, and Manish Boys flopped—despite the latter's "I Pity the Fool" (1965) featuring soon-to-be star Jimmy Page. A name change to the evocative "**Bowie**" did little to improve his fortunes, though he scored a fluke hit with 1969's "Space Oddity" (featuring future Yes star Rick Wakeman, who returned on *Hunky Dory*). Unbowed, Bowie recruited producer Tony Visconti, guitarist **Mick Ronson**, bassist **Trevor Bolder** (later of Uriah Heep), and drummer **"Woody" Woodmansey**.

The Man Who Sold the World and *Hunky Dory*, coupled with provocative interviews, brought Bowie enviable press coverage but negligible sales. That ended with *The Rise and Fall of Ziggy Stardust and the Spiders from Mars*, the first of a sequence of albums from 1972 to 1977 that—for variety, innovation, and influence—is eclipsed only by The Beatles. Unleashed at a now unthinkable rate, *Aladdin Sane*, *Diamond Dogs*, *Young Americans*, *Station to Station*, and an extraordinary 1977 quartet—*Low*, "*Heroes*," and Iggy

Pop's *The Idiot* and *Lust for Life* (both as much Bowie's work as Iggy's)—proved influential for generations. Even the throwaway *Pin Ups* hit the U.K. No. 1, while *David Live* went Top Ten on both sides of the Atlantic.

An array of musicians gave life to his music. After the dismissal of the band with whom Bowie had found fame, Ronson was replaced by **Earl Slick**, then **Carlos Alomar**, who co-wrote the star's first U.S. chart-topper, "Fame." (Alomar had been in the Harlem Apollo's house band. His replacement in that lineup was Nile Rodgers.) "Fame" was written with John Lennon, who played on it and a cover of "Across the Universe" on *Young Americans* (which also starred Luther Vandross).

Diamond Dogs featured bassist Herbie Flowers, who had played on "Space Oddity" and Lou Reed's Bowie-produced "Walk on the Wild Side," while *Aladdin Sane* and *Young Americans* showcased the piano of **Mike Garson**. The latter stayed until usurped on *Station to Station* (1976) by Springsteen keyboardist Roy Bittan and on tour by Yes man Tony Kaye.

The "Berlin trilogy"—*Low*, "*Heroes*," and *Lodger*—ushered in new musical foils. **Brian Eno** influenced their

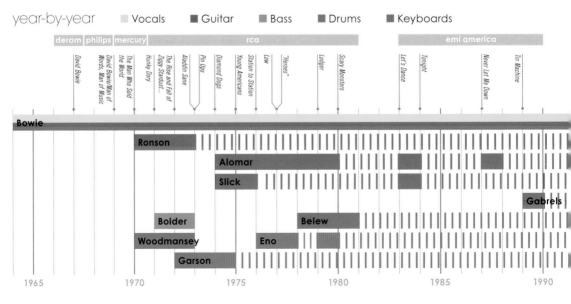

year-by-year ▢ Vocals ■ Guitar ■ Bass ■ Drums ■ Keyboards

7.5M	**9.5M**	**2.5M**	**3.5M**
The Rise and Fall of Ziggy Stardust... (1972)	*Let's Dance* (1983)	*Tonight* (1984)	*Best of Bowie* (2002)

B

Earl Slick
b. October 1, 1952

Brian Eno
b. May 15, 1948

Adrian Belew
b. December 23, 1949

Reeves Gabrels
b. June 4, 1956

Gail Ann Dorsey
b. November 20, 1962

experimentation, but producer Visconti was equally important, creating unique sounds such as the treated drums on *Low* and *The Idiot*. King Crimson's Robert Fripp played guitar on *"Heroes"* and Frank Zappa guitarist **Adrian Belew** featured on *Lodger* and 1978's live *Stage* (before joining Crimson in 1981). Meanwhile, Iggy's *Lust for Life* featured bassist and drummer Hunt and Tony Sales, later Tin Machine's rhythm section.

Scary Monsters—featuring Fripp, Bittan, and Pete Townshend—bookended Bowie's "classic" period. He replaced rock with acting for two years but created the splendid "Under Pressure" with Queen and "Cat People" with pioneering producer Giorgio Moroder.

By 1982, Bowie had no record deal (he had fled RCA, the label he shared with another star born on January 8: Elvis Presley) and a modest profile in the U.S. (where he last troubled the Top Ten with *Station to Station*). Accordingly, his brief to new producer Nile Rodgers (latterly of Chic) was simple: "Make hits." Blessed with a key Bowie discovery—the then-unknown guitarist Stevie Ray Vaughan—*Let's Dance* duly became his greatest commercial success.

The ensuing years saw the patchy *Tonight* and *Never Let Me Down*, the ill-fated Tin Machine, a hits-recycling 1990 tour (featuring Belew), and a reunion with Rodgers and Ronson for *Black Tie White Noise*. The latter topped the U.K. chart but failed to revive his again waning U.S. fortunes. Blissfully unconcerned, Bowie produced the beautifully uncommercial *The Buddha of Suburbia*, featuring Lenny Kravitz, and the often splendid Eno and Garson reunion, *1. Outside*.

Bowie rounded off the nineties with the dancey *Earthling* and dour *Hours...* Associates included guitarist **Reeves Gabrels**, who first appeared with him in 1988 before graduating to Tin Machine, and bassist **Gail Ann Dorsey**, a Tears for Fears alumnus. Bowie's fortunes were revived by a reunion with Visconti—exiled after *Scary Monsters*—for *Heathen* (featuring Townshend and Dave Grohl) and *Reality* (with Garson, latterly a Smashing Pumpkin). A 2003–2004 tour, cut short by ill health, preceded a lengthy sabbatical, broken only by cameos with Arcade Fire and David Gilmour. However, he made a triumphant return in 2013 with the Visconti-produced *The Next Day*. **BM**

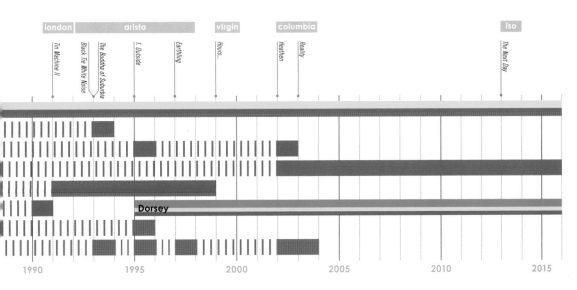

london   arista   virgin   columbia   iso

Tin Machine II   *Black Tie White Noise*   *The Buddha of Suburbia*   *I. Outside*   *Earthling*   *Hours...*   *Heathen*   *Reality*   *The Next Day*

Dorsey

1990   1995   2000   2005   2010   2015

The Man Who Sold the World (1970)

Hunky Dory (1971)

The Rise and Fall of Ziggy Stardust... (1972)

Aladdin Sane (1973)

Diamond Dogs (1974)

Low (1977)

Scary Monsters (1980)

Let's Dance (1983)

Earthling (1997)

Heathen (2002)

The fresh-faced "Space Oddity" star, shortly before donning a dress.

Entertaining DJ Rodney Bingenheimer's party guests in L.A. in 1971.

Straight from the glitter galaxy to the heart of London, Ziggy Stardust poses in June 1972.

The *Aladdin Sane* look continued on the artwork for the covers collection *Pin Ups*. "A lovely man," was the verdict of supermodel Twiggy, his co-star in this shot.

Performing the anthemic "Rebel Rebel" in Holland's Top Pop Studios in February 1974.

With actress and Andy Warhol associate Monique van Vooren at a 1977 movie premiere.

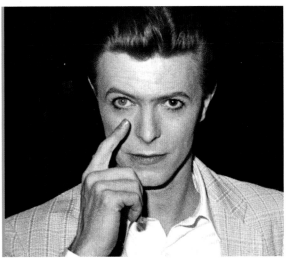

At the Broadway opening of *The Elephant Man*, one of his post-*Scary Monsters* acting roles.

Bowie opens his set at Britain's Phoenix festival in July 1997 with *Hunky Dory*'s "Quicksand."

Live in London with bassist Carmine Rojas and **Carlos Alomar** on 1983's blockbuster Serious Moonlight tour.

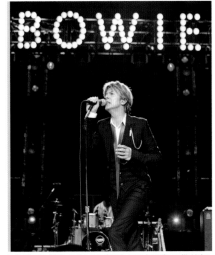

In California, 2002, on the Area:2 tour—a co-headliner with Moby.

buffalo springfield 1966–2011

B

Neil Young
b. November 12, 1945

Stephen Stills
b. January 3, 1945

Bruce Palmer
b. September 9, 1946
d. October 1, 2004

Richie Furay
b. May 9, 1944

Dewey Martin
b. September 30, 1940
d. January 31, 2009

Jim Messina
b. December 5, 1947

The best sixties band never to make it big began in a traffic jam. Stuck on L.A.'s Sunset Boulevard in early 1966, ex-folkies **Stephen Stills** (a failed auditionee for The Monkees) and **Richie Furay** spotted a hearse with Ontario plates. Its driver was **Neil Young**, whom Stills knew, and his passenger was bassist **Bruce Palmer**. They hitched up, added drummer **Dewey Martin** (ex-The Dillards) within the week, and named themselves after a steamroller parked in the street where Stills and Furay lived. Seasoned musicians all, they gelled swiftly and caused a buzz in L.A., cemented by a residency at the Whisky a Go Go club and a tour with The Byrds.

Stills and Young were standout guitarists and—along with Furay—singular songwriters. A self-titled 1966 debut set was re-released in March 1967 to include Stills's "For What It's Worth"—a compelling tale of rioters clashing with cops on Sunset Strip in 1966 that provided their biggest hit (U.S. No. 7).

But cracks were already appearing. Palmer was busted in early 1967 and deported back to Canada. Sessions for the follow-up album, *Stampede*, were fractious, and it was eventually shelved. Palmer returned but then Young briefly quit; David Crosby of The Byrds filled in for him when the group played at the Monterey Pop festival in June 1967.

Remarkably, late 1967's *Buffalo Springfield Again* (U.S. No. 44) was a masterpiece, though more a "White Album"-style collection of solo works than an ensemble piece. Aided by producer Jack Nitzsche, Young created the orchestrated epics "Expecting to Fly" and "Broken Arrow"; Stills shone on "Rock'n'Roll Woman" and "Bluebird"; and Furay contributed three tracks, notably "A Child's Claim to Fame" and Motown-style belter "Good Time Boy."

Then Palmer was busted again—to be replaced by **Jim Messina**—and Young began drifting toward a solo career; the cover of their swan song *Last Time Around* (1968) showed him facing away from the others. However, the record itself contained a handful of gems, including Young's disarming "I Am a Child." After another bust in spring 1968, the band folded.

Together for just two years, Buffalo Springfield pioneered country rock and paved the way for the likes of the Eagles and Poco (featuring Furay and Messina). "That was a great group, man," Young reflected fondly in 1975. "I'd love to play with that band again, just to see if the buzz was still there." Remarkably, they did exactly that—minus Palmer and Martin, who died in 2004 and 2009, respectively—for well-received gigs in 2010 and 2011. **RD**

year-by-year ▧ Vocals ▪ Guitar ▪ Bass ▪ Drums

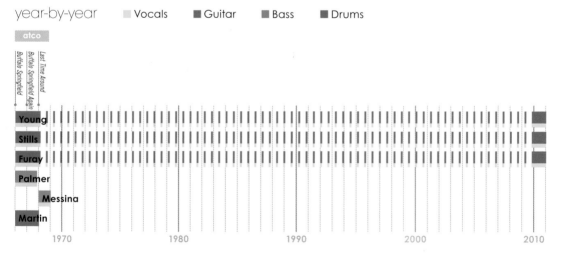

bush 1992–present

Gavin Rossdale
b. October 30, 1965

Robin Goodridge
b. September 10, 1966

Dave Parsons
b. July 2, 1965

Nigel Pulsford
b. April 11, 1963

Chris Traynor
b. June 22, 1973

Corey Britz
b. July 5, 1979

It is one of music's great mysteries: why were British rock band Bush not bigger in their home country? In 1992, when their mutual love of the Pixies got them chatting at a London club, **Gavin Rossdale** and **Nigel Pulsford** had the world in their sights. British rock fans were clamoring for homegrown talent to compete with the American grunge movement, while the charts were bursting with a conveyor belt of boy bands and female warblers. The duo formed Future Primitive with **Dave Parsons** and **Robin Goodridge**, then rebranded themselves as Bush after Shepherd's Bush, the area of London they called home.

Bush's debut, *Sixteen Stone*, failed to gain a foothold in their homeland in 1994, but it was a completely different story in America. Attracting the same passionate fans that put grunge heavyweights Nirvana and Pearl Jam on the map, and with cuts like "Comedown" and "Glycerine" in heavy rotation on radio, *Sixteen Stone* would eventually breach the Top Five and sell six million copies.

With one album, Bush had set the blueprint for modern British rock (notably Radiohead and Coldplay) to make inroads in America, although few would admit it, given the perplexing "uncool" tag stapled to Rossdale's charges in the intervening years.

The group's career peak arrived at the tail-end of 1996 and the beginning of 1997 when *Razorblade Suitcase* crowned the U.S. album chart and made No. 4 in the United Kingdom. Regarded by some as the death knell of grunge in the aftermath of Kurt Cobain's suicide, the abrasive *Suitcase* featured "Swallowed," their only U.K. Top Ten single. (The album was knocked off the U.S. top spot by Bush's Trauma Records labelmates No Doubt, featuring Rossdale's future wife, Gwen Stefani.)

Despite bagging a fourth No. 1 on the U.S. Modern Rock Tracks chart with "The Chemicals Between Us," the post-grunge era made casualties of *The Science of Things* (1999) and *Golden State* (2001), an ill-timed attempt at a return to their riff-laden glory days. In 2002, Pulsford left and was replaced by **Chris Traynor**, who appeared on one tour before Bush disbanded.

Following the split, Rossdale showcased his vocal prowess with Institute, released a solo album (*Wanderlust*), and delved into acting. However, after a nine-year hiatus, Bush returned in 2010 with **Corey Britz** replacing Parsons. Allmusic described *The Sea of Memories* (2011) as "easily the most enjoyable collection of songs released under Bush's name."

Bush maintain an uneasy relationship with the U.K., where visitors to their website are greeted with videos that are "unavailable in your country"—but type "bush" into any search engine and they still come out ahead of Kate, George W., and all manner of shrubs. With *The Sea of Memories* hinting at a bright future, Bush should keep it that way for years to come. **MW**

year-by-year ■ Vocals ■ Guitar ■ Bass ■ Drums ■ Other percussion

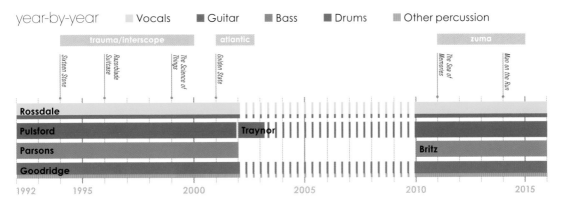

trauma/interscope   atlantic   zuma

Sixteen Stone
Razorblade Suitcase
The Science of Things
Golden State
The Sea of Memories
Man on the Run

Rossdale

Pulsford   Traynor

Parsons   Britz

Goodridge

1992   1995   2000   2005   2010   2015

the byrds 1964–1973

Jim (Roger) McGuinn
b. July 13, 1942

Gene Clark
b. November 17, 1944
d. May 24, 1991

David Crosby
b. August 14, 1941

Chris Hillman
b. December 4, 1944

Michael Clarke
b. June 3, 1946
d. December 19, 1993

Kevin Kelley
b. March 25, 1943
d. April 6, 2002

They were America's Beatles, matching freewheeling studio experimentation with top-notch songwriting and blissful harmonies. The Byrds' heyday lasted only from 1965 to 1968; their influence is lasting far longer.

Jim (later **Roger**) **McGuinn**, **Gene Clark**, and **David Crosby** had been folkies and initially teamed up as The Jet Set. After The Beatles hit America in 1964, though, all that changed. Invigorated by the Fabs' *A Hard Day's Night*, they briefly became The Beefeaters (an Anglophile nod to the U.K. pop invasion of the States). Joined by bassist **Chris Hillman**, whose background was in bluegrass, and drummer **Michael Clarke** (recruited because of his Brian Jones haircut), on November 26, 1964, they became The Byrds.

Initially, they grumbled over the choice of Bob Dylan's "Mr. Tambourine Man" for their first single, but mellowed when it became a worldwide No. 1. The debut album *Mr. Tambourine Man* (1965) showcased Gene Clark's songwriting skill, notably on the delirious

stomp "Feel a Whole Lot Better" and the wistful "I Knew I'd Want You." With their louche on-stage cool, McGuinn's tinted sunglasses and Crosby's whimsical grin, The Byrds swiftly became teenybop faves.

Turn! Turn! Turn! (1965) was marginally less ecstatic, though the title track secured their last U.S. No. 1 hit. But problems were brewing. There was resistance to Clark's material within the group, touring exhausted him, and he was afraid of flying. After a hit-and-miss tour of the U.K., he quit—though not before co-writing the jazz-and-raga-influenced "Eight Miles High," based on their U.K. tour and among their finest cuts.

Initially, the four-piece Byrds maintained the momentum. The diverse *Fifth Dimension* (1966) augured well, while *Younger Than Yesterday* (1967) was a triumph: studio magic sprinkled over stand-out tunes, including Crosby's divinely melancholy "Everybody's Been Burned." Alas, Crosby was now increasingly unpredictable, given to on-stage rants

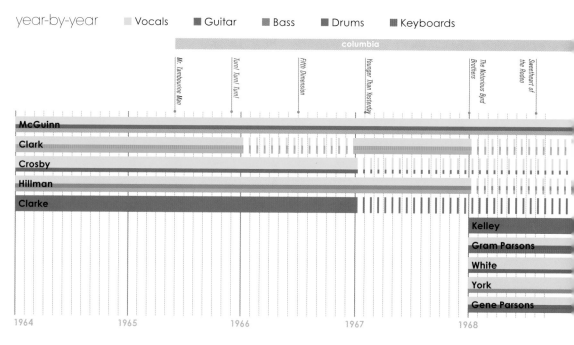

year-by-year   ■ Vocals   ■ Guitar   ■ Bass   ■ Drums   ■ Keyboards

3.5M	2M	1M	4M
Mr. Tambourine Man (1965)	**Turn! Turn! Turn!** (1965)	**Fifth Dimension** (1966)	**The Byrds Greatest Hits** (1967)

B

Gram Parsons
b. November 5, 1946
d. September 19, 1973

Clarence White
b. June 7, 1944
d. July 14, 1973

John York
b. August 3, 1946

Gene Parsons
b. September 4, 1944

Skip Battin
b. February 18, 1934
d. July 6, 2003

and poor playing, and engaged in a power struggle with McGuinn. *The Notorious Byrd Brothers* (1968) was another strong set but, by its release, Crosby and Clarke had been dismissed, the latter replaced by Hillman's cousin **Kevin Kelley**. Crosby went on to form Crosby, Stills and Nash (and, occasionally, Young), one of rock's most successful supergroups.

The newly recruited **Gram Parsons** led The Byrds into country music, though it had influenced their work since at least "Satisfied Mind" on *Turn! Turn! Turn!*. On *Sweetheart of the Rodeo* (1968), they embraced country ballads and standards—dismaying many fans. The willful Parsons left prior to an ill-fated tour of South Africa, and The Byrds' next incarnation saw McGuinn and Hillman joined by country guitarist **Clarence White** and bassist **John York**. The four-piece recorded *Dr. Byrds and Mr. Hyde* (1960)—country meets psychedelia—and *Ballad of Easy Rider* (1969)—which had little to do with *Easy Rider* (1969) the movie.

Hillman left to join Parsons in The Flying Burrito Brothers (with ex-Byrd Michael Clarke), and the final incarnation of the group saw drummer **Gene Parsons** (no relation to Gram) and bassist **Skip Battin** replace Kelley and York respectively. They recorded the well-received *Untitled* (1970), featuring "Chestnut Mare," a U.K. Top Twenty hit, though *Byrdmaniax* (1971) and *Farther Along* (1971) were poorly received.

The Byrds finally folded in 1973. Hopes were high when the original five-piece reunited for that year's *Byrds*, but only "Full Circle" and a cover of Neil Young's "(See The Sky) About To Rain" hinted at past magic.

Latterly, individual members performed together —and issued lawsuits against each other for touring fake "Byrds" outfits—while the original five reunited for their inauguration into the Rock and Roll Hall of Fame in 1991. Revisit their music from 1965 to 1968—then listen to jingly-jangly descendants like Tom Petty and R.E.M.—and you'll see why they matter so much. **RD**

■ Aerophones   ■ Other percussion   ■ Strings

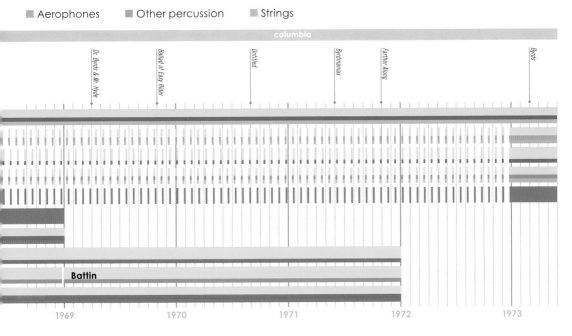

the byrds 93

can 1968–1991

Holger Czukay
b. March 24, 1938

Jaki Liebezeit
b. May 26, 1939

Irmin Schmidt
b. May 29, 1937

Michael Karoli
b. Apr 29, 1948
d. Nov 17, 2001

Malcolm "Desse" Mooney
b. Unknown

Kenji "Damo" Suzuki
b. January 16, 1950

Rosko Gee
b. Unknown

"Reebop" Kwaku Baah
b. Feb 13, 1944
d. Jan 12, 1983

"I felt they had picked up the gauntlet that The Velvet Underground had thrown down," Brian Eno observed in 1997. A glowing testament—and totally warranted when, as Can did, you re-write the rules of rock.

Like the Velvets, Can had one foot in the avant-garde—**Holger Czukay** (bass) and **Irmin Schmidt** (keyboards) had even studied with classical *enfant terrible* Karlheinz Stockhausen. **Michael Karoli** (guitar), a pupil of Czukay, alerted him to Hendrix and the twisted rock of the Velvets. **Jaki Liebezeit** provided their locked beat and **Malcolm "Desse" Mooney** added spontaneous vocals and off-kilter energy.

Monster Movie (1969) was a wildly original debut; for "Yoo Do Right," Mooney sang a letter he had received from his girlfriend. Alas, a nervous breakdown obliged the singer to return to the U.S. for help. Czukay and Liebezeit found his replacement, **Kenji "Damo" Suzuki**, busking in Munich. After a highly confrontational show, only thirty of the 1,500 crowd were left—including, oddly, actor David Niven.

Having refined their sound on *Soundtracks* (1970), Can delivered their first masterpiece with *Tago Mago* (1970), produced by Conny Plank. It boasted the funky, eighteen-minute "Hallelujah" and "Augmn"— like a farther out-there "Interstellar Overdrive."

Ege Bamyasi (1972) was more approachable and featured an unlikely German No. 1 in "Spoon," while the gentle *Future Days* (1973) offered myriad delights, from the shuffling beat of the title track to the shape-shifting closer, "Bel Air." Suzuki subsequently departed to become a Jehovah's Witness; Karoli and Schmidt shared vocals on the ambient *Soon Over Babaluma* (1974) and *Landed* (1975). By now, Can's avant-garde edge had been somewhat dulled. Newcomers **Rosko Gee** (bass) and **"Reebop" Kwaku Baah** (percussion) were good musicians, but perhaps too conventional for Can, though *Flow Motion* (1976) gave the band their sole U.K. hit (No. 26) with "I Want More."

Increasingly drawn toward more left-field music making, Czukay drifted from the group and was gone by their final set, 1978's *Can* (aka *Inner Space*), by which time elements of world music had filtered in. In 1986, the five core members (including a more stable Mooney) reconvened for *Rite Time* (1989), while a 1991 reunion saw them contribute a track to Wim Wenders's 1991 movie *Until the End of the World*.

Can's brew of improvisation, hypnotic rhythms, and enigmatic vocals continues to fascinate. Those smitten have included David Bowie, Brian Eno, The Fall, The Flaming Lips, and Primal Scream. **RD**

year-by-year ■ Vocals ■ Guitar ■ Bass ■ Drums ■ Keyboards ■ Other percussion ■ Strings ■ Programming

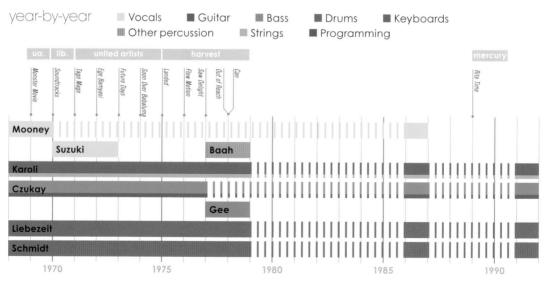

canned heat 1965–present

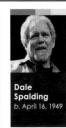

Bob "The Bear" Hite
b. Feb 26, 1943
d. Apr 5, 1981

Alan "Blind Owl" Wilson
b. July 4, 1943
d. September 3, 1970

Frank Cook
b. Unknown

Henry "Sunflower" Vestine
b. Dec 25, 1944
d. Oct 20, 1997

Larry "The Mole" Taylor
b. June 26, 1942

Fito de la Parra
b. February 8, 1946

Harvey "The Snake" Mandel
b. Mar 11, 1945

Dale Spalding
b. April 16, 1949

Canned Heat were five white Americans who wanted to play the blues, popularize it, and raise awareness of its black roots. The band was the brainchild of frontman **Bob "The Bear" Hite** and guitarist **Alan "Blind Owl" Wilson**, who hired drummer **Frank Cook**, former Frank Zappa guitarist **Henry "Sunflower" Vestine**, and former Jerry Lee Lewis bassist **Larry "The Mole" Taylor**. The name of the band was inspired by "Canned Heat Blues" by guitarist Tommy Johnson—"canned heat" being a colloquial term for Sterno, a cooking fuel drunk by impoverished alcohol dependents.

The band attracted attention at 1967's Monterey Pop festival even before their self-titled debut album. Their covers of long-forgotten blues numbers and almost encyclopedic knowledge of the music's roots gave them a good-time worthiness that built an appreciative audience. Canned Heat soon made headlines—not all of them desirable. They were notorious for their excesses, and a drug bust in Denver precipitated the departure of Cook. He was replaced by **Fito de la Parra**. However, *Boogie with Canned Heat* (1968) featured two transatlantic Top Twenty hits with which they remain forever associated: "On the Road Again" and "Going Up the Country."

The final year of the sixties was Canned Heat's annus mirabilis as they consolidated their fanbase with new albums and broadened it with a strong set at the Woodstock festival. In 1970, their definitive cover of "Let's Work Together"—originally by Wilbert Harrison—hit No. 2 in the U.K. and No. 26 in the U.S. But just as the band was about to embark on a British tour in September, Blind Owl died of a drug overdose, shaking the band to its core.

Now under Hite's sole direction, Canned Heat began to recover when a session with John Lee Hooker was released as 1971's *Hooker 'n Heat*, giving a welcome wake-up to the blues master's career. They would collaborate with two more blues stars in 1973: Clarence "Gatemouth" Brown (*Gate's on the Heat*) and Memphis Slim (*Memphis Heat*).

From the early seventies, as musicians came and went, the only constant was Hite. His fatal heroin-induced heart attack in 1981 seemed to spell the end of the band, but de la Parra kept it going. In the twenty-first century, Canned Heat's participation in the Heroes of Woodstock Tour, marking the fortieth anniversary of the festival, brought guitarist **Harvey Mandel** and Larry Taylor back into the fold. In 2010, the official lineup comprised Mandel, Taylor, de la Parra, and harmonica player **Dale Spalding**. They continue to tour, and the band's motto, "Don't forget to boogie!," holds as true as ever. **GL**

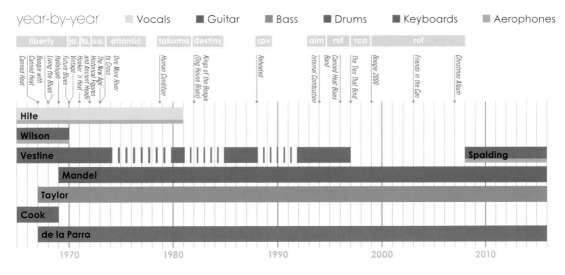

year-by-year ▪ Vocals ▪ Guitar ▪ Bass ▪ Drums ▪ Keyboards ▪ Aerophones

captain beefheart and his magic band

Don Van Vliet (Captain Beefheart)
b. January 14, 1941
d. December 17, 2010

Ry Cooder
b. March 15, 1947

Alex St Clair
b. September 14, 1941
d. January 5, 2006

John French
b. September 29, 1948

Jerry Handley
b. Unknown

Jeff Cotton
b. May 31, 1948

In rock's pantheon of great eccentrics, Captain Beefheart stands alone. His uncompromising music has inspired successive generations; his surreal pronouncements have baffled, infuriated, and entertained. And, after abandoning music altogether, he achieved enormous success as a painter: prior to his death in December 2010, his works were among the highest priced of any living artist.

Born in Glendale, California in 1941, Don Glen Vliet was a child prodigy who, by the age of eleven, had won first prizes in sculpture and featured on local television. Although Vliet's blue-collar father was not comfortable with his son's interests, he was indulged by his mother and allowed to spend his teens sculpting, painting, and listening to blues and modern jazz, with little interruption from the outside world.

Having met Frank Zappa at high school, Vliet teamed up with him in a group known as the Soots. Vliet's deep bass Howlin' Wolf growl, Zappa's distorted electric guitar, and song titles such as "Metal Man Has Won His Wings" found the duo well adrift of the prevailing musical styles of the period. Although this collaboration was brief, Zappa would play a pivotal role in the Captain Beefheart story.

In early 1965, guitarist Alex Snouffer invited Vliet to sing with an R&B group he was assembling. With the singer now **Don Van Vliet**, they became known as Captain Beefheart and his Magic Band and signed with A&M to produce two singles in 1966, one a cover of Bo Diddley's "Diddy Wah Diddy." Unimpressed by the group's lack of success and the "negative" sound of their demos, A&M promptly dropped them.

Two important new arrivals appeared at the end of 1966. Drummer **John French** took on the critical task of interpreting "non-musician" Van Vliet's creative ideas. Meanwhile, twenty-year-old guitar prodigy **Ry Cooder** honed and rearranged the band's material for what would become their 1967 debut album, *Safe as Milk*. Recorded for the Buddah label, this contorted slab of blues-rock made little commercial impact in the U.S., but affected an influential group of musicians in Europe—not least John Lennon, who tried briefly to sign the Magic Band to the Apple label.

Cooder's tenure in the band was a brief one, **Jeff Cotton** joining in time for sessions for an album/ design concept intended to be called *It Comes in a Plain Brown Wrapper*. Once again, initial recordings— more overtly "period" sounds with psychedelic audio

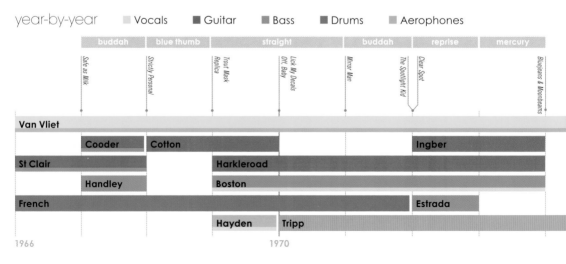

year-by-year   ▨ Vocals   ■ Guitar   ■ Bass   ■ Drums   ▨ Aerophones

750,000	450,000	300,000	300,000
Trout Mask Replica (1969)	*Lick My Decals Off Baby* (1970)	*Mirror Man* (1971)	*The Spotlight Kid* (1972)

C

Bill Harkleroad	**Mark Boston**	**Victor Hayden**	**Art Tripp**	**Elliot Ingber**	**Roy Estrada**
b. December 12, 1948	*b.* 1949	*b.* Unknown	*b.* September 10, 1944	*b.* Unknown	*b.* April 17, 1943

effects—were not appreciated by the pop-oriented Buddah. The Magic Band were dropped and the album emerged as *Strictly Personal* on a tiny label owned by the band's producer, Bob Krasnow.

The year 1969 proved pivotal for the Magic Band. With no record deal in place, Van Vliet's old friend Frank Zappa—now successful with the Mothers of Invention—stepped in, offering to produce an album for his own newly created Straight label. At this time, Van Vliet began to assert his domination of the group. Living communally in a rented house in a Los Angeles suburb, the Magic Band spent eight months learning Van Vliet's new music: a complex, avant-garde hybrid of blues, rock, and free jazz. A dramatic shift in compositional style came about as Van Vliet created new material at the piano, an instrument for which he had no training or knowledge. He would "play" until he found the required sounds, chords, or rhythms, which drummer French would articulate to the others.

The conditions were, claimed French, "cult-like," as the broke and starving musicians were drilled fourteen hours a day, continually berated by Van Vliet to perfect what may have sounded like a group free improvisation, yet in truth was anything

but. The double album that emerged, *Trout Mask Replica*, made no immediate impact in America and spent one week in the U.K. chart—largely on the strength of producer Zappa's involvement. But, to be appreciated, *Trout Mask Replica* requires multiple close listens. It is now revered as a landmark in rock.

The same process was matured on 1970's self-produced *Lick My Decals Off, Baby*, which provided the Magic Band with their only Top Twenty album in the United Kingdom. In spite of its predecessor's stature, Van Vliet rated *Decals* as his best work.

Throughout the seventies, Captain Beefheart, with an ever-changing Magic Band, continued to release albums that increasingly mined a more accessible, blues-oriented rock furrow. After a falling-out with Zappa, Van Vliet reunited with him for 1975's *Bongo Fury*, a blend of live and studio recordings.

Ice Cream for Crow, released in 1982, would be Van Vliet's final studio album before music finally gave way to his love of abstract expressionist painting. Wheelchair-bound with multiple sclerosis, Van Vliet made few public appearances over the two decades before his death, three weeks before his seventieth birthday, on December 17, 2010. **TB**

▓ Other percussion

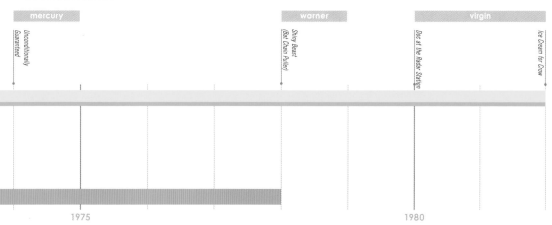

mercury	warner	virgin
Unconditionally Guaranteed	Shiny Beast (Bat Chain Puller)	Doc at the Radar Station	Ice Cream for Crow

1975

1980

From Her to Eternity (1984)

Kicking Against the Pricks (1986)

Tender Prey (1988)

The Good Son (1990)

Henry's Dream (1992)

Murder Ballads (1996)

The Boatman's Call (1997)

No More Shall We Part (2001)

Abattoir Blues/The Lyre of Orpheus (2004)

Dig, Lazarus Dig!!! (2008)

Feel his pain: **Nick Cave** performs at de Meervaart in Amsterdam, the Netherlands, in 1984.

Cave mid-performance at Utrecht, the Netherlands, in 1986.

Cave onstage with **Blixa Bargeld** at London's Town and Country Club in October 1988.

A 1990 portrait of a man who transforms dark thoughts into fine songs.

Cave plays the Ritz Club, New York, in November 1986.

Cave sings with fellow dark balladeer PJ Harvey on U.K. TV show *The White Room* in 1996.

Cave outstares the camera in 2001.

Cave performs again on the U.K. TV show *The White Room* in 1997.

Cave plays Amsterdam in the Netherlands during a European tour in 2004.

Cave and the Bad Seeds appear on the U.S. TV show *Late Night with Conan O'Brien* on October 3, 2008.

the clash 1976–1986

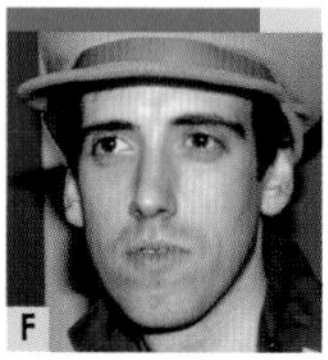

Mick Jones
b. June 26, 1955

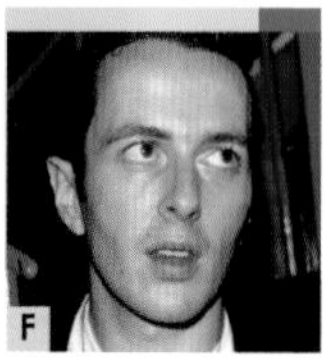

Joe Strummer
b. August 21, 1952
d. December 22, 2002

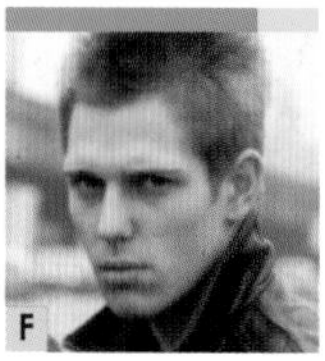

Paul Simonon
b. December 15, 1955

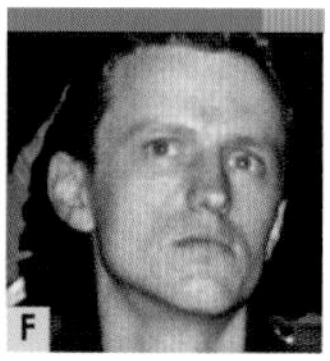

Terry Chimes
b. July 5, 1956

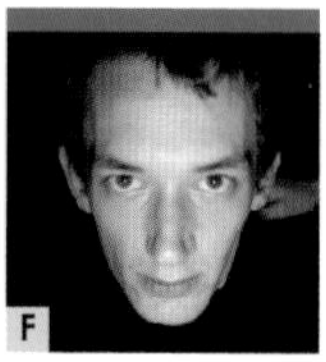

Keith Levene
b. July 18, 1957

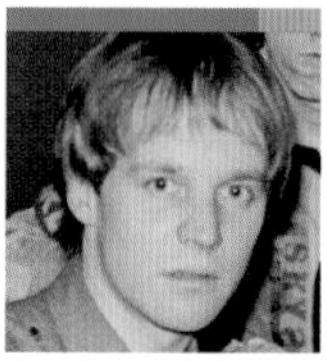

Rob Harper
b. Unknown

Purveyors of muscular, exciting punk rock, The Clash were the most political of all the major groups of the era. As Pete Townshend of The Who put it, "When you listen to The Clash, you're facing up to life, and at the same time being given strength to deal with it."

The Clash formed in London in 1976. Guitarist **Mick Jones**'s manager, Bernie Rhodes, who had already recruited **Paul Simonon** so that Jones could teach him to play bass, brought in **Joe Strummer** from pub rock stalwarts The 101'ers on vocals. Guitarist **Keith Levene** (who later joined John Lydon in Public Image Ltd) and drummer **Terry Chimes** completed the lineup, although Levene was soon fired.

If 1976 was the year that changed the direction of rock music because of the punk explosion, then the principal U.K. providers of the dynamite were The Clash and Sex Pistols. One of punk's credos was that boring "musicianship" led to earnest navel-gazing of the "multiple concept album with endless solos" variety. So punk championed a DIY "pick up and play" ethos in response, with sometimes rudimentary results. Yet the members of The Clash could play.

After a premature opening gig supporting the Sex Pistols, they rehearsed furiously before going on an infamous tour with the same headliners, where nearly every other concert was called off. Chimes quit, disgusted by the punk habits of spitting and bottle throwing, to be replaced by **Rob Harper**, although he returned to play on their first album. Soon afterwards **Nicky "Topper" Headon** took over on drums.

Their debut LP *The Clash* came out in the U.K. in 1977. It was an instant hit in their homeland, the adrenaline rush of the opening lyrics to the first track "Janie Jones" ("he's in love with a rock 'n' roll world") never letting go of the listener. Not released in the U.S., allegedly because of the lack of radio-friendly songs, the album eventually came out there in 1979 after it had become the highest ever seller on import. *Give 'Em Enough Rope*—produced by Sandy Pearlman, best known for his work with New York's sophisticated heavy metal outfit Blue Öyster Cult—followed in 1978 and solidified the group's appeal.

The Clash's third (double) album came out in December 1979 in the United Kingdom and a month later in the United States. Heralded by its anthemic title track, *London Calling* was produced by Guy Stevens, who had guided the early career of Mott the Hoople. It was a break-out hit in the U.S. after

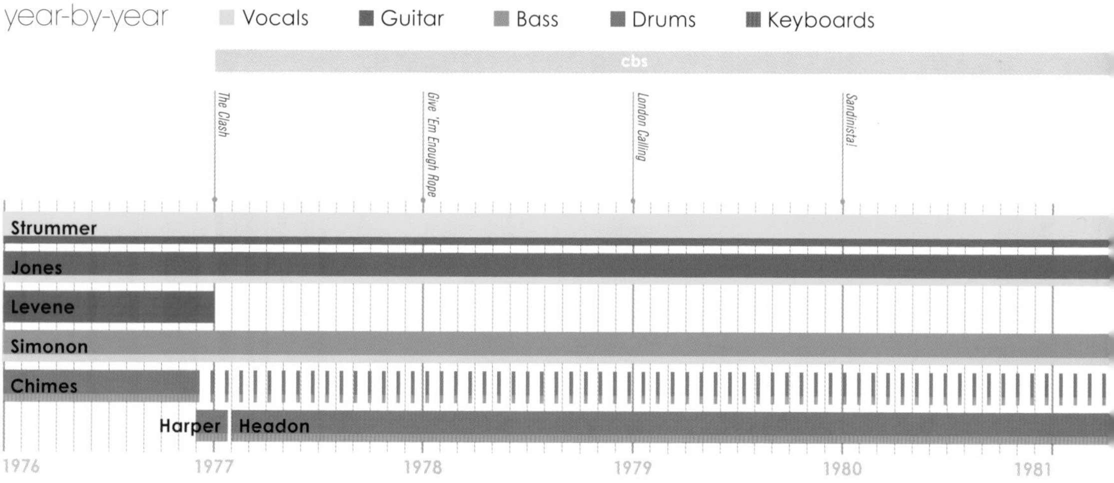

1.4M
The Clash
(1977)

 750,000
*Give 'Em
Enough Rope*
(1978)

2.1M
London Calling
(1979)

3.7M
Combat Rock
(1982)

**Nicky "Topper"
Headon**
b. May 30, 1955

Pete Howard
b. Unknown

Nick Sheppard
b. 1960

Vince White
b. 1960

C

receiving extravagant praise, and is still regarded as their most artistically successful statement. By contrast, *Sandinista!*, released at the end of 1980 in the U.K. (and, again, a month later in the U.S.) was more diffuse and experimental. The irony that this was a triple album was not lost on diehard and former punks, although the sprawling record contained many good songs. In typical fan-friendly style, both these albums cost only the price of a single LP.

Years of constant touring were beginning to take their toll. Headon was fired in April 1982 because of his addiction to heroin. Chimes, perhaps relieved that bottles and spitting were no longer prevalent, briefly returned. The group's fifth album, *Combat Rock*, was released later that same year. It turned out to be their most successful commercially and also spawned two hits, "Rock the Casbah" and "Should I Stay or Should I Go?" Jones confessed that the latter song, which would go on to become the band's only chart-topping record, described his tempestuous relationship with American singer Ellen Foley.

However, tensions between the two chief songwriters had been steadily rising and something had to give. Jones left The Clash in 1983 and formed

Big Audio Dynamite two years later, after dabbling with the group General Public. Chimes quit for the final time; Strummer and Simonon recruited **Pete Howard** on drums, and **Nick Sheppard** and **Vince White** on guitars, to carry on.

Despite some belligerence on behalf of the miners in 1984 (there was a huge U.K. strike), the best days of the group were now over. After a chaotic recording schedule, *Cut the Crap* came out in 1985—it turned out to be The Clash's final studio album. Although they put on The Busking Tour to support its release, the material was not as strong as in their heyday. The Clash had always relied more than most on fire and brimstone, and Strummer and Simonon no longer had the will to keep going. The group split in 1986, leaving a body of work remarkable for its consistency and memories of a tremendous stage presence. Their reputation has grown in the years since then.

Strummer died from heart complications in 2002. That same year, the group and director Don Letts received a Grammy for *Westway to the World* in the Best Long Form Video category, followed by Rock and Roll Hall of Fame induction a year later—belated recognition for their enduring popularity. **MiH**

■ Other percussion

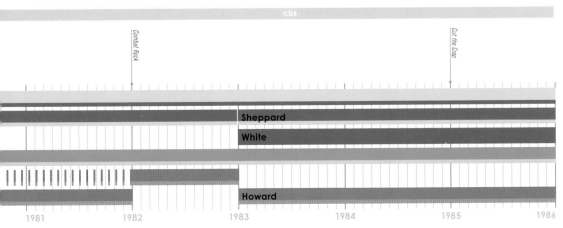

The Clash (1977)

Give 'Em Enough Rope (1978)

London Calling (1979)

Sandinista! (1980)

Combat Rock (1982)

Cut the Crap (1985)

Left to right **Paul Simenon, Joe Strummer, Topper Headon,** and **Mick Jones** in 1977.

Jones, Strummer, and **Simenon** hold the frontline at Rafters, Manchester, on July 3, 1978.

Strummer plays the New York Palladium on September 20, 1979.

London posing: The Clash outside the city's Notre Dame Hall off Leicester Square.

Doing the business: **Jones, Strummer,** and **Simenon** set things to rights in 1980.

Jones and **Strummer** at the Warfield Theater, San Francisco, on March 2, 1980.

Jones, Simenon, Terry Chimes, and **Strummer** at JFK Stadium, Philadelphia, in 1982.

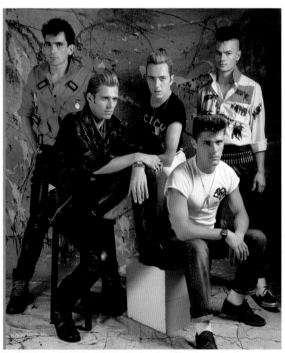

The Clash in the mid-eighties, following the departure of founder member **Jones.**

joe cocker 1959–2014

Joe Cocker
b. May 20, 1944
d. December
22, 2014

Chris Stainton
b. March 22,
1944

Alan Spenner
b. May 7, 1948

Neil Hubbard
b. Unknown

Henry McCullough
b. July 21, 1943

Bruce Rowland
b. May 22, 1941

Leon Russell
b. April 2, 1942

Standing still while whirling his arms has made this Yorkshireman's performing style widely parodied, but his gritty vocals are inimitable and unforgettable— and his soulful delivery was credited with raising Beatles material to an even more exalted plane.

Cocker formed his first band in 1959. By the early sixties they were playing pubs in his native Sheffield as Vance Arnold and The Avengers. Signed by Decca in 1964, their debut single—a cover of The Beatles' "I'll Cry Instead" (featuring session guitarist Jimmy Page)— was a flop. Cocker, having given up his day job as a gas fitter, opted to try his luck in London. There, he and keyboardist **Chris Stainton**, a fellow Sheffield lad, formed The Grease Band—also featuring bassist **Alan Spenner**, guitarists **Neil Hubbard** and **Henry McCullough**, and drummer **Bruce Rowland**—then co-wrote "Marjorine," a minor U.K. hit.

The breakthrough came with their version of Lennon and McCartney's "With a Little Help from My Friends" (featuring Page and Steve Winwood), which hit No. 1 in the U.K. An album of the same name reached the U.S. Top Forty, then a stunning performance at the 1969 Woodstock festival propelled a second album, *Joe Cocker!* (featuring **Leon Russell**), to No. 11. Another Beatles song, "She Came in Through

the Bathroom Window," was a Top Thirty hit in the U.S., while the live *Mad Dogs and Englishmen* got to No. 2.

As Cocker's career took off, his health deteriorated, mainly through alcohol abuse, and his decline enabled Russell to steal the show when on tour. After 1974's *I Can Stand a Little Rain*, sales waned, and Cocker became notorious for vomiting on stage. Having returned home to live quietly with his family, he had got his act together by the early eighties. He re-established himself with an Oscar-winning, platinum-selling duet with Jennifer Warnes— "Up Where We Belong" (from the soundtrack of the 1982 movie *An Officer and a Gentleman*)—which topped the U.S. chart in 1982. His troubles seemingly behind him and his vocal power undiminished, Cocker, now popular globally, has enjoyed even greater success the second time around.

In 1996 he released *Organic*, a Don Was-produced album of new material, with contributions from a host of big-name guests, including Jim Keltner, Billy Preston, and Randy Newman. Cocker has since continued to do what he does best—interpreting great pop, blues, and soul and making them sound sublime. His admirers agree that, no matter how good the original version of any song, Joe Cocker's is even better. **GL**

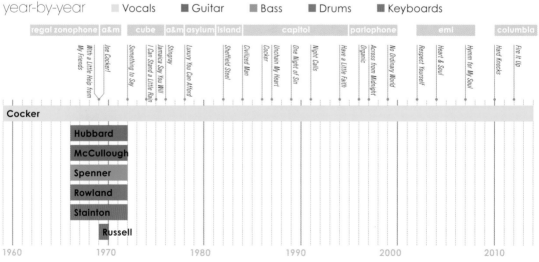

year-by-year   ■ Vocals   ■ Guitar   ■ Bass   ■ Drums   ■ Keyboards

cold chisel 1973–present

Jimmy Barnes
b. April 28, 1956

Don Walker
b. November 29, 1951

Ian Moss
b. March 20, 1955

Phil Small
b. Unknown

Ray Arnott
b. Unknown

Les Kaczmarek
b. 1955
d. December 5, 2008

Steve Prestwich
b. March 5, 1954
d. Jan 16, 2011

Charley Drayton
b. May 9, year unknown

Cold Chisel evolved as the ultimate hardworking, hard-drinking, hard-rocking Aussie bar band. Largely unknown to non-Antipodean audiences, they are a national institution in their home country. Formed in Adelaide in 1973, Cold Chisel began life as a blues-rock cover band. They gigged relentlessly, relocating first to Melbourne, then Sydney, but found little success until 1977 when they were signed by WEA.

The band's self-titled debut appeared a year later. Ranging from jazz- and blues-based ballads to hard pub rock, it scraped into the Top Forty. The first single, **Don Walker**'s "Khe Sanh," was named after a battle in the Vietnam War and detailed the struggles of an Australian veteran returning home. It should have been a major hit, but was thwarted by Australian censors deeming it unfit for airplay because of its sex and drugs references. It struggled to reach No. 48 in the chart at the time, but in 2001 was voted No. 8 in a list of the greatest Australian songs.

Breakfast at Sweethearts (1979) gave Cold Chisel their commercial breakthrough. A new, radio-friendly sound helped take the album into the Top Five, but the band disliked its smooth production. Bluff frontman **Jimmy Barnes** was characteristically forthright: "*Breakfast at Sweethearts* stunk—and you can spell that F-U-C-K-E-D!"

East (1980) was notable as the first album on which the whole band contributed to the songwriting—every member would eventually write one of their hits. *East* was also the first album on which Cold Chisel were able to achieve a commercial sound that retained the raw edge of their powerful live shows. It was the biggest-selling album of the year in Australia and provided them with their only overseas success, briefly scraping into *Billboard*'s Top 200. By 1981 Cold Chisel were enormously popular, but they were notorious for their unruly behavior: live on TV, they smashed up the stage at that year's music business *Countdown* award show.

Circus Animals (1982) was another massive success at home, yielding three hits. But continued lack of success outside of Australia and New Zealand fed a mood of growing despondency and, by 1984's *Twentieth Century,* the band were barely on speaking terms. Although the album shot straight to the top of the chart, Cold Chisel announced their break-up.

In the aftermath, Barnes enjoyed a solo career that, commercially speaking, eclipsed his old band, with nine chart-topping albums. Personality issues having thawed over time, in 1998 Cold Chisel re-formed to record *The Last Wave of Summer*, which, supported by a tour, once more topped the chart. **TB**

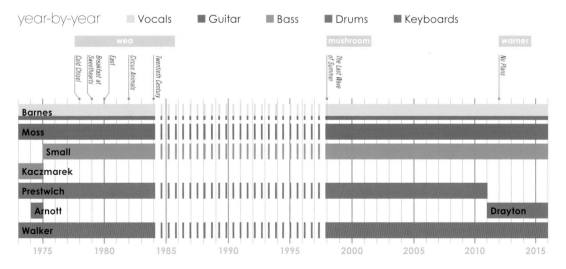

year-by-year ■ Vocals ■ Guitar ■ Bass ■ Drums ■ Keyboards

coldplay 1998–present

Chris Martin
b. March 2, 1977

Jonny Buckland
b. September 11, 1977

Guy Berryman
b. April 12, 1978

Will Champion
b. July 31, 1978

From tentative, daydreamy roots at University College London in 1996, Coldplay have become one of the biggest bands in the world. They have effortlessly filled arenas and soundtracked lives all over the globe with their universal but increasingly ambitious music. Only five albums into their career, they stand shoulder to shoulder with U2 and have in truth taken even less time to achieve world domination than Bono and company—Bono said of singer **Chris Martin**, "Chris is a songwriter in the high British line of Paul McCartney, Ray Davies, and Noel Gallagher."

Chris Martin and guitarist **Jonny Buckland** met at UCL in the mid-nineties and kicked around the idea of forming a band from the first moment. Shaky starts as Pectoralz and Starfish were soon brushed under the carpet as bassist **Guy Berryman**, then drummer **Will Champion**, joined in 1998 to form a unit that has remained rock solid ever since.

Their debut release, the *Safety* EP in 1998, was a limited issue designed to reach out to labels, but their break soon came when they performed at the Falcon pub in Camden, London, that December. In attendance, Fierce Panda Records chief Simon Williams was seriously impressed and the young band were signed up to record their *Brothers and Sisters* EP in the new year. That release tickled the U.K. Top 100 and—completing an extraordinary trajectory—

Coldplay signed to Parlophone within a few months, pausing only briefly to finish their university degrees.

Another EP—*The Blue Room*—followed, as well as a debut performance at the Glastonbury festival, an event that they would come to dominate, before they recorded debut album *Parachutes*. Their first proper single, "Shiver," made the lower reaches of the U.K. Top Forty in spring 2000, but it was the follow-up "Yellow" that got them noticed, becoming Coldplay's first Top Ten hit. The groundwork was complete for *Parachutes*,which duly topped the U.K. chart, stopped just short of the Top Fifty in the U.S., and was later nominated for the U.K.'s Mercury Prize.

Parachutes' worldwide success was initially a source of pressure, but a strong work ethic and early satisfaction with what would be its first single, "In My Place," kept the band focused on the second album *A Rush of Blood to the Head* (2002). They trailed its release with a feverishly received Glastonbury headline slot, where they aired their new, assured songs—including the stunningly melodic "Clocks" and piano ballad "The Scientist"—to a wider TV audience for the first time. The band's fresh confidence was well placed. On its August release, the muscular, stadium-filling material propelled *A Rush of Blood to the Head* to the top spot in the U.K., Top Five in the U.S., and multi-million global sales in a few months.

year-by-year ▪ Vocals ▪ Guitar ▪ Bass ▪ Drums ▪ Keyboards

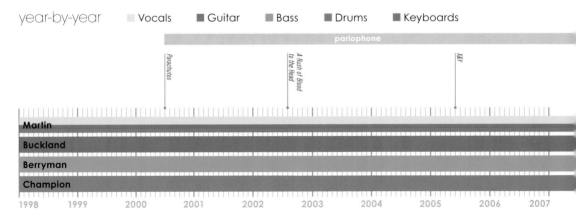

Then there were the awards: Best British Album at the Brits, Best Alternative Music Album at the Grammys, and further Grammys for the singles "In My Place" and "Clocks." If the hardworking Coldplay had not quite conquered all before them in 2000, they certainly had now. Marking the end of their relentless tour cycle, Martin was to cap his rise to super-stardom when he married Hollywood actress Gwyneth Paltrow in December 2003.

When the hectic schedule let up for a year, Coldplay cooked up a third album. *X&Y* (2005) topped the chart in every territory and became the best-selling album worldwide that year. A good thing, too—the story was that EMI's share price depended on it—but critics did not give it an easy ride. There was fierce scrutiny of Martin's everyman style of lyric, and disquiet at a perceived lack of killer tunes (despite the inclusion of the anthemic "Fix You," which reached the Top Five in the U.K. and the Top Twenty in the U.S. Martin was unsettled, too, by EMI's obsession with its bottom line: "Shareholders, stocks—all that stuff—it has nothing to do with me." Still, EMI were undoubtedly delighted with the results.

But something must have stung because, next time out, Coldplay went for a change of direction. Taking the well-worn U2 route, they co-opted super-producer Brian Eno to add magic dust to *Viva La Vida or Death and All His Friends* (2008) and the results were dramatic. The more ordinary lines of their mass-appeal rock were bent out of shape, songs were extended, risks taken—and the audience went with them. The title track went to No. 1 in the U.K. on downloads alone when released exclusively via iTunes; it would later achieve a kind of notoriety after American virtuoso guitarist Joe Satriani claimed it had appropriated portions of his "If I Could Fly." That case was eventually settled, and the song went on to gain two Grammy awards. The bold move to bring in Eno certainly paid off, as once more Coldplay topped album charts all over the world.

Similar accolades greeted 2011's *Mylo Xyloto*, another Eno collaboration, which delved further into a brighter pop style and included a duet with R&B star Rihanna (Martin had long professed a love of pop—Jay-Z and Girls Aloud supported Coldplay in the U.K. in 2009). The album's path was eased by the sparkling single "Every Teardrop Is a Waterfall" in the summer and a return to top billing at Glastonbury, and Coldplay dominated the global charts yet again. Martin coquettishly hinted that it might be Coldplay's last album, perhaps in the belief that their stock might never be higher. But any concerns that fans may have had about the band splitting were proved unfounded with the release of *Ghost Stories* in 2014. **MaH**

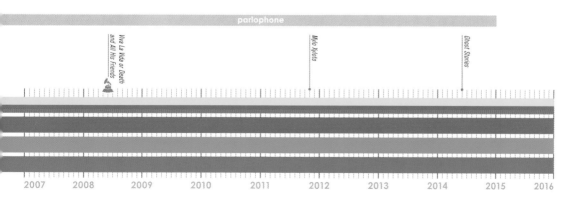

Parachutes (2000)

A Rush of Blood to the Head (2002)

X&Y (2005)

Viva La Vida or Death and All His Friends (2008)

Mylo Xyloto (2011)

Ghost Stories (2014)

Ivy-clad Coldplay (left to right) **Guy Berryman**, **Will Champion**, **Chris Martin**, and **Jonny Buckland** in July 2000.

Champion, Martin, and **Berryman** at the KROQ-FM Almost Acoustic Xmas XI annual concert at Universal City, California, on December 16, 2000.

Buckland, Martin, Champion, and **Berryman** perform in October 2002 beneath large images for the benefit of those at the back.

Champion swaps drums for piano during a special hour-long concert performed for the *Austin City Limits* TV program on December 13, 2005.

Martin plays piano at the Manchester Evening News Arena on December 11, 2008.

Martin and **Buckland** perform in a paper storm at Cologne, Germany, in December 2011.

Buckland, **Martin**, and **Berryman** perform live for fans at the Enmore Theatre in Sydney, Australia, on June 19, 2014.

Love It to Death
(1971)

Killer (1971)

School's Out
(1972)

**Billion Dollar
Babies** (1973)

**Welcome to My
Nightmare** (1975)

Constrictor (1986)

Trash (1989)

**The Last
Temptation** (1994)

**Along Came a
Spider** (2008)

**Welcome 2 My
Nightmare** (2011)

Alice Cooper goes into a typically arresting "straitjacket" routine in 1971.

Cooper with (left to right) **Dennis Dunaway, Glen Buxton, Michael Bruce,** and **Neal Smith.**

Cooper addresses his audience from an "electric chair" in 1971.

Cooper about to apply his career-enhancing eye makeup.

Cooper plus that famous python in 1986.

Cooper makes a theatrical entrance in a 1975 stage show, aided by an assortment of helium-filled balloons.

Taking prisoners in 1989.

Cooper plays the Olympiahalle in Munich, Germany, in November 2008.

You get the joke, right? A portrait from 1994.

Still scary after all these years at the Cobb Energy Center, Atlanta in December 2011.

My Aim Is True
(1977)

This Year's Model
(1978)

Armed Forces
(1979)

Get Happy!! (1980)

Imperial Bedroom
(1982)

King of America
(1986)

Spike (1989)

**All This Useless
Beauty** (1996)

The Delivery Man
(2004)

National Ransom
(2010)

Elvis Costello with Attractions bassist **Bruce Thomas** in England, October 1977.

Attractions **Steve Naïve, Pete Thomas,** and **Bruce Thomas,** with **Costello,** on tour in the U.S. in 1979.

Richard Hell and **Costello** at New York's CBGB club in October 1978.

Costello performs live onstage in Boston, Massachusetts, 1980.

Costello in New York as part of an extensive world tour.

On tour in the Netherlands in April, 1996.

With Cait O'Riordan, former Pogue and his then-wife, in London, 1986.

Nick Lowe, June Carter Cash, and Johnny Cash, join **Costello** onstage in London, 1989.

With Dave Grohl and Bruce Springsteen at the Grammys, shortly before recording *The Delivery Man*.

A relaxed **Costello** with Norah Jones in 2010.

cream / eric clapton 1966–present

Eric Clapton
b. March 30, 1945

Jack Bruce
b. May 14, 1943
d. October 25, 2014

Ginger Baker
b. August 19, 1939

Steve Winwood
b. May 12, 1948

Albert Lee
b. December 21, 1943

Chris Stainton
b. March 22. 1944

"We set out to change the world," **Eric Clapton** noted of the band that confirmed his star status, "to upset people, and to shock them… Our aim was to get so far away from the original line that you're playing something that's never been heard before."

Cream were arguably the first and the finest, and undoubtedly the most lauded, of all the supergroups. Their name perfectly evoked their individual prowess, and their fusing of blues and jazz roots created a new kind of powerhouse rock. The trio was born when Eric Clapton (who had quit The Yardbirds) and John Mayall's Bluesbreakers joined up with Bluesbreakers bassist **Jack Bruce** (who arrived after a short stint with Manfred Mann) and **Ginger Baker**, who had drummed alongside Bruce in bands fronted by Alexis Korner and Graham Bond.

The group made their live debut at Manchester's Twisted Wheel nightclub in on July 29, 1966, ahead of their formally advertised debut two days later at the Windsor Jazz & Blues Festival. Signed to entrepreneur Robert Stigwood's Reaction label (and to Atlantic in the U.S.), they debuted on vinyl with the U.K. Top Forty hit "Wrapping Paper," written by Bruce and rock and folk poet Pete Brown (and, according to Baker, "the most appalling piece of shit I've ever heard"). Around this time, Clapton had become *the* must-see

guitarist about town, but met his match at a London Polytechnic College gig in October 1966 when newly arrived U.S. guitarist Jimi Hendrix joined Cream for an unannounced and memorable blues jam.

The group's debut album, *Fresh Cream* (1966) shot to No. 6 in the U.K., establishing the band's blend of high-volume blues and rock at the forefront of the music scene. A second Bruce/Brown composition, "I Feel Free," was another hit in early 1967. Meanwhile, Stateside shows—featuring loud and massively extended versions of album tracks—eventually propelled *Fresh Cream* into the U.S. Top Forty.

Cream rose to new heights with *Disraeli Gears*, released in November 1967. It charted at No. 5 in the U.K., went one better in the U.S. (where it went on to sell a million copies), and spawned classics such as "Strange Brew" (U.K. No. 17) and "Sunshine of Your Love" (U.S. No. 5). But, by early 1968, there were stories of strife within the band—particularly between Bruce and Baker—and a split looked inevitable.

Despite the rumors, 1968's double *Wheels of Fire*— the live half of which was recorded at San Francisco's Fillmore West, and included Baker's seventeen-minute drum showcase "Toad"—earned Cream their sole U.S. No. 1. "The band probably was dead already, but it didn't know it," Bruce admitted to author Craig Rosen.

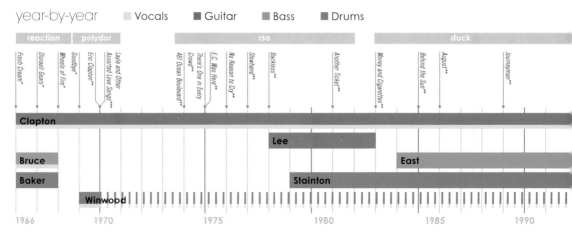

year-by-year   ▨ Vocals   ■ Guitar   ■ Bass   ■ Drums

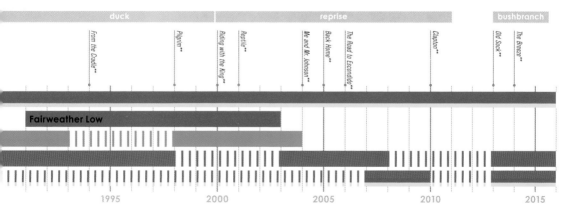

6.2M	11.8M	24M	6.6M
Slowhand	*Time Pieces*	*Unplugged*	*From the Cradle*
(1977)	(1982)	(1992)	(1994)

Nathan East
b. December 8, 1955

Andy Fairweather Low
b. August 2, 1948

* Cream
** Eric Clapton
*** Derek & the Dominos

"There were things going down through those sessions that probably led to the demise of Cream… Eric didn't do very much writing, and I didn't do much more."

In September the band finally made their much-anticipated "Cream split" announcement after little more than two years together. A farewell U.S. tour, during which "White Room" hit No. 6, was followed by two sign-off shows at London's Royal Albert Hall in November 1968, at which 10,000 fans paid homage. The band's final studio set, *Goodbye,* turned out to be their first and only British No. 1 (U.S. No. 2), aided by the George Harrison co-write "Badge."

Life after Cream saw a series of live sets and compilations surface throughout the seventies and eighties, while Clapton and Baker teamed up with Steve Winwood and Ric Grech to form the album chart-topping supergroup Blind Faith. Bruce forged an enduring solo career, co-founding West, Bruce, and Laing and BLT along the way. Baker went on to form Airforce, followed by the Baker-Gurvitz Army, and Clapton went spinning off into a host of hugely successful ventures involving Delaney and Bonnie and Friends, Derek and the Dominos, and a host of hugely successful solo recordings.

The man known to the rock fraternity as "God" and "Slowhand" survived addiction to drink and drugs while adding to his catalog of classics with the imperious "Layla," the reggaefied "I Shot The Sheriff," and the emotional "Tears in Heaven." *461 Ocean Boulevard* (1974) topped the U.S. chart and hit the U.K. Top Three, while 1980's live *Just One Night* and 1991's *Journeyman* continued his success into new decades. The Grammy-winning *Unplugged* (1992) topped the U.S. chart, and a collection of blues standards, 1994's *From the Cradle,* hit No. 1 on both sides of the Atlantic. More recently, rock albums such as *Pilgrim* (1998) and *Reptile* (2001) have punctuated journeys back to the blues, like *Riding with the King* (a 2000 collaboration with B.B. King) and *Me and Mr. Johnson* (2004).

In 1993, Cream were inducted into America's Rock and Roll Hall of Fame, with all three members reunited for the first time in decades. Bruce and Baker teamed up with guitarist Gary Moore for the faux-Cream of *Around the Next Dream* (1994), but a more serious comeback occurred in May 2005 when Clapton, Bruce, and Baker returned to the Royal Albert Hall to play four shows—all sold out in less than an hour. They completed the revival with three dates in New York's Madison Square Garden in October, to critical acclaim and a rapturous reception from fans. A year later, the trio earned the Lifetime Achievement Grammy for their all too brief period as Cream. **BS**

Fresh Cream
(1966)

Disraeli Gears
(1967)

Wheels of Fire
(1968)

Goodbye (1969)

461 Ocean Boulevard (1974)

August (1986)

Journeyman
(1989)

From the Cradle
(1994)

Pilgrim (1998)

**Me and Mr
Johnson** (2004)

Left to right: **Eric Clapton, Jack Bruce, Ginger Baker** in October 1966.

Cream pose for a portrait in Central Park, New York, in November 1968.

Studio portrait taken in 1969 featuring, from left to right, **Clapton, Baker,** and **Bruce.**

Cream on the streets of London in 1967.

Clapton chills with *461 Ocean Boulevard* in 1974.

Clapton gets lost in a guitar solo in 1986.

Clapton with Ozzy Osbourne and Grace Jones in 1989.

Bonnie Raitt joins Clapton onstage at Birmingham NEC Arena on October 13, 1998.

A live TV performance for Saturday Night Live in 1994.

Clapton with bassist Nathan East, in Barcelona in 2004, on the Me and Mr. Johnson tour.

Crosby, Stills, & Nash (1969)

Déjà Vu (1970)

4 Way Street (1971)

So Far (1974)

CSN (1977)

Daylight Again (1982)

American Dream (1988)

Live It Up (1990)

After the Storm (1994)

Looking Forward (1999)

At Stephen Stills' house in Los Angeles, the **Crosby**, **Stills**, **Nash & Young** *Déjà Vu* lineup in 1969, augmented by drummer **Dallas Taylor** (far left) and bassist **Greg Reeves** (far right).

Joni Mitchell guests with **Crosby** and **Nash** at Wembley Stadium, London, in 1971.

Nash, **Crosby** (fingers crossed it works, man), and **Stills** rehearse backstage before a concert in 1970.

CSN&Y with drummer **Johnny Barbata** in 1970, the year they taped the live *4 Way Street*.

"Captain Manyhands" **Stills** at Berkeley's Bread & Roses Festival, 1978.

Nash steps up to the mike in November 1982.

Foreground, left to right: **Nash**, **Crosby**, and **Stills** perform for Atlantic Records' 40th Anniversary Celebration at Madison Square Garden, New York, in May 1988.

Left to right **Crosby**, **Young**, **Nash**, and **Stills** play at a concert held to benefit the California Environmental Protection Initiative in April 1990.

Crosby performs at Woodstock II in 1994.

Looking Forward: (clockwise from top left) **Young**, **Stills**, **Nash**, and **Crosby** in April 2000.

Three Imaginary Boys (1979)

Seventeen Seconds (1980)

Faith (1981)

The Top (1984)

The Head on the Door (1985)

Kiss Me Kiss Me Kiss Me (1987)

Disintegration (1989)

Wish (1992)

Bloodflowers (2000)

The Cure (2004)

Robert Smith at Birmingham Odeon, England, in September 1979.

Smith and **Lol Tolhurst** with Blondie's Debbie Harry in New York, in April 1980.

Simon Gallup, Smith, and **Tolhurst** in the U.S. in mid 1981.

Implausible pop stars The Cure in all their backcombed glory in November 1984.

Bringing *The Head on the Door* to Rotterdam in November 1985.

Gallup, Smith, Tolhurst, Boris Williams (on floor), and Porl Thompson in Brazil in March 1987.

Smith on the road in the U.S. on 1992's Wish tour.

Smith in Chicago on the Prayer tour in 1989.

The Cure bring Bloodflowers to Brisbane in October 2000.

Roger O'Donnell, Smith, Gallup, and Perry Bamonte perform live in London in September 2004.

the damned 1976–present

Dave Vanian
b. October 12, 1956

Captain Sensible
b. April 24, 1954

Rat Scabies
b. July 30, 1955

Brian James
b. February 18, 1955

Roman Jugg
b. July 25, 1957

Stu West
b. December 24, 1964

Pinch
b. September 5, 1965

Monty Oxy Moron
b. September 27, 1961

British punk milestones for The Damned flew by at the same breakneck speed as the songs they spewed out: first to release a single, first to release an album, first to tour the U.S., first to split, all in eighteen amphetamine-fueled months. This was after **Brian James** met drummer **Rat Scabies** at an unsuccessful audition for the London SS, which included Mick Jones. Scabies knew a south London janitor who swapped his toilet brush for bass guitar and the name Ray Burns for **Captain Sensible**. Cemetery worker **Dave Vanian** rose from the grave to lend vampiric vocals.

Damned, Damned, Damned (1977) was recorded in a blur, with Sensible recalling that producer Nick Lowe bought them "bottle after bottle of scrumpy cider." Time was not wasted on the introductory single "New Rose." "The whole thing was written in fifteen minutes," said James. In the studio, Scabies "smashed his drum kit apart." U.K. punk was born.

Syd Barrett was mooted to produce the follow-up. In the end, Nick Mason oversaw *Music for Pleasure*. Right Floyd, wrong member. Among the touring replacements for the departed Scabies was future Culture Clubber Jon Moss, but the band fell apart. Individual projects did not ignite, so Sensible, Scabies, and Vanian re-united, with Algy Ward on bass and Sensible replacing James as guitarist/songwriter. Speed remained key on *Machine Gun Etiquette*, but psychedelia weighed heavier than garage rock.

Those interests were further explored on *The Black Album* (1980), a seductive delight whose highlight was "Curtain Call." Ex-Eddie and the Hot Rods bassist Paul Gray stayed through this and *Strawberries* (1982) as the band pulled ahead of their 1976 contemporaries.

With Sensible unable to juggle band commitments with his solo career (including 1982's U.K. No. 1 "Happy Talk"), **Roman Jugg** moved from keyboards to guitar, recommending Bryn Merrick for bass. Success arrived with the ghoulish goth of *Phantasmagoria* in 1985 and single "Eloise," a U.K. No. 3. But in the world The Damned inhabit, good times rarely last. *Anything* (1986) was a critical and commercial disappointment.

Scabies and Vanian were the only founder members on *I'm Alright Jack & the Beanstalk* (U.S. title *Not of This Earth*), which drew on ex-members of New Model Army and The Godfathers. Keeping track of comings and goings was a full-time job. Out: Scabies, Moose, Kris Dollimore, Allan Lee Shaw. In: Patricia Morrison, **Monty Oxy Moron**, **Pinch**. Back in: Sensible. Offspring frontman Dexter Holland bankrolled *Grave Disorder*, which was more like peak-period Damned. Morrison—aka Mrs Vanian—handed bass duties to **Stu West**, who featured on *So, Who's Paranoid?* (2008). Its singular sound summed up The Damned's bloodyminded attitude. Recalled Sensible: "We were just doing what we wanted to hear, because there was nothing around at the time that we liked." **CB**

year-by-year   ■ Vocals   ■ Guitar   ■ Bass   ■ Drums   ■ Keyboards

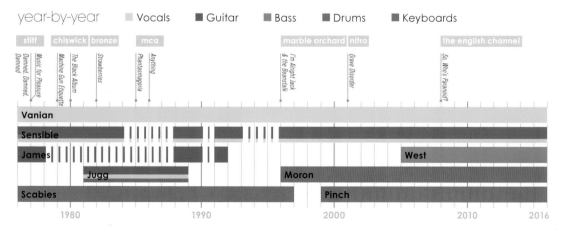

dead kennedys 1978–present

East Bay Ray
b. November
17, 1958

**Klaus
Flouride**
b. May 30, 1949

Jello Biafra
b. June 17, 1958

D.H. Peligro
b. July 9, 1959

Ted
b. unknown

6025
b. unknown

One of the greatest U.S. punk bands was formed in the former hippie haven of San Francisco in 1978. Dead Kennedys started out as a quintet, all adopting *noms de guerre*. Frontman Eric Boucher became **Jello Biafra**. He was joined by **East Bay Ray** (aka Raymond Pepperell) on lead guitar, **Klaus Flouride** (Geoffrey Lyall) on bass, **Ted** (Bruce Slesinger) on drums, and **6025** (Carlos Cadona) on second guitar.

6025 left before the June 1979 release of debut single, "California Über Alles," a withering attack on Californian governor Jerry Brown. Their follow-up "Holiday in Cambodia," was a roller-coaster of a song that lampooned Communist totalitarianism and the delusions of privileged Americans with equal venom. Next came critically lauded *Fresh Fruit for Rotting Vegetables* (1980), on which pure punk sonic assault met speeded-up surf pop and scathing social satire.

Ted left at the end of 1980 to be replaced by future Red Hot Chili Peppers drummer **D.H. Peligro** (Darren Henley). The new lineup debuted with "Too Drunk to Fuck," which reached the U.K. Top Forty despite predictable airplay restrictions. December 1981 brought the *In God We Trust Inc.* EP, dominated by full-tilt hardcore punk. *Plastic Surgery Disasters* (1982) was a more varied collection, the lyrics becoming even more caustic as the music diversified.

Dead Kennedys then took an extended break from recording as Biafra and Ray developed their Alternative Tentacles label into a home for a variety of underground acts. They returned with the well-received *Frankenchrist* (1985), but the melodically menacing music on the album was overshadowed by obscenity charges arising from a free print included in its packaging: *Penis Landscape*, an image of rows of copulating genitalia, created by *Alien* artist H.R. Giger. Biafra vigorously contested the charges and was eventually acquitted, but the lengthy legal proceedings—coupled with growing disillusionment with the hardcore punk scene—drained energy from the band. They split before the November 1986 release of their swansong album, *Bedtime for Democracy*. A gold-selling compilation of non-album tracks, *Give Me Convenience or Give Me Death*, followed in 1987.

In the late nineties Biafra was successfully sued by Flouride, Ray, and Peligro over underpayment of royalties. The resultant bad feeling was one of the reasons that Biafra declined to join in the Dead Kennedys reunion instigated by his former colleagues in 2001. Even without Biafra, however, Dead Kennedys remained a popular live act. Their first new front-man was former child actor Brandon Cruz, followed by Jeff Penalty and then Skip McSkipster. In 2011, Flouride declared that their original singer could return if he wished, but instead Biafra has devised new variations on the Dead Kennedys sound with his own band, Jello Biafra and the Guantanamo School of Medicine. **DJ**

year-by-year ■ Vocals ■ Guitar ■ Bass ■ Drums

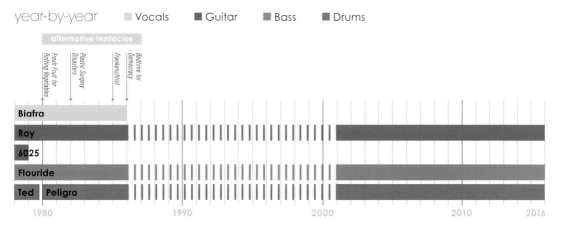

Shade of Deep Purple (1968)

In Rock (1970)

Fireball (1971)

Machine Head (1972)

"Who Do We Think We Are" (1973)

Burn (1974)

Come Taste the Band (1975)

Perfect Strangers (1984)

Slaves and Masters (1990)

Abandon (1998)

Mark I: **Rod Evans, Jon Lord, Ritchie Blackmore, Nicky Simper** and **Ian Paice** in London.

Mark II: **Roger Glover, Ian Gillan, Blackmore, Paice,** and **Lord.**

Blackmore and Glover at work on *Fireball* in London in September 1970.

Gillan unleashes his earthshaking voice in Denmark in March 1972.

The Mark II lineup rocks the Rainbow in London, February 1973.

Mark III: **Lord**, singer **David Coverdale**, bassist **Glenn Hughes**, **Blackmore**, and **Paice** in 1974.

Blackmore at the Mark II's U.K. comeback show at the Knebworth Fayre, in 1985.

Tommy Bolin, Blackmore's brilliant but doomed successor, in 1975. Less than five months after Purple disbanded in 1976, the guitarist died of a drug overdose, aged twenty-five.

Former Rainbow bandmates **Joe Lynn Turner** and **Blackmore** reunited in Purple.

Blackmore's second successor, **Steve Morse**, performs live in Melbourne, Australia.

On Through the Night (1980)

High 'n' Dry (1981)

Pyromania (1983)

Hysteria (1987)

Adrenalize (1992)

Slang (1996)

Euphoria (1999)

X (2002)

Yeah! (2006)

Songs from the Sparkle Lounge (2008)

Leppard's **Joe Elliott** at the U.K.'s Reading Festival in August 1980.

Rick Savage, **Elliott**, **Pete Willis**, **Rick Allen**, and **Steve Clark** in July 1981.

Savage, **Clark**, new recruit **Phil Collen**, and **Elliott** storm the stage on the *Pyromania* tour.

The resilient thunder god **Allen** onstage in 1987 with his specially adapted drum kit.

Elliott at the Freddie Mercury tribute show in London, in 1992.

Elliott and Collen during a tour promoting the group's sadly underrated *Slang* album.

Savage and Vivian Campbell continue to proudly defy fashion.

Leppard's resident teetotaler Collen rocks Britain's Bournemouth on the *Euphoria* tour.

Campbell, once a protégé of Ronnie James Dio, now firmly established in Leppard.

Elliott onstage at London's Wembley Arena during a co-headlining tour with Whitesnake.

the doobie brothers 1970–present

F

F

F

F

John Hartman
b. March 18, 1950

Tom Johnston
b. August 15, 1948

Dave Shogren
b. Unknown
d. December 14, 1999

Patrick Simmons
b. January 23, 1950

Tiran Porter
b. September 26, 1949

Michael Hossack
b. Sept 17, 1946
d. Mar 12, 2012

Keith Knudson
b. October 18, 1952
d. Feb 8, 2005

Bill Payne
b. March 12, 1949

It has been a *Long Train Runnin'* (as the Doobies' thirty-year retrospective box set aptly called it) for a band who garnered two U.S. No. 1 singles (five years apart), one U.S. No. 1 album, and considerable personnel and stylistic changes along the way. But perhaps the greatest accolade is an unlikely namecheck by arch funksters Parliament in their "P.Funk (Wants to Get Funked Up)" song, which notes that listening to the band is "cool—but can you imagine Doobiein' your funk?" Recreational drugs were the lifeblood of seventies California, so a band name based on slang for a marijuana joint seemed cool—and the vibe felt like they were brothers even though they weren't.

Drummer **John Hartman** had come to San José to re-form Moby Grape with guitarist Skip Spence. Instead, he formed a power trio, Pud, with lead guitarist **Tom Johnston**—still leading the band today—and bassist Gregg Murphy. With the replacement of the latter by **Dave Shogren**, and the addition of singer and bluegrass-influenced guitarist **Patrick Simmons**, the quartet became The Doobie Brothers.

They started as a roadhouse boogie band popular with Hells Angels, but their musical direction was steered by the pristine production of Ted Templeman. His vocals on the 1967 hit "59th Street Bridge Song (Feelin' Groovy)" by Harpers Bizarre gave few future pointers, but his drumming abilities injected impetus into the Doobies, as did his cooperative style of producing. As a producer at Warner Bros., he heard the Doobies' demo tape and persuaded his boss Larry Waronker to sign them. Their self-titled 1971 debut album was a dud—but, with Templeman having refined his production skills on Van Morrison's *Tupelo Honey,* he was ready to roll on the second Doobies set, *Toulouse Street.* The band now had a second drummer, **Michael Hossack**, and a new bassist, **Tiran Porter**. The radio-friendly "Listen to the Music"—with its then-novel flanging effect on the vocals—became their first hit, reaching No. 11 in the U.S.

Templeman twiddled the knobs on all their studio albums until 1980 (and returned for 2010's *World Gone Crazy*). He helped create a Spector-esque "wall

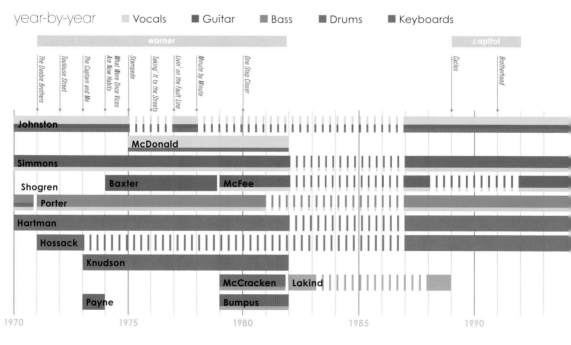

1970   1975   1980   1985   1990

Jeff "Skunk" Baxter
b. December 13, 1948

Michael McDonald
b. February 12, 1952

John McFee
b. November 18, 1953

Chet McCracken
b. July 17, 1952

Cornelius Bumpus
b. January 13, 1952
d. Feb 4, 2004

Bobby Lakind
b. April 28, 1945
d. June 14, 1992

of sound" (double power drumming, interlocking guitars, and high-rise vocals) that hit the listener full-on with their third album and finest hour, *The Captain and Me* (1973). Every track is a standout, but "Without You" and "Dark Eyed Cajun Woman"—with **Jeff "Skunk" Baxter** guesting on pedal steel guitar (he later joined full-time after leaving Steely Dan) are pure uncut Doobies. An obvious chart-topper eluded them, however; instead, *What Were Once Vices Are Now Habits* (1974) gave the band their first U.S. No. 1 in "Black Water," a country rock oddity. Originally relegated to a B-side, this part *a capella* song (**Keith Knudson** had joined the band on vocals) unravels slowly with drums overdubbed onto a rhythm machine (and not very well either). But Southern U.S. music stations picked it up and the Mississippi-inspired song grabbed the airwaves nationally.

The ...*Vices*... album title was misleading, as the band played it safe with this and 1975's countrified *Stampede*. What did change was the influence of versatile guitarist Jeff Baxter and, crucially, the arrival

of another Steely Dan dropout, keyboardist **Michael McDonald**, for 1976's *Takin' It to the Streets*. Its title track revealed that McDonald had one of the planet's best blue-eyed soul falsettos. His songwriting skills hit paydirt in 1979 with the U.S. chart-topping "What a Fool Believes." Thanks to McDonald's mellifluous vocals and the band willingness to stretch out under the guiding light of Templeman, The Doobie Brothers became polished purveyors of a more urbane, light soul-funk—more Steely Dan than Allman Brothers. The set that spawned "What a Fool Believes," *Minute by Minute*, became the band's only U.S. No. 1 album, reigning at the summit for five consecutive weeks in 1979. (Oddly, it failed to chart at all in the U.K.)

The Doobies were now pretty much Michael McDonald's backing band. His star was in the ascendancy, but Simmons's guitar-led songs had nowhere to go, and the group split in 1982 with their *Farewell Tour* live album. After a five-year hiatus, they re-formed under Johnston but without McDonald. The good time boogie band was back. **JaH**

■ Aerophones　▧ Other percussion

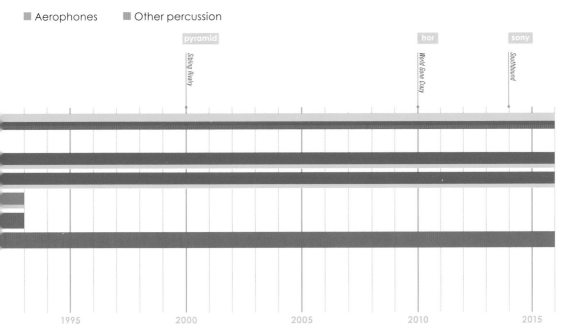

the doors 1965–1973

Jim Morrison
b. December 8, 1943
d. July 3, 1971

Ray Manzarek, Jr.
b. February 12, 1939
d. May 20, 2013

John Densmore
b. December 1, 1944

Robby Krieger
b. January 8, 1946

Few bands polarize opinion like The Doors. For some, the six studio albums they released between 1967 and 1971 burn with a seductive fire of hallucinatory imagery, paeans to sex and incitements to riot. For others, they represent an overrated grab-bag of proto-prog rock pretension. How you feel about the band's singer tends to decide which side you are on.

In 1965, The Doors—formed in Los Angeles—were just another group playing mostly cover versions in clubs. Drummer **John Densmore** provided supple, jazz-inflected rhythms. **Robby Krieger**'s sinuous guitar lines drew on flamenco, blues, and tough rock 'n' roll. **Ray Manzarek**'s chirpy Vox Continental keyboards gave the band its signature sound (he used another keyboard, a Fender Rhodes piano bass, to provide bass lines in concert). What ultimately distinguished them, though, was **Jim Morrison**: strikingly handsome; gifted with a versatile baritone that could rise from a sonorous croon to a startling blues shriek; and a poet to boot. Morrison's lyrics were informed by his voracious reading (Existentialist philosophy, French Symbolism, the Beats, avant-garde theater)—and by drugs, particularly LSD.

Having built a fearsome live reputation—the intrinsically shy Morrison developed into a powerful, if unpredictable, front-man—the band were signed to the Elektra label in August 1966. Their assured debut album *The Doors* (1967) featured a wealth of Morrison's trademark dark visions, none darker than the shocking, Oedipal-themed "The End." But it was the jazzy "Light My Fire," written mostly by Krieger, that launched the band. Edited down from the seven-minutes-plus album version, it topped the *Billboard* Hot 100 in April 1967. The follow-up, *Strange Days* (1967), explored similar territory, and included the haunting "People Are Strange" and the lengthy, apocalyptic workout "When the Music's Over." Krieger's slide guitar scintillated on "Moonlight Drive."

The Doors were banned from Hollywood club the Whisky a Go Go after Morrison littered "The End" with profanities, while an on-stage rant against local cops in New Haven, Connecticut, saw him jailed. Increasingly untogether, he made the sessions for *Waiting for the Sun* (1968) hard work for everyone, and the album suffered accordingly. "Hello, I Love You" (another U.S. No. 1) sounded too poppy for the Nietzschean Doors—and a little too like The Kinks' "All Day and All of the Night." However, their originality still shone out on the anti-war "The Unknown Soldier" and the strident Us vs. Them call-to-arms "Five to One."

The Soft Parade (1969) added strings and brass, but lacked inspiration. "Touch Me" returned the band to the U.S. Top Three, but lightweight efforts ("Easy Ride"), inoffensive singalongs ("Tell All the People"),

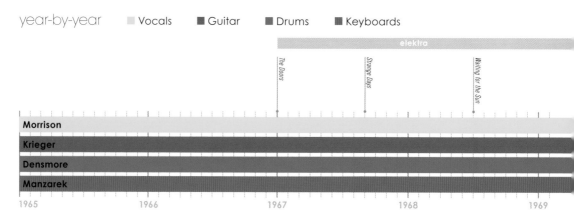

year-by-year   ■ Vocals   ■ Guitar   ■ Drums   ■ Keyboards

elektra

The Doors

Strange Days

Waiting for the Sun

Morrison

Krieger

Densmore

Manzarek

1965   1966   1967   1968   1969

D

and the long, lackadaisical title track further dented the band's image. A drunken, bearded, chubbier Morrison may or may not have exposed himself on stage at an overheated Miami concert in 1969—but, either way, the result was disastrous for the band, with panicked venues pulling engagements. Morrison now had a court case hanging over him. (He was finally pardoned, posthumously, in 2010.)

Morrison Hotel (1970) saw a return to form, the band embracing a hard, funky edge on "Roadhouse Blues" and the stark "Peace Frog," and sounding positively bouncy on "Ship of Fools" and "Land Ho!" The same year, Absolutely Live confirmed that The Doors could be a supple and powerful live act.

L.A. Woman (1971) maintained the momentum. Strong material—from the blues (including John Lee Hooker's "Crawling King Snake") to the boogie-friendly "The WASP"—earned it their eighth gold album in a row (including 1970's hits set 13). Two longer tracks dominate: the chug-along title track and the muted, melancholy closer, "Riders on the Storm," highlighted by Manzarek's brooding keyboards. Morrison's vocals are ragged but riveting throughout, though heavy smoking had shredded his voice.

Shortly before its release in April 1971, Morrison left for Paris with his partner, Pamela Courson. Three months later he was dead—probably of a heart attack while bathing, although the myth surrounding his demise endures to this day. The remaining three Doors struggled on for two years—issuing Other Voices and Full Circle (on which Manzarek and Krieger sang lead vocals)—and reunited in 1978 to set some of Morrison's poetry to music for An American Prayer.

The music was not over, though. Francis Ford Coppola's atmospheric use of "The End" in Apocalypse Now (1979), and the following year's uncritical but enjoyable Morrison biography No One Here Gets Out Alive by Jerry Hopkins and Danny Sugarman, sparked renewed interest in The Doors in the eighties. In 1981, Morrison graced a Rolling Stone cover—its headline, "Jim Morrison: He's hot, he's sexy and he's dead." The live compilation Alive, She Cried (1983) garnered strong sales and reviews. Oliver Stone's movie The Doors (1991)—featuring a startlingly convincing performance by Val Kilmer as Morrison—also did much to keep the flame alive. Manzarek and Krieger even toured as "The Doors of the 21st Century," with Ian Astbury of The Cult on vocals, and The Police's Stewart Copeland, then Ty Dennis, on drums.

More than forty years after Morrison's death, the band has shifted around 100 million albums worldwide (A 2007 hits set gave them their first Australian No. 1). It seems songs about sex and death will always sell—when the band is as good as The Doors. **RD**

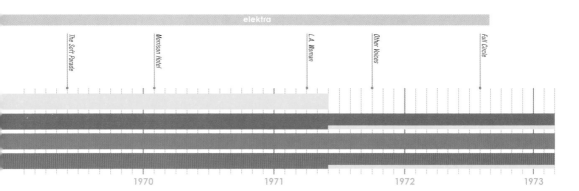

The Soft Parade · Morrison Hotel · elektra · L.A. Woman · Other Voices · Full Circle

1970   1971   1972   1973

The Freewheelin'
Bob Dylan (1963)

The Times They
Are a-Changin'
(1964)

Highway 61
Revisited (1965)

Bringing It All Back
Home (1965)

Blonde on Blonde
(1966)

Blood on the
Tracks (1975)

Desire (1976)

Oh Mercy (1989)

Time Out of Mind
(1997)

Modern Times
(2006)

A fresh-faced **Dylan** in 1963.

Performing at the Newport Folk Festival in 1964.

Sporting arguably his most iconic look at a 1966 press conference.

Dylan plays both harmonica and piano while recording in 1965.

Playing a Fender Jazz bass while recording *Bringing It All Back Home*.

At Kezar Stadium in San Francisco, California, 1975.

With Joan Baez in Houston on 1976's Rolling Thunder Revue tour.

Cruising the amps at Palau d'Esports in Barcelona, Spain, in 1989.

With The Band's **Rick Danko** (left) at the Oakdale Theatre in Connecticut.

At the New Orleans Jazz and Heritage Festival in 2006.

Eagles (1972)

Desperado (1973)

On the Border (1974)

One of These Nights (1975)

Hotel California (1976)

The Long Run (1976)

Long Road Out of Eden (2007)

Glenn Frey, Don Felder, Bernie Leadon, and, on drums, **Don Henley** perform in 1972.

Randy Meisner, Leadon, Henley, and **Frey** endure a photoshoot in 1973.

Henley captured during the *On the Border* tour in 1974.

Leadon swaps his guitar for a banjo in 1975.

Henley, Felder, Meisner (kneeling), **Leadon,** and **Frey** in 1976.

Felder, Henley, **Joe Walsh**, **Frey**, and **Meisner** in 1976.

Walsh solos on stage in New York in October 1979.

Frey at the Day on the Green concert in Los Angeles, in 1977.

Frey, **Walsh**, and **Henley** are reunited in 2007.

A new Eagles frontline of **Timothy B. Schmit**, **Henley**, **Frey**, and **Walsh** plays at the IndigO2 in London on October 31, 2007—an intimate show to launch *Long Road Out of Eden*.

einstürzende neubauten 1980–present

Blixa Bargeld
b. January 12, 1959

Alexander Hacke
b. October 11, 1965

N.U. Unruh
b. June 9, 1957

F.M. Einheit
b. December 18, 1958

Mark Chung
b. June 3, 1957

Jochen Arbeit
b. June 26, 1961

"You must draw on the musical past," said Billy Bragg in 1984. "You can't just spring out of nowhere. Unless you're Einstürzende Neubauten." Or, as a review in U.K. music paper *Sounds* put it: "I have seen the death of rock and roll and its name is Einstürzende Neubauten."

March 7, 1983 saw London's Lyceum Ballroom hosting the debut British concert by this largely unknown band of noise terrorists, who had spent the previous two years playing small art venues in their native Berlin. Strangled and screamed vocals, slow throbbing bass, and discordant guitar feedback were the only vague nods to rock convention: the rest of the performance was filled with sheets of metal, gigantic aluminum duct pipes, industrial springs, chains, slabs of concrete, and a pneumatic drill. Reports of the band's exploits attracted a large crowd, eager for a first taste of "industrial" music.

Formed by Berlin school friends **Blixa Bargeld** (Hans Christian Emmerich) and **N.U. Unruh** (Andrew Chudy), Einstürzende Neubauten—which translates as "collapsing new buildings"—played their first show on April Fools' Day, 1980. Adding **Mark Chung, F.M. Einheit** (Frank Martin Strauß), and **Alexander Hacke** (a.k.a. Alexander von Borsig)—a stable lineup for the next fifteen years—the band abandoned drums in favor of the loud crash of "found" metal percussion.

Their earliest recordings were cassettes. "The battery-operated tape recorder was an indispensable gadget..." wrote Bargeld. "We recorded discussions, music improvisation, TV, day to day noises—we yelled, looped, we kissed the microphone and threw it on long suspenders across the Wall..."

The Neubauten sound is well represented on 1981's debut album *Kollaps* ("Collapse"), issued before they had been heard outside of Berlin's post-punk scene. However, *Zeichnungen des Patienten O.T.* ("Drawings of Patient O.T.")—emerging in 1983 during their first flush of notoriety, when they were banned from venues (including Manchester's Haçienda club) because of the damage they unleashed—indicated a desire to progress beyond beating metal.

Controversy surrounding Neubauten peaked in January 1984 when they played *Concerto for Voice and Machinery* at the ICA—London's leading venue in the promotion of cutting-edge art. Before a disbelieving (albeit appreciative) crowd, the band attacked the concrete stage with jackhammers and pneumatic drills. Twenty years later, Hacke claimed the plan had been "to dig through the stage into the tunnel system underneath the venue," rumored to link up with the nearby Buckingham Palace. Officials pulled the plug after twenty minutes, but tens of

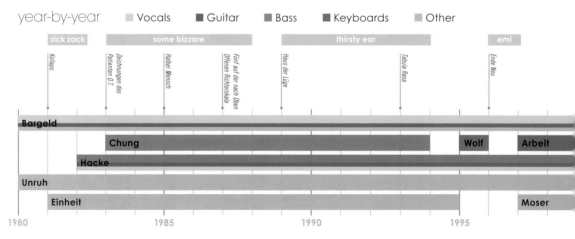

year-by-year ◼ Vocals ◼ Guitar ◼ Bass ◼ Keyboards ◼ Other

○   ○   ○   ○

100,000
Zeichnungen des
Patienten O. T.
(1983)

100,000
Halber Mensch
(1985)

100,000
Haus der Lüge
(1989)

100,000
Tabula Rasa
(1993)

Rudolf Moser
b. Unknown

Roland Wolf
b. 1965
d. March 29, 1995

E

thousands of pounds' worth of damage had already been incurred. The event duly received coverage well outside of the weekly music press. (*Concerto for Voice and Machinery* gradually acquired such a legendary status that, in 2004, the venue staged a reconstruction —albeit one with a less drastic outcome.)

By 1985, Neubauten were undisputed leaders of an industrial scene that had spawned many imitators, most inspired by the band's percussive proclivities. (Depeche Mode's live sets were clearly influenced by the German band. "Hitting bits of metal," observed Martin Gore, "is very visual.") But industrial hammering was a diminishing component of their sound, which shifted toward more conventional structures, most evident in Bargeld's newly restrained vocals and lyrics. This new approach was illustrated in the 1986 movie *Halber Mensch* ("Half Men"), which documented the band's successful visit to Japan. The same period saw Neubauten visiting the United States, where *Fünf auf der nach Oben Offenen Richterskala* ("Five on the Open-Ended Richterscale") and *Haus der Lüge* ("House of the Lie") enjoyed cult success.

The nineties saw a further softening of the band's industrial sound, with 1993's *Tabula Rasa* heralding a greater use of electronic sounds. The same year, Neubauten provided unlikely support on U2's Zoo

TV tour. Received with extreme hostility, their tenure lasted for one performance, ending when an iron bar was allegedly thrown from the stage into the booing crowd. For the remainder of the decade, an ever-shifting personnel—revolving around the hub of Bargeld, Unruh and Hacke—saw Neubauten maintain a diehard following in Europe, America, and Japan.

The new millennium witnessed Neubauten issuing a series of subscriber albums and DVDs. This approach was extended in 2005 with the launch of the *Musterhaus* project, a series of quarterly album releases intended to "give the band an outlet for more experimental impulses and exploration."

In addition to this prolific output, individual members continued a wide array of side interests and collaborations. Notably, Bargeld gave speech-based solo performances and was a long-standing guitarist with Nick Cave and the Bad Seeds.

In 2010, Einstürzende Neubauten celebrated the thirtieth anniversary of their first performances in Berlin with a sold-out tour of Europe (a U.S. leg was abandoned owing to visa problems). Few who witnessed those early venue-crushing events would have predicted such a vibrant and varied career for what is one of the most influential bands to have emerged from Europe in the past three decades. **TB**

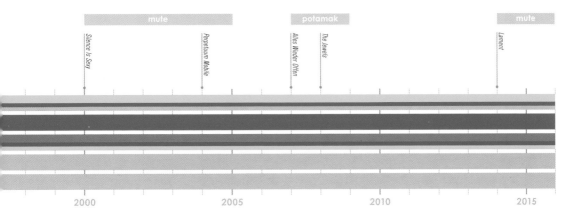

mute   potomak   mute

Silence Is Sexy   *Perpetuum Mobile*   *Alles Wieder Offen*   *The Jewels*   *Lament*

2000   2005   2010   2015

electric light orchestra 1970–present

Jeff Lynne
b. December 30, 1947

Roy Wood
b. November 8, 1946

Bev Bevan
b. November 24, 1944

Richard Tandy
b. March 26, 1948

Mike De Albuquerque
b. June 24, 1947

Kelly Groucutt
b. September 8, 1945
d. February 19, 2009

England's second city, Birmingham, has always made for something of a low-key cultural center. During the sixties, while London swung and Liverpool and Manchester produced a seemingly endless supply of chart acts, the "Brum Beat" scene was altogether more insular. The first breakout band was The Move, founded by **Roy Wood**, former guitarist with the city's leading beat group, The Nightriders. The Move hit the charts with such delightful slabs of period pop psychedelia as "I Can Hear the Grass Grow."

In 1970, with that band in decline, Wood and another former Nightrider, **Jeff Lynne**, conceived a new project that took as its template the baroque string sounds of The Beatles' "Eleanor Rigby." With Lynne joining Wood and drummer **Bev Bevan** for the final days of The Move, the trio began recording as the Electric Light Orchestra. Replete with violins, cellos, and horns overdubbed by Wood, a self-titled debut album (re-christened No Answer in the U.S.) emerged a year later. Tensions, however, appeared from the start, and Wood stepped back: he went on to enjoy an illustrious pop career of his own.

The new-look ELO—now including classically trained keyboard player **Richard Tandy**—emerged at the start of 1973 with ELO II. A rather unsatisfying, schizophrenic affair, its long, symphonic passages of progressive rock were interrupted by a rendition of Chuck Berry's "Roll Over Beethoven." As a single this was a sizable hit in the U.K., but it ensured that ELO would struggle to be treated as a serious entity in their homeland. Nine months later, On the Third Day appeared. On an album of shorter pieces, the same symphonic rock gestures were in place—violins and cellos, classical piano and Moog synthesizers—but the overall effect was this time far more cohesive. Significantly, though, it was their first album to achieve a chart placing in the U.S.

Consolidating this success with a heavy touring schedule, 1974's Eldorado (the source of "Can't Get It Out of My Head") and 1975's Face the Music impressed American critics and audiences, earning their first U.S. gold albums. These were also the first ELO albums to feature a full orchestra and choir, with arranger Louis Clark playing a key role in the sound.

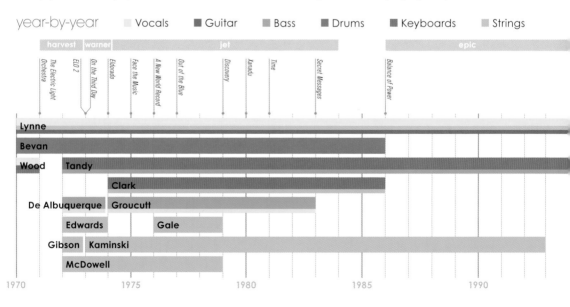

year-by-year □ Vocals ■ Guitar ■ Bass ■ Drums ■ Keyboards □ Strings

Mike Edwards
b. May 31, 1948
d. September 3, 2010

Wilf Gibson
b. February 28, 1945

Mik Kaminski
b. September 2, 1951

Hugh McDowell
b. July 31, 1953

Louis Clark
b. February 27, 1947

Melvyn Gale
b. January 15, 1953

A New World Record (1976) saw the emergence of a global phenomenon. A magnificent symphonic pop set, the album oozed confidence, and—thanks to the hit "Livin' Thing"—gave them a first U.K. Top Ten entry.

Now on a creative roll, Lynne took the potentially dangerous step of consolidating his band's popularity with a double album. Emerging in the fall of 1977, *Out of the Blue* turned out to be an album that had fans struggling to find adequate praise. A monumental hit, it yielded four international hits, among them the enduring "Mr Blue Sky."

To support the album, ELO set out on an epic nine-month world tour, accompanied by an opulent stage show. Billed in the U.S. as *The Big Night*, it became the highest grossing concert series up to that time. *Out of the Blue* remains ELO's benchmark achievement, and is regarded as one of *the* pop albums of the decade.

It would prove a tough act to follow. While 1979's *Discovery* topped the U.K. chart, it received criticism, especially for the disco feel of several tracks. Yet "Last Train to London" showed that few writers mastered the art of the irresistible hook as well as Lynne.

The group worked with Olivia Newton-John on the soundtrack of the film *Xanadu*, then 1981's *Time* saw ELO stepping back from overt commercialism with a concept album about a time-traveler from the eighties stuck a century in the future. Despite its gentle prog-rock—well out of sync with what was then fashionable—*Time* was the year's sixth-biggest seller.

Commercial success began to recede with *Secret Messages* in 1983. Conceived as a double album but forcibly cut back by the record label, it sounded tired and half-hearted. It would be a further three years before the "contractual obligation" of *Balance of Power* confirmed ELO as a spent force.

Zoom (2001) was essentially a Lynne solo album, rather than the ELO it purported to be. Bevan founded ELO Part Two—effective as a tribute band but a rather hollow experience without the man who wrote and sang the songs. However, in 2014—twenty-eight years after ELO's last full concert performance—Lynne and Tandy reunited for a charity concert in London's Hyde Park. The overwhelming success of the performance confirmed the band's official revival. **TB**

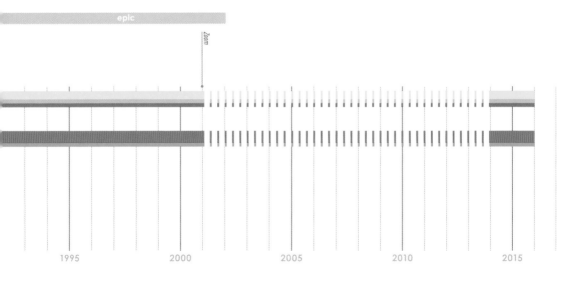

eurythmics 1980–2005

Annie Lennox
b. December 25, 1954

Dave Stewart
b. September 9, 1952

The British charts of the early eighties were flooded with synthesizer-dominated bands, as fashion turned against the guitar groups that had ruled during the preceding punk and new wave boom. Singer **Annie Lennox** and multi-instrumentalist **Dave Stewart** met in 1976 through a mutual friend and began a personal relationship while playing in one such guitar-pop band. They started out as The Catch before enjoying moderate success as The Tourists between 1977 and 1980, notably with a cover of Dusty Springfield's "I Only Want to Be with You."

The Tourists disbanded at the start of the eighties, and Lennox and Stewart ended their romantic relationship but decided to maintain their musical partnership. They named their new act Eurythmics after a method of classical musical tuition that Lennox had undergone as a child, and went to Cologne, Germany, to work on their debut album. The result was *In the Garden* (1981): a mix of psychedelic, krautrock, and electropop elements featuring contributions from Blondie drummer Clem Burke (who later toured with the duo), and Can's Holger Czukay and Jaki Liebezeit. It was warmly reviewed but sold slowly. Meanwhile, another Dave Stewart enjoyed short-lived U.K. chart success, prompting the Eurythmics' founding member to begin styling himself as David A. Stewart.

Sweet Dreams (Are Made of This), released in January, 1983, was recorded in the more humble surroundings of the duo's own tiny eight-track studio in Chalk Farm, London, though this was not apparent from the glossy production. "Love Is a Stranger" explicitly dealt with erotic obsession and took the duo to No. 6 in the British singles chart, but it was the brooding title track that brought Eurythmics their international breakthrough.

Built around a staccato synthesizer riff, "Sweet Dreams" (later covered by artists from Marilyn Manson to Leona Lewis) darkly reflected on the manipulative and masochistic elements in human interaction. It was accompanied by a startling video in which Lennox appeared in a man's suit, her hair cropped short and dyed bright orange. Heavy MTV rotation followed, helping to push the single to No. 1 in the U.S. Lennox's striking androgynous styling became her trademark and soon promoted her to pop icon status. Her image went on to grace numerous magazine covers, including *Rolling Stone*.

The video for "Who's That Girl?," the lead single from *Touch* (1983), saw Lennox take the gender-bending a stage further. She appeared as a blonde chanteuse in a club attended by Stewart, who was seen swilling champagne with a succession of different female companions, several of whom were British music stars of the time. In the video, Lennox also portrayed a moody male customer, complete with greasy rocker's haircut and stubbly chin. The two Lennoxes finally leave together, and slick editing allowed them to kiss. *Touch* yielded two more hits: the dramatic orchestral ballad "Here Comes the Rain Again" and the atypically joyous "Right by Your Side."

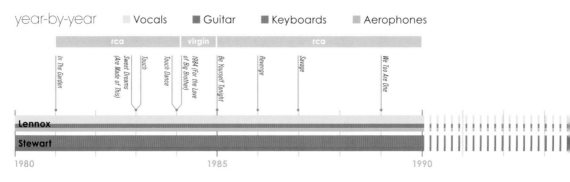

year-by-year   ■ Vocals   ■ Guitar   ■ Keyboards   ■ Aerophones

rca   virgin   rca

In The Garden | Sweet Dreams (Are Made of This) | Touch | Touch Dance | 1984 (For the Love of Big Brother) | Be Yourself Tonight | Revenge | Savage | We Too Are One

Lennox

Stewart

1980   1985   1990

3.7M
Touch
(1983)

4.1M
*Be Yourself
Tonight*
(1985)

3.4M
Revenge
(1986)

8.9M
Greatest Hits
(1991)

E

Controversy attended two Eurythmics releases in 1984. *Touch Dance* was a remix album assembled with little input from the duo; Lennox admitted to disliking it. *1984 (For the Love of Big Brother)* was a soundtrack for Michael Radford's film, based on George Orwell's dystopian novel. Eurythmics' music was commissioned by Virgin without Radford's approval—the director wanted to use an orchestral score, and publicly voiced his anger when the studio insisted on using some of Eurythmics' music in his film. The hits, however, continued with "Sexcrime (Nineteen Eighty-Four)."

Be Yourself Tonight (1985) moved away from electronica toward soul and yielded the duo's only U.K. No. 1 single: "There Must Be an Angel (Playing with My Heart)" for which Stevie Wonder provided a harmonica solo. Lennox duetted with Aretha Franklin on another international hit, the cautiously pro-feminist "Sisters Are Doin' It for Themselves."

Revenge (1986) continued Eurythmics' progress toward commercial pop-rock, with big choruses that suited the world tour the duo undertook in its support. The fans' favorite, *Savage* (1987), returned to a more experimental sound and saw a sharper feminist focus in Lennox's lyrics. *We Too Are One* (1989) did much to reinstate Eurythmics' commercial pop gloss and sold strongly despite its lack of major hits. The title proved ironic: though Eurythmics never formally disbanded, *We Too Are One* preceded a decade-long hiatus.

Greatest Hits (1991), featuring smashes from 1982 to 1990, went triple platinum in America and sextuple platinum in the U.K. The duo had, however, effectively split and embarked on a lengthy hiatus. Lennox launched herself as a solo singer in spectacular style in 1992 with *Diva*, which received Best British Album at the 1993 Brit Awards and three Grammy nominations, while earning the singer quadruple platinum in the U.K. and double platinum awards in the U.S.

Stewart formed Dave Stewart and the Spiritual Cowboys in 1990, with whom he recorded two albums before embarking on a solo career. (A parallel career as a producer has included Tom Petty's *Southern Accents* in 1985, Mick Jagger's *Primitive Cool* in 1987, Jon Bon Jovi's *Destination Anywhere* in 1997, and Stevie Nicks' *In Your Dreams* in 2011.)

Eurythmics finally reunited for *Peace* (1999), a lushly orchestrated collection and final album marked by a wistful, reflective atmosphere. The duo went on a worldwide tour to promote it, donating all profits to Amnesty International and Greenpeace.

A further reunion took place in 2005 when Lennox and Stewart recorded two new songs—"I've Got a Life" and "Was It Just Another Love Affair?"—for a new hits compilation, *The Ultimate Collection*. "I've Got a Life" is a song of defiance in the face of life's cruelties, featuring a particularly powerful vocal performance from Lennox. For the accompanying video, she once again donned a man's business suit, shirt, and tie, returning to the androgynous image that did much to launch the extraordinary career chronicled on *The Ultimate Collection*. **DJ**

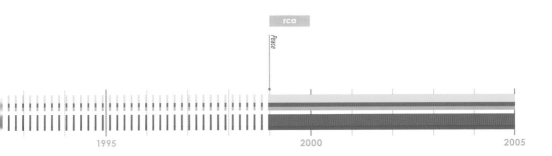

extreme 1985–present

Gary Cherone
b. July 26, 1961

Nuno Bettencourt
b. September 20, 1966

Pat Badger
b. July 22, 1967

Kevin Figueiredo
b. January 12, 1977

Paul Geary
b. July 24, 1961

Mike Mangini
b. April 18, 1963

Not quite fitting into the late-eighties wave of glam-metal but never straying that far from it either, thanks to their pretty cheekbones and penchant for tight stagewear, Massachusetts quartet Extreme scored two memorable hits in 1990 and 1991… then sank into relative obscurity. However, their reformation in recent years is testament to their impressive songs—after all, their hits still soundtrack weddings to this day—and also demonstrates the band's position somewhere outside the usual genre categories. While most glam bands of the eighties (Warrant, Cinderella, Britny Fox, we are looking at you) sound as relevant today as The Sweet, "More Than Words" and "Hole Hearted" receive as much airplay now as in those far-off days.

And let us be clear: ninety percent of Extreme's reputation rests on those two songs. Although their four first-round albums contain plenty of singable compositions, and their comeback album from 2008 is a solid effort, "More Than Words" and "Hole Hearted" define Extreme. Neither song conforms to the lightweight, diet-metal parameters established in the mid-eighties by the many hairsprayed acts whose dearest wish was to be the next Guns N' Roses or Mötley Crüe. Both songs avoided those clichés—the former because it was a wholly acoustic ballad; the

latter because it was effectively a chunk of folk rock: slide solos, twelve-string acoustic guitars, and all.

Indeed, guitars were the key ingredient in Extreme's approach. Portugal-born guitarist and founder member **Nuno Bettencourt** was and remains an awe-inspiringly gifted master of his instrument, delivering a range of styles from country picking to all-out metallic shredding at world-class standards. Nowadays he is a regular feature of guitar magazines rather than rock publications, which reveals much about the nature of Extreme's appeal to its followers.

His early band Sinful first came into contact with The Dream, featuring vocalist **Gary Cherone** and drummer **Paul Geary**, on the local rock-club scene of Malden, Massachusetts. After adding bassist **Pat Badger**, the new band was formed. Its name was derived from "ex-Dream," and inevitably, given that this took place in an era when thrash metal was at its peak, the new foursome were often thought to be an extreme metal band. Nothing could be further from the truth: Extreme's primary influences were Queen and Van Halen, with Bettencourt's clean, melodic guitar sound directly shaped by that of the former's guitarist Brian May, and his virtuoso fusillades of notes an obvious nod to Eddie Van Halen.

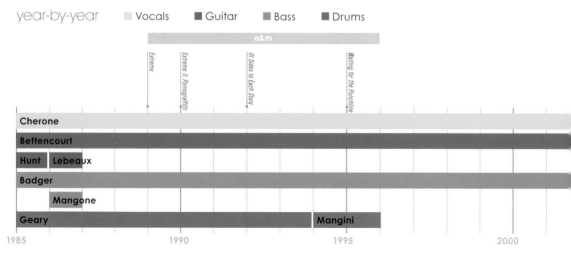

year-by-year ▪ Vocals ▪ Guitar ▪ Bass ▪ Drums

1M	5M	3M	1M
Extreme (1989)	*Extreme II: Pornograffitti* (1990)	*Ill Sides to Every Story* (1992)	*Waiting for the Punchline* (1995)

Peter Hunt
b. Unknown

Hal Lebeaux
b. Unknown

Paul Mangone
b. Unknown

A self-titled debut album came and went in 1989 without attracting much attention in the saturated rock scene. However, when Bettencourt extended his songwriting chops for its follow-up, *Extreme II: Pornograffitti* (1990), audiences responded en masse to its catchy, funky melodies and choruses—such as the saucy "Get the Funk Out." The stars aligned for the two hits, released in 1990 and 1991, which conquered charts with ease. Fans responded to the simple, heartfelt sentiments of "More Than Words" (a U.S. chart topper and No. 2 in the U.K.) and enjoyed the sly humor of its video, in which the temporarily redundant Badger and Geary lounged around with nothing to do. As for "Hole Hearted," its brisk, energetic riffage and layers of infectious vocals were difficult to resist.

Extreme were among the star attractions at 1992's Freddie Mercury Tribute Concert in London, and *Ill Sides to Every Story* (on which Geary was replaced by ex-Annihilator drummer **Mike Mangini**) hit Top Tens in the U.S., the U.K., and Japan. *Waiting for the Punchline* (1995), however, struggled to secure a foothold in an era when grunge, alternative rock, and the nascent nü-metal movement were occupying consumers. Even a knowing single from 1995 titled "Hip Today" could not slow the band's slide. The same year,

Cherone joined Van Halen, a move that endeared him to neither VH fans nor his own followers. "It was," he admitted, "very intimidating." By the time he quit in 1999, Extreme were long gone, with Bettencourt forming a series of low-key side projects. His collaboration with Perry Farrell of Jane's Addiction— Satellite Party's *Ultra Payloaded*—saw the light in 2007.

A reformation in 2004 was greeted with enthusiasm, and Extreme (now featuring drummer **Kevin Figueiredo**, another Satellite Party veteran) found themselves a niche once more. Their 2008 studio album *Saudades de Rock* (which, roughly translated from Portuguese, means "rock nostalgia") was never likely to match up to their early work, but respect for the band remains high and Extreme seem likely to be able to make a living as a touring and festival band for the foreseeable future.

Perhaps the best way to approach Extreme nowadays is on stage, where Bettencourt's guitar pyrotechnics can most easily be appreciated: happily, *Take Us Alive*—recorded at Boston's House of Blues in August 2010—was released for that very purpose. "We really live to challenge ourselves and challenge our audience," said Cherone, "and it happens every time we hit the stage." **JM**

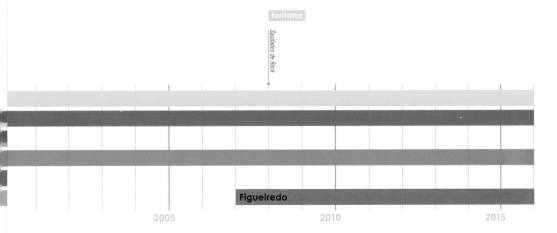

faith no more 1982–present

Mike "Puffy" Bordin
b. November 27, 1962

Roddy Bottum
b. July 1, 1963

Billy Gould
b. April 24, 1963

Mike Patton
b. January 27, 1968

Jon Hudson
b. April 13, 1968

Chuck Mosely
b. January 27, 1958

Faith No More covers Black Sabbath's "War Pigs." A musical pigeonhole is immediately identified for the band to fill, especially after tours with Metallica and Guns N' Roses. But the ever-restless outfit finds the metal label restrictive. "We were being packaged into something we weren't," says bassist **Billy Gould**. The obvious solution is found, naturally enough, at a bar. "Easy" by the Commodores plays. "We looked at each other and said, 'That's it! This'll get us out of this mess.'" Among fans, much head-scratching ensues.

It was ever thus with these brilliantly perverse Californians, a group that started in the early eighties in San Francisco, coming together around the nucleus of Gould, **Roddy Bottum** on keys, and drummer **Mike "Puffy" Bordin**. The inhabitants of other roles within the band were originally regarded as interchangeable from show to show. One of the many who came and went in the early days was future Hole front-woman **Courtney Love**, demonstrating early signs of a devotion to the spotlight that was so apparent later on. "When we played a show and there was only five people in the audience," said Gould, "she'd make sure they were all paying attention to her."

Chuck Mosely lasted longer than anyone else at this stage as front-man, while an icon of sorts came to them recommended by Metallica bassist Cliff Burton: **Jim Martin**—heavy of guitar and big of beard. "Subtlety is for old people," he rumbled to *Kerrang!* magazine. "Subtlety is for people who blow their noses into handkerchiefs in the bathroom."

The title track of 1985 studio album *We Care a Lot* caused ripples as it ticked off most boxes in its anti-everything stance. That and the pockets of intensity and invention elsewhere on the band's debut release were enough for a step over from an independent to a major label. "We Care a Lot" was re-recorded for *Introduce Yourself* (1987). The release was another leap forward ("Anne's Song" is a twisted highlight) but Mosely sometimes had trouble carrying a tune, and had a similar lack of control with his substances.

For all the promise shown so far, Faith No More needed something to set the band apart from the pack. Enter **Mike Patton**. His larynx was much more elastic than the departed Mosely's, switching lanes from style to style, while his lyrics were often things of dark beauty. It required the rock-rap crossover "Epic" to go Top Ten for America to wake up to *The Real Thing* (1989), after which record buyers discovered that they dug albums that sounded like being caught up in propeller blades.

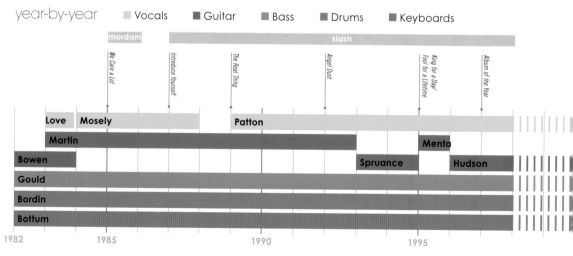

| 3M | 2M | 1M | 1M |
| The Real Thing (1989) | Angel Dust (1992) | King for a Day/ Fool for a Lifetime (1995) | Album of the Year (1997) |

Jim Martin
b. July 21, 1961

Trey Spruance
b. August 14, 1969

Dean Menta
b. Unknown

Courtney Love
b. July 9, 1964

Mark Bowen
b. Unknown

At this point, one of the biggest bands in the rock world switched to the status of one of the most interesting groups in any genre. "We can't go where we've been before," said Patton, referring to 1992's genre-bending *Angel Dust*. "It's boring and it's insulting." What one reviewer called "a baroque pomp-punk brew closer to Rush on acid than the acerbic funk-thrash fans had come to expect" included the tracks "Caffeine" and "Land of Sunshine," which benefited from a self-imposed sleep-deprivation experiment undergone by Patton.

The band and Martin parted—not on the best of terms—in 1993. Gould's reflective comment "people get tired of compromising with each other" was probably the most diplomatic way of summing up a difficult time internally. Much of it allegedly centered around a clash between Patton and Martin—ironic since the latter had recommended the former for the band in the first place, after hearing his work with the uncategorizable experimental band Mr. Bungle. To complicate things further, it was that band's **Trey Spruance** who came in to take Martin's place on 1995's *King for a Day/Fool for a Lifetime*, an album that might have lacked the out-there feel of its predecessor but conceded nothing in quality.

As far as Patton was concerned, Spruance's CV would read "great guitarist lacking any sense of responsibility." To go out on a seven-month world tour, **Dean Menta**—previously part of Faith No More's interchangeable backup team—was viewed as a safer bet for on-the-road guitarist. What was needed, however, was someone to work both on stage *and* in the studio. Gould's compadre, **Jon Hudson**, came in for 1997's *Album of the Year*. Such a title invites accusations of overarching ambition, but "Last Cup of Sorrow," "Ashes to Ashes," and the threatening electronica of "Stripsearch" made it a contender for the crown, if not the outright winner.

The band's effect on the world was good, bad, and obviously completely out of its hands. The likes of Limp Bizkit aped the style of the pioneering "Epic" but pretty much missed the point completely, so it was eleven long years before Faith No More returned in 2009—with the *Album of the Year* lineup—to show the young pretenders how it should be done. But how to reintroduce Faith No More onstage in Brixton, south London (the location used for the group's 1991 live album) for their first gig since 1998? With none other than an easy-listening U.S. No. 1 from 1978: "Reunited" by Peaches & Herb. **CB**

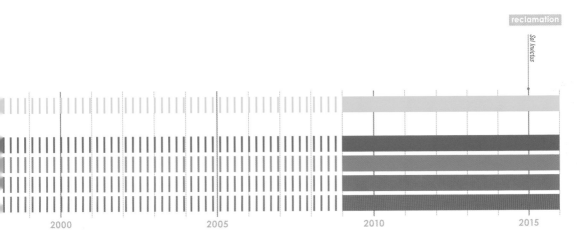

reclamation

Sol Invictus

2000   2005   2010   2015

the fall 1976–present

Mark E. Smith
b. March 5, 1957

Tony Friel
b. May 4, 1958

Una Baines
b. April 1957

Martin Bramah
b. September 18, 1957

Karl Burns
b. 1958

Marc Riley
b. July 10, 1961

Steve Hanley
b. May 29, 1959

Craig Scanlon
b. December 7, 1960

Where to start with **Mark E. Smith**'s revolving-door employment exchange? Instead of former members of The Fall, it is probably better to think of casualties of war. Those who have passed through—and, to date, that number exceeds fifty—often talk like battle-scarred veterans returned from tours of duty. They have escaped with their lives, but not always their sanity. In the same breath, many speak of unforgettable creative experiences.

At the center of this maelstrom is Smith. While seminal Sex Pistols shows inspired many to form bands, Smith saw it differently: "Whatever I did would have to be better than most of the so-called punk shite."

Named after a novel by French philosopher Albert Camus, The Fall's lineup included **Martin Bramah** (guitar), **Tony Friel** (bass), and **Una Baines** (keyboards). A drummer not around long enough for anyone to remember his name—posthumously identified as Steve Ormrod—was ejected for writing a song praising British prime minister Margaret Thatcher. Enter **Karl Burns** for the first of several stints. And, when it was time to refresh the lineup, musical proficiency was not a prerequisite. "It's like, 'You're on bass, so get cracking,'" Smith told *The Guardian*. "Seems to work."

The Fall's music is a distillation of Smith: lacerating, cruel, darkly humorous, compelling. The group's debut album, 1979's *Live at the Witch Trials*—not, in fact, live—was recorded in a single day, with future BBC DJ **Marc Riley** on bass (later guitar). A pivotal addition was **Steve Hanley**, on bass from 1979's second album, *Dragnet*. In a rare example of Smith mentioning a band member for reasons other than reminding them of their disposability, he said: "He is the Fall sound."

With *Hex Enduction Hour* (1982), the band became a chart concern, albeit a minor one. Having joined in 1983, **Brix Smith** brought qualities thus far unfamiliar to the band (and became Smith's first wife). Early Fall songs were memorable for punching holes in your brain. Now the same effect was achieved by melody. *The Wonderful and Frightening World of...* (1984), *This Nation's Saving Grace* (1985), and *Bend Sinister* (1986) are classics, with tunes to match the band's attack.

Comings and goings were relatively rare at this time. **Craig Scanlon** was a guitar rock, although the departure of **Paul Hanley** took away the pulverizing double-drummer assault at gigs. He lasted five years, commendable in itself, but still short of the nineteen years eventually served by his brother, Steve.

year-by-year

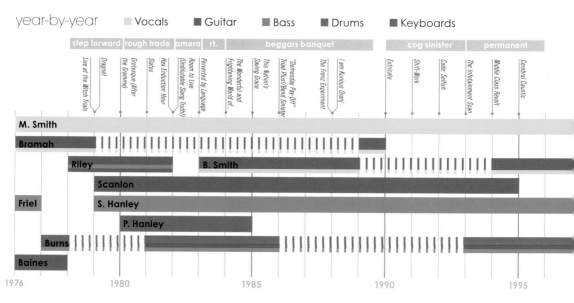

250,000
Bend Sinister
(1986)

 250,000
The Frenz Experiment
(1988)

250,000
Extricate
(1990)

250,000
The Infotainment Scan
(1993)

Paul Hanley
b. February 18, 1964

Brix Smith
b. November 12, 1962

Spencer Birtwistle
b. Unknown

Ben Pritchard
b. Unknown

Elena Poulou
b. Unknown

Steve Trafford
b. February 12, 1976

Tim Presley
b. Unknown

F

There were even charting singles, including covers of "Victoria" by The Kinks and R. Dean Taylor's "There's a Ghost in My House." In 1993, *The Infotainment Scan* gave the band what is likely to be its only U.K. Top Ten album. Divorce did not prevent Brix from reappearing for a couple of albums in the mid-nineties, while Bramah also made a brief return. Scanlon was dismissed for his "slovenly appearance" at the end of 1995, but more serious meltdowns followed.

New York, 1998: at Brownies, on April 7, Smith's noted tendency to mess with band members' instruments was taken too far for Karl Burns's liking. The drummer had allegedly been set on fire in Public Image Ltd by bass guitarist Jah Wobble, but even he had his breaking point. According to one eyewitness, he "grabbed Mark's head, which he looked like he was completely capable of crushing." Backstage, Smith was arrested, and the group packed their bags.

With Steve Hanley, guitarist Tommy Crooks, and Burns out, the fresh meat for *The Marshall Suite* (1999) included drummer Tom Head, guitarist Neville Wilding, and bassists Karen Leatham and Adam Helal. As BBC DJ—and Fall evangelist—John Peel commented: "I don't know if Smith is killing them or what."

Smith reserved special contempt for sticksmen. "You are only a drummer. I am Mark Smith," he told **Spencer Birtwistle**. The Chemical Brothers' manager Nick Dewey was drafted in at minutes' notice to play Britain's Reading festival in 1999. "After a while in The Fall, you're no longer normal," said Steve Hanley. Launching a sort of defense, guitarist **Ben Pritchard** said: "I have nightmares, but it's never boring."

There have been more Fall fallouts and walkouts (Birtwistle, **Steve Trafford**, and Pritchard left in 2006, again in the U.S.) but Mrs. Smith No. 3 (after a doomed second marriage to Safron Pryor and relationship with keyboardist Julia Nagle) arrived in the shape of **Elena Poulou**. Three releases from 2008—*Imperial Wax Solvent, Your Future Our Clutter*, and *Ersatz GB*—all feature guitarist Peter Greenway, Dave Spurr on bass, drummer Keiron Melling, and Poulou on keyboards.

The albums continue to divide the world: those who believe, as John Peel said, that The Fall is "the band against which all others are judged," and those for whom any charms stay hidden. It is fair to say that one group is larger than the other, but plowing a middle ground has never been an option. As Hanley observed: "Smith doesn't do average." **CB**

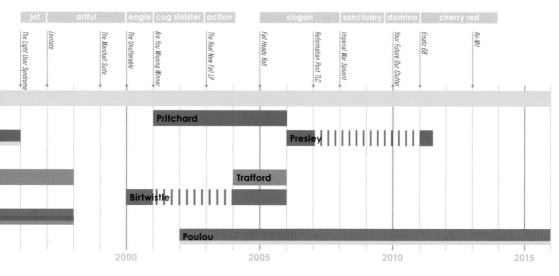

fall out boy 2001–present

Patrick Stump
b. April 27, 1984

Pete Wentz
b. June 5, 1979

Joe Trohman
b. September 1, 1984

T.J. "Racine" Kunasch
b. Unknown

Andy Hurley
b. May 31, 1980

By 2005, pop-punk was in trouble. Blink-182 were falling apart, Simple Plan had split, and pioneers New Found Glory were battling comparisons to bandwagon-jumpers Good Charlotte. Green Day had reinvented themselves as a twenty-first-century version of The Who, and the genre's youthful angsty zest was being swamped by corporate soundalikes.

Happily, saviors awaited in the forms of Paramore, who hit with *All We Know Is Falling,* and Fall Out Boy, who scored a double platinum U.S. smash with "Sugar We're Going Down." Having pin-ups in their ranks—Hayley Williams in Paramore, bassist **Pete Wentz** in Fall Out Boy—did not hurt, and neither did the fact that they were not much older than many of the fans.

Wentz and guitarist **Joe Trohman** first united in Chicago, recruiting drummer Mike Pareskuwicz and singer **Patrick Stump**. Their name referred to a comic strip character in *The Simpsons*—in Wentz's self-deprecating view, said Stump, the band would "always be the Fall Out Boy to somebody else's Radioactive Man." Their first full-length release—*Fall Out Boy's Evening Out with Your Girl*—indeed troubled no charts, but secured them a deal with Florida indie label Fueled by Ramen (the home of Paramore). It also attracted major label Island, who bankrolled 2003's *Take This to Your Grave* (featuring a

new drummer, Wentz's friend **Andy Hurley**). Touring, coupled with airplay for *Grave*'s "Grand Theft Autumn/Where Is Your Boy" and "Saturday" laid the groundwork for 2005's *From Under the Cork Tree.* The album smashed into the U.S. Top Ten, as did "Sugar We're Going Down" and "Dance Dance." The band earned a Grammy nod, and toured with Wentz's protégés Panic! at the Disco. The latter were signed to the bassist's label Decaydance, also home to Gym Class Heroes, on whose "Cupid's Chokehold" Stump appeared (he bolstered his hip-hop discography with cameos on cuts by The Roots, Lupe Fiasco, and Tyga).

Now fully fledged stars, Fall Out Boy scored a U.S. No. 1 and global smash with 2007's *Infinity on High.* The ensuing tour was commemorated by **** *Live in Phoenix,* featuring a cover of Michael Jackson's "Beat It." However, ambition bested them on 2008's *Folie à Deux.* Featuring Elvis Costello, Pharrell Williams, and Blondie singer Debbie Harry, it left all but the most devoted fans cold. With Wentz's marriage to pop star Ashlee Simpson attracting more interest than his music, Fall Out Boy were put on ice in 2009. "When you do it for seven years straight, you start grating on each other," the bassist told MTV. However, they regrouped in 2012, recorded *Save Rock and Roll* in secret, and returned to well-received live duties in 2013. **BM**

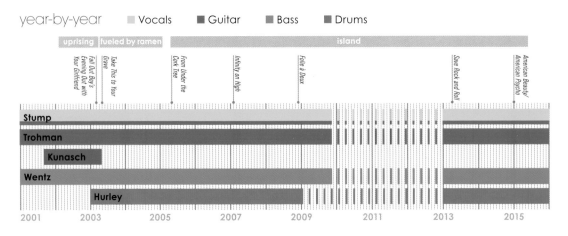

faust 1971–present

Uwe Nettelbeck
b. August 7, 1940
d. January 17, 2007

Werner "Zappi" Diermaier
b. Unknown

Hans Joachim Irmler
b. 1950

Jean-Hervé Péron
b. Unknown

Rudolf Sosna
b. Unknown

Gunter Wüsthoff
b. Unknown

In 1973, before his empire ballooned, record label owner Richard Branson introduced avant-garde German rock to the masses by selling an LP for the price of a single. As a marketing idea it was a triumph: more than 100,000 paid pennies for *The Faust Tapes*. Many buyers doubtless got no further than ten minutes into side one before consigning the record to its jacket, never again to be disturbed. But for a minority it was a life-changing entry point to an alien universe.

Faust were formed in 1971 in the rural German town of Wümme by producer and "overseer" **Uwe Nettelbeck** and musicians **Hans Joachim Irmler, Jean-Hervé Péron, Werner "Zappi" Diermaier, Rudolf Sosna, Gunther Wüsthoff,** and Armulf Meifert. Nettelbeck negotiated an advance from the Polydor label to convert a schoolhouse into a studio. The *modus operandi* was initially simple: Faust would experiment and record at their leisure, without being charged by the hour. The results would be studied and tapes chopped labor-intensively into musical fragments, to create the band's noisy sound collages.

Faust's self-titled 1971 debut LP, pressed on clear vinyl, sold poorly but won the group a passionate cult following. *Faust So Far* (1972) was another commercial failure that lost the band its existing deal but earned a new one as an early signing to Branson's Virgin label.

As a condition of the new contract, as negotiated by Nettlebeck, Faust gave an album to Branson free of charge on the condition that it was sold as cheaply as possible. Hence 1973's *The Faust Tapes* became arguably the biggest-selling avant-garde rock album of all time, and earned the band not a single pfennig.

That same year, Faust collaborated at their studio in Wümme with American avant-garde musician and filmmaker Tony Conrad on the minimalist classic *Outside the Dream Syndicate*. Meanwhile, hoping to capitalize on the wide circulation of *The Faust Tapes*, Virgin issued *Faust IV*. Sales suggested that few buyers desired a second helping: Faust were dropped from Branson's growing roster and disbanded.

Little more was heard until, in 1990, Irmler, Péron, and Diermaier re-formed for European performances and, in 1993, their first U.S. shows, with old friend Tony Conrad. New releases *Rien* and *You Know FaUSt* were hailed as the return of genuine musical pioneers.

Faust continue to function, albeit as two bodies: one headed by Irmler, the other by Péron and Diermaier. Both remain worthy of investigation. **TB**

year-by-year

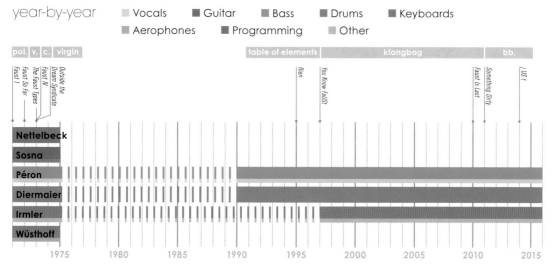

the flaming lips 1983–present

Wayne Coyne
b. January 13, 1961

Michael Ivins
b. March 17, 1963

Richard English
b. Unknown

Nathan Roberts
b. Unknown

Jonathan Donahue
b. May 6, 1966

Ronald Jones
b. November 26, 1970

"If you think you're going to hear an utterly original, powerful, and freaky record when you put on *Nevermind*…" **Wayne Coyne** complained to *The Guardian*, "Christ, you're going to be disappointed. You're going to think, 'Who is this band that sounds like Nickelback? What are these drug addicts going on about?'" This desire to buck prevailing trends has clearly informed his own band, who blazed a Technicolor trail for acts like MGMT and Passion Pit.

The Flaming Lips are the premier purveyors of modern psychedelia, employing colorful and eccentric methods of making and presenting music. They formed in Oklahoma City in 1983 as a trio: Coyne on guitar, his brother Mark Coyne on vocals, and bassist **Michael Ivins**. Their first regular drummer, **Richard English**, joined in 1984, in time to feature on a self-titled debut EP. Wayne took over as singer after his sibling quit in 1985, and the lineup produced three albums that moved from straightforward indie rock to something stranger: *Hear It Is* (1986), *Oh My Gawd!!!* (1987), and 1989's *Telepathic Surgery*.

In 1989, English was replaced by drummer **Nathan Roberts** and the Lips were joined by guitarist **Jonathan Donahue**, also a member of Mercury Rev. *In A Priest Driven Ambulance* (1990) introduced the fragile falsetto that became one of Coyne's vocal trademarks, earning comparisons to Neil Young.

Signed to Warner, the Lips made their major-label debut in 1991 with an EP whose title hardly suggested corporate compromise: *Yeah I Know It's a Drag… But Wastin' Pigs Is Still Radical*. The album *Hit to Death in the Future Head* followed in 1992, after a delay caused by clearing the use of a sample. By the time it hit stores, Donahue and Roberts had been replaced by guitarist **Ronald Jones** and drummer **Steven Drozd**. (Donahue returned to Mercury Rev, whose drummer Dave Fridmann produced many of the Lips' albums.)

The band's first commercial success came when MTV's *Beavis and Butt-head Show* belatedly picked up on the jokey single "She Don't Use Jelly," from 1993's *Transmissions from the Satellite Heart*. It took The Flaming Lips into the *Billboard* Hot 100 for the first and only time, and earned them an improbable guest spot on the teen drama *Beverly Hills 90210*.

After *Clouds Taste Metallic* (1995) sold less well despite positive reviews, Jones quit. Drozd began to contribute guitar and keyboards as well as drums and, with Coyne and Ivins, embarked on sonic experiments that culminated in *Zaireeka* (1997), a set of four CDs intended to be played simultaneously.

year-by-year   ■ Vocals   ■ Guitar   ■ Bass   ■ Drums   ■ Keyboards

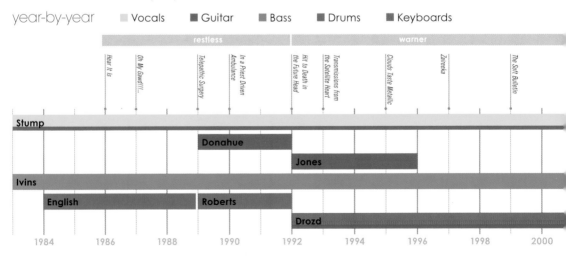

Steven Drozd
b. June 11, 1969

Kliph Scurlock
b. June 16, 1973

The Soft Bulletin (1999) boasted lush, symphonic arrangements that drew comparisons to The Beach Boys' *Pet Sounds*. The Lips expanded their live show into a colorful carnival involving dancers in animal costumes, special effects, video screens, and confetti.

Yoshimi Battles the Pink Robots (2002) added more electronica and weightier words. After its release, the band toured with Beck both as the opening act and as Beck's backing musicians. "Do You Realize??" and part one of the title track both became U.K. hits, and in 2003 the Lips collected the Grammy for Best Rock Instrumental performance for "Approaching Pavonis Mons by Balloon (Utopia Planitia)." *At War with the Mystics* (2007) featured simpler, poppier music, allied to direct and sometimes polemical lyrics. It received a mixed response but earned two more Grammys.

Typically, the Lips reacted to this acceptance by becoming outré again. In 2008, they premiered the quirky, low-budget, sci-fi movie *Christmas on Mars* that they had worked on since 2001. Then came the often cacophonous *Embryonic* (2009), on which jazz-influenced freak-outs were more in evidence than psychedelic pop. Later the same year, they teamed up with another Oklahoma band, Stardeath and White Dwarfs, plus electroclash queen Peaches and

hardcore legend Henry Rollins to remake Pink Floyd's *Dark Side of the Moon.*

The Lips spent 2011 releasing new songs in bizarre formats, such as flash drives encased in a jelly fetus or a jelly skull. In September 2011, they issued *Strobo Trip*, a package consisting of three songs—including the six-hour-long "I Found a Star on the Ground"—and a set of discs that produced visual effects when spun and lit with an enclosed strobe.

For Halloween, the Lips went to a new extreme: a twenty-four-hour song on a hard drive inside a real human skull. Only five of these macabre packages were created, but the track soon found its way online. In the same highly productive year, the band issued a series of limited-edition collaborative EPs. Four tracks from these releases were included on 2012's vinyl-only double album *The Flaming Lips and Heady Fwends*. It included collaborations with Coldplay's Chris Martin, Ke$ha, Yoko Ono, Nick Cave, and Erykah Badu—an impressive list reflecting the widespread respect that the bands enjoys worldwide. The Lips continued the collaborative theme on 2014's *With A Little Help From My Fwends*, a track-for-track tribute to The Beatles' *Sgt. Pepper's Lonely Hearts Club Band* (1967) that featured two songs with Miley Cyrus. **DJ**

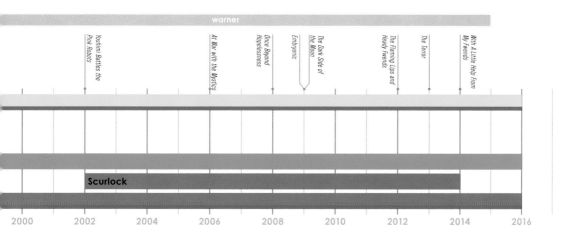

fleetwood mac 1967–present

Mick Fleetwood
b. June 24, 1947

Peter Green
b. October 29, 1946

Jeremy Spencer
b. July 4, 1948

Bob Brunning
b. June 29, 1943
d. October 18, 2011

John McVie
b. November 26, 1945

Danny Kirwan
b. May 13, 1950

Christine McVie
b. July 12, 1943

Bob Welch
b. August 31, 1945
d. June 7, 2012

Perhaps "Fleetwood Macs" would be nearer the mark than "Fleetwood Mac," for there have been many incarnations through the years. Drummer **Mick Fleetwood** had joined John Mayall's Bluesbreakers in 1967. **Peter Green** was part of that band (having replaced Eric Clapton in 1966) but, within a month of Fleetwood joining, Mayall fired him and Green. The duo promptly formed their own outfit, with Green on vocals and lead guitar, alongside guitarist **Jeremy Spencer** (ex-The Levi Set). **Bob Brunning** played bass, until he left to form The Brunning Sunflower Blues Band in September 1967, to be replaced by another former Bluesbreaker, **John McVie** (Mayall had fired him, too).

Joined in mid-1968 by third guitarist **Danny Kirwan** (ex-Boilerhouse), the quintet became shining lights of the U.K.'s blues boom, aided by Green's outstanding musicianship and songwriting chops. From 1968, they enjoyed a run of hit albums, including Top Tens *Fleetwood Mac*, *Mr. Wonderful* (featuring Chicken Shack's Christine Perfect, the future Christine McVie), and *Then Play On*. The Peter Green-penned "Albatross," "Man of the World," "Oh Well," and "The Green Manalishi (with the Two-Prong Crown)" (later covered by Judas Priest) were also British Top

Ten hits, though their melancholic tinge suggested their composer was not a happy man. Unsettled by their success and destabilized by LSD use, Green announced his departure from the group in 1970, withdrawing from the world and releasing only the occasional solo album before reappearing with his Splinter Group in the late nineties (he left them in 2004 and joined The British Blues All Stars). More positively, however, keyboard player **Christine McVie** joined.

On a U.S. tour in 1971, Spencer went out for a newspaper and never returned; he had joined a cult, The Children of God. (He later released a 1979 album, *Flee*, with the Jeremy Spencer Band.) His replacement was guitarist **Bob Welch**, who, with Christine McVie, helped steer the band in a more melodic direction.

The Mac played across the U.S. in the early seventies, with frequent lineup changes. The unreliable Kirwan was fired in 1972, to be replaced by **Dave Walker** (formerly of The Idle Race, and Savoy Brown) and **Bob Weston**, though they only lasted one album— 1973's *Penguin*. (Walker went on to form Hungry Fighter with the ejected Kirwan, then to join Raven and Mistress, and was briefly a contender to replace Ozzy Osbourne in Black Sabbath.) Meanwhile, an affair with

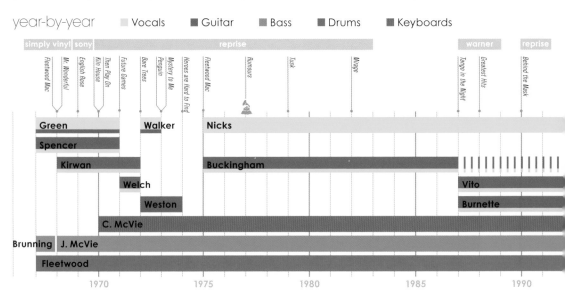

year-by-year ■ Vocals ■ Guitar ■ Bass ■ Drums ■ Keyboards

Dave Walker
b. January 25, 1945

Bob Weston
b. Nov 1, 1947
d. January 3, 2012

Lindsey Buckingham
b. October 3, 1949

Stevie Nicks
b. May 26, 1948

Rick Vito
b. October 13, 1949

Billy Burnette
b. May 8, 1953

Bekka Bramlett
b. April 19, 1968

Dave Mason
b. May 10, 1946

Fleetwood's wife Jenny saw Weston fired in September 1973. Then, toward the end of 1974, Welch departed to form Paris and embark on a successful solo career.

With Fleetwood and the McVies now settled in California, the drummer's interest was piqued by a tape of an album by **Lindsey Buckingham** and **Stevie Nicks**. The duo were invited to join the band, creating the band's tenth and most successful incarnation.

After a slow climb, the West Coast-flavored *Fleetwood Mac* made No. 1 in the U.S. in 1976. By the next year, the relationships between Fleetwood and his wife, the McVies, and Nicks and Buckingham were collapsing. "A complete disaster zone…" Fleetwood told writer Craig Rosen. "Emotional hell laced with musical pleasure." Despite (and even inspired by) their friction and cocaine habits, 1977's melodic *Rumours* became one of rock's all-time best-sellers.

Eager to avoid making *Rumours Pt II*, Buckingham pushed for an experimental approach for *Tusk* (1979). The title track and "Sara" were both hits, but the band returned to less controversial waters for *Mirage* (1982).

With Nicks having launched a platinum-selling solo career with 1981's *Bella Donna*, the Mac went their separate ways for three years. They re-formed in

late 1985 to create *Tango in the Night* (1987), which proved another huge hit. However, plans for a tour broke down and Buckingham quit, to be replaced by guitarist **Rick Vito** and vocalist **Billy Burnette** (who had played with Fleetwood in the latter's band The Zoo).

The six-strong lineup cut 1990's *Behind the Mask*, but Nicks and McVie quit at the end of the year. The full return of the Mac came in 1993, at the request of President Bill Clinton: Buckingham, Nicks, Fleetwood, and the McVies performed *Rumours*' "Don't Stop" at his inauguration party. However, it proved a one-off—instead, Fleetwood and the McVies recruited vocalist **Bekka Bramlett** and former Traffic guitarist **Dave Mason** for 1995's disappointing *Time*.

The famous five re-grouped again for 1997's live *The Dance* (1997). Coupling originals with old hits, it returned them to the multi-platinum status of old, and preceded a spectacularly successful reunion tour.

Christine McVie departed again in 2003, but the remaining four produced that year's *Say You Will* (despite renewed tension between Buckingham and Nicks) and mounted a tour in 2009. In 2013, just a year after Fleetwood said, "I don't believe Fleetwood Mac will ever tour again," they hit the road once more. **RD**

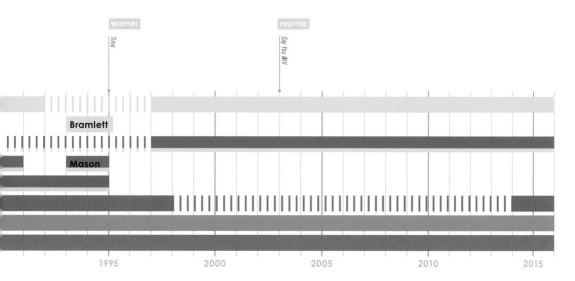

Mr. Wonderful (1968)

Then Play On (1969)

Bare Trees (1972)

Mystery to Me (1973)

Fleetwood Mac (1975)

Rumours (1977)

Tusk (1979)

Tango in the Night (1987)

Behind the Mask (1990)

Say You Will (2003)

Left to right: **Mick Fleetwood, Jeremy Spencer, John McVie,** and **Peter Green** in 1968.

Danny Kirwan (bottom left) with Fleetwood Mac in 1969.

Fleetwood plays at the Sundown, a converted cinema in Mile End, London, in 1972.

From top: **Fleetwood, Bob Weston, Bob Welch, Dave Walker, John McVie,** and **Christine McVie** in 1973.

John McVie, Lindsey Buckingham, Christine McVie, Stevie Nicks, and **Fleetwood**—Fleetwood Mac's most commercially successful lineup—in 1975.

McVie performs onstage with **Buckingham** in 1977.

Nicks, Fleetwood, Rick Vito, Christine McVie, John McVie, and **Billy Burnette**—the lineup that took *Tango in the Night* on the road after Buckingham declined to tour.

Nicks wearing characteristically other-worldly finery in 1979.

Christine McVie, Fleetwood, Nicks and **Burnette** in 1990.

Fleetwood performs with his band on *The Tonight Show with Jay Leno* in April 2003.

the flying burrito brothers 1968–2000

Gram Parsons
b. November 5, 1946
d. September 19, 1973

Chris Hillman
b. December 4, 1944

Michael Clarke
b. June 3, 1946
d. December 19, 1993

Sneaky Pete Kleinow
b. Aug 20, 1934
d. January 6, 2007

Chris Ethridge
b. February 10, 1947
d. April 23, 2012

Bernie Leadon
b. July 19, 1947

John Beland
b. July 24, 1949

Gib Guilbeau
b. September 26, 1937

When the experimental International Submarine Band petered out owing to a lack of success, bassist Ian Dunlop dreamed up a name for a new band (featuring ex-ISB drummer Mickey Gauvin) that reflected the soul, jump, rock 'n' roll, and western swing they wanted to play. The Flying Burrito Brothers were born, but the name was soon adopted by another two former ISB members, **Gram Parsons** and the short-stayed John Nuese. Parsons buried old animosity with **Chris Hillman** (with whom he had played in The Byrds) and the two set about writing the country rock classic *The Gilded Palace of Sin* in 1968.

The Parsons/Hillman partnership flourished at a house—nicknamed "Burrito Manor"—shared by the two in L.A. An A&M contract followed and *The Gilded Palace of Sin*, despite only minor chart success in 1969, proved to be an album of enduring quality, reflected by its rank in the top half of *Rolling Stone*'s 500 Greatest Albums of All Time list. "Christine's Tune (Devil in Disguise)" was typical of the Burritos'souped-up country music. Parsons' laidback interpretation and persistent love of the genre extended to the band's extraordinary stage apparel: Nudie suits boasting traditional embroidery, with Gram's depicting marijuana leaves and naked women.

Another ex-Byrd, **Michael Clarke** joined and, before the end of 1969, **Chris Ethridge** left. Guitarist

Bernie Leadon arrived ahead of *Burrito Deluxe* (1970). The harmony Hillman and Parsons had enjoyed was now compromised by the latter's drug dependency. Parsons went solo, and Rick Roberts joined for *The Flying Burrito Bros* (1971). The revolving door hadn't stopped yet: **Sneaky Pete Kleinow** left, replaced by pedal steel legend Al Perkins. Kenny Wertz filled the void left by Leadon, who hooked up with the new kids in town, the Eagles. The live *Last of the Red Hot Burritos* (1972) seemed to signal the end, leaving Hillman to close down the band. Rick Roberts soldiered on with a Burritos tour of Europe in 1973 while 1974's *Close Up the Honky Tonks* compilation kept the flag flying.

The death of Parsons in 1973 heightened interest in his past recordings, and a reconvened band—featuring the returning Kleinow and Ethridge, with new additions Gene Parsons, **Gib Guilbeau**, and Joel Scott Hill—released the appropriately titled *Flying Again* (1975). A year later, *Airborne* saw former Byrd Skip Battin replacing Ethridge. A less rock-oriented, more countrified Burritos wowed fans and critics.

With Guilbeau and newly joined **John Beland**, supported by veteran Burrito Kleinow (and a long line of the finest country musicians), they soared toward a *Billboard* award in 1981 for Best New Country crossover group—exactly what early Burritos Parsons and Hillman had been striving for in 1968. **DR**

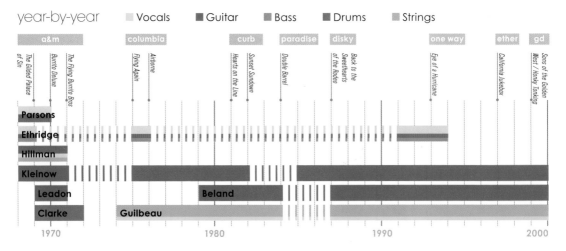

year-by-year ▢ Vocals ▮ Guitar ▮ Bass ▮ Drums ▢ Strings

focus 1969–present

Thijs van Leer
b. March 31,
1948

Jan Akkerman
b. December 24, 1946

Hans Cleuver
b. Unknown

Pierre van der Linden
b. February 19, 1946

Cyril Havermans
b. Unknown

Bert Ruiter
b. November 26, 1946

David Kemper
b. 1947 or 1948

A talented bunch of progressive jazz-rockers, the Dutch group Focus came together in 1969, comprising **Thijs van Leer** (keyboards, flute, vocals), **Jan Akkerman** (guitar), Martin Dresden (bass), and **Hans Cleuver** (drums). The alternative title of *Focus Plays Focus*, their 1970 debut—*In and out of Focus*—proved prophetic: Akkerman promptly left to play with **Cyril Havermans** (bass) and **Pierre van der Linden** (drums). But when Dresden and Cleuver also departed, van Leer swiftly teamed up with Akkerman's trio to form a new Focus.

This lineup recorded *Focus II*—also known as *Moving Waves*. It bore a surprise hit in the exhilarating, yodeling "Hocus Pocus," which rose to No. 9 in the U.S., balanced by the classically inspired, sidelong "Eruption." The album peaked at No. 2 in the U.K.

Havermans then left to be replaced by bassist **Bert Ruiter**. *Focus 3* (1972), a U.K. No. 6, featured another hit, "Sylvia," a U.K. No. 4, as well as another full-length workout, "Anonymous II." The live *At the Rainbow* (1973) caught Focus near the group's zenith.

British drummer Colin Allen replaced van der Linden before their next studio recording, *Hamburger Concerto* (1974). It boasted a lengthy title track based on a Brahms variation on a Haydn theme, yet still made the U.K. Top Twenty. The lighter, poppier *Mother Focus* (1975) followed with twelve radio-friendly songs,

with **David Kemper** now on drums. *Ship of Memories* was released in 1976, although all the tracks had been originally recorded for release in 1973 and 1974.

Akkerman, who apparently never liked those sessions, departed once more, with guitarists Philip Catherine and Eef Albers coming in to play on the next album, as did drummer Steve Smith. Never a predictable group, Focus then united with flamboyant American singer P.J. Proby for *Focus con Proby* (1977).

Van Leer and Akkerman created *Focus*—confusingly, not a group album—in 1985 and briefly reunited with Ruiter in 1990. After 1994's *The Best of Focus: Hocus Pocus*, van Leer made another attempt at re-forming the group in 1999, with Ruiter, Cleuver, and new guitarist Menno Gootjes. It did not last.

Finally, van Leer successfully re-formed the group in 2001, with Jan Dumeé (guitar), Bobby Jacobs (bass), and Ruben van Roon (drums), although the latter was soon replaced by Bert Smaak. This new incarnation recorded *Focus 8* (2002) and toured extensively—hence 2003's *Live in America* and 2004's *Live in South America*—before van der Linden returned in place of Smaak. Nils van der Steenhoven came in on guitar for Dumeé to record *Focus 9/New Skin* (2006) to the group's satisfaction, although Gootjes reappeared to oust him in 2010. In and out of Focus, indeed! **MiH**

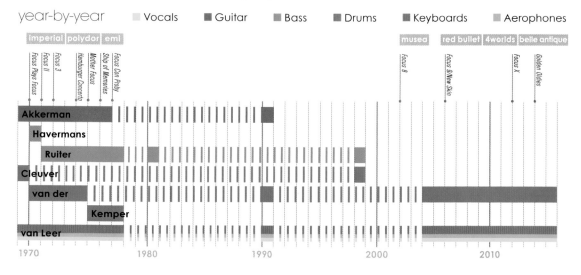

year-by-year　■ Vocals　■ Guitar　■ Bass　■ Drums　■ Keyboards　■ Aerophones

Nursery Cryme
(1971)

Foxtrot (1972)

Selling England by the Pound (1973)

The Lamb Lies Down on Broadway (1974)

A Trick of the Tail (1976)

And Then There Were Three (1978)

Abacab (1981)

Invisible Touch (1986)

We Can't Dance (1991)

Calling All Stations (1997)

Peter Gabriel's sense of theater helped draw attention to Genesis.

Peter Gabriel and **Mike Rutherford** on the *Lamb* tour.

The classic incarnation in concert in the early seventies, now with **Phil Collins** on drums.

Steve Hackett appears with Genesis at Newcastle City Hall, England, in October 1973.

In New York in 1976: **Hackett, Phil Collins,** King Crimson drummer **Bill Bruford (who guested for the A Trick of the Tail tour), Tony Banks,** and **Rutherford.**

Rutherford silhouetted against Collins in Rotterdam, The Netherlands, in September 1978.

Collins and Banks at The Spectrum, Philadelphia, on the *Abacab* tour, in November 1981.

Genesis take a bow at Wembley Stadium, London, on July 3, 1987. Left to right Collins, Chester Thompson, Banks, Rutherford, and Daryl Stuermer.

Collins sings in 1992; he took over vocal duties from Gabriel in 1975.

Ex-Stiltskin vocalist Ray Wilson performs with Banks in 1997.

gilberto gil 1964–present

Gilberto Gil
b. June 26, 1942

Caetano Veloso
b. August 7, 1942

Maria Bethânia
b. June 18, 1946

Gal Costa
b. September 26, 1945

Tom Zé
b. October 11, 1936

One of the giants of Brazilian music, singer, songwriter, and guitarist **Gilberto Gil** established a reputation for innovation that began with his central role in the Tropicália movement. He eventually emerged as one of the country's biggest-selling artists, incorporating an eclectic range of influences, including rock, samba, bossa nova, reggae, and music from Africa. Gil's lifelong commitment to Brazilian politics saw him first exiled by the country's military leadership in the seventies and then, thirty years later, taking a senior ministerial position in the government of President Luiz Inácio Lula da Silva.

Gilberto Gil was born in Salvador, an industrial city in the northeast of Brazil. He came from a solidly middle-class background: his father was a doctor and his mother a school teacher. Gil was prodigiously talented—by the age of ten he was already playing the drums and trumpet, as well as studying classical accordion. At high school, Gil joined his first band, Os Desafinados ("The Out of Tunes"), but hearing guitarist João Gilberto led him to abandon the accordion and learn to play bossa nova on the acoustic guitar. (Fellow vocalist Robert Palmer later described him as "the most tender of all the bossa nova singers.")

In 1963, while a business student at the Federal University of Bahia in Salvador, Gil met singer and guitarist **Caetano Veloso**. A year later, with Veloso, **Maria Bethânia**, **Gal Costa**, and **Tom Zé**, Gil took part in *Nos Por Exemplo* ("Us, For Example"), a show of bossa nova and traditional Brazilian songs, eventually becoming its musical director. This collective, under the leadership of Gil and Caetano, came together once again on the landmark *Tropicália: Ou Panis et Circensis* ("Tropicália: Or Bread and Circuses") in 1968, one of Brazilian music's most important albums, and, according to Gil, the birth of Tropicália, an artistic movement based on the idea of *antropofagia*—the taking of cultural influences from different genres to create something unique. The stars of Tropicália, among them Os Mutantes, would play a dominant role in Brazilian culture over the coming decades.

Gil enjoyed his first personal success in 1965 when singer Elis Regina had a hit with his song "Louvação." He also began to establish a name for himself as a protest singer at this time, and in 1967 he recorded his debut album, also called *Louvaçao*. A year later, he produced a characteristic Tropicália follow-up with his second album, *Gilberto Gil*, which blended traditional Brazilian styles such as samba and bossa nova with electric rock music provided by Os Mutantes.

The antics of the Tropicálistas did not sit well with Brazil's right-wing military regime, and in February 1969

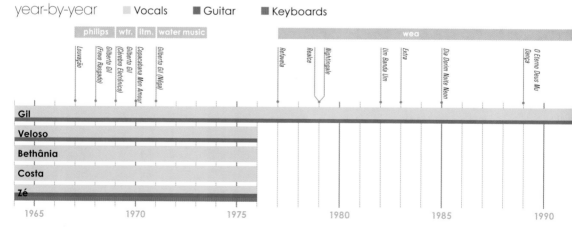

year-by-year   ■ Vocals   ■ Guitar   ■ Keyboards

both Gil and Veloso were arrested; they spent three months in prison and a further four under house arrest. No official reasons were ever given but Gil would maintain that the authorities saw the emergence of their new culture as a threat.

Released from custody, Gil, Veloso, and their wives were exiled to London, where they remained for three years. (They lived in Chelsea with singer Terry Reid, and the Tropicália influence can be clearly heard on his 1973 album *River.*) As a songwriter, this period gave Gil plenty of ammunition for his new material and, while in London, Jimmy Cliff and Burning Spear also provided his first exposure to reggae, which would have a profound effect on his future music.

Returning to Brazil in 1972, Gil recorded *Expresso 2222*—which yielded two major hits, "Back in Bahia" and "Oriente"—before beginning a period of collaborations. This culminated in a 1976 "supergroup" tour with Veloso, Costa, and Bethânia—by then three of the biggest stars in Brazilian musical history— documented on the massive-selling live album *Doces Báraros.* During the seventies and eighties, much of Gil's work followed contemporary trends and production methods, and it can sound rather dated. Songs from this period are generally better appreciated on his many live recordings.

Until 1977, Gil's success had largely been restricted to his homeland. An international deal with the WEA group of labels enabled him to establish a broader following, touring extensively throughout the U.S., his albums no longer restricted to the specialist import bins. In 1982 he enjoyed a huge crossover success with the joyous, sophisticated jazz funk of "Palco," a dance hit that led to greater exposure of his music in Europe.

Back in Brazil, Gil had become increasingly politically active as a prominent spokesman for black rights within his country. He was also largely responsible for the introduction of reggae to Brazil when his 1980 cover of Bob Marley's "No Woman No Cry" topped the chart, selling over 750,000 copies.

During the nineties, Gil found increasing support for his growing involvement in social and political causes, and he was elected to office in his hometown, Salvador. In 2003, he became Brazil's Minister of Culture, before stepping down in 2008, citing health reasons. His music had taken a back seat during this period, but in 2010 he signaled a return with *Fé Na Festa*—an album of original songs performed in traditional forró style—marking the São João festival celebrated in his native northeast Brazil.

Gil continues to tour, and features in Spike Lee's 2012 documentary, *Go Brazil, Go!* **TB**

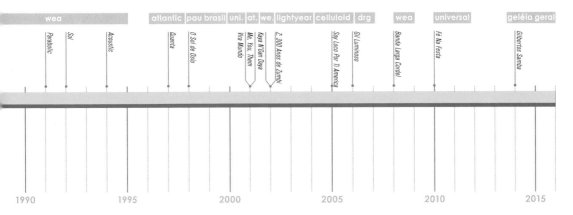

grateful dead 1965–1995

Jerry Garcia
b. August 1, 1942
d. August 9, 1995

Bob Weir
b. October 16, 1947

Phil Lesh
b. March 15, 1940

Ron "Pigpen" McKernan
b. September 8, 1945
d. March 8, 1973

Bill Kreutzmann
b. May 7, 1946

Mickey Hart
b. September 11, 1943

Of all the groups to emerge from America's West Coast in the sixties, The Grateful Dead managed to combine different musical styles with long-lasting success better than any, while epitomizing with panache what the hippie counter-culture stood for.

Jerry Garcia (guitar), **Bob Weir** (guitar), **Phil Lesh** (bass), **Ron "Pigpen" McKernan** (keyboards), and **Bill Kreutzmann** (drums) formed The Warlocks in San Francisco in early 1965, becoming the Grateful Dead a year later. Ken Kesey's contemporary Robert Hunter, who was to become lyricist for many of the group's songs, was partly instrumental in bringing them together. From their commune in Haight-Ashbury, San Francisco, the band's reputation—based on lengthy, improvisational live shows and their enthusiastic espousal of psychedelic drugs—grew rapidly.

The Grateful Dead (1967) was a solid debut, although the group felt it was not fully representative of their free-form spirit. **Mickey Hart** (drums) joined later in 1967, and **Tom Constanten** (keyboards) was added before *Anthem of the Sun* (1968). It was rather too experimental for commercial success (and is the

only one of their early albums yet to go gold) but, artistically, the group were happy with it. *Aoxomoxoa* (1969), including "St. Stephen," featured further interesting experimentation and the Dead were now established as an outstanding live draw.

Live/Dead (1969) proved their unrivaled ability to improvise on blues rock and acid rock themes, with Garcia's extended lead solos and Weir's sympathetic interplay to the fore. Constanten left at the start of 1970, which was to prove the *annus mirabilis* of their studio output. *Workingman's Dead* (1970) was another change in direction, with more succinct songs in a country rock vein, and gave the Dead their first taste of the U.S. Top Thirty. *American Beauty* came out later the same year, broke into the Top Thirty again, and gave the band their highest U.K. chart placing, No. 27.

Typically, the group followed these triumphs with a bout of solo projects and further upheavals. Hart left—possibly because his father, who had been the Dead's manager, absconded with a lot of their cash. Around the same time, Pigpen's narcotic and alcohol habits were causing problems and the jazz-leaning

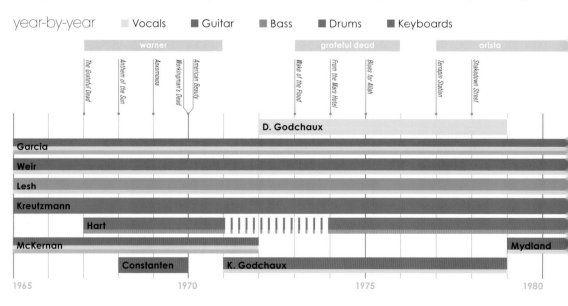

| 1.5M | 3.2M | 4.1M | 3M |
| *Workingman's Dead* (1970) | *American Beauty* (1970) | *Skeletons from the Closet* (1974) | *In the Dark* (1987) |

Tom Constanten
b. March 19, 1944

Keith Godchaux
b. July 19, 1948
d. July 23, 1980

Donna Godchaux
b. August 22, 1947

Brent Mydland
b. October 21, 1952
d. July 26, 1990

Vince Welnick
b. February 21, 1951
d. June 2, 2006

Bruce Hornsby
b. November 23, 1954

Keith Godchaux joined as another keyboard player. Two more live albums emerged, the second of which, *Europe '72*, reached No. 12 in the U.S. By this time, **Donna Godchaux** (vocals) had joined her husband in the group. Meanwhile, Pigpen quit the band; he died from liver complications in 1973.

Wake of the Flood, released just afterward, was the group's first studio album for three years, and reached No. 18 on the *Billboard* chart. *From the Mars Hotel* (1974) went one place better and Hart rejoined in time for *Blues for Allah* (1975), a U.S. No. 12.

The lush *Terrapin Station* (1977), featuring "Estimated Prophet" and the long title track, and *Shakedown Street* (1978), produced by Little Feat's Lowell George, fell short of the Top Twenty, although both subsequently reached gold status. With the pressures of endless touring, they increasingly turned to harder drugs. Keith and Donna Godchaux left, replaced by **Brent Mydland** (keyboards) in 1979.

Go to Heaven (1980) was the Dead's last studio album for seven years, while they continued to play live and wrestle with their demons. Garcia became

so seriously ill in 1985 that he was forced to clean up. Their comeback album, *In the Dark* (1987), was their biggest seller, reaching No. 6. Its single, "Touch of Grey," became their only Top Forty single, peaking at No. 9 as they toured with Bob Dylan (hence 1989's gold-selling but rotten live album *Dylan & the Dead*).

Built to Last (1989) proved to be the Dead's final studio album: Mydland died in 1990, replaced by **Vince Welnick**, formerly of The Tubes; **Bruce Hornsby** also played piano from 1990 to 1992. The Dead were inducted into the Rock and Roll Hall of Fame in 1994, but the end was near. Garcia died in 1995, and the rest of the group called it a day, although there have been various revivals since. The band's numbers were further depleted when Welnick tragically took his own life in 2006. As a belated testimonial, the surviving members of the Grateful Dead were given a Grammy Lifetime Achievement Award in 2007. "The Dead," observed Warren Haynes (who has played with later versions of the band), "redefined success. They created this following that grew and grew, and they did it without compromising themselves." **MiH**

■ Aerophones ▓ Other percussion

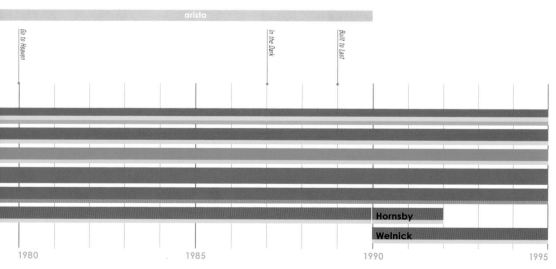

green day 1987–present

Billie Joe Armstrong
b. February 17, 1972

Mike Dirnt
b. May 4, 1972

Al Sobrante
b. July 11, 1969

Tré Cool
b. December 9, 1972

Green Day helped drive the rebirth of U.S. punk in the nineties, and evolved in the twenty-first century to appeal to a whole new generation of fans. The band began as a hobby of Californian teens **Billie Joe Armstrong** and Mike Pritchard (known to his friends as **Mike Dirnt**) in 1987, at a time when bands like Guns N' Roses and Mötley Crüe were the characters—and performers—that most kids like them were idolizing. But Armstrong and Dirnt preferred punk heroes, in particular fellow Californians Rancid, a punk outfit set up by Tim Armstrong and Matt Freeman, and set about forming a group in the same vein, originally known as Sweet Children. Billie Joe assumed vocal duties and guitar while Mike took up bass.

A year later, they met drummer John Kiffmeyer, better known as **Al Sobrante** (the nickname was a reference to his hometown of El Sobrante, California), who was a couple of years older and assumed the role of manager. A party derailed by snow would prove to be the band's big break. Scheduled to play with fellow local band, the Lookouts, adverse weather conditions saw Sweet Children playing to a handful of friends. Lookouts' singer Larry Livermore was impressed and signed them to his independent label for their first EP, *1,000 Hours*, released in April 1989.

Renamed Green Day, the band issued their debut album *39/Smooth* in 1990. "They were in bands when they were fourteen and put out their own record when the lead singer was seventeen..." observed

R.E.M.'s guitarist Peter Buck, admiringly. "They're heirs to a tradition: you're sixteen, you write punk songs, you make your own record on a small label, you tour."

Sobrante's college commitments saw him leave the band in 1990, with Lookouts' drummer **Tré Cool** (born Frank Edwin Wright III) stepping in. With him, Green Day's sophomore album, *Kerplunk!*, released in April 1992, featured an early version of their signature song "Welcome to Paradise." The trio's underground momentum was building, and they opted to sign to Reprise, a subsidiary of Warner.

Backed by a major label, Green Day hit the big time with *Dookie* (1994), as the trio became poster boys for the emerging punk generation (even old hands like Elton John and Patti Smith expressed their liking for them). Tracks such as "When I Come Around," "Longview," and "Basket Case" helped *Dookie* to No. 2 in the U.S. chart and No. 13 in the U.K., with sixteen million copies eventually shifted worldwide. A mudfight with the audience at August 1994's Woodstock II festival provided one of the event's most memorable performances.

Insomniac followed a year later, and equaled *Dookie*'s U.S. position of No. 2 (U.K. No. 8). The album—whose working title, Armstrong later claimed, was *Jesus Christ Supermarket*—could not match the runaway success of its predecessor, but nonetheless went double platinum on the back of tracks like "Geek Stink Breath" and "Walking Contradiction."

year-by-year ▢ Vocals ▪ Guitar ▪ Bass ▪ Drums

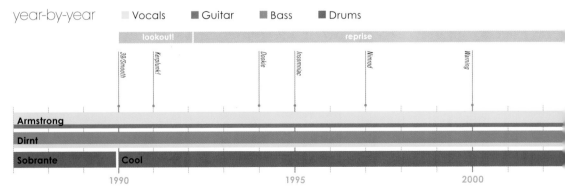

With a loyal fanbase sustaining the group once the hype had dissipated, *Nimrod* (1997) made the U.S. Top Ten (U.K. No. 11). The album is notable for the acoustic gem "Good Riddance (Time of Your Life)," which became a lighter-raising moment at live shows.

Warning (2000) proved a watershed for Green Day. After a three-year gap between albums, it rocketed to No. 4 in both the U.S. and the U.K., but sales were no match for previous efforts. Critics were beginning to sharpen their pens, with *NME* describing the album as "the sound of a band losing its way." More embarrassingly, in 2002, Green Day found themselves supporting Blink-182, a punk trio who had originally followed in their footsteps.

The band busied themselves with *Money Money 2020*, recorded with friends and issued under the band name The Network in 2003, and a new album, *Cigarettes and Valentines*. When the latter began to look like just another entry in their dwindling career, they abandoned it and instead, with producer Rob Cavallo, created the greatest album of their career.

With a new image and sound, the unashamedly grandiose *American Idiot* (2004) was a rock opera whose energy never flagged—even with two tracks, "Jesus of Suburbia" and "Homecoming," clocking in at over nine minutes each and split into "acts." *American Idiot* rocketed to No. 1 in both the U.S. and the U.K., ultimately becoming the band's second-biggest seller. Five of its songs were hits, with "Boulevard of Broken Dreams" and "Wake Me Up When September Ends" both making the U.S. Top Ten (and, in the former's case, going double platinum).

American Idiot earned a Grammy nomination for album of the year. Ultimately, it picked up the trophy for best rock album, while "Boulevard of Broken Dreams" took the prestigious Record of the Year award (its video won six trophies at the MTV Video Music Awards in 2005). The album even spawned a musical of the same name—a move into the mainstream that emphasized the gulf between Green Day and their former contemporaries. The *American Idiot* tour was commemorated by *Bullet in a Bible*, a 2005 CD/DVD set recorded at massive shows in Britain.

The follow-up would always be a big ask, but Green Day cemented their position in punk and rock history with *21st Century Breakdown* in 2009. Despite the longest gap between albums of the trio's career, it picked up where *American Idiot* left off, hitting No. 1 around the world. (The ensuing stadium tour was cherry-picked to create another CD/DVD set, 2011's modestly monickered *Awesome as F**k*.)

Carrying on its predecessor's social commentary, *21st Century Breakdown*—their fifth Grammy-winner— underlined Green Day's enviable position as a band with something to say and an audience that would listen. The *¡Uno!, ¡Dos!, ¡Tré!* trilogy emerged in 2012, and the band remain stadium-fillers—a long way from two kids with a dream in a Californian garage. **DH**

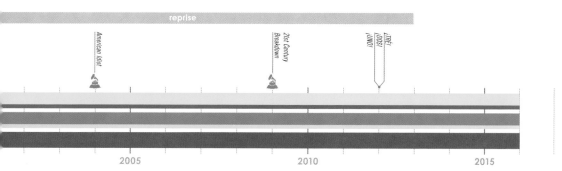

39/Smooth
(1990)

Kerplunk!
(1991)

Dookie
(1994)

Insomniac
(1995)

Nimrod
(1997)

Billie Joe Armstrong at one of Green Day's formative punk shows.

Mike Dirnt, **Armstrong**, and **Tré Cool** make their punk roots clear in a promotional shot.

Continuing to deplete California's hair dye reserves at the Shoreline Amphitheater in 1994.

Armstrong rocks the Lowlands festival in the Netherlands, in 1995.

Warning
(2000)

American Idiot
(2004)

21st Century Breakdown
(2009)

¡Uno! (2012)

Armstrong and **Dirnt** live in L.A., shortly before the release of *Nimrod*.

Dirnt defies their decline as the twenty-first century dawns.

Say cheese: **Dirnt**, **Cool**, and **Armstrong** circa *Warning*.

Displaying a new sense of purpose as the *American Idiot* era begins.

At 2009's American Music Awards, where the trio played *21st Century Breakdown*'s opening hit, "21 Guns."

Armstrong performs onstage during the iHeartRadio Music Festival in Las Vegas on September 21, 2012.

Appetite for Destruction (1987)

Use Your Illusion I (1991)

Use Your Illusion II (1991)

"The Spaghetti Incident?" (1993)

Chinese Democracy (2008)

Duff McKagan and **Slash** rock the Ritz club in New York: a 1988 concert shown on MTV.

Axl Rose, possibly still a farm-boy from Indiana·at heart, in 1987.

Still standing—just—after a series of dates supporting Mötley Crüe in late 1987, the classic line-up of **McKagan**, **Slash**, **Rose**, **Izzy Stradlin**, and **Steven Adler**.

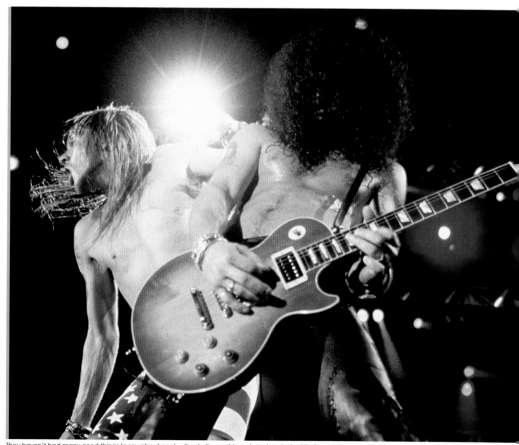

They haven't had many good things to say about each other in the past two decades—but, at their peak, **Rose** and **Slash** were rock's most exciting double act.

McKagan, Slash, Rose, and **Gilby Clarke** at 1992's Freddie Mercury tribute show, at Wembley Stadium.

Slash handled most press promotion for *"The Spaghetti Incident?"*.

Axl with Adler's replacement, former Cult drummer **Matt Sorum**, at the Freddie Mercury tribute show.

Reunited with **Stradlin** (and Ronnie Wood) in Britain in 1993.

Rose: still nuts and still incapable of arriving onstage on time, but still packing in the crowds.

Ron **"Bumblefoot" Thal**, in Ottawa, Canada, 2010.

jimi hendrix 1966–1970

Jimi Hendrix
b. November 27, 1942
d. September 18, 1970

Noel Redding
b. December 25, 1945
d. May 11, 2003

Mitch Mitchell
b. June 9, 1947
d. November 12, 2008

Buddy Miles
b. September 5, 1947
d. February 26, 2008

Billy Cox
b. October 18, 1941

Larry Lee
b. March 7, 1943
d. October 30, 2007

Born in Seattle, Washington, Johnny Allen Hendrix arrived in Britain in 1966 and began his transformation from a side player on the "chitlin' circuit"—the venues at which African American acts played—to the guitar wielding, global superstar known as **Jimi Hendrix.**

After leaving the U.S. Army in 1962, he toured with Little Richard, Ike and Tina Turner, and the Isley Brothers. In 1965, Hendrix cut his first records for PPX Productions, which resulted in a five-year legal dispute. While playing around New York as Jimmy James & the Blue Flames, Hendrix was spotted by Chas Chandler, bassist with British band The Animals, who suggested that he become part of London's swinging sixties scene. Hendrix adopted the name Jimi, reportedly en route to the U.K., and in October 1966 recruited bassist **Noel Redding** and drummer **Mitch Mitchell** to create The Jimi Hendrix Experience.

Having signed a deal with the new Track label, their debut single "Hey Joe" peaked at No. 6 in early 1967. Following a series of club gigs in Europe, the Experience joined The Walker Brothers on a tour around Britain, during which Hendrix was criticized for setting fire to his guitar and for his "erotic" stage act.

Now a fully-fledged sensation in Britain, the band scored Top Three hits with "Purple Haze" and *Are You Experienced*, despite the latter including neither of their British hit singles. The album was, however, packed with classics, like "Fire," "Foxy Lady," "Manic Depression," and "3rd Stone from the Sun."

Ten months after leaving America, Hendrix returned to the States when The Experience played at the Monterey International Pop Festival alongside The Who and the Grateful Dead. The band were also booked to support pop sensations The Monkees on a U.S. tour—but, after eight shows, they departed amid protests about the guitarist's act. "Hendrix would be up there belting out 'Foxy Lady'," marveled drummer Micky Dolenz to *Livewire*, "and the kids would be screaming for The Monkees. It was kinda strange!"

After "The Wind Cried Mary" and "Burning of the Midnight Lamp" provided further British hits, Hendrix made his U.S. chart debut with "Purple Haze." Then *Are You Experienced?* began a 100-week run on the *Billboard* chart, including sixty weeks in the Top Ten.

After a British tour (on which Motörhead's Lemmy was a roadie) supported by The Move, The Nice, and

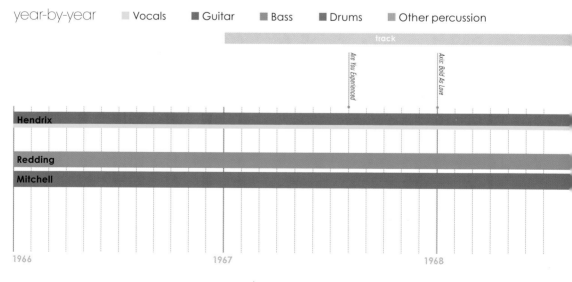

year-by-year   ■ Vocals   ■ Guitar   ■ Bass   ■ Drums   ■ Other percussion

7.5M	4.5M	2M	4.5M
Are You Experienced (1967)	*Smash Hits* (1968)	*Electric Ladyland* (1968)	*Band of Gypsys* (1970)

Juma Sultan
b. April 13, 1942

Jerry Velez
b. August 15, 1947

Pink Floyd, the band scored another Top Five hit on both sides of the Atlantic with *Axis: Bold as Love* (1967). Its clutch of classics included the lovely "Little Wing," "Wait Until Tomorrow," and "Castles Made of Sand," although its only (minor) hit was "Up from the Skies."

Hendrix relocated to New York to develop his career in America with a series of tours and a third album, *Electric Ladyland.* Reaching No. 6 in the U.K.—where the original sleeve featured twenty naked women—it hit No. 1 in the U.S., where the cover was changed to a less controversial psychedelic design.

The compilation *Smash Hits* reached the U.K. Top Five in 1968. A year later, a different collection of the same name—featuring the Experience's first U.S. hit single, an acclaimed cover of Bob Dylan's "All Along The Watchtower"—hit the U.S. Top Ten.

Hendrix, Redding, and Mitchell played a last show together in Denver, in June 1969. While Redding formed the band Fat Mattress, Mitchell continued to support Hendrix—including a dramatic closing spot that summer at the legendary Woodstock festival with guitarist **Larry Lee**, bassist **Billy Cox**, and percussionists **Juma Sultan** and **Jerry Velez**. This temporary band—dubbed Gypsy Sun & Rainbows—evolved into Band of Gypsys (Hendrix, Cox, and drummer **Buddy Miles**) for the live album *Band of Gypsys*. (Miles resurfaced as lead vocalist for TV sensation the California Raisins.)

In August 1970, Hendrix returned to Britain for only the second time in three years to play the Isle of Wight festival (for which his sound was mixed by Pink Floyd's David Gilmour). But after jamming with Eric Burdon at a London club on September 17, he returned to his girlfriend's flat, where he was found unconscious and rushed to hospital. He died, aged just twenty-seven, as a result of inhalation of vomit caused by barbiturate intoxication. Two months later, he topped the U.K. singles chart with "Voodoo Child." In early 1971, his final official studio album, *The Cry of Love,* was a Top Three hit in both America and Britain.

The ensuing decades saw a slew of live albums, and compilations of archive material—with 2010's *Valleys of Neptune,* featuring unreleased tracks spanning 1967 to 1970, billed as a "lost" studio album.

Despite myriad guitar heroes emerging in his wake, Hendrix remains the ultimate. "He did things," observed Pete Townshend, "which were magical." **BS**

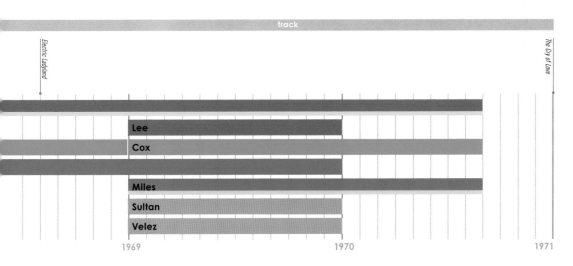

Are You Experienced
(1967)

Axis: Bold as Love
(1967)

Electric Ladyland
(1968)

The Cry of Love
(1971)

Jimi Hendrix finding his groove at the Star Club, Hamburg, 1967.

The Jimi Hendrix Experience: **Mitch Mitchell, Hendrix,** and **Noel Redding**.

In the midst of psychedelia in 1967.

Performing a trademark **Hendrix** move in the late sixties.

Hendrix, Mitchell, and **Redding** at London's legendary Marquee Club in London, 1967.

Making history at the Woodstock festival, where he was the highest-earning performer.

The guitar hero rocks London's Royal Albert Hall in February 1969.

Playing in his last concert, at the Isle of Fehmarn, Germany, in September 1970.

Rock and roll and afros. Left to right **Mitchell**, **Hendrix**, and **Redding**.

los hermanos 1997–present

Marcelo Camelo
b. April 2, 1978

Rodrigo Amarante
b. September 6, 1976

Bruno Medina
b. August 10, 1978

Rodrigo Barba
b. January 23, 1979

Patrick Laplan
b. Unknown

Los Hermanos is a multi-faceted quartet based in Rio de Janeiro. They started out in 1997 as an indie-rock band with punk and ska influences and a tendency to concentrate on romantic matters in their lyrics, drawing comparisons to U.S. acts such as Weezer. Despite their Brazilian origins, the group's name is Spanish for "the brothers." The first stable lineup consisted of singer/guitarists **Marcelo Camelo** and **Rodrigo Amarante**, keyboard player **Bruno Medina**, drummer **Rodrigo Barba**, and bassist **Patrick Laplan**.

Appearances at some of Brazil's biggest music festivals won Los Hermanos a reputation as a powerful live act and a contract with Sony BMG followed. Their self-titled debut album, released in 1999, was propelled by the hit "Anna Júlia," a melodic slice of indie-pop whose huge success overshadowed their career. The song was covered by artists including Jim Capaldi, whose English version featured guitar by George Harrison—one of his last recordings.

Bloco do Eu Sozinho (2001) established a fresh direction: moving away from the noisier elements of their debut and incorporating samba rhythms. The brooding, musically complex single "Todo Carnaval Tem Seu Fim" ("Every Carnival Has Its End") was a world away from the chirpy pop of "Anna Júlia." The album was positively reviewed, but the lack of a major hit meant it failed to match the success of their debut.

Minus Laplan (who resurfaced as a member of the dance act Eskimo), 2003's *Ventura* further developed Los Hermanos' distinctive Brazilian identity, adding choro and bossa nova to the rhythmic mix. The album earned further critical acclaim and expanded their following in their homeland. However, they alienated some fans and reviewers with the melancholy mood of their fourth album, released in 2006 and simply titled *4*. By this point Los Hermanos were seen as leading lights of MPB (Musica Popular Brasiliera), a loosely knit cultural movement encompassing all popular music with traditional Brazilian characteristics.

Los Hermanos toured extensively over the next two years, and the compilation *Perfil* was released to healthy sales in 2006. Then, in April 2007, Los Hermanos announced that they would be going on hiatus after a series of homecoming dates in Rio de Janeiro in June. The band explained that the split was entirely amicable, prompted by nothing more than the need for a break. Accordingly, they reunited in 2009 for two festival dates in Rio and São Paulo. Another short series of shows in their home nation followed in 2010.

As the fifteenth anniversary of their formation approached, the group revealed that they would be marking the occasion with a full tour of Brazil in April and May 2012. The public response demonstrated that they remained among Brazil's most beloved bands. **DJ**

year-by-year ■ Vocals ■ Guitar ■ Bass ■ Drums ■ Keyboards

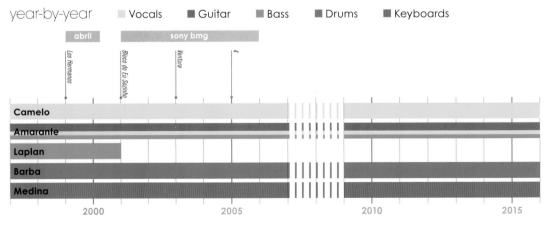

abril · sony bmg

Los Hermanos · Bloco do Eu Sozinho · Ventura · 4

Camelo
Amarante
Laplan
Barba
Medina

2000 · 2005 · 2010 · 2015

héroes del silencio 1984–2007

| **Enrique Bunbury** | **Juan Valdivia** | **Joaquin Cardiel** | **Pedro Ardreu** | **Alan Boguslavsky** | **Gonzalo Valdivia** |
| b. August 11, 1967 | b. December 3, 1965 | b. June 2, 1965 | b. April 15, 1966 | b. May 18, 1965 | b. October 3, 1972 |

Héroes del Silencio were one of the most successful rock bands ever to emerge from continental Europe. Formed in Zaragoza, Spain, in 1984, their loyalty to their native tongue made them major contributors to the Rock en Español movement of the nineties. Their dramatic, bombastic style brought them lasting popularity in Europe and Latin America, their Goth-tinged sound and visual image drawing comparisons to British post-punk acts like The Cult and The Mission.

Guitarist **Juan Valdivia** and singer **Enrique Bunbury** first performed together in another Zaragoza-based band, Zumo de Vidrio ("Glass of Juice"). Born Enrique Ortiz de Landázuri Izardui, Bunbury took his stage name from a character in the Oscar Wilde play *The Importance of Being Earnest*. The first HDS lineup was completed by Juan's drummer brother Pedro, with Bunbury on bass. By the end of 1985, the former had been replaced by **Pedro Andreu** and the band had expanded to a quartet with bassist **Joaquin Cardiel**.

Their debut was the well-received EP *Héroe de Leyenda*, released in 1988. The four tracks on the EP included "El Mar No Cesa," also the title of the Héroes' first full-length album, although the eponymous song does not appear on the album. By the time of that debut album's release in February 1989, HDS had built up a sizable following via extensive touring. *El Mar No Cesa* proved to be a platinum-selling hit in Spain.

Produced by Roxy Music guitarist Phil Manzanera, *Senderos de Tración* (1990) became their greatest commercial success, selling more than two million copies. It also drew positive reviews from the Spanish music press, who were not always supportive of HDS's efforts. "Entre Dos Tierras" became an international hit and the band's best known song, aided by a sepia-toned video in which their performance was intercut with scenes of domestic violence.

El Espíritu del Vino followed in 1993, with Manzanera again producing. Second guitarist **Alan Boguslavsky** was added to the lineup for the tour that followed its release. Another hit album arrived in the form of 1995's *Avalancha*, produced by Bob Ezrin.

A decade of touring led to increasing tensions within the band, and they went on hiatus in October 1996. The final date on their farewell tour came to an ignominious end when the band was forced off stage in Los Angeles by missiles thrown by the audience.

In the years that followed, Bunbury launched a successful solo career, and various compilations and live albums have enjoyed healthy sales. The group reunited in 2007 for a tour that took them to South America and the U.S. before concluding with a triumphant homecoming in Spain. A CD and DVD taken from the tour, titled simply *Tour 2007*, were released just in time for Christmas of that year. **DJ**

year-by-year — Vocals ■ Guitar ■ Bass ■ Drums

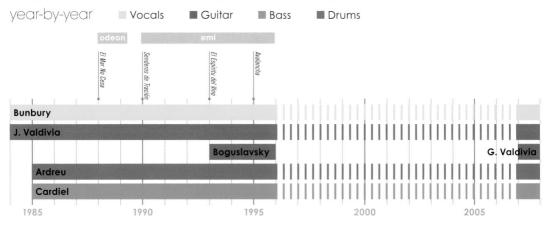

hole 1989–2012

Courtney Love
b. July 9, 1964

Eric Erlandson
b. January 9, 1963

Caroline Rue
b. Unknown

Jill Emery
b. May 1, 1962

Patty Schemel
b. April 24, 1967

Kristen Pfaff
b. May 26, 1967
d. June 16, 1994

"She's almost a genius," remarked Smashing Pumpkins figurehead Billy Corgan of **Courtney Love**, "in an insane kind of way." This insane genius had graced the cover of the Grateful Dead's *Aoxomoxoa* (via her father, Hank Harrison, briefly the Dead's manager), hung out with Julian Cope and The Teardrop Explodes, fronted Faith No More in 1982, and formed Sugar Babydoll with Jennifer Finch and Kat Bjelland (latterly of L7 and Babes in Toyland, respectively).

After Love's heroin use caused Sugar Babydoll to implode, she moved on to movie work, starring in Alex Cox's *Sid & Nancy* (1986) and *Straight to Hell* (1987), the latter also featuring Joe Strummer. Neither project made her famous, and Love returned to an intermittent stripping career. In 1989, she settled in L.A. for a final stab at stardom. Thanks to an ad declaring, "My influences are Big Black, Sonic Youth, and Fleetwood Mac," she snared guitarist **Eric Erlandson**.

Dubbing themselves Hole, the duo enlisted bassist Lisa Roberts, drummer **Caroline Rue**, and guitarists Mike Geisbrecht and Errol Stewart. In 1990, the band solidified with Love, Erlandson, Rue, and bassist **Jill Emery**. Abrasive singles foreshadowed *Pretty on the Inside*, released in 1991 and co-produced by Sonic Youth's Kim Gordon. Despite including a cover of Joni Mitchell's "Clouds," the album was, Erlandson noted, "really obnoxious and in your face and noisy."

On tour in 1991, Hole played Leadbelly's "Where Did You Sleep Last Night?"—an idea that clearly resonated with Love's soon-to-be boyfriend, Kurt Cobain (whom she met after a liaison with Corgan). Love and Cobain married in February 1992, Emery quit Hole, and Rue was reportedly fired. Hole regrouped with drummer **Patty Schemel** and temporary bassist Leslie Hardy, although producer Jack Endino played bass on their next single, "Beautiful Son."

Songs for Hole's sophomore album were road-tested in 1993 with new bassist **Kristen Pfaff**. But, with tragic timing, *Live Through This* was released just days after Cobain's suicide in April 1994. The nightmare was compounded by Pfaff's fatal overdose in June.

Corgan recommended Hole's new bassist, **Melissa Auf der Maur**. "I am gonna enter the dark side," she acknowledged, "and be living in close proximity to people who play with death." The new lineup debuted, messily, at Britain's Reading festival, then toured the U.S. with Nine Inch Nails. Love's criticism of NIN, and an alleged fling with their leader Trent Reznor, sparked an undying war between the two.

In 1995, Love oversaw the *Tank Girl* film soundtrack and, on Valentine's Day, Hole performed tellingly dark cuts such as Donovan's "Season of the Witch" and The Crystals' "He Hit Me (and It Felt Like a Kiss)" for MTV's *Unplugged*. Amid a controversy-plagued tour, Love

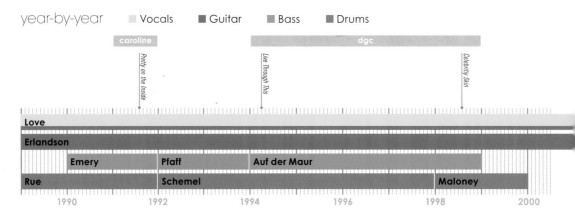

year-by-year　■ Vocals　■ Guitar　■ Bass　■ Drums

Melissa Auf der Maur
b. March 17, 1972

Samantha Maloney
b. December 11, 1975

Micko Larkin
b. October 13, 1986

Stuart Fisher
b. circa 1975

Shawn Dailey
b. Unknown

conceived the artwork for the archive-plundering EP *Ask for It:* a woman's slashed wrists.

Reinvention came in 1996. While Hole covered Fleetwood Mac's "Gold Dust Woman"—produced by Cars singer Ric Ocasek—for the soundtrack of *The Crow: City of Angels,* Love starred in the movies *Feeling Minnesota* and *The People Vs. Larry Flynt.* As Hollywood embraced her, further archive releases plugged the gap in Hole's output: 1997's *The First Session* and *My Body, the Hand Grenade.*

To complete a love letter to the West Coast, Hole undertook a writing project with Billy Corgan. The result was *Celebrity Skin* (1998), which turned platinum three times faster than *Live Through This.* However, as Auf der Maur observed, "A lot of blackness went into it." At producer Michael Beinhorn's behest, Schemel's parts were played by former Bad English (and future Journey) drummer Deen Castronovo. Although pictured on the album's artwork, Schemel quit in protest. Hole hired a lookalike for the "Celebrity Skin" video, then installed drummer **Samantha Maloney.**

After the ensuing tour, including a rancorous stint with Marilyn Manson, Auf der Maur joined The Smashing Pumpkins and Maloney jumped ship to Mötley Crüe. Then Love and Erlandson fell out, finally declaring Hole defunct in 2002. In the interim, Love formed "punk rock femme supergroup" Bastard with

Schemel and Veruca Salt's Louise Post and Gina Crosley. The project collapsed amid, Post reported, "unhealthy and unprofessional working conditions."

With her life in freefall, Love assembled the sadly underrated solo album *America's Sweetheart* (2004) with producer Linda Perry. Contributions came from Elton John's lyricist Bernie Taupin and members of the Distillers, the Pixies, and Girls Against Boys. None could save it from barbed reviews and poor sales.

Finally, after years in which her personal notoriety eclipsed her music, including an attempted second solo album (with Corgan and Perry), Love revived the Hole banner—to the absent Erlandson's annoyance—for *Nobody's Daughter* (2010). Guitarist **Micko Larkin**, formerly of British band Larrikin Love, headed the new lineup. (Former Red Hot Chili Peppers/Pearl Jam drummer Jack Irons also contributed.)

Hopes for a genuine reunion were raised when Love, Erlandson, and Auf der Maur attended a 2011 screening of *Hit So Hard,* P. David Ebersole's documentary about Patty Schemel—essential viewing for Hole and Nirvana fans.

Regarding Hole, Erlandson admitted that "Nothing has been resolved, but I'm open to all possibilities." With customary defiance, Love declared, "Madonna wakes up every day and someone wants to be her. Nobody wants to be me. Which is awesome!" **BM**

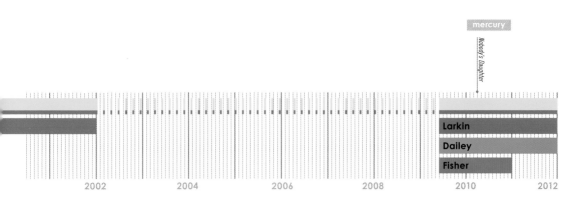

mercury

Nobody's Daughter

Larkin

Dailey

Fisher

2002   2004   2006   2008   2010   2012

buddy holly & the crickets 1957–1959

Buddy Holly
b. September 7, 1936
d. February 3, 1959

Niki Sullivan
b. June 23, 1937
d. April 6, 2004

Jerry Allison
b. August 31, 1939

Joe B. Mauldin
b. July 8, 1940

Sonny Curtis
b. May 9, 1937

H

Buddy Holly was one of the most prolific musicians to emerge during America's fifties rock 'n' roll boom. Born in Texas, he began performing at thirteen with his school pal Bob Montgomery—as Buddy & Bob, they graced local country/bluegrass concerts. After adding bass player Larry Welborn, Buddy & Bob supported Bill Haley & His Comets and found themselves doing the same for Elvis Presley in 1955.

In 1956, Holly was offered a solo deal by Decca and recruited guitarist **Sonny Curtis**, bassist Don Guess, and drummer **Jerry Allison**. As Buddy Holly & The Three Tunes, they released "Blue Days, Black Nights" and "Modern Don Juan" before Decca let them go.

In 1957, with Allison, Welborn, and guitarist **Niki Sullivan,** Holly recorded "That'll Be the Day" with producer Norman Petty. With **Joe B. Mauldin** replacing Welborn, they took on the name The Crickets and were assigned to Brunswick, which issued the single. It reached No. 1 in the U.S. and the U.K.

The group came to Britain in March 1958 for a twenty-five-date tour, which made hits of "Listen to Me" and "Maybe Baby." But in October that year, Holly left The Crickets to pursue a solo career. (His first single—"Early in the Morning"—had been released in August.) The twenty-two-year-old moved to New York. He ended his association with Petty and passed rights to the Crickets name to Allison and Mauldin.

(Their career as The Crickets would extend well into the nineties, and include collaborative efforts such as 1962's *Bobby Vee Meets the Crickets* and, with singer Nanci Griffith, 1996's *Too Much Monday Morning*).

Holly recorded in Coral's studios in New York in 1958 and entered the charts with "Heartbeat" on the eve of a U.S. tour with The Big Bopper, Richie Valens, and Dion & The Belmonts. On February 2, 1959, Holly played in Iowa then, with Valens and the Big Bopper, boarded a plane to fly to North Dakota. Minutes after takeoff, the plane crashed, killing all three stars.

Within two months of his death, a track from his last session in November 1958—Paul Anka's "It Doesn't Matter Anymore"—hit No. 13 in the U.S. and topped the U.K. charts. During his ten years as a professional musician Holly made over 120 recordings—releasing less than fifty of them in his lifetime. Two years after his death, *That'll Be the Day*—a collection of his early Decca recordings—charted in the U.K. at No. 5. It was among a host of compilations that have appeared since 1959, with both *20 Golden Greats* (1978) and *Words of Love* (1993) topping the U.K. chart.

"He was one of the first to get away from the Tin Pan Alley songwriting factory and communicate directly, honestly with his audience," observed John Mellencamp in *Rolling Stone*. "The magic that Buddy Holly created was nothing short of a miracle." **BS**

year-by-year   ▫ Vocals   ■ Guitar   ■ Bass   ■ Drums

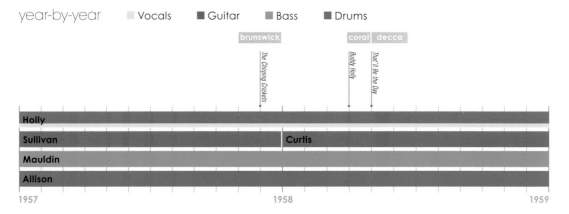

1957   1958   1959

hootie & the blowfish 1986–present

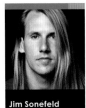

Darius Rucker
b. May 13, 1966

Mark Bryan
b. May 6, 1967

Dean Felber
b. June 9, 1967

Jim Sonefeld
b. October 20, 1964

If you are one of the sixteen million Americans who bought a copy of *Cracked Rear View*, you will need no introduction to Hootie & the Blowfish. If you live anywhere else in the world, you might be forgiven for asking "Who's Hootie?" or "What's a blowfish?"

Hootie & the Blowfish (**Darius Rucker, Mark Bryan, Dean Felber**, and **Jim Sonefeld**, who replaced Brantley Smith in 1989) were one of a number of feel-good, melody-driven rock groups to emerge in the early nineties—alongside the Dave Matthews Band, Gin Blossoms, Blues Traveler, and Hootie's rivals in nominal daftness, Toad the Wet Sprocket.

The band were named after friends of Rucker: Hootie (nicknamed on account of his round face and glasses making him look like an owl) and Blowfish (whose chubby cheeks inspired his pseudonym). Having formed in 1986 in South Carolina, they issued the self-released EP *Kootchypop* in 1993; "We sold so many copies…" Rucker told *Billboard* writer Craig Rosen, "people couldn't believe it."

But it was their debut album that really shook the music industry to its core. *Cracked Rear View* (1994) has been outsold by only fifteen albums in U.S. chart history, and it yielded a string of hits that radio could not get enough of. "Hold My Hand" (featuring backing vocals by David Crosby), "Let Her Cry," "Only Wanna Be with You," and "Time"—all of which had

originally appeared on *Kootchypop*—cracked the Top Twenty, with "Let Her Cry" winning a Grammy.

The quartet appeared on the soundtrack to the sitcom *Friends* with "I Go Blind" after being named in an episode (Courteney Cox's character, having met the band, admits a love-bite is "the work of a Blowfish"). They also contributed to the 1995 Led Zeppelin tribute album *Encomium*.

After founding the short-lived Breaking Records label, they released their second U.S. No. 1, *Fairweather Johnson*, featuring the hits "Old Man & Me (When I Get to Heaven)" and "Tucker's Town."

In 1998, Hootie released some of their finest work on the platinum-selling *Musical Chairs*—namely the single "I Will Wait" and the glorious ballad "Only Lonely." Then they drifted off into relative obscurity with the covers album *Scattered, Smothered & Covered* (2000) and two further studio sets, *Hootie & the Blowfish* (2003) and *Looking for Lucky* (2005).

Rucker reinvented himself as a country singer in 2008—six years after his R&B album *Back to Then*—and has country chart-topping albums (*Learn to Live, Charleston, SC 1966*, and *True Believers*) and singles to his credit. While his solo projects seemed to mark the end of the Blowfish and their exhaustive charity work, the versatile singer-songwriter has hinted at a revival of the band "some time down the road." **MW**

year-by-year   ▨ Vocals   ■ Guitar   ■ Bass   ■ Drums   ■ Keyboards
    ■ Aerophones   ▨ Other percussion

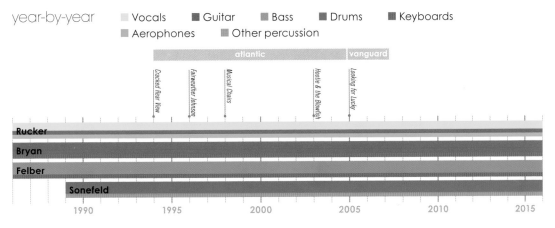

humble pie 1968–2002

Steve Marriott
b. Jan 30, 1947
d. April 20, 1991

Peter Frampton
b. April 22, 1950

Greg Ridley
b. Oct 23, 1947
d. November 19, 2003

Jerry Shirley
b. February 4, 1952

Clem Clempson
b. September 5, 1949

Anthony "Sooty" Jones
b. Aug 24, 1953
d. Sept 21, 1999

Bobby Tench
b. September 21, 1944

Formed at the end of 1968 in Essex, England, the "supergroup" Humble Pie combined the talents of Small Faces front-man **Steve Marriott**, The Herd's **Peter Frampton**, and Spooky Tooth bass player **Greg Ridley**. Their hard-edged blues-rock sound featured three lead vocalists, two of whom were also highly accomplished guitarists. Signed to the Immediate label, Humble Pie quickly found themselves in the U.K. Top Five with their 1969 debut, "Natural Born Bugie." This was followed by an eclectic but successful mix of blues-rock and acoustic whimsy, As Safe as Yesterday.

Before the year was out, a sophomore effort had appeared. Town and Country reduced the rock quotient, introducing a gentler folk-inspired sound. The timing was unfortunate: with Immediate filing for bankruptcy, the album emerged with no promotion and went largely unnoticed.

New management encouraged Marriott to direct Humble Pie toward the lucrative heavy rock market, and his raw, bluesy vocals began to dominate the band's albums. By 1971, Humble Pie were in greater demand from U.S. rock audiences than they were in their homeland, cementing their growing success with 1971's live Performance—Rockin' The Fillmore, which took the band into the Billboard Top Twenty for the first time. Frampton, however, was unhappy at the band's musical direction and decided to go it alone.

With Marriott in sole control, the group grew even heavier. "He was one of my heroes," said Kiss's Paul Stanley. "I saw Marriott perform live with Humble Pie and it was like being at a church revival." Smokin' (1972) proved to be the band's commercial peak— later albums declined in quality and sales. Marriott's personal habits had become problematic and, with their finances in chaos, Humble Pie disbanded in 1975. Marriott reformed them in the eighties with little success: he died in a house fire in 1991. Bassist Ridley, drummer **Jerry Shirley**, and guitarist **Bobby Tench** reunited for 2002's Back on Track, featuring former Bad Company man Dave "Bucket" Colwell.

Having left Humble Pie in 1972, Frampton embarked on what looked to be a low-key solo career. Albums like Wind of Change and Frampton's Camel made little headway, but persistent touring in the U.S. paid off with his breakthrough—1975's Frampton, an album of appealing pop/rock that highlighted his growing confidence as a songwriter.

Songs from Frampton would reappear a year later on Frampton Comes Alive!, a slow burner that debuted at No. 191 on the Billboard chart. Few could have predicted that this live recording would turn him into a star and become the biggest-selling album of 1976. Frampton would never recapture this level of success, but remained a popular concert draw. **TB**

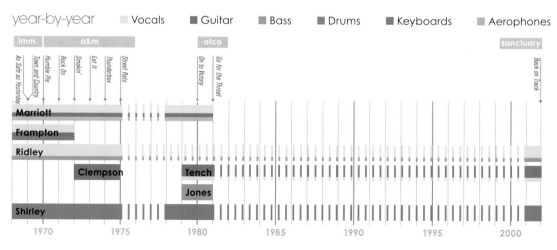

year-by-year ■ Vocals ■ Guitar ■ Bass ■ Drums ■ Keyboards ■ Aerophones

hüsker dü 1979–1987

Bob Mould
b. October 16, 1961

Grant Hart
b. March 18, 1961

Greg Norton
b. March 13, 1959

"It was clear who was taking over the world," sang **Bob Mould** in 2002. "It wasn't going to be me." The man behind two of alternative rock's greatest groups did indeed remain largely on the sidelines while the likes of the Pixies and Nirvana reaped the rewards of his endeavors—but that makes much of his back catalog a treasure chest of mostly unheard classics.

Mould rose to fame (of sorts) with drummer and singer **Grant Hart** and bassist **Greg Norton**. As Minneapolis-based hardcore trio Hüsker Dü, they were first famed more for the speed at which they played than for their music. But bitter competition between Mould and Hart drove each to write ever finer songs. After 1984's *Zen Arcade*—an extraordinary, albeit incomprehensible, concept album recorded in mostly first takes over forty hours—the pair packed 1985's *New Day Rising* and *Flip Your Wig*, 1986's *Candy Apple Grey*, and 1987's *Warehouse: Songs and Stories* with an embarrassment of songwriting riches.

Unfortunately, not even the backing of Warner Bros. in their latter years could promote the trio from critical acclaim to mainstream success. "Hüsker Dü are making quite important music now," observed former Led Zeppelin singer Robert Plant, "and people aren't hearing it because it never gets played."

More damage was done to the group by Mould and Hart's rivalry, exacerbated by the latter's drug problem. The suicide of their manager was the final straw, and the band fell apart on tour at the end of 1987. The coruscating live album *The Living End* (1994)—a *de facto* best of—proved a fine epitaph.

In the aftermath, Norton moved into the catering business, and Hart pursued a mostly low-key solo career, of which the highlights are 1989's *Intolerance* and 1991's ambitious *Last Days of Pompeii* (the latter recorded with the short-lived Nova Mob).

Mould recorded two increasingly gloomy solo albums before uniting with bassist David Barbe and drummer Malcolm Travis as Sugar. With their leader belatedly acknowledged as a "godfather of grunge"—although "grumpy uncle of grunge" is more fitting—Sugar made good on Hüsker Dü's potential. The classic *Copper Blue* (1992) slammed into the British Top Ten, as did 1993's brutal *Beaster* and 1994's melodious *File Under: Easy Listening*. But after four years of touring and recording—compounding Mould's hearing problems—Sugar dissolved.

Mould returned to the sidelines, grumbling "I hate alternative rock" on his self-titled 1996 solo album. After a nominally final foray into poppy hardcore—1998's self-mockingly titled *The Last Dog and Pony Show*—he pursued an increasingly electronic career, before bringing guitars back to the forefront on 2005's *Body of Song*. He is increasingly amenable to recognizing his past, with his solo shows often heavy on Hüsker and Sugar classics—2012 even found him playing the whole of *Copper Blue*. And while a frosty relationship with Hart ensures Hüsker Dü's patchily produced catalog remains un-remastered and often unavailable, Mould seems to have made peace with acts who made his formula their own, guesting on Foo Fighters' *Wasting Light* (2011) and at their shows. **BM**

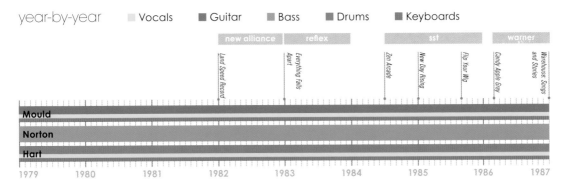

inxs 1977–2012

Michael Hutchence
b. January 22, 1960
d. November 22, 1997

Andrew Farriss
b. March 27, 1959

Jon Farriss
b. August 10, 1961

Tim Farriss
b. August 16, 1957

Garry "Gary" Beers
b. June 22, 1957

Kirk Pengilly
b. July 4, 1958

"There's no drugs or drinking problems. So I think, 'Phew, I've survived.' I really have." A bold claim from **Michael Hutchence** in 1992, just five years before he took his own life with cocaine, alcohol, and prescription drugs. But then what did the world expect from the lead singer of a band called INXS?

At the time of his death, Hutchence had been touring and promoting the Australian band's tenth album *Elegantly Wasted*—whose title alone, reports said, was further evidence of the singer's hedonistic tendencies. While his partner Paula Yates claimed later that Hutchence had died accidentally trying for the sexual high only possible through "auto-asphyxiation," it was actually—according to the coroner's report—frustration about not having access to his daughter that drove the singer to suicide.

INXS had started out in Sydney in 1977 as The Farriss Brothers. **Andrew**, **Jon**, and **Tim Farriss** were the siblings in question. Looking outside the family, they drafted in **Garry "Gary" Beers**, **Kirk Pengilly** and Andrew's school pal, Hutchence.

Despite non-Farrisses equaling the number of brothers, everyone seemed happy enough with the band tag—until, that is, they met Gary Morris,

manager of fellow Australian act Midnight Oil. Morris offered the "Brothers" a support slot and suggested they changed their name. On September 1, 1979, a "new" band called INXS made their live debut.

Around thirteen months later, a low-budget album of the same name was released on the independent Deluxe label. It did not exactly make headlines—or hits—but was promising enough for Deluxe to invest a little more in its successor. *Underneath the Colours* justified the expense, reaching No. 15 in Australia.

Hearing their songs on jukeboxes, on the radio, and whistled in the street gave INXS the confidence to look further afield. By the time *Shabooh Shoobah* was released in 1982, it was with major-label distribution. As a result, the album charted in the U.S., where it earned a gold award, and the single "The One Thing" cracked the Top Thirty. (Back home, it made No. 5.)

American tours supporting Adam and the Ants, Hall & Oates, and The Go-Go's helped build the kind of audience INXS had down under, while a stint as opener for compatriots Men at Work proved Antipodean roots need not be a barrier to U.S. success. They just needed the right record... Unfortunately, 1984's *The Swing* was not it, making little

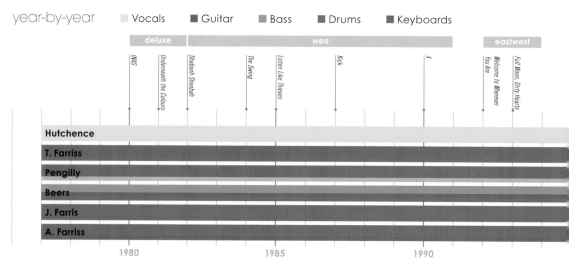

year-by-year   ■ Vocals   ■ Guitar   ■ Bass   ■ Drums   ■ Keyboards

Jon Stevens
b. October 8, 1961

JD Fortune
b. September 1, 1973

Ciaran Gribbin
b. 1976

impression in America and even less in the U.K. It did, however, chart well in France, Argentina, Canada, and elsewhere, and became INXS's first No. 1 in Australia. So, not a flop by any means, but still not a smash in the "major" territories. And then, in 1985, they released *Listen Like Thieves* and everything changed.

While the album's first single, "This Time," sank without trace, its follow-up, "What You Need," gained huge airplay in the States and rocketed into the Top Five. As the rest of the world (bar the U.K.) followed suit, the band thanked their lucky stars that producer Chris Thomas (whose resume included mixing Pink Floyd's *Dark Side of the Moon*) had forced them into a few days' extra work. "We'd already finished the album but Chris told us there was still no 'hit'," Andrew Farriss recalls. "We left the studio that night knowing we had one day left to deliver a 'hit'. Talk about pressure." In desperation, Farriss pulled out all his old demos and, forty-eight hours later, "Funk Song No. 13" had evolved into the powerful "What You Need."

With Britain's *NME* calling INXS "a depressingly definitive example of excruciating, boring, incredibly unimaginative MTV rock," it was always going to take longer to break into the U.K. market. But with

Kick (1987), they managed it. And this time they were not taking any chances with the hits. "We wanted to make an album where all the songs were possible singles," Pengilly explained. With "New Sensation," "Never Tear Us Apart," "Devil Inside," and "Need You Tonight" charting worldwide, they clearly succeeded.

Ten years after the Farrisses had set out, INXS was one of the biggest acts in the world—and with that came new pressures. Hutchence could not move without someone taking his picture. His relationship with fellow Australian pop star Kylie Minogue arguably resulted in an increased public demand for concert tickets and copies of the band's *X* (1990).

However, despite the eclectic gems on *Welcome to Wherever You Are* and cameos by Ray Charles and Chrissie Hynde on *Full Moon, Dirty Hearts*, sales had waned by the time of Hutchence's death. (*Elegantly Wasted* even fell short of the Australian Top Ten.)

New singers **Jon Stevens** (briefly) and **JD Fortune**—the latter hired after he won the *Rock Star: INXS* reality TV show—and albums *Switch* and *Original Sin* failed to lead the band back to former heights. Despite the addition of fourth front-man **Ciaran Gribbin** in 2011, INXS announced their retirement in 2012. **JaH**

■ Aerophones

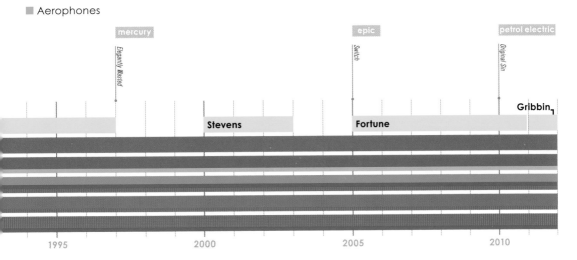

iron butterfly 1966–present

Doug Ingle
b. September 9, 1945

Danny Weis
b. September 28, 1948

Ron Bushy
b. December 23, 1945

Erik Braunn
b. August 11, 1950

Lee Dorman
b. September 15, 1942
d. Dec 21, 2012

Larry Reinhardt
b. July 7, 1948
d. Jan 2, 2012

Mike Pinera
b. September 29, 1948

Philip Taylor Kramer
b. July 12, 1952
d. Feb 12, 1995

Few acts in rock are so closely tied to one song as Iron Butterfly are to "In-A-Gadda-Da-Vida." It is mentioned in every conversation about the San Diego act—usually as the main topic. Often, such conversations lead to heated debates: one side proclaiming "In-A-Gadda-Da-Vida" to be a prime example of sixties psychedelia, the other arguing that it is nothing more than bloated nonsense. (A third party might counter that there is little difference between the two.)

There is, however, no debating that "In-A-Gadda-Da-Vida" is quite a song: a spiraling opus of excess that took up the entire second side of the Butterfly's 1968 album of the same title. It clocked in at over seventeen minutes—nineteen on 1970's Live—and featured church organ, one of the stoniest grooves ever recorded, a nonsensical chorus, and a lengthy drum solo. And it was just what the public wanted to hear: "In-A-Gadda-Da-Vida" was a worldwide hit, especially with the emerging album-oriented rock radio format, and earned its parent album the first-ever platinum certification in the U.S.

Vocalist and keyboardist **Doug Ingle**, the song's author, had been prepping for that success for most his life—the Nebraska native got his musical education from his father, a church organist, prior to his family moving to San Diego. He formed Iron Butterfly in 1966, quickly shuffling through a variety of lineups before striking upon the one—featuring guitarist **Danny Weis**, tambourine player Darryl DeLoach, bassist Jerry Penrod, and drummer **Ron Bushy**—heard on 1968's debut Heavy.

It was easy to hear the influence of predecessors Jefferson Airplane and The Doors (both of whom Iron Butterfly had opened for) on that first record, but there was something else going on—a movement from acid rock toward what would later become known as heavy metal. DeLoach, Weis, and Penrod had left the band (DeLoach to become a gourmet chef, Weis and Penrod to form Rhinoceros) by the time Heavy began climbing the U.S. chart, on its way to No. 78. Bassist **Lee Dorman** and guitarist **Eric Braunn** came in to complete Iron Butterfly's classic lineup.

That was the cast that went into the studios to record the sophomore set In-A-Gadda-Da-Vida. They came up with solid songs to kick off the album—notably "Termination," released as an overseas single—but all of side one seemed a mere prelude to what was waiting for fans once they flipped the

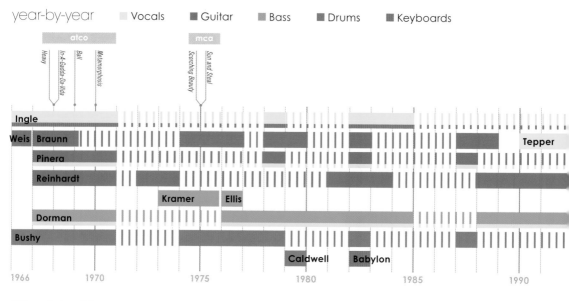

year-by-year ▪ Vocals ▪ Guitar ▪ Bass ▪ Drums ▪ Keyboards

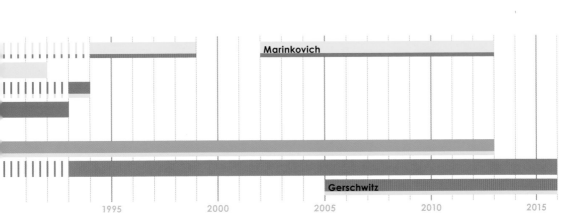

Keith Ellis
b. March 19, 1946
d. Dec 12, 1978

Bobby Caldwell
b. unknown

Guy Babylon
b. December 20, 1956
d. Sept 2, 2009

Robert Tepper
b. unknown

Charlie Marinkovich
b. October 7, 1959

Martin Gerschwitz
b. unknown

record over. Ironically, the song that was to become the band's calling card was not supposed to be titled "In-A-Gadda-Da-Vida"—it was written as "In the Garden of Eden." But Ingle slurred the words in the studio and everyone liked the results.

A ridiculously edited version (chopping off more than fourteen minutes) was released as a single in the U.S.—where it climbed into the Top Thirty—but that would not cut it for the devoted fans who eventually pushed the parent album to multi-million sales. *In-A-Gadda-Da-Vida* became the Atlantic label's biggest seller, holding that claim until the fourth album by Led Zeppelin (who had supported and upstaged the Butterfly on the British quartet's first American tour in late 1968 and early 1969).

The band remained intact for 1969's more melodic *Ball*, which hit No. 3 in the U.S. and yielded two Top 100 hits, "Soul Experience" and "In the Time of Our Lives." They were even scheduled to play at the Woodstock festival, and duly despatched a telegram containing a list of directives to the stage manager: "You will send helicopter to LaGuardia. Pick us up, bring us back. We will go immediately onstage, in front of everybody else, and then we will be given

a helicopter and flown back." The stage manager's reply? "Fuck off." They did not play.

Braunn left before 1970's *Metamorphosis*, which hit U.S. No. 16, but a bigger blow came when Ingle split after its release. The group trudged on for another year, before calling it quits in 1971. A revised lineup—with Braunn, Bushy, and keyboardist **Philip Taylor Kramer**—returned with *Scorching Beauty* (1975) and *Sun and Steel* (1976). Unfortunately, both records failed to crack the Top 100.

The group has since gone through more than three dozen lineup changes but remained active in every year except 1986. Iron Butterfly have spent decades living off past success—and have yet to record a follow-up to *Sun and Steel*.

But perhaps they do not need to. "In-A-Gadda-Da-Vida," in all of its notoriously excessive grandeur, continues to fascinate to this day. Slayer covered it for 1987's *Less Than Zero* soundtrack, rapper Nas sampled it on "Hip Hop Is Dead," and it has been used in such films as *Freddy's Dead: The Final Nightmare*. And, in 1995, the band received pop culture's greatest nod of approval when "In-A-Gadda-Da-Vida" was featured in an episode of *The Simpsons*. **JiH**

Marinkovich

Gerschwitz

1995   2000   2005   2010   2015

iron maiden 1975–present

Steve Harris
b. March 12, 1956

Bruce Dickinson
b. August 7, 1958

Adrian Smith
b. February 27, 1957

Dave Murray
b. December 23, 1956

Janick Gers
b. January 27, 1957

Nicko McBrain
b. June 5, 1952

Paul Day
b. April 19, 1956

Ron "Rebel" Matthews
b. Unknown

Alongside Black Sabbath and Metallica, Iron Maiden are one of the most influential metal bands ever to don spandex. The London group—a six-piece since 1999—have demonstrated for over three decades that what most fans want is a consistent entity with an iconic image, an instantly recognizable sound, and songs about warfare, conquest, and science fiction.

It is a testament to founder member, bassist, and chief songwriter **Steve Harris**'s determination that Maiden existed for over four years before coming close to commercial success. After forming the band in 1975, Harris went through a carousel of guitarists, singers, and drummers before hitting on a relatively stable lineup, comprising singer **Paul Di'Anno**, guitarists **Dave Murray** and **Dennis Stratton**, and drummer **Clive Burr**. The self-released *Soundhouse Tapes* EP from 1979 was snapped up by Maiden's fanbase, a core of devotees who had been attracted by the band's ambitious live show and powerful, melodic tunes.

Maiden's self-titled 1980 debut album hit No. 4 in the U.K. and spearheaded the "New Wave Of British Heavy Metal" (NWOBHM). This new sound took the old demons-and-wizards tropes of traditional, Sabbath-style metal and added the speed and aggression of punk. Alongside Def Leppard, Saxon, and Diamond Head, Maiden were this new wave's obvious leaders, with fans including future Metallica founder Lars Ulrich: "My heart and soul were in England with Iron Maiden."

Like Leppard, Maiden went on to transcend the NWOBHM genre tag. After *Killers* (1981), for which Stratton was replaced by **Adrian Smith**, the band fired Di'Anno and recruited the operatically throated **Bruce Dickinson** (ex-Samson) for Maiden's first true classic and first U.K. chart-topper, *The Number of the Beast*. Controversy engulfed certain parts of the U.S. owing to the album's splendidly Satanic cover art, which depicted Maiden's horrific mascot Eddie as a devilish puppet-master. However, the music was what counted, and songs such as "The Prisoner," "Children of the Damned," and "Run to the Hills" (the latter a U.K. Top Ten hit) ensured that Maiden made a huge impact on the international rock scene.

As the decade unfolded, the unstoppable group issued a sequence of essential albums. Their live shows (propelled by new drummer **Nicko McBrain**, who took over from Burr in 1982) were as memorable as their music, with high points including 1984–85's World Slavery Tour (leading to 1985's fine in-concert set *Live*

year-by-year
■ Vocals ■ Guitar ■ Bass ■ Drums

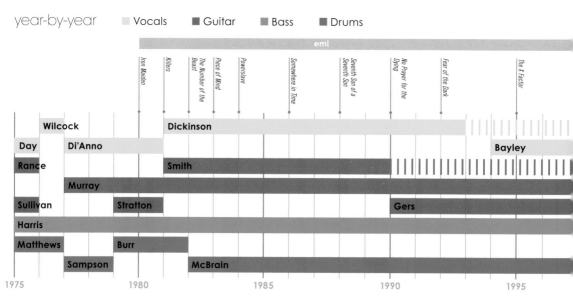

5.1M
The Number of the Beast (1982)

3.9M
Piece of Mind (1983)

3.9M
Somewhere in Time (1984)

3.7M
Powerslave (1986)

Terry Rance
b. Unknown

Dave Sullivan
b. Unknown

Dennis Wilcock
b. Unknown

Doug Sampson
b. June 30, 1957

Paul Di'Anno
b. May 17, 1958

Dennis Stratton
b. Nov 9, 1954

Clive Burr
b. March 8, 1957
d. March 12, 2013

Blaze Bayley
b. May 29, 1963

After Death) and a triumphant headline slot at the Donington Monsters of Rock festival in 1988, then the world's most prestigious metal fixture. With that year's semi-progressive, U.K. chart-topping *Seventh Son of a Seventh Son*, Maiden's songwriting hit a new peak.

While they remained enviably successful, the following decade was a period of turmoil. Dickinson, the band's most outspoken and visually important character, had always been a man of many faces—novelist, airline pilot, and world-class fencer among them. But after a third U.K. chart-topper (1992's *Fear of the Dark*) and even a No. 1 single (1990's "Bring Your Daughter… to the Slaughter"), he quit in 1993 to launch a moderately successful solo career.

Smith also departed, obliging Harris to recruit ex-Gillan guitarist **Janick Gers** alongside Wolfsbane singer **Blaze Bayley**. This lineup released *The X Factor* (1995) and *Virtual XI* (1998), neither of which matched up to Maiden's previous work. Fans found it hard to accept Bayley, a competent but unremarkable singer, and many felt that Harris's songwriting lacked the raw excitement of Maiden's eighties albums.

This period in the doldrums came to an end in 1999, when Dickinson and Smith returned to the fold.

Gers remained on board, making Maiden that rare thing, a three-guitar band. Since then, they have plowed an acclaimed furrow as a classic metal act, one of the few to survive the great cull of the nineties, and certainly the only metal band (apart from Metallica) that tours on a truly grandiose scale.

The revived lineup instantly reversed the pattern of waning chart placings with a trio of big-hitters: 2000's solid comeback *Brave New World*, 2003's stirring *Dance of Death*, and 2006's war-dominated *A Matter of Life and Death*. In recent years, however, the focus has been less on albums and more on their live show, which is a spectacle like no other. Between 2008 and 2011, Dickinson actually piloted the band and twelve tons of equipment around the world on a custom-painted Boeing 757 (dubbed "Ed Force One"), as documented in the 2009 documentary *Flight 666*.

The title of 2010's *The Final Frontier* attracted inevitable speculation that it would be the group's last album, but Harris and his troops have made it clear that Eddie will be stalking the Earth for some years yet. Iron Maiden remain one of the world's truly unique acts: a band with their own sound, their own image, and their own mission. Long may they reign. **JM**

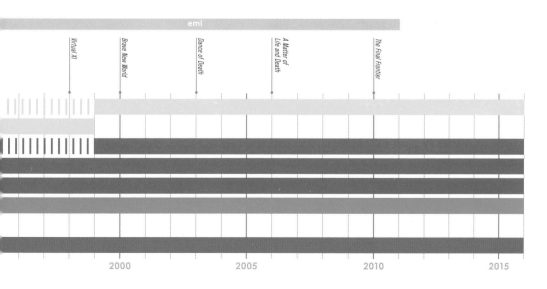

emi

Virtual XI

Brave New World

Dance of Death

A Matter of Life and Death

The Final Frontier

2000   2005   2010   2015

Iron Maiden (1980)

The Number of the Beast (1982)

Piece of Mind (1983)

Powerslave (1984)

Somewhere in Time (1986)

Seventh Son of a Seventh Son (1988)

Fear of the Dark (1992)

The X Factor (1995)

A Matter of Life and Death (2006)

The Final Frontier (2010)

Steve Harris is flanked by the debut's singer **Paul Di'Anno** and guitarist **Dennis Stratton.**

Harris, Clive Burr, Dave Murray, Adrian Smith, and **Bruce Dickinson.**

Murray on the World Piece Tour with the band's mascot, Eddie.

Burr's successor **Nicko McBrain** enjoys the gold and platinum haul.

Dickinson and **Harris,** who often jostled for space centerstage, on the World Slavery Tour.

Dickinson rocks Toronto on the A Matter of Life and Death Tour.

Dickinson with **Janick Gers** on his penultimate tour before quitting the Irons in 1993.

Harris and **Murray** *in extremis* as the Seventh Tour of a Seventh Tour hits New Jersey in 1988.

Murray and **Harris** (with **Gers** peeking out) marvel at new singer **Blaze Bayley**'s dancing…

Gers celebrates twenty years as the "new boy" at the Sonisphere festival in 2010.

In the City (1977)

This Is the Modern World (1977)

All Mod Cons (1978)

Setting Sons (1979)

Sound Affects (1980)

The Gift (1982)

Paul Weller backstage, one month after the release of *In the City*.

Rick Buckler, **Weller**, and **Bruce Foxton**, around the time of *This Is the Modern World*.

Having started the year playing the capital's clubs, the trio ended 1977 playing at London's prestigious Hammersmith Odeon on December 18.

The Jam hit the United States in March 1978 for their second set of dates in the country.

The Jam at the Palladium in New York, February 1980. "American audiences are more into that rock 'n' roll thing; 'Yeah, let's just rock out,'" observed **Weller**, adding "It's just not my scene."

The sharp suits get a rest in 1980, the year of the trio's first No. 1 hits.

The Jam rock the Rainbow in London, May 1979.

Weller wows the crowd at The Jam's last British TV appearance, on Channel 4's *The Tube*.

Elton John (1970)

Honky Chateau (1972)

Goodbye Yellow Brick Road (1973)

Blue Moves (1976)

Too Low for Zero (1983)

Sleeping with the Past (1989)

The One (1992)

Made in England (1995)

Songs from the West Coast (2001)

The Union (2010)

Elton John in 1970, at the start of his prolific recording career as a solo artist.

The newly-arrived superstar at home in Windsor, England, in 1972.

With *Goodbye Yellow Brick Road* having provided a third U.S. and second U.K. No. 1, **Elton** was on a high at London's Hammersmith Odeon in December 1973.

With **Davey Johnstone** on 1976's Louder Than Concorde (But Not Quite As Pretty) tour.

With fellow superstar Rod Stewart at a Liza Minnelli show in 1983.

John during the Victoires de la Musique awards ceremony, France, in 1989.

At the Oakland Coliseum, Los Angeles, on October 30, 1992, on a tour for *The One*.

John plays "Candle in the Wind" at the funeral of Diana, Princess of Wales, in 1997.

At Andre Agassi's Grand Slam for Children fundraiser in Las Vegas, in 2001.

Elton and Leon Russell, with whom he cut *The Union*, on U.S. TV's *Good Morning America*.

journey 1973–present

Neal Schon
b. February 27, 1954

Gregg Rolie
b. June 17, 1947

Ross Valory
b. February 2, 1949

George Tickner
b. September 8, 1946

Prairie Prince
b. May 7, 1950

Steve Smith
b. August 21, 1954

Aynsley Dunbar
b. January 10, 1946

Robert Fleischman
b. Unknown

Journey are *the* American AOR band, selling millions in the seventies and eighties without many record-buyers having a clue as to the members' individual identities. Appropriately, they began life as a group of sessionmen—the Golden Gate Rhythm Section—playing around the Bay Area of San Francisco.

Keyboardist **Gregg Rolie** and guitarist **Neal Schon** had been mainstays of Santana, while bassist **Ross Valory** and rhythm guitarist **George Tickner** had played in psychedelic group Frumious Bandersnatch. Drummer **Prairie Prince**, on loan from The Tubes, completed the original quintet. Rechristened Journey, and with Prince replaced by **Aynsley Dunbar** (latterly a Frank Zappa sidekick), they signed to the Columbia label and issued their self-titled debut in early 1975.

On *Journey*—and its successors *Look Into the Future* (1976) and *Next* (1977)—lyrics and vocals were very much secondary to instrumental rock, just as in Santana. But the record label issued an ultimatum: they wanted a front-man. **Robert Fleischman** proved a short-stayed solution in 1977, making way for **Steve Perry** (who joined the band on the road while the Fleischman-fronted incarnation were supporting Emerson Lake & Palmer) to become the final piece of the Journey jigsaw. His anguished falsetto became much-imitated by American singers of the era.

Infinity (1978) redefined their sound and took them to the edge of the pop Top Twenty. It benefited from Perry's presence and also that of U.K. producer Roy Thomas Baker, fresh from making his name with Queen and supervising their "Bohemian Rhapsody" period. While most of the band members were happy with the commercial rewards their new style brought them, Dunbar packed his sticks and quit for Jefferson Starship, leaving drum duties to **Steve Smith**.

Schon admitted the metamorphosis was a learning curve for him. Writing with Perry was a different discipline from anything he had done before. But the reward came in a string of early eighties hits—dubbed the "dirty dozen" by the band—that projected Journey into the pomp-rock stratosphere.

Evolution (1979) gave the band their first *Billboard* Top Twenty hit, "Lovin', Touchin', Squeezin'," while 1980's *Departure* reached No. 8 on the album chart and included the Top Thirty hit "Any Way You Want It."

Rolie left after 1981's live *Captured* (dedicated to recently deceased AC/DC front-man Bon Scott), to be replaced by **Jonathan Cain** from the Babys. Determined to streamline and modernize the band's sound, Cain muscled into the Schon-Perry songwriting team, and replaced organs with synthesizers. Their defining statement was on its way.

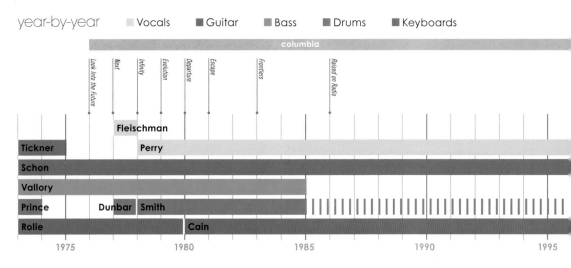

year-by-year   ▪ Vocals   ▪ Guitar   ▪ Bass   ▪ Drums   ▪ Keyboards

5.8M
Departure
(1980)

12.4M
Escape
(1981)

9.9M
Frontiers
(1983)

19.5M
Greatest Hits
(1988)

Steve Perry
b. January
22,1949

Jonathan Cain
b. February 26,
1950

Steve Augeri
b. January 30,
1959

Jeff Scott Soto
b. November
4, 1965

Arnel Pineda
b. September
5, 1967

Deen Castronovo
b. August 17,
1965

Escape—the band's eighth and biggest-selling original album—topped the U.S. album chart in 1981 and went nine times platinum, thanks to three Top Ten hits: "Who's Cryin' Now," "Don't Stop Believin'," and "Open Arms." Journey also graced the soundtracks for the movies *Heavy Metal* (1981) and *Tron* (1982).

1983's *Frontiers* cemented their status, reaching No. 2 on the U.S. chart (and providing the group's first and last U.K. Top Ten album chart entry). Thanks to four hits—"Separate Ways (Worlds Apart)," "Faithfully," "Send Her My Love," and "After the Fall"—it sold six million copies in their homeland.

Success brought inevitable attempts at solo stardom. In 1984, Schon united with Sammy Hagar, Kenny Aaronson, and another Santana alumnus, Michael Shrieve as HSAS, for *Through the Fire*. But when Perry's *Street Talk* (also 1984) proved he did not need Journey behind him to sell millions of albums, the writing was on the wall. Replacing Smith and Valory with Mike Baird and Randy Jackson, the band managed a final album, *Raised on Radio*, in 1986, then splintered. Their epitaph, 1988's *Greatest Hits*, sold around a million a year for the ensuing decade.

Schon, Perry, Cain, Smith, and Valory reunited for 1996's *Trial by Fire*, scoring a first Grammy nomination in the process. But Perry's health problems cut the comeback short. After a less lengthy wait, the band carried on without him, which both parties have done with varying degrees of success to this day.

Front-men **Steve Augeri** and **Jeff Scott Soto** came and went, but the band played on, benefiting from their faceless image. A 2008 tour with Filipino singer **Arnel Pineda** made Journey one of the year's top-grossing live acts, while a second album with him, *Eclipse*, hit U.S. No. 13 in 2011.

Journey invited critical wrath in their heyday with many now-common practices like selling their images for video games, making commercials for beer, and being filmed for fly-on-the-wall documentaries. "There's nothing wrong with being commercial," Schon instructed *Kerrang!* magazine. "It's just another way of saying you're successful, getting a wider audience." Figures back up his conviction: forty-seven million album sales in the U.S. make them one of the nation's top thirty best-selling bands.

Journey undertook a U.S. tour in 2005 to celebrate the thirtieth anniversary of their first album, playing songs from their entire career. Meanwhile, "Don't Stop Believin'" took on a life of its own: its use in TV shows *The Sopranos*, *Scrubs*, and *Glee* propelled cover versions and the original into international charts. When it comes to arena rock, Journey still rule. **MHe**

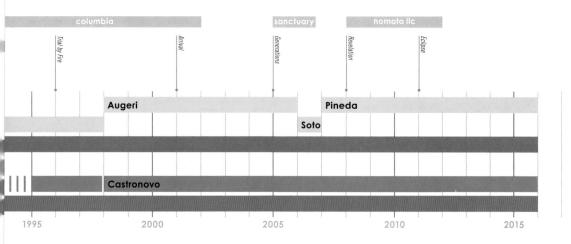

Unknown Pleasures (1979)

Closer (1980)

Movement (1981)

Power, Corruption and Lies (1983)

Low-life (1985)

Brotherhood (1986)

Technique (1989)

Republic (1993)

Get Ready (2001)

No

Waiting for the Sirens' Call (2005)

Joy Division—left to right: **Bernard Sumner**, **Stephen Morris**, **Ian Curtis**, and **Peter Hook**—perform at Bowdon Vale Youth Club, Altrincham, England, on March 14, 1979.

Gillian Gilbert, **Morris**, **Sumner**, and **Hook** perform for the U.K.'s ITV channel in 1981.

Curtis sings at the Lyceum, London, on February 29, 1980.

New Order in the eighties (clockwise from top): **Hook**, **Morris**, **Gilbert**, and **Sumner**.

Sumner, Stratocaster in hand, takes the mike in 1983.

Gilbert, **Sumner**, **Morris**, and **Hook** perform on British TV's *The Tube* in 1986.

Artful distortion in 1989 (clockwise from right): **Gilbert, Sumner, Hook,** and **Morris.**

Gilbert plays the Reading festival, England, in 1993.

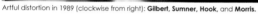

A New Order BBC TV performance on October 11, 2001; **Phil Cunningham** (left) replaced **Gilbert** earlier that year.

Hook gets down but not necessarily dirty with New Order in 2005.

Cunningham onstage at the Wireless Festival, Hyde Park, London, on June 24, 2005.

kiss 1972–present

Gene Simmons
b. August 25, 1949

Paul Stanley
b. January 20, 1952

Peter Criss
b. December 20, 1945

Ace Frehley
b. April 27, 1951

Bob Kulick
b. January 16, 1950

Anton Fig
b. August 8, 1952

The power of the Kiss brand—hammered home via merchandise from condoms to coffins—has powered them through years of lineup changes. New Yorkers **Gene Simmons** and **Paul Stanley** had envisaged a power trio in the hit-making mold of Mountain and Grand Funk Railroad, hence their enlisting drummer **Peter Criss** in 1972. But when the format's limitations became apparent they sought a guitarist. Among those to audition was **Bob Kulick**, who re-entered the story later, but the successful applicant was **Ace Frehley**. (Criss and Frehley's views on drink and drugs diverged—to career-crippling effect—from those of Simmons and Stanley, who made up for their abstinence by bedding groupies by the thousand.)

With the lineup settled, Kiss developed their now-trademark makeup. Fans of The Beatles and Alice Cooper, Simmons and Stanley wanted a band where each member had a recognizable identity. They became the Demon and Starchild, Criss the Cat and Frehley the Spaceman. Their heavy rock 'n' roll was honed on 1974's Kiss and Hotter Than Hell, and 1975's Dressed to Kill. But, as they toured the U.S., their blood-spitting, fire-breathing show provoked more comment and sales than their music. "They're a good band,"

Alice Cooper noted drily after seeing Kiss at a record label showcase in 1974. "All they need is a gimmick."

The quartet's big break came with Alive! (1975), a touchstone for future stars from Slash of Guns N' Roses to Dimebag Darrell of Pantera. Being a member of the Kiss Army became de rigueur among U.S. teens. This fanbase, married to the Casablanca label's over-the-top promotion, made Kiss seem bigger than they actually were. For three years in the seventies—despite being outsold by the Stones, Led Zeppelin, and Pink Floyd—they were voted America's most popular act.

While critics hated them, fans lapped up Destroyer and Rock and Roll Over (both 1976), and Love Gun and Alive II (both 1977). But, by 1978, cracks were showing. Frehley and Criss resented Simmons and Stanley's control, while the founders despaired of their partners' indulgences. (Kulick had deputized for an incapacitated Frehley on studio cuts for Alive II.)

After 1978's hits set Double Platinum, in a mad mix of publicity stunt and damage limitation, the band issued simultaneous solo albums. Criss's was the worst, Stanley's the best, Simmons's the most star-studded (from Joe Perry and Bob Seger to Donna Summer and Cher), and, surprisingly, Frehley's the most successful.

year-by-year

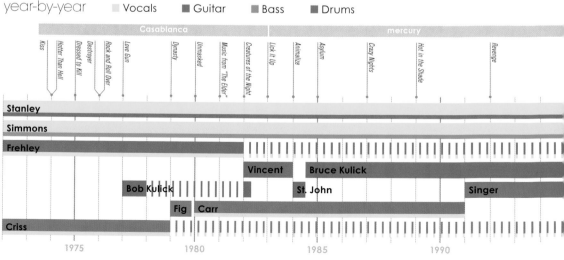

| 3.5M
Destroyer
(1976) | 1.9M
Alive II
(1977) | 2.7M
Crazy Nights
(1987) | 2.9M
*Smashes,
Thrashes & Hits*
(1988) |

Eric Carr
b. July 12, 1950
d. November 24, 1991

Vinnie Vincent
b. August 6, 1953

Mark St. John
b. February 7, 1956
d. April 5, 2007

Bruce Kulick
b. December 12, 1953

Eric Singer
b. May 12, 1958

Tommy Thayer
b. November 7, 1960

Still together in name if not spirit, they recorded 1979's *Dynasty* before Criss (whose duties on *Dynasty* and 1980's *Unmasked* were filled by **Anton Fig**) was replaced by **Eric Carr**. The band's star had waned at home, but an Australian tour was rapturously received. Nevertheless, a re-think was needed, hence 1981's baffling rock opera *Music from "The Elder"* (the soundtrack to a never-made movie). Exasperated by this shift from hard rock, Frehley quit, although his image graced the sleeves of 1982's compilation *Killers* (on new cuts for which he was again replaced by Kulick) and the skull-crushing *Creatures of the Night*.

Among guitarists on the latter was **Vinnie Vincent**. Enlisted full-time, he was part of the excitement when Kiss shed their makeup to promote 1983's *Lick It Up*. But by 1984 he was out—replaced first by **Mark St. John**, then by **Bruce** "brother of Bob" **Kulick**, both of whom played on 1984's platinum-selling *Animalize*.

Asylum (1985), *Crazy Nights* (1987), *Smashes, Thrashes, & Hits* (1988), and *Hot in the Shade* (1989) kept sales ticking over, but Kiss were eclipsed by acts they had inspired, such as Mötley Crüe. "Forever," written with Bruce Kulick's former employer Michael Bolton, was a hit but, by the nineties, Kiss were again a cult concern. Carr's death from cancer (on the same day as Freddie Mercury) compounded their woes.

They forged ahead with Alice Cooper/Black Sabbath drummer **Eric Singer**, but *Revenge* (1992) and *Alive III* (1993)—despite their heavier feel and U.S. Top Ten placings—were overshadowed by grunge-era acts that they had also inspired. In 1995, Simmons and Stanley bowed to the inevitable: enlisting Criss and Frehley for *MTV Unplugged* (1995), then a blockbusting reunion. *Psycho Circus* (1998) gave them a new U.S. chart high (No. 3), but neither Criss nor Frehley contributed much to it. By 2001, after a so-called "farewell" tour, Singer was filling in for the former.

In February 2003, Kiss returned to the road. For the orchestra-embellished recording of *Kiss Symphony: Alive IV* (2003), Criss was back but Frehley had been replaced by band associate **Tommy Thayer**. On a tour that year with Aerosmith, the lineup settled: Simmons, Stanley, Thayer (in Frehley's makeup), and, yet again, Singer (in Criss's makeup). Confounding skeptics, 2009's rollicking *Sonic Boom*—their first new album in a decade—was kept off the U.S. No. 1 spot only by Michael Bublé. And, in 2012, Kiss launched another assault on senses and sensibilities with *Monster*. **BM**

K

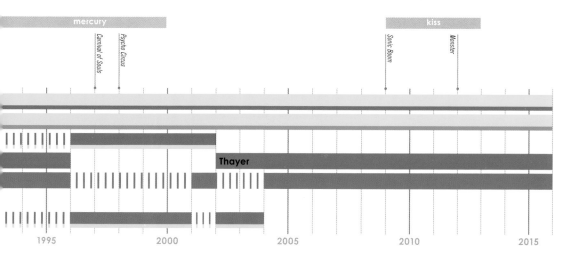

mercury — kiss — Carnival of Souls — Psycho Circus — Sonic Boom — Monster — Thayer

1995   2000   2005   2010   2015

Kiss (1974)

Destroyer (1976)

Love Gun (1977)

Dynasty (1979)

Music from "The Elder" (1981)

Creatures of the Night (1982)

Lick It Up (1983)

Revenge (1992)

Psycho Circus (1998)

Sonic Boom (2009)

Gene Simmons gets into character, backstage in 1974.

Paul Stanley lends a hand with preparations, backstage in 1977.

Stanley (top), **Peter Criss**, **Ace Frehley**, and **Simmons**, in Westminster, London.

Frehley and **Stanley**—the guitarists who powered most of the band's most seminal songs—in a moment of harmony in Chicago in September 1979.

Simmons, Frehley, new drummer **Eric Carr**, and **Stanley**—the lineup responsible for 1981's musically excellent but commercially doomed *Music from "The Elder."*

Simmons and new guitarist **Vinnie Vincent**, who debuted on *Creatures of the Night*.

Vincent and **Stanley** in Chicago, on the *Lick It Up* tour—their first without makeup.

Simmons, guitarist **Bruce Kulick**, and Stanley exact *Revenge* on London in 1992.

The reunited originals—who would later cut *Psycho Circus*—with rapper **Tupac Shakur**.

With **Eric Singer** in Criss's stage makeup, and new guitarist **Tommy Thayer** in Frehley's, **Stanley** and **Simmons** rock Britain's Download festival the year before the quartet cut *Sonic Boom*.

Led Zeppelin
(1969)

Led Zeppelin II
(1969)

Led Zeppelin III
(1970)

Led Zeppelin IV
(1971)

Houses of the Holy
(1973)

Physical Graffiti
(1975)

Presence (1976)

In Through the Out Door (1979)

The band's first public performance together—(left to right) **John Paul Jones**, **Robert Plant**, **Jimmy Page**, and **John Bonham** were billed as The New Yardbirds.

Bonham, Plant, and **Jones** sleep between shows on a 1969 tour of the U.S.

Plant with Fairport Convention's Sandy Denny, who provided the only guest vocal in their catalog: 1971's "The Battle of Evermore."

Plant and **Page** hold court at a press conference before a show at the Forum, Los Angeles, on September 4, 1970.

Page (with Plant in the background) at Madison Square Garden, New York, July 29, 1973.

Plant and Page at Madison Square Garden during Led Zeppelin's 1977 U.S. tour.

Plant, Page, and Bonham at one of five shows at London's Earls Court in May 1975. Thereafter, the original lineup played only two more concerts in their home country, both in 1979.

Jones, Plant, Page, and Bonham in Rotterdam on June 21, 1980, on their final tour. "Morale was very high," Jones told TheCelebrityCafe.com in 2000. "We were in really good spirits."

legião urbana 1982–1996

Renato Russo
b. March 27, 1960
d. October 11, 1996

Dado Villa-Lobos
b. June 29, 1965

Marcelo Bonfá
b. January 30, 1965

Renato Rocha
b. May 27, 1961

Eduardo Paraná
b. Unknown

Bone disease is rarely a catalyst for rock superstardom. However, following surgery for epiphysiolysis in 1975, fifteen-year-old Brazilian Renato Manfredini Jr. spent six months immobile in bed, doing little but listening to music and fantasizing about becoming a musician.

In his late teens, under the stage name **Renato Russo**—inspired by philosophers Bertrand Russell and Jean-Jacques Rousseau, and painter Henri Rousseau—he formed the punk rock group Aborto Eletrico ("Electric Abortion"). Four years, several arguments, and zero albums later, the group split.

Russo briefly performed as a solo artist before founding Legião Urbana (Portuguese for "Urban Legion") with **Marcelo Bonfá** (drums), **Eduardo Paraná** (guitars), and Paulo Paulista (keyboards) in Brasília in 1982, although Paraná and Paulista were band members for barely five minutes. **Dado Villa-Lobos**, the great-grandnephew of noted composer Heitor Villa-Lobos, replaced Paraná on guitar, and in 1985 **Renato Rocha** completed the quartet on bass.

As frontman and vocalist, Russo quickly found himself as a new voice of eighties youth. Poetry, literature, and politics informed his lyrics and Russo became one of Brazil's most significant songwriters. He sparked a connection with the country's disaffected young generation, exasperated with recession and debt, poor health, and education, and tales of corrupt politicians.

Russo had been influenced by British rock bands of the late seventies in his Aborto Eletrico days, and he was now likewise moved by downbeat new wave and post-punk acts from across the Atlantic, such as The Smiths, The Cure, and PiL. Joy Division fans must surely have thought "Ainda É Cedo" from Legião Urbana's self-titled 1985 debut album owed more than a nod to the Manchester group's "A Means to an End."

After the modest success of Legião Urbana's debut, the follow-up *Dois* appeared in 1986. Its title, meaning "Two," referred to the band's intended number of discs before their record label, EMI-Odeon, rejected the idea of a double album.

Russo had written most of the songs on their third album *Que País É Este* (1987) almost a decade earlier, performing some solo or as part of Aborto Eletrico. Despite including one track about a nuclear power plant, and a nine-minute epic about a murdered drug trafficker, with 168 lines and no chorus ("Faroeste Caboclo"), the album shifted over 500,000 copies.

As the band's popularity soared, their fans' enthusiasm led to chaotic shows. A crush at a gig in Brasília left one female fan dead. At another concert, a crazed fan chased the band off stage, causing a

year-by-year ■ Vocals ■ Guitar ■ Bass ■ Drums

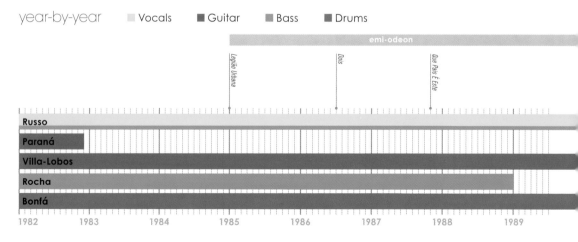

emi-odeon

Legião Urbana

Dois

Que País É Este

Russo

Paraná

Villa-Lobos

Rocha

Bonfá

1982 1983 1984 1985 1986 1987 1988 1989

riot that saw dozens of people injured. The violent disturbances heightened Russo's stage fright and subsequently the band played live as little as possible.

Rocha quit before the release of the fourth album, 1989's *As Quatro Estações*, and Russo took over bass duties. Some fans were alienated by songs about love and family, and lyrics hinting at Russo's bisexuality. He came out as gay during an interview the following year and briefly lost some followers, but the album went on to be one of Legião Urbana's most successful.

V (1991) saw a return to bleaker subjects, with tales of drug abuse and reflections on Brazil's economic crisis. By then, Russo had been diagnosed with AIDS, although this was not made public while he was alive, and his increasing dependency on alcohol ensured *V*'s promotional tour in 1992 was short.

Música P/ Acampamentos ("Music for camping," 1992)—a collection of rarities, including a cover of The Rolling Stones' "Gimme Shelter," and a medley of The Righteous Brothers' "You've Lost That Lovin' Feelin'," John Lennon's "Jealous Guy," and The Beatles' "Ticket to Ride"—preceded a sixth studio set, *O Descobrimento do Brasil* ("The discovery of Brazil," 1993). This, Russo explained, was about his drug rehabilitation ("I was almost following Cobain's steps, but I have found people to help me"). Russo then

proved himself to be quite the prolific multilinguist, releasing two solo albums: a set of cover versions in English, *The Stonewall Celebration Concert,* which included tracks as diverse as Stephen Sondheim's "Send In The Clowns" and Madonna's "Cherish"; and the Italian-language album *Equilibrio Distantei,* which helped to popularize Italian music in Brazil.

The self-produced *A Tempestade, ou O Livro dos Dias* ("The Tempest, or The Book of Days") was released in September 1996, but Russo died three weeks later, having stopped taking his AIDS medication. His bandmates dissolved Legião Urbana eleven days after his passing, revealing that much of that last album had been recorded "in a lot of pain" because of Russo's illness.

In 1997, unreleased tracks from the *A Tempestade* sessions, completed with additional musicians—including former member Rocha—appeared on the posthumous *Uma Outra Estação*. A collection of songs left off Russo's two solo albums was also released.

Compilations and live albums, including the successful *Acústico MTV,* have kept Legião Urbana in the Brazilian charts in the years since they disbanded. Total sales of around twenty million have helped establish them as one of the biggest bands in the music-loving country's history. **RJ**

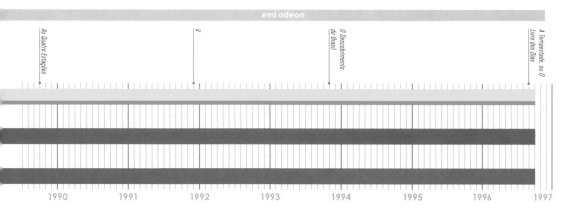

john lennon 1968–1980

John Lennon
b. October 9, 1940
d. December 8, 1980

Yoko Ono
b. February 18, 1933

Klaus Voorman
b. April 29, 1942

Nicky Hopkins
b. February 24, 1944
d. September 6, 1994

Alan White
b. June 14, 1949

Jim Keltner
b. April 27, 1942

"He had just come from being in the biggest group on the planet," Lenny Kravitz told *Rolling Stone* of **John Lennon**'s solo career. "Most people in his position would say, 'How do I keep this up? I don't want to come down off this pedestal.' He didn't care. He got butt naked… with his dick hanging out."

Lennon's solo discography in fact began while he was still a Beatle, with November 1968's *Unfinished Music No.1—Two Virgins*. But it is indeed remembered for its nude picture of the star and his soon-to-be wife, **Yoko Ono**. Neither that album nor 1969's *Unfinished Music No.2—Life with the Lions* and *Wedding Album* made much impression on charts, but the summer's "Give Peace A Chance" hit the U.K. Top Three and U.S. Top Twenty. The single was credited to the Plastic Ono Band, a name used again when Lennon played in Toronto in September with Eric Clapton, bassist **Klaus Voorman** and future Yes drummer **Alan White** (hence the Top Ten album *Live Peace in Toronto 1969*).

Featuring the talents of George Harrison and producer Phil Spector, 1970's "Instant Karma" was a Top Five success on both sides of the Atlantic. At the end of the year, the stark *John Lennon/Plastic Ono Band* followed it into the charts' upper reaches. "The attitude and emotion of that album are harder than any punk rock I've ever heard," remarked Kravitz.

In August 1971, Lennon left Britain for the last time. *Imagine*—completed before his departure and issued a month later—hit No. 1 around the world. Celebrated for its lovely title track and "Jealous Guy," the album also included the vicious "Crippled Inside" and "How Do You Sleep?"—the latter a barely veiled attack on Paul McCartney, featuring Harrison on slide guitar.

When Lennon and Ono were threatened with deportation from the U.S. (allegedly related to a 1968 cannabis bust), they left "sugar-coated" sounds behind. "Women is the Nigger of the World" was the sole, minor hit from 1972's *Some Time in New York City*, a political/avant garde double album made with Voorman, drummer **Jim Keltner** (who had also played on *Imagine*), New York band Elephant's Memory, and Frank Zappa's Mothers of Invention. It was, inevitably, out-sold by 1973's more song-oriented *Mind Games*.

Lennon's battle to remain in America—which extended to him seeking a pardon from the Queen for the drug offence—ran until October 1975, when

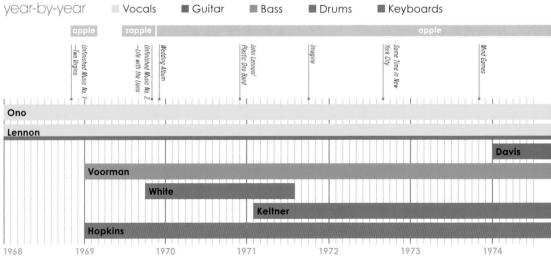

year-by-year ▫ Vocals ▪ Guitar ▪ Bass ▪ Drums ▪ Keyboards

Jesse Ed Davis
b. September 21, 1944
d. June 22, 1988

the deportation order was reversed. In the intervening years, he embarked on his infamous "lost weekend," often in the company of singer Harry Nilsson, whose *Pussy Cats* (1974) he produced.

Nilsson, Elton John, and Lennon's eleven-year-old son Julian contributed to *Walls and Bridges* (1974), which returned him to the U.S. No. 1. Elton played on "Whatever Gets You Thru' The Night" and made Lennon promise that he would guest at a live show if the song topped the chart. This it duly did, and a terrified Lennon joined the star onstage at New York's Madison Square Garden in November 1974, to play that song, plus "Lucy in the Sky with Diamonds" and "I Saw Her Standing There." His first live appearance in over two years would also be his last.

Rock 'n' Roll (1975)—a set of fifties and sixties covers—gave Lennon a No. 6 hit on both sides of the Atlantic. Later that year, David Bowie's "Fame"—co-written by Lennon—topped the U.S. chart, and the hits set *Shaved Fish* rounded off this first phase of the former Beatle's solo career. Following the birth of his son Sean in October, Lennon "retired," to focus on fatherhood in his and Ono's New York apartment.

He was finally granted a green card, confirming his U.S. residency, in 1976, and returned to the studio in the summer of 1980, with Ono, to make the album *Double Fantasy*. But in December, a week after its release, Lennon was shot dead by Mark Chapman—who, hours earlier, had collected his autograph on a copy of the new album. *Double Fantasy* promptly topped international charts, as did its "(Just Like) Starting Over." Subsequent hits "Woman" and "Watching the Wheels" shared charts with reissues of 1971's "Imagine" and "Happy Xmas (War is Over)."

Lennon was honored for his Outstanding Contribution to British Music by both the Brit and Ivor Novello awards, while *Double Fantasy* won the 1982 Grammy for Album of the Year. Unreleased songs were compiled on 1984's gold-selling *Milk and Honey*, while an August 1972 show was issued as *Live in New York City* (1986). A host of compilations included the multi-platinum *The John Lennon Collection* (1982) and *Lennon Legend: The Very Best of John Lennon* (1997).

His legacy, for all its inconsistencies, continues to inspire contemporary rock stars, perhaps most notably Kurt Cobain and Oasis's Gallagher brothers. **BS/BM**

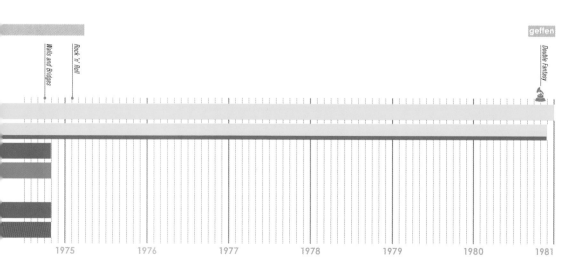

Unfinished Music No.1—Two Virgins (1968)

Unfinished Music No.2—Life with the Lions (1969)

Wedding Album (1969)

John Lennon/ Plastic Ono Band (1970)

Imagine (1971)

Some Time in New York City (1972)

Mind Games (1973)

Walls and Bridges (1974)

Rock 'n' Roll (1975)

Double Fantasy (1980)

John Lennon and Yoko Ono in a London studio in 1968.

During their seven-day protest against war and violence, **Lennon** and **Ono** receive the press in the Presidential Suite of the Hilton Hotel, Amsterdam, on March 27, 1969.

Lennon sleeps on a hospital floor beside **Ono**. The scene appears on the sleeve of *Unfinished Music No.2—Life with the Lions* (1969).

Lennon and **Ono** perform with the newly formed and experimental Plastic Ono Band in 1969.

Black Power leader Michael X trades a pair of Muhammad Ali's bloodied boxing shorts for the newly cut hair of **Lennon** and **Ono** on February 19, 1970.

Lennon and **Ono** pose at their home, Tittenhurst Park, Berkshire, England, during the making of *Imagine* in 1971.

On August 30, 1972, **Lennon** and **Ono** perform at New York's Madison Square Garden, to benefit a facility for children with learning difficulties.

Lennon enjoys a night out in Los Angeles with Alice Cooper.

In the last live performance of his career, **Lennon** appears with Elton John at Madison Square Garden, on November 28, 1974.

Left to right: Art Garfunkel, Paul Simon, **Ono**, and **Lennon** at the Grammys on March 1, 1975, at the Uris Theater, New York.

Fans cluster around **Lennon** as he leaves the Hit Factory recording studio in Times Square, New York, after a session for his final album *Double Fantasy* in August 1980.

limp bizkit 1994–present

Fred Durst
b. August 20, 1970

Sam Rivers
b. September 2, 1977

John Otto
b. March 22, 1977

Wes Borland
b. February 7, 1975

DJ Lethal
b. December 18, 1972

Mike Smith
b. October 11, 1973

Equally lauded and despised, Limp Bizkit succeeded where so many others failed: they took the rap-rock genre and turned it into a commercial juggernaut. They were not first to the party, which had been going on at least since Aerosmith and Run-D.M.C. collaborated on "Walk This Way" in 1986, but they were the band that carried the party to the next level. Limp Bizkit quickly became as popular as any act in rap or rock—and, for a few years, challenged the biggest names in pop for chart supremacy.

None of that impressed most critics, who slammed the group, reserving extra venom for outspoken vocalist **Fred Durst**. But negative reviews could not stop fans—some thirty-three million records were sold.

Durst had worked in a number of Jacksonville area bands before he starting an outfit that would combine both of his musical passions—metal and hip-hop—in 1994. He first joined forces with two cousins, bassist **Sam Rivers** and drummer **John Otto**, then guitarist **Wes Borland** and turntablist **DJ Lethal**, aka Leor Dimant. Limp Bizkit developed a die-hard local following with a high-energy live show, but it was not until Durst met Korn that they got their first big break. Durst played the band some demos and they landed an opening slot on the nü-metal superstars' tour.

Consequently, Flip/Interscope signed them up to record their first full-length album, *Three Dollar Bill, Yall$*.

Released in 1997, the debut generated impressive sales—eventually peaking at U.S. No. 22. Fans were hooked by its powerful hybrid sound and it went on to double-platinum sales. *Significant Other*, released in 1999, debuted at No. 1 in the U.S. and established Limp Bizkit as one of the top new bands in the world.

Chocolate Starfish and the Hot Dog Flavored Water (2000) sold more than a million in its first week and was eventually certified six times platinum. Critics, however, despised it, with *Entertainment Weekly* naming it the year's worst album. All the negative criticism—not just of the band, but of the rap-rock genre as a whole—began to catch up with Limp Bizkit by the time they released 2003's *Results Might Vary* (minus Borland). It went platinum, but the writing was on the wall and—after 2005's *The Unquestionable Truth (Part 1)* (with Borland)—the Bizkit went on hiatus.

While the intervening years have not changed critics' views on Durst, Limp Bizkit acquired a nostalgic appeal. The comeback album *Gold Cobra* (2011) restored them to the U.S. Top Twenty, and their shows have been well-received. A new album, *Stampede of the Disco Elephants*, is threatened for 2015. **JiH**

year-by-year ▢ Vocals ◼ Guitar ◼ Bass ◼ Drums ◼ Programming

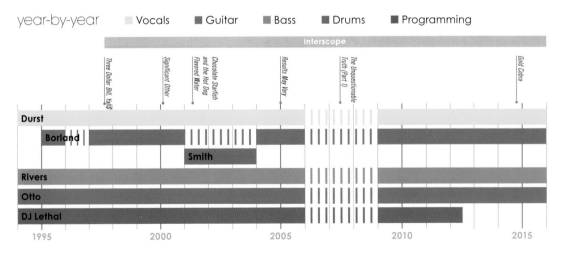

linkin park 1999–present

Mike Shinoda
b. February 11, 1977

Rob Bourdon
b. January 20, 1979

Brad Delson
b. December 1, 1977

Joe Hahn
b. March 15, 1977

Phoenix Farrell
b. February 8, 1977

Chester Bennington
b. March 20, 1976

"I'm very happy when I hear new stuff like Linkin Park," remarked Rudolf Schenker of the Scorpions in 2001. His enthusiasm was not shared by everyone: the group's overnight success and MTV ubiquity led to suggestions that they were nü-metal's very own Backstreet Boys. Fast forward a decade, however, and Linkin Park have three international chart-topping albums under their belts, can still headline stadium shows, and have left all their nü contemporaries in the commercial dust.

The band began as Xero, a post-high school project for **Mike Shinoda**, **Rob Bourdon**, and **Brad Delson**. With **Joe Hahn**, **Dave "Phoenix" Farrell**, and **Chester Bennington**, Xero became Hybrid Theory, then Linkin Park (a reference to Lincoln Park, Santa Monica, in the band's home state of California).

Dazzling videos, the might of Warner Bros., and songs that effortlessly bridged any remaining gaps between metal and hip hop ensured that Linkin Park were an immediate success. *Hybrid Theory* became the best-selling album of 2000, and spawned a platinum-selling remix set, *Reanimation* (2002). Guests on the latter included Korn's Jonathan Davis, Staind's Aaron Lewis, Deftones' Stef Carpenter, Sneaker Pimps' Kelli Ali, Taproot's Stephen Richards, and rappers Pharaohe Monch and Black Thought.

Relentless touring confirmed their international appeal, and *Meteora* (2003) duly smashed in at the top of charts around the world. Illustrating the twin foundations of their sound, Linkin Park toured with Metallica and united with Jay-Z for 2004's mash-up mini-album *Collision Course*—inevitably, another U.S. No. 1 and million-seller. "The whole group, as far as how professional they were in putting this together, was very impressive," Jay noted. "I'm used to having to carry people and they showed me something else."

After a variety of side projects, the group reconvened, with Midas-touch producer Rick Rubin, for *Minutes to Midnight* (2007). The nü-metal bubble had long since burst, but Linkin Park's ability to storm to No. 1 in every major territory remained unchanged. This massive international popularity was confirmed by stadium shows, including one in Britain immortalized on 2008's *Road to Revolution: Live at Milton Keynes* (featuring a collaboration with Jay-Z).

The double platinum single "New Divide" (from a *Transformers* movie soundtrack) and *A Thousand Suns* (2010), again helmed by Rubin, maintained their defiance of commercial trends. With the release of *Living Things* (2012) and *The Hunting Party* (2014), their supremacy seems unassailable. **BM**

year-by-year ▪ Vocals ▪ Guitar ▪ Bass ▪ Drums ▪ Keyboards ▪ Programming

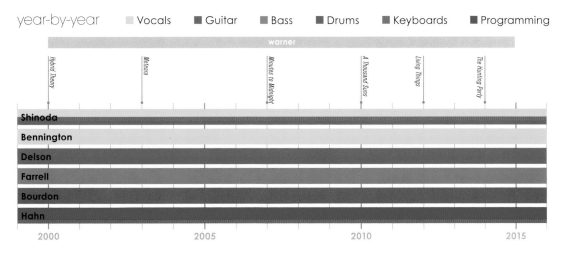

warner

Hybrid Theory · *Meteora* · *Minutes to Midnight* · *A Thousand Suns* · *Living Things* · *The Hunting Party*

Shinoda
Bennington
Delson
Farrell
Bourdon
Hahn

2000 · 2005 · 2010 · 2015

little feat 1969–present

Lowell George
b. April 13, 1945
d. June 29, 1979

Bill Payne
b. March 12, 1949

Richie Hayward
b. February 6, 1946
d. August 12, 2010

Roy Estrada
b. April 17, 1943

Paul Barrere
b. July 3, 1948

Kenny Gradney
b. February 25, year
unknown

With their intoxicating blend of rock 'n' roll, country, folk, and southern fried boogie, Little Feat were—in their day—one of the most intelligent, innovative, and exciting bands around.

Lowell George (vocals/guitar) started the band with **Bill Payne** (keyboards/vocals) in Los Angeles in 1969. The guitarist had served a short stint in Frank Zappa's Mothers of Invention, after Zappa produced tracks for his earlier band The Factory, a combo that also featured **Richie Hayward** (drums). After Payne unsuccessfully auditioned for Zappa's band, he and George formed Little Feat, with Hayward and former Mothers bassist **Roy Estrada**.

George had already cut a demo of his signature song, "Willin'," with his friend Ry Cooder. This track would serve as both inspiration and direction for the new band's sound, major features of which were George's slide guitar and world-weary, soulful vocals.

With Zappa's help, they signed to Warner Bros. and recorded two critically acclaimed but poorly selling albums, the fumbling *Little Feat* (1971) and the more refined *Sailing Shoes* (1972). Estrada left soon

after to join Captain Beefheart's Magic Band, and the group expanded to include **Paul Barrere** (guitar) and former Delaney and Bonnie musicians **Kenny Gradney** (bass) and **Sam Clayton** (congas).

The new lineup added a New Orleans funk swagger to their ever-growing pallet of influences and soon proved to be a spectacular live act. With George as producer, they recorded *Dixie Chicken* (1973)—now considered a landmark release—but it sold no better than its predecessors and, demoralized, the band split. Payne joined The Doobie Brothers' touring band, while the others went into session work.

But, eventually, Warner realized how superb Little Feat really were. With the promise of the label finally putting some serious promotional muscle behind the band, the group reconvened and recorded the successful *Feats Don't Fail Me Now* (1974).

At the start of 1975, the band played two gigs at the Rainbow in London as part of a Warner package tour and impressed everyone with their stunning live sets. Their reputation, particularly in England, as one of rock's most vital and important bands was enhanced

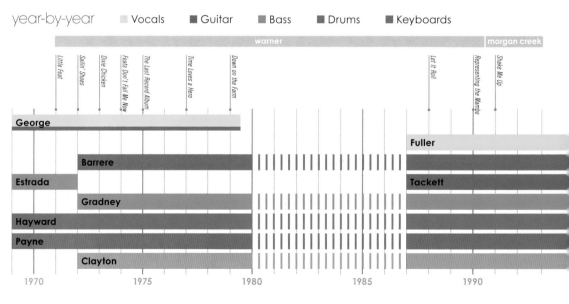

year-by-year   ▢ Vocals   ■ Guitar   ■ Bass   ■ Drums   ■ Keyboards

1M
Dixie Chicken
(1973)

1M
Feats Don't Fail
Me Now
(1974)

1M
Time Loves
a Hero
(1977)

2.7M
Waiting for
Columbus
(1978)

Sam Clayton
b. September 15, year
unknown

Fred Tackett
b. August 30, 1945

Craig Fuller
b. unknown

Shaun Murphy
b. unknown

Gabe Ford
b. June 8, 1973

even further by a legendary bootleg album of a killer live radio broadcast, *Electrif Lycanthrope*.

Little Feat had finally arrived but, on The *Last Record Album* (1975) and *Time Loves a Hero* (1977), with his own songwriting contributions now at a bare minimum, George felt Payne and Barrere had too much influence within the band. He disliked intensely the pair's new progressive jazz-rock leanings, and relations between them degenerated into antagonism and ill-feeling.

The spectacular live double *Waiting for Columbus* was their best-selling album yet. However, George—with both his health and interest in the band declining fast—walked out of the recording sessions for the next album, declaring his intentions to disband Little Feat and then reform the group without Payne and Barrere.

The label had just released *Thanks, I'll Eat It Here*, George's first, and as it turned out only, solo album, put together mostly from covers he had recorded in previous years. In the summer of 1979, he set out on tour in support of its release. But that outing ended abruptly with his untimely death on June 29 from a

drug-induced heart attack, aged just thirty-four. The remaining members completed the recordings for *Down on the Farm* (1979) before disbanding altogether. *Hoy-Hoy!* (1981), a double album of outtakes and archive live material, highlighted their undoubted brilliance but George's death inevitably spelt the end of them as a true creative force.

They re-formed in 1987 with guitarist **Fred Tackett** and vocalist **Craig Fuller**, recording the commercially successful *Let It Roll* (1988). But Warner, unhappy with the jazz-rock elements of the follow-up, *Representing the Mambo* (1990), dropped the band.

After one more album, Fuller left in 1993 to be replaced by female vocalist **Shaun Murphy**. This new lineup lasted sixteen years, releasing live albums and occasional studio efforts on various small labels.

As a hugely popular fixture on the live jam band circuit, Little Feat have continued to this day. Murphy, after five albums and over 1,400 live appearances, departed in 2009. And, sadly, Hayward succumbed to cancer in August 2010; he was replaced by **Gabe Ford**, the band's drum technician. **MD**

■ Other percussion

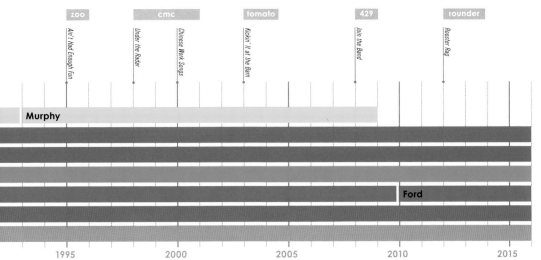

loudness 1981–present

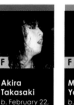

Minoru Niihara
b. March 12, 1960

Akira Takasaki
b. February 22, 1961

Masayoshi Yamashita
b. November 29, 1961

Munetaka Higuchi
b. Dec 24, 1958
d. November 30, 2008

Masayuki Suzuki
b. 1973

Many believed that Loudness would be the Japanese hard rock act to finally conquer America. The band, who became a hit in their homeland within months of forming in Osaki in 1981, had all the elements—incredible players (especially shredder-supreme **Akira Takasaki**), a powerful vocalist (**Minoru Niihara**), a metal sound that echoed the popular flavor of the day, solid songs, and a glam metal wardrobe (which could have been lifted straight out of Ratt's closet).

Loudness would get their shot in 1985, when they became the first Japanese hard rock act to sign an international deal with a major U.S. label—Atco Records. It turned out to be a modest victory, with two Loudness albums charting in the U.S. Top 100, but what was at risk of being lost was equally significant. Loudness's fascination with America, which led to the band replacing Niihara with Yankee vocalist Michael Vescera, did not go over well with fans in the Land of the Rising Sun. In fact, Loudness would eventually give up on America, a few years after the country gave up on the band, and return to courting its longtime fan base. The group, with some two-dozen full-length studio efforts under their belt, are now considered one of the all time great Japanese metal acts.

Given the band's mighty work ethic, it is ironic that Loudness emerged from a group dubbed Lazy. Guitarist Takasaki and drummer **Munetaka Higuchi** toiled away in that mainstream pop-rock outfit from 1977 to 1981, before bolting to join the rising tide of Japanese metal artists like Bow Wow. They hooked up

with Niihara and bassist **Masayoshi Yamashita** and Loudness were born, quickly landing a record deal and dropping the Japanese-language debut *The Birthday Eve* (1981). The band released three albums over the next three years, a pace they have kept for much of their career. The fifth album, 1985's *Thunder in the East*, was a thoroughly Western affair—recorded in Los Angeles with producer Max Norman and sung entirely in English. Thanks to "Crazy Nights" (Loudness's biggest American hit), *Thunder in the East* became the first offering from a Japanese act to chart in the *Billboard* 200, peaking at No. 74. The following year's *Lightning Strikes* did even better—No. 64—but U.S. listeners were clearly losing interest by 1987's *Hurricane Eyes*, which stalled at *Billboard* No. 190.

Former Obsession front man Michael Vescera replaced Niihara at the microphone in 1988, but the clear ploy to entice more U.S. listeners was ineffective, and EZO front-man Masaki Yamada took the mic for much of the nineties. Although some fans were dismayed by the band's new direction—which embraced radio-friendly pop-metal—Loudness continued to sell well in their homeland.

Niihara returned to the fold for *Spiritual Canoe* (2001), but Higuchi died in 2008 after a lengthy battle with liver cancer. In 2011, the band released its twenty-fourth studio album, *Eve to Dawn*. However, the best introductions to their discography remain the storming first two of their eight live albums, 1983's *Live-Loud-Alive: Loudness in Tokyo* and 1987's *8186 Live*. **JiH**

year-by-year ■ Vocals ■ Guitar ■ Bass ■ Drums

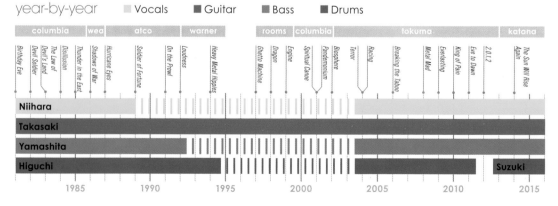

love 1965–2005

Arthur Lee
b. March 7, 1945
d. August 3, 2006

Johnny Echols
b. February 21, 1947

Bryan MacLean
b. Sept 25, 1946
d. December 25, 1998

Kenny Forssi
b. March 30, 1943
d. January 10, 1998

Alban "Snoopy" Pfisterer
b. September 27, 1946

Michael Stuart
b. July 29, 1944

Tjay Cantrelli
b. unknown
d. unknown

Love are best remembered for acid rock masterpiece *Forever Changes*, ranked fortieth on *Rolling Stone's* 500 Greatest Albums of All Time and inducted, eventually, into the Grammy Hall of Fame in 2008.

Performing as The Grass Roots in 1965 and with a lineup of **Arthur Lee**, **Johnny Echols**, Don Conka, **Bryan MacLean**, and John Fleckenstein, they competed with another Los Angeles band with the same name until Lee's outfit eventually called themselves Love. In November 1965, Fleckenstein was replaced by **Kenny Forssi**, then drummer Conka left to be replaced by **Alban "Snoopy" Pfisterer**. With the lineup now stabilized, Love released their self-titled folk-rock debut album in March 1966.

By August, with Pfisterer switching from drums to keyboards and with new drummer **Michael Stuart** and woodwind player **Tjay Cantrelli**, the band had concocted a John Coltrane-influenced sound that resulted in the release of *Da Capo*. The music was described as a free form blending of jazz and rock before the term "fusion" was familiar. Although the album spawned Love's biggest U.S. single, "7&7 Is," in January 1967, Pfisterer and Cantrelli were fired: the material Lee and MacLean were writing for the next album demanded an orchestral sound, played by a five-man group with strings and horns. Orchestral pop

was the dazzling hallmark of Love's acclaimed third album, *Forever Changes*. The title was a prophetic one because, in August 1968, the band fractured and Lee put together a new blues-rock lineup, adding Frank Fayad, Jay Donnellan, and George Suranovich. That fall, Suranovich was briefly out of the band after a disagreement with Lee over money, and was temporarily replaced by Drachen Theaker. With Theaker on board, the band cut tracks that surfaced on their next two albums, *Four Sail* and *Out Here*.

With Gary Rowles added and Suranovich returning, the band delivered *False Start* (1970), notable for a guest appearance by Jimi Hendrix. After recording the lackluster *Love Lost* in 1971, the band broke up. Lacking much of his earlier inventiveness, Lee nevertheless created a new soul and R&B-oriented Love featuring Robert Rozelle, Melvan Whittington, and Joe Blocker and set about recording *Black Beauty* (released, after Lee's death, in 2011).

In 1974, the band released *Reel to Real*, before yet another break-up in 1975. Not until the early nineties did Lee resurrect the Love brand, when Rozelle, Whittington, Gary Stern, and Tony Mikesell got together to make the final album, *Arthur Lee and Love*. Their ever-popular live appearances continued until a year before Lee's death in 2006. **BC**

year-by-year   ■ Vocals   ■ Guitar   ■ Bass   ■ Drums   ■ Keyboards

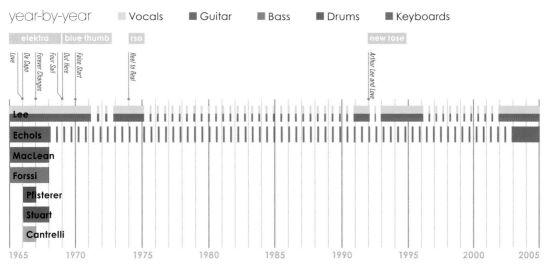

lynyrd skynyrd 1964–present

Gary Rossington
b. December 4, 1951

Ronnie Van Zant
b. Jan 15, 1948
d. October 20, 1977

Allen Collins
b. July 19, 1952
d. January 23, 1990

Bob Burns
b. November 24, 1950

Larry Junstrom
b. June 22, 1949

Rickey Medlocke
b. February 17, 1950

Ed King
b. September 14, 1949

Artimus Pyle
b. July 15, 1948

It was a good thing Lynyrd Skynyrd immediately taught fans how to say their unusual name—the title of 1973's debut record was *(Pronounced 'leh-'nérd 'skin-'nérd)*—because listeners would repeat it often from that point forward. The band practically burst out of the gate as the definitive Southern rock act, arguably flying past the Allman Brothers on the back of the almighty cut "Free Bird"—and their stranglehold on the genre would tighten over the next four years. There is really no telling how high Lynyrd Skynyrd could have eventually soared had a 1977 air crash not claimed the lives of three band members and shattered the worlds of those left behind.

How it began, however, can be traced back to 1964, when a trio of childhood pals—charismatic vocalist **Ronnie Van Zant**, guitarist **Gary Rossington**, and **Allen Collins**—formed the Noble Five in Jacksonville, Florida. One year later, the troupe, which by then included drummer **Bob Burns** and bassist **Larry Junstrom**, was going by the moniker My Backyard. Then, in 1970, the group began calling itself "Leonard Skinnerd"—a backhanded compliment to the musicians' former gym teacher, Leonard Skinner, at

Robert E. Lee High School—and the name eventually morphed into the current one.

Touring through the South into the early seventies, Skynyrd were distinguished by a hard-hitting, guitar-drenched sound heavily influenced by British rockers like Cream, The Rolling Stones, and The Yardbirds. Unlike the Allmans' jazz-influenced improvisational workouts, which at times seemed built to thrill the tie-dyed masses at Bill Graham's Fillmore clubs, this was real Deep South boogie, drawing inspiration from backwoods blues and real-deal country.

Having cut demos in 1971 in Alabama's Muscle Shoals studio, the group snared Al Kooper, who would produce Skynyrd's first three albums. The Blood, Sweat & Tears founder encountered them during a week-long residency at an Atlanta club. "Each night I'd hear another great original song…" he told *Rolling Stone,* "and knew I'd found the band I was searching for."

(Pronounced 'leh-'nérd 'skin-'nérd) (1973) was nothing less than one of the greatest debut records of the era. The album, which rose to No. 27 in the U.S., produced four of the group's signature songs—the mournful "Tuesday's Gone," the reflective "Simple

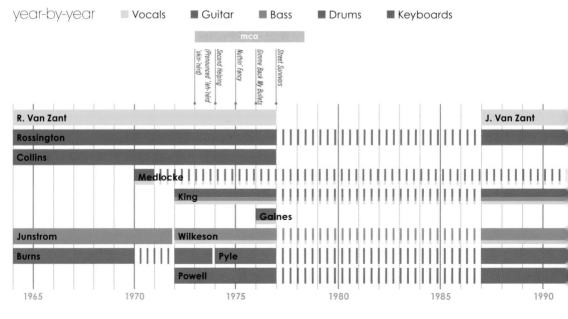

4.1M	3.2M	3.3M	8.9M
(Pronounced 'leh-'nérd 'skin-'nérd) (1973)	*Second Helping* (1974)	*Street Survivors* (1977)	*Skynyrd's Innyrds* (1989)

Steve Gaines
b. September 14, 1949
d. October 20, 1977

Leon Wilkeson
b. April 2, 1952
d. July 27, 2001

Billy Powell
b. June 3, 1952
d. January 28, 2009

Johnny Van Zant
b. February 27, 1960

Michael Cartellone
b. June 7, 1962

Peter Keys
b. May 30, 1965

Hughie Thomasson
b. Aug 13, 1952
d. September 9, 2007

Ean Evans
b. September 16, 1960
d. May 6, 2009

Man," the ruckus-raising "Gimme Three Steps," and the anthemic "Free Bird." The latter has long stood as one of rock's most famous songs—its status cemented, for better or worse, by fans who yell "Freeeee Biiiiiiiird!" at concerts, no matter who is on stage. Ironically, the song, perhaps best known for its epic three-guitar showdown, would not become a Top Twenty hit until 1975—one year after the band's sophomore effort, the appropriately named *Second Helping*, hit shelves. By that point, Lynyrd Skynyrd was already a star act, thanks in no small part to the irresistible "Sweet Home Alabama," which gave the band its first Top Ten hit.

The good times kept right on rolling, as 1975's *Nuthin' Fancy* finally admitted the band into the U.S. album chart Top Ten. A fourth album, *Gimme Back My Bullets*, stalled at No. 20, but Skynyrd reached their chart peak with 1977's *Street Survivors*, which hit No. 5. However, three days after its release, disaster struck.

On October 20, 1977, the band's tour plane—nicknamed, of course, "Free Bird"—crashed in Mississippi, killing founding member Van Zant, guitarist **Steve Gaines**, and backup vocalist **Cassie Gaines**. The loss—especially of Van Zant, widely considered the heart and soul of the band—was too much to take, and Lynyrd Skynyrd would call it quits. *Gold & Platinum*, released in 1979 and eventually certified triple-platinum in the U.S., served as an excellent summation of all the band had accomplished in the span of five studio albums. And that appeared to be it for the Lynyrd Skynyrd saga, until the surviving members came together on the tenth anniversary of the crash and embarked on a major tour. Decades later, Lynyrd Skynyrd—fronted by Ronnie's brother, **Johnny Van Zant**, on vocals—is still trucking right along and delighting fans in concert. Among the members is former Blackfoot leader **Rickey Medlocke**, who had briefly sung and drummed for Skynyrd in 1970.

That the ever-rotating cast of players would find work on the road is really no surprise in the nostalgia-driven classic rock world. More of a shock is that the group has maintained such a healthy recording career. Lynyrd Skynyrd have released seven studio albums since reforming in 1987, and these have done well on the charts. Indeed, the group's twelfth studio album, 2009's *God & Guns*, was Skynyrd's first Top Twenty offering since *Street Survivors*. **JiH**

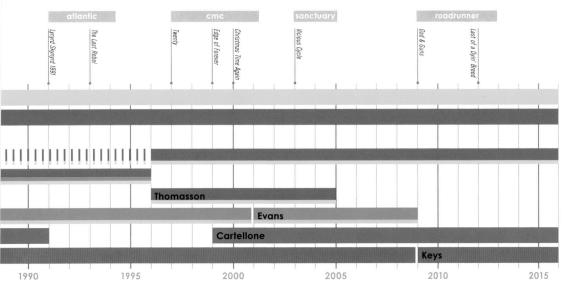

manic street preachers 1986–present

James Dean Bradfield
b. February 21, 1969

Nicky Wire
b. January 20, 1969

Sean Moore
b. July 30, 1968

Richey Edwards
b. December 22, 1967
d. February 1, 1995

Manic Street Preachers had No. 1 singles about the Spanish Civil War ("If You Tolerate This Your Children Will Be Next"); No. 1 albums named after speeches made by long-dead politicians (*This Is My Truth Tell Me Yours*); and audiences with Cuban leader Fidel Castro (in 2001). If its members had remained faithful to their manifesto, the group would have imploded after just one huge hit album. But then we would have been denied one of the U.K. music scene's most intriguing, contrary, politicized, and polarizing careers. Oh, and a load of great, incendiary, and intelligent music.

After a false start in the mid-eighties with a lineup that included Miles Woodward, known as "Flicker," on bass, the us-against-the-world quartet from south Wales was settled—**James Dean Bradfield** (guitar/vocals), **Nicky Wire** (bass), **Richey Edwards** (rhythm guitar), and **Sean Moore** (drums). Early singles such as "Motown Junk" (1991) and "You Love Us" (1992) seemed to verge on punk pastiche, with heavy debts to The Clash. With its metal guitars, their debut album *Generation Terrorists* (1992) swam against the tide of indie shoegazing, but did so successfully enough to reach U.K. No. 13. In a career that was to be characterized by confounding expectations, the album ultimately proved to be a calling card rather than a signing-off. "At least we broke our own rules," remarked Bradfield in 2004.

Two 1992 singles edged the Manics toward the mainstream: "Motorcycle Emptiness," whose yearning guitar was a clear nod to their heroes Guns N' Roses' "Sweet Child o' Mine," and a U.K. Top Ten cover of the theme from the TV show *M*A*S*H*, "Suicide is Painless."

Gold Against the Soul (1993) is not greatly loved by the band, but it became their first Top Ten album entry in the U.K. Said Chemical Brother Ed Simons of "La Tristesse Durera (Scream to a Sigh)"—one of four Top Forty singles from it—"What it really has, like all great dance records, is that integral sense of transcendent melancholy."

Success and *Gold Against the Soul*'s smoother sound could not disguise the worsening personal problems experienced by Richey Edwards. These had been most publicly demonstrated in an act of self-mutilation during an interview with then-NME writer Steve Lamacq: to show that deeds were as important to the band as words, he carved "4 REAL" into his arm. Lamacq, complained Edwards, "couldn't conceive that people can be so frustrated and pissed off that they're prepared to hurt themselves."

The Holy Bible came out in the U.K. in early 1994, but was overshadowed later the same year by two albums that came to define the era—*Definitely Maybe* by Oasis and Blur's *Parklife*. Where those sold millions, the only place *The Holy Bible* reached No. 1

M

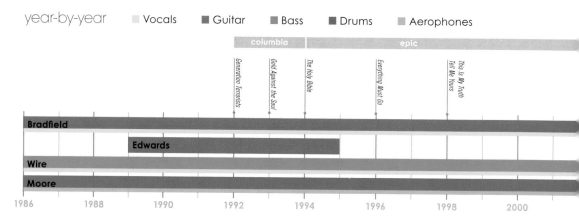

year-by-year — ■ Vocals ■ Guitar ■ Bass ■ Drums ■ Aerophones

columbia | epic

Generation Terrorists
Gold Against the Soul
The Holy Bible
Everything Must Go
This Is My Truth Tell Me Yours

Bradfield

Edwards

Wire

Moore

1986 1988 1990 1992 1994 1996 1998 2000

was on *NME*'s Fifty Darkest Albums Ever. Nicky Wire described the album as "full of disgust with humanity."

A destructive gig in London at the end of 1994 was Edwards's last stage appearance. Just weeks later, he was missing, presumed dead. Even by Manics standards, the future was bleak. "We are haunted by ghosts," reflected Wire. Out of this, though, appeared the almost total triumph of *Everything Must Go* (1996). Although Edwards received credits on a handful of tracks, the lyrical focus fell on Wire. "I'm not pretending to be the same kind of lyricist as Richey," he admitted. "I don't reach the depths of madness and self-hatred that he did." However, an arresting opening line—"Libraries gave us power"—allied to "a bit of R.E.M., a bit of Ennio Morricone" from Bradfield made "A Design for Life" an instant anthem.

This Is My Truth Tell Me Yours (1998) completed their transformation from a purely U.K. chart concern—albeit triple platinum-selling one—to a band with a strong international profile. For the Manics, a purity of purpose always co-exists with a need for popularity. "I couldn't survive on critical acclaim alone," said Wire. After the success of *This Is My Truth...* the pendulum swung the other way for 2001's back-to-basics *Know Your Enemy* (featuring a cameo by My Bloody Valentine's Kevin Shields). However, the non-album single "The Masses Against the Classes" gave them a second U.K. chart-topper (after 1998's "If You Tolerate This Your Children Will Be Next").

Lifeblood (2004) did not live up to its title, its polite posturing marking a band whose life force seemed to be ebbing away—more the Middle-Aged than Manic Steet Preachers. *Send Away the Tigers* (2007) was a partial return to form, notably in its hit duet with the Cardigans' Nina Persson, "Your Love Alone is Not Enough." But in more typical Manics fashion, it took the lyrics of a dead man (at his parents' instigation, Edwards was legally declared deceased in November 2008) to revive a spirit that was at best dormant and, concluded many, gone for good. Thirteen years separated Edwards bequeathing a folder of lyrics and the band using its contents as the basis for the best—read most uncompromising—Manics album in years, *Journal for Plague Lovers*, released in 2009.

The exit that was planned for 1992 came to pass—sort of—almost two decades on, with the band announcing a hiatus in the slipstream of the hook-heavy *Postcards from a Young Man* (2010) and the singles collection *National Treasures* (2011). "You're only this hateful and angry once, really," Wire had said in 1991. Like everything the Manics do, this is subject to debate and revision. Thankfully, nothing much has changed. Said Wire in 2011: "There's just so much hate within this band." And we love them for it. **CB**

M

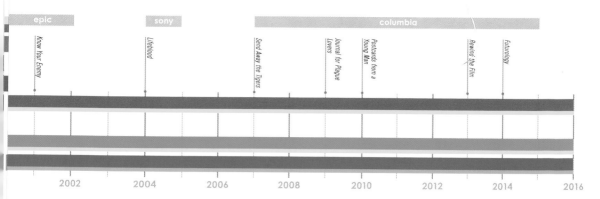

McCartney (1970)

Band on the Run (1973)

Back to the Egg (1979)

McCartney II (1980)

Pipes of Peace (1983)

Flowers in the Dirt (1989)

Flaming Pie (1997)

Run Devil Run (1999)

Driving Rain (2001)

Memory Almost Full (2007)

Linda and **Paul McCartney** in a New York studio in 1970.

Wings' last lineup: (back) **Paul**, Laurence Juber, (front) Steve Holley, **Denny Laine**, **Linda**.

Paul at home in Britain's Sussex, after his deportation from Japan for marijuana possession.

In 1973, the year of *Red Rose Speedway* and *Band on the Run*.

Michael Jackson, Kim Wilde, Pete Townshend, and **Paul** in 1983.

With Pete Townshend at The Concert for New York City.

Back on the road for the first time in a decade, in August 1989.

Promoting The Beatles' *Anthology* retrospective with **Ringo** and George, just after starting work on *Flaming Pie*.

Back at the Cavern club in Liverpool, promoting *Run Devil Run*, with Pink Floyd's David Gilmour, Deep Purple's Ian Paice, and guitarist Mick Green.

Live in London for *Memory Almost Full*'s launch, looking as remarkably youthful as ever...

meat loaf 1967–present

Meat Loaf
b. September 27, 1947

Shaun "Stoney" Murphy
b. Unknown

Steve Buslowe
b. Unknown

Bob Kulick
b. January 16, 1950

Paul Jacobs
b. Unknown

Mark Alexander
b. December 26, 1963

A cursory glance at Michael Lee Aday's vital stats—including that once hefty waistline—confirms that the Texas native is not your average rock star. With a blown fuse (quite literally) here and a near-death experience there, **Meat Loaf**'s rock and roll dreams have come through and made him one of the most admired, yet most ridiculed, icons in rock.

Michael (born Marvin) had music in his veins from the get-go courtesy of a mother who sang in a gospel quartet. In the summer of 1967, after relocating to California as a nineteen-year-old, he formed his first band, Meatloaf Soul. Surviving a fall from a balcony at a house the group used for rehearsals, the "Man of Steel" was destined to rub shoulders with the likes of The Who, Pink Floyd, Janis Joplin, and Alice Cooper as "ringmaster" of The Floating Circus (the third incarnation of Meatloaf Soul), wearing—in the words of bandmate Rick Bozzo—"his soon-to-be signature tuxedo with red cummerbund; barefoot of course."

By 1969, with many of the musicians (in Bozzo's words) "surfing, mentally messed up from drugs," or bagging "cushy jobs working for their dads," Meatloaf was going nowhere fast and turned to theater,

landing a role in a Detroit production of the musical *Hair*. Then, alerted to his vocal prowess, the Motown label signed him up, with fellow cast member **Shaun "Stoney" Murphy**. The pair briefly raided the U.S. chart with the *Stoney and Meatloaf* album cut "What You See Is What You Get." (Murphy would later sing with Eric Clapton before joining Little Feat in 1993.)

Meatloaf returned to the stage with the Broadway cast of *Hair*, but it was the audition for his next acting role (The Public Theater's *More Than You Deserve*) that transformed his life. There, he met Jim Steinman—composer, lyricist, producer, and the man who would be instrumental in shaping Meat's career.

Still a couple of years from his first association with those creatures that hang upside-down in caves, Meatloaf played "ex-delivery boy"-turned-zombie Eddie in *The Rocky Horror Show*, reprising his role for the 1975 movie version. But the larger-than-life star of more than fifty movies and TV shows was now ready to ditch his "Hot Patootie" for a full-blown rock career, initially providing guest vocals on Ted Nugent's Top Forty album *Free-for-All*. However, it was a second slice of Meat Loaf—now two words rather than one—

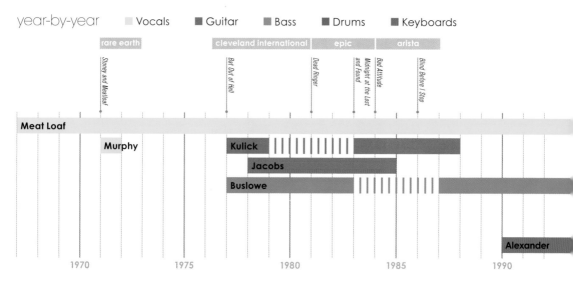

year-by-year ▪ Vocals ▪ Guitar ▪ Bass ▪ Drums ▪ Keyboards

28.6M	**14.8M**	**5.2M**	**2.5M**
Bat Out of Hell (1977)	*Bat Out of Hell II: Back Into Hell* (1993)	*Welcome to the Neighbourhood* (1995)	*Couldn't Have Said It Better* (2003)

John Miceli
b. May 29, 1961

Kasim Sulton
b. December 8, 1955

Paul Crook
b. February 12, 1966

Randy Flowers
b. Unknown

Dave Luther
b. Unknown

that spectacularly exposed him to a worldwide audience, when 1977's *Bat Out of Hell* took flight.

Rolling out a few numbers barely does the album justice, but here goes: approaching thirty million copies sold worldwide, including fourteen million in the U.S. alone, and more than *nine* years on the U.K. chart, including 244 weeks in the Top Forty—an achievement unmatched by any other solo artist. No mean feat considering the seven-track album peaked modestly at No. 14 in the U.S. and No. 9 in the U.K.

Despite an epic, million-selling single ("Two Out of Three Ain't Bad") from *Bat Out of Hell*, Meat Loaf's U.S. career was frequently all revved up with no place to go. Incredibly, *Bat*'s title track has failed to chart on three occasions, and early eighties albums *Dead Ringer* (source of the rousing Cher duet, "Dead Ringer for Love"), *Midnight at the Lost and Found*, and *Bad Attitude*—all Top Ten hits in the U.K.—fell short of the Top Forty in his homeland. Meat has spoken candidly about his struggle to be taken seriously as a rock musician, and one might argue that negative publicity toward his theatrical stage antics and "silly" songs blunted his post-*Bat* sales potential.

However, in 1993, armed with some of the longest and daftest titles in rock history—"Life Is a Lemon and I Want My Money Back," "Objects in the Rear View Mirror May Appear Closer Than They Are"—and with Steinman back by his side, Meat scored his first transatlantic No. 1s with the long-awaited *Bat* sequel, *Back Into Hell*, and its Grammy-winning lead single, "I'd Do Anything for Love (But I Won't Do That)."

After two more mega-sellers—1995's *Welcome to the Neighbourhood* and 2003's *Couldn't Have Said It Better*—the final album of the *Bat* trilogy, *The Monster Is Loose*, returned Meat to global Top Tens in 2006. And despite announcing his retirement in 2007, Meat was back in 2010 with the U.K. platinum puller *Hang Cool Teddy Bear* and in 2011 with *Hell in a Handbasket*.

Meat has triumphed over adversity throughout his life. He endured an alcoholic father and a catalog of creative differences with Steinman, was branded a "circus clown," and has survived Wolff-Parkinson-White Syndrome, cocaine, vocal malfunctions, being hit on the head during shot put at high school, and starring in a Spice Girls movie. You could say he has been to hell and back several times over. **MW**

■ Aerophones   **■** Other percussion

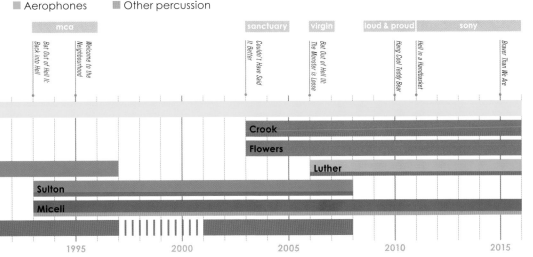

megadeth 1984–present

Dave Mustaine
b. September 13, 1961

David Ellefson
b. November 12, 1964

Chris Broderick
b. March 6, 1970

Shawn Drover
b. May 5, 1966

Chris Poland
b. December 1, 1957

Gar Samuelson
b. Feb 18, 1958
d. July 22, 1999

Jeff Young
b. March 31, 1962

Marty Friedman
b. December 8, 1962

Alongside Metallica, Slayer, and Anthrax, Megadeth form a quarter of the so-called Big Four, an elite group that popularized thrash metal in the eighties. Thrash—a faster, more aggressive form of the heavy metal that had influenced all the bands—found a commercial home thanks to its combination of melodic hooks and uncompromising riffage. And no band mastered this trick as ably as Megadeth.

Founded by ex-Metallica guitarist **Dave Mustaine** with bassist **David Ellefson** (nicknamed "Junior" to avoid confusion, to his irritation) in 1984, Megadeth started life with the aim of being faster, heavier, and generally more "metal" than Mustaine's former band, against whom he harbored a very public grudge.

While this was a futile ambition (Metallica went on to become metal's biggest band of all time), the band nonetheless unleashed a sequence of classic albums, fueled by their leader's world-class guitar pyrotechnics and knack for a catchy chorus. After what Mustaine described as a "$4,000 piece of crap first album" (1985's *Killing Is My Business… and Business Is Good*), the group's first major hit was *Peace Sells… but Who's Buying?* (1986). The album was a stormer, despite tensions between the two Daves, guitarist **Chris Poland**, and drummer **Gar Samuelson** that threatened to derail it, exacerbated by all four being drug abusers at the time. A side-effect of Mustaine's habit was that he often derided his contemporaries in public, establishing feuds against a raft of bands including Slayer and Pantera. (In later years, he

claimed—with some justification—that the media encouraged and promoted these disagreements.)

Megadeth stepped up their game with *So Far, So Good… So What?* (1988) and *Rust in Peace* (1990), by their most commercially successful lineup, featuring guitarist **Marty Friedman** and drummer Nick Menza. This platinum-selling period of success peaked with the U.S. Top Five albums *Countdown to Extinction* (1992) and *Youthanasia* (1994), but fashions were changing in metal and Megadeth found it difficult to expand their profile through the rest of the decade.

After a final U.S. Top Ten million-seller—1997's *Cryptic Writings*—they made an ill-advised switch to a softer sound with *Risk* (1999) and *The World Needs a Hero* (2001). Then Mustaine injured his arm, rendering him unable to play guitar, and dissolved the band. A lawsuit from Ellefson seemed to spell the end, but Mustaine returned after a year's physiotherapy with a new lineup and album, *The System Has Failed* (2004).

Since then Megadeth have rebuilt their profile with admirable speed, releasing acclaimed albums that adhere to the technical thrash template that made them famous. Now clean and sober and with the feud with his old band (mostly) resolved, Mustaine has become an elder statesman of thrash, revered once more for his musical and songwriting skills.

Against all expectations, Ellefson rejoined Megadeth in 2010 in time for a Big Four tour series initiated by Metallica, and the two Daves' comeback album, *Th1rt3en*, marked a welcome return to form. **JM**

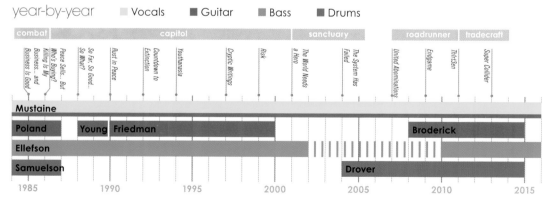

year-by-year ▢ Vocals ■ Guitar ■ Bass ■ Drums

men at work 1979–2012

Colin Hay
b. June 29, 1953

Ron Strykert
b. August 18, 1957

Greg Ham
b. September 27, 1953
d. April 19, 2012

Jerry Speiser
b. 1953

John Rees
b. unknown

There are plenty of argumentative bands in this book, but Men at Work hold a special place: the lead guitarist was arrested in 2009 for threatening to kill the lead vocalist. But let us start in happier times.

Colin Hay, born in Scotland, emigrated to Australia with his parents when he was fourteen. He later formed an acoustic duo with **Ron Strykert**, who he had met while working on a stage musical. In 1979, they expanded into a pub band with **Greg Ham** (keyboards), **Jerry Speiser** (drums), and classical violinist **John Rees** (bass). Influenced by The Police and The Cars, they called themselves Men at Work and secured a residency at a hotel in Melbourne. A CBS accountant spotted them there and recommended them to the A&R division. As a result, they made *Business as Usual* with U.S. producer Peter McIan.

Hay said that he wrote "Who Can It Be Now" "in the middle of the bush with my girlfriend." The song, a study in paranoia, topped the charts in Australia and, after a successful tour supporting Fleetwood Mac, in the U.S. The follow-up, "Down Under," was about Australians who go overseas and want to return, parodying Aussie life with its "fried-out combies" and Vegemite sandwiches. McIan suggested the reggae rhythm and its promotion was helped by a comic video, heavily rotated on MTV. (When the publishers of a 1934 song, "Kookaburra," sued for plagiarism, the judge ruled that only Ham's flute line was similar and they were awarded five per cent of the royalties.)

Having achieved the rare feat of topping the U.K. and U.S. albums and singles charts simultaneously, the stage was well set for *Cargo* (1983). A bleak album, lacking the distinctiveness of *Business as Usual*, it nonetheless promptly went platinum, thanks to its hits "Overkill" and the anti-war "It's a Mistake."

Rees and Speiser left during the making of 1985's *Two Hearts*. The album was completed with session musicians and synthesizers, and even managed to be certified gold in the U.S., but arguments over management and songwriting royalties left Hay on his own, including a tour of China with a makeshift band. He developed a solo career with *Looking for Jack* (1987), *Wayfaring Sons* (1990), *Peaks and Valleys* (1993), and *Topanga* (1995), appeared in films, and toured in Ringo Starr's All-Starr Band in 2003.

Hay and Ham reformed a version of Men at Work for a South American tour, which led to the live *Brazil* (1996). The lineup has varied ever since. They appeared at the 2000 Summer Olympics in Sydney with actor Paul Hogan of *Crocodile Dundee* fame, but Strykert did not join them because he felt he had been cheated out of royalties. Instead, he worked with the Nudist Funk Orchestra, cut a solo album, *Paradise* (2009), and was arrested when he threatened to kill Hay. The singer assured fans that Strykert did not mean it—but, like the protagonist of "Who Can It Be Now," he may be wary when somebody knocks at his door. **SL**

M

year-by-year ■ Vocals ■ Guitar ■ Bass ■ Drums ■ Keyboards ■ Aerophones

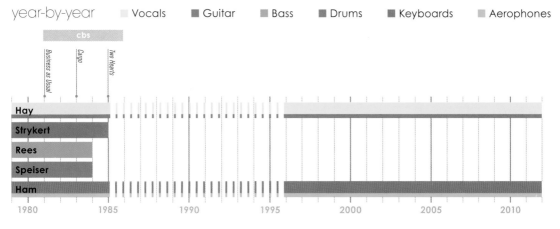

cbs

Business as Usual
Cargo
Two Hearts

Hay
Strykert
Rees
Speiser
Ham

1980　　1985　　1990　　1995　　2000　　2005　　2010

metallica 1981–present

James Hetfield
b. August 3, 1963

Lars Ulrich
b. December 26, 1963

Kirk Hammett
b. November 18, 1962

Robert Trujillo
b. October 23, 1964

Dave Mustaine
b. September 13, 1961

Ron McGovney
b. November 2, 1962

San Francisco-based quartet Metallica are metal's biggest-selling band and have been since the mid-nineties, when their expert combination of anthemic songs and dynamic live performances first elevated the band to the top of the international music scene. Some have labeled the group "this generation's Led Zeppelin," with good reason: the number of Metallica albums (five of which topped the U.S. chart) sold over the band's three decades is approaching 100 million, and they continue to play the biggest stadiums with little indication that any members are slowing down.

Those members' every move is scrutinized in the rock media these days, a scenario that could scarcely have been imagined when the first incarnation of Metallica gathered in Los Angeles in late 1981. Guitarist and singer **James Hetfield**, a fan of stadium rock acts such as Aerosmith, had been through a series of high-school bands, but only made headway when he met Danish drummer **Lars Ulrich** through a musicians-wanted ad in a local magazine.

The pair had jammed before and parted ways, but their second meeting was driven by Ulrich's need to form a band: he had offered to provide a song for a compilation, *Metal Massacre*. Adding Hetfield's room-mate **Ron McGovney** on bass and recruiting session guitarist Lloyd Grant, the group cut "Hit the Lights."

Metallica replaced Grant with hotshot guitarist **Dave Mustaine** and began to tour the Los Angeles area. Demo recordings appeared, the most widely-distributed of which was 1982's *Power Metal*, but the group made serious progress when McGovney was replaced by San Francisco native **Cliff Burton**. A move north to Burton's home town followed and, in early 1983, the band traveled to New York, where record-store owner Jon Zazula had offered to help them find a deal. After fruitless attempts to raise industry interest, Zazula founded the Megaforce label to release Metallica's debut album, *Kill 'Em All*, recorded after they replaced the erratic Mustaine with Exodus guitarist **Kirk Hammett**. The album's fast, aggressive blend of intensity and melody established the thrash metal sound in America: within a couple of years, Metallica were the leaders of the genre's so-called Big Four, alongside Slayer, Anthrax, and Megadeth (the last of these formed by a very bitter Mustaine).

The Hetfield/Hammett/Burton/Ulrich lineup—Metallica's most critically acclaimed incarnation—unleashed scene-redefining albums in *Ride the Lightning* (1984) and *Master of Puppets* (1986). Their profile exploded on a U.S. tour with Ozzy Osbourne, but a tragic setback occurred in September 1986 when Burton died in a tour-bus accident in Sweden.

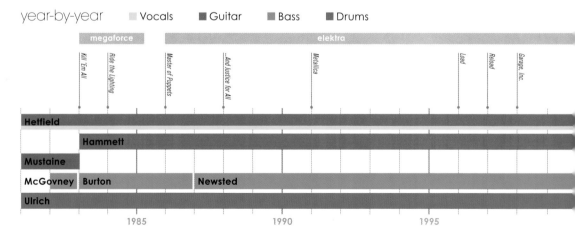

year-by-year ▢ Vocals ▪ Guitar ▪ Bass ▪ Drums

Cliff Burton
b. February 10, 1962
d. September 27, 1986

Jason Newsted
b. March 3, 1963

The originator of many of Metallica's most musically beguiling passages and an authority within the band, Burton had taught Hetfield elements of musical theory that informed 1988's ...And Justice for All. The brutal album—a Top Ten smash on both sides of the Atlantic—featured (albeit barely audibly) their new bassist, former Flotsam and Jetsam man **Jason Newsted** (who had made his Metallica debut with 1987's jolly The $5.98 E.P.—Garage Days Re-Revisited).

In 1991 Metallica took a giant leap toward the mainstream with their fifth, self-titled set, aka "The Black Album." This dispensed with the thrashier elements of their earlier work and, unlike Justice, placed Newsted's bass high in the mix for a rich sound that paid enormous dividends. As the album soared towards fifteen million sales in the U.S. alone, Metallica became a touring machine, embarking on global jaunts that lasted years. (A bad-tempered excursion with Guns N' Roses in 1992 left Metallica the clear winners). Meanwhile, even two albums held in lesser regard by fans—Load (1996) and ReLoad (1997)—topped charts around the world and sold millions.

A covers album, Garage, Inc. (1998), and a live set recorded with the San Francisco Symphony, S&M (1999)—though both enjoyable and multi-million-selling—suggested Metallica's innovatory spirit was waning. When they did pursue a new direction, it was with 2003's deliberately under-produced St. Anger (which went multi-platinum around the world despite being very hard to listen to). The album's self-destructive conception was documented in the gripping movie Some Kind of Monster, which followed the band's experiences with rehab and therapy and the replacement of Newsted by former Suicidal Tendencies and Ozzy Osbourne bassist **Robert Trujillo**.

Metallica returned from the abyss with the above-average Death Magnetic (2008) and toured as part of a Big Four of Thrash package in 2010, also the year of their induction into the Rock and Roll Hall of Fame. A collaboration with Lou Reed—2011's Lulu—met with universal horror, but the group's thirtieth anniversary in December of that year occasioned celebratory shows, whose guests included Dave Mustaine, Ozzy Osbourne, Black Sabbath's Geezer Butler, Alice in Chains' Jerry Cantrell, and Judas Priest's Rob Halford.

Long a constant on the international summer festival circuit, Metallica launched their own event, Orion Music + More, in 2012. As illustrated by 2009's phenomenal DVDs Français pour une nuit (2009) and Orgullo, Pasión Y Gloria: Tres Noches en la Ciudad de México, the band and their classic-packed repertoire remain a force to be reckoned with on stage. **JM**

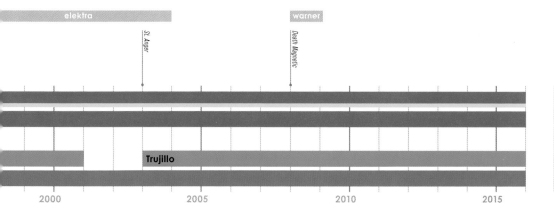

Kill 'Em All (1983)

Ride the Lightning (1984)

Master of Puppets (1986)

...And Justice for All (1988)

Metallica (1991)

Load (1996)

Reload (1997)

Garage, Inc (1998)

St. Anger (2003)

Death Magnetic (2008)

Cliff Burton and **James Hetfield** in 1981, playing the songs that would become *Kill 'em All*.

Burton, **Lars Ulrich**, Hetfield, and **Kirk Hammett** ride the lightning.

Burton, whose death in 1986 dealt the band a tragic blow.

With bassist **Jason Newsted** (far left) and mascot "Doris" on the Damaged Justice tour.

Now one of the biggest bands on the planet, Metallica rock Britain's Sheffield Arena in November 1992, on the mammoth Wherever We May Roam tour.

Hetfield and Ulrich in Illinois in June 1996, on the Lollapalooza leg of the Poor Touring Me tour for *Load*.

Hetfield and Ulrich—the band's founders and creative driving forces—rockin' Worcester, Massachusetts, in 1997.

Hammett on the Garage Remains the Same tour in 1999.

Rob Trujillo channeling the spirit of Cliff Burton on the Madly in Anger with the World tour, in Belgium in 2003.

With The Kinks' Ray Davies on a break from *Death Magnetic* duties.

midnight oil 1976–2002

Rob Hirst
b. 1955

Andrew James
b. Unknown

Jim Moginie
b. May 18, 1956

Peter Garrett
b. April 16, 1953

Martin Rotsey
b. February 18, year unknown

Peter Gifford
b. 1955

Bones Hillman
b. 1958

Australian rock band Midnight Oil created music that appealed to both mind and body. Their sound was energetic and danceable, while the lyrics dealt sensitively with nuclear proliferation, the environment, and the plight of Australia's indigenous people.

Based in Sydney, drummer **Rob Hirst**, bassist **Andrew James**, and keyboard player/guitarist **Jim Moginie** were performing under the name Farm when, in 1972, they were joined by law student **Peter Garrett**. Playing a set that drew heavily on English progressive rock, Farm remained a part-time occupation until Garrett completed his degree in 1976, from which time they became known as Midnight Oil. With a new name came a departure in their music, the addition of second guitarist **Martin Rotsey** heralding a shift toward a faster, more aggressive rock style.

Midnight Oil gigged furiously in their early days, playing over 200 shows a year. They quickly built up a solid following on the Sydney bar circuit based on a reputation for loud, high-energy performances. Their 1978 debut, *Midnight Oil*, was less successful in capturing the essence of the band's live work, but their growing cult following nonetheless pushed it into the lower reaches of the Australian chart.

Signed to CBS, the band were expected to reap international rewards with *Place Without a Postcard*. The experience, however, was not a happy one: the dilution of their new wave sound for a more

commercial style placed an uncomfortable emphasis on Garrett's vocals. A balance between adventurous modern pop and Garrett's increasingly political lyrics was finally struck on 1982's *10, 9, 8, 7, 6, 5, 4, 3, 2, 1*. This proved to be "The Oils"' breakthough, hitting the Australian Top Three, remaining on the chart for the next four years, and providing an opportunity for the band to broaden their fanbase for the first time.

Peter Garrett was now becoming newsworthy in his own right. Cutting an imposing, shaven-headed figure, he ran a high-profile—if ultimately unsuccessful—campaign as a candidate for the Nuclear Disarmament Party at elections in 1984.

In 1987, Midnight Oil produced their defining album, *Diesel and Dust*. It topped the chart at home, and hit the Top Thirty in Europe and the U.S., thanks to "Beds Are Burning," a global smash that dealt with the return of Australia's desert lands to Aboriginal tribes. The band cemented their international success with heavy touring and similarly styled big-sellers such as *Blue Sky Mine*, *Earth and Sun and Moon*, and *Breathe*.

In 2002, committing himself to Australian politics, Garrett announced he was leaving the band. As a candidate for the Australian Labor Party, he won a seat at the 2004 elections, and three years later was named Minister for the Environment, Heritage, and the Arts. The Midnight Oil name was laid to rest, and is now revived only for one-off benefit concerts. **TB**

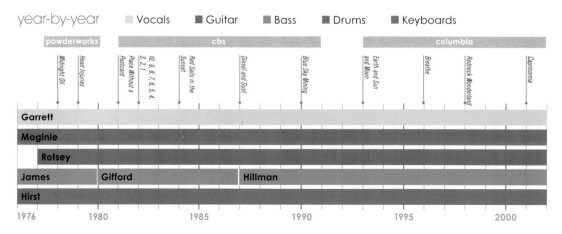

year-by-year ⬜ Vocals ⬛ Guitar ⬛ Bass ⬛ Drums ⬛ Keyboards

powderworks | cbs | columbia

Midnight Oil — Head Injuries — Place Without a Postcard — 10, 9, 8, 7, 6, 5, 4, 3, 2, 1 — Red Sails in the Sunset — Diesel and Dust — Blue Sky Mining — Earth and Sun and Moon — Breathe — Redneck Wonderland — Capricornia

Garrett
Moginie
Rotsey
James | Gifford | Hillman
Hirst

1976 · 1980 · 1985 · 1990 · 1995 · 2000

steve miller 1966–present

Steve Miller
b. October 5, 1943

Lonnie Turner
b. February 24, 1947

Tim Davis
b. November 29, 1943

Gary Mallaber
b. October 11, 1946

Byron Allred
b. October 27, 1948

David Denny
b. February 5, 1948

Norton Buffalo
b. Sept 28, 1951
d. Oct 30, 2009

Gerald Johnson
b. Unknown

"Enter **Steve Miller**: man without a face" ran the headline on a *Rolling Stone* feature in 1976. It was not a jibe. On all his albums, his visage had been blurred, even masked, and the laid back blues-jazz-rock guitarist himself had said: "I want people to enjoy my music. I don't want to be a personality." So there you have it: one of rock's "A-list," happy to give the limelight to his alter egos—"The joker," "The space cowboy," "The gangster of love," and, er, "Maurice."

Little Steve had a formative upbringing. At five years old, he was given advice and encouragement by guitar legend Les Paul. Bluesman T-Bone Walker played guitar at his house when Miller was nine. At fourteen, Miller backed electric blues pioneer Jimmy Reid in a Dallas bar. This was a boy with pedigree, even before he hustled gigs in Chicago with Muddy Waters, Howlin' Wolf, and The Butterfield Blues Band.

But blues was not a happening scene, whereas San Francisco's psychedelia was. The guitarist played at the Matrix club on the same night Grace Slick joined Jefferson Airplane on stage. This good omen was sealed by a record-breaking $50,000 deal with no artistic strings. Steve headed to London to hang out with The Beatles' engineer Glyn Johns, who gave Miller's albums segued tunes and the best effects that two four-track machines could muster. Jamming with Paul McCartney one night led to two cuts

on *Brave New World,* on which Macca is credited as Paul Ramon. (Nearly thirty years later, the two collaborated again on McCartney's *Flaming Pie.*)

The Steve Miller Band went through myriad personnel shifts—college friend Boz Scaggs played guitar on the first two albums—as they charged through albums and tours (supporting Hendrix and the Grateful Dead). It was a blur of rushed deadlines, band tensions, marriage, divorce, a broken neck, hepatitis, and having his guitar overdubbed by Jesse Ed Davis (because Miller had to do a promo tour). At one point he retreated home for eight months, only to re-emerge to self-produce his 1973 *Billboard* No. 2 album *The Joker* and its chart-topping title track.

After another hiatus, Miller emerged with his best songs yet, of which "Rock 'n Me," referencing Free's "All Right Now," gave him another U.S. No. 1. His third, "Abracadabra," came in 1982, but Miller's standout song is *Circle of Love*'s sixteen-minute "Macho City"—which, with its funky feel and trippy effects, made him an unlikely New York disco darling of the eighties.

Tired of playing the songs that comprised his thirteen million-selling *Greatest Hits 1974–78,* Miller took time out again before returning with *Bingo!* (2010) and *Let Your Hair Down* (2011). "Never in my wildest dreams," he admitted, "did I think that I'd be the guy on the radio that you can't move." **JaH**

M

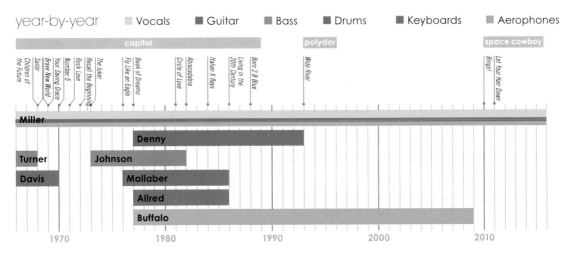

year-by-year   Vocals   Guitar   Bass   Drums   Keyboards   Aerophones

capitol   polydor   space cowboy

Children of the Future / Sailor / Brave New World / Your Saving Grace / Number 5 / Rock Love / Recall the Beginning... / The Joker / Fly Like an Eagle / Book of Dreams / Circle of Love / Abracadabra / Italian X Rays / Living in the 20th Century / Born 2 B Blue / Wide River / Bingo! / Let Your Hair Down

Miller

Denny

Turner   Johnson

Davis   Mallaber

Allred

Buffalo

1970   1980   1990   2000   2010

the moody blues 1964–present

Denny Laine
b. October 29, 1944

Ray Thomas
b. December 29, 1942

Graeme Edge
b. March 30, 1942

Mike Pinder
b. December 27, 1941

Clint Warwick
b. June 25, 1940
d. May 15, 2004

John Lodge
b. July 20, 1945

In one of rock's earliest brand sponsorship deals, five musicians from Britain's Midlands adopted the name MB Five in return for two thousand pounds' worth of sponsorship from local brewers Mitchells & Butlers. However, the Birmingham-based group—keyboardist **Mike Pinder**, guitarist **Denny Laine**, flautist and vocalist **Ray Thomas**, drummer **Graeme Edge**, and bassist **Clint Warwick**—soon became The Moody Blues.

At the tail-end of a British tour with Chuck Berry in January 1965, their aching "Go Now"—a cover of an R&B song by Bessie Banks—topped the U.K. chart. It also hit No. 10 in the U.S., although follow-up releases and their debut album, 1965's *The Magnificent Moodies*, failed to make much impact.

The quintet supported The Beatles on their final British tour in December 1965, but the following year saw the exits of Warwick (replaced for a Danish tour by Rod Clarke) and Laine (later to reappear alongside ex-Move man Trevor Burton in the splendidly named Balls, then Paul McCartney's Wings).

The group split in October 1966... only to re-form the following month, with bassist/vocalist **John Lodge** (who had played with Thomas and Pinder in their pre-Moodies band Ed Riot & the Rebels) and guitarist/ vocalist **Justin Hayward** (who had asked singer Eric Burdon for a job in a new lineup of The Animals, only

for Burdon to recommend him to Ray Thomas instead). The new band moved to Belgium to avoid punitive U.K. taxes and plotted their evolution from pop into conceptual progressive rock.

The first result, unveiled over a year later, could not have been more jaw-dropping: the sumptuous, transatlantic Top Ten hit "Nights in White Satin." The conceptual *Days of Future Passed* (1967), based on themes of different times of day and night, made No. 3 in the U.S. and No. 27 at home, and heralded a fruitful, decade-long relationship with producer Tony Clarke.

With a modest stealth that made Pink Floyd look like Led Zeppelin, the next ten years saw The Moody Blues become one of Britain's most internationally successful acts. "There was a lot of pressure," Hayward told writer Craig Rosen. "The nature of the business was that every record you made was tremendously important." "Tremendously important" wasn't a view shared by the rock press, who dismissed the band when they paid them any attention at all. "Moody Blues devotees seemed to think they were getting something higher toned than mere rock," sneered *Rolling Stone*. "They were kidding themselves."

Nonetheless, of the seven studio albums the group issued between 1968 and 1978, three topped the U.K. chart (1969's *On the Threshold of a Dream*, 1970's

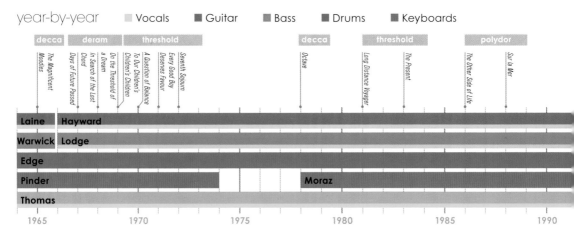

year-by-year   ■ Vocals   ■ Guitar   ■ Bass   ■ Drums   ■ Keyboards

Justin Hayward
b. October 14, 1946

Patrick Moraz
b. June 24, 1948

A Question of Balance, and 1971's *Every Good Boy Deserves Favour*), and one (1972's *Seventh Sojourn*) hit No. 1 in the States. The latter's path to success was smoothed by the belated Stateside success of "Nights in White Satin," which in turn sent *Days of Future Passed* into the U.S. Top Ten, just weeks before *Seventh Sojourn*. The latter bequeathed "I'm Just a Singer (in a Rock 'n' Roll Band)," their first major hit since "Question" from *A Question of Balance*.

After a nine-month world tour, with Mike Pinder exhaused, the Moodies split in early 1974. Hayward and Lodge forged ahead with 1975's *Blue Jays*, another transatlantic success that yielded the U.K. Top Ten hit "Blue Guitar" (eclipsing Pinder's *The Promise*, Ray Thomas's *From Mighty Oaks*, and The Graeme Edge Band's *Kick Off Your Muddy Boots*).

The band re-formed in 1978 but, by the time *Octave* (1978) was released, producer Tony Clarke—effectively "the sixth Moody"—had quit. Nonetheless, the album took them straight back into transatlantic best-seller charts. Meanwhile, Hayward scored a hit with "Forever Autumn" from Jeff Wayne's *War of the Worlds* album. Their profile was maintained by a successful world tour—before which Pinder quit and was replaced by former Yes keyboard player **Patrick Moraz**—and a U.K. hit reissue of "Nights in White Satin."

Long Distance Voyager (1981) produced by Pip Williams (he joined them after a run of success with Status Quo, whose resemblance to the Moodies ended at nationality), took a year of work. The effort was rewarded when the album followed *Seventh Sojourn* to the top of the U.S. and Canadian charts, and went Top Ten at home. "It was like being in a gang again," Hayward told Craig Rosen. "We had that feeling again of all being together."

When the follow-up, 1983's *The Present,* flopped, it seemed the Moodies' time had passed. However, *The Other Side of Life* (1986)—produced by David Bowie sidekick Tony Visconti—restored them to the big league, thanks to the U.S. hit "Your Wildest Dreams."

Subsequent albums traced a gentle commercial decline. After Moraz's acrimonious departure in 1991, Bias Boshell and Paul Bliss were recruited to complete *Keys of the Kingdom* (1991). Neither that nor *Strange Times* (1999) were major successes, but the band remained a reliable draw on the live circuit.

Thomas retired in 2002, leaving Edge, Hayward, and Lodge as the band's nucleus. (Flautist Norda Mullen graced 2003's Christmas-themed *December*). With new keyboard player Alan Hewitt they continue to tour successfully, while live sets and compilations add to their multi-million-selling legacy. **BS/BM**

M

■ Aerophones

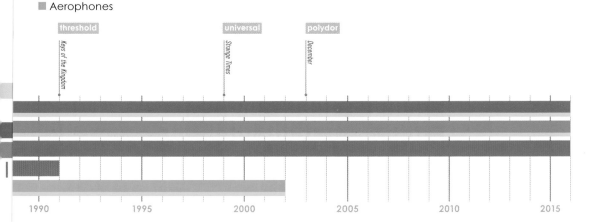

Too Fast for Love
(1981)

Shout at the Devil
(1983)

Theatre of Pain
(1985)

Girls, Girls, Girls
(1987)

Dr. Feelgood
(1989)

Mötley Crüe (1994)

Generation Swine
(1997)

New Tattoo (2000)

Saints of Los Angeles (2008)

Singer **Vince Neil** emulates the *Too Fast for Love* cover pose.

With Ozzy Osbourne, clutching gold awards for *Shout at the Devil*.

Nikki Sixx rocks New York on the *Girls, Girls, Girls* tour.

Neil's replacement, **John Corabi**, gets into the Motley spirit.

Tommy Lee's kit tilts on the *Theatre of Pain* tour. The album's cover is on his bass drums.

Mick Mars—the band's "musical heartbeat," says **Vince Neil**—onstage.

The late **Randy Castillo**, drummer on the under-rated *New Tattoo*.

The reunited **Mars**, **Lee**, **Sixx**, and **Neil** make an impression at the Guitar Center's RockWalk in Hollywood, in 1997.

The inaugural Crüe Fest explodes at the Verizon Wireless Music Center, in Noblesville, Indiana, in 2008.

motörhead 1975–present

Lemmy
b. December 24. 1945

Phil Campbell
b. May 7, 1961

Mikkey Dee
b. October 31, 1963

Larry Wallis
b. May 19, 1949

Lucas Fox
b. Unknown

Phil Taylor
b. September 21, 1954

Occupying an uncategorizable space somewhere between heavy metal, biker rock, and rock 'n' roll, Motörhead have been making music that is loud and violent—but still intelligent—since 1975. At the time of writing, the band—led, as ever, by singer and bassist Ian **"Lemmy"** Kilmister—have released no fewer than twenty studio albums and a similar number of live records, compilations, and EPs. Motörhead are an international rock institution—and, when their time is up, as it no doubt will be within the next decade or so, they will be irreplaceable.

Lemmy, as he is universally known, is the band's linchpin and a man whose opinions and image have allowed him to transcend the status of mere musician to become a genuine icon. While the contributions of the many other talents who have passed through Motörhead should not be underestimated, in many ways the story of Lemmy and his band are one and the same. He earned his dues in the mid-sixties, playing in a variety of R&B and psychedelic rock bands and roadieing for none other than Jimi Hendrix, before joining space-rock experimentalists Hawkwind.

Drugs rapidly became a way of life for Lemmy, whose consumption of speed and acid became legendary: however, they also led to his departure from Hawkwind, who fired him in 1975 after a drugs

bust in North America. Irritated, he formed a new group, Motörhead, named after the last song he had written for his old band: the name is biker slang for a speed user (and was a much better choice than his defiant initial idea, Bastard).

It took two years for Motörhead to find their feet. After a brief dalliance with guitarist **Larry Wallis** and drummer **Lucas Fox**, the Motörhead lineup stabilized as Lemmy plus **"Fast" Eddie Clarke** on guitar and **Phil "Philthy Animal" Taylor** on drums. This trio has become regarded as the classic Motörhead, and it is certainly true that most of the band's best-known songs were written by that lineup. By 1982, however, both backing musicians were gone, leading Lemmy to state in one interview: "Did I leave them or did they leave me?" The legacy of the Clarke/Taylor lineup remains impressive all these years later, with albums such as *Overkill* (1979), *Ace of Spades* (1980), and the U.K. chart-topping *No Sleep 'Til Hammersmith* (1981) among the era's most essential rock releases.

Joined by ex-Thin Lizzy guitarist **Brian Robertson** and sometime Saxon drummer **Pete Gill**, Lemmy soldiered on, releasing a sequence of albums in the eighties that contained many a classic song, although they lacked the raw attitude of Motörhead's earlier work. Robertson did not last long: ejected in 1983 after

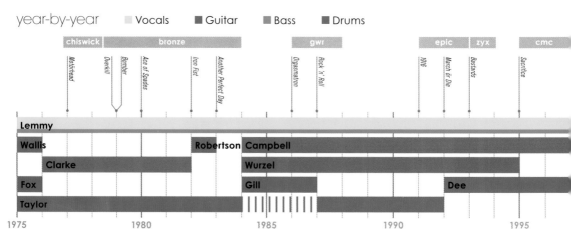

year-by-year ▪ Vocals ▪ Guitar ▪ Bass ▪ Drums

250,000	750,000	250,000	250,000
Ace of Spades (1980)	*No Sleep 'Til Hammersmith* (1981)	*Iron Fist* (1982)	*1916* (1991)

"Fast" Eddie Clarke
b. October 5, 1950

Pete Gill
b. June 9, 1951

Brian Robertson
b. September 12, 1956

Würzel
b. October 23, 1949
d. July 9, 2011

arguments over his stage attire and reluctance to play old material, he was replaced by two six-stringers, **Phil Campbell** (ex-Persian Risk) and Michael "**Würzel**" Burston, the latter a complete unknown who had sent Lemmy an audition cassette. However, plagued by unreliable managers and record companies, the band struggled to find a niche, even when the erratic but frequently brilliant Taylor returned in 1987 (his comeback album, *Rock 'n' Roll,* also featured a spoken cameo by Monty Python's Michael Palin).

According to Lemmy, who wrote about Motörhead's ever-changing fortunes in his 2002 autobiography *White Line Fever,* the band would have split had he not moved to live in Los Angeles in the early nineties. With easier access to the rock 'n' roll industry (not to mention bourbon and groupies), he took his group to a new level, attracting deals with labels including Sony and recording a series of above-average albums (powered from 1993's *Bastards* onward by drummer **Mikkey Dee**).

Since then Motörhead has plowed a profitable furrow, releasing albums every couple of years and benefiting immensely from its leader's presence in the media—he appears in the occasional film and television commercial and was the subject of a self-titled biopic in 2010. Lemmy was even invited to address the Welsh Assembly in 2007 on the evils of heroin, the drug that killed the love of his life, Susan Bennett, back in the seventies.

Since 1995, Motörhead have been a trio: when Wurzel left (sadly, he succumbed to heart disease in 2011), Campbell took over the guitar playing. However, the band's music continues to be critically and commercially applauded. In recent years, their albums have been produced by Cameron Webb, an American console-tweaker who has given the music a polished, but still heavy, sound. Although Motörhead's naysayers claim that their albums tend to sound the same (not true), those who take the time to listen know that Lemmy and his troops are still firing on all cylinders. Axe-man extraordinaire Steve Vai guested on *Inferno* (2004), while *Kiss of Death* (2006) boasted cameos by Poison guitarist CC DeVille and Alice in Chains bassist Mike Inez. Incredibly, over thirty years after the band's formation, *Motörizer* (2008) and *The Wörld Is Yours* (2010) were their first releases to sneak into the Top 100 of *Billboard*'s album chart.

Now that he is in his mid-sixties, Lemmy's time as a touring musician may end sooner rather than later, but he refuses to relinquish the rock 'n' roll lifestyle and may die on stage, if he dies anywhere—some believe him to be immortal. His best songs certainly are. **JM**

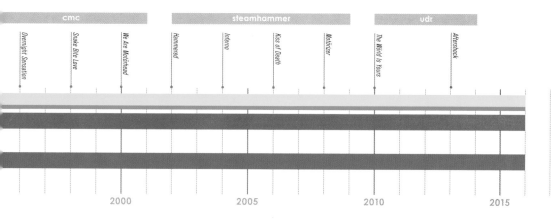

mott the hoople 1969–2013

Overend Watts
b. May 13, 1947

Dale "Buffin" Griffin
b. October 24, 1948

Mick Ralphs
b. March 31, 1944

Verden Allen
b. May 26, 1944

Ian Hunter
b. June 3, 1939

Morgan Fisher
b. January 1, 1950

Mott the Hoople released seven interesting albums and a series of excellent singles between 1972 and 1974, but generally only dented the U.K. charts. However, their influence far outstrips their success.

The group had its origins in Hereford, England. **Overend Watts** (bass) and **Dale "Buffin" Griffin** (drums) were joined in 1968 by **Mick Ralphs** (guitar) and **Verden Allen** (organ) in The Silence after they had played in rival local bands. They were snapped up by producer Guy Stevens, and singer **Ian Hunter** completed the lineup (original vocalist Stan Tippins generously became their road manager). Stevens was determined to manage a group called Mott the Hoople after reading Willard Manus's novel of that title—the band reluctantly adopted the name in 1969.

Their self-titled debut album (1969) was a fascinating mix of hard rock ("Rock and Roll Queen") with Hunter's Dylanesque inflections ("Half Moon Bay") and fine cover versions ("At the Crossroads"). As the group toured, it crept into the lower reaches of the charts in the U.S. and U.K., and was followed by *Mad Shadows* (1970). The latter's songs were dark

and evocative—Hunter's introspective musings, such as "When My Mind's Gone," were juxtaposed with straightforward rockers like Ralphs's "Thunderbuck Ram." But it was as a live outfit that the group built their reputation, with fanatical followers at every U.K. show. The challenge was to translate that live energy and feeling of excitement onto vinyl.

Wildlife (1971) contained songs that were closer to lush country rock, including "Waterlow" and "Angel of Eighth Avenue," but did not achieve a breakthrough. *Brain Capers* (also 1971) showed signs of the strains on the group and, despite the live favorite "Sweet Angeline," yielded similarly disappointing sales.

Two things kept the group together when they were on the verge of splitting. The first was the adulation of fans at concerts; the second was the intervention of David Bowie. Fresh from stardom with *Ziggy Stardust,* Bowie generously gave the group a new song, "All the Young Dudes." It gave Mott a massive hit, which Bowie underlined by producing their album. Also called *All the Young Dudes* (1972), the record was uneven, but "One of the Boys,"

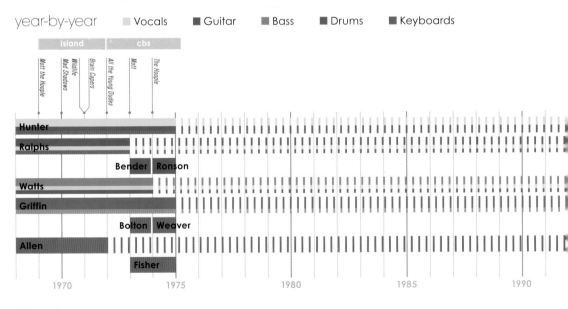

year-by-year   ■ Vocals   ■ Guitar   ■ Bass   ■ Drums   ■ Keyboards

250,000	750,000	750,000	250,000
All the Young Dudes (1972)	Mott (1973)	The Hoople (1974)	Mott the Hoople Live (1974)

Mick Bolton
b. 1948

Ariel Bender
b. December 23, 1946

Mick Ronson
b. May 26, 1946
d. April 29, 1993

Blue Weaver
b. March 11, 1947

Martin Chambers
b. September 4, 1951

"Ready for Love/After Lights" and a version of The Velvet Underground's "Sweet Jane" (Bowie was championing Lou Reed in similar fashion at the time) helped make it their biggest to date.

This triumph boosted the group's confidence, and *Mott* (1973) contained a sharp selection of songs, including "Ballad of Mott the Hoople" (Hunter was always keen on chronicling their adventures, in diaries and on record). Its hits, "Honaloochie Boogie" and "All the Way from Memphis," climbed to No. 12 and No. 10, respectively, in the U.K. Yet the band's bonds were loosened by their transformed fortunes. The disillusioned Verden Allen was replaced by pianist **Morgan Fisher** in time for *Mott,* then Mick Ralphs left to form Bad Company. Spooky Tooth guitarist Luther Grosvenor, calling himself **Ariel Bender** for obscure legal reasons, came in, as did organist **Mick Bolton**.

The group's final studio album, *The Hoople* (1974) revisited their winning formula. The magnificent singles "The Golden Age of Rock 'n' Roll" and "Roll Away the Stone" were its cornerstones, although "Marionette" perhaps told the real story. Bar a live set

later that year, it was their highest-charting U.S. album (No. 28), but the end was close at hand. Bolton and Bender were replaced by former Strawb **Blue Weaver** (keyboards) and Bowie's guitarist, **Mick Ronson**. But after two wonderful yet underperforming singles— "Foxy Foxy" and "Saturday Gigs"—and another U.S. tour, the group decided to split up at the end of 1974.

Fisher, Watts, and Griffin persisted for a while with a version of the group called Mott, recording *Drive On* (1975) and *Shouting and Pointing* (1976), but it was not the same. Hunter and Ronson played together for many years, until the latter's cruelly premature death in 1993. In the meantime, the group's name was kept alive by admirers like Mötley Crüe's Nikki Sixx and Def Leppard's Joe Elliott. But that seemed to be that.

However, in October 2009, the group re-formed for triumphant shows at London's Hammersmith Apollo. Watts, Ralphs, Allen, Hunter, and Griffin (with **Martin Chambers** from the Pretenders assisting with drumming owing to the latter's Alzheimer's disease) earned a rapturous response, captured in the 2011 documentary *The Ballad of Mott the Hoople.* **MiH**

 Other percussion

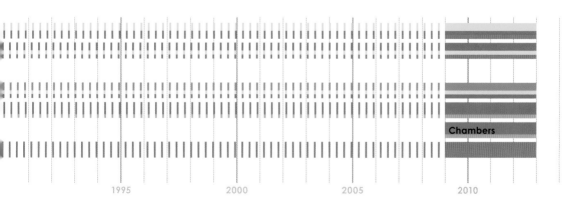

Chambers

1995   2000   2005   2010

mudhoney 1988–present

Mark Arm
b. February 21,
1962

Steve Turner
b. March 28,
1965

Dan Peters
b. August 18,
1967

Matt Lukin
b. August 16,
1964

Guy Maddison
b. March 31,
1965

Perennial bridesmaids Mudhoney were the forefathers of grunge, leading the way on Seattle's Sub Pop label before stablemates Nirvana grabbed the glory. They rose from the ashes of local band Green River (also the alma mater for Jeff Ament and Stone Gossard of Pearl Jam): front-man **Mark Arm** (formerly Mark McLaughlin) and guitarist **Steve Turner** (who had left earlier) hooked up with drummer **Dan Peters** and ex-Melvins bassist **Matt Lukin** to broker the new band.

Taking their name from a Russ Meyer movie, the nascent Mudhoney made a splash with the 1988 EP *Superfuzz Bigmuff*—named, somewhat disappointingly, after Turner's preferred effects pedal—and the short, sharp, shocking "Touch Me I'm Sick." They struck up a rapport with the daddies of U.S. alt. rock, Sonic Youth, covering each other's songs and touring the U.K. together. There, Mudhoney gained a reputation for shows that spun out of control—Arm once memorably invited the entire audience to join the band on stage. In the U.K., *Superfuzz Bigmuff* made its mark on the independent charts before the band's self-titled 1989 debut album cemented their caustic, calculatedly messy sound.

Every Good Boy Deserves Fudge followed in 1991 and gave the band a healthy chart placing (U.K. No. 34) as grunge became rock's one true path (Peters had played on Nirvana's 1990 single "Sliver" before Dave Grohl became their drummer). Mudhoney were broadening their palette, with Arm adding organ to his instrumental mix. The natural next step came with

a break from Sub Pop: the band signed to the Warner imprint Reprise in 1992 and conjured up *Piece of Cake*, another U.K. Top Forty album.

Their next set would come at a crossroads for the grunge scene, following Nirvana front-man Kurt Cobain's suicide in 1994. *My Brother the Cow* (1995) featured a meditation on Cobain, "Into Your Schtick," as disaffected critics began to turn their backs on Mudhoney and their ilk. It would be another three years before *Tomorrow Hit Today* (1998) turned up with a recalibrated, more bluesy style.

The turn of the century saw Lukin leave, to be replaced—after short stints by Wayne Kramer (of the MC5) and Steve Dukich—by bassist **Guy Maddison**. There were more changes afoot, as Mudhoney returned to Sub Pop for 2002's *Since We've Become Translucent*. Confrontational and ambitious in equal measure, this was a return to form, and paved the way for 2006's warmly received *Under a Billion Suns*. (In the interim, Arm deputized for Rob Tyner on an MC5 revival tour in 2004.) After 2008's *The Lucky Ones*, Mudhoney turned full circle, putting out a deluxe *Superfuzz Bigmuff* and playing it in full at New York's All Tomorrow's Parties festival in 2010.

Rolling back the years again, they joined Pearl Jam on the latter's PJ20 anniversary tour in 2011, in the process celebrating their common roots. It was a festival of nostalgia but—more than two decades down the line—Mudhoney's searing, distorted take on punk had lost none of its potency. **MaH**

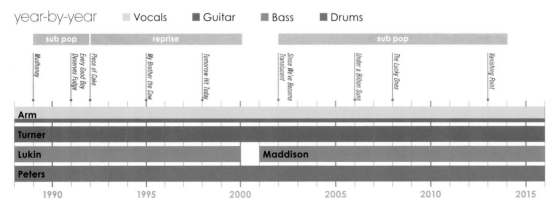

year-by-year ■ Vocals ■ Guitar ■ Bass ■ Drums

muse 1994–present

Matt Bellamy
b. June 9, 1978

Chris Wolstenholme
b. December 2, 1978

Dominic Howard
b. December 7, 1977

"They're very good boys and extremely talented," declared Brian May of Queen. "And, like us, they have their tongue in cheek a lot of the time." One of contemporary hard rock's most exciting acts, Muse have amassed a vast following through a combination of magnificent live shows and stirring anthems that touch on conspiracy and catastrophe.

Matt Bellamy (guitars, keyboards, vocals), **Chris Wolstenholme** (bass), and **Dominic Howard** (drums) met at school in the seaside town of Teignmouth, Devon, in southwest England. Although they had played together before, the genesis of the group dates to 1994 when, as Rocket Baby Dolls, they won a local "battle of the bands" competition. Deciding to get serious, they settled on the name Muse (because, they claimed, it looked good on posters).

The group spent several years formulating their vision and rehearsing, while playing live and building a fan base. They had released two EPs before their first album, Showbiz, emerged in 1999. Crammed with interesting material, such as "Sunburn" and the title track, it established Muse as a group to watch.

Origin of Symmetry (2001)—featuring the gems "Plug in Baby," "Feeling Good," and "New Born"— confirmed their potential and sold well in the U.K. However, their American record label felt Bellamy's histrionic vocal style would harm its prospects, and demanded a re-mix. The group refused, and the album was not released in the U.S. until 2005.

Meanwhile, Muse had broken into the front ranks with Absolution (2003). Powerful mini-epics such as

"Time Is Running Out" and "Stockholm Syndrome" were juxtaposed with restrained hymns of brooding splendor like "Sing for Absolution." The group's supersonic onslaught framed Bellamy's alternately yearning and overwrought vocals to immaculate effect. The whole package was wrapped in artwork by Pink Floyd's sleeve designer, Storm Thorgerson.

Muse also established a reputation for delivering huge, imaginative shows. They defied the impossible, using a trio format to soundtrack the apocalypse.

Stomping into international Top Tens, Black Holes and Revelations (2006) supercharged their blueprint of punchy, dramatic songs into an extravagant space opera. "Supermassive Black Hole," "Starlight," and "Knights of Cydonia" were unsettling yet uplifting standouts. The superb live recording HAARP (2008) testifies to their grandeur.

The Resistance (2009), another worldwide smash, solidified their status as one of rock's greatest groups and biggest draws. Songs like "Uprising," "Resistance," and the ambitious "Exogenesis: Symphony" raised their standard to a new level, and shows on the accompanying tour were even more spectacular than before. Amid a welter of awards that the group has won over the past decade, The Resistance earned a Grammy for Best Rock Album of 2010.

There was no scaling down of ambitions in 2012: "Survival" was the official song of the Olympics and The 2nd Law was another international smash. In 2014, Muse announced that they were working on a new album with AC/DC producer Mutt Lange. **MiH**

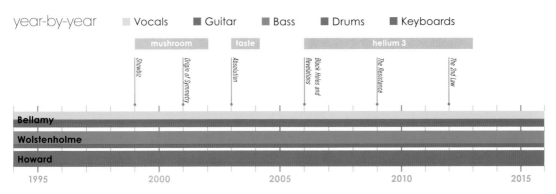

year-by-year — Vocals — Guitar — Bass — Drums — Keyboards

mushroom | taste | helium 3

Showbiz | Origin of Symmetry | Absolution | Black Holes and Revelations | The Resistance | The 2nd Law

Bellamy

Wolstenholme

Howard

1995 | 2000 | 2005 | 2010 | 2015

os mutantes 1966–present

Sérgio Dias Baptista
b. December 1st, 1951

Rita Lee
b. December 31st, 1947

Arnaldo Baptista
b. July 6th, 1948

Liminha
b. 1951

Dinho Leme
b. Unknown

Antonio Pedro
b. Unknown

Rui Motta
b. Unknown

Túlio Mourão
b. January 18, 1952

On April 1, 1964, armed forces seized control of Brazil, initiating twenty years of martial law. From this harsh environment arose a late sixties counter-revolution: Tropicália, a cultural movement that encompassed theater, music, and poetry, and from which many artists would emerge—including Caetano Veloso and Gilberto Gil. Central to the movement's manifesto was *antropófago* ("cannibalism") that encouraged cross-genre pollination to create something unique. Arguably the most visible example was Os Mutantes.

Formed in 1966 by brothers **Sérgio Dias** and **Arnaldo Baptista** with vocalist **Rita Lee**, Os Mutantes ("The Mutants") brought a sense of playfulness to the sometimes earnest Tropicália circle. By the time they recorded their 1968 debut album, Os Mutantes had melded American psychedelia with Brazilian samba and bossa nova, a sound both of its time yet unique. The experiment was repeated with greater critical and commercial success on 1969's *Mutantes* and a third period classic, 1970's *A Divina Comédia ou Ando Meio Desligado* ("A Divine Comedy or I Am a Bit Disconnected"). However, while popular among Brazilian teens, Os Mutantes would remain little known to the outside world for another two decades.

In 1972, Lee—the band's focal point—left to pursue a solo career that would encompass rock,

disco, and her own TV show. Arnaldo Baptista followed shortly afterward. Os Mutantes began to veer toward progressive rock, although works such as 1974's *Tudo Foi Feito Pelo Sol* ("Everything Is the Sun") remained just as curious to Western ears.

Disbanding in 1978, the group would have stayed a solely Brazilian phenomenon were it not for a cult that evolved over the following decade. Original Brazilian LPs, particularly the first three albums, began filtering into Europe and the U.S. By the early nineties, Os Mutantes were being cited as an influence on artists with no visible South American connections: in 1993 Kurt Cobain wrote to Arnaldo Baptista calling for Os Mutantes to reform; five years later, Beck enjoyed a hit with "Tropicália," his own tribute to the group. Recordings from 1973 and 1970, respectively, were issued as *A e o Z* (1992) and *Tecnicolor* (2000).

Outside interest in Os Mutantes was a surprise to Sérgio Dias. In 2006, he formed a new version of the band, which played to acclaim on the global festival circuit—new vocalist Bia Mendes proving an effective substitute for Rita Lee. *Haih… or Amortecedor,* the first new Os Mutantes album in over thirty years, illustrated that the reappearance of Dias was no exercise in cheap nostalgia but the return of a creative artist who had merely taken an unusually long break. **TB**

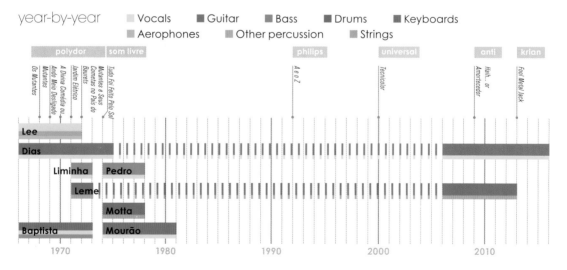

year-by-year ■ Vocals ■ Guitar ■ Bass ■ Drums ■ Keyboards ■ Aerophones ■ Other percussion ■ Strings

my bloody valentine 1983–present

Kevin Shields
b. May 21, 1963

Colm Ó Ciosóig
b. October 31, 1964

Dave Conway
b. Unknown

Debbie Googe
b. October 24, 1962

Bilinda Butcher
b. September 16, 1961

Take Phil Spector's Wall of Sound. Raise it. Add dreamy melodies. Then bury them under exquisitely crafted noise. And you might have My Bloody Valentine.

Drummer **Colm Ó Ciosóig**, New York-born **Kevin Shields**, vocalist **Dave Conway**, and his keyboardist girlfriend Tina Durkin quit Dublin first for Holland, then (inspired partly by The Birthday Party) Berlin. There, they recorded their debut mini-LP *This Is Your Bloody Valentine* (1985), whose dark post-punkery made little impression. The band relocated to London, where Durkin left and bassist **Debbie Googe** joined. But after a series of EPs and another mini-LP (1987's *Ecstasy*), My Bloody Valentine—named for a 1981 slasher movie—were still, as Shields reflected in 1991, merely a "Jesus and Mary Chain rip-off band."

Guitarist/singer **Bilinda Butcher** replaced Conway in 1987. This, coupled with extended studio time, resulted in a breakthrough: the crackling EP *You Made Me Realise*. Building on the momentum, their debut album *Isn't Anything* (1988) boasted waves of fuzzy, reverb-soaked guitar and soft harmonies blanketing Butcher's languorous vocals. These brutal and beautiful soundscapes—couple with their infamously loud shows—saw the Valentines become figureheads for the U.K.'s "shoegazing" scene.

Two years in the making, involving countless engineers in nearly twenty studios, *Loveless* (1991) proved another landmark. Masterminded by Shields—the sole musician on most of the album—it was recorded in mono, for greater punch. Rather than employing hordes of effects, Shields used the tremolo arm of his guitar to shape and twist pitch and timbre.

Q magazine hailed *Loveless* as "a virtual reinvention of the guitar," and Brian Eno declared that its closer, "Soon," "set a new standard for pop." (Accordingly, Coldplay's Eno-produced "Chinese Sleep Chant" is a fine Valentines pastiche.) The supporting tour was provocative—volumes were so loud they hurt, the band hammering on one chord in "You Made Me Realise" for ten minutes at a time.

However, with recording costs estimated at £250,000, *Loveless* nearly sank the Creation label. Then it only made U.K. No. 24, and the Valentines found themselves label-less. They moved to Island and began a third album, but Shields's perfectionism proved too much and the others slipped away. Shields busied himself with home recordings, emerging to play with Dinosaur Jr., Yo La Tengo, and Primal Scream (he appeared on 2000's *Xtrmntr* and toured with them). He also provided music for the 2003 movie *Lost in Translation* and Patti Smith's *The Coral Sea* (2005/6).

In 2008, the Valentines kicked off a reunion tour with deafening sets at London's ICA (earplugs were dispensed to the crowd). In 2012—the year Googe began moonlighting with Primal Scream—long-mooted remastered versions of *Isn't Anything* and *Loveless* appeared alongside a compilation of their early EPs. Most remarkably of all, long after even the most dogged fans had stopped holding their breath, 2013 brought the decades-in-the-making *m b v*. **RD**

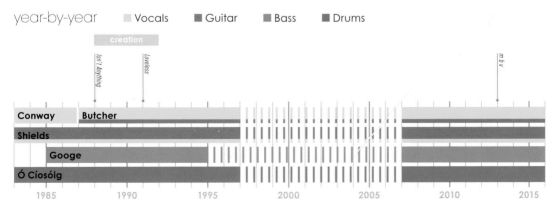

year-by-year ▦ Vocals ▪ Guitar ▪ Bass ▪ Drums

creation

Isn't Anything *Loveless* *m b v*

Conway | Butcher

Shields

Googe

Ó Ciosóig

1985   1990   1995   2000   2005   2010   2015

neu! 1971–1975

Klaus Dinger
b. March 24, 1946
d. March 21, 2008

Michael Rother
b. September 2, 1950

Thomas Dinger
b. October 28, 1952
d. April 9, 2002

Hans Lampe
b. Unknown

Emerging in 1971 from Düsseldorf in Germany, the duo Neu! ("New!") were among the founding fathers of "krautrock," influencing the course of punk and new wave and inspiring artists such as David Bowie and Radiohead. Prior to forming Neu!, **Klaus Dinger** and **Michael Rother** were original members of Kraftwerk—whose importance in modern music is indisputable.

Having left Kraftwerk during abortive sessions for the band's second album, drummer Dinger and guitarist Rother regrouped in Hamburg with German studio legend Conny Plank. Their 1972 debut album, Neu!, is widely regarded as one of the high points of the krautrock genre. The tone was set from the opening track, "Hallogallo," which heralded the first appearance of Dinger's "motorik" beat, a simple, uninterrupted four-four rhythm with few fills or other embellishments that became a defining characteristic of the band's sound. Atop the driving beat sat Rother's spacious, pulsing bass lines and atmospheric guitar soundscapes. A seminal piece of work, even today Neu! still sounds remarkably fresh.

A year later, Neu! 2 followed the same formula, the exhilarating eleven minutes of "Für immer" remaining one of the band's recorded highlights. The album's genesis took a curious turn when Dinger and Rother discovered they had used their entire recording budget with only one side of material completed. Refused a further advance, they came up with the ingenious solution of filling up side two by mechanically manipulating the tapes of an earlier single. While by no means an easy listen, the result could be considered a prototype "remix"—the post-production of multiple versions of the same track later popular in reggae and dance music.

Having completed Neu! 2, the duo took a two-year hiatus, regrouping for Neu! '75. During this time, however, their musical interests had begun to diverge. What emerged was a split album: side one, recorded as a duo, was gentler than its predecessors, dominated by Rother's fluid guitar and keyboard textures; side two, however, was driven by Dinger's newly acquired interest in rock music. Handing over the drumming duties to his brother **Thomas** and **Hans Lampe**—who were instructed to play simultaneously—Klaus Dinger switched to guitar and vocals. The heavily distorted beat and his sneering voice on the track "Hero" would influence the U.K. punk scene as well as David Bowie. (The latter divided his own Low into distinct halves, reminiscent of Neu! '75.)

Although Neu! performed as a four-piece, the widening chasm between Rother and Dinger made it impossible to continue; shortly after the release of Neu! '75 the band dissolved. Rother went on to enjoy a prolific solo career, also collaborating with Cluster and Brian Eno; the Dinger brothers and Lampe formed the much-touted La Düsseldorf. **TB**

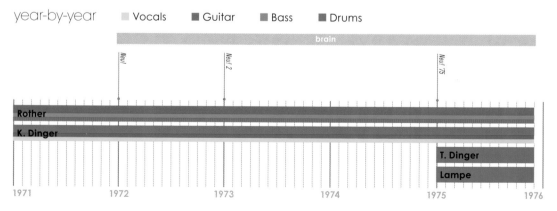

year-by-year ■ Vocals ■ Guitar ■ Bass ■ Drums

brain

Neu! / Neu! 2 / Neu! 75

Rother

K. Dinger

T. Dinger

Lampe

1971 1972 1973 1974 1975 1976

the new york dolls 1971–present

Sylvain Sylvain
b. February 14, 1951

Billy Murcia
b. 1951

Johnny Thunders
b. July 15, 1952
d. April 23, 1991

Arthur "Killer" Kane
b. February 3, 1949
d. July 13, 2004

David Johansen
b. January 9, 1950

Jerry Nolan
b. May 7, 1946
d. January 14, 1992

Straddling glam and punk, the Dolls were commercial non-starters—but as influential as an earthquake.

Sylvain Sylvain, **Billy Murcia**, and **Johnny Thunders** united in 1970, naming themselves Dolls after the New York Dolls' Hospital, a toy repair shop. Thunders and Murcia hooked up in another band with **Arthur "Killer" Kane** in 1971, as did **David Johansen** in October. Sylvain replaced original guitarist Rick Rivets and the New York Dolls were born. By summer 1972, they had a weekly spot at the Mercer Arts Center.

The Dolls played scrappy, livewire rock 'n' roll, Johansen and Thunders an out-there parody of Jagger and Richards. In 1972, they embarked on a U.K. tour, to the delight of fledgling Sex Pistol Steve Jones, whose verdict was "out-of-control kind of stuff that I'd never seen before." In London, however, a comatose Murcia drowned in a bath. The shell-shocked band drafted in new drummer **Jerry Nolan**.

Todd Rundgren took charge of their self-titled debut album. The band hated his production but "Looking for a Kiss," "Trash," and "Personality Crisis" still sound deliriously fresh. "The last rock 'n' roll band," trumpeted the U.K.'s Melody Maker, though the album won zero airplay. But their 1973 European tour proved a pivotal inspiration for U.K. punks; anticipating Vicious

and Siouxsie, Thunders even sported a swastika armband. Future Smiths front-man Morrissey adored them, becoming president of their British fan club.

Johansen persuaded Shangri-Las mastermind Shadow Morton to produce Too Much Too Soon (1974); applauded today, it was panned at the time. Quarrels ensued, notably between Johansen and Thunders. Throw in Kane's alcoholism and Thunders and Nolan's fondness for heroin, and the end seemed nigh.

Cue Malcolm McLaren, a Dolls devotee who clad them in red leather and gave them a hammer-and-sickle backdrop onstage. In 1975, Thunders quit, going back to New York to form The Heartbreakers with Nolan. The unsteady Kane was summarily fired, and Johansen and Sylvain called it a day in late 1976.

Thunders overdosed in 1991; Nolan followed a year later. But the surviving Dolls enjoyed a reunion, at Morrissey's request, for 2004's Meltdown festival in London—a triumph and a wish come true for Kane, who died of leukemia the next month. Sylvain and Johansen struck on with new Dolls (including Blondie's Frank Infante, Hanoi Rocks' Sami Yaffa, and Bowie guitarist Earl Slick), completing three solid albums, and even playing iconic punk venue CBGBs (for the first time) in 2006. They've earned their happy ending. **RD**

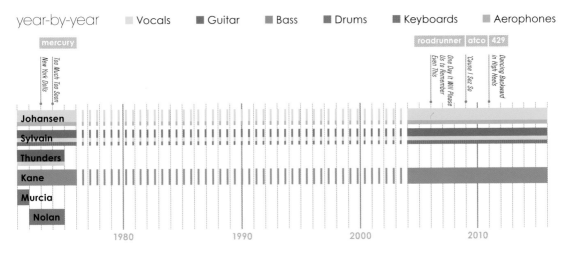

year-by-year   ■ Vocals   ■ Guitar   ■ Bass   ■ Drums   ■ Keyboards   ■ Aerophones

mercury   roadrunner | atco | 429

New York Dolls
Too Much Too Soon

One Day It Will Please
Us to Remember
Even This
'Cause I Sez So
Dancing Backward
in High Heels

Johansen
Sylvain
Thunders
Kane
Murcia
Nolan

1980   1990   2000   2010

nickelback 1995–present

Chad Kroeger
b. November 15, 1974

Mike Kroeger
b. June 25, 1972

Ryan Peake
b. March 1, 1973

Mitch Guindon
b. March 10, 1970

Ryan Vikedal
b. May 9, 1975

Daniel Adair
b. February 19, 1975

"We all just wanna be big rock stars / And live in hilltop houses, drivin' fifteen cars…" Forty-five million records sold worldwide? Four multi-platinum albums in the United States? More awards than a standard trophy cabinet can hold? Wish granted. Someone find these guys a garage big enough for fifteen automobiles!

Nickelback were, of course, established musicians long before the tongue-in-cheek "Rockstar" and its star-studded video saturated radio and television in 2006. Let us remind ourselves how it happened.

The group broke out of Alberta, Canada, in 1995, consisting of three Kroegers—brothers **Chad** and **Mike**, and their cousin Brandon—and **Ryan Peake**. Mike's job as a cashier at Starbucks handed the group their name on a plate: customer buys coffee, hands over cash, Mike does his stuff, dishes out change: "Here's a nickel back, sir."

A limited-edition seven-track EP, *Hesher* (1996), was the first Nickelback material offered for public consumption. Despite front-man Chad Kroeger's subsequent desire to "bury that album as fast as I can," one copy changed hands for over $400 on eBay in 2001—approximately sixty times its original value.

Nickelback's first full-length album, 1996's *Curb*, found the quartet in an uncompromising mood: distorted guitar riffs, Chad's raw vocals, and a disturbing Nirvana-esque ditty about a boy wanting

to shoot himself to discover if he goes to Heaven or Hell ("Fly"). In the first of the band's Spinal Tap-esque personnel turnovers, *Curb* marked the end of the road for Brandon Kroeger, whose replacement was drummer **Mitch Guindon**. In 1998, Guindon quit for a "real" job and **Ryan Vikedal** climbed on board.

The State, issued at the turn of the century, kicked off a prolific period for the self-managing Nickelback. Over the course of six years and four albums, the boys went from post-grunge also-rans to world-conquering, radio-friendly rock heavyweights—much to the chagrin of a number of short-sighted music critics.

Silver Side Up (2001) featured a trio of airplay monsters: "Never Again," "Too Bad," and their Grammy-nominated signature tune, "How You Remind Me." All three crowned the Mainstream Rock Tracks chart (for a combined nineteen weeks), while "How You Remind Me"—incredibly, the last No. 1 rock record on the *Billboard* Hot 100 until 2007—bothered Top Ten charts across the globe *and* became the most played song on U.S. radio in the 2000s, with 1.2 million spins. On the Silver Side Up tour, the band headlined over Jerry Cantrell, the then solo guitarist from their most obvious musical ancestors, Alice in Chains. "I had the guys come up and play with us on some Alice in Chains tunes…" Cantrell recalled. "We had a real fun time on the tour. It was a good thing."

year-by-year   ■ Vocals   ■ Guitar   ■ Bass   ■ Drums   ■ Other percussion

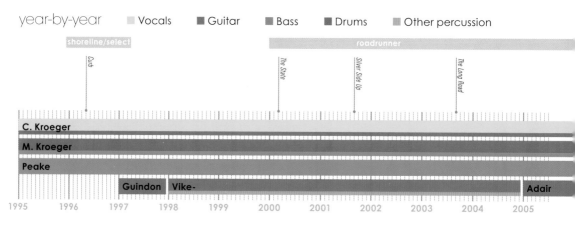

shoreline/select   roadrunner

Curb   The State   Silver Side Up   The Long Road

C. Kroeger
M. Kroeger
Peake
Guindon | Vike-   Adair

1995   1996   1997   1998   1999   2000   2001   2002   2003   2004   2005

In 2002, Chad Kroeger temporarily ditched his day job to provide a lead track for the *Spider-Man* movie soundtrack. The resulting "Hero"—essentially a duet with Saliva's Josey Scott but also featuring the talents of Matt Cameron (Pearl Jam/Soundgarden), Tyler Connolly (Theory of a Deadman), and Nickelback's very own Mike Kroeger—was summed up by the *NME*: "commercial grunge + MOR sensibility = Nu-MOR hit." To that we add: winning formula = worldwide smash.

Back in Nickelback's world, *The Long Road* (2003) turned triple platinum in the U.S. within six months of its release, and its lead single, "Someday," gave them a second No. 1 in Canada.

Nickelback's next two albums, 2005's *All the Right Reasons* (their first with 3 Doors Down graduate **Daniel Adair** on drums) and 2008's *Dark Horse*, each spawned an incredible *seven* U.S. singles. Among them were "Gotta Be Somebody" and "If Today Was Your Last Day" from *Dark Horse* and "Photograph," "Far Away," and the aforementioned "Rockstar" from the eight million-selling *Right Reasons*. "Rockstar" has the distinction of being one of only twenty-five singles to accumulate fifty weeks in the U.K. Top Seventy-Five. Its witty video—starring, among others, Gene Simmons of Kiss, Ted Nugent, Kid Rock, ZZ Top's Billy Gibbons, pop star Nelly Furtado, and rapper Lupe Fiasco—undoubtedly helped.

The success of *Right Reasons* led to a World Music Award for the World's Best-Selling Rock Artist of 2006, two American Music Awards, three *Billboard* Music Awards, and two Juno Awards, including a third Group of the Year accolade. In 2006, Nickelback became the first non-British or Irish winner of the U.K.'s coveted Record of the Year Award. They have claimed a huge thirty-one major awards since 2001.

If ever the world needed to feel good again, that time is *Here and Now*. Cutting through the hyperbole of the Roadrunner label's press release that accompanied Nickelback's seventh studio album in 2011, *Here and Now* shifted 226,714 first-week copies in the United States to debut at No. 2, just 419 units shy of Michael Bublé's chart-topping *Christmas*.

Negative headlines have plagued the group for the past decade, but for every "Why Nickelback is the world's most hated band" or "Nickelback named No. 1 musical turnoff" article, there are plenty of fans willing to pay homage to their idols, among them admirers like Coldplay's Chris Martin and rapper/producer Timbaland. One thing is for sure: Nickelback have paid their dues and have nothing to prove.

Just one ambition remains for "Rockstar" Chad Kroeger and his associates: "My own star on Hollywood Boulevard / Somewhere between Cher and James Dean is fine for me." Watch this space. **MW**

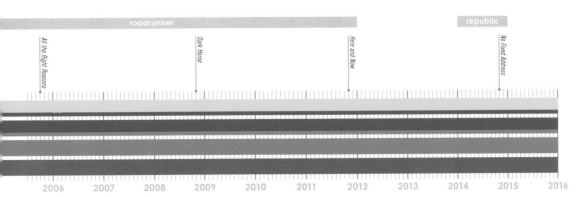

nine inch nails 1988–present

Trent Reznor
b. May 17, 1965

Chris Vrenna
b. February 23, 1967

Richard Patrick
b. May 10, 1968

Jeff Ward
b. Nov 18, 1962
d. March 19, 1993

James Woolley
b. Unknown

Danny Lohner
b. December 13, 1970

Robin Finck
b. November 7, 1971

Charlie Clouser
b. June 28, 1963

"A small lad with a tuba," as David Bowie described him in *Rolling Stone,* Michael **Trent Reznor** grew up to study engineering and fuse influences from Depeche Mode to Public Enemy. The result: Nine Inch Nails, in which Reznor would be the only constant.

A first tour in 1988 found him accompanied by drummer Ron Musarra and keyboardist **Chris Vrenna**. The latter contributed to *Pretty Hate Machine* (1989), which, recalled Bowie, "birthed the first real mainstream breakthrough for industrial rock." In the year of touring that made NIN famous, Vrenna switched to drums (replaced temporarily by **Jeff Ward** for stints on the Lollapalooza festival and with Guns N' Roses), future Filter front-man **Richard Patrick** played guitar, and keyboard duties switched from Nick Rushe to David Haymes, Lee Mars, then **James Woolley**.

Broken (1992)—featuring PiL drummer Martin Atkins—took NIN into the U.S. Top Ten and spawned the remixed *Fixed*. Then came *The Downward Spiral* (1994), NIN's commercial zenith. Guests included Bowie's guitarist Adrian Belew, drummer Andy Kubiszewski (leader of Reznor's pre-NIN band Exotic Birds), and Jane's Addiction sticksman Stephen Perkins. Additional guitar was by **Danny Lohner**—who, alongside **Robin Finck**, bolstered a new live lineup.

The ensuing tour included Reznor, Finck, Lohner, Woolley, and the returning Vrenna's scene-stealing

set at August's Woodstock '94 event. That same month, Reznor's ascendancy to alt-rock godhead was secured by his *Natural Born Killers* soundtrack, which zigzagged brilliantly from Patsy Cline to Dr. Dre.

After Woodstock and the *Further Down the Spiral* re-mix album, *Downward Spiral* programmer **Charlie Clouser** replaced Woolley. The band co-headlined twenty-six dates with—and arguably upstaged—Bowie, promoting his industrial-influenced *1. Outside*.

In 1996, Reznor bequeathed his crown to Marilyn Manson. Having signed Manson to his Nothing label, Reznor co-produced his protégé's *Portrait of an American Family* (1994) and *Smells Like Children* (1995) and took his band on tour. This endorsement, coupled with the gruesome crooner's own fanbase, sent the Reznor co-produced *Antichrist Superstar* (1996) into the U.S. Top Three. (Manson and Bowie featured on Reznor's second soundtrack, 1997's *Lost Highway*. NIN also overhauled Bowie's single "I'm Afraid of Americans," the video for which starred Reznor.)

The Fragile (1999), sequenced by producer Bob Ezrin, boasted new drummer **Jerome Dillon** and NIN's largest supporting cast. Guests included Belew, Bowie's pianist Mike Garson, Helmet's Page Hamilton, Pop Will Eat Itself man turned film soundtracker Clint Mansell, and former Ministry/future R.E.M. drummer Bill Rieflin. The ensuing tour—captured on 2002's *And All*

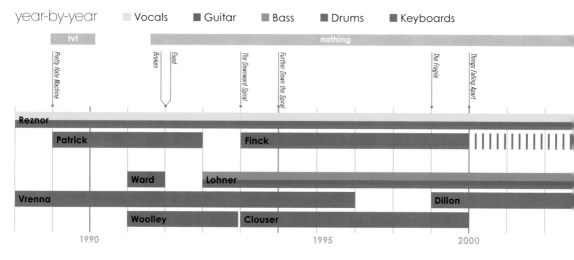

year-by-year · Vocals · Guitar · Bass · Drums · Keyboards

tvt · nothing

Pretty Hate Machine · *Broken* · *Fixed* · *The Downward Spiral* · *Further Down the Spiral* · *The Fragile* · *Things Falling Apart*

Reznor

Patrick · Finck

Ward · Lohner

Vrenna · Dillon

Woolley · Clouser

1990 · 1995 · 2000

Jerome Dillon
b. July 16, 1969

Alessandro Cortini
b. May 24, 1976

Aaron North
b. March 22, 1979

Jeordie White
b. June 20, 1971

Josh Freese
b. December 25, 1972

Justin Meldal-Johnsen
b. Mar 26, 1970

Ilan Rubin
b. July 7, 1988

That Could Have Been—featured Clouser, Lohner, and Dillon alongside the returning Finck. The latter had spent 1997–1999 as Slash's replacement in Guns N' Roses, a position to which he returned in 2006/2007.

Thereafter, Reznor tinkered with Tapeworm, a side-project with Lohner and Clouser. Years of on-off work attracted names such as Page Hamilton, Pantera's Phil Anselmo, and Tool's Maynard James Keenan. But, bar two songs performed by Keenan's own side-projects A Perfect Circle and Puscifer, no results emerged. Instead, *With Teeth* (2005) saw Reznor shedding most names from his past, bar drummer Dillon and co-producer Alan Moulder. Dave Grohl drummed on half of its songs, but the key contributor was programmer Atticus Ross, an associate of film composer Barry Adamson (whose music had graced *Natural Born Killers* and *Lost Highway*).

With Teeth followed *The Fragile* to No. 1 in the U.S., and gave Reznor his highest U.K. chart placing, No. 3. A new touring lineup featured punk band The Icarus Line's guitarist **Aaron North**, bassist **Jeordie White** (née Twiggy Ramirez of Marilyn Manson), and keyboardist **Alessandro Cortini** (formerly of The Mayfield Four, the group that spawned Alter Bridge's Myles Kennedy). Six months into the tour, Dillon was replaced on drums by stand-in Alex Carapetis, then **Josh Freese**, latterly of Guns N' Roses and A Perfect Circle.

The North-White-Cortini-Freese lineup toured in support of *Year Zero* (2007), which promoted Atticus Ross to co-producer. Its Public Enemy-esque noise included brass—a NIN first—and hip-hop poet Saul Williams, whose coruscating *The Inevitable Rise and Liberation of NiggyTardust!* (2007) was produced and largely co-written by Reznor.

Fulfilling contractual obligations with a *Year Zero* re-mix album, Reznor embraced self-released, download albums. In quick succession came 2008's sprawling *Ghosts I-IV*—featuring Belew and Dresden Dolls' drummer Brian Viglione—and taut *The Slip*. The ensuing tour saw Finck return once more, with Cortini, Freese, and bassist **Justin Meldal-Johnsen**, a long-time associate of Beck. Finck and Meldal-Johnsen remained for a four-man lineup on what Reznor claimed would be NIN's final tour, in 2009, alongside ex-Lostprophets drummer **Ilan Rubin**. Jane's Addiction completed a dream double bill on part of the trek.

In the aftermath, Reznor recorded with his wife Mariqueen Maandig and Atticus Ross, christening the project *How to Destroy Angels*. Meanwhile, he and Ross won an Academy Award for their soundtrack for *The Social Network* (2010) and scored *The Girl with the Dragon Tattoo* (2011). However, he reassured fans, "Nine Inch Nails is not dead"—as confirmed by 2013's *Hesitation Marks* and subsequent worldwide tour. **BM**

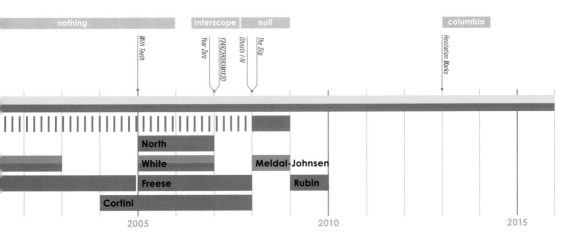

nirvana 1987–1994

Kurt Cobain
b. February 20, 1967
d. April 5, 1994

Krist Novoselic
b. May 16, 1965

Dave Grohl
b. January 14, 1969

Aaron Burckhard
b. November 14, 1963

Dale Crover
b. October 23, 1967

Dave Foster
b. Unknown

There are not many acts in the history of rock 'n' roll that seemed to change everything: what people listened to, what they wore, and even how they acted. Count The Beatles and Elvis among that number, for sure. But the pickings grow mighty slim after that. Nirvana, however, was one of those acts. The pride of Aberdeen, Washington—a city located roughly 100 miles outside of Seattle—made one of the biggest splashes of all time with 1991's *Nevermind*. The ripple touched all corners of pop culture, from fashion (flannel shirts and knitted caps, shockingly, would be seen on Paris runways) to film (the Seattle music scene was the backdrop to 1992's hit *Singles*).

Nevermind represented the coming of age of grunge, the term used to label all the new bands— some worthy, some not so much—that embraced a hardcore sound built on throat-tearing vocals, muddy guitars, contrasting tempos, and, often, a heavy sense of angst. It was the moment that many alt-rockers thought they had been waiting for, when they got to kick aside the "cool kids" and run the party. The rise of Nirvana and other similar acts—notably, Pearl Jam, Alice in Chains, and Soundgarden—caused a drastic

flip in public taste and, for a few years, made Seattle the center of the musical universe. It also cut short the careers of countless pop-metal acts—if not for Nirvana, hairsprayed, spandex-clad acts like Skid Row might still be enjoying commercial success.

Grunge would experience its own backlash, thanks to a deluge of hastily signed inferior acts, and was pretty much passé by the late nineties. However, Nirvana's music—but not, unfortunately, the band itself—was strong enough to outlast the trend and rise above the label. Vocalist **Kurt Cobain** committed suicide on April 5, 1994 at the age of twenty-seven, leaving behind one of rock's truly essential songbooks as well as one eternal question: What could this band have accomplished if they had had more time?

Cobain was an avid music fan growing up in Washington, with tastes ranging from The Beatles and Led Zeppelin to The Stooges and Velvet Underground. He then discovered the act that most influenced his own. "When I heard the Pixies for the first time," he said, "I connected with that band so heavily I should have been *in* that band—or at least in a Pixies cover band." Instead, he toiled briefly in the short-lived punk

year-by-year ■ Vocals ■ Guitar ■ Bass ■ Drums ■ Strings

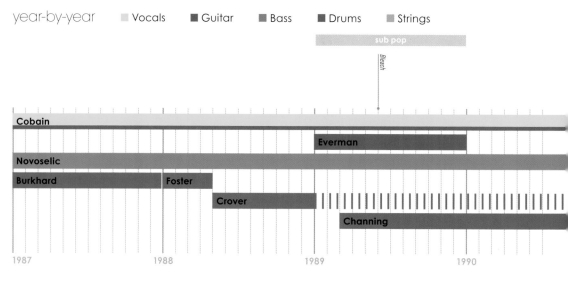

sub pop

Bleach

Cobain				
Everman				
Novoselic				
Burkhard	Foster			
	Crover			
		Channing		

1987   1988   1989   1990

3.7M
Bleach
(1989)

24.6M
Nevermind
(1991)

10.8M
In Utero
(1993)

14.2M
*MTV Unplugged
in New York*
(1994)

Chad Channing
b. January 31, 1967

Jason Everman
b. August 16, 1967

Dan Peters
b. August 18, 1967

Pat Smear
b. August 5, 1959

Lori Goldston
b. 1963

act Fecal Matter, before hooking up with bassist **Krist Novoselic** to start Nirvana in 1987. They first enlisted drummer **Aaron Burckhard** (one of a half-dozen men to carry the beat for the band), but had switched to **Chad Channing** and (on three tracks) **Dale Crover** for their full-length debut on the Sub Pop label. Released in 1989, *Bleach* showcased a heavy Black Sabbath influence and did respectable business for an indie release over the next two years.

That was enough to earn the band—by then featuring future Foo Fighter **Dave Grohl** on drums— a contract with David Geffen's new DGC label: a signing that was tantamount to catching lightning in a bottle. Propelled by "Smells Like Teen Spirit"—which quickly became Generation X's definitive anthem— 1991's *Nevermind* became a runaway smash, moving some 400,000 copies per week in the U.S. by year-end. The record pushed Michael Jackson's *Dangerous* from No. 1 in America and topped the charts in several other countries, on its way to eventual worldwide sales of almost twenty-five million.

Three more Top Twenty U.S. hits, including the brooding "Come as You Are," established Cobain as a writer of great significance and had commentators referring to him as "the voice of a generation." "That kid," remarked Bob Dylan, "has heart."

Cobain, to put it mildly, was uncomfortable with the attention. He was torn between his roots in the underground and the demands of success, which seemed to play havoc with his already fragile health (including an undiagnosed stomach problem). He sought relief in heroin and a relationship, then marriage, with Hole's Courtney Love (seen by many, fairly or not, as Nirvana's Yoko Ono).

None of that would stop Nirvana from releasing what some see as their crowning achievement. *In Utero*, a ragged, unexpected counterpoint to the polish of *Nevermind*, topped the U.S. charts upon release. It was a work of fragile beauty, untamed will, and unmistakable genius, highlighted by such achingly personal tracks as "All Apologies" and "Pennyroyal Tea." It turned out be the band's swansong, one tragically punctuated when Cobain put a shotgun to his head some six months later. The posthumous *MTV Unplugged in New York* would precisely underscore what was lost on April 5, 1994. **JiH**

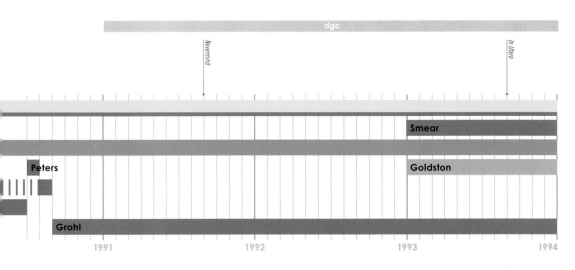

Bleach (1989)

Nevermind (1991)

In Utero (1993)

Kurt Cobain meets his public in Cambridge, Massachusetts, on April 18, 1990.

Cobain records at the Hilversum studio, the Netherlands, in 1991.

Cobain is captured seeking sustenance in 1990.

Dave Grohl records with Nirvana in Los Angeles in 1992.

Cobain enjoys backstage hospitality in Belfast, Northern Ireland, in 1992.

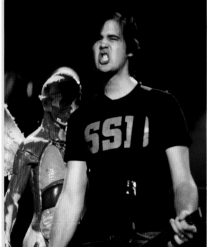

Krist Novoselic performs for MTV *Live and Loud* at Pier 28 in Seattle, Washington, in December 1993.

Novoselic, veteran crooner Tony Bennett, **Grohl**, and touring guitarist **Pat Smear** at the MTV Awards in 1994.

Cobain takes center stage with cellist **Lori Goldston, Novoselic, Grohl,** and **Smear** to record *MTV Unplugged in New York* at Sony Studios on November 18, 1993.

Definitely Maybe
(1994)

**(What's the Story)
Morning Glory**
(1995)

Be Here Now
(1997)

**Standing on the
Shoulder of Giants**
(2000)

Heathen Chemisty
(2002)

**Don't Believe the
Truth** (2005)

Dig Out Your Soul
(2008)

Paul "Guigsy" McGuigan, Paul "Bonehead" Arthurs, Tony McCarroll, and **Liam Gallagher** at their first London show, at the Water Rats' Splash club. January 1994.

Liam Gallagher, headlining Britain's Glastonbury festival in 1995.

Brothers grim **Liam** and **Noel Gallagher** on stage at Earls Court in London in 1997.

In the aftermath of *Standing on the Shoulder...*, the band celebrate "ten years of noise and confusion" at London's Shepherd Bush Empire in October 2001.

Gem Archer, Liam Gallagher, and Andy Bell at the Coachella festival, California, in 2002.

Noel, a.k.a. "The Chief," at Melbourne's Festival Hall in 2005.

On August 28, 2009, six months after this gig in Munich, Germany, Noel Gallagher quit the band.

The Piper at the Gates of Dawn (1967)

Ummagumma (1969)

Meddle (1971)

Dark Side of the Moon (1973)

Nick Mason, **Roger Waters**, **Rick Wright**, and **Syd Barrett** laying down tracks—a far cry from the sophisticated studio scenarios of later years.

Wish You Were Here (1975)

Animals (1977)

The Wall (1979)

Pretty in Pink: **Mason**, **David Gilmour**, **Wright** and **Waters**.

Wright, **Waters**, and **Mason** live in Rotterdam, shortly before beginning to record *Meddle*.

The Final Cut (1983)

A Momentary Lapse of Reason (1987)

Touring *Dark Side...* with backing singers and, second from right, saxophonist **Dick Parry**.

Waters and **Mason** at Nassau Coliseum, New York, in June 1975.

The Division Bell (1994)

Touring bassist and guitarist **Snowy White, Mason,** and **Waters** on the In The Flesh tour for the *Animals* album at Wembley Empire Pool in London, in March 1977.

The teacher and the band, including extra drummer Willie Wilson, at a final *Wall* concert.

Bob Geldof in a still from the 1982 *Wall* movie. *The Final Cut* was originally its soundtrack.

The Floyd's iconic pig returns on the extended Momentary Lapse tour, in Belgium in 1989.

Two pigs? Check. Lots of lights? Check. Explosions? Check. The Floyd bring their full artillery for a performance of "One of These Days (I'm Going to Cut You Into Little Pieces)" in 1994.

Outlandos d'Amour (1978)

Reggatta de Blanc (1979)

Zenyatta Mondatta (1980)

Ghost in the Machine (1981)

Synchronicity (1983)

Left to right: **Andy Summers, Stuart Copeland, and Sting** police one of the passages at Waterloo station on the London Underground in 1978.

Copeland and **Sting** sweating in '78.

In a harbinger of later tension, **Sting** and **Copeland** pretend to push **Summers** into the River Thames during a London photoshoot in 1979.

Summers plays a Telecaster with The Police in 1979.

Copeland, Sting, and Summers during a photoshoot for the sleeve of *Zenyattà Mondatta*.

The Police live on the *Ghost in the Machine* tour in 1982.

Sting and Summers at the Sports Arena, Los Angeles, in January 1981.

Police work continues with a U.S. performance in 1983; more than eight million copies of that year's album, *Synchronicity*, have been sold in the United States.

iggy pop / the stooges 1967–present

Iggy Pop
b. July 21, 1947

Ron Asheton
b. July 17, 1948
d. January 4,
2009

Scott Asheton
b. August 16,
1949
d. March 15,
2014

**Dave
Alexander**
b. June 3, 1947
d. February 10,
1975

**James
Williamson**
b. October 29,
1949

**Scott
Thurston**
b. January 10,
1952

**Brian
Glascock**
b. July 17, 1948

Hunt Sales
b. March 2, 1954

One of rock's most mesmeric performers, **Iggy Pop** had (and retains) the wild qualities of an intelligent, hyperactive child following unfettered instincts. Originally he fronted The Stooges, purveyors of sleaze-filled garage rock, before going solo for nearly thirty years. The group recently re-formed but, for both Pop and the Stooges, sales have never approached the heights of their formidable reputation.

First known as the Psychedelic Stooges, vocalist James Osterberg (known as Iggy from one of his earlier groups, the Iguanas), guitarist **Ron Asheton**, drummer **Scott Asheton**, and bassist **Dave Alexander** were all from Detroit. They came together late in 1967, inspired partly by local hard rock gods the MC5, and partly by Chicago blues musicians. Signed when the Elektra label came to seal a deal with headliners the MC5, the group seemed ready for take-off.

It was not to be. *The Stooges* came out in 1969 to mixed critical reaction and relatively few sales. But cuts such as "No Fun" and "I Wanna Be Your

Dog" crystallized their sneering boredom and wild sexuality—punk before its time. *Fun House* was issued in 1970 with much the same lack of effect. Despite more great tracks—"TV Eye" and "Loose"—the album was only later recognized as a seminal masterpiece.

So it was not success that ripped the group apart, but overindulgence. Most of the members were on heroin. By contrast, Alexander was an alcoholic and had to quit in 1970 (he died in 1975), replaced briefly by Thomas "Zeke" Zettner, then Jimmy Recca. Iggy persuaded saxophonist **Steve Mackay**, who had played on *Fun House*, to join their tour, and **James Williamson** came in as a second guitarist, but the brief magic was over and the Stooges split up in 1971.

While Iggy was nursing his own heroin habit, he met **David Bowie**, who persuaded him to come to London to record. They were joined by Williamson and, eventually, the Asheton brothers, with Ron relegated to playing bass. The result was *Raw Power*, whose phenomenal songs were somewhat diluted

P

year-by-year ▢ Vocals ■ Guitar ■ Bass ■ Drums ■ Keyboards

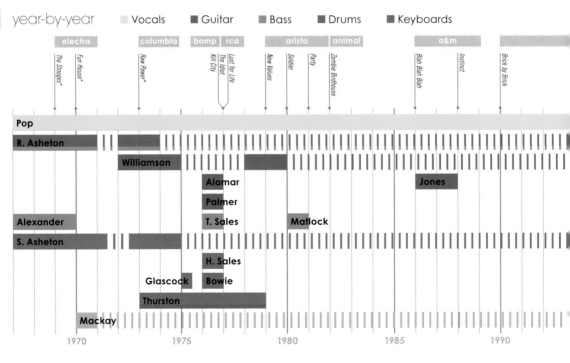

250,000	250,000	1M	500,000
The Stooges (1969)	Raw Power (1973)	Lust for Life (1977)	The Idiot (1977)

Tony Sales
b. June 26, 1951

David Bowie
b. January 8, 1947

Carlos Alomar
b. January 9, 1951

Phil Palmer
b. September 9, 1952

Glen Matlock
b. August 27, 1956

Steve Jones
b. September 3, 1955

Mike Watt
b. December 20, 1957

Steve Mackay
b. September 25, 1949

by Bowie's primitive recording techniques that no amount of re-mixing has ever been able to put right.

Touring for another year was enough to finish off the vulnerable group. Iggy was admitted to rehab in 1974 and kept quiet for a couple of years, despite escaping to record excellent songs with Williamson in 1975 (issued as 1977's *Kill City*). Then Bowie whisked him away to Berlin and they began prospecting.

Iggy's golden year was 1977. Both of his influential collaborations with Bowie, *The Idiot* and *Lust for Life*, were commercially and critically successful. Meanwhile, Iggy toured with a band that included **Hunt Sales** (drums), **Tony Sales** (bass), and **Carlos Alomar** (guitar), plus Bowie playing keyboards.

Williamson was back to produce *New Values* (1979) and *Soldier* (1980), although he was fired for wanting a fuller sound on the latter (featuring ex-Sex Pistol **Glen Matlock**) than Iggy would allow.

For a notorious hellraiser, Iggy turned out a run of consistent albums with guests. Blondie's Chris Stein produced Zombie Birdhouse (1982), and another Sex Pistol, **Steve Jones**, underpinned the success of *Blah Blah Blah* (which saw the return of Bowie). Jones can also be heard on *Instinct* (1988). *Brick by Brick* (1990) boasted stars including Slash and Duff of Guns N' Roses and Kate Pierson, and *American Caesar* (1993) expanded on its themes. Among the subsequent albums, *Naughty Little Doggie* (1996) included the gorgeous Johnny Thunders tribute "Look Away," and *Skull Ring* (2003) featured a reformation of the original Stooges with **Mike Watt** on bass, plus contributions from Green Day, Peaches, and Sum 41.

Recent sightings prove that Iggy is still one of the most riveting live performers around. His longevity has been enhanced by the rebirth of the Stooges in 2003 and a series of impressive gigs. (The Stooges entered the Rock and Roll Hall of Fame in 2010.) When Ron Asheton died in 2009, Williamson returned to the fray. Meanwhile, Iggy diverted onto a jazzy path that yielded *Préliminaires* (2009) and *Après* (2012). **MiH**

■ Aerophones

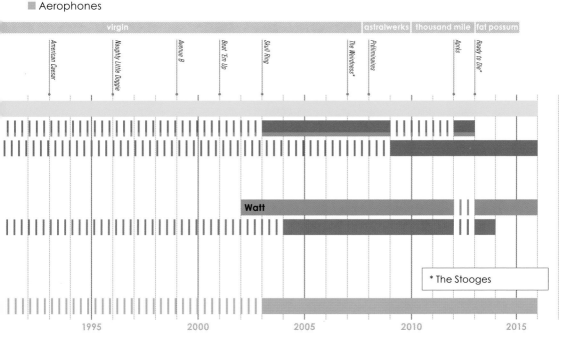

virgin | astralwerks | thousand mile | fat possum

American Caesar · Naughty Little Doggie · Avenue B · Beat 'Em Up · Skull Ring · The Weirdness* · Préliminaires · Après · Ready to Die*

Watt

* The Stooges

1995 2000 2005 2010 2015

The Stooges (1969)

Fun House (1970)

Raw Power (1973)

The Idiot (1977)

Lust for Life (1977)

Blah Blah Blah (1986)

Brick by Brick (1990)

Skull Ring (2003)

The Wierdness (2007)

Préliminaires (2008)

The Stooges and MC5 pose with friends and executives after both groups signed to the Electra label in 1969.

Clockwise from bottom left **Iggy Pop**, **Scott Thurston**, **Ron Asheton**, **James Williamson**, and **Scott Asheton** on October 30, 1973.

Meeting of minds: **Iggy** and **David Bowie** in Germany in 1977.

Iggy and **Bowie** perform in 1977.

Iggy rides the crowd at Crosley Field, Cincinnati, Ohio, in June 1970.

With **Bowie**, backstage after an Iggy concert at The Ritz, New York, in 1986.

With Guns N' Roses guitarist Slash in 1990.

Iggy and James Hetfield of Metallica during the MTV Video Music Awards at Radio City Music Hall, New York, on August 28, 2003.

Mike Watt, Iggy, Scott Asheton, and **Ron Asheton** perform in New York in 2007.

Iggy takes centerstage at Studio 105, La Maison de la Radio, Paris, on May 28, 2009.

popol vuh 1969–2001

Florian Fricke
b. February 23,
1944
d. Dec 29, 2001

Daniel Fichelscher
b. March 7, 1953

Holger Trulzsch
b. unknown

Frank Fiedler
b. unknown

Conny Veit
b. unknown

Robert Eliscu
b. unknown

Djong Yun
b. unknown

Klaus Wiese
b. January 18,
1942
d. Jan 27, 2009

Popol Vuh was not so much a group in the usual sense as a vehicle for the influential experimentations of **Florian Fricke**. The music is often bundled into the krautrock category, but it is more accurate to think of it as the forerunner of today's new age and electronic music. Like most forerunners, Fricke was the best, but increasingly his music came to be devotional in form and content, harking back to older Christian traditions and utterly separate from the rock explosion. "Popol Vuh is a mass for the heart," he told writer Gerhard Augustin in 1996. "It is music for fove."

Fricke founded Popol Vuh—it means "meeting place" or "gathering under the sign of the sun" in Mayan—in Munich with **Holger Trulzsch** (drums) and **Frank Fiedler** (synthesizers) in 1969. He preferred to work in the studio, so Popol Vuh seldom played live.

It is true that their first two albums, *Affenstunde* (1970) and *In den Gärten Pharaos* (1971), had links to what came to be known as krautrock and, in particular, to the waves of sound associated with Tangerine Dream. For their *Zeit* (1972), remembered band leader Edgar Froese, "We invited Florian Fricke to the sessions. He owned the only big modular Moog

synth in Germany, but we didn't know how to use it that well. So we were forced into learning how the thing worked." (Amon Düül II also borrowed the Moog for their own 1972 album, *Wolf City*).

By *Hosianna Mantra* (1972), Fricke had moved away from such electronic instrumentation and reverted to acoustic sounds, with himself on piano. His meeting with singer **Djong Yun** was partly the reason— he claimed her voice was so perfect for his work that it ended his attempts to imitate vocal sounds with electronics. There were other new musicians: guitarist **Conny Veit**, oboe player **Robert Eliscu**, and tamboura player **Klaus Wiese**.

Shortly afterward, guitarist and drummer **Daniel Fichelscher** (from Amon Düül II) signed up. He proved to be the longest-serving collaborator, starting with the uplifting *Seligpreisung* (1973), on which Fricke sang for the first time, as Yun was not available. The music was pouring out of Fricke at that time, and he followed up with *Einsjäger und Siebenjäger* (1974) and *Das Hohelied Salomos* (1975), with vocals coming from Yun once again and sitar by **Alois Gromer**.

Aguirre (1975) saw a partial return to the heavenly

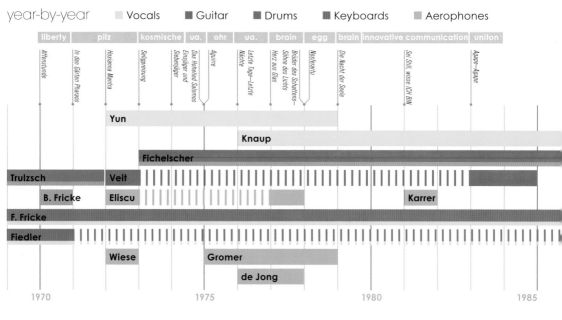

year-by-year ▪ Vocals ▪ Guitar ▪ Drums ▪ Keyboards ▪ Aerophones

| 250,000
Affenstunde
(1970) | 250,000
Aguirre
(1975) | 250,000
Herz aus Glas
(1977) | 250,000
Nosferatu
(1978) |

Renate Knaup
b. unknown

Alois Gromer
b. unknown

Ted de Jong
b. unknown

Chris Karrer
b. unknown

Bernd Wippich
b. unknown

Bettina Fricke
b. unknown

choral effects of the first two albums. But Fricke was not backtracking. Some of the music was more than three years old and had been used, to supreme effect, as the soundtrack to Werner Herzog's *Aguirre, Wrath of God* (1972), a magnificent study of Spanish conquistadors at the end of their tether in South America. It proved to be the start of a very fruitful artistic relationship, with Fricke scoring three further Herzog movies—*Herz aus Glas* (1977), *Nosferatu* (1978), and *Cobra Verde* (1987)—and contributing to *The Enigma of Kaspar Hauser* (1974) and *Fitzcarraldo* (1982). However, Herzog was unusual in that he would often use music already written, rather than asking his composers to write music to suit the action.

Meanwhile, the general trend toward a modern style of sacred music was maintained and Popol Vuh continued to produce albums at a prolific rate. After the slightly rockier *Letzte Tage, Letzte Nachte* (1976) came the more somber *Brüder des Schattens—Söhne des Lichts* (1978) and *Die Nacht der Seele* (1979), both of which had Yun singing on them, with **Renate Knaup**, another refugee from Amon Düül II, joining her. On the latter, Fricke took up singing once again and,

with Amon Düül's **Chris Karrer** on soprano sax and Yun gone, he maintained vocal duties for *Sei Still, wisse ICH BIN* (1981), *Agape—Agape* (1983) and *Spirit of Peace* (1985), albeit supported by Knaup.

The group had produced sixteen albums in as many years. Output now started, almost inevitably, to diminish. *For You and Me* came out in 1991 and was the last album to feature Fichelscher, although he guested on *City Raga* (1995), a suite of songs based on Indian rhythms. These two releases showed the influence of guitarist and keyboard player Guido Hieronymus, as did the final studio album, *Shepherd's Symphony*, in 1997.

The last Popol Vuh release, *Messa di Orfeo* (1998), was, uncharacteristically, a live recording from the Time Zones festival in Molfetta, near Bari, Italy. But no one ever suggested that Fricke did things in a conventional manner. To the end, he remained almost impossible to categorize, conceding only that his songs could be defined as "magic music." His group managed the difficult feat of repeating key themes over many different albums yet always moving ahead. Tragically, he died following a stroke late in 2001. **MiH**

P

■ Other percussion   ■ Strings

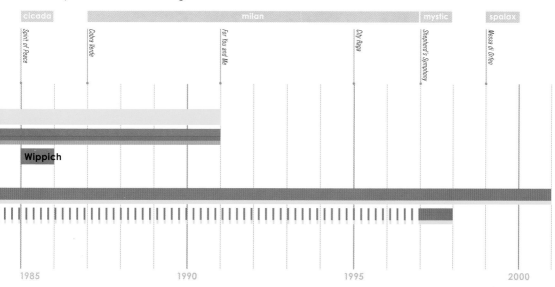

elvis presley 1954–1977

Elvis Presley
b. January 8, 1935
d. August 16, 1977

Scotty Moore
b. December 27, 1931

Bill Black
b. September 17, 1926
d. October 21, 1965

D.J. Fontana
b. March 15, 1931

James Burton
b. August 21, 1939

"This was punk rock…" marveled U2's Bono to *Rolling Stone*. "**Elvis** changed everything—musically, sexually, politically." There had been rhythm and blues before Elvis, and country music, too. But in July 1954, he cut a cover of Arthur Crudup's R&B hit "That's All Right Mama" with guitarist **Scotty Moore** and bassist **Bill Black**—and gave it a country twang. He coupled it with Bill Monroe's bluegrass waltz "Blue Moon of Kentucky"—pepped up with an R&B beat. From that fusion grew rockabilly, and from *that* rose rock 'n' roll. "Before Elvis, everything was in black and white," said Keith Richards. "Then came Elvis. Zoom, glorious Technicolor." For John Lennon, the distinction was even more stark: "Before Elvis, there was nothing."

The joyous adrenalin rush of the five singles Presley cut for Sam Phillips's Sun label between July 1954 and August 1955 (drummer **D.J. Fontana** was hired in late 1954) marked a seismic shift in popular music. In their course, he morphed from an unknown artist with a penchant for crooning into a rising star. By 1956, RCA had snapped him up—a deal masterminded by new manager Colonel Tom Parker. From then until his draft into the U.S. Army in 1958, Presley cut definitive singles, including the reverb-drenched "Heartbreak Hotel" (his first U.S. No. 1 and the top-selling single of 1956), the poppy "All Shook Up," and the staggering "Hound Dog"—which sparked an inspired relationship with

songwriters Jerry Leiber and Mike Stoller. "Hound Dog" also sparked controversy when Presley performed a hip-grinding rendition on *The Milton Berle Show*.

The draft slowed the star's momentum—though the Colonel had stockpiled material to release during Presley's military service in Germany. On his return, the fine *Elvis Is Back!* (1960) demonstrated a broader stylistic range. Initially, the quality of Presley's records—such as the semi-operatic "It's Now or Never" (a worldwide, multi-million-selling No. 1) and the heartfelt "Are You Lonesome Tonight?"—suggested business as usual (with Moore and Fontana returning for studio work). The soundtrack to his film *Blue Hawaii* (1961)—featuring the enduring "Can't Help Falling in Love with You"—was outsold in the sixties only by that for the musical *West Side Story* (1961).

Within a few years, however, the stream of movies that an increasingly out-of-shape Elvis churned out—at the Colonel's insistence—during the sixties lowered his standing considerably. (Only 1964's comic *Viva Las Vegas* came anywhere close to fulfilling the promise of his greatest on-screen role, 1958's *King Creole*.)

Presley's comeback stemmed from his deeply rooted love of gospel music. Originally recorded in 1960, "Crying in the Chapel" gave him a U.S. Top Three hit in 1965. Its success spawned an album in the same vein—*How Great Thou Art*—that earned Presley his

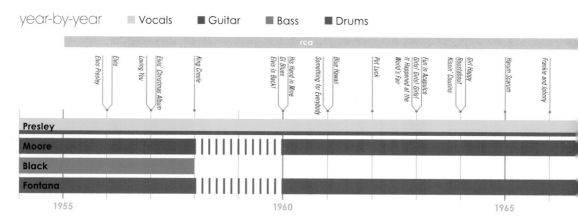

year-by-year   ■ Vocals   ■ Guitar   ■ Bass   ■ Drums

rca

Elvis Presley | Elvis | Loving You | Elvis' Christmas Album | King Creole | His Hand in Mine | El Blues | Elvis Is Back! | Something for Everybody | Blue Hawaii | Pot Luck | Fun in Acapulco | Girls! Girls! Girls! | It Happened at the World's Fair | Kissin' Cousins | Roustabout | Girl Happy | Harum Scarum | Frankie and Johnny

Presley

Moore

Black

Fontana

1955   1960   1965

5M
Elvis
(1956)

15M
Elvis' Christmas Album
(1957)

9M
Elvis' Golden Records
(1958)

5M
Blue Hawaii
(1961)

first Grammy (for Best Sacred Performance). It led to a TV show—subsequently known as "the comeback special"—in 1968 in which the leather-clad, slimmed-down star injected his early hits with a new vibrancy. He closed with "If I Can Dream," a plea for universal brotherhood sung with throat-shredding intensity. Afterward, he told the show's producer that he would never again record a song he did not believe in.

He did, of course. But the late sixties and early seventies marked a genuine second coming. The superb *From Elvis in Memphis* (1969) featured the sobering "In the Ghetto," while the same sessions produced his final U.S. No. 1, "Suspicious Minds." Booked for shows at the Las Vegas Hilton, he set new attendance records. Backed by the TCB ("Taking Care of Business") band, led by guitarist **James Burton**, he delivered high-energy, funky sets—witness the exhilarating "Polk Salad Annie" on 1970's *On Stage*.

The hits continued apace. In 1972, "Burning Love" even saw a return to rock 'n' roll, and the epic concert staple "American Trilogy"—melodramatic overkill in other hands—succeeded because of Presley's disarming sincerity. Increasingly, however, he turned to reflective, bittersweet ballads such as "Always on My Mind" (1972)—perhaps to broaden his audience, but also informed by the disintegration of his marriage (he had wed Priscilla Ann Wagner in 1967).

Presley packed out New York's Madison Square Gardens for four shows in 1972, while *Aloha from Hawaii* (1973) saw a show broadcast to an estimated 1.5 billion people. An album of the latter provided his first U.S. No. 1 since *Roustabout* was knocked off the top by The Beatles in 1965, but he was now a troubled man. Relentless touring, Vegas residencies, an addiction to prescription drugs, and a burgeoning weight problem saw him become a parody by mid-decade, often given to rambling on-stage monologues. Miraculously, he could still cut it sometimes: his take on "Unchained Melody," from *Moody Blue* (1977) was brave, and the funky "Way Down" gave him a U.K. No. 1—posthumously. Elvis Presley's tired body finally gave out on August 16, 1977.

Re-releases, tourism to his Graceland home, shows such as the *Cirque du Soleil Viva Elvis* extravaganza, and the revitalization of the 1968 soundtrack off-cut "A Little Less Conversation" have made Elvis more commercially successful than ever. He is currently the second-richest dead celebrity, according to Forbes, with profits of $55 million in the year to October 2011.

Rock critic Lester Bangs, for one, knew that—despite his long, sad decline—Presley's impact would be imperishable: "I can guarantee you one thing," he wrote in his obituary for *Village Voice*, "We will never agree on anything as we agreed on Elvis." **RD**

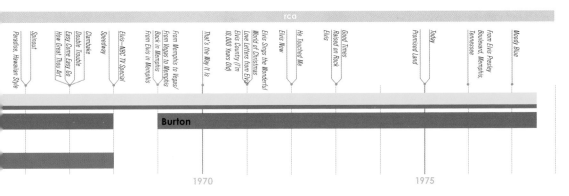

Elvis Presley (1956)

King Creole (1958)

Elvis Is Back! (1960)

Blue Hawaii (1961)

Elvis—NBC TV Special (1968)

From Elvis in Memphis (1969)

That's the Way It Is (1970)

He Touched Me (1972)

Today (1975)

Moody Blue (1977)

The King's Cadillac gets a parking ticket on January 29, 1956.

Working on the soundtrack to *King Creole*, on January 15, 1958.

Frank Sinatra welcomes back a hero from military service on May 12, 1960.

Strolling with Joan Blackman in the 1961 movie *Blue Hawaii*.

The black biker's jacket is dusted off for the comeback special on June 27, 1968.

Presley chats with his father, Vernon, following a Las Vegas performance in August 1969.

Backstage with Sammy Davis, Jr. on August 10, 1970—the opening night of his third season at the Showroom International Hotel, Las Vegas.

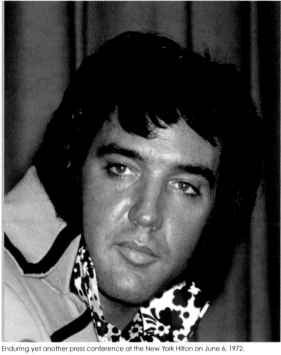
Enduring yet another press conference at the New York Hilton on June 6, 1972.

Presley in concert at the Nassau Coliseum, Uniondale, New York, on July 19, 1975.

Sporting his "Arabian" jumpsuit in Austin, Texas, on March 28, 1977.

Dirty Mind (1980)

1999 (1982)

Purple Rain (1984)

Around the World in a Day (1985)

Parade (1986)

Sign 'o' the Times (1987)

Diamonds and Pearls (1991)

The Gold Experience (1995)

Musicology (2004)

20Ten (2010)

Prince (right) and **André Cymone** at the Bottom Line, New York, on Feburary 15, 1980.

With guitarist **Dez Dickerson**—who would sing on 1999's title track—at the Palladium, New York, on December 2, 1981.

The Revolution—**Brown Mark**, **Doctor Fink**, **Bobby Z**, **Prince**, **Lisa Coleman**, and **Wendy Melvoin**—at the Forum in Inglewood, California, on February 19, 1985.

Intense guitar from the regal one in 1985.

Prince focuses on some knob work at Wembley Arena, London, in 1986.

A high-energy performance in Rotterdam, Netherlands, in 1987.

On 1991's Nude tour, when he took to playing "Nothing Compares 2 U" for the first time.

"Love Symbol" with then-wife **Mayte Garcia** at Wembley Arena, London, in 1995.

Beyoncé and **Prince** perform his hits at the 2004 Grammy Awards show in Los Angeles.

His stage outfit adorned with the *20Ten* album artwork, **Prince** performs at the fortieth Roskilde Festival, in Denmark, on July 4, 2010.

Experience (1992)

Music for the Jilted Generation (1994)

The Fat of the Land (1997)

Always Outnumbered, Never Outgunned (2004)

Invaders Must Die (2009)

Liam Howlett (left) and **Leeroy Thornhill** in an atmospheric 1992 photo.

The band collect the first of four MTV "Best Dance" awards they won from 1994 to 1998

Maxim and **Flint** unveil their demonic personae at 1996's Phoenix festival.

Howlett, **Keith Flint**, **Thornhill**, and **Maxim Reality** on the "Voodoo People" video shoot.

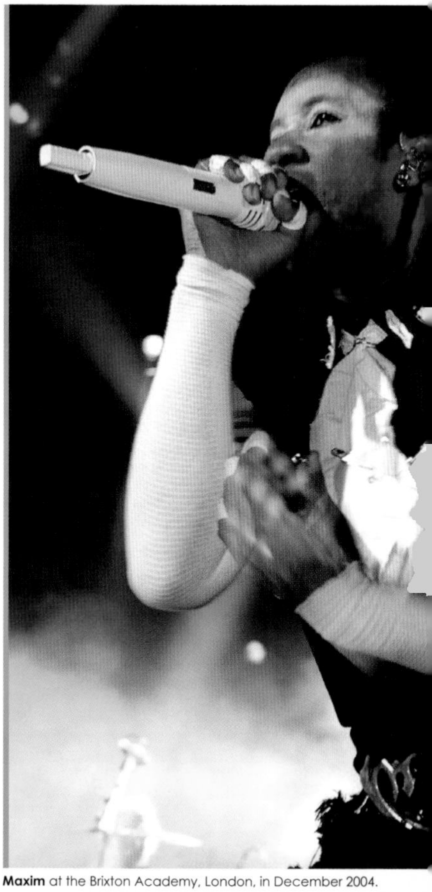

Maxim at the Brixton Academy, London, in December 2004.

Flint's lunatic persona helped to sweep The Prodigy onto the world stage.

Nearly twenty years after their formation, The Prodigy perform at Britain's Download festival in 2009.

Queen (1973)

Sheer Heart Attack (1974)

A Night at the Opera (1975)

A Day at the Races (1976)

News of the World (1977)

The Game (1980)

The Works (1984)

A Kind of Magic (1986)

The Miracle (1989)

The Cosmos Rocks (2008)

Left to right: Ian Hunter, **Freddie Mercury**, Overend Watts, Morgan Fisher, and **Roger Taylor** at a 1973 party with Mott the Hoople.

Brian May, Mercury, Taylor, and **John Deacon** appear on BBC TV's *Top of the Pops* in November 1974.

Deacon's bass underpins **Mercury** in a 1975 performance.

Mercury bestrides the world like a pop colossus in 1977.

Taylor and **Mercury** at a free concert in Hyde Park, London, on September 18, 1976.

Mercury sings in his memorable harlequin garb in 1977.

Mercury in fabulous pants at Wembley Arena, London, in 1984.

Queen onstage at Leiden, Netherlands, on November 27, 1980.

Mercury and **May** etch themselves into legend at Live Aid in 1985.

Mercury at London's Wembley Stadium—the venue for 1985's Live Aid and a 1992 tribute show for him—in 1986.

May records with Black Sabbath's Tony Iommi in July 1989.

Paul Rodgers sings at the 46664 Concert in Celebration of Nelson Mandela's Life in London on June 27, 2008.

radiohead 1991–present

Thom Yorke
b. October 7, 1968

Jonny Greenwood
b. November 5, 1971

Colin Greenwood
b. June 26, 1969

Ed O'Brien
b. April 15, 1968

Phil Selway
b. May 23, 1967

Panic, alienation, disgust, despair—just because the personnel in Radiohead has been settled for more than two decades does not indicate an absence of darker, more destructive emotions. For most of that time, the band has enjoyed unbroken success, yet there has been as much conflict as in much more volatile lineups. The difference here? It is intertwined with personal consciences, internal battles that have bled into the work of one of music's game-changers.

Before Radiohead, first came Oxfordshire five-piece On a Friday. Different name, same faces: singer (and occasional guitarist and keyboard player) **Thom Yorke**, guitarist **Jonny Greenwood**, his older brother and bassist **Colin**, second guitarist **Ed O'Brien**, and drummer **Phil Selway**. A switch to a moniker inspired by a Talking Heads song was followed by their debut, *Pablo Honey* (1993). Some bands burst out fully formed; it was not so here, with an album that owed too much to grunge influences, and which sold more than it deserved to after "Creep," with Greenwood Jr's crunching guitar, picked up airplay in America. (There, the song forged a link between grunge and emo—a micro-genre known, thanks to a quote about Radiohead in the movie *Clueless,* as "mope rock.")

"Creep" reached the U.K. Top Ten, but the tag of one-hit wonders did not dangle around the band's

necks for too long: *The Bends* (1995) was rapturously received. *Rolling Stone* praised its "exploded emotional palette," and the notoriously self-critical Yorke conceded that his lyrics for "Fake Plastic Trees"—one of five U.K. hits from the album—were the first with which he was almost content. Radiohead, said Michael Stipe of R.E.M. (with whom they toured in 1995), were "so good they scare me."

Having scarred audiences by playing new songs while supporting Alanis Morissette in 1996, Radiohead lurched into the leftfield the following year. Disdain for politicians, dislocation from technology, and dismay at what the group saw as the easy musical options exercised by the Britpop movement all informed *OK Computer*. It was immediately hailed as the band's masterpiece, despite Yorke previewing it as "sort of skiffle-Pink Floyd that sounds like Queen." (Floyd's Roger Waters said that he "really liked" the album, while their unsurprisingly different-minded David Gilmour expressed a preference for *The Bends*.)

Given that the pre-teen Yorke's first song was called "Mushroom Cloud," his grim themes came as little surprise, but the album tapped into fears about the approaching new millennium. It is debatable whether the U.K. Top Three has, before or since, been home to anything as weird as "Paranoid Android."

year-by-year ■ Vocals ■ Guitar ■ Bass ■ Drums ■ Keyboards

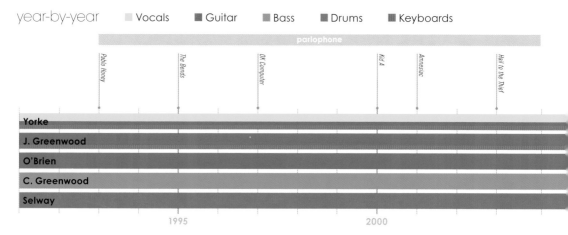

Still the internal doubts remained, even after a headline slot at Britain's Glastonbury festival in 1997 that is regarded as one of the event's greatest-ever performances. "We thought we'd blown it in the biggest possible way," said Colin Greenwood.

Having documented their unease on 1998's video *Meeting People Is Easy,* the band determined to veer even further away from rock orthodoxy. *Kid A* (2000) and its companion piece *Amnesiac* (2001) came at no small cost to the band's internal dynamics. "There was a lot of turning up and hanging around and wondering what to do next and not doing anything, and then going home," said Greenwood Sr. "Every day. For weeks and weeks. It's very soul sapping."

But the stranger they became, the more the world loved them. *Kid A* took the U.S. No. 1 slot to kick off a run of Top Three albums. Yorke's battle to open *Kid A* with "Everything in its Right Place" was an ideal way of signposting its cold love for electronica, but influences across the two albums even included jazz from British trumpeter Humphrey Lyttelton. Yorke's keening voice was one of the band's unique selling points, so it was a characteristically contrary next step to play it down. Underpinning everything was the imperative to shed what Yorke saw as the straitjacket of "it's not a song unless it's got a guitar in it, or whatever nonsense."

Ironically, *Hail to the Thief* (2003) returned the band to a more conventional approach, but charges of water-treading did not come only from outside the band. Of the band's fourth U.K. chart-topper, Yorke said: "What we were doing was becoming routine. It felt like we were doing it because we didn't really know what else to do." The frontman stepped outside the band for the gorgeous *The Eraser* (2006) while Jonny Greenwood redefined film soundtracks with 2007's *There Will Be Blood.*

Like its predecessor, 2007's beautiful *In Rainbows* did not rip up the rule book, but saved its innovation for its system of pay-what-you-want downloads. And after 2009's heartbreaking "Harry Patch (In Memory Of)," there was no consideration for slipping into comfortable and unchallenging middle age with *The King of Limbs* (2011). On a record dominated by skittering and unsettling rhythms, Phil Selway sounded on some cuts as if he were aiming to personify the title of his band's most opinion-dividing album.

The restless search for bars to raise and boundaries to push continues. "We always have a feeling that we can do better. There's always acres and acres of room for improvement," said Jonny Greenwood. "Maybe that's what keeps us going. Imagine being satisfied with something." **CB**

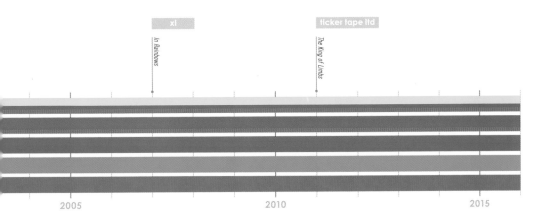

Pablo Honey
(1993)

The Bends (1995)

OK Computer
(1997)

Kid A (2000)

Amnesiac (2001)

Hail to the Thief
(2003)

In Rainbows (2007)

The King of Limbs
(2011)

Ed O'Brien, **Thom Yorke**, **Phil Selway**, **Jonny Greenwood** and **Colin Greenwood** in 1993.

Yorke backstage in Cambridge, England, in November 1995.

Jonny Greenwood, his arm in a brace, on stage in 1997.

Yorke, the driving force behind *Kid A*'s unconventional sound, in the Netherlands in 2000.

By now regarded as one of rock's finest live bands, Radiohead hit Florida's Cruzan Amphitheatre on the *In Rainbows* tour, in May 2008.

Jonny Greenwood, **Yorke**, **Selway**, **Colin Greenwood**, and **Ed O'Brien** in London, in a shoot to promote *Kid A*'s "sequel," *Amnesiac*—the third of five consecutive U.K. No. 1 albums.

After a sensational set at Britain's Glastonbury festival in 1997, **Yorke** and **O'Brien** feature in Radiohead's second headlining slot, in 2003.

Yorke at New York's Roseland Ballroom in 2011—one of a series of shows that preceded a world tour for *The King of Limbs* in 2012.

rage against the machine 1990–present

Zack de la Rocha
b. January 12, 1970

Tom Morello
b. May 30, 1964

Tim Commerford
b. February 26, 1968

Brad Wilk
b. September 5, 1968

Los Angeles quartet Rage Against the Machine are rather political in the same way that the surface of the sun is rather warm. Their intense drive has sustained them for their twenty years as a band, and provided them with endless targets for lyrical inspiration. Although critics have sneered at the group's willingness to sign with a major label for its resolutely anti-corporate albums, RATM continue to plough a furrow that places message resolutely over medium.

Formed by guitarist **Tom Morello** in 1991, Rage Against the Machine also features rapper **Zack de la Rocha**, whose politically active parents had given him a high-octane zeal; bassist **Tim Commerford**, a school friend of de la Rocha; and drummer **Brad Wilk**, who had auditioned for Morello's previous band, Lock Up. In that earlier group, the guitarist had honed an unusual, hard-hitting guitar style based on inventive effects and razor-sharp riffs. This approach became the core of RATM's music, committed to demo tape after club gigs and submitted to the Epic label. The subsequent deal did not represent an ideological clash, said Morello, because it allowed the musicians complete control over their music.

The band's self-titled debut, issued in 1992, was a breathtaking piece of work. Its stern, uncompromising view of the modern world as a media-controlled hell, populated by zombies and governed by a callous military-industrial complex, spoke to the slacker generation just as much as Rage's contemporaries like Nirvana. The band's most striking songs—"Killing in the Name," "Bullet in the Head," "Know Your Enemy" and "Wake Up"—became regulars on MTV and radio, a remarkable achievement given their raw anger and frequently graphic language.

Although Rage recorded two more albums (*Evil Empire* and *The Battle of Los Angeles*) and a covers collection (*Renegades*) before calling it a day in 2000, they never really equaled that stunning first record. Latterday singles such as "Bulls on Parade" and "People of the Sun" had power, certainly, but after the rise of nü-metal—in many ways, the logical extension of RATM's signature sound—fans had other, heavier bands to follow, each with its own lyrical fury.

In the hiatus before their much-publicized reunion in 2007, Morello, Wilk and Commerford united with Soundgarden singer Chris Cornell for three U.S. Top Ten albums as Audioslave. But there was a palpable sense of expectation for the original band to reform and, when they did so, crowds surged to their shows.

A splendid dose of publicity came at the end of 2009 when "Killing in the Name" became a Christmas No. 1 in the U.K. after a Facebook campaign was set up in protest against the usual chart domination by a reality TV winner. RATM repaid the compliment by playing a free concert in London the following summer. As modern-day protests go, this one had all the right elements: a modern, technological platform for the people; a corporate adversary; and an anthem for a generation. Somehow it seemed to sum up the band's entire career in one stroke. **JM**

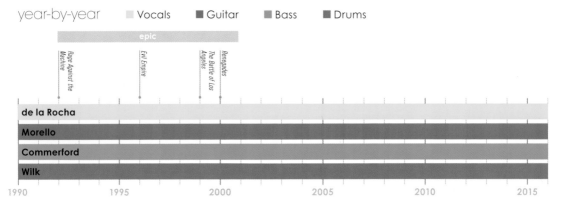

year-by-year ■ Vocals ■ Guitar ■ Bass ■ Drums

rainbow 1975–1997

Ritchie Blackmore
b. April 14, 1945

Ronnie James Dio
b. July 10, 1942
d. May 16, 2010

Graham Bonnet
b. December 23, 1947

Cozy Powell
b. December 29, 1947
d. April 5, 1998

Roger Glover
b. November 30, 1945

Joe Lynn Turner
b. August 2, 1951

Bobby Rondinelli
b. July 27, 1955

Doogie White
b. March 7, 1960

Ritchie Blackmore is one of classic rock's most accomplished guitarists, and a man who resolutely treads his own path. So when his band Deep Purple changed its sound in 1974 and that change was not to his liking, he left to form Rainbow. Purple were among the planet's biggest bands at the time, touring in a private jet and playing to stadiums. Simply walking away to found a new band took serious conviction.

But Blackmore's gamble paid off. Enlisting Elf singer **Ronnie James Dio** and Dio's bandmates Craig Gruber (bass), Gary Driscoll (drums), and Micky Lee Soule (keyboards) and cutting *Ritchie Blackmore's Rainbow*, the guitarist established the band as a credible project. He also quickly gained a reputation as a man not to be trifled with, firing the entire band bar Dio for the follow-up. The classic *Rainbow Rising* (1976) featured Jimmy Bain (bass), Tony Carey (keyboards) and **Cozy Powell** (drums). Musicians came and went over the next few years, notably former Purple bassist **Roger Glover**. Dio decamped for Black Sabbath when Blackmore made it clear that he wanted Rainbow to drop its sword-and-sorcery focus and move into commercial rock territory.

Ex-Marbles singer **Graham Bonnet** came aboard for the new era, which—as Blackmore predicted— saw Rainbow meet with significant success, thanks to a new sound. The group will always be remembered for "Since You Been Gone," a 1979 radio-rock anthem.

Subsequent albums with Bonnet's successor **Joe Lynn Turner** maintained Rainbow's transatlantic commercial superiority over rival post-Purple projects Whitesnake and Gillan. However, the re-formation of the classic Mark II lineup of Deep Purple put Rainbow on ice in 1984.

When Purple fractured once again a decade later, Blackmore reconvened Rainbow, with Scottish singer **Doogie White** and session musicians. *Stranger in Us All* (1995) was a decent slab of modern rock, albeit one unlikely to compete with *Rainbow Rising*. While the new band enjoyed a three-year run, Blackmore became fixated on performing Renaissance music, and called time on Rainbow in 1997 to do exactly that. His new band, Blackmore's Night, has toured ever since to a rather unusual niche market of audiences wearing leather jerkins and other medieval garments.

Despite the absence of Blackmore from the rock scene and exhortations from fans for reunions of Rainbow (and indeed a Blackmore-led Purple), his band's songs have only grown in popularity. A touring tribute band called Over the Rainbow is led by Blackmore's son Jürgen, and several of the group's best-known songs were performed live by groups such as Dio and the Hughes-Turner Project. Many fans petitioned for a reunion of Blackmore with Ronnie James Dio but, sadly, the vocalist's death to stomach cancer in 2010 rendered such a dream impossible. **JM**

R

year-by-year   ◻ Vocals ■ Guitar ■ Bass ■ Drums

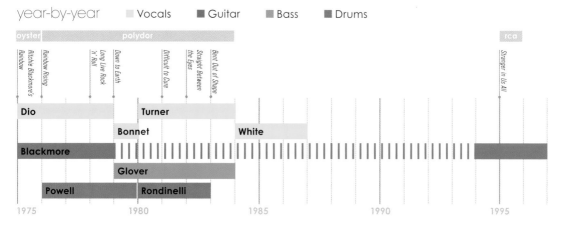

rammstein 1993–present

Till Lindermann
b. January 4, 1963

Paul H. Landers
b. December 9, 1964

Christian "Flake" Lorenz
b. November 16, 1966

Richard Z. Kruspe
b. June 24, 1967

Oliver Riedel
b. April 11, 1971

Christoph "Doom" Schneider
b. May 11, 1966

Rammstein were among the progenitors of what in 1995 was dubbed by the music press in Europe as "Neue Deutsche Härte"—"New German Hardness." It describes a crossover style combining groove metal with elements of techno and industrial electronica. In Rammstein's case, that meant a brutally intense form of hard rock with lyrics sung in German in a deep, domineering male voice, with visual presentations that skirt pornography, homoeroticism, and military chic. Oh, and lots of explosions.

Formed in 1993, Rammstein's roots were in the East Berlin punk band Feeling B. Active for a decade, the band had featured guitarist **Paul H. Landers** and keyboard player **Christian "Flake" Lorenz**. They were joined briefly in the early nineties by Leipzig-born drummer **Till Lindermann**, a former swimmer once in contention for a place in the East German Olympic team. The trio formed Rammstein: with Lindermann as lead singer, they entered and won a competition to make a professional demo. Provocative from the beginning, the band took their name from a 1988 German air show disaster at the Ramstein USAF air base in which seventy spectators were killed and many more injured: aptly, given the band's sound, the word also describes a medieval stone battering ram.

Expanding to a six-piece lineup, with lead guitarist **Richard Z. Kruspe**, bassist **Oliver Riedel** and drummer **Christoph "Doom" Schneider**, Rammstein quickly established a reputation for powerful and theatrical live performances.

After the band's first single, "Du riechst so gut," their debut album *Herzeleid* ("Heartbreak") appeared in September 1995, its powerful electro-metal striking an immediate chord with German youth. The ingredients of the characteristic Rammstein sound—stomping drums, rolling bass, cascades of feedback, clipped electronic beats, and over-enunciated vocals (seemingly presented without a flicker of irony)—were in place from the very beginning, and the album effortlessly sailed into the German Top Ten. Some critics may have been uncomfortable with song titles such as "Der Meister" ("The Master") and "Weißes Fleisch" ("White Flesh"), sleeve artwork showing the musclebound band posing bare-chested and stern-faced, and a video that included excerpts from the 1936 Berlin Olympics by Hitler's filmmaker of choice, Leni Riefenstahl—but Rammstein would always be firm in their denial of fascist tendencies.

German bands—especially those singing in their native tongue—have rarely made a lasting impression

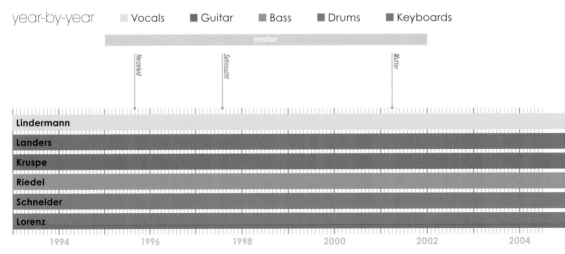

year-by-year ■ Vocals ■ Guitar ■ Bass ■ Drums ■ Keyboards

motor

Herzeleid *Sehnsucht* *Mutter*

Lindermann

Landers

Kruspe

Riedel

Schneider

Lorenz

1994   1996   1998   2000   2002   2004

○ 3.4M
Sehnsucht
(1997)

○ 1.5M
Mutter
(2001)

○ 1.5M
Reise, Reise
(2004)

○ 1.1M
Rosenrot
(2005)

on the international music scene. By the beginning of 1996, Rammstein were already setting themselves up as an exception by performing in London as part of MTV's *Hanging Out* series. Their exposure was further broadened when Nine Inch Nails' Trent Reznor selected two songs from *Herzeleid* in his capacity as music director for David Lynch's movie *Lost Highway*.

In November 1996, Rammstein decamped to the Mediterranean island of Malta to record their critical second album. Two singles released in the first half of 1997—"Engel" ("Angel") and "Du Hast" ("You Have")—went gold and hit the German Top Five.

When *Sehnsucht* ("Longing") emerged in the summer of 1997, it entered Germany's chart at No. 1 while, in a frenzy of exposure, two earlier singles surged back into the Top Twenty. *Sehnsucht* featured six different front covers, each depicting a member of the band wearing bizarre facial equipment constructed from kitchen utensils. As the band toured the U.S. with Ice Cube, Korn, and Limp Bizkit, the album gave Rammstein their first *Billboard* chart success, reaching No. 45 and earning the band a Grammy nomination. It remains the only album sung entirely in German to be certified platinum in the U.S. (later Rammstein albums incorporated some English lyrics).

After 1999's concert album *Live aus Berlin*, Rammstein retreated to the south of France to record *Mutter* (2001)—their third album to top the German charts. By now, they were a huge international live draw, their shows increasingly outlandish spectacles. Indeed, vocalist Lindemann became a licensed pyrotechnician, his signature trick being to perform entire songs while engulfed head to toe in flames. Kruspe describes their often misinterpreted shows as "a combination of humor, theater, and our East German culture," acknowledging that "ninety-nine per cent of the people don't understand the lyrics, so you have to come up with something to keep the drama in the show."

With the success of 2004's *Reise, Reise* ("Journey, Journey") and 2005's *Rosenrot* ("Rose Red"), Rammstein were acknowledged by *Billboard* as the biggest-selling German-language band of all time. This position was cemented in 2009 with the band's crowning achievement, *Liebe ist für alle da* ("Love Is There for Everyone") which topped charts throughout continental Europe and reached the Top Twenty for the first time in both the U.K. and U.S. The 2011 "greatest hits" collection *Made in Germany 1995–2011* summed up their extraordinary career so far. **TB**

■ Programming

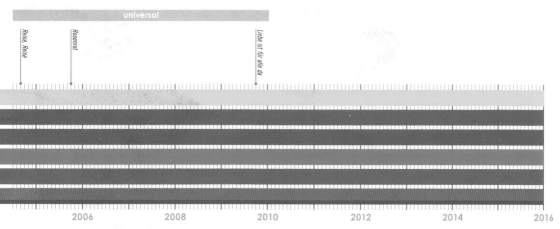

red hot chili peppers 1983–present

Anthony Kiedis
b. November 1, 1962

Josh Klinghoffer
b. October 3, 1979

Flea
b. October 16, 1962

Chad Smith
b. October 25, 1961

John Frusciante
b. March 5, 1970

Hillel Slovak
b. April 13, 1962
d. June 25, 1988

Jack Irons
b. July 18, 1962

Dave Navarro
b. June 7, 1967

The enormous success and longevity of the Red Hot Chili Peppers could never have been predicted. When they formed in 1983, punk bands played small clubs, funk was a niche musical genre, and slapping bass guitars was almost criminally unfashionable. That this Los Angeles foursome combined those elements and met with worldwide acclaim is one of rock's most unusual outcomes—even more so given that their progress has been hindered by addiction and death.

It all began when L.A. high school students **Anthony Kiedis** (vocals) and Australian-born Michael "**Flea**" Balzary (nicknamed for his energetic stage moves) began playing songs together, united by a love of hardcore punk and seventies funk bands such as Sly & the Family Stone and Parliament-Funkadelic. "Funk," Flea assured *Kerrang!* magazine, "is as heavy as shit." The pair recruited drummer **Hillel Slovak** (guitar) and **Jack Irons** (drums), although the latter duo were also in a band called What Is This? This dual commitment was the first contributor to a constantly shifting lineup through much of their career. In fact, after the band, which began life as Tony Flow & The Miraculously Majestic Masters of Mayhem, renamed themselves the Red Hot Chili Peppers and scored a deal with EMI America, Slovak and Irons did not play on their self-titled debut album in 1984. Instead, **Jack**

Sherman and **Cliff Martinez** played guitar and drums respectively. Slovak returned for 1985's *Freaky Styley* (produced by funk godfather George Clinton) and Irons in 1987 for *The Uplift Mofo Party Plan*.

These early albums established the Chili Peppers' idiosyncratic funk-punk, propeled by Kiedis's semi-rapped, semi-sung vocals and Flea's expert slap bass. The group's profile rose impressively, thanks to the 1987 hit "Fight Like a Brave" and the Beatles-spoofing "socks on cocks" cover of 1988's *The Abbey Road E.P.*

However, tragedy struck when Slovak succumbed to a heroin overdose in 1988. Grieving, Irons left the band (he later joined Pearl Jam), and—after a period of uncertainty in which P-Funk guitarist **DeWayne McKnight** and Dead Kennedys drummer **D. H. Peligro** filled in—permanent replacements **John Frusciante** and **Chad Smith** were added. The former was a Slovak disciple who claimed to have learned everything he knew about funk guitar from his late idol, and the latter brought a strong rock style that gave the Chilis a much-needed commercial edge. *Mother's Milk* (1989) was the new lineup's first release, and became the band's most notable success yet, largely thanks to a hit cover of Stevie Wonder's "Higher Ground."

Greater exposure came in 1991, however, when production guru Rick Rubin agreed to tweak the

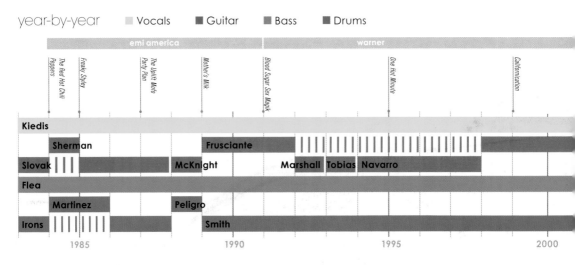

year-by-year ■ Vocals ■ Guitar ■ Bass ■ Drums

Cliff Martinez
b. February 5, 1954

D.H. Peligro
b. July 9, 1959

Arik Marshall
b. February 13, 1967

Jack Sherman
b. January 18, 1956

DeWayne McKnight
b. April 17, 1954

Jesse Tobias
b. April 1, 1972

faders on the Chilis' *Blood Sugar Sex Magik*. Along with Nirvana's *Nevermind* and Metallica's *Metallica*, both released mere months beforehand, *Blood Sugar* became one of the alternative rock generation's must-have albums, leading to hits such as "Give It Away" and the ballad "Under the Bridge."

But while on tour to promote the album, Frusciante began to buckle under the stresses of fame and developed a crippling heroin addiction, just as his predecessor had done before him. In May 1992, he quit, to be replaced first by Zander Schloss, then **Arik Marshall** (who lasted for the band's headlining slot on the Lollapalooza tour and *Simpsons* cameo in 1993), then **Jesse Tobias** (who would subsequently resurface alongside Alanis Morissette and, later, Morrissey).

Kiedis, Flea and Smith returned in 1994 with a new guitarist, **Dave Navarro** of Jane's Addiction. However, the resultant *One Hot Minute*—despite containing fine songs and going double platinum in the U.S.—failed to match the impact of *Blood Sugar Sex Magik*. As the funk-rock that the Chilis had pioneered was evolving into the heavier nü-metal sound, it seemed that the band might fade. Navarro was ousted after rumors of more drug addiction—but, just as all hope seemed gone, Frusciante returned to the fold, now cleaned up after a life-threatening few years of addiction.

Once again Rick Rubin enabled a rebirth for the Chili Peppers: one of equally giant proportions to their breakthrough almost a decade earlier. The intermittently pretty *Californication* (1999) and utterly gorgeous *By the Way* (2002) established the band as a stadium-sized force to be reckoned with, especially in the U.K. and Europe, where the Chilis topped charts and headlined at arenas and festivals—*Live in Hyde Park* gave the band their second U.K. No. 1 in 2004. Perhaps the new sound lacked the raw danger of the eighties albums and the stripped-down emotion of the *Blood Sugar Sex Magik* era, but the Chilis' smoother sound was welcomed by a new audience—combined worldwide sales of *Californication* and *By the Way* approach twenty-five million.

Greatest Hits (2003) helped fill the gap before 2006's *Stadium Arcadium*, a bloated set that earned middling reviews yet yielded the platinum-selling U.S. hit "Snow (Hey Oh)." Wisely, the group embarked on a long hiatus, during which Smith joined Van Halen's Sammy Hagar and Michael Anthony in Chickenfoot, Flea played with Radiohead's Thom Yorke and Blur's Damon Albarn, and Frusciante departed once more.

I'm with You (2011) was cut with new guitarist Josh Klinghoffer and contained the sort of radio-friendly rock that ensures the band are set for the future. **JM**

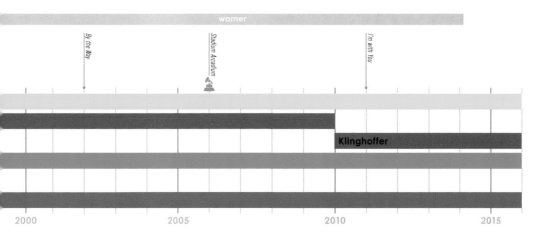

The Red Hot Chilli Peppers (1984)

Freaky Styley (1985)

The Uplift Mofo Party Plan (1987)

Mother's Milk (1989)

Blood Sugar Sex Magik (1991)

One Hot Minute (1995)

Californication (1999)

By the Way (2002)

Stadium Arcadium (2006)

I'm with You (2006)

Left to right: **Flea**, **Cliff Martinez**, and **Anthony Kiedis** perform at The Roxy, Hollywood, on September 9, 1984.

Martinez, Flea, Kiedis, and **Hillel Slovak** ham it up for the camera in 1985.

Flea, Slovak, and Kiedis pose with **Jack Irons** in Minneapolis, in January 1987.

Kiedis with new guitarist **John Frusciante** (right).

Flaming headgear distinguishes a Peppers performance in Stanhope, New Jersey, in August 1991.

Kiedis and **Navarro** at the Cow Palace, San Francisco, on April 6, 1996.

Brilliant lightbulb costumes conceal **Dave Navarro** (left) and **Kiedis** at the Woodstock festival, August 14, 1994.

Chad Smith (drums) and **Kiedis** at the Shoreline Amphitheater in Mountain View, California, on June 18, 1999.

Flea and **Frusciante** perform in Belgium in 2002.

A laid-back **Flea, Kiedis,** and **Frusciante** entertain at the Grammy Awards, Los Angeles, on February 8, 2006.

Flea with **Josh Klinghoffer** in Sunrise, Florida, on April 2, 2012.

r.e.m. 1980–2011

Michael Stipe
b. January 4, 1960

Peter Buck
b. December 6, 1956

Mike Mills
b. December 17, 1958

Bill Berry
b. July 31, 1958

In the early eighties, when overpowering ballads, "hair metal," and bombastic production values dominated the charts, R.E.M. provided a much-needed antidote: mystery. From the eerie shot of kudzu vines on their debut album cover to **Michael Stipe**'s blurred vocal delivery, this band intrigued.

Formed in Athens, Georgia, R.E.M. evolved an idiosyncratic, ringing sound built on **Peter Buck**'s Rickenbacker guitar—he favored subtle arpeggios over power chords—and Stipe's rootsy vocals. **Mike Mills** supplied melodic bass and backing vocals, with **Bill Berry** on drums and vocals. The band cut their debut single, "Radio Free Europe," for indie label Hib-Tone in mid-1981. A sizzling slice of post punk, it attracted critical plaudits and record company interest. The *Chronic Town* E.P. followed, marking their debut for the I.R.S. label. A re-recorded "Radio Free Europe" kicked off the debut album *Murmur* (1983), but other pleasures abounded—notably the brooding "Talk About the Passion," the carefree "Shaking Through," and the quietly sublime "Perfect Circle." *Rolling Stone* made it their album of the year (over Michael Jackson's *Thriller*).

Reckoning (1984), an assured follow-up, boasted the wistful wonders "So. Central Rain (I'm Sorry)," "Camera," and "Time After Time (AnnElise)," and a hit-that-never-was in "(Don't Go Back To) Rockville."

Fables of the Reconstruction (1985) was cut in London with Fairport Convention/Nick Drake producer Joe Boyd. Ill at ease in an unfamiliar country, the group were in low spirits, hence the album's subdued sound (exceptions being the funked-up "Can't Get There from Here" and "Driver 8"). The mythology of the South pervades the album, notably on "Old Man Kensey" and the plaintive, banjo-led "Wendell Gee."

Lifes Rich Pageant (1986) was bigger and bolder—witness the clarion-call "Begin the Begin," the euphoric "These Days," and an uplifting take on The Clique's "Superman," sung by Mills. (The group peppered their live sets and B-sides with cover songs; *Document* boasts a fine version of Wire's "Strange.") Subtler delights included the richly melodic "Fall on Me" and the touching Civil War memento "Swan Swan H." The result was their first U.S. gold album.

As R.E.M. grew in confidence and stature—aided by intensive touring and college-radio support—their songs graduated from reflections on personal relationships to the wider world, with Stipe's lyrics becoming less impressionistic, more direct. *Document* (1987), their first platinum album, addressed a dark period of past U.S. politics—with implications for the Reagan era—on "Exhuming McCarthy." "The One I Love"—a twisted rejection note—gave the band a first genuine hit (U.S. No. 9), while another standout

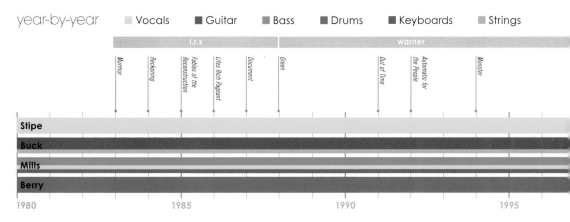

year-by-year ▪ Vocals ▪ Guitar ▪ Bass ▪ Drums ▪ Keyboards ▪ Strings

16.4M	**13.9M**	**10.2M**	**5.4M**
Out of Time (1991)	*Automatic for the People* (1992)	*Monster* (1994)	*In Time: The Best of R.E.M. 1988-2003* (2003)

was "It's the End of the World as We Know It (And I Feel Fine)," whose helter-skelter imagery recalled Bob Dylan's "Subterranean Homesick Blues."

Green (1988) marked the band's debut for Warner, and saw them shake up proceedings by regularly switching instruments. (It is also the first to feature Buck playing mandolin, on the spine-tingling trio "Hairshirt," "The Wrong Child," and "You Are the Everything.")

Despite the rap-friendly opener "Radio Song" (featuring KRS-One), *Out of Time* (1991) was a country-tinged affair. Boosted by the worldwide smash "Losing My Religion," and featuring Kate Pierson of The B-52's on three cuts (including "Shiny Happy People"), it proved a career high and sold over sixteen million copies, providing the band with their first U.S./U.K. No. 1 and bagging three Grammys in the process.

Another multi-platinum smash, *Automatic for the People* (1992), confirmed R.E.M. as superstars, despite their failure to tour and the album's downbeat atmosphere—prompting (unfounded) rumors about Stipe's health. From the sobering "Drive"—which references David Essex's 1973 hit "Rock On"—to the Andy Kaufman tribute "Man on the Moon," and the inspiring "Everybody Hurts," quality abounded.

Having decided to return to the road for the first time since the end of the *Green* tour, the group created 1994's crunchy *Monster*. In complete contrast

to the subdued palette of *Out of Time* and *Automatic For the People*, this transatlantic No. 1 nodded to grunge, rocking out engagingly on "Star 69," and paying tribute to Stipe's late friend Kurt Cobain on "Let Me In." Now stadium-fillers, R.E.M. renewed their Warner contract in a deal said to be worth $80 million. However, the gamely experimental *New Adventures in Hi-Fi* (1996), a U.S. No. 2 and U.K. No. 1, sold "only" five million copies. More damagingly, Berry—weary of the rock-star treadmill—announced his departure. (The *Monster* tour had seen him collapse on stage from a brain aneurysm, while Mills and Stipe were hospitalized with less serious ailments.)

Subsequent albums charted well without enjoying the acclaim heaped on earlier efforts. However, *Up* (1998) and *Around the Sun* (2004)—while frustratingly inconsistent—included some of their most affecting songs (including the former's "At My Most Beautiful" and the latter's "I Wanted to Be Wrong"). The jingly-jangly *Reveal* (1999) played it straighter, while the feisty *Accelerate* (2008) provided their seventh U.K. chart-topper, and restored them to the U.S. Top Three.

After 2011's *Collapse into Now* sank faster than any of its predecessors (despite featuring Peaches, Eddie Vedder, and Patti Smith), R.E.M. split on September 21 that year. Their heyday may have been long gone, but during that heyday they were untouchable. **RD**

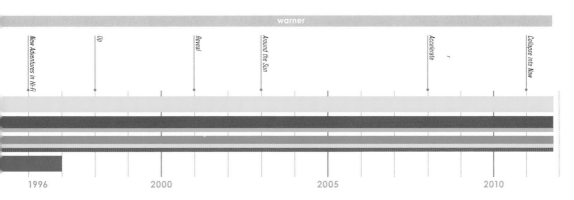

Murmur (1983)

Lifes Rich Pageant (1986)

Green (1988)

Out of Time (1991)

Automatic for the People (1992)

Monster (1994)

Up (1998)

Reveal (2001)

Around the Sun (2004)

Accelerate (2008)

Michael Stipe and **Peter Buck** opening for The Police at New York's Shea Stadium in 1983.

Stipe on the *Green* tour, at the Netherlands' Pinkpop festival, in 1989.

Buck, **Mike Mills**, **Bill Berry**, and **Stipe** around the time of *Lifes Rich Pageant*.

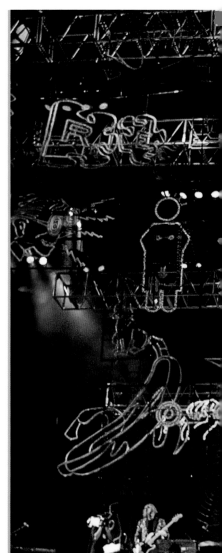

Stipe and **Buck** film a Dutch TV appearance on the day *Out of Time* is released.

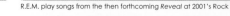

R.E.M. play songs from the then forthcoming *Reveal* at 2001's Rock in

Mills and Stipe with 1992's "Best International Group" BRIT award.

Clutching belated MTV Video Music awards for "Everybody Hurts" in the year of Monster.

Stipe at a Tibet Freedom show where they debuted songs from Up.

Rockin' with Bruce Springsteen on 2004's Vote for Change tour.

Recording a U.S. TV appearance in New York, in 2008.

the rolling stones 1962–present

Mick Jagger
b. July 26, 1943

Keith Richards
b. December 18, 1943

Brian Jones
b. February 28, 1942
d. June 3, 1969

Bill Wyman
b. October 24, 1936

Charlie Watts
b. June 2, 1941

Ian Stewart
b. July 18, 1938
d. December 12, 1985

Dick Taylor
b. January 28, 1943

Mick Taylor
b. January 17, 1948

"The Stones are a different kind of group," observed **Mick Taylor**. "I realized that when I joined them. It's not really so much their musical ability, it's just they have a certain kind of style and attitude which is unique."

Mick Jagger, **Keith Richards**, and **Brian Jones** formed The Rolling Stones in 1962 with bassist **Dick Taylor** and pianist **Ian Stewart**. By 1963 Taylor had gone (to resurface fronting The Pretty Things) and the rhythm section consisted of bassist **Bill Wyman** and drummer **Charlie Watts**. (The latter succeeded future Kinks sticksman Mick Avory, who rehearsed with the band, and Tony Chapman, with whom the Stones played their first show, in London, on July 12, 1962.)

Their name taken from the Muddy Waters song "Rollin' Stone," the group were regulars at London clubs before they signed to the Decca label—minus Stewart, who was relegated to become chief roadie and a studio-only musician. Three hits—"Come On" (the first of several Chuck Berry covers), "I Wanna Be Your Man" (written for them by Paul McCartney and John Lennon), and "Not Fade Away" (by Buddy Holly)—preceded their self-titled debut album, which topped the British chart. In America it was re-titled *England's Newest Hit Makers* and peaked at No. 11.

By the end of 1966, the group had racked up six U.K. No. 1s. "(I Can't Get No) Satisfaction" also topped the U.S. chart, while *Out of Our Heads* became their first *Billboard* album chart No. 1 in 1965. The Stones stumbled only with 1967's *Their Satanic Majesties Request,* an attempt to board *Sgt. Pepper*'s psychedelic bandwagon (though it bequeathed the fine "2,000 Light Years from Home" and "2000 Man").

A more productive reinvention yielded 1968's hard-rockin' "Jumpin' Jack Flash" and bluesy *Beggars Banquet,* paving the way for 1969's hard-rockin', bluesy, and brilliantly nasty *Let It Bleed*. The latter proved the swansong for Brian Jones, who drowned in 1969. Mick Taylor, of John Mayall's Bluesbreakers, replaced him and hence graced the 1970 live album *Get Yer Ya-Yas Out!* (drawn from a 1969 tour that effectively invented arena rock as we know it now).

As the band became superstar tax exiles, their golden era continued, thanks to 1971's cocaine-infused *Sticky Fingers*—the first of eight consecutive U.S. No. 1 studio albums. *Exile on Main St* (1972) hit a standard they could only hope to match, never exceed. *Goats Head Soup* (1973) and *It's Only Rock 'n Roll* (1974) are less celebrated, although each has their

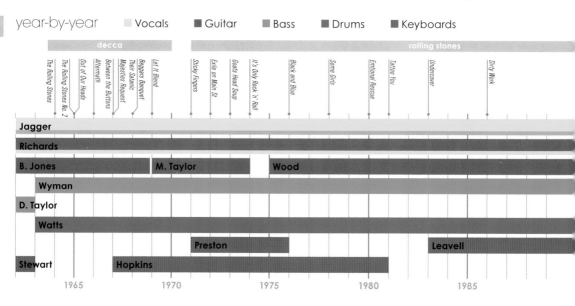

R year-by-year ▪ Vocals ▪ Guitar ▪ Bass ▪ Drums ▪ Keyboards

Ronnie Wood b. June 1, 1947	**Billy Preston** b. September 2, 1946 d. June 6, 2006	**Nicky Hopkins** b. Feb 24, 1944 d. Sept 6, 1994	**Chuck Leavell** b. April 28, 1952	**Darryl Jones** b. December 11, 1961

share of classics (the former's "Angie" and "Coming Down Again" and the latter's title track and "Time Waits for No One"). However, with heroin having made life with the band increasingly less fun, Taylor quit in 1975. Harvey Mandel and Wayne Perkins, who applied for his job, wound up on 1976's underrated *Black and Blue*, although its artwork featured the man who got the job: ex-Faces guitarist **Ronnie Wood**.

The Stones survived Richards' career-threatening drug bust in 1977 to score the biggest-selling album of their career: *Some Girls* (1978), boosted by the U.S. chart-topping "Miss You." *Emotional Rescue* (1980) continued their success into the new decade, but was eclipsed by *Tattoo You* (1981) and an ensuing stadium tour that set a visual and commercial yardstick for all that followed. (Throughout much of their career, and especially post-1980, the Stones' success has been based more on sales of tickets than of albums.)

After the live *Still Life* (1982), the Stones floundered. With even Watts dabbling in heroin, Jagger grew impatient with the band, and plotted a solo career that yielded 1985's million-selling *She's the Boss*. The Stones eked out 1983's platinum *Undercover* but, by *Dirty Work* (1986), the singer and Richards were at

each other's throats. In the ensuing hiatus, the guitarist made the excellent *Talk Is Cheap* (1988), before the Stones regrouped for *Steel Wheels* (1989). The tour that followed—the band's first in seven years—again raised the bar for everyone else. (The Stones broke their own money-making records in 1994 and 2005.)

Jagger and Richards—the "Glimmer Twins"—were jointly inducted into the American Songwriters Hall of Fame in 1993. That same year, Bill Wyman quit, to be replaced by **Darryl Jones**, only for *Voodoo Lounge* (1994) to return the Stones to the top of the U.K. chart for the first time in fourteen years.

Bridges to Babylon (1997), the best-of *Forty Licks* (2002, the year that saw Jagger knighted for services to music), and *A Bigger Bang* (2005) each prompted huge sales and tours. And, after years of hit-and-miss live albums and videos, the Stones got the memorial they deserved in the form of Martin Scorsese's movie *Shine a Light* in 2008. Two years later, a reworked version of *Exile on Main St* topped the U.K. chart and hit U.S. No. 2, a full thirty-eight years after the original had headed both lists. And, continuing to defy all naysayers, they returned to the road in late 2012 for the "50 & Counting" tour. **BS/BM**

■ Aerophones

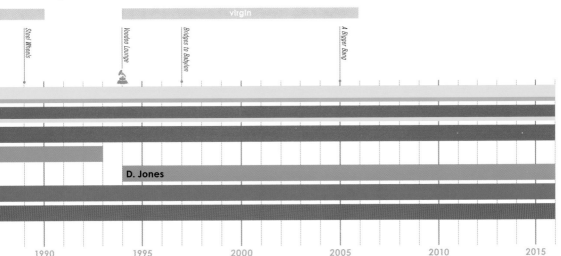

The Rolling Stones (1964)

Aftermath (1966)

Beggars Banquet (1968)

Let It Bleed (1969)

Sticky Fingers (1971)

Exile on Main St (1972)

Some Girls (1978)

Tattoo You (1981)

Voodoo Lounge (1994)

A Bigger Bang (2005)

Performing "Not Fade Away" on U.K. TV's *Ready Steady Go!*, 1964.

Brian Jones's sitar was key to the *Aftermath* classic "Paint It Black."

Guitarist **Mick Taylor**, who took over from Jones on *Let It Bleed*.

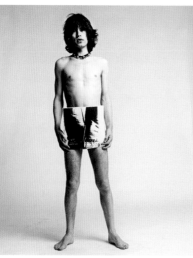

Jagger poses with the Andy Warhol–designed *Sticky Fingers* sleeve.

Jones and **Mick Jagger** recording the brilliant *Beggars Banquet* in London, June 1968.

Jagger, **Richards**, and eternal "new boy" **Ronnie Wood** on the *Tattoo You* tour in 1982.

Taylor and **Jagger** at New York's Madison Square Garden in 1972.

Wood backstage at a show in New York with Paul McCartney.

Jagger and **Richards** on a stage set designed by Japanese artist Kazuhide Yamazaki.

Jagger on the spectacular *Voodoo Lounge* stage set in 1994.

Wood, **Jagger**, and **Richards** at the prestigious Super Bowl half-time show at Ford Field in Detroit, in 2006.

the saints 1974–present

Chris Bailey
b. 1959

Ed Kuepper
b. December 20, 1955

Ivor Hay
b. not known

Kym Bradshaw
b. May 21, 1954

Algy Ward
b. July 7, 1959

Barry Francis
b. not known

The Saints stake a claim to be among the founding fathers of punk, their influence far exceeding their sales. **Chris Bailey** (vocals), **Ed Kuepper** (guitar), and **Ivor Hay** (drums)—schoolmates in Brisbane, Australia —founded the group in 1974 and brought in Jeffrey Wegener (drums). Hay switched to bass until **Kym Bradshaw** joined, after a cameo by Doug Balmanno.

In 1976, their superb debut single, "(I'm) Stranded," earned rave reviews in the U.K. and prompted EMI to sign them. Reminiscent of the Stooges and New York Dolls, they epitomized doomed punk alienation without slavishly following the fashions that pervaded the English scene. Their first album, *(I'm) Stranded* (1977)—also containing the single "Erotic Neurotic"— is a fine, rough example of the genre. They moved to London soon afterward, where **Algy Ward** (later to join The Damned) replaced Bradshaw on bass.

"This Perfect Day," a minor U.K. hit, featured on the excellent *Eternally Yours* (1978), which had a slightly smoother sound. The horn-embellished "Know Your Product" and haunting "Memories Are Made of This" pointed the way for the same year's more soulful, jazzier *Prehistoric Sounds*. "The whole punk rock thing was going on," marveled Nick Cave to

writer Barney Hoskyns, "and they did things with brass sections." Confounding their fans' expectations of a straightforward punk approach, it was not a success, despite critical acclaim. Dropped by their label, the original version of The Saints split in 1979. Hay and Kuepper (who has enjoyed a thriving solo career with a series of other bands) returned to Australia.

Re-forming the group almost immediately, Bailey recruited new disciples **Janine Hall** (bass), **Mark Birmingham** (drums), Bruce Callaway (guitar) and **Barry Francis** (guitar). Bailey brought back the prodigal Hay on drums and keyboards for *The Monkey Puzzle* (1981), while Iain Shedden (drums) came in for 1982's *I Thought This Was Love, But This Ain't Casablanca* (known outside Australia as *Out in the Jungle… Where Things Ain't So Pleasant*). Brian James of The Damned guested on guitar. Both albums had relatively commercial aims that remained mostly unrealized. Meanwhile, guitarists Chris Burnham and Laurie Cuffe had joined, the Saints apparently having a revolving door policy for personnel. (Iain Shedden was to have five separate spells with the group.)

By the time of *A Little Madness to Be Free* (1984), Bailey had released 1983's solo *Casablanca* and

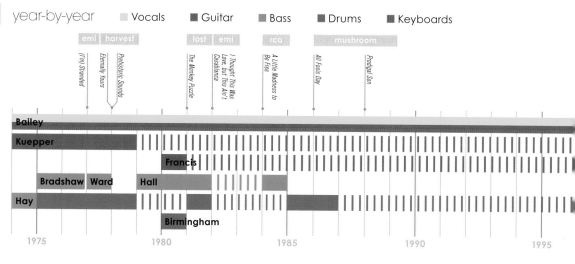

year-by-year   ▨ Vocals   ■ Guitar   ■ Bass   ■ Drums   ■ Keyboards

Janine Hall
b. not known
d. May 2008

Mark Birmingham
b. not known

moved back to Australia, where Bradshaw and (yet again) Hay rejoined. A 1984 tour also saw cameos by Kuepper and The Birthday Party's Tracy Pew.

After short stints by Louise Elliott (saxophone) and Richard Burgman (guitar), bassist Arturo LaRizza joined for the first of four spells. Sales of *All Fools Day* (1986) were boosted by the strong single "Just Like Fire Would," which belatedly won The Saints recognition in the U.S. Joe Chiofalo came in on keyboards, Hay left again, and Shedden rejoined before their next recording. *Prodigal Son* (1988)—including the singles "Grain of Sand" and "Music Goes Round My Head," an old Easybeats number—bolstered their newfound popularity. However, never ones to follow a straightforward path, the Saints made no attempt to follow it up. More changes of personnel in 1991 saw Chiofalo joined by Dror Erez on keyboards, Tony Faehse (guitar), and Peter Jones (drums). After these lineup switches, they went into abeyance once more while Bailey concentrated on further solo projects.

In 1994, he moved to Sweden and assembled a new lineup, with drummer Andreas Jornvill, bassist Joakim Tack, and guitarists Mans Wieslander and Ian Walsh. Neither *Howling* (1996), after which the lineup

changed again, nor *Everybody Knows the Monkey* (1998) generated the original excitement, although both had stripped-back production and contained characteristically thought-provoking songs. A new incarnation—with drummer Martin Bjerregaard, bassist Michael Bayliss, and guitarist Andy Faulkner—became a fairly stable unit, by Saints standards.

By the time of *Spit the Blues Out* (2002)—its title a fair summary of its more blues-based content—the group, with Pete Wilkinson (drums) replacing Bjerregaard and alternating with Shedden, had moved to Amsterdam in the Netherlands. They stayed there for the resolutely punkish *Nothing Is Straight in My House* (2005), the players now consisting of Bailey, guitarist Marty Willson-Piper (formerly of The Church and All About Eve), bassist Caspar Wijnberg (latterly succeeded by Jane Mack), and drummer Wilkinson.

Thirty years after their debut, *Imperious Delirium* (2006)—on which Bailey played all the guitars after Willson-Piper departed—proved the fire was still burning. Not the least remarkable aspect of the Saints' long career is how consistent their output has been despite all the changes—a tribute to Bailey's enduring vision. **MiH**

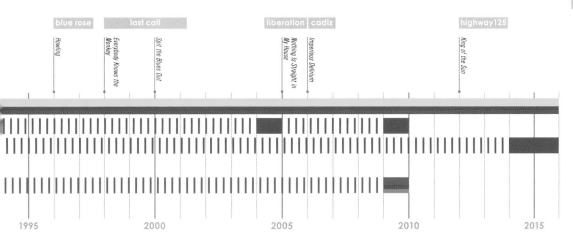

santana 1966–present

Carlos Santana
b. July 20, 1947

Gregg Rolie
b. June 17, 1947

David Brown
b. February 15, 1947

Michael Shrieve
b. July 6, 1949

José "Chepito" Areas
b. July 25, 1946

Michael Carabello
b. November 18, 1947

Bob Livingston
b. November 26, 1948

Neal Schon
b. February 27, 1954

Smooth by name, smooth by nature, **Carlos Santana** enjoyed his biggest hit ever with "Smooth," which reached No. 1 in October 1999—exactly thirty years after his powerhouse percussive Afro-Latin rock band had a first entry in the U.S. Top 100 with "Jingo." Sung by Matchbox Twenty's Rob Thomas, "Smooth" stayed at the top for twelve weeks, going on to win Grammys for Song of the Year, and Best Pop Collaboration with Vocals. (Its parent album, *Supernatural,* bagged Album of the Year). From the first bars, you know it can only be Carlos on guitar: the timbre and style of his effortlessly smooth and rounded samba-blues is instantly recognizable. Other Santana trademarks include long, even sustains, alongside occasional psychedelic wails and high-speed jazz licks.

"Smooth" was the first of two smashes from *Supernatural* ("Maria Maria" hit No. 1 for ten weeks), which has sold fifteen million copies in the U.S. alone. It earned so many Grammy nominations that, when Sheryl Crow won Best Female Rock Vocal in 2000, she thanked Carlos for not being in that category.

It was all a long way from the guitarist's humble Mexican beginnings, when—with his mariachi musician father—he played in Tijuana brothels and saloons. His mother took the family to San Francisco, where Carlos formed the Santana Bluesband in 1966.

In the best of its ever-changing incarnations, the band showcased **Gregg Rolie**'s rich organ sound, **David Brown** on bass, **Michael Shrieve** on drums, and **José "Chepito" Areas** on percussion. Concert promoter/producer Bill Graham was an early fan, hence their early shows at San Francisco's Fillmore West and Carlos's first live recording (from the same venue), as part of 1968's *The Live Adventures of Mike Bloomfield and Al Kooper.*

At Graham's insistence, Santana—newly signed to the Columbia label—were enlisted for the Woodstock festival in August 1969. The most significant concert of its generation brought the group to international attention. Millions saw the movie of the event—in which their "Soul Sacrifice" accompanied the audience's mud-soaked antics—and heard the soundtrack triple album. "All of a sudden we went from the streets of San Francisco to arenas," Santana told *Billboard* book author Craig Rosen. "It was kind of like riding the rapids with everything going by so fast."

A self-titled debut album was a straightforward Latin-blues-rock calling card, but *Abraxas* (1970)

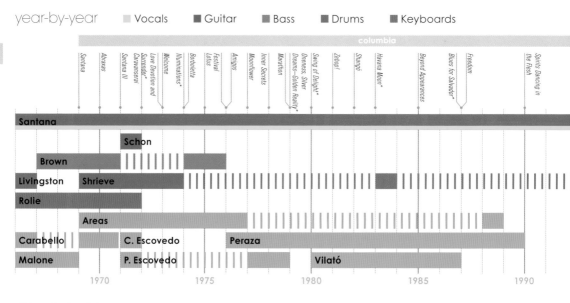

year-by-year   ■ Vocals   ■ Guitar   ■ Bass   ■ Drums   ■ Keyboards

Coke Escovedo
b. Apr 30, 1941
d. Apr 30, 1985

Pete Escovedo
b. October 13, 1935

Armando Peraza
b. May 30, 1924

Marcus Malone
b. Unknown

Orestes Vilató
b. May 4, 1944

established the Santana sound, with songs such as Fleetwood Mac's blues-drenched "Black Magic Woman," Tito Puente's salsa "Oye Como Va," and the self-penned instrumental "Samba Pa Ti." The album soared into the U.K. Top Ten and to No. 1 in the U.S.

Neal Schon was added on guitar and vocals and **Coke Escovedo** on percussion for 1971's *Santana* (known as *Santana III,* to distinguish it from the band's identically-titled debut). This also made No. 1 in the U.S., despite tensions that had arisen between the band members. "We would fight like cats and dogs to create that chemistry," Santana told Craig Rosen. "You could hear us cussing at each other between takes." Rolie and Schon quit after the album's release, to later find fame and fortune with Journey.

Caravanserai (1972) saw Santana move toward jazz fusion, as Shrieve's influence grew—he and Carlos shared a passion for players like Miles Davis, John Coltrane, and Herbie Hancock. A 1972 version of "In a Silent Way" was a tribute to Davis, and Carlos later guested on fusion stars Weather Report's *This Is This* (1986). The latter was one of more than fifty collaborations that Carlos has undertaken, from 1972's *Carlos Santana and Buddy Miles, Live!* and 1973's

Love Devotion Surrender (with jazz-fusion guitarist John McLaughlin), to 1989's "The Healer," from John Lee Hooker's comeback of the same name. Carlos collected a Grammy for *Blues for Salvador* (1987), a solo album featuring Willie Nelson, Booker T. Jones, and The Fabulous Thunderbirds. He also wrote the score for 1986's Ritchie Havens biopic *La Bamba,* which brought Latin pop to a new generation.

After the career-revitalizing *Supernatural*—which featured Eric Clapton and Dave Matthews, alongside Rob Thomas—the all-star formula was re-applied on *Shaman* (2002). The album (boasting Nickelback's Chad Kroeger, among others) gave Santana a fourth U.S. No.1 and saw the return of Shrieve.

Over eighty side-men have come and gone but Carlos's smooth guitar sound remains. This influential guitarist (not least on Prince) also dared to put his stamp on a clutch of hard rock standards on 2010's *Guitar Heaven.* Amid star turns by Joe Cocker, Rob Thomas, Chris Cornell of Soundgarden, Scott Weiland of Stone Temple Pilots—on songs by the likes of Led Zeppelin and the Stones—the implausible highlight was an audacious and typically idiosyncratic take on AC/DC's "Back in Black," featuring rapper Nas. **JaH**

■ Other percussion

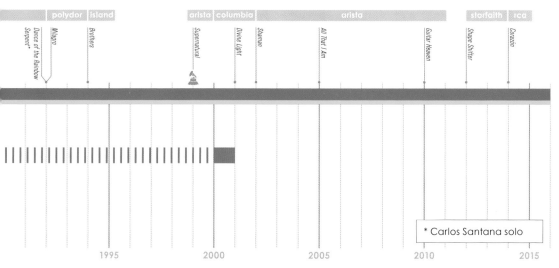

* Carlos Santana solo

scorpions 1965–present

Klaus Meine
b. May 25, 1948

F

Rudolf Schenker
b. August 31, 1948

Matthias Jabs
b. October 25, 1955

James Kottak
b. December 26, 1962

Pawel Maciwoda
b. February 20, 1967

Francis Buchholz
b. February 19, 1954

Herman Rarebell
b. November 18, 1949

Michael Schenker
b. January 10, 1955

German hard rock has rarely been harder or more rocking than in the hands of the Scorpions, the Hanover quintet that has straddled stages for an astounding forty-seven years and counting. Although in 2010 the group announced plans to retire after a final tour, it would be unwise to write them off.

Guitarist **Rudolf Schenker** formed the band in 1965, with an initial lineup that had mostly dissipated by the release of their debut album, *Lonesome Crow*, seven years later. Musicians passing through the ranks since then have included guitarists extraordinaire **Uli Jon Roth** and Schenker's younger brother **Michael**. But the most commercially successful lineup featured Rudolf Schenker, singer **Klaus Meine**, guitarist **Matthias Jabs**, bassist **Francis Buchholz**, and drummer **Herman Rarebell**. This quintet was responsible for many of the Scorpions' biggest hits in a golden era stretching from the late seventies to the early nineties.

The band first impacted on the public outside Germany thanks to their controversial album artwork. *Virgin Killer* depicted a naked ten-year-old girl, *Lovedrive* boasted a female breast, and *Animal Magnetism* featured a woman sitting faithfully to attention alongside a dog. Once these follies were discarded, however, the Scorpions were revealed as a powerful group of serious musicians. On guitar, they boasted two successive stars: Michael Schenker, then, when he was poached by British rockers UFO, Uli Jon Roth (known at the time as Ulrich Roth). The latter debuted on *Fly to the Rainbow* (1974), but made his mark on *In Trance* (1975), the best of their early albums (not least because he suggested its cover, on which a model with an exposed breast holds his Stratocaster).

However, by the time of 1977's *Taken by Force*, reported new drummer Rarebell, "The band was divided between Ulrich Roth and the others. To me, the band really started to work as a unit after he left."

Having secured a loyal following at home and in Japan (hence 1978's live *Tokyo Tapes*, Roth's swansong), the Scorpions' popularity exploded when they ditched the last lingering acid rock elements of their formative years in favor of big-chorused arena anthems. *Lovedrive* (1979)—the debut of Matthias Jabs (although Michael Schenker, who had fled UFO, guested on three cuts)—charted internationally, winning fans including the young Metallica and Billy Corgan of The Smashing Pumpkins. (The latter would later guest on 2007's *Humanity: Hour 1*.)

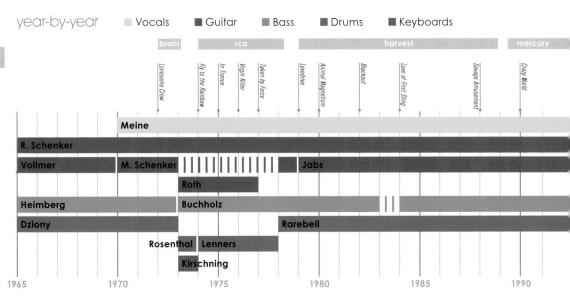

year-by-year   ■ Vocals   ■ Guitar   ■ Bass   ■ Drums   ■ Keyboards

brain | rca | harvest | mercury

Lonesome Crow | Fly to the Rainbow | In Trance | Virgin Killer | Taken by Force | Lovedrive | Animal Magnetism | Blackout | Love at First Sting | Savage Amusement | Crazy World

Meine

R. Schenker

Vollmer | M. Schenker | Jabs

Roth

Heimberg | Buchholz

Dziony | Rarebell

Rosenthal | Lenners

Kirschning

1965   1970   1975   1980   1985   1990

Lothar Heimberg b. Unknown **Wolfgang Dziony** b. 1949 **Karl-Heinz Vollmer** b. Unknown **Uli Jon Roth** b. December 18, 1954 **Jürgen Rosenthal** b. July 29, 1948 **Achim Kirschning** b. Unknown **Rudy Lenners** b. Unknown **Ralph Rieckermann** b. August 8, 1962

The group's escalating fortunes saw a run of multi-platinum albums, beginning with *Animal Magnetism* (1980) and *Blackout* (1982). They hit a peak with 1984's *Love at First Sting,* which yielded the hits "Rock You Like a Hurricane" (which even found its way into the formative Green Day's repertoire), "Still Loving You," and "Big City Nights." The charms of the Scorpions' live show (the visual highlight of which came when the members formed a human pyramid) was brilliantly captured on 1985's gonzoid *World Wide Live.* "We give the people all our energy every night," Meine told *Kerrang!*. "We'll go onstage and rock our ass off."

Inevitably, such momentum could last only for so long, and 1988's *Savage Amusement*—home to the hit "Rhythm of Love"—seemed to bookend the band's time in the big league. However, an unexpected leap into the mainstream came three years later, courtesy of Meine's ballad "Wind of Change." The song, heralded by the singer's whistled melody, had been inspired by the group's trip to Russia in 1988, where they played to 150,000 people in Leningrad. "We had never experienced anything like it..." Meine reported. "Soldiers cried when we played [the *Lovedrive* ballad] 'Holiday'." The song was recorded in the summer

of 1990—when the Scorpions participated in Roger Waters's epic re-staging of Pink Floyd's *The Wall* in Berlin, and returned to Russia as conquering heroes for a show alongside Bon Jovi, Ozzy Osbourne, and Mötley Crüe—and appeared on that winter's *Crazy World*. The following year, "Wind of Change" became a sort of unofficial anthem for the fall of the Soviet Union and German reunification. With global sales running into millions, it became the best-selling single of all-time by a German act. This success also ensured the band's survival at a point when grunge was poised to eradicate many traditional rockers.

Thereafter, the Scorpions occupied a respected position as a classic rock band, despite an unsettling foray into pop territory (1999's *Eye II Eye*), an orchestral folly (2000's *Moment of Glory*), and an unplugged live album (2001's *Acoustica*). *Sting in the Tail* (2010) even restored them to the U.S. Top Thirty after a seventeen-year absence. A 2012 album of re-recorded classics, *Comeblack,* was alleged to be their last—but, after so many years, it seems the Scorpions as a concept is bigger than any individual or group of musicians. After all, as Meine remarked, "We are not in this for the fashion or the fame or any of that shit." **JM/BM**

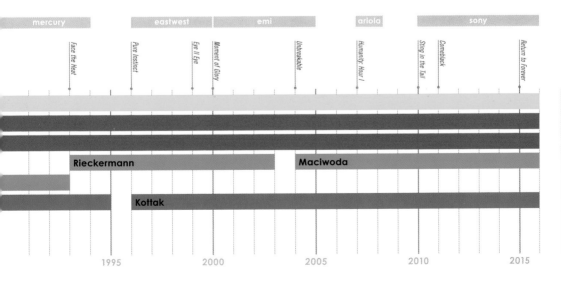

Taken by Force (1977)

Lovedrive (1979)

Animal Magnetism (1980)

Love at First Sting (1984)

Savage Amusement (1988)

Crazy World (1990)

Eye II Eye (1999)

Unbreakable (2004)

Humanity Hour 1 (2007)

Comeblack (2011)

Vintage Scorpions: guitarist **Uli Jon Roth**, bassist **Francis Buchholz**, guitarist **Rudy Schenker**, singer **Klaus Meine**, and drummer **Herman Rarebell**.

New guitarist **Matthias Jabs** rocks Britain's Reading festival in 1979.

Schenker, Meine, and Jabs: no one ever accused them of being subtle.

Buchholz, **Schenker**, **Meine**, and **Jabs** with the world at their feet.

Rarebell, Meine, Buchholz, Schenker, and Jabs in the hair metal era in which *Savage Amusement* was released.

With Roger Waters at his 1990 performance of *The Wall* in Berlin.

Schenker stings at the Universal Amphitheatre in Los Angeles, in November 2004.

Schenker rocks Le Zenith in Paris on the Eye II Eye tour.

Schenker and Jabs at France's Vieilles Charrues Festival in 2011.

Pawel Maciwoda proves he's the man for the job as the *Unbreakable* tour hits London.

Meine at the Bercy in Paris, in 2011, on what the Scorpions claimed was their final tour.

bob seger 1968–present

Bob Seger
b. May 6, 1945

Chris Campbell
b. Unknown

Drew Abbott
b. January 13, 1947

Charlie Allen Martin
b. June 6, 1952

Alto Reed
b. Unknown

Robyn Robbins
b. 1951

"Bob Seger is the voice of the working man," enthused Kid Rock, "and living proof of the American dream."

Michigan native Seger was a nomadic veteran of Detroit's music scene by the time he formed The Silver Bullet Band in 1974. Blessed with a timeless voice that would strike a chord with the "heartland" rock movement, the singer-songwriter began his journey as a sixteen-year-old with The Decibels (a key influence on another Detroit star, Iggy Pop). After a decade-long apprenticeship with a handful of hopefuls, The Bob Seger System infiltrated the U.S. Top Twenty with "Ramblin' Gamblin' Man" (from a 1969 album of the same name)—but it was six years before Seger returned to the singles chart, riddled with Silver Bullets.

The original Bullets—guitarist **Drew Abbott**, bassist **Chris Campbell**, keyboard player Rick Manasa (replaced by **Robyn Robbins** in 1975), drummer **Charlie Allen Martin** (replaced by **David Teegarden** in 1977), and saxophonist **Alto Reed**—appeared, uncredited, on Seger's Seven (1974) and Beautiful Loser (1975). As the celebrated Silver Bullet Band, they were first officially billed on 1976's blockbusting Live Bullet. Like Kiss's Alive!, it was recorded at Detroit's Cobo Hall

and—again like Alive!—it broke into the big time an act more famous for their shows than their records.

Night Moves (1976) took the band into the U.S. Top Ten—although four of its nine tracks were recorded with Seger's "other" group, the Muscle Shoals Rhythm Section (the R&B collective who had backed stars like Aretha Franklin and Wilson Pickett). The album's title song rose into the U.S. and Canadian Top Fives, and gave Seger a first, albeit minor, hit in the U.K.

In 1978, Stranger in Town added more classics to his repertoire: "Still the Same," "Hollywood Nights," "We've Got Tonite," and "Old Time Rock and Roll." (The latter's iconic status was secured when Tom Cruise mimed to it in the 1983 movie Risky Business.)

The group reached a commercial peak in 1980 with the two-time Grammy winner Against the Wind, featuring Eagles stars Glenn Frey, Don Henley, and Timothy B. Schmidt on the hit "Fire Lake." (Seger had written the chorus for, and sung backing vocals on, the Eagles' 1979 hit "Heartache Tonight.") Despite scathing reviews, Against the Wind ended Pink Floyd's fifteen-week run at No. 1 with The Wall on the way to six chart-topping weeks of its own.

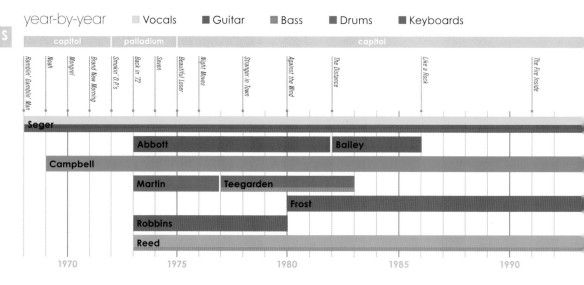

year-by-year ▢ Vocals ▪ Guitar ▪ Bass ▪ Drums ▪ Keyboards

capitol | palladium | capitol

Ramblin' Gamblin' Man | Noah | Mongrel | Brand New Morning | Smokin' O.P.'s | Back in '72 | Seven | Beautiful Loser | Night Moves | Stranger in Town | Against the Wind | The Distance | Like a Rock | The Fire Inside

Seger

Abbott · Bailey

Campbell

Martin · Teegarden

Frost

Robbins

Reed

1970 · 1975 · 1980 · 1985 · 1990

David Teegarden
b. Unknown

Craig Frost
b. April 20, 1948

Dawayne Bailey
b. Unknown

Seger's charges returned to the Top Ten with each of their next four releases: 1981's live *Nine Tonight*, 1982's *The Distance* (including the hit "Shame on the Moon," featuring Glenn Frey), 1986's *Like a Rock* (featuring Don Henley and Timothy B. Schmidt), and 1991's *The Fire Inside* (featuring Bruce Hornsby and members of Was Not Was, Tom Petty's Heartbreakers, the Eagles, and Bruce Springsteen's E Street Band).

In 1983, Kenny Rogers and Sheena Easton took "We've Got Tonite" to No. 1 on the U.S. and Canadian country charts. Meanwhile, Prince found himself on a U.S. jaunt at the same time as the Silver Bullet Band were touring *The Distance*. Intrigued by Seger's country-tinged anthems, Prince wrote his own: "Purple Rain." In 1987, a solo Seger squeezed in his first (and, to date, only) U.S. chart-topping single, "Shakedown," from the Eddie Murphy movie *Beverly Hills Cop II*.

In 1994 came *Greatest Hits*, featuring a previously unreleased Chuck Berry song ("C'est la Vie") and iconic cover art showing Seger—guitar in hand—standing on a Californian railroad. In 2009, *Billboard* named it the biggest-selling catalog album of the decade, ahead of The Beatles and Michael Jackson.

Among *Greatest Hits'* gems is the *Live Bullet* version of "Turn the Page" (originally from 1973's *Back in '72*), a song that became a 1998 hit in the heavy hands of Metallica. (It had previously been covered by country star Waylon Jennings in 1985. Jennings also tackled "Against the Wind" that year, with Willie Nelson, Kris Kristofferson, and Johnny Cash.) Other rockers to tackle Seger songs include Thin Lizzy (*Back in '72*'s "Rosalie" on their *Fighting*, 1975), Status Quo (*Seven*'s "Get Out of Denver" on 1996's *Don't Stop* and "Old Time Rock and Roll" on 2000's *Famous in the Last Century*), and Rod Stewart ("Still the Same" on his 2006 U.S. chart-topping album of the same name). "I try to write about what I know, maybe with a little content," the modest Seger told *Q* magazine. "Songwriting is miniature work; you don't have a lot of time with your material, so you have to pinpoint it."

Seger was inducted into the Rock & Roll Hall of Fame in 2004, while *Face the Promise*, the Silver Bullet Band's first studio album since 1995, returned them to familiar Top Ten territory in 2006. A new hits set, *Rock & Roll Never Forgets* (2011), is testament to one of the most underrated groups in rock 'n' roll history. **MW/BM**

■ Aerophones   ▨ Other percussion

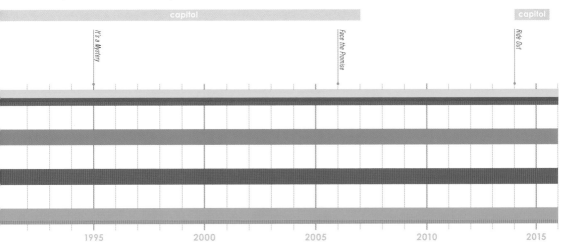

sepultura 1984–present

Max Cavalera
b. August 4, 1969

Igor Cavalera
b. September 4, 1970

Paulo Jr.
b. April 30, 1968

Wagner Lamounier
b. Unknown

Jairo Guedz
b. November 25, 1968

Andreas Kisser
b. August 24, 1968

Back in 1985, with Brazil emerging from the grip of a twenty-year military dictatorship, the country's most celebrated metal exponents (congratulations if you can name any of the less celebrated ones) adopted "scary" names and stepped out of the shadows.

Rocked by the death of their diplomat father and influenced by Led Zeppelin, Black Sabbath, and Deep Purple, school drop-outs **Max** "Possessed" **Cavalera** (lead vocals) and **Igor** "Skullcrusher" **Cavalera** (drums) channeled their grief into music making. The brothers from Belo Horizonte hired **Jairo** "Tormentor" **Guedz** (lead guitar) and **Paulo** "Destructor" **Jr.** (bass) and called themselves Sepultura, Portuguese for "grave." Apparently, Max opted for the name while translating Motörhead's "Dancing on Your Grave" into Portuguese—"Dançando em sua sepultura."

The four-piece first put their fearsome attitude and indecipherable lyrics on record with the self-produced "Bestial Devastation" EP. Recorded in just two days, the release featured "Antichrist," written by founding member and original vocalist **Wagner** "Antichrist" **Lamounier**, who left Sepultura in 1985 to form the long-running extreme metal outfit Sarcófago (and, later, to become a professor of economics).

Sepultura's first full-length release, *Morbid Visions*, followed in 1986. With the band as yet unable to write in English, the album was shaped by the Satanic verses of influential British metallers Venom. "After we got acquainted with Venom, we stopped listening to Iron Maiden and all that lighter stuff," confirmed Igor.

The group relocated to São Paulo, and Guedz was replaced by **Andreas Kisser**. They forged ahead with *Schizophrenia* (1987) and *Beneath the Remains* (1989). "Total fuckin' hate!" enthused *Kerrang!* magazine in a coveted 'five K' review of the latter, a thrash classic.

By the time they got to Phoenix, Arizona—the host of an early date on 1990's U.S. and European *Beneath the Remains* tour—Brazil's finest were making all the right noises (albeit severely loud ones). "If it's heavier," Max Cavalera told *Kerrang!*, "we're happier."

Homeward bound in early 1991, they entertained 100,000 headbangers at the Rock in Rio festival before unleashing *Arise*, whose title track was shunned by MTV America owing to its apocalyptic religious imagery. The socially adept *Chaos A.D.* (1993), infused with industrial and hardcore punk, gave Sepultura their first Top Forty hit in America and, bizarrely, a Top Ten single ("Territory") in Ireland.

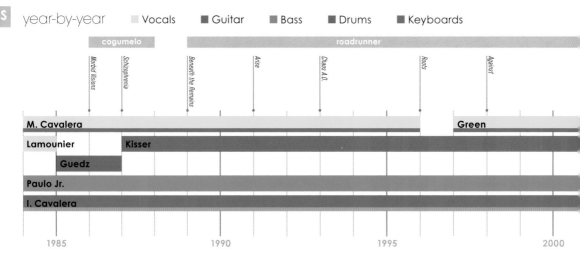

year-by-year   ▧ Vocals   ■ Guitar   ■ Bass   ■ Drums   ■ Keyboards

Derrick Green
b. January 20, 1971

Jean Dolabella
b. May 14, 1978

Eloy Casagrande
b. January 29, 1991

The group hit a creative pinnacle with *Roots* (1996), which introduced native Brazilian percussion and influences to their ferocious musical styling. Peaking at No. 4 in the U.K. and smashing into Top Tens across Europe, *Roots*'s defining moments were the singles "Roots Bloody Roots," which narrowly missed the top spot in the heavy metal haven of Finland, and the throbbing, tribal "Ratamahatta," complete with the best music video you have probably never seen.

"Ratamahatta" also marked the departure of Soulfly-bound frontman Max Cavalera, sparked by the death of his stepson with Gloria Bujnowski—his wife and the group's manager—in an automobile accident. Weeks after the tragedy, when the rest of the group confronted the singer about replacing her with a new manager, the still traumatized Max quit in disgust. His replacement was the incendiary Cleveland, Ohio-born vocalist **Derrick Green**.

In the midst of an apparently terminal sales decline, Green slowly won over the skeptics—and no doubt a fair few Max Cavalera fans—with passionate, powerhouse vocals on *Against* (1998), *Nation* (2001), *Roorback* (2003), and *Dante XXI* (2006), the latter the final Sepultura album to feature Igor Cavalera. When Igor reunited with brother Max to form the Cavalera Conspiracy, drumming duties were handled by **Jean Dolabella**, who, in turn, made way for twenty-year-old **Eloy Casagrande** in November 2011.

Post-Cavaleras Sepultura still had a few tricks up their sleeves. In 2008, in a departure from their heavy/death/thrash roots, they starred in a Brazilian TV commercial for Volkswagen, performing a bossa nova track. Toward the end of the same year, they appeared at the Latin Grammy Awards to promote their concept album *A-Lex* (2009). Green, Paulo Jr., Kisser, and Dolabella kicked off 2010 in São Paulo sharing the stage with Metallica in front of 100,000 people, while their album *Kairos* (2011) features a compelling version of The Prodigy's "Firestarter."

Sepultura have sold millions of albums worldwide, impressive given that their lyrics and "machine-gun-tempo mayhem," as the *Phoenix New Times* put it, are impenetrable to the average human ear. MTV even described Sepultura as "perhaps the most important heavy metal band of the nineties," which speaks volumes given that the odds were stacked against them from the start in terms of nationality, language, and the extreme nature of their music. **MW**

■ Other percussion

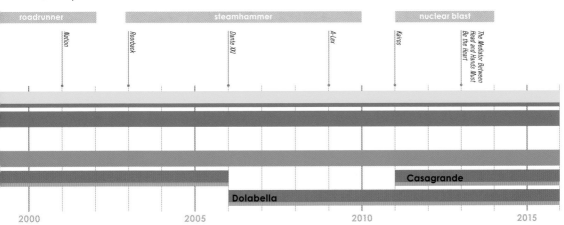

roadrunner | steamhammer | nuclear blast

Nation | Roorback | Dante XXI | A-Lex | Kairos | The Mediator Between Head and Hands Must Be the Heart

Casagrande

Dolabella

2000 | 2005 | 2010 | 2015

sex pistols 1975–present

Johnny Rotten
b. January 31, 1956

Sid Vicious
b. May 10, 1957
d. February 2, 1979

Steve Jones
b. September 3, 1955

Paul Cook
b. July 20, 1956

Glen Matlock
b. August 27, 1956

Britain of the mid-seventies seemed a country drained of color. Gray and grainy it may have been, but many people still had an attachment to the status quo, which explains the impact of the band that came to be seen as the public face of punk. "I hate hippies," said **Johnny Rotten** in April 1976. "I hate long hair. I hate pub bands." What he thought of another staple of the day—progressive rock—was earlier made clear when, still known as John Lydon, he walked into the shop owned by entrepreneur Malcolm McLaren and designer Vivienne Westwood wearing a Pink Floyd t-shirt self-amended with "I hate."

That was around the point when youthful alienation started to coalesce into something more. However, **Steve Jones**, in his days as a frontman, and drummer **Paul Cook** had been messing around since the beginning of the decade. Bassist **Glen Matlock** entered the frame in 1974, the same year that trendspotter *par excellence* McLaren was sensing something in the air. A short stint as manager of the New York Dolls whetted his appetite.

It was clear that Jones was better suited to a prominent supporting role, so he shunted across to guitar. That left a vacancy to front a band—by now known as QT Jones & His Sex Pistols—that Richard Hell and Dolls rhythm guitarist Sylvain Sylvain turned down.

Instead, Rotten, as he was soon to be known, became a home-grown legend more celebrated than either.

Controversy was to follow the band everywhere. Whether this was the grand design of McLaren or events that, with hindsight, he credited himself with manipulating, depends on your view of him. With 1976's "Anarchy in the UK" laid down as a marker, the group was passed around like a bomb about to go off: within six months, EMI and A&M signed, paid, then dropped them (both labels were namechecked in "EMI," issued by Virgin.) Then Matlock was dismissed—allegedly for liking Abba and The Beatles—and Rotten's friend John "**Sid Vicious**" Ritchie was brought in. All image and attitude, the latter proved better at making headlines than making music. (Motörhead's Lemmy, who tried to tutor Vicious, told Q magazine: "He had no aptitude for the bass whatsoever… He didn't play it, he hit it. He might as well have been playing air guitar with a broom." Steve Jones played bass on much of the Pistols' post-Matlock output.)

Most of the population had little understanding of the band's method of communication. But opponents deciphered enough of the language used during an early-evening TV appearance—and then brandished on the cover of *Never Mind the Bollocks Here's the Sex Pistols*—to recoil in horror and even take their hysteria

year-by-year ■ Vocals ■ Guitar ■ Bass ■ Drums

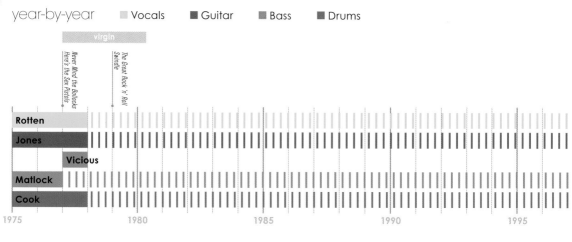

3.7M
*Never Mind the Bollocks,
Here's the Sex Pistols*
(1977)

250,000
*Flogging a Dead
Horse*
(1980)

500,000
Kiss This
(1992)

250,000
Filthy Lucre Live
(1996)

into courtrooms. With all this free publicity, how could the album not assume the U.K. No. 1 slot? *Rolling Stone* saw the changing of the guard: "The rock wars of the 1970s have begun." When *Never Mind...* topped the long-player charts, justice was served after Rod Stewart's "I Don't Want to Talk About It" had denied the Pistols the same spot in the singles rundown for 1977's "God Save the Queen." (Jones later admitted that a Stewart album was the first record he bought.)

Tours were announced and canceled; members were beaten up—in Rotten's case, by aggrieved royalists. As Jones later recalled, without Matlock's melodies, "We were just slung in the deep end and didn't have the time to breathe, much less think about writing songs." With the band in bad shape, shows on Christmas Day 1977 in Britain's Yorkshire (one, oddly, in front of an audience mainly of children) preceded a U.S. tour that was never likely to pass without incident. In midwest and southern states especially, the atmosphere was more hostile than harmonious.

Six months earlier, Rotten had said, "As soon as it gets really boring is when I'm going to fucking stop." Come the last day of the U.S. tour, Vicious was in drug disintegration and, recalled Jones, "I was hating it." From the Winterland Ballroom stage in San Francisco, a version of the Stooges' "No Fun" was a fitting finale.

Staring at the audience, Rotten hammered the point home: "Ever get the feeling you've been cheated?"

The band was dead in the water, but even a corpse can be squeezed for cash. *The Great Rock 'n' Roll Swindle* of early 1979, directed by Julien Temple, took a motley crew of characters (including on-the-run Great Train Robber Ronnie Biggs), an even motlier collection of covers (which made for bizarrely successful singles, such as Vicious's version of "My Way"), and a few fabulous ideas for a double album that preceded McLaren's self-mythologizing film of the same name. It was time that everyone went off and did their own thing: Rotten reverted to Lydon and formed PiL; Cook and Jones became The Professionals. Vicious's sudden death surprised no one.

Just shy of twenty years since the unleashing of "Anarchy in the UK," Lydon, Jones, Cook, and Matlock reunited for a tour. Its third date—in the singer's home territory, London's Finsbury Park—was recorded for 1996's surprisingly fiery *Filthy Lucre Live*.

The group has since belched back into life for further comebacks. And while they may claim otherwise, the expiry of their outsider status was confirmed by a 2006 induction into the Rock and Roll Hall of Fame. "Sex Pistols is a business," admitted Jones, "and we have to keep the ball rolling." **CB**

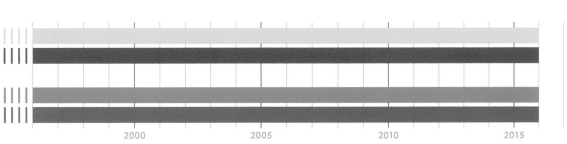

siouxsie and the banshees 1976–2002

Siouxsie Sioux
b. May 27, 1957

Steve Severin
b. September 25, 1955

Kenny Morris
b. February 1, 1957

Peter "P.T." Fenton
b. unknown

John McKay
b. unknown

Budgie
b. August 21, 1957

"I don't embrace the 'legacy' thing," **Siouxsie Sioux** declared in 2007, punk to the last. "I just want to do what I do, and leave me the fuck alone." Fellow stars begged to differ. Her band's songs have been covered by LCD Soundsystem ("Slowdive"), The Mars Volta ("Pull to Bits"), Simple Minds ("Christine"), and Tricky ("Tattoo"), and their influence can be detected in acts from the Cocteau Twins and U2 to Radiohead and Florence and the Machine.

But back in 1976, Sue Dallion and Steven Bailey were just disaffected youths, living outside London and obsessed by the nascent punk movement, led by the Sex Pistols. When they heard that a band had dropped out of a showcase at London's 100 Club, they stepped in. Dallion adopted the name Siouxsie Sioux, with a group inspired by the witch-hunting movie *The Cry of the Banshee* (1970), starring Vincent Price. Bailey picked up a bass for the first time and, with Marco Pirroni (guitar) and Sid Vicious (drums), they jammed a version of The Lord's Prayer (incorporating "Twist and Shout" and "Knockin' on Heaven's Door") for twenty minutes.

Having met an enthusiastic response, Bailey became **Steve Severin** (a reference to the hero of the

book *Venus im Pelz,* as namechecked in The Velvet Underground's "Venus in Furs") and the Banshees installed guitarist **John McKay** (after the short-stayed **Pete Fenton**) and drummer **Kenny Morris**. As their following increased, record labels showed interest but balked at the group demanding control of their work.

Eventually Polydor granted their wishes, with the extraordinary *The Scream* being unleashed in 1978. Siouxsie's powerhouse wailing was well suited to The Beatles' "Helter Skelter" and the band hit the U.K. Top Ten with the stand-alone single "Hong Kong Garden." Siouxsie dressed provocatively and exploded the boundaries for female singers. Her ice-queen image and the bleak songs of *Join Hands* (1979) helped create a template for Goths. Meanwhile, **McKay** and **Morris** walked out on the band just after the start of a 1979 tour. **Robert Smith**, from support band The Cure, deputized on guitar, while **Budgie** joined on drums.

With new guitarist **John McGeoch**, formerly of Magazine, the Banshees took flight. "I could say, 'I want this to sound like a horse falling off a cliff,' and he would know exactly what I meant," enthused Siouxsie. The results were 1980's experimental *Kaleidoscope,* 1981's voodoo-inspired *Ju Ju,* and 1982's orchestral

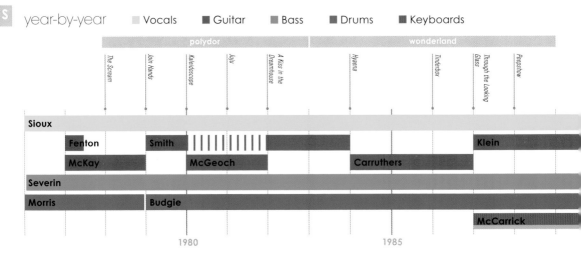

year-by-year   ■ Vocals   ■ Guitar   ■ Bass   ■ Drums   ■ Keyboards

250,000	250,000	250,000	250,000
The Scream (1978)	*Kaleidoscope* (1980)	*Juju* (1981)	*Once Upon a Time: The Singles* (1981)

Robert Smith
b. April 21, 1959

John McGeoch
b. August 25, 1955
d. March 4, 2004

John Carruthers
b. 1958

Jon Klein
b. May 9, 1960

Martin McCarrick
b. July 29, 1962

Knox Chandler
b. unknown

and more romantic (by Siouxsie's standards) *A Kiss in the Dreamhouse*. A hits collection, *Once Upon a Time* (1981), became their biggest seller in Britain.

Meanwhile, Siouxsie and Budgie formed the percussion-dominated duo, The Creatures. Debuting with the *Wild Things* EP in 1981, they scored a U.K. hit with a mock big band take on Mel Tormé's "Right Now" in 1983, and produced *Feast* (1983), *Boomerang* (1989), *Anima Animus* (1999), and *Hai!* (2003).

When McGeoch quit in 1982 (later to join Public Image Ltd), Smith returned to the Banshees, doing double time with The Cure (plus a one-off, drug-crazed collaboration with Severin, called The Glove, making 1983's *Blue Sunshine*). With Smith, they cut the live *Nocturne* (1983), *Hyœna* (1984), and a U.K. Top Ten-charting cover of The Beatles' "Dear Prudence."

Smith fled back to The Cure (much to Siouxsie's irritation) and guitarist **John Carruthers** joined in time for the Banshees' U.S. Top 100 debut, *Tinderbox* (1986). The new lineup paid tribute to their inspirations with the covers collection *Through the Looking Glass* (1987), featuring a hit version of "This Wheel's on Fire."

The success continued with 1988's *Peepshow*, featuring multi-instrumentalist **Martin McCarrick** (who

had played on The Glove's album) and new guitarist **Jon Klein** (formerly of Specimen). *Superstition* (1991) yielded their sole U.S. Top Forty single ("Kiss Them for Me"), while the Banshees secured high billing on the first Lollapalooza tour in 1991. They also provided the lead single for the 1992 movie *Batman Returns*: "Face to Face," co-written with Danny Elfman.

After Siouxsie's 1994 duet with Morrissey on a cover of Yma Sumac's "Interlude," the band bowed out with 1995's *The Rapture*, co-produced by the Velvets' John Cale. Disheartened by a lack of record company support, the Banshees disbanded in 1996.

In 2002, Siouxsie, Budgie, and Severin—with former Psychedelic Fur **Knox Chandler**, who had replaced Klein for their last outing, in 1995—reformed for a tour that coincided with *The Very Best of Siouxsie and the Banshees* and led to the live *Seven Year Itch* (2003).

In 2007, Siouxsie released her splendid solo debut, *Mantaray*. With seemingly little chance of another reunion, the box set *At the BBC* (2009) was left to prove just how versatile this influential band were. "We were genuinely miffed when we didn't change the face of pop music," Budgie admitted to *Record Collector*, "but maybe we added another facet to it." **SL**

■ Strings

polydor   wonderland

Superstition   *The Rapture*

Chandler

1990   1995   2000

Mate. Feed. Kill. Repeat. (1996)

Slipknot (1999)

Iowa (2001)

Vol 3: (The Subliminal Verses) (2004)

All Hope is Gone (2008)

Anders Colsefni—the band's frontman in the *Mate. Feed. Kill. Repeat.* era.

Shawn Crahan entertains at Ozzfest, Vancouver, in 1999.

"The Nine" in Grand Rapids, Michigan, in 1999.

Slipknot hit Ozzfest at the Shoreline Amphitheater, Mountain View, California, on June 29, 2001.

Corey Taylor in frightening form during Slipknot's Pledge of Allegiance tour in 2001.

Bassist and founder member **Paul Gray** performs in 2004; he died in 2010.

Percussionist **Chris Fehn** at the Astoria, London, in May 2004.

Guitarist **Jim Root** onstage at the Hammersmith Apollo, London, on December 8, 2008.

Joey Jordison on drums as Slipknot headline the Rockstar Energy Mayhem Festival at the Verizon Wireless Amphitheater, San Antonio, Texas, on July 26, 2008.

the small faces / the faces 1965–present

Ronnie Lane
b. April 1, 1945
d. June 4, 1997

Kenney Jones
b. September 16, 1948

Jimmy Winston
b. April 20, 1945

Steve Marriott
b. January 30, 1947
d. April 20, 1991

Ian McLagan
b. May 12, 1945
d. 3 December, 2014

Rick Wills
b. December 5, 1947

When **Ronnie Lane**, **Kenney Jones**, **Steve Marriott**, and **Jimmy Winston** formed The Small Faces, they could never have imagined that their "Mod" group would eventually turn into the ultimate good time rock 'n' roll band and launch a singer's forty-year solo career.

Even as the four young Londoners celebrated their first hit, "Whatcha Gonna Do About It," in 1965, their lineup changed with keyboard player **Ian McLagan** replacing Winston. With a second hit, "Sha La La La Lee," under their belts, The Small Faces spent more than six months in the U.K. album chart with their self-titled debut, peaking at No. 3.

With the Mod movement thriving, The Small Faces topped the U.K. chart with "All or Nothing" in 1966. In complete contrast to that rabble-rouser was 1967's psychedelic "Itchycoo Park" in 1967, which took the four-piece into the U.S. chart for the first time. "I lifted it from a hymn, 'God Be In My Head'" Lane confessed to *Record Collector*, "and I also got the theme to the words in a hotel in Bath or Bristol. There was a magazine in the room with a rambling account of some place in the country and it was about 'dreaming spires' and a 'bridge of sighs'."

The U.K. chart-topping concept album *Ogden's Nut Gone Flake* (1968) included the group's final Top Ten hit, "Lazy Sunday." In January 1969, Marriott left to form Humble Pie, leaving the remaining three members to recruit The Jeff Beck Group's singer **Rod Stewart** and guitarist **Ronnie Wood**. "We got together with Rod and Ron at the Stones' rehearsal studio one afternoon and played a bit," McLagan told *Circus*, "then we just saw more and more of each other. So the five of us decided to stay together. As soon as Steve left, it was a breath of fresh air." Re-christened The Faces, they signed to Warner, while Stewart pursued a solo career on the Mercury label.

The Faces' debut *Long Player* charted in both the U.K. and the U.S., and for the next six years they and the singer enjoyed parallel careers. However, as Stewart topped charts in Britain and America with "Maggie May," the group came to be billed as Rod Stewart & The Faces, which caused some rancor.

The 1971 Top Ten album *A Nod's as Good as a Wink… to a Blind Horse* featured the hit "Stay with Me." It was quickly followed by the U.K. No. 1 *Ooh La La*, but with Stewart apparently more focused on his solo

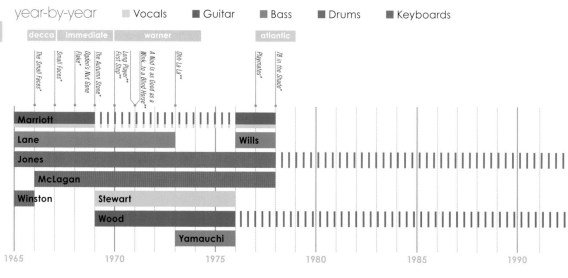

year-by-year   ■ Vocals   ■ Guitar   ■ Bass   ■ Drums   ■ Keyboards

500,000	750,000	1.3M	500,000
Small Faces*	Ogden's Nut	A Nod Is as Good	Ooh La La
(1966)	Gone Flake*	as a Wink...**	(1973)
	(1968)	(1979)	

Rod Stewart
b. January 10, 1945

Ronnie Wood
b. June 1, 1947

Tetsu Yamauchi
b. October 21, 1946

Mick Hucknall
b. June 8, 1960

Glen Matlock
b. August 27, 1956

career—his *Never A Dull Moment* reached No. 1 in the U.K. and No. 2 in the U.S.—Lane left The Faces, to be replaced by former Free bassist **Tetsu Yamauchi.**

In 1974 came the live *Coast to Coast Overtures and Beginners*—credited to Rod Stewart & The Faces—and the band's final hit, "You Can Make Me Dance or Anything." Although members of the band supported Stewart on a solo U.S. tour to promote his smash *Atlantic Crossing* (U.S. No. 9 and U.K. No. 1), The Faces finally came to an end in December 1975, by which time Wood had begun working with The Rolling Stones.

In 1976—as the re-released "Itchycoo Park" and "Lazy Sunday" hit the U.K. chart—Jones, McLagan, and Marriott reformed The Small Faces (with former David Gilmour/Peter Frampton associate **Rick Wills** on bass). However, after two failed singles, the band split for the final time. Jones replaced Keith Moon in The Who, McLagan joined The Rolling Stones' touring band, Wills joined Foreigner, and Marriott returned to the U.K. pub circuit until his death in a fire in 1991.

When Stewart bagged a Lifetime Achievement Award at the U.K. Brit Awards in 1993, The Faces reunited for a one-off appearance at the show. The Rolling Stones' bassist Bill Wyman deputized for Lane, who had developed multiple sclerosis (he eventually died from the disease in 1997).

Stewart had continued to hit new heights as a solo star: *A Night on the Town* (1976), *Foot Loose and Fancy Free* (1977), and *Blondes Have More Fun* (1978) made the Top Three in the U.K. and U.S. In 1993, he reunited with Wood for MTV's *Unplugged,* which became a multi-platinum album featuring The Faces' "Stay with Me." The following year, he was inducted into the Rock and Roll Hall of Fame (as were The Faces in 2012.)

In the new millennium, Stewart's career received a major boost when he moved to RCA's J label and began his series of *American Songbook* albums. All five were Top Ten hits on both sides of the Atlantic, with *Volume III* and the *Still The Same... Great Rock Classics of Our Time* collection hitting No. 1 in the U.S.

In 2010 and 2011, a new Faces lineup—minus Stewart—hit the road. Originals Jones, McLagan, and Wood were joined by Simply Red singer **Mick Hucknall** and former Sex Pistols bassist **Glen Matlock.** "They were my all-time favourite band," Matlock told *The Telegraph,* "so to be in them for a bit is great." **BS**

* The Small Faces
** The Faces

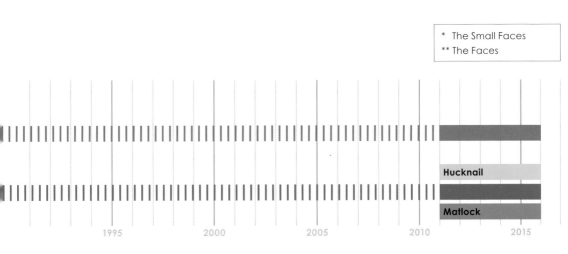

Hucknail

Matlock

1995   2000   2005   2010   2015

The Small Faces
(1966)

Small Faces (1967)

Ogden's Nut Gone Flake (1968)

First Step (1970)

Long Player (1971)

A Nod Is as Good as a Wink... to a Blind Horse (1971)

Ooh La La (1973)

Playmates (1977)

78 in the Shade (1978)

Left to right: **Ronnie Lane, Kenney Jones, Steve Marriott,** and **Ian McLagan** in 1966.

McLagan, Marriott, Lane, and **Jones** with P.P. Arnold (center).

The Small Faces on camera: a color-coordinated portrait of **Marriott, Lane, Jones,** and **McLagan** in 1968.

Group huddle: The Faces conceal theirs in Copenhagen in 1970.

The Faces play the Weeley Festival, England, on August 29, 1971.

Faces **Ronnie Wood** and **Rod Stewart** perform in 1972.

Left to right: **McLagan, Marriott, Rick Wills,** and **Jones** in 1977.

Left to right: **McLagan, Wood, Stewart, Lane,** and **Jones** perform as The Faces on BBC TV's *Top of the Pops* in February 1973.

Clockwise from bottom left: **Marriott, Jones, Wills, McLagan,** and Jimmy McCulloch on tour in 1978.

the smashing pumpkins 1988–present

Billy Corgan
b. March 17, 1967

James Iha
b. March 26, 1968

D'arcy Wretsky
b. May 1, 1968

Jimmy Chamberlin
b. June 10, 1964

Melissa Auf der Maur
b. March 17, 1972

Jeff Schroeder
b. February 4, 1974

"The guitars are every bit as loud as anything you'd want," observed Kiss mainman Gene Simmons of The Smashing Pumpkins, "and on top of that there are pop melodies with all sorts of interesting subject matters." Mighty riffs, potentially chart-busting tunes, and lyrical poetry have indeed dominated the Pumpkins discography—as has a penchant for female bassists.

Guitarists **Billy Corgan** and **James Iha** created the band in Chicago in 1988. After a first show with just a drum machine, they enlisted bassist **D'arcy Wretzky**—with whom Iha had a short-lived romance—then drummer **Jimmy Chamberlin**. In 1990, they began playing outside Chicago and recording their debut album with future Nirvana producer Butch Vig. *Gish* (1991) proved a slow-burner while the Pumpkins toured relentlessly. However, a stint with Pearl Jam and the Red Hot Chili Peppers—plus speculation about Corgan's relationship with a pre-Kurt Cobain Courtney Love—boosted their profile. (Corgan and Love's two decades of recriminations and reconciliations would see him contributing to, then disowning, *Celebrity Skin* and *Nobody's Daughter* by her group Hole.)

The Pumpkins became famously dysfunctional: Chamberlin developed a drug problem, and the megalomaniacal Corgan replaced parts recorded by Wretzky and Iha for *Siamese Dream* (1993). But the turmoil was rewarded when the album—featuring piano by Mike Mills of R.E.M. and violin by David Ragsdale of Kansas—smashed into the U.S. Top Ten.

Pisces Iscariot (1994), a compilation of offcuts and radio sessions, hit No. 4 before the Pumpkins shot to the top with *Mellon Collie and the Infinite Sadness* (1995). This ambitious double set sold five million in its first three months, a figure boosted by the hit "Tonight, Tonight," featuring the Chicago Symphony Orchestra. Keyboardist Jonathan Melvoin, who had worked with Prince alongside his sisters Wendy and Susannah, augmented the Pumpkins' touring lineup. However, when Melvoin fatally overdosed in July 1996, Chamberlin—with whom he had been using heroin—was fired. Just over a month later, the tour resumed, with former Filter drummer Matt Walker and keyboardist Dennis Flemion of The Frogs. (The former also played on Iha's 1998 album, *Let It Come Down*.)

The appropriately downbeat *Adore* (1998) featured guest drummers including Soundgarden's Matt Cameron and Beck's Lenny Waronker. It turned platinum in a month, but the Pumpkins reverted—to Corgan's frustration—to being a cult band, albeit an arena-filling one. On tour, it took three people to fill Chamberlin's place: John Mellencamp's drummer Kenny Aronoff and two percussionists.

year-by-year   ■ Vocals   ■ Guitar   ■ Bass   ■ Drums   ■ Keyboards

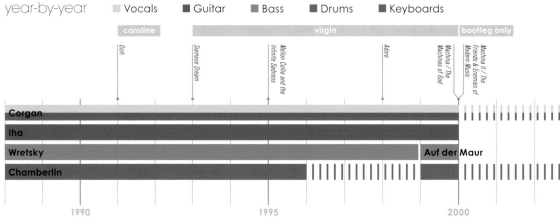

| 6.8M | 2M | 7.1M | 4M |
| *Siamese Dream* (1993) | *Pisces Iscariot* (1994) | *Mellon Collie and the Infinite Sadness* (1995) | *Adore* (1998) |

Ginger Reyes
b. April 22, 1980

Lisa Harriton
b. November 18, 1980

Mike Byrne
b. February 6, 1990

Nicole Fiorentino
b. April 8, 1979

Chamberlin rejoined in early 1999, only for Wretzky to quit later that year. Corgan forged ahead with 2000's gorgeous *Machina / The Machines of God*, featuring David Bowie's keyboardist Mike Garson, but its underwhelming sales prompted the band's label, Virgin, to stymie plans for a sequel. Corgan duly disseminated *Machina II / The Friends & Enemies of Modern Music* via fans and the internet, and announced that the Pumpkins' next tour would be their last. Garson, keyboardist Chris Holmes, and former Hole bassist **Melissa Auf der Maur** completed the lineup that disbanded in December 2000.

After a stint as New Order's tour guitarist, Corgan formed Zwan in 2002 with Chamberlin, indie cult heroes Matt Sweeney and David Pajo, and another female bassist, A Perfect Circle's Paz Lenchantin. (Iha joined A Perfect Circle the following year.) Zwan's gloriously colorful *Mary, Star of the Sea* (2003) hit U.S. No. 3 but the band imploded on tour.

In interviews promoting his largely electronic 2005 solo album *The Future Embrace*—featuring The Cure's Robert Smith duetting on a cover of the Bee Gees' "To Love Somebody"—Corgan blamed Iha for the Pumpkins' demise and denounced Wretzky as a drug casualty, yet announced plans to revive the group. Unsurprisingly, he and Chamberlin proved the sole survivors of the original lineup: the duo are the only musicians credited on 2007's lumpen *Zeitgeist*, the tour for which featured guitarist **Jeff Schroeder**, keyboardist **Lisa Harriton**, and bassist **Ginger Reyes**. The live lineup was augmented in 2008 by No Doubt brass players Stephen Bradley and Gabrial McNair, Reyes' husband Kristopher Pooley on accordion and keyboards, and violinist Gingger Shankar.

With *Zeitgeist* stalling and fans' patience eroded by a self-indulgent twentieth anniversary tour, Corgan announced in 2009 that he had fired Chamberlin and would issue the conceptual *Teargarden by Kaleidyscope* one song at a time. He also dallied with a psychedelic side project, Spirits in the Sky, featuring Jane's Addiction guitarist Dave Navarro, Catherine drummer (and Wretzky's ex-husband) Kerry Brown, and Electric Prunes bassist Mark Tulin.

By the end of 2011, the self-defeating nature of this nuttiness appeared to have dawned on Corgan. With new bassist **Nicole Fiorentino** and drummer **Mike Byrne**, he laid the groundwork for *Oceania* (2012). Its follow-up, *Monuments to an Elegy* (2014), somewhat surprisingly featured Mötley Crüe's Tommy Lee on drums, and the lineup for the supporting tour included Mark Stoermer of The Killers and Brad Wilks of Rage Against the Machine. **BM**

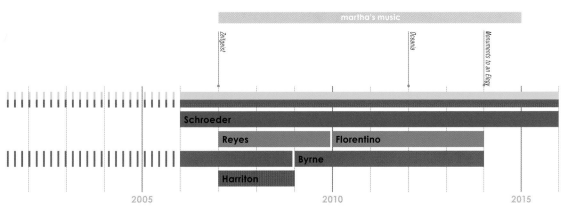

patti smith 1974–present

Patti Smith
b. December 30, 1946

Lenny Kaye
b. December 27, 1946

Richard Sohl
b. May 26, 1953
d. June 3, 1990

Ivan Kral
b. May 12, 1948

Jay Dee Daugherty
b. March 22, 1952

Bruce Brody
b. Unknown

Patti Smith broke the mold in two ways: she proved that an accomplished poet could forge a successful career in rock music, and that a young woman, a noted style icon, could front a major group without trading on her looks. The Patti Smith Group was an excellent hard rock/new wave band that managed to be both experimental and traditional.

The group began in New York City in 1971 when Smith (vocals) united with **Lenny Kaye** (guitar) to play (mainly poetry) gigs. With **Richard Sohl** (keyboards), they cut a 1974 single coupling a cover of "Hey Joe" with Smith's "Piss Factory." (Smith also wrote songs for boyfriend Allen Lanier's Blue Öyster Cult). With guitarist/bassist **Ivan Kral** and drummer **Jay Dee Daugherty**, the Patti Smith Group came into existence.

Their first album, *Horses* (1975), was a sensation and remains a classic. Smith was on the poetic cutting edge of New York's punk movement and the songs were superb: "Land," "Gloria," "Redondo Beach," and the marathon "Birdland" (Smith would often write one long track for each album). "The most exciting rock album of the year…" enthused the then seventeen-year-old Morrissey in a letter to *Sounds*. "Patti is intriguing without being boring." *Horses* hit U.S. No. 47.

The follow-up, *Radio Ethiopia* (1976), was greatly underrated. Smith said the songs were influenced by Detroit hard rockers the MC5 (whose guitarist **Fred "Sonic" Smith** she was to marry), and Aerosmith's producer Jack Douglas was brought in to beef up the group's muscle. "Ask the Angels" and "Pumping (My Heart)" in particular delivered the goods. However, the album was less commercially successful.

The group built a reputation for exciting shows, with Smith's unpredictability a particular draw. Sometimes she could be a little too unpredictable: in a Florida concert in January 1977, supporting Bob Seger, she fell offstage and broke her neck. During her recuperation, she had time to reassess her career.

Easter (1978) was her resurrection, taking her into the U.S. and U.K. Top Twenty. Its success was boosted by the exhilarating hit "Because the Night," cowritten with Bruce Springsteen. The rollicking "Till Victory," heartfelt "Privilege (Set Me Free)," and provocative "Rock N Roll Nigger" also rode the line between commercial appeal and artistic edge. **Bruce Brody** played keyboards on most of the record—produced by Jimmy Iovine—although Sohl and Allen Lanier also contributed (as did Television's Tom Verlaine).

year-by-year   Vocals   Guitar   Bass   Drums   Keyboards

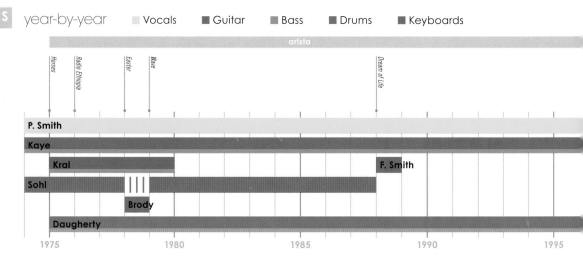

Fred "Sonic" Smith
b. September 13, 1949
d. November 4, 1994

Tony Shanahan
b. Unknown

Oliver Ray
b. Unknown

Jackson Smith
b. 1982

There was another critical reaction against *Wave* (1979), which now seems unjustified. The joyful opener "Frederick" (a paean to the man Smith was to marry), the euphoric "Dancing Barefoot" (later covered by U2) and the stirring "Broken Flag" set up the spoken title track, which seemed to announce her retirement. The album again reached the U.S. Top Twenty.

Nevertheless, the group played their last show in 1979 and Smith committed herself to marriage and motherhood, giving birth to son Jackson and daughter Jesse. Shortly after the latter was born, she made an unexpected return with *Dream of Life* (1988), another underrated album that included "People Have the Power" and "Where Duty Calls." The group reformed without Kaye and Kral; Fred Smith played guitar and shared production duties with Iovine. And then silence once more, as Smith received a series of shattering blows. Great friend and photographer Robert Mapplethorpe, whose label Mer had first released "Piss Factory," died in 1989, followed by keyboard player Sohl in 1990. Worse yet, her husband Fred and brother Todd died in 1994.

After intermittent live appearances in 1995, Bob Dylan invited her on tour at the the end of the year.

Gone Again (1996) came to terms with her grief, in the title song, "Dead to the World," and "About a Boy," a tribute to the late Kurt Cobain. **Tony Shanahan** (bass) and **Oliver Ray** (guitar) joined founding stalwart Kaye.

The same personnel recorded *Peace and Noise* (1997), which also boasted a cameo by Michael Stipe (with whom she had sung on R.E.M.'s 1996 hit "E-bow the Letter"). After another tour with Dylan in 1998 came *Gung Ho* (2000), whose title track was an attack on militarism. The group was still together for the excellent *Trampin'* (2004) with its epic songs "Gandhi" and "Radio Baghdad," as well as "Mother Rose" and "Peaceable Kingdom," both hymns to Patti's mother, who had recently died. Guitarist Ray departed in 2006, to be replaced by **Jackson Smith**, Patti's son.

In 2007, the Patti Smith Group were inducted into the Rock and Roll Hall of Fame. Appropriately, *Twelve* (2007) saw Smith covering her favorite rock songs, from Neil Young to Nirvana. Two poetry and music performances with My Bloody Valentine's Kevin Shields were issued as *The Coral Sea* in 2008, a year that also saw the star-studded documentary *Patti Smith—Dream of Life*. An eleventh studio album, *Banga* (2012), confirms that her fire still burns. **MiH**

■ Other percussion

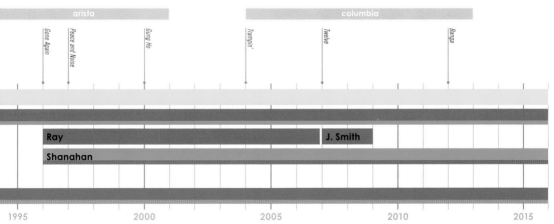

| | | |
| arista | | columbia |

Gone Again | Peace and Noise | Gung Ho | Trampin' | Twelve | Banga

Ray — J. Smith

Shanahan

1995 — 2000 — 2005 — 2010 — 2015

the smiths 1982–1987

Morrissey
b. May 22, 1959

Johnny Marr
b. October 31, 1963

Andy Rourke
b. January 17, 1964

Mike Joyce
b. June 1, 1963

Craig Gannon
b. July 30, 1966

Noel Gallagher of Oasis once observed that The Beatles, The Smiths, and the Sex Pistols said everything about British music that anyone ever needed to know. He was right: each group brought a unique world view that touched a nerve within millions of listeners. Perhaps unexpectedly in The Smiths' case, a large American fanbase was able to connect with their haunting lyrics, based on life in working-class England.

So the music is bleak? Make no mistake, **Stephen Morrissey**'s songs were often exactly that. Heartfelt, bittersweet, depressing, impotent, suicidal, self-indulgent—all these adjectives were liberally applied by both Morrissey's supporters and detractors during and after his group's relatively brief career. But far from being a mere miserablist, he injected his songs with a powerful, knowing sense of humor (in particular about matters sexual and cultural), often adding a dose of anger when it came to subjects that he felt strongly about, including vegetarianism and warfare.

His foil, musically and personally, was guitarist **Johnny Marr** (born John Maher), whose unearthly, textural playing made him a guitar hero and progenitor of the modern indie sound. Backed by bassist **Andy Rourke** (recruited after Dale Hibbert was briefly considered) and drummer **Mike Joyce** (who followed a fleeting stint by future Fall sticksman

Simon Wolstencroft)—Morrissey and Marr set about redefining pop, not from a cultural epicenter such as London but from depressed, rundown Manchester.

The Smiths, who chose their mundane name to contrast with ostentatious contemporary band names such as Spandau Ballet, began by writing songs about the agonies of teenage life. "Hand in Glove," "What Difference Does It Make?," and "Heaven Knows I'm Miserable Now" all addressed the troubles of the particular time and place in which they were written.

Although critics scoffed at Morrissey's unusual, intoned vocals, none could deny the plangent beauty of Marr's guitar playing nor the professionalism of the arrangements on *The Smiths*, their No. 2 debut on the U.K. chart in 1984. Controversy flared over the song "Suffer Little Children," which addressed the Moors Murders in the mid-sixties, in which five children were abducted, murdered, and buried near Manchester, a recent memory for many in the area. However, Morrissey weathered the storm and his band moved rapidly toward British domination.

Entering the chart at No. 1, *Meat Is Murder* (1985) was more assured, with Morrissey targeting both meat-eaters and brutal headmasters. A single, "That Joke Isn't Funny Anymore," fell outside the Top Forty, but has gone on to epitomize the band's career: even

year-by-year ■ Vocals ■ Guitar ■ Bass ■ Drums

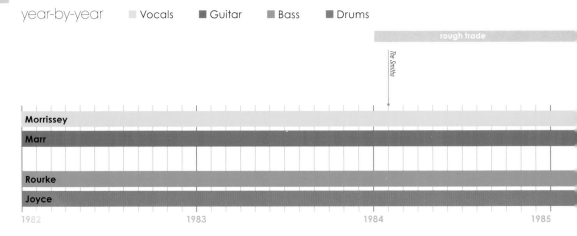

1.1M
Hatful of Hollow
(1984)

1.5M
The Queen is Dead
(1986)

1.5M
Strangeways, Here We Come
(1987)

1.4M
"Singles"
(1995)

without a repeated riff or chorus to hang radio play on, or indeed a topic that would appeal to anyone other than the most miserable, lovelorn youth, "That Joke..." is now regarded as a classic. That could well be said about The Smiths themselves, as a group at least a decade ahead of its time, doomed to be more read about than listened to during its active career, and only fully appreciated several years after the members went their separate ways. (Although Robert Smith, of the equally morbid The Cure, remained unswayed, telling *The Face* in 1989: "I hate The Smiths and everything they've ever done... Morrissey is precious, effete, glib, out-of-touch and a million other vile things that I can't be bothered to list.")

Regret, a longing for security, and a wistfulness for times long gone pervaded *The Queen is Dead* (1986). "Frankly, Mr. Shankly" and "Some Girls Are Bigger Than Others" evoked a view of vintage kitchen-sink England; "There Is a Light That Never Goes Out" reached directly into the hormonal instability of every suffering listener who heard it; and "The Boy with the Thorn in His Side" revealed better than ever the trials of life at this stage of English history.

Although *Strangeways, Here We Come* (1987) was The Smiths' last studio album, there were no signs that inspiration had started to wane. Immortal songs such as "Girlfriend in a Coma" and "I Started Something I Couldn't Finish" still had the power to captivate the listener. But Morrissey and Marr—the Lennon and McCartney of the eighties—had begun to tire of each other, and a split came later the same year. The live *Rank* (1988) provided a strong epitaph, but no fewer than ten compilations gleaned from the four original albums, live tracks, and single B-sides have appeared in the quarter-century since then. However, *Hatful of Hollow* (1984) remains perhaps their strongest collection (including the epic "How Soon is Now?").

Morrissey's solo debut, *Viva Hate*, was the first of his three U.K. chart-topping albums, to be followed by *Vauxhall and I* (1994) and *Ringleader of the Tormentors* (2006). Marr's post-Smiths career tended to be more collaborative, with roles in a succession of new bands—The The, Electronic, Modest Mouse, The Cribs, and his own Johnny Marr and The Healers.

Few bands have carried the weight of a reunion expectation as constantly as The Smiths. The yearning among disciples for them to reunite is ongoing, but the freedom Morrissey and Marr have secured in solo projects means that this wish is likely to remain unfulfilled. "I would rather eat my own testicles than reform The Smiths," the singer told *Uncut* in 2006, "and that's saying something for a vegetarian." **JM**

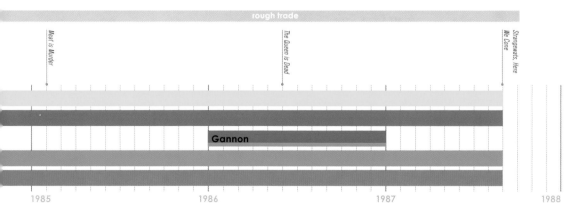

soft machine 1966–1984

Robert Wyatt
b. January 28, 1945

Mike Ratledge
b. April 1943

Kevin Ayers
b. August 16, 1944
d. February 18, 2013

Daevid Allen
b. January 13, 1938

Andy Summers
b. December 31, 1942

Hugh Hopper
b. April 29, 1945
d. June 7, 2009

Phil Howard
b. Unknown

Elton Dean
b. October 28, 1945
d. February 8, 2006

When progressive rock was at its peak in the early seventies, bands such as Yes, Genesis, and Emerson, Lake & Palmer were among the biggest-selling album artists. Paving the way for the progressive era, the "Canterbury Scene" comprised an intermingling group of musicians whose work melded complex jazz-style improvisation with psychedelic rock, catchy pop melodies, and whimsical lyrics celebrating prosaic aspects of English life—drinking tea, for example. None of the bands enjoyed enormous commercial success, but surely influenced the cultural mood.

This particular tale began in 1964 with The Wilde Flowers, a teenage pop group from the city of Canterbury, southeast England. Variously featured were **Kevin Ayers** (vocals), **Robert Wyatt** (drums, vocals), **Daevid Allen** (guitar), **Hugh Hopper** (bass), Richard Sinclair (guitar, vocals), and Pye Hastings (guitar, vocals). The Wilde Flowers enjoyed no success in the conventional sense, and none of their music appeared on record at the time. And yet its members would go on to form the axes of The Soft Machine and Caravan, two of the most vital forces in English rock in the early seventies; Allen would found Anglo-French experimentalists Gong; and both Ayers and Wyatt would enjoy cult solo careers.

Formed during 1966 by Wyatt, Ayers, Allen, and **Mike Ratledge**—a young jazz pianist with a fondness for the avant-garde tinkling of Cecil Taylor—the band named themselves after a William Burroughs novel, *The Soft Machine*. Ratledge had earlier left Canterbury to study at Oxford University, and so had not joined his friends in The Wilde Flowers.

Playing what was essentially psychedelic rock, The Soft Machine made a mark on the same London underground circuit as the Syd Barrett-era Pink Floyd, at the UFO and Middle Earth clubs. (Wyatt, Hopper, and Ratledge graced Barrett's 1970 solo album *The Madcap Laughs*.) Ratledge's instrumental skill during unusually complex extended improvised sequences set "the Softs" apart from other bands of the time. After an appearance at the French *Nuits Psychédéliques* in the summer of 1967, this unusually cerebral bunch became darlings of the Parisian Left Bank. On their return, however, Australian passport holder Allen was refused entry to Britain. He remained in France (where he formed Gong), and was briefly replaced by future Police-man **Andy Summers**.

The Soft Machine were fortunate in sharing the same management as The Jimi Hendrix Experience, whom they supported on their first major U.S. tour

year-by-year

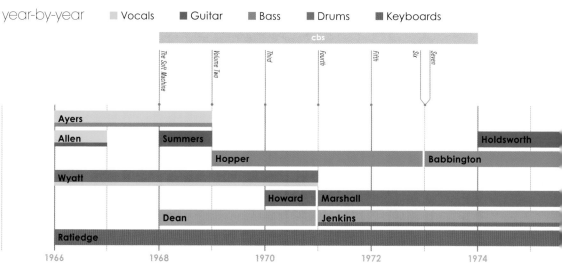

year-by-year   ■ Vocals   ■ Guitar   ■ Bass   ■ Drums   ■ Keyboards

John Marshall
b. August 28, 1941

Karl Jenkins
b. February 17, 1944

Roy Babbington
b. July 8, 1940

Allan Holdsworth
b. August 6, 1946

John Etheridge
b. January 12, 1948

Ric Sanders
b. December 8, 1952

Percy Jones
b. December 3, 1947

Steve Cook
b. Unknown

in 1968. While in New York, they recorded their eponymous debut album, a classic of its type that took psychedelic rock into uncharted complexity, at the same time ushering in progressive rock. The U.S. experience was turbulent for the band, however; after their final U.S. date, at the Hollywood Bowl, both Ayers and Wyatt left and The Soft Machine folded.

At the start of 1969, to fulfill a contractual obligation, Ratledge, Wyatt, and composer/bassist Hugh Hopper regrouped to record a second album. Inspired in part by Frank Zappa's *Absolutely Free*, the acclaimed *Volume Two* was very different to the band's debut, heralding a transition to entirely instrumental music. (Softs fan Bryan Ferry would later concede that "They were short of a melody or two.") This was even more marked on *Third* (1970), which appeared in the wake of Miles Davis's crossover milestone *Bitches Brew*. By now, Soft Machine (having lost the definite article) had augmented the core lineup with saxophone player **Elton Dean**, who can be heard to outstanding effect on *Third*'s centerpiece, the eighteen-minute suite "Slightly All the Time."

Following 1971's similarly styled *Fourth*, Wyatt was fired, possibly because of his poppier leanings. "We're English, so we never talked about it," he told

the *Daily Telegraph*. Wyatt formed Matching Mole, who enjoyed two years of critical acclaim before, at a party in June 1973, the drummer fell from an upstairs window. Paralyzed from the waist down and wheelchair-bound, Wyatt terminated Matching Mole and began a solo career of extraordinary breadth and distinction. He remains a much-loved cult icon.

Soft Machine albums became increasingly jazz-oriented. On *Six* (1973), Dean was replaced by reeds/keyboard player **Karl Jenkins**. On *Bundles* (1975), with Ratledge now the only remaining original member, the Soft Machine sound took a dramatic turn with the introduction of high-speed guitar wizard **Allan Holdsworth**. That was Ratledge's final appearance in the band; in the following decade he would concentrate on composition.

Thereafter, Soft Machine ceased to exist as a live entity, but for a brief revival in 1984. However, Jenkins, Holdsworth, and drummer John Marshall created a final studio album, 1981's *Land of Cockayne,* with hired hands including Cream bassist Jack Bruce and jazz pianist John Taylor.

Because the band generally performed at its best in the concert environment, many live recordings have been issued since the group's demise. **TB**

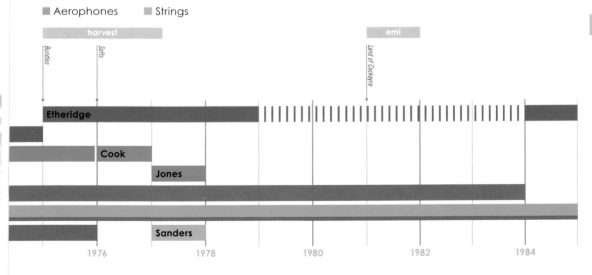

■ Aerophones   ■ Strings

soft machine 471

Greetings from
Asbury Park, N.J.
(1973)

Born to Run (1975)

Darkness on the
Edge of Town
(1978)

The River (1980)

Born in the U.S.A
(1984)

Tunnel of Love
(1987)

The Ghost of Tom
Joad (1995)

The Rising (2002)

Devils & Dust
(2005)

Wrecking Ball
(2012)

Bruce Springsteen poses in New Jersey in 1973.

Springsteen with vocalist Ronnie Spector at the Bottom Line Club, New York, in 1975.

Clarence "The Big Man" **Clemons** with Springsteen in San Francisco, in 1978.

Springsteen and future *Friends* star Courteney Cox filming the video for "Dancing in the Dark" in June 1984.

Clemons, **Springsteen**, bassist **Garry Tallent**, and guitarist **Steven Van Zandt** ham it up at The Spectrum, Philadelphia, on December 8, 1980.

Springsteen welcomes Roy Orbison as an inductee to the Rock and Roll Hall of Fame, in New York, in 1987.

Springsteen's "Streets of Philadelphia" won four Grammys in 1995, including Song of the Year and Best Rock Song.

Performing with wife **Patti Scialfa** in the Netherlands in 2002.

With U2's Bono at the annual Rock and Roll Hall of Fame induction ceremony in 2005.

Springsteen and **Van Zandt** perform with the E Street Band at Madison Square Garden, New York, on April 9, 2012.

status quo 1967–present

Francis Rossi
b. May 29, 1949

Rick Parfitt
b. October 12, 1948

John Coghlan
b. September 19, 1946

Alan Lancaster
b. February 7, 1949

Roy Lynes
b. October 25, 1943

Pete Kircher
b. January 21, 1945

Francis Rossi and **Rick Parfitt** first united as front-men in the mid-sixties, little knowing that they would still be rocking nearly five decades later. Ironically, they were regarded as one-hit wonders after they found it hard to recapture the magic of their 1968 U.K. chart debut "Pictures of Matchstick Men," a classic piece of pop psychedelia (and their sole U.S. success). Instead, they adopted a twelve-bar blues formula, bending it to their skills as guitarists and songwriters. The result was a denim-clad brand of heads-down, no-nonsense boogie not dissimilar to that of America's Grand Funk Railroad. This was a working man's band.

The roots of Quo were in south London, where they came together in 1962 as the Spectres. Guitarist/singer Rossi was initially abetted by bassist **Alan Lancaster** and drummer **John Coghlan**. Parfitt was added in 1965 when his cabaret band the Highlights shared a stage with them at a holiday camp in Somerset. Until the summer of 1970, when he quit en route to a gig in Glasgow, organist **Roy Lynes** made up the numbers. Another crucial figure was road manager Bob Young, who has played harmonica onstage with the band and written many hits with Rossi.

After recording as the Spectres and Traffic Jam, the band adopted their Latin name. The chirpy "Ice in the Sun," made No. 8, one place below "Matchstick Men," but extensive work in continental Europe saw Quo choose the rock road. The band made major steps toward stardom when they traded their frilly shirts for denim and the Pye label for Vertigo in 1972. Scruffy jeans and dirty trainers somehow projected a "men of the people" image that broke down the barrier between performers and their audience. And Vertigo—the launchpad for Black Sabbath, among others—had its finger on the pulse of seventies rock in a way that Pye (home of Petula Clark) clearly did not.

Quo based their success on a hard-rocking live act and shrewd pop sensibilities. Their singles sold as well as their albums—unusual for the time. A street-level image won them a sponsorship deal with Levi's jeans, and their sound became more sophisticated in the later seventies, when they started working with outside producers. Three U.K. chart-topping albums, *Hello* (1973), *On the Level* (1975), and *Blue for You* (1976), were impressive—Quo were happy to vary the formula just enough to attract outsiders while keeping hard-core fans satisfied. Punk made little impact.

"Down Down" became their one and only U.K. chart-topping single in 1975, but many more graced the Top Twenty. Highlights from the seventies included "Paper Plane" (1972), "Caroline" (1973), "Rain" (1976), and "Whatever You Want" (1979). "Rockin' All Over

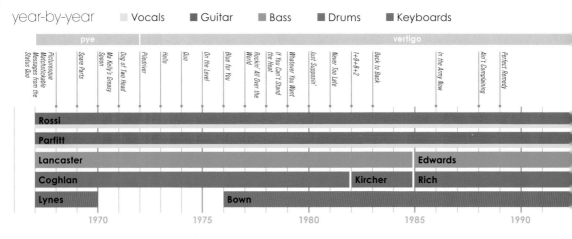

year-by-year ▪ Vocals ▪ Guitar ▪ Bass ▪ Drums ▪ Keyboards

	pye							vertigo											
Albums	Picturesque Matchstickable Messages from the Status Quo	Spare Parts	Ma Kelly's Greasy Spoon	Dog of Two Head	Piledriver	Hello	Quo	On the Level	Blue for You	Rockin' All Over the World	If You Can't Stand the Heat	Whatever You Want	Just Supposin'	Never Too Late	1+9+8+2	Back to Back	In the Army Now	Ain't Complaining	Perfect Remedy

Rossi

Parfitt

Lancaster / Edwards

Coghlan / Kircher / Rich

Lynes / Bown

1970   1975   1980   1985   1990

Jeff Rich
b. June 8, 1953

Andy Bown
b. March 27, 1946

Matt Letley
b. March 29, 1961

John "Rhino" Edwards
b. May 9, 1953

Leon Cave
b. September 24, 1978

the World," a cover of a John Fogerty song released as a Quo single in 1977, was the opening number in 1985's Live Aid global jukebox when Quo kicked off proceedings at London's Wembley Stadium.

Keyboardist **Andy Bown** joined in 1976 (having appeared as a session player since 1973), splitting his time between Quo and Pink Floyd in 1980 and 1981. Otherwise, the lineup stayed solid until the eighties, when—in time for the U.K. chart-topping *1+9+8+2*—drum duties passed from Coghlan to **Pete Kircher**, then in 1985 to **Jeff Rich**. Bassist **John "Rhino" Edwards** joined in 1986 when the group reunited after a two-year break. Lancaster launched a legal action from his new home in Australia; it was settled out of court, and Rossi and Parfitt were able to carry on as Quo.

While their shows remained unremittingly boogie-based, the band endeavored to vary their sound in the eighties. "In the Army Now," an atypical ballad, reached U.K. No. 2 in 1986, and an album of the same name maintained an extraordinary run of seventeen U.K. gold records that stretched from 1973's *Hello* to 1988's *Ain't Complaining* (including 1977's thunderous *Live!* and 1980's hit-packed *12 Gold Bars*).

The nineties saw the band struggle, with them recording two whole albums of cover versions and taking on BBC Radio 1 in a battle to have their singles played (Quo were seen as passé by the broadcasting establishment). But 1996's *Don't Stop* narrowly missed the No. 1 slot, and 2002's *Heavy Traffic* was another strong seller. By 2009, when they played the Glastonbury festival, they were established as grand old men of British rock and a national institution. Indeed, a plaque was erected at the site of their first gig in Eltham, south London, back in 1967.

Parfitt has survived health scares that included quadruple bypass surgery and suspected throat cancer. With Rossi, he was awarded the Order of the British Empire in 2010 for services to music.

It is fitting that Quo's twenty-ninth studio album, *Quid Pro Quo* (2011), was first sold as an exclusive edition through a leading U.K. supermarket—the band remain as quintessentially British as fish and chips. To fans' delight, Lancaster and Coghlan reunited with Rossi and Parfitt in 2012 for the filming of a fiftieth anniversary documentary, *Hello Quo.*

The following year, the quartet embarked on a "Frantic Four" reunion tour, with Leon Cave taking over from Matt Letley on drums. The huge success of these concerts saw further dates added in 2014. Rossi described their "Final Fling" as "an opportunity to kick it up a notch and to get the gang back together for one final blast." **MHe**

S

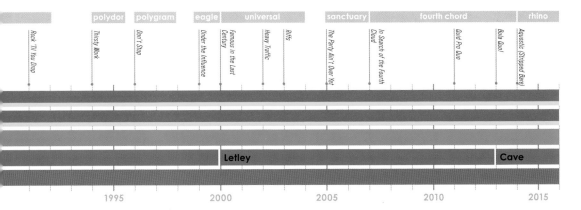

| | polydor | polygram | eagle | universal | | | sanctuary | | fourth chord | | rhino |

Rock 'Til You Drop · Thirsty Work · Don't Stop · Under the Influence · Famous in the Last Century · Heavy Traffic · Riffs · The Party Ain't Over Yet · In Search of the Fourth Chord · Quid Pro Quo · Bula Quo! · Aquostic (Stripped Bare)

Letley · Cave

1995 · 2000 · 2005 · 2010 · 2015

steely dan 1972–present

Donald Fagen
b. January 10, 1948

Walter Becker
b. February 20, 1950

Denny Dias
b. December 1, 1946

David Palmer
b. Unknown

Jeff "Skunk" Baxter
b. December 13, 1948

Jim Hodder
b. December 17, 1947
d. June 6, 1990

Peerless pimps of the coolest studio band of the early seventies, **Donald Fagen** and **Walter Becker** were always happiest writing their sophisticated songs, scoring their jazz-fusiony rhythm charts, and twiddling their production knobs for sonic perfection. If the band could not quite lay down the sound they were looking for, the duo simply hired sessionmen to do it.

School friends from Bard, upstate New York, the young songwriters knocked on New York's Brill Building door, wrote a song for Barbra Streisand, and also one for a movie soundtrack (*You Gotta Walk It Like You Talk It*...), recorded with later Dan member **Denny Dias** on guitar. It was produced by Kenny Vance, who got them a few gigs backing his harmony vocal group Jay and The Americans. Through Vance they met producer Gary Katz, who brought them to ABC/Dunhill Records in Los Angeles to write.

Tucked away in a side office, they rehearsed their own new songs for a debut album with Dias, **Jeff "Skunk" Baxter** (guitar), and **Jim Hodder** (drums). Although Fagen could sing, he preferred to bring in

"Daltreyesque" vocalist **David Palmer** to add a pop veneer to some of the songs. Session guitarist Elliot Randall was also hired to deliver the blistering guitar intro and solo for the upbeat pop of "Reelin' in the Years" (which Jimmy Page once said was his favorite). They had the songs, now they needed a band name; they chose that of a squirting dildo from William Burroughs' junkie novel *Naked Lunch*.

Can't Buy a Thrill yielded two surprise hits: the seductive, Latin-tinged vibe "Do It Again" (U.S. No.6) and "Reelin' in the Years" (U.S. No.11), so the record label pushed the band out on the road to promote it, and into the studio for 1973's *Countdown to Ecstasy*. Fagen took the lead on all the vocals (Palmer quit) and the band performed an assured set of songs including "Show Biz Kids," enhanced by powerful slide guitar from Rick Derringer. This song also demonstrated the duo's tireless pursuit of studio sound perfection: having decided that Hodder's percussive pulse was not sufficiently metronomic, they ran thirty feet of tape loop via recording equipment to outside

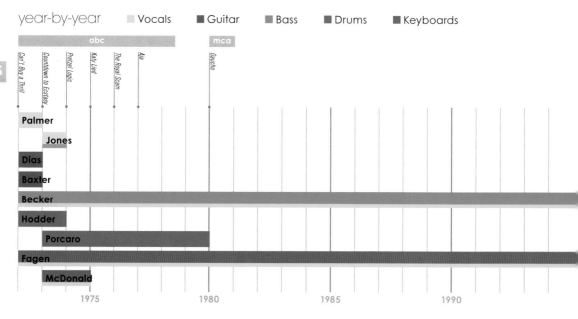

year-by-year   ■ Vocals   ■ Guitar   ■ Bass   ■ Drums   ■ Keyboards

2M	**2.5M**	**5M**	**2M**
Can't Buy a Thrill	*Pretzel Logic*	*Aja*	*A Decade of*
(1972)	(1974)	(1977)	*Steely Dan*
			(1985)

Jeff Porcaro
b. April 1, 1954
d. August 5, 1992

Michael McDonald
b. February 12, 1952

Royce Jones
b. December 15, 1954

the control room and back to achieve the hypnotic effect that drives the song so superbly.

A single from 1974's *Pretzel Logic*, "Rikki Don't Lose That Number," was their biggest chart success—U.S. No. 4. The band's jazz influences were now out in the open: the song's riff was very reminiscent of a Horace Silver piano number, while other tunes included a quirky like-for-like rendition of Duke Ellington's "East St. Louis Toodle-oo," with Becker mimicking a growling trumpet on his wah-wah guitar.

By *Katy Lied* (1975), Becker and Fagen, whose live lineup was augmented by **Jeff Porcaro** on drums and **Michael McDonald** on backing vocals and keyboards, were tired of touring. When they opted to become a purely studio-based unit, Baxter and Hodder quit, followed later by McDonald (to The Doobie Brothers).

The Royal Scam (1976) was the definitive Steely Dan guitar album, driven by Larry Carlton's fluid jazz-blues playing. It was also the only one on which the duo shared songwriting credits—thanks to Paul Griffin's organ work on "The Fez." But it was *Aja* (1977)

that confirmed Steely Dan's shimmering production credentials. It became a definitive laid-back FM-jazz fusion crossover, with Joe Sample, Wayne Shorter, and Tom Scott adding a cool L.A. vibe.

Gaucho (1980) acquired a *Spinal Tap* quality, what with contractual difficulties, Becker being hit by a car, and a version of "The Second Arrangement" being accidentally wiped. It was a recording nightmare, epitomized by fifty-five takes to sign off the mix for a fifty-second fade out on "Babylon Sisters."

Such perfectionism could not be sustained, and the duo split in 1981 to concentrate on solo projects, of which the best-loved is Fagen's *The Nightfly* (1982). When Becker produced his partner's *Kamakiriad* (1993), a transatlantic Top Ten success, fans clamored for a Dan reunion. After a well-received return to the road (hence 1995's *Alive in America*), the pair revived the group name for *Two Against Nature* (2000) with a new backing band. It won four Grammies including Album of the Year, and set the scene for an ongoing series of successful world tours. **JaH**

▓ Other percussion

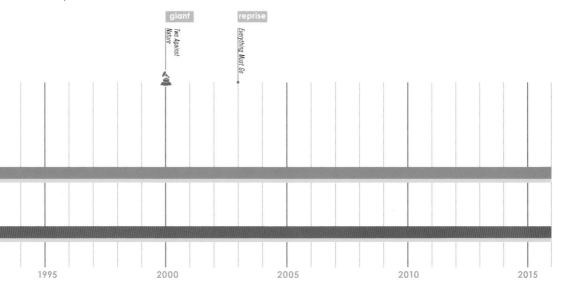

giant	reprise
Two Against Nature	*Everything Must Go*

1995 2000 2005 2010 2015

S

steppenwolf 1967–present

John Kay
b. April 12, 1944

Michael Monarch
b. July 5, 1950

Rushton Moreve
b. November 6, 1948
d. July 1, 1981

Goldy McJohn
b. May 2, 1945

Jerry Edmonton
b. Oct 24, 1946
d. November 28, 1993

Nick St. Nicholas
b. September 28, 1943

Larry Byrom
b. December 27, 1948

George Biondo
b. September 3, 1945

The Canadian-American Steppenwolf enjoyed huge success in the late sixties, partly because two great songs from their first album—"The Pusher" and "Born to be Wild"—graced the road movie *Easy Rider* (1969).

John Kay (vocals), **Goldy McJohn** (keyboards), and **Jerry Edmonton** (drums)—then in a Toronto-based group, called Sparrow, on the cusp of breaking through—recruited **Michael Monarch** (guitar) when they moved to California. The group split but reconstituted itself as Steppenwolf—the title of Herman Hesse's novel allegedly suggested by producer Gabriel Mekler—with the addition of **Rushton Moreve** in 1967. Success came instantly.

Steppenwolf (1968) soared to U.S. No. 8, on the back of the bikers' anthem "Born to Be Wild" (written by Edmonton's brother, Dennis), which accelerated to No. 2. *The Second* (also 1968) rose to No. 3 on the *Billboard* chart and contained another smash, "Magic Carpet Ride." Steppenwolf were flying high.

However, internal frictions were tearing the group apart. Moreve left (he later died in a 1981 bike accident) and was replaced by Rob Black, briefly, then **Nick St. Nicholas**, another ex-Sparrow. **Larry Byrom** (guitar) replaced Monarch.

Meanwhile, *At Your Birthday Party* (1969) went Top Ten, and the ambitiously political *Monster* (1969) and *Steppenwolf 7* (1970) kept them in the Top Twenty. The latter was indeed their seventh album, their discography being bolstered by two live albums, 1968's *Early Steppenwolf* and 1970's *Steppenwolf Live*.

By 1971, bassist **George Biondo** and guitarist Kent Henry had joined the group, but the next offering, *For Ladies Only*, fell short of their customary sales. One compilation album later, Steppenwolf broke up in 1972, only to re-form in 1974, now with Bobby Cochran, Eddie's nephew, on guitar. McJohn also quit; Andy Chapin, then Wayne Cook, took over keyboard duties. They rapidly recorded three albums: *Slow Flux* (1974), *Hour of the Wolf* (1975), and *Skullduggery* (1976), before splintering in 1976. Various members, each purporting to represent the real Steppenwolf, toured concurrently in different lineups until 1980.

Negotiations determined Kay's right to the name, leading to *Wolftracks* (1982), *Paradox* (1984), *Rock & Roll Rebels/Feed the Fire* (1987/1996), and *Rise & Shine* (1990). Kay tours with Michael Wilk (keyboards), Gary Link (bass), Danny Johnson (guitar), and Ron Hurst (drums) in a still compelling live act. **MiH**

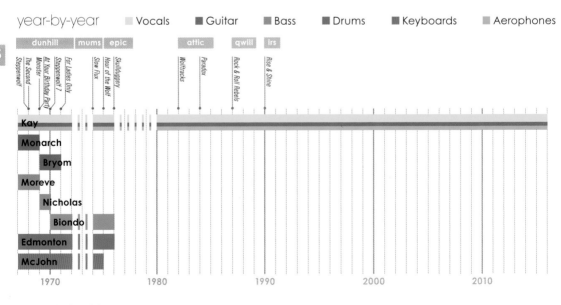

year-by-year ■ Vocals ■ Guitar ■ Bass ■ Drums ■ Keyboards ■ Aerophones

dunhill | mums | epic | attic | qwill | irs

Steppenwolf
The Second
At Your Birthday Party
Monster
Steppenwolf 7
For Ladies Only
Slow Flux
Hour of the Wolf
Skullduggery
Wolftracks
Paradox
Rock & Roll Rebels
Rise & Shine

Kay
Monarch
Bryom
Moreve
Nicholas
Biondo
Edmonton
McJohn

1970   1980   1990   2000   2010

stereophonics 1992–present

Kelly Jones
b. June 3, 1974

Adam Zindani
b. March 5, 1972

Richard Jones
b. May 23, 1974

Javier Weyler
b. July 3, 1975

Stuart Cable
b. May 19, 1970
d. June 7, 2010

Emerging on the heels of Britpop but with a more rock-oriented approach, power trio Stereophonics became Wales's most successful act since the Manic Street Preachers. Like the Manics, **Kelly Jones** (vocals, guitar), **Richard Jones** (no relation; bass), and **Stuart Cable** (drums) created songs that gripped listeners with their tales of the joys and anguish of modern life. Solid riffs and Kelly Jones's hoarse, Rod Stewart-indebted vocals distinguished their delivery.

Word Gets Around (1997), and their first U.K. chart-topper, *Performance and Cocktails* (1999), established them as a force to be reckoned with, thanks to their defiantly anthemic choruses and infectious melodies. The hits—"Local Boy in the Photograph," "A Thousand Trees," "The Bartender and the Thief," and "Pick a Part That's New" among them—pulsated with energy and a full-sized, polished production that made fans and media all the more curious about the group's roots in the tiny valley village of Cwmaman. With groups such as Catatonia emerging at the same time, the new Welsh rock scene became a talking point and Stereophonics benefited from huge press exposure.

By *Just Enough Education to Perform* (2001), the group had diversified its approach to an extent, incorporating balladry and acoustic instrumentation and scoring a major hit with a cover of Mike D'Abo's "Handbags and Gladrags." As with so many groups, however, the initial impetus became a little diffused, and fans reacted uncertainly to the sacking of Cable in 2003 for spending too much time away from the

group in his other role as a media personality. But after Black Crowes drummer Steve Gorman filled in, Cable's permanent replacement, **Javier Weyler**, gave renewed energy to the band. Stereophonics scored a U.K. No. 1 with "Dakota" from 2005's *Language. Sex. Violence. Other?* (the song also gave them a second moderate U.S. hit, after 2001's "Have a Nice Day"). Guitarist **Adam Zindani** was recruited in 2008 to enhance the group's live sound.

Although the hysteria that once surrounded them has receded, Jones and company have reached a comfortable commercial plateau. After 2006's *Live from Dakota*, 2007's *Pull the Pin* gave them a fifth U.K. No. 1 album, and 2008's *Decade in the Sun: The Best of Stereophonics* (2008) went double platinum. Fans' grief at Cable's alcohol-related death in 2010 was both genuine and widespread.

The band now have two decades of experience behind them and, while their career has waxed and waned over that time, they still command a considerable live following. *Keep Calm and Carry On* (2009) kept their sales at a gold-selling level, while in July 2012 they were chosen to represent Wales at a London show to mark the start of the Olympics. Weyler parted company with the band shortly before the concert, and his replacement was announced in September as Jamie Morrison of the Noisettes. *Graffiti on a Train* (2013) saw Stereophonics' sound take on a more cinematic style, with "Indian Summer" becoming their first U.K. Top 40 single since 2007. **JM**

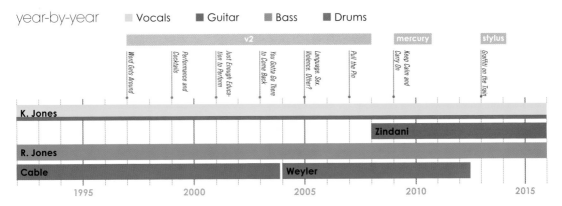

year-by-year ▪ Vocals ▪ Guitar ▪ Bass ▪ Drums

v2 | mercury | stylus

Word Gets Around | *Performance and Cocktails* | *Just Enough Education to Perform* | *You Gotta Go There to Come Back* | *Language. Sex. Violence. Other?* | *Pull the Pin* | *Keep Calm and Carry On* | *Graffiti on the Train*

K. Jones

Zindani

R. Jones

Cable | Weyler

1995 | 2000 | 2005 | 2010 | 2015

the stone roses 1983–present

Ian Brown
b. February 20, 1963

John Squire
b. November 24, 1962

Pete Garner
b. Unknown

Simon Wolstencroft
b. Unknown

Reni
b. April 10, 1964

Mani
b. November 16, 1962

With only two albums to their name, The Stone Roses enjoy a near mythic reputation for their transcendent flowering and huge impact on groups such as Oasis.

Ian Brown (vocals), **John Squire** (guitar), Andy Couzens (rhythm guitar), **Pete Garner** (bass), and **Simon Wolstencroft** (drums) formally became The Stone Roses in the Manchester area in 1983, although they had played together around Altrincham (a town in Cheshire, near Manchester) since 1980.

The Stone Roses always took their time, and their path to success was checkered. Wolstencroft departed in 1984, to be replaced by Alan "**Reni**" Wren on drums. Couzens quit in 1986 and was not replaced. When Garner left in 1987, Rob Hampson, then Gary "**Mani**" Mounfield, took over on bass. They recorded but shelved an album they were unhappy with, making the singles "Sally Cinnamon" (1987) and "Elephant Stone" (1988) their first real calling cards.

The group's debut album, *The Stone Roses*, came out in 1989 to immediate U.K. critical acclaim. From the magnificent chutzpah of opener "I Wanna Be Adored," to the closing "I Am the Resurrection" (Brown and Squire were big on Messianic imagery), it was a statement of intent. The fragile beauty of the singles "She Bangs the Drums," "Made of Stone," and "Waterfall" showed what the group could achieve.

With the Happy Mondays bringing up the rear, the Roses spearheaded the "Madchester" movement, and the success of the single "Fools Gold" meant they entered 1990 with a seemingly bright future. But the group became locked in legal wrangles over a change of record company, then took an unconscionable time to record their second album. "One Love," a 1990 single, was the last anyone heard for four years. Their triumphant live shows ceased.

Second Coming finally emerged in 1994, but was not what fans were expecting. Years of seclusion had made their sound rougher and more guitar-heavy. "Love Spreads," "Ten Storey Love Song," and "Begging You" were all U.K. hits, but their moment had passed.

When their shows flopped, a round of changes ensued. Reni left and Robbie Maddix deputized on drums, while Nigel Ipinson-Fleming (keyboards) varied the sound. When Squire left to form The Seahorses, the writing was on the wall. Although Aziz Ibrahim joined on guitar, the group split in late 1996. Brown's solo career proved successful and Mani joined Primal Scream, while The Seahorses broke up in 1999.

In 2011, oft-mooted rumors and long-held dreams bore fruit: the classic lineup of Brown, Squire, Reni, and Mani reunited for instantly sold-out stadium shows and a slew of headline slots at festivals in 2012. **MiH**

year-by-year   ▢ Vocals   ■ Guitar   ■ Bass   ■ Drums

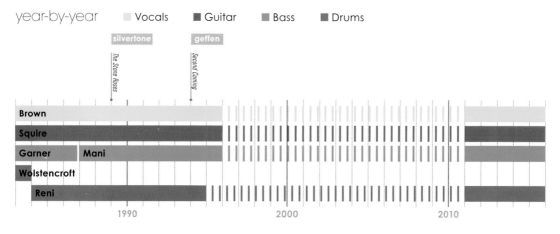

Grunge   Hard Rock

stone temple pilots 1986–present

F

Scott Weiland
b. October 27, 1967

F

Dean DeLeo
b. August 23, 1961

F

Robert DeLeo
b. February 2, 1966

F

Eric Kretz
b. June 7, 1966

Stone Temple Pilots were viewed as bandwagon-jumpers when they threw their weight behind the Seattle sound's mainstream success in 1992. Yet the group—hailing from San Diego, some 1,255 miles down the coast from grunge's heartland—predated Nirvana and Pearl Jam, and their diverse songs set them apart from their angst-ridden peers.

The Pilots took off in 1986 when singer **Scott Weiland** and bassist **Robert DeLeo** met at a Black Flag concert. When the conversation turned to women, they discovered they were dating the same one—but, rather than fighting over her affections, they dumped the Texas-bound beauty, moved into her San Diego apartment, hired drummer **Eric Kretz** and Robert's guitar-playing older brother **Dean**, and started jamming.

Their 1992 debut, *Core*, afforded them a U.S. No. 3 hit, a Grammy for Best Hard Rock Performance, and simultaneous nods for Best and Worst New Band from *Rolling Stone*'s readers and critics, respectively. Reportedly the only Pilots album Weiland wrote sober, *Core* was certified eight times platinum in 2001.

The group dodged the sophomore slump with *Purple* (1994). "Interstate Love Song" and "Vaseline" followed "Plush" to No. 1 on the U.S. Mainstream Rock Tracks listing, and the album enjoyed three chart-topping weeks en route to an eventual six million sales.

In 1995, however, Weiland pushed the self-destruct button with heroin and crack cocaine, resulting in numerous convictions, probation violations, stints in rehab, and ultimately jail. Despite this, he contributed to *Tiny Music… Songs from the Vatican Gift Shop* (1996), a sixties-influenced set that preserved their platinum sales. However, most of an accompanying tour was canceled due to Weiland's problems.

When disbandment inevitably occurred in 1997, Kretz and the DeLeo brothers formed Talk Show, while Weiland, against all the odds, released a solo album, *12 Bar Blues*. When both bombed, the Pilots reformed, returning to their hard rock roots on *No. 4* (1999).

With tensions simmering, the bossa nova-infused *Shangri-La Dee Da* (2001) marked the beginning of the end. In 2003 Weiland joined three-fifths of Guns N' Roses in Velvet Revolver, making the U.S. No. 1 *Contraband* (2004) and *Libertad* (2007). Meanwhile, the DeLeos formed Army of Anyone.

In 2008, a new chapter began. Mellowed by fatherhood, they embarked on a North American tour as a prelude to their self-titled sixth studio album. Legal wrangles with Atlantic aside, the Pilots were flying high again and celebrating the twentieth anniversary of *Core* in 2012. Things came crashing down the following year, however, when Weiland was fired from the band—a split that resulted in lawsuits from both sides. Chester Bennington of Linkin Park stepped into the breach as frontman, promising to do his "best to honor the legacy of the music." **MW**

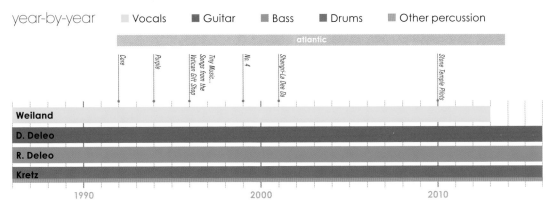

year-by-year   ▢ Vocals   ■ Guitar   ■ Bass   ■ Drums   ▨ Other percussion

atlantic

Core | *Purple* | *Tiny Music… Songs from the Vatican Gift Shop* | *No. 4* | *Shangri-La Dee Da* | *Stone Temple Pilots*

Weiland

D. Deleo

R. Deleo

Kretz

1990   2000   2010

the stranglers 1974–present

Jean-Jacques Burnel
b. February 21, 1952

Jet Black
b. August 26, 1938

Dave Greenfield
b. March 29, 1949

Baz Warne
b. March 25, 1964

Hugh Cornwell
b. August 28, 1949

Hans Wärmling
b. July 22, 1943
d. October 12,1995

Even if they did drive to early shows in an ice-cream van, there was a definite fear factor at work where The Stranglers were concerned. Punk, the movement with which they were closely associated, prized youth above most other qualities, but three of the quartet—singer/guitarist **Hugh Cornwell**, keyboardist **Dave Greenfield**, and drummer **Jet Black**—were already too old to be "bad boys" in 1977 (Black was three years older than even Charlie Watts). "Mad men" was closer to the mark. Combative bassist **Jean-Jacques Burnel**—an accomplished martial artist—completed a lineup that often had journalists ducking for cover: kidnap, abandonment in the desert, and, on one occasion, being taped to the Eiffel Tower were regarded as amusing distractions. "We're clean wholesome boys…" said Burnel. "Just like the boys next door—if you happen to live next door to a morgue."

Were they punk or not? Their background as The Guildford Stranglers suggests not. Churning out soft rock covers on the club circuit was not the coolest of credentials, and it left them with few friends on either side of the music spectrum. "We missed that pub rock thing—we were too young and not good enough to be a part of it," said Cornwell. "When the punk thing happened, we were too good and too old… We were a class of one. But it didn't stop our success."

When that success came, it was considerable: three albums in just fourteen months lodged in the U.K. Top Five. The band avoided many of the obligatory names—New York Dolls, MC5, The Stooges—dropped by punk groups with whom they were misleadingly grouped. On *Rattus Norvegicus* and *No More Heroes* (both 1977), and *Black and White* (1978), Greenfield's keyboards (replacing the guitar of the departed **Hans Wärmling**) made The Doors a more obvious musical touchstone. The requisite garage aesthetic came from Black, who sounded to one critic as though "he was hammering the roof on a garden shed."

The songs were often dark vignettes from society's underbelly. The likes of "London Lady," "Hanging Around," and "I Feel Like a Wog," featured lyrics that, contrarily, combined acute intelligence with attitudes (especially toward women) that might have embarrassed a bad hair-metal outfit. The Stranglers were a hit-singles machine, too. The loping "Peaches," the driving "Something Better Change," and the vicious "No More Heroes" all crashed the U.K. Top Ten, with "Five Minutes" and "Nice 'n' Sleazy" close behind. One of the covers that survived from the cull after the group's days as The Guildford Stranglers became an extraordinary reading of Bacharach and David's "Walk on By" that just missed the Top Twenty.

year-by-year ■ Vocals ■ Guitar ■ Bass ■ Drums ■ Keyboards

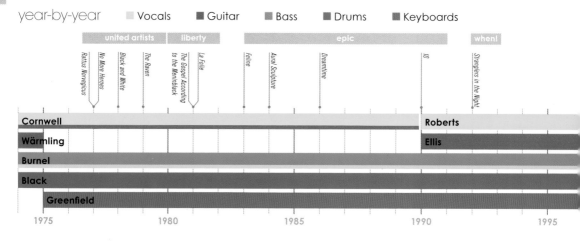

1M
Rattus
Norvegicus
(1977)

500,000
No More Heroes
(1977)

500,000
Black and White
(1978)

1M
Greatest Hits
1977–1990
(1990)

Paul Roberts
b. December 31, 1959

John Ellis
b. June 1, 1952

A group that relished baiting pretty much everyone at every available opportunity could hardly avoid controversy. There were the strippers hired to appear at a 1978 show in south London, Cornwell's three-month jail term for drugs possession in 1980, and a group arrest after a show in Nice, France, later that year (for allegedly inciting a riot). In the studio, the band were moving further away from punk. The change that was noticeable on a fourth smash, *The Raven* (1979), was unmistakeable by the time of *The Gospel According to the Meninblack* (1981), a concept album. The latter, however, won few friends. "Unanimous slagging," recalled Burnel to *Select* magazine. "Even the fans said it was fucking horrible."

Their renaissance had unlikely origins. "I've listened to everything," said Cornwell. "When I was fifteen, I was really getting off on Mose Allison." "Golden Brown," from *La Folie* (1981), duly betrayed jazz influences. Tongue firmly in cheek, Cornwell introduced the band's biggest hit (U.K. No. 2) at the Reading festival as a "heavy metal classic." In reality, it was a hazy, waltz-like paean to heroin.

The Stranglers always sounded less abrasive than most contemporaries. After *Feline* (1983), those edges were smoothed away further on *Aural Sculpture* (1984) and *Dreamtime* (1986), with funk flirtations and bursts of brass. However, although those albums yielded the sublime hits "Skin Deep" and "Always the Sun," it took a couple of sixties covers to revive real interest: "All Day and All of the Night," originally by The Kinks, and "96 Tears," by ? and the Mysterians.

The latter featured on *10* (1990), which proved a swansong for Cornwell, who departed after a gig in August 1990. The rest of the group moved quickly to fill a huge gap left by their first major lineup change in a decade and a half. Duties were split, with **John Ellis**—formerly of The Vibrators and a touring presence with The Stranglers dating back to Cornwell's stint in prison—taking on the guitar and **Paul Roberts** on vocals. As a five-piece, the band recorded four albums, with *Stranglers in the Night* (1993), *About Time* (1995), *Written in Red* (1997), and *Coup de Grace* (1998) all seeming to confirm Cornwell's parting shot that "no chances were being taken any more."

That was accurate until a confounding return to form on the band's thirtieth anniversary with *Norfolk Coast* (2004). More chopping and changing had taken place, with former Toy Doll **Baz Warne** replacing Ellis. And with *Suite XVI* (2006) and *Giants* (2012)— despite being down to a lean four-piece again (Roberts had departed)—The Stranglers showed that not all the life had been squeezed out of them yet. **CB**

S

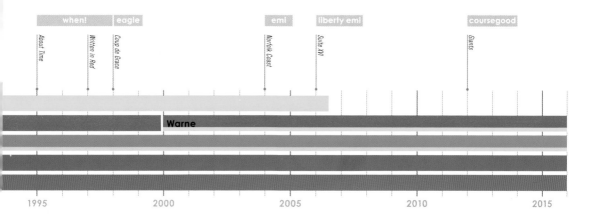

supertramp 1970–present

Rick Davies
b. July 22, 1944

Roger Hodgson
b. March 21, 1950

Dave Winthrop
b. November 27, 1948

Bob Millar
b. February 2, 1950

Richard Palmer-James
b. June 11, 1947

Kevin Currie
b. Unknown

Supertramp began as a progressive group but came to prominence only after they softened their heavy rock with easy-listening elements. They were formed in London, England, when Dutch millionaire Sam Miesgaes wearied of The Joint, a group he had bankrolled, and decided instead to back the new band of one of its members, **Rick Davies**. The new enterprise started life with the name Daddy, featuring Davies on keyboards and vocals and **Roger Hodgson** on bass; with the additions of saxophonist **Dave Winthrop**, drummer **Bob Millar**, and guitarist **Richard Palmer-James** the group became Supertramp.

The failure of their self-titled debut album led to the replacement of Millar by drummer **Kevin Currie** and the addition of bassist **Frank Farrell** (Hodgson having switched to guitar). But Supertramp again made little impression with Indelibly Stamped (1971).

When all the recent recruits left, Miesgaes teamed Davies and Hodgson with former Alan Bown Set players **Dougie Thomson** (bass) and **John Helliwell** (saxophone), plus American **Bob Siebenberg** (drums), and gave them a year to get their act together. The group duly tempered their more outré progressive

elements with poppier melodies and irresistible hooks. The result was worth the wait and the investment: after a slow start, Crime of the Century (1974) climbed to U.K. No. 4 and yielded the lilting hit "Dreamer."

Hodgson's distinctive falsetto and electric piano gave a trademark sound to his delivery of lyrics that, in a decidedly post-Dark Side of the Moon spirit, touched on madness and melancholy. Supertramp had the Floyd beat on one front, though: the album's indignant opener, "School," predated "Another Brick in the Wall" by five years. The gruffer Davies sang the album's second hit, the wry "Bloody Well Right."

Although the group themselves did not rate it, Crisis? What Crisis? (1975), with fan favorite "Ain't Nobody But Me," maintained their success. The far better Even in the Quietest Moments… (1977), opening with Hodgson's gorgeous "Give a Little Bit," broke Supertramp into the U.S. Top Twenty and secured their first U.S. gold award. (The revitalized Crime of the Century finally earned gold status two months later.)

Having relocated to the United States, the band took their time preparing a new album. "Supertramp at that time was a very easy band to be in," Davies

year-by-year   ■ Vocals   ■ Guitar   ■ Bass   ■ Drums   ■ Keyboards

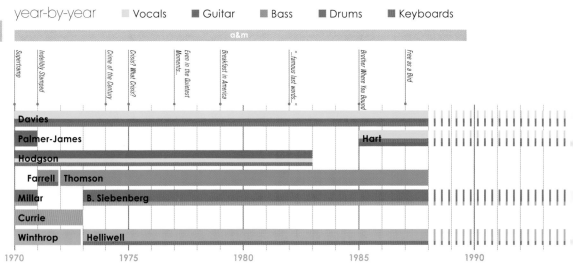

Dougie Thomson
b. March 24, 1951

John Helliwell
b. February 15, 1945

Bob Siebenberg
b. October 31, 1949

Mark Hart
b. July 2, 1953

Jesse Siebenberg
b. February 1977

Frank Farrell
b. March 31, 1947
d. July 19, 1997

told *Billboard* writer Craig Rosen. "We still weren't that big saleswise to start causing the usual friction when the songwriter gets more money than the drummer." The result was *Breakfast in America* (1979), which topped the U.S. chart within two months of its release. Four singles—"The Logical Song," the title track, "Goodbye Stranger," and "Take the Long Way Home"—propelled the album to multi-million sales. This immense popularity drowned the voices of cynics who bemoaned Supertramp's lack of character.

However, differences between Davies and Hodgson became a rift during the demanding world tour that ensued. (The resulting live album—1980's *Paris*—bequeathed a version of "Dreamer" that became a U.S. Top Twenty hit.) The tension between Davies's blues preferences and Hodgson's poppier approach was clearly audible on 1982's *"...famous last words..."*—the source of the band's last major hit, "It's Raining Again"—and there was little surprise when Hodgson left to go solo soon after its release.

After a moderately successful solo album, *In the Eye of the Storm* (1984), Davies revived the band for the well-received *Brother Where You Bound* (1985),

whose epic title track boasted guitar work by Thin Lizzy's Scott Gorham and Pink Floyd's David Gilmour. But as he experimented with synthesized sound, *Free as a Bird* (1987) fell short of the U.S. Top 100—despite "I'm Beggin' You," somewhat implausibly, topping *Billboard*'s Hot Dance Club Play chart—and fared little better at home. Supertramp duly fragmented.

Eight years later, Davies re-formed the group with Helliwell, Siebenberg (whose percussionist son **Jesse** later joined the band too), bassist Cliff Hugo, guitarist Carl Verheyen, brass player Lee Thornburg, and, on keyboards and guitar, former Crowded House associate **Mark Hart**. The resultant *Some Things Never Change* (1997) was a belated return to their most successful style. "We've had entire pop movements come and go between our albums," Davies noted, "and we haven't even noticed."

After another tour in 2002, the band again lapsed into silence. Hopes that a 2010 tour—celebrating the fortieth anniversary of their first album—would feature Hodgson proved in vain. "You need harmony, both musically and personally," said Davies. "Unfortunately, that doesn't exist between us anymore." **GL**

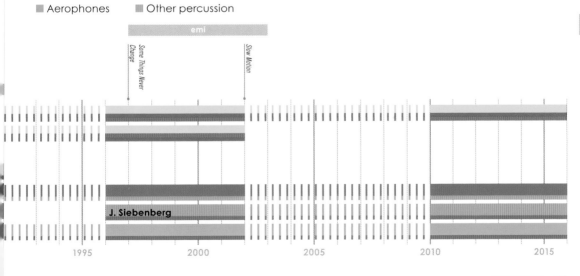

■ Aerophones   ■ Other percussion

emi

Some Things Never Change

Slow Motion

J. Siebenberg

1995   2000   2005   2010   2015

talking heads 1975–1991

David Byrne
b. May 14, 1952

Chris Frantz
b. May 8, 1951

Tina Weymouth
b. November 22, 1950

Jerry Harrison
b. February 21, 1949

One of the most influential bands of the new wave era, Talking Heads actually came together several years before punk's heyday. Founder members **David Byrne**, **Chris Frantz**, and **Tina Weymouth** had been friends at the Rhode Island School of Design (Byrne and Frantz were briefly in a band called The Artistics; Frantz's girlfriend Weymouth would cart the band around) and moved to Manhattan together in 1974.

Byrne and Frantz decided to supplement their fresh New York lifestyle with a fresh New York sound. Weymouth was persuaded to join on bass and the name Talking Heads followed almost as swiftly as their debut gig, a dream slot supporting the Ramones at New York's punk mecca CBGB. That show in June 1975—launching their alien, clean, clipped style—attracted the attention of Seymour Stein, who signed them to his Sire label. (During their CBGB days, Weymouth later recalled, "Lou Reed would take us aside and give us some hilarious tips... Then he'd say, 'Smart move getting a chick in the band—wonder where you got that idea.'") The Heads' debut single, "Love > Building on Fire," was released in February 1977, shortly before they fully realized their sound with the recruitment of **Jerry Harrison** (ex-Jonathan Richman and the Modern Lovers) on keyboards.

With the fiery ostentation of punk around them, Talking Heads' "straight" image stood out. Their debut

album, *Talking Heads: 77,* was happy to deal with distinctly un-rock 'n' roll subject matter: out went high-living, nihilism, sex, and drugs; in came songs about, well, buildings and food. Weymouth and Frantz's taut funk rhythm section provided the perfect vessel for the panicky austerity of Byrne's jerky vocal tics, and the debut struck a chord. It and the single "Psycho Killer" were modest U.S. and U.K. hits, but crucially they caught the attention of Brian Eno, ex-Roxy Music, now producer of intriguing sonic adventures.

On tour with the Ramones in spring 1977, Talking Heads met Eno in London and hit it off. Eno recorded a song called "King's Lead Hat" (an anagram of Talking Heads, no less) for his *Before and After Science* (1977) and moved on to produce the Heads' second album, *More Songs About Buildings and Food* (1978). The Eno effect further tightened the band's sound on what is otherwise an unabashedly pop album, even culminating in an enthusiastic take on Al Green's "Take Me to the River." But if Talking Heads were flirting around the edges of the mainstream, their next collaboration with Eno would shy away while paradoxically providing their biggest hit yet.

Fear of Music emerged in 1979, wild and paranoid as ever—that title's no fluke. It almost reached the *Billboard* Top Twenty, as record buyers' appetite for sickly noise and mental breakdown spread.

year-by-year   ■ Vocals   ■ Guitar   ■ Bass   ■ Drums   ■ Keyboards

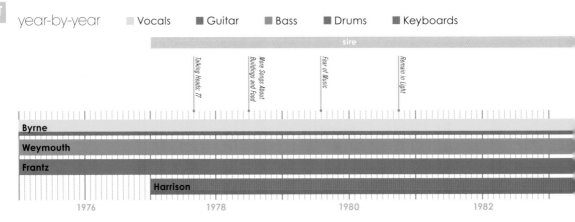

1.8M
**More Songs About
Buildings and Food**
(1978)

3.3M
**Speaking in
Tongues**
(1983)

4.9M
**Stop Making
Sense**
(1984)

4.2M
Little Creatures
(1985)

But beyond the studio trickery, and in spite of all the crazed innovation, *Fear of Music* piled on the tunes.

Even more of a studio product was *Remain in Light* (1980). "Ambient music and strong lyrics and incredibly inventive percussion and bass parts," enthused Dave Sitek, fêted producer and leader of TV on the Radio, to *Rolling Stone*. "I was a kid, but I still thought, 'I should have been involved in that record!' It was amazing." The last of Eno's production jobs, the album was a fascinating document of intra-band tension. Basic tracks were enlivened by layer after layer as Byrne jammed his way from bare bones to full songs, resulting in odd classics like "Once in a Lifetime."

But these working methods only shed light on the band's fractious state. Byrne and Eno had become their own little club, with Frantz and Weymouth on the other side and Harrison somewhere in between. There were tangible benefits to this, of course: the Byrne/Eno love-in also produced their loop-led masterpiece *My Life in the Bush of Ghosts*, while Frantz and Weymouth formed the Tom Tom Club, blending hip-hop, soul, and funk—plus substantially more sunshine than the day-job—to glorious effect on songs like "Genius of Love."

Still at loggerheads, the band regrouped for 1983's *Speaking in Tongues*. Even as internal relations deteriorated, they bagged their biggest U.S. hit, "Burning Down the House," which peaked at No. 9.

Revitalized if not quite reconciled, they followed this in 1984 with *Stop Making Sense*, a double whammy of live film—directed by Jonathan Demme, later an Oscar winner for *The Silence of the Lambs*—and soundtrack album, featuring (on record) choice cuts from the previous decade and (on celluloid) David Byrne's unfeasibly wide suit.

Talking Heads were now, commercially, at a high watermark and capitalized with their most accessible effort yet, 1985's *Little Creatures*, including the U.K. hit "Road to Nowhere." This found a sleek Talking Heads comfortably tucked into the MTV era, with similar fare to follow on the following year's *True Stories*, a quasi-soundtrack to the movie of the same name. (A song on the latter album bequeathed a new name to an Oxford quintet then known as On a Friday, later to conquer the world as Radiohead.)

They would manage one more album together, taking a different tack on *Naked* (1988) and embracing world music rather the crisp video-age sound that had fattened their wallets. It was a U.K. Top Three and U.S. Top Twenty hit, but their coming asunder was made permanent in 1991. Although they regrouped for a performance when their questing funk received a richly deserved induction into the Rock 'n' Roll Hall of Fame in 2002, there is, sadly, scant likelihood that we will see them again. **MaH**

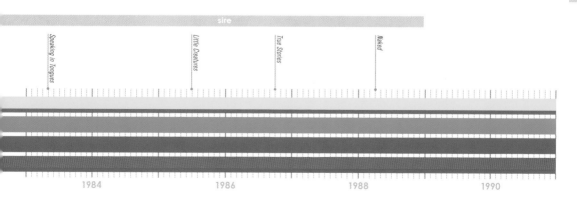

tangerine dream 1967–2014

Edgar Froese
b. June 6, 1944
d. January 20, 2015

Klaus Schulze
b. August 4, 1947

Conrad Schnitzler
b. 1937
d. August 4, 2011

Peter Baumann
b. January 29, 1953

Chris Franke
b. April 6, 1953

Klaus Krieger
b. Unknown

Steve Jolliffe
b. April 28, 1949

Johannes Schmölling
b. November 9, 1950

Compiling a definitive list of Tangerine Dream's albums is not a task for the weak-willed: since 1970, almost one hundred studio albums have been released under their moniker—*not* including over thirty soundtracks and forty compilations. But among them are gems that are still proving influential today.

The experimental music scene in sixties Germany produced pioneering bands who championed electronic sound, and owed more to the postwar European classical tradition than American blues or rock 'n' roll. The British music press came up with a description for these new bands: for better or for worse, "krautrock" entered the musical lexicon.

Tangerine Dream emerged from West Berlin's Zodiak Free Arts Lab. There, art student **Edgar Froese** and experimental musicians, including **Klaus Schulze** and **Conrad Schnitzler**, staged multimedia events, mixing music, literature, and visual arts.

Released in 1970, Tangerine Dream's debut, *Electronic Meditation,* featured tape collages and drones. The following year, Froese unveiled a very different version of Tangerine Dream. Schulze and Schnitzler were out (to Ash Ra Tempel and Cluster, respectively), and **Chris Franke** and Steve Schroyder were in. Bearing almost no resemblance to its predecessor, 1971's *Alpha Centauri* was reliant on atmospheric organ, swirling electronic sounds, and flute. The first step toward what Froese described as "kosmische (cosmic) musik," it sold a respectable 20,000 copies to a core audience of German stoners. ("Fly and Collision of Comas Sola" proved a favorite of future Sisters of Mercy main-man Andrew Eldritch, who indulged his Tangerine Dream leanings on the unreleased 1997 album *Feel No Pain*.)

With Schroyder relegated to "guest" status and **Peter Baumann** added, 1972's ambitious double set *Zeit* ("time" in German) comprised four LP side-long songs. The sound was more overtly electronic, with heavy use of the VCS3 synthesizer (best known for The Who's "Won't Get Fooled Again" and Pink Floyd's "On the Run"). Florian Fricke of Popul Vuh guested on his Moog synth, and, with no clear melodies and rhythms, the music seemed out of this world.

The following year's *Atem* ("Breath" in German) was just as experimental, introducing the Mellotron, an electronic keyboard that played pitched tape loops of recorded instruments—in effect, an analog precursor to today's digital samplers. Airplay on BBC DJ John Peel's show introduced Tangerine Dream to a British audience. "We started getting requests for all these German records by people we'd never heard of," Simon Draper, who ran the chain of Virgin record stores with Richard Branson, told *Mojo*. "Of all of them, Tangerine Dream were far and away the most interesting—and the level of interest in them was huge." The Tangs were duly signed to the Virgin label.

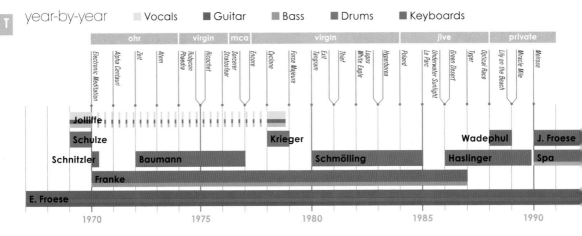

year-by-year ▢ Vocals ■ Guitar ■ Bass ■ Drums ■ Keyboards

| ohr | virgin | mca | virgin | jive | private |

Electronic Meditation · *Alpha Centauri* · *Zeit* · *Atem* · *Rubycon* · *Phaedra* · *Ricochet* · *Sorcerer* · *Stratosfear* · *Encore* · *Cyclone* · *Force Majeure* · *Exit* · *Tangram* · *Thief* · *Logos* · *White Eagle* · *Hyperborea* · *Poland* · *Underwater Sunlight* · *Le Parc* · *Green Desert* · *Tiger* · *Optical Race* · *Lily on the Beach* · *Miracle Mile* · *Melrose*

Jolliffe
Schulze · Krieger · Wadephul · J. Froese
Schnitzler · Baumann · Schmölling · Haslinger · Spa
Franke
E. Froese

1970   1975   1980   1985   1990

Paul Haslinger
b. Demember 11, 1962

Ralph Wadephul
b. 1958

Jerome Froese
b. November 24. 1970

Linda Spa
b. September 4, 1968

Thorsten Quaeschning
b. Unknown

The investment was rewarded when *Phaedra* (1974) hit the U.K. Top Twenty. (Young fans included not only future progressive rockers like Marillion, but also members of other Virgin acts like The Human League and OMD.) A benchmark in electronic music, *Phaedra* made extensive use of sequencers creating repeating patterns of synthesizer notes. It all but gave birth to the "Berlin School"—a group of artists whose sequenced, synthesized soundscapes typically fitted entire sides of LPs. Among those paying attention was producer Giorgio Moroder, who told *NME*: "I used to know these guys very well, and loved their *Phaedra* album very much." The band's influence is obvious in Moroder's early, often epic work with Donna Summer.

Tangerine Dream hit a commercial peak with 1975's *Rubycon*. Continuing in the "Berlin" style, it followed *Phaedra* into the U.K. Top Twenty. The band toured throughout Europe, improvising loosely in the manner of their studio albums, and their sound evolved to incorporate multilayered sequencer patterns and a greater use of percussion and electric guitar, documented effectively on 1975's live *Ricochet*.

Toward the end of the seventies, the band experimented with more melodic compositions and, on occasion, vocals. After an abortive attempt to make an album with Pink Floyd drummer Nick Mason, they reworked the material as 1976's *Stratosfear*. Then 1977's live *Encore* proved Baumann's swansong

(he later founded the New Age label Private Music). Singer **Steve Jolliffe** and drummer **Klaus Krieger** brought a stronger rock influence to 1978's *Cyclone*, but by 1979's *Force Majeure* the pair had been dropped and the "Berlin" sound had been restored.

Cinema and TV had long provided a fertile setting for Tangerine Dream; 1977's *Sorcerer* became better known for its soundtrack than for the film itself. The band scored more than twenty-five movies in the eighties—memorably, 1981's *Thief* opens with their accompaniment to James Caan's safe-cracking, and 1983's *Risky Business* became as indelibly linked with them as with Bob Seger's "Old Time Rock and Roll."

Thereafter, mainstream popularity waned. But touring throughout Europe and America, and an uninterrupted release schedule ensured that the band remained unchallenged in their field well into the nineties—at which point their influence once again became clear, thanks to latterday ambient acts such as The Orb. Froese promptly created his own TDI label, to issue a bewildering series of original and remix sets. Many feature his son **Jerome**, who joined in 1990.

Froeses's sidekicks now include saxophonist **Linda Spa** (more of a presence at shows than on albums) and keyboardist **Thorsten Quaeschning**, whose work recalls classic-period Tangerine Dream (the band's recorded output is largely down to him and Froese). There are no signs of the phenomenon ending. **TB/BM**

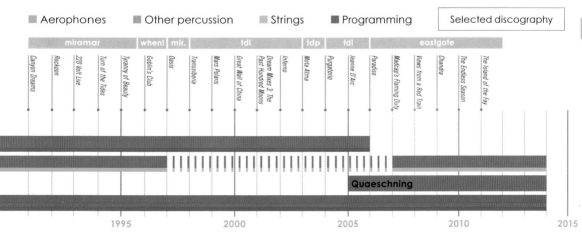

■ Aerophones   ■ Other percussion   ■ Strings   ■ Programming   Selected discography

miramar   when!   mir.   tdi   tdp   tdi   eastgate

Canyon Dreams · Rockoon · 220 Volt Live · Turn of the Tides · Tyranny of Beauty · Goblin's Club · Oasis · Transsiberia · Mars Polaris · Great Wall of China · Dream Mixes 3. The Past Hundred Moons · Inferno · Mota Atma · Purgatorio · Jeanne D'Arc · Paradiso · Madcap's Flaming Duty · Views from a Red Train · Chandra · The Endless Season · The Island of the Fay

Quaeschning

1995   2000   2005   2010   2015

Boy (1980)

War (1983)

The Unforgettable Fire (1984)

The Joshua Tree (1987)

Achtung Baby (1991)

Zooropa (1993)

Pop (1997)

All That You Can't Leave Behind (2000)

How to Dismantle an Atomic Bomb (2004)

No Line on the Horizon (2009)

Left to right: **The Edge, Larry Mullen Jr., Bono,** and **Adam Clayton** perform in Belgium on October 18, 1980, during their *Boy* tour.

Clayton and **Bono** at the 1984 Band Aid recording session.

Bob Dylan joins U2 onstage in L.A. on the Joshua Tree tour in 1987.

Bono and **The Edge** on British TV's *The Tube* in 1983.

Bono—in the character of MacPhisto that he used for songs such as "Lemon"—performs in Paris, France, in June 1993, during U2's *Zooropa* tour.

Bono as The Fly: the first and most enduring of the alter-egos that he adopted for U2's reinvention on *Achtung Baby*.

The visually extraordinary Popmart tour reaches the Netherlands in the summer of 1997.

Larry Mullen Jr. performs in San Diego on March 28, 2005, at the start of U2's Vertigo tour of that year.

Bono and The Edge in one of their Elevation tour set pieces, 2001.

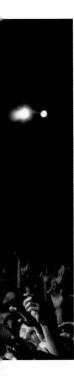

The band perform under New York's Brooklyn Bridge in late 2004.

The record-breaking 360° Tour reaches New Jersey's New Meadowlands Stadium in 2011.

univers zéro 1974–present

Daniel Denis
b. 1953

Roger Trigaux
b. Unknown

Michel Berckmans
b. September 1, 1955

Christian Genet
b. Unknown

Kurt Budé
b. Unknown

In 1978, British avant-garde rock band Henry Cow initiated a London concert featuring similar-minded artists from continental Europe—among them, Univers Zéro from Belgium. The show's slogan was simple: "The bands the record companies don't want you to hear." Its name, Rock in Opposition (RIO), became that of a genre—less of related musical styles than of a progressive, politically minded attitude.

Having worked with French progressive rockers Magma, Belgian drummer and composer **Daniel Denis** formed Univers Zéro in 1974. Initially influenced by avant-garde classical music and electronic jazz, the band's sound had evolved by the time of their 1977 debut. *Univers Zéro* was a mix of progressive rock and free jazz, but presented by a chamber ensemble with largely acoustic instrumentation: bassoon, viola, violin, harmonium, spinet. The compositions, by Denis or guitarist **Roger Trigaux**, were often dark in tone and showed the influence of Béla Bartók; Denis also championed Albert Huybrechts, a little-known Belgian composer active in the twenties. The sound is encapsulated in the fifteen-minute "Ronde": tightly structured chamber music with asymmetrical rhythms and elements of post-bop jazz. (The album was remixed and reissued in the eighties as *1313*.)

Univers Zéro continued in this vein with 1979's *Heresie*. Denis and Trigaux's songs mined darker depths, with a bleak, dissonant sound that showcased the oboe and bassoon of **Michel Berckmans**.

1981's *Ceux du dehors* ("Those from the outside") witnessed a change in tone following the departure of Trigaux, who left to form his own progressive group, Present. (The album was issued internationally on the Recommended label, itself an influential base for RIO artists, founded in the late seventies by Henry Cow's drummer, Chris Cutler.) With a lighter, less brooding sound than previous works, the album saw the introduction of electronics into the band's music.

Having toured throughout Europe, Univers Zéro resurfaced on record with 1984's *Uzed*, which showed a significant stylistic departure. Synthesizers took an increasingly prominent role, as did the cello textures of new member André Mergen. Denis's compositions had also taken on an increasingly Middle Eastern flavor, most evidently on the opener "Présage."

Working outside the conventional music industry offered Univers Zéro artistic freedom, but there was a commercial corollary: with little in the way of business management, finances were a persistent struggle and, in 1986, Denis decided to fold the band. He made two solo albums before relaunching Univers Zéro in 1999 with Berckmans. Subsequent work has seen the band moving away from their early sound toward more traditional progressive rock territory. **TB**

year-by-year   ■ Vocals   ■ Guitar   ■ Bass   ■ Drums
■ Keyboards   ■ Aerophones   ■ Strings

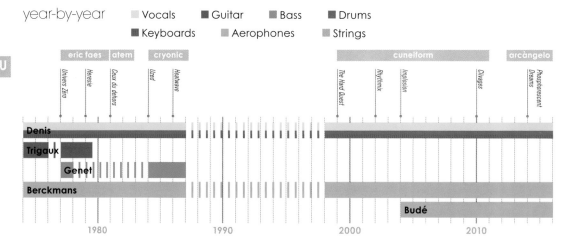

uriah heep 1969–present

Mick Box
b. June 9, 1947

Ken Hensley
b. August 24, 1945

David Byron
b. Jan 29, 1947
d. February 28, 1985

Paul Newton
b. February 21, 1948

Alex Napier
b. Unknown

Gary Thain
b. May 15, 1948
d. December 8, 1975

Trevor Bolder
b. June 9, 1950
d. May 21, 2013

Lee Kerslake
b. April 16, 1947

You can't stop the Heep. The British act have endured myriad lineup changes and bad reviews. (Famously, *Rolling Stone*'s Melissa Mills wrote, "If this group makes it, I'll have to commit suicide.") Along the way, they've issued more than fifty studio, live, and compilation albums. In their 1971–1975 heyday, Heep were among the most popular hard rock acts in the U.S. and U.K. When those countries stopped buying their records, the band focused on other nations—notably, Norway and Germany—until their renaissance with *Abominog* in 1982. Today, though they rarely trouble charts, they still tour and put out albums that add to their legacy.

Uriah Heep's roots stretch back to the Stalkers, a group that rocked pubs in England's Essex in the mid-sixties. When the Stalkers split, guitarist **Mick Box** and vocalist **David Byron** enlisted keyboardist-guitarist **Ken Hensley** and bassist **Paul Newton** in a new band, Spice, which became Uriah Heep (after a character in Charles Dickens' *David Copperfield*). Starting with Alex Napier, the band would go through drummers at a Spinal Tap-style rate, utilizing at least four different players in its first six years. (Others to feature in the ranks include **Lee Kerslake**, who also drummed in the first incarnation of Ozzy Osbourne's Blizzard of Ozz, **Trevor Bolder**, former bassist in David Bowie's Spiders from Mars, and Bernie Shaw, Heep's singer since 1986.)

Heep made little noise on the charts with 1970's debut *Very 'Eavy... Very 'Umble* (issued as a self-titled affair in the U.S.), but the response from critics was deafening. "From the first note," critiqued Mills, "you know you don't want to hear any more." But Heep didn't make that an option. The band charged ahead at an astounding pace, releasing a dozen studio albums in its first nine years. They were never shy about showing their grand ambitions on such cuts as the title track to 1971's *Salisbury*, which ran to sixteen minutes and featured a twenty-four-piece orchestra.

The band broke out with *Look at Yourself* (1971), a mostly prog-free rocker that cracked the Top 100 in the U.S. (where fans included future Metallica man Lars Ulrich). The next three albums all went gold in the U.S. Then, just as their popularity waned in America, Heep finally conquered Britain, landing in the Top Ten for the first time with 1975's *Return to Fantasy*. And, as their domestic following faded, the group began to experience great success elsewhere—in Germany, 1977's *Innocent Victim* was a million-seller.

Heep have continued to cultivate new fan bases as old ones slip away: in 1987, they became the first Western band to perform in Soviet Russia. More than forty years into their career, Heep—with Box the sole remaining original member—remain unbowed. **JiH**

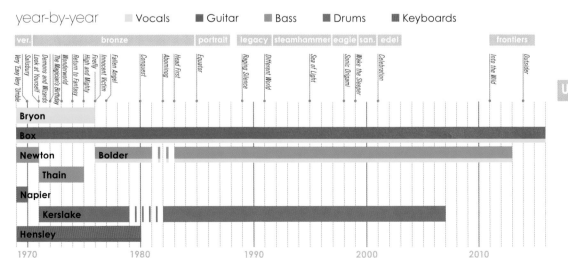

year-by-year   ■ Vocals   ■ Guitar   ■ Bass   ■ Drums   ■ Keyboards

Van Halen (1978)

Van Halen II (1979)

Women and
Children First
(1980)

Fair Warning
(1981)

1984 (1984)

5150 (1986)

For Unlawful
Carnal Knowledge
(1991)

Balance (1995)

Van Halen III
(1998)

A Different Kind of
Truth (2012)

Michael Anthony, Alex Van Halen, David Lee Roth, and Eddie Van Halen in London, 1978.

Roth—arguably *the* rock star of his time—at the Palladium, New York, in May 1979.

Eddie performs at the Dutch Pinkpop Festival in May 1980.

Roth limbers up for another scene-stealing performance in 1981.

Eddie with Michael Jackson, on whose "Beat It" he soloed, in 1984.

Alex Van Halen with fellow drumming legends Carmine Appice (left) and Ginger Baker (cente

With new singer **Sammy Hagar** (second from left) at **Eddie**'s house in Los Angeles.

Hagar and **Eddie** perform at Mountain View, California, on October 14, 1995.

Roth at a warm-up show for his second reunion tour with Van Halen, at The Forum in Inglewood, California, in February 2012.

Anthony, new singer (and former Extreme front-man) **Gary Cherone**, and **Eddie** live in California in 1998.

the velvet underground / lou reed

Lou Reed
b. March 2, 1942
d. October 27, 2013

John Cale
b. March 9, 1942

Sterling Morrison
b. August 28, 1942
d. August 30, 1995

Angus MacLise
b. March 4, 1938
d. June 21, 1979

Moe Tucker
b. August 26, 1944

Nico
b. October 16, 1938
d. July 18, 1988

Drawing on avant-gardisms, Brill Building-style pop, and primal rock 'n' roll, The Velvet Underground are a keystone of rock. Their sonic world is frequently dark, but occasionally pretty—and always engrossing.

Lou Reed united with the classically trained **John Cale** in The Primitives, later adding guitarist **Sterling Morrison**, who had known Reed at Syracuse University. Inspired by a paperback about S&M found in the street, they renamed themselves The Velvet Underground. Drummer Maureen "**Moe**" Tucker— whose monolithic thumping became central to their sound—joined when original percussionist **Angus MacLise** dropped out prior to a gig.

After seeing them at New York's Cafe Bizarre in late 1965, artist Andy Warhol became their patron, drafting in chanteuse **Nico** for a touch of European cool. Warhol also financed their debut LP—and designed its iconic "banana" sleeve. It sold zilch (U.S. No. 171—the highest position of any of their studio sets), but became one of rock's Rosetta stones. No one sang about drugs ("Heroin," "Waiting for the Man," "Run, Run, Run") with such arresting nonchalance, or made sado-masochism ("Venus in Furs") so mesmerizing. The churning "All Tomorrow's Parties" became Warhol's favorite Velvets song.

The follow-up *White Light, White Heat* (1968) was lo-fi, distorted—deliberately so: the band recorded at maximum volume, in the red. "The kind of record you have to be in the mood for," mused The Strokes' Julian Casablancas to *Rolling Stone*. "You have to be in a shitty bar, in a really shitty mood." The title track was a chugalong paean to amphetamine, "The Gift" a twisted love story with a shock ending, narrated in John Cale's melodious Welsh tones. The remorseless, seventeen-minute "Sister Ray" was a jam with odd lyrics, many of them muffled—like "Louie Louie."

Tensions within the band saw Cale depart in 1968—to be replaced by **Doug Yule**—and *The Velvet Underground* (1969) lacked the avant-garde edge he would have supplied. In its place was a renewed emphasis on melody and harmony. "I'm Set Free" and "Beginning to See the Light" were jubilant confessionals, "What Goes On" a joyous jam, and the beautiful "Pale Blue Eyes" simply transfixing.

By *Loaded* (1970)—minus Tucker, then pregnant— a disillusioned Reed was set to quit. As a parting gift, he said, "I gave them an album loaded with hits." Wistful reflections ("New Age," "Oh! Sweet Nothin'") sat alongside rockers like "Sweet Jane" and "Rock 'n' Roll"—both of which Reed would incorporate into his

year-by-year

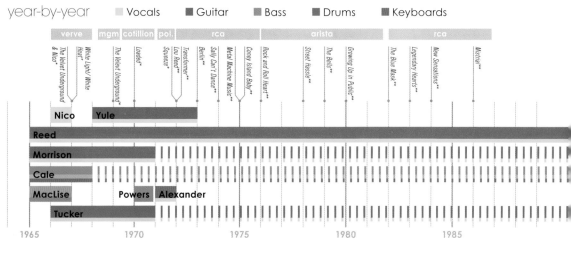

Vocals Guitar Bass Drums Keyboards

verve | mgm | cotillion | pol. | rca | arista | rca

The Velvet Underground & Nico* · White Light/ White Heat* · The Velvet Underground* · Loaded* · Squeeze* · Lou Reed** · Transformer** · Berlin** · Sally Can't Dance** · Metal Machine Music** · Coney Island Baby** · Rock and Roll Heart** · Street Hassle** · The Bells** · Growing Up in Public** · The Blue Mask** · Legendary Hearts** · New Sensations** · Mistrial**

Nico · Yule

Reed

Morrison

Cale

MacLise · Powers · Alexander

Tucker

1965 · 1970 · 1975 · 1980 · 1985

Doug Yule
b. February 25, 1947

Walter Powers
b. August 4, 1946
d. Unknown

Willie Alexander
b. January 13, 1943

solo act. Sterling Morrison left in 1971 to study English literature. In his wake, the Doug Yule-helmed Velvets had little to offer, but endured until 1973.

Reed's first solo album revisited unreleased Velvets tunes and was largely overlooked. His second, *Transformer* (1972), co-helmed by long-term admirer David Bowie and his sidekick Mick Ronson, was a resounding success, alternately strident ("Vicious," "I'm So Free"), quirky ("Andy's Chest," "New York Telephone Conversation"), and plainly enchanting ("Perfect Day"). "Walk on the Wild Side" gave Reed his first and biggest hit, receiving generous airplay despite its near-the-knuckle lyrics.

He followed it with the memorable but harrowing *Berlin* (1973), a concept album about a doomed relationship, taking in "The Bed" (captivating, but mighty bleak) and ending with the oddly uplifting "Sad Song." *Sally Can't Dance* and the live *Rock 'n' Roll Animal* (both 1974) maintained Reed's profile, which he destroyed with *Metal Machine Music* (1975), a double album of shrill feedback that fans returned in their droves. The mellow, melodic *Coney Island Baby* (1975) redressed the balance, while *Street Hassle* (1978) carried a harder edge, reflecting the rise of punk—of which the Velvets were seen as godfathers.

Reed's career stalled somewhat in the eighties, although *The Blue Mask* (1982) and *New York* (1989) were well received. The death of friend and former mentor Andy Warhol in 1987, however, prompted a reunion with his ex-Velvet bandmate John Cale on the moving *Songs for Drella* (1990)—its title a nickname for Warhol ("Dracula" meets "Cinderella").

In 1990, the original four-piece Velvets reunited for a one-off benefit gig, and by 1992 they were once again a gigging concern—hence *LIVE MXMXCIII* (1993). The group played in Europe to acclaim, though arguments between Reed and Cale ruined plans for a U.S. tour. After Morrison passed away in 1995, Cale, Reed, and Tucker performed "Last Night I Said Goodbye to My Friend" at their Rock and Roll Hall of Fame induction in 1996, drawing the story of The Velvet Underground to a respectful close.

The Velvets' vast legacy can be heard in the chugging rhythms of Jonathan Richman's Modern Lovers and Arcade Fire, the art rock of Roxy Music and David Bowie, the dark energy of Joy Division, and the sparseness of Prince's "The Cross." They fed The Jesus and Mary Chain's white noise, Sonic Youth's aural avalanche, and The Strokes' deadpan drawl. "Influential" doesn't begin to cover it. **RD**

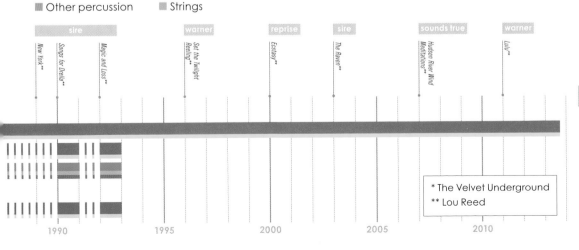

■ Other percussion   ■ Strings

sire | warner | reprise | sire | sounds true | warner

*New York*** | *Songs for Drella*** | *Magic and Loss*** | *Set the Twilight Reeling*** | *Ecstasy*** | *The Raven*** | *Hudson River Wind Meditations*** | *Lulu***

* The Velvet Underground
** Lou Reed

1990 | 1995 | 2000 | 2005 | 2010

the verve 1989–2009

Richard Ashcroft
b. September 11, 1971

Simon Jones
b. May 29, 1972

Nick McCabe
b. July 14, 1971

Peter Salisbury
b. September 24, 1971

Simon Tong
b. July 9, 1972

The Greater Manchester town of Wigan and the words "hotbed of musical creativity" have been uneasy bedfellows since the birth of rock 'n' roll in the fifties, but the ripple of excitement caused by Kajagoogoo/Limahl in the mid-eighties turned into a tidal wave a decade on when **The Verve** arrived on the scene with their bittersweet symphonies.

In truth, only fifty percent of the group's original lineup—"lips and cheekbones" frontman **Richard Ashcroft** and bass guitarist **Simon Jones**—were actually born in the town. But the Wigan Casino (once dubbed the "best disco in the world" by *Billboard* magazine), rugby league, and the pier made famous by writer George Orwell were all shifted down the search engine pecking order from the moment the psychedelic shoegazers established a foothold in the charts and minds of the record-buying public. They first locked horns in 1989 as students at Wigan's Winstanley College, and made their live debut in 1990.

Ashcroft, Jones, guitarist **Nick McCabe**, and drummer **Peter Salisbury** were signed to Hut Records (a subsidiary of Virgin) as Verve in 1991, and among their first recordings was the single "She's a Superstar." With *A Storm in Heaven* (1993) brewing, Verve called on producer John Leckie—who masterminded The Stone Roses' self-titled debut—and embraced

psychedelic rock. However, their first album failed to ignite at retail despite favorable publicity for their Glastonbury appearance in 1993 and shows with Manchester band Oasis.

In 1994, after a legal tussle with Verve Records, the group gained the definite article but lost their heads at the nomadic Lollapalooza festival in the United States. In a drink- and drug-induced haze, The Verve returned home to begin work on their second album, *A Northern Soul* (1995). Described by one critic as "a traumatic realization of the hopelessness of human existence, a document of fractured mentalities, the sound of four young men old before their time," *A Northern Soul* was released to mixed reviews. Nonetheless, it continued their upward trajectory, peaking at No. 13 in the U.K.

Ashcroft dissolved The Verve, riddled by internal conflict, at Britpop's zenith in the summer of 1995. But he swiftly revived them—initially with **Simon Tong** as McCabe's replacement and then with McCabe and Tong strumming in harmony—ahead of their career-defining third studio album, *Urban Hymns* (1997).

In the summer of 1997, "Bitter Sweet Symphony" ended America's futile resistance to the lads' northern charm with a Top Twenty berth on the *Billboard* Hot 100. The song's Walter Stern-directed video presented

year-by-year ■ Vocals ■ Guitar ■ Bass ■ Drums ■ Keyboards

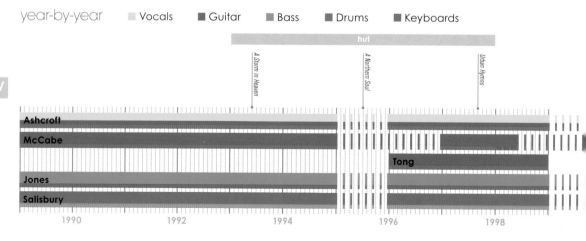

hut

A Storm in Heaven *A Northern Soul* *Urban Hymns*

Ashcroft
McCabe
Tong
Jones
Salisbury

1990   1992   1994   1996   1998

Ashcroft, loaded with attitude, barging his way along London's Hoxton Street in homage to Massive Attack's "Unfinished Sympathy." Ashcroft labeled "Bitter Sweet Symphony" "the best song Jagger and Richards have written in twenty years"—a reference to a prominent sample of the Andrew Oldham Orchestra's rendition of the Stones' "The Last Time." Accused of plagiarism, The Verve reluctantly surrendered their writing credits, plus 100 percent of the royalties, to the wrinkly duo. "It's a bitter sweet symphony, this life / Try to make ends meet / You're a slave to money then you die…"

Urban Hymns' one-two punch was completed by "The Drugs Don't Work," a title clearly at odds with the fuzzy, room-trashing experimentation of their formative years, or perhaps one tinged with regret and a sign of their growing maturity. The poignant yet depressing ballad (writer Ashcroft compared growing old to "a cat in a bag waiting to drown") debuted at No. 1 in the U.K. on September 7, 1997, and captured the somber mood of the nation following the death of Diana, Princess of Wales, exactly one week earlier.

The Verve were nominated for four Brit Awards in 1998 (winning Best British Group and Best British Album) and *Urban Hymns* was a no-brainer for the Mercury Prize shortlist in the year their homecoming gig attracted 33,000 fans to the Haigh Fest in Greater Manchester. In 2010, *Hymns* was nominated for the Brits' Best British Album of the Last Thirty Years, but the prize went to *(What's the Story) Morning Glory?* The irony was not lost on Noel Gallagher, who years earlier had dedicated *Morning Glory*'s "Cast No Shadow" to "the brilliance of Richard Ashcroft."

The Verve disbanded for a second time in 1999, scattering members far and wide. McCabe had already quit in 1998, to be replaced by pedal steel veteran B.J. Cole. Ashcroft launched a successful solo career, scoring three consecutive U.K. Top Three albums (including the No. 1 Alone with Everybody in 2000). Jones and Tong formed The Shining with John Squire prior to Tong replacing Graham Coxon in Blur and playing alongside Damon Albarn in The Good, The Bad & The Queen. Salisbury drummed with Black Rebel Motorcycle Club, and McCabe jammed with John Martyn and The Music. But in 2007 the original lineup buried their differences to mastermind comeback gigs that sold out in twenty minutes, along with an arena tour, headline festival appearances, and, in 2008, another British chart-topper (*Forth*).

Wigan's warriors were terminated for a third time in August 2009, but do not rule out a chapter four. Perhaps, to quote "The Drugs Don't Work," Ashcroft will offer to "sing in your ear again." **MW**

■ Other percussion

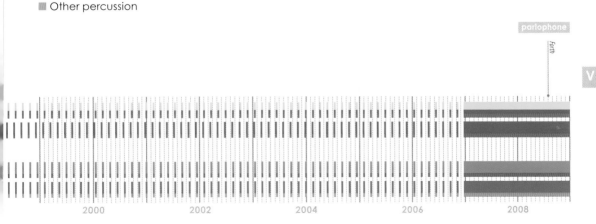

Trouble (1978)

Lovehunter (1979)

Ready an' Willing (1980)

Saints & Sinners (1982)

Slide It In (1984)

Whitesnake (1987)

Slip of the Tongue (1989)

Restless Heart (1997)

Good to Be Bad (2008)

Forevermore (2011)

Neil Murray, Bernie Marsden, David Coverdale, Micky Moody, David Dowle, and **Jon Lord** in August 1978.

Marsden, who sang lead on *Lovehunter*'s standout track "Outlaw."

Coverdale at the Reading Festival, England, in 1980.

Cozy Powell arrived in time to promote, but not play on, *Saints & Sinners*.

Powell, Murray, John Sykes, and **Coverdale** in Rio.

'Snake video star Tawny Kitaen with boyfriend **Coverdale** in 1987.

Tommy Aldridge, Rudy Sarzo, Coverdale, and Adrian Vandenberg make Steve Vai (far right) blush at a Minnesota date on the *Slip of the Tongue* tour, in 1990.

Coverdale onstage with Whitesnake to promote *Restless Heart*.

Drummer Brian Tichy, Coverdale, and Doug Aldrich in Bournemouth, England, on June 18, 2011.

A customarily rampant peformance from Coverdale as the *Good to Be Bad* tour hits the Enmore Theater in Sydney, Australia, on March 28, 2008.

the who 1962–present

Pete Townshend
b. May 19, 1945

Roger Daltrey
b. March 1, 1945

John Entwistle
b. October 9, 1946
d. June 27, 2002

Doug Sandom
b. February 26, 1930

Keith Moon
b. August 23, 1947
d. September 7, 1978

Kenney Jones
b. September 16, 1948

In 1962, a surly bunch of young musicians got together in Shepherd's Bush, west London, and created one of rock's greatest and most influential groups. "They smashed through the door of rock 'n' roll," Pearl Jam's Eddie Vedder told *Rolling Stone*, "leaving rubble and not much else for the rest of us to lay claim to."

Pete Townshend (guitar), **Roger Daltrey** (vocals), **John Entwistle** (bass), and **Doug Sandom** (drums) were The Detours—but, in April 1964, everything changed. Out went the older Sandom and in came the younger and wilder **Keith Moon**. After an ignored single as The High Numbers, they reverted to The Who (as they had been known for a few weeks before Sandom's exit).

The quartet forged a reputation for explosive live shows, culminating in the smashing of equipment by the volatile Townshend (whose destruction began as an accident) and Moon (whose destruction was invariably meticulously plotted). The band's first two hits—1965's "I Can't Explain" and "My Generation"—had no less of an earth-shaking impact.

The Who's debut, *My Generation* (issued in the U.S. as *The Who Sings My Generation*) hit the U.K. Top Five. But their reputation was founded more on singles, including 1965's "Anyway, Anyhow, Anywhere," 1966's "Substitute," and 1967's "Pictures of Lily."

Neither of their albums of the time made the same impact, but both are key components of The Who's legacy. *A Quick One* (1966, issued in the U.S. as *Happy Jack* in 1967) contained what Townshend called a mini-opera, "A Quick One While He's Away," and the favorites "Boris the Spider" and "So Sad About Us." *The Who Sell Out* (1967) boasted another mini-opera, "Rael," plus "Armenia, City in the Sky," "Mary Anne with the Shaky Hand," and the soaring, transatlantic Top Ten hit "I Can See for Miles."

In 1967, The Who took their game-changing rock template to the U.S. In June, they stormed the Monterey International Pop Festival in California, upstaging everyone bar Jimi Hendrix. Three months later, on TV's *The Smothers Brothers Comedy Hour*, Moon detonated his drumkit, leaving fellow guest Bette Davis aghast and Townshend with tinnitus.

The Who hit their stride with 1969's ambitious *Tommy* (1969). In this double concept album, the young protagonist—born deaf, dumb, and blind—is dragged through a series of picaresque adventures, including becoming revered as a "Pinball Wizard." The album soared into the U.S. and U.K. Top Five, but its iconic status was secured by The Who's epochal performance at that year's Woodstock festival. The

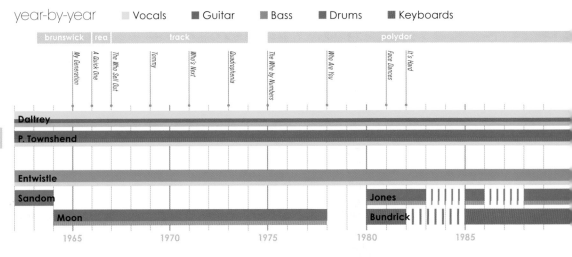

year-by-year ▢ Vocals ▪ Guitar ▪ Bass ▪ Drums ▪ Keyboards

John "Rabbit" Bundrick
b. November 21, 1948

Zak Starkey
b. September 13, 1965

Simon Townshend
b. October 10, 1960

Pino Palladino
b. October 17, 1957

Simon Phillips
b. February 6, 1957

awesome power of the band's onstage attack can be heard in their legendary *Live at Leeds* (1970)—after which they were regularly and justifiably billed as the world's greatest live rock and roll band.

From the remnants of an abandoned conceptual piece called *Lifehouse* came *Who's Next* (1971), their sole U.K. No. 1 album. From the fluttering introduction of "Baba O'Riley" to the crashing chords of the epic "Won't Get Fooled Again," it was the quintessential rock album. It also, unfortunately, set a standard that chief composer and conceptualist Townshend would find impossible to top. Emerging amid stage and film versions of *Tommy*, 1973's equally ambitious *Quadrophenia* (1973)—the quasi-spiritual story of a young Mod—boasted gems like "5.15" and "Love Reign O'er Me," but, on stage, it often proved incomprehensible and technologically disastrous. (Nonetheless, it inspired a much-loved *Quadrophenia* movie in 1979, and was a clear influence on Green Day's contemporary rock opera *American Idiot*.)

The Who by Numbers (1975) was the exhausted Townshend's self-mocking title for their seventh studio album—a less grand affair, exemplified by the perky "Squeeze Box." By the end of a 1976 tour, The Who had entered the record books as the world's loudest band,

only for Townshend to fret that they had nothing left to say. Amid the advent of punk (including ardent Who fans like The Jam's Paul Weller), the band stayed off the road. They returned in 1978 with *Who Are You*, but then Moon died from an overdose of prescription drugs that he was taking for his alcoholism.

With **Kenney Jones** of The Faces, The Who returned to stadiums, and cut *Face Dances* (1981) and *It's Hard* (1982). But Townshend was finding it harder to write material for Daltrey's voice, and called time in 1982. Bar one-off reunions in 1985 and 1988, that was it until 1989, when a much-expanded lineup undertook the biggest-grossing tour of their career. Within the ranks were keyboard player **John "Rabbit" Bundrick**, Pete's brother **Simon Townshend** on rhythm guitar, and, on drums, the phenomenal **Simon Phillips**.

Subsequent outings—with Ringo Starr's son **Zak Starkey** on drums—kept the flame alive until, on the eve of a 2002 U.S. tour, Entwistle was found dead. Townshend and Daltrey soldiered on with bassist **Pino Palladino** and, in 2006, issued their first new album for twenty-four years, *Endless Wire*. It proved no disgrace, but The Who's latter-day legacy is best exemplified by show-stealing performances at 2001's The Concert for New York City and 2010's Super Bowl. **MiH/BM**

▪ Aerophones ▪ Other percussion

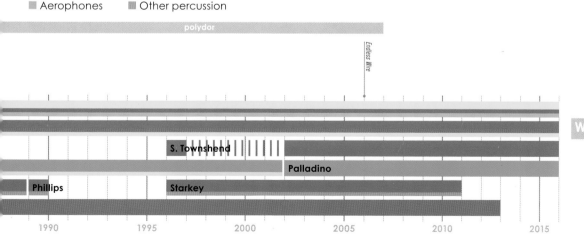

My Generation
(1965)

The Who Sell Out
(1967)

Tommy (1969)

Who's Next (1971)

Quadrophenia
(1973)

**The Who by
Numbers** (1975)

Who Are You
(1978)

Face Dances
(1981)

Endless Wire (2006)

Pete Townshend strikes an iconic pose on the 1966 tour that followed *My Generation*.

Roger Daltrey caught pneumonia from this *...Sell Out* cover shoot.

Daltrey in his *Tommy*-era glory, in Britain's Redcar, in February 1969.

John Entwistle, Steve Winwood, **Daltrey**, Billy Idol, Patti Labelle, Elton John, Phil Collins, and **Townshend** at a 1989 performance of 1969's *Tommy* at the Royal Albert Hall, London.

Townshend and **Keith Moon** help to write the rulebook for arena rock in the 1970s.

Daltrey, **Townshend**, **Moon** and **John Entwistle** in Surrey, England, promoting *Who's Next*.

The Who with Moon's replacement, former Faces drummer **Kenney Jones** (second left).

Elton John with **Entwistle** and **Daltrey** in the *Tommy* movie, issued in 1975, the same year as *The Who by Numbers*.

Townshend and **Moon** in August 1978; Moon died a month later.

Townshend, in the shadow of **Moon**, in California in 2006.

Yes (1969)

Fragile (1971)

Close to the Edge (1972)

Relayer (1974)

Going for the One (1977)

Drama (1980)

90125 (1983)

Union (1991)

Magnification (2001)

Fly from Here (2011)

The formative Yes: **Peter Banks**, **Tony Kaye**, **Chris Squire**, **Bill Bruford**, and **Jon Anderson**

With new drummer **Alan White** at London's Crystal Palace in 1972.

Bruford, Squire, **Steve Howe**, Anderson, and keyboard wizard **Rick Wakeman** creating *Fragile* at London's Advision Studios in August 1971.

Anderson live in Rotterdam on the *Going for the One* tour.

Howe, White (top), Anderson, Squire, and Wakeman's doomed successor **Patrick Moraz**.

White, **Geoff Downes**, Squire, **Trevor Horn**, and Howe in 1980.

South African songwriter and guitarist **Trevor Rabin**—the key to the band's renaissance and survival—on the successful 9012Live tour.

Wakeman, **Squire**, **Bruford**, **Anderson**, and **White**: five-eighths of the *Union* incarnation.

Yes live in Britain, on the Symphonic tour that followed the release of *Magnification*.

Benoît David—the man with the unenviable task of replacing Jon Anderson—in 2011.

Everybody Knows This Is Nowhere (1969)

Harvest (1972)

Tonight's the Night (1975)

Rust Never Sleeps (1979)

Trans (1982)

Ragged Glory (1990)

Mirror Ball (1995)

Greendale (2003)

Living with War (2006)

Americana (2012)

Neil Young (right) with CSN&Y harmonizers Graham Nash and David Crosby at the ill-fated Altamont Speedway Free Festival, California, on December 6, 1969.

Young at his California ranch during the recording of *Harvest*.

With Bob Dylan and The Band at the SNACK (Students Need Athletics, Culture, and Kicks) benefit show at San Francisco's Golden Gate Park, on March 23, 1975.

With singer Nicolette Larson at the premiere for his *Rust Never Sleeps* movie in 1979.

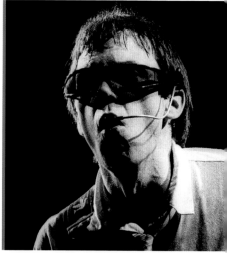

The "Transformer Man" on stage in Rotterdam in 1982.

Young returns to acoustic guitar for a concert in Indianapolis on April 7, 1990.

With young disciple Eddie Vedder, whose group Pearl Jam would back him on *Mirror Ball*.

With Aerosmith's Steven Tyler at the Rock and Roll Hall of Fame induction ceremony, New York, in 2003—the year of *Greendale*.

For the 2006 CSN&Y Freedom of Speech tour, **Young** reunites with, from left, **Stills**, Nash, and Crosby, here in Concord, California.

Young inducts Paul McCartney onto the Hollywood Walk of Fame in 2012, the year that also saw the star looking back on the Crazy Horse album *Americana*.

frank zappa 1965–1993

Frank Zappa
b. December 21, 1940
d. December 4, 1993

Ray Collins
b. November 19, 1936

Roy Estrada
b. April 17, 1943

Jimmy Carl Black
b. February 1, 1938
d. Nov. 1, 2008

Don Preston
b. September 21, 1932

Aynsley Dunbar
b. January 10, 1946

Mark "Flo" Volman
b. April 19, 1947

Howard "Eddie" Kaylan
b. June 22, 1947

Frank Zappa was a musical genius of the rarest kind. Over a thirty-year career as a songwriter, guitarist, composer, innovator, producer, and sardonic observer of the human condition, he never stopped creating brilliant and often challenging music.

In the early sixties, Zappa created soundtracks for B-movies. But things really began to happen when he took over R&B band The Soul Giants and transformed them into The Mothers of Invention. The group's debut album, *Freak Out!* (1966)—with its ambitious palette of rock, doo-wop, R&B, jazz, classical, avant-garde, and biting social commentary—was ten steps ahead of anything else issued that year. *Absolutely Free* (1967) was equally innovative, characterized by extended yet tight performances, abrupt time changes, and brilliant lyrics. (Zappa never bought into the counterculture and satirized it as mercilessly as he did the establishment.) Live performances mixed theatrical improvised sections with cutting-edge playing.

By the time he split the Mothers of Invention in late 1969, he had put out ten albums, both with the band and—beginning with 1967's *Lumpy Gravy*—solo. (Relationships between Zappa and his former

bandmates would rarely be cordial, but drummer **Jimmy Carl Black** would guest at subsequent shows and reappear on 1981's vicious *You Are What You Is*. The latter also included the Mothers of Invention's madcap saxophonist Jim "Motorhead" Sherwood.)

A new lineup—now called simply The Mothers—debuted in 1970, with vocalists **Mark "Flo" Volman** and **Howard "Eddie" Kaylan** from pop band The Turtles, and brilliant new players **George Duke** and **Aynsley Dunbar**. This more theatrical lineup, renowned for outrageous epics about life on the road, lasted until the end of 1971, when an audience member pushed Zappa off a stage in London, causing serious injuries.

He had recovered by 1973, and assembled a new band. **Ruth Underwood** (percussion), drummer Chester Thompson (later of Genesis), and **Napoleon Murphy Brock** (saxophone/vocals) featured in a lineup—continuing as the Mothers until their disbandment in 1974—of breathtaking virtuosity and warmth. Zappa hit new heights on 1973's *Over-Nite Sensation*, 1974's *Apostrophe (')*—featuring Cream's Jack Bruce—and 1975's *One Size Fits All* and *Bongo Fury* (the latter a collaboration with his old friend Captain Beefheart).

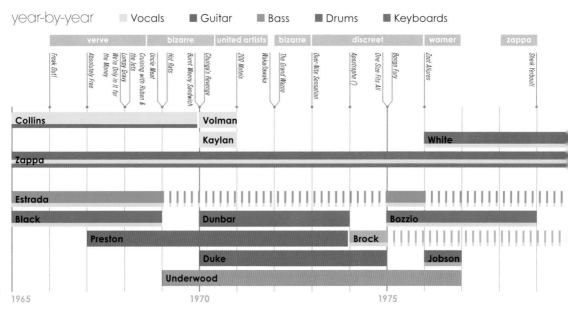

year-by-year   ■ Vocals   ■ Guitar   ■ Bass   ■ Drums   ■ Keyboards

George Duke
b. January 12, 1946

Ruth Underwood
b. May 23, 1946

Napoleon Murphy Brock
b. April 23, 1943

Terry Bozzio
b. December 27, 1950

Eddie Jobson
b. April 25, 1955

Ike Willis
b. November 14, 1951

Ray White
b. July 11, 1945

Steve Vai
b. June 6, 1960

After the rock-oriented *Zoot Allures* (1976), Zappa mooted a four-album set entitled *Läther*. The Warner label refused to indulge this expensive folly, hence the separate releases of the live *Zappa in New York* and *Studio Tan* in 1978 and *Sleep Dirt* and *Orchestral Favorites* in 1979. Zappa duly set up his own label and scored his highest-charting album in five years with *Sheik Yerbouti* (1979). That paved the way for the rock opera *Joe's Garage*, issued in two installments in 1979.

Star musicians graduating from his group included guitarists Adrian Belew (later to join Talking Heads, Bowie, and King Crimson), Warren Cuccurullo (who founded Missing Persons with Zappa drummer **Terry Bozzio**, then joined Duran Duran), and **Steve Vai** (who would play with Public Image Ltd, David Lee Roth, and Whitesnake). Bozzio joined the progressive band U.K. alongside King Crimson's John Wetton and former Roxy Music keyboard player **Eddie Jobson**, who had played with him in Zappa's touring band back in 1976. As a musician, however, Zappa was equal to the best of them, as *Shut Up 'n Play Yer Guitar* (1981) testifies.

Zappa's eclectic projects continued up to his untimely death from prostate cancer in 1993. After

"rock" albums such as *Ship Arriving Too Late to Save a Drowning Witch* (1982)—the source of his biggest hit, "Valley Girl," featuring his daughter Moon on vocals—and *The Man from Utopia* (1983) came the dazzling electronic experimentation of *Jazz from Hell* (1986). Thereafter, his discography exploded with live albums, including *Broadway the Hard Way* (1988), featuring Sting; orchestral pieces, such as *The Yellow Shark* (1993); and archive releases, including the six-volume series *You Can't Do That on Stage Anymore* (1988–1992) and the *Beat the Boots* series (1991–2009).

Zappa was posthumously inducted into the Rock and Roll Hall of Fame by Lou Reed in 1995 and given a Grammy Lifetime Achievement Award. His estate has nearly doubled his outsized discography with further archive releases. His son, guitarist Dweezil, keeps his father's music alive with Zappa Plays Zappa, a touring band that debuted in 2006 and occasionally features guests from his father's original lineups.

"Zappa gave me the faith that anything in music was possible," enthused Phish's Trey Anastasio. For Matt Groening, creator of *The Simpsons*, it was even more straightforward: "Frank Zappa was my Elvis." **MD**

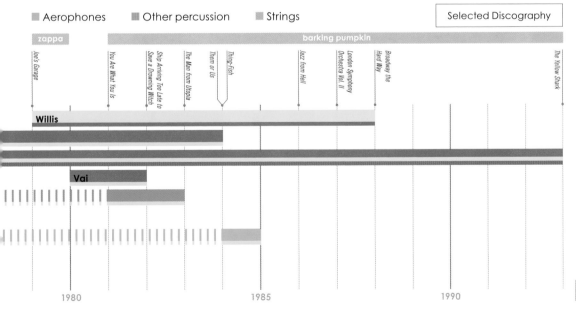

■ Aerophones ■ Other percussion ■ Strings | Selected Discography

zappa | barking pumpkin

Joe's Garage · *You Are What You Is* · *Ship Arriving Too Late to Save a Drowning Witch* · *The Man from Utopia* · *Them or Us* · *Thing-Fish* · *Jazz from Hell* · *London Symphony Orchestra Vol. II* · *Broadway the Hard Way* · *The Yellow Shark*

Willis

Vai

1980 · 1985 · 1990

Freak Out! (1966)

We're Only in It for the Money (1968)

Hot Rats (1969)

Waka/Jawaka (1972)

Apostrophe (') (1974)

Zoot Allures (1976)

Joe's Garage, Act I (1979)

Ship Arriving Too Late to Save a Drowning Witch (1982)

Them or Us (1984)

Broadway the Hard Way (1988)

Frank Zappa circa *Freak Out!*, whose sleevenotes advised fans to "Drop out of school before your mind rots."

Zappa at the Newport Jazz Festival in 1969 —the year of his first solo album, *Hot Rats*.

Zappa with his second wife Gail, at the Oval cricket ground in London, in 1972.

Top: Bunk Gardner, James "Motorhead" Sherwood, **Roy Estrada**, **Jimmy Carl Black**, and Art Tripp. Bottom: Ian Underwood, **Zappa**, and **Don Preston**.

Zappa in Rotterdam on the extensive tour that followed the triumphant *Apostrophe (')*. On *Saturday Night Live*, shortly after the release of *Zoot Allures*.

In March 1979, the month he began recording *Joe's Garage*. With daughter Moon Unit, who sang on *Drowning Witch's* "Valley Girl," and son Dweezil.

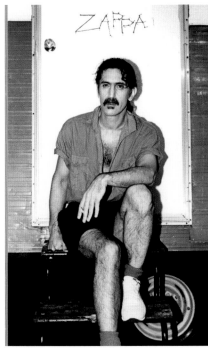

Backstage during the 1984 tour to promote *Them or Us*. Zappa's 1988 tour reaches Rotterdam (Financial losses and inter-band conflicts meant he never toured again).

zz top 1969–present

Billy Gibbons
b. December 16, 1949

Dusty Hill
b. May 19, 1949

Frank Beard
b. June 11, 1949

"The heartbeat of the whole country," according to Keith Richards, this blues rock trio formed in Houston, Texas. **Billy Gibbons** (vocals and guitar), Joseph **"Dusty" Hill** (vocals, bass, and keyboards), and **Frank Beard** (drums) created one of the longest-running stable lineups in rock. Until September 2006, they even kept the same manager, Bill Ham.

The men of the magnificent ZZ Top had played in other Texas-based groups—Gibbons in Moving Sidewalks and Hill and Beard in American Blues (once known as The Warlocks). By 1969, both of these groups had disbanded, and Gibbons invited Beard to join his new enterprise. Beard suggested that Hill join them, and thus the ZZ lineup was finalized.

Their name was speculated to be a combination of two popular brands of rolling papers, Zig Zag and TOP. However, the mischievous Gibbons has also described it as a tribute to bluesmen B.B. King and Z.Z. Hill, and even to the Z-shaped beams in a hay loft.

Having hooked up with Ham and issued their first single, "Salt Lick," on the Scat label, ZZ Top played their first show in February 1970. Incessant touring—centered on Texas, Louisiana, and Mississippi—made them an arena-filling sensation in the American South long before the rest of the U.S. even knew their name.

Issued on London Records, neither *ZZ Top's First Album* (1971) nor *Rio Grande Mud* (1972) made much of an impression outside Texas, although the latter's "Francine" became their first U.S. Top 100 hit.

In January 1973, ZZ Top opened for three Rolling Stones shows in Hawaii. "I remember walking out on stage in our standard attire of cowboy boots and a cowboy hat…," Gibbons told *Classic Rock*, "and someone in the front row shouted out, 'Oh my God, they're a country band!'" With the band's profile duly raised, *Tres Hombres* (1973) climbed into the U.S. Top Ten and eventually went gold. Its classic "La Grange" was written about the Chicken Ranch, a famous bordello at La Grange, Texas. (The same establishment became the subject of Burt Reynolds and Dolly Parton's 1982 movie *The Best Little Whorehouse in Texas*.) The album's "Waitin' for the Bus" and "Jesus Just Left Chicago," joined "La Grange" as fan favorites and rock-radio staples.

Fandango! (1975) contained a mixture of live and studio recordings. One of the new studio cuts, "Tush," became ZZ Top's first Top Forty single, while the album again went Top Ten. *Tejas* (1976)—its title an earlier spelling of the Texas state name—continued their gold-selling streak, and prompted The Worldwide Texas Tour, on which the band performed amid sand, cacti, and even examples of Texan wildlife.

That excursion complete, the road-weary band opted to take a break. During the two-year vacation, Gibbons and Hill grew their trademark chest-length beards. "I thought, 'I hope these guys are not on the run,'" remembered Keith Richards, "'cause that disguise is not gonna work." (In 1984, the Gillette razor

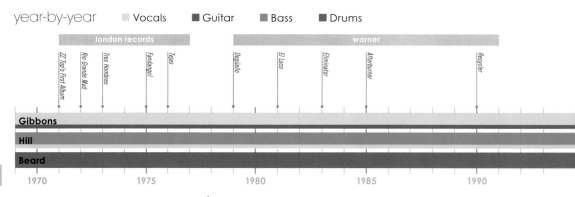

year-by-year   ■ Vocals   ■ Guitar   ■ Bass   ■ Drums

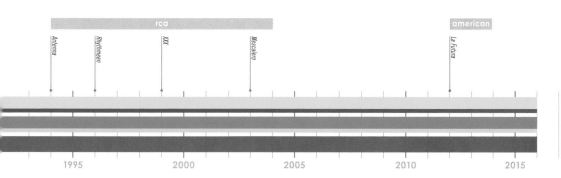

3M	17.1M	8.4M	5.7M
The Best of ZZ Top (1977)	Eliminator (1983)	Afterburner (1985)	Greatest Hits (1992)

company reportedly offered the trio a million dollars each to shave their beards for a TV commercial. They declined, Gibbons declaring, "We're too ugly.")

The beards were not the only visual marker. The trio almost always appear wearing sunglasses, with Gibbons and Hill also sporting similar black clothing (usually motorcycle leathers) and stetsons or baseball caps. Their eyewear inspired "Cheap Sunglasses," the best-known track from their first album for Warner Bros, *Degüello* (1979). But the biggest U.S. hit from the album was a cover of Sam & Dave's "I Thank You." *El Loco* (1981) sustained the group's success with risqué party anthems like "Pearl Necklace."

However, *Eliminator* (1983) represents ZZ Top's commercial and critical peak. The trio flavored their old-school boogie with sequenced beats, a formula that spawned the hits "Gimme All Your Lovin'," "Legs," "Sharp Dressed Man," and "TV Dinners." *Eliminator*—their first international success (it went quadruple platinum in Britain)—also made them MTV favorites, thanks to videos featuring the customized 1933 Ford coupe that appeared on its cover. In the clips, this gleaming retro-styled vehicle was driven by a trio of glamorous young women (Danièle Arnaud and *Playboy* models Jeana Tomasino and Kymberly Herrin) who appeared as muses to help various troubled people. The band members took a background role as unsuccessful hitchhikers and observers of a running narrative featuring a wide-eyed young gas attendant.

The only blip in their fortunes came in 1984, when Hill accidentally shot himself in the abdomen while removing his boot. "I was in France," Gibbons told *Creem* magazine, "and the operator said, 'Your partner Dusty has been shot.' I said, 'How is he?' and she said, 'I'm sorry monsieur, I don't speak English.'"

Afterburner (1985) and *Recycler* (1990) both sold strongly, although some critics complained that the group were indeed simply recycling the elements that had made *Eliminator* so successful. A cover of Elvis's "Viva Las Vegas," from 1992's *Greatest Hits,* was an international success and, after signing to RCA, they scored another million-seller with *Antenna* (1994).

ZZ Top's commercial fortunes gracefully declined with *Rhythmeen* (1996), *XXX* (1999), and *Mescalero* (2003), although the latter earned critical praise for its adventurousness; alongside the group's familiar gritty boogie were forays into country and Tex-Mex music. (The title refers to Apache Native Americans who depended on the mescal agave as a food source.)

Inducted by Keith Richards into the Rock and Roll Hall of Fame in 2004, the band plotted a new album with producer Rick Rubin. Meanwhile, Gibbons kept himself busy with cameos on work by Queens of the Stone Age, Ministry, Kid Rock, Nickelback, and Everlast. As for what has held the band together for so long, Hill told *Classic Rock*, "It's down to the three of us genuinely enjoying playing together. We still love it, and we still get a kick out of being on stage." **DJ**

rca · american

Antenna · Rhythmeen · XXX · Mescalero · La Futura

1995 · 2000 · 2005 · 2010 · 2015

(L)   Live album
(ST)   Soundtrack album
(*)   Winner of both the Album of the Year and the Best Rock Album Grammy categories

ALBUM OF THE YEAR

Awarded to rock acts featured in *Rock Chronicles*.

1968	*Sgt. Pepper's Lonely Hearts Club Band—* The Beatles	**1982**	*Double Fantasy—*John Lennon & Yoko Ono
		1988	*The Joshua Tree—*U2
1970	*Blood, Sweat & Tears—*Blood, Sweat & Tears	**1998**	*Time Out of Mind—*Bob Dylan
1973	*The Concert for Bangla Desh* (L)— George Harrison and Friends	**2000**	*Supernatural* (*)—Santana
		2001	*Two Against Nature—*Steely Dan
1978	*Rumours—*Fleetwood Mac	**2006**	*How to Dismantle an Atomic Bomb—*U2
1979	*Saturday Night Fever* (ST)— Bee Gees and Various Artists	**2011**	*The Suburbs—*Arcade Fire
		2015	*Morning Phase* (*)—**Beck**

BEST ROCK ALBUM

This Grammy award was first presented in 1995. Entries that appear in *Rock Chronicles* are indicated in **bold**

1995	*Voodoo Lounge—***The Rolling Stones**	**2006**	*How to Dismantle an Atomic Bomb—***U2**
1996	*Jagged Little Pill—*Alanis Morissette	**2007**	*Stadium Arcadium—***Red Hot Chili Peppers**
1997	*Sheryl Crow—*Sheryl Crow	**2008**	*Echoes, Silence, Patience & Grace—* **Foo Fighters**
1998	*Blue Moon Swamp—*John Fogerty		
1999	*The Globe Sessions—*Sheryl Crow	**2009**	*Viva La Vida or Death and All His Friends—* **Coldplay**
2000	*Supernatural* (*)—**Santana**		
2001	*There Is Nothing Left to Lose—***Foo Fighters**	**2010**	*21ˢᵗ Century Breakdown—***Green Day**
2002	*All That You Can't Leave Behind—***U2**	**2011**	*The Resistance—***Muse**
2003	*The Rising—***Bruce Springsteen**	**2012**	*Wasting Light—***Foo Fighters**
2004	*One by One—***Foo Fighters**	**2014**	*Celebration Day—***Led Zeppelin**
2005	*American Idiot—***Green Day**	**2015**	*Morning Phase* (*)—**Beck**

BEST ROCK SONG

This Grammy award was first presented in 1992. Entries that appear in *Rock Chronicles* are indicated in **bold**

1992	"The Soul Cages"—Sting	**2004**	"Seven Nation Army"—The White Stripes
1993	"Layla" (Unplugged)—**Eric Clapton**	**2005**	"Vertigo"—**U2**
1994	"Runaway Train"—Soul Asylum	**2006**	"City of Blinding Lights"—**U2**
1995	"Streets of Philadelphia"—**Bruce Springsteen**	**2007**	"Dani California"—**Red Hot Chili Peppers**
1996	"You Oughta Know"—Alanis Morissette	**2008**	"Radio Nowhere"—**Bruce Springsteen**
1997	"Give Me One Reason"—Tracy Chapman	**2009**	"Girls in Their Summer Clothes"—**Bruce Springsteen**
1998	"One Headlight"—The Wallflowers	**2010**	"Use Somebody"—**Kings of Leon**
1999	"Uninvited"—Alanis Morissette	**2011**	"Angry World"—**Neil Young**
2000	"Scar Tissue"—**Red Hot Chili Peppers**	**2012**	"Walk"—**Foo Fighters**
2001	"With Arms Wide Open"—Creed	**2014**	"Cut Me Some Slack"—**Dave Grohl,** **Paul McCartney, Krist Novoselic, Pat Smear**
2002	"Drops of Jupiter (Tell Me)"—Train		
2003	"The Rising"—**Bruce Springsteen**	**2015**	*"Ain't It Fun"*—Hayley Williams & Taylor York

rock and roll hall of fame inductees

Inductees in the performer category of the Rock and Roll Hall of Fame, Cleveland, Ohio
Entries that appear in *Rock Chronicles* are indicated in **bold**

1986
Chuck Berry
James Brown
Ray Charles
Sam Cooke
Fats Domino
The Everly Brothers
Buddy Holly
Jerry Lee Lewis
Little Richard
Elvis Presley

1987
The Coasters
Eddie Cochran
Bo Diddley
Aretha Franklin
Marvin Gaye
Bill Haley
B.B. King
Clyde McPhatter
Ricky Nelson
Roy Orbison
Carl Perkins
Smokey Robinson
Big Joe Turner
Muddy Waters
Jackie Wilson

1988
The Beach Boys
The Beatles
The Drifters
Bob Dylan
The Supremes

1989
Dion
Otis Redding
The Rolling Stones
The Temptations
Stevie Wonder

1990
Hank Ballard
Bobby Darin
The Four Seasons
The Four Tops
The Kinks
The Platters
Simon & Garfunkel
The Who

1991
LaVern Baker
The Byrds
John Lee Hooker
The Impressions
Wilson Pickett
Jimmy Reed
Ike & Tina Turner

1992
Bobby Blue Bland
Booker T. & The M.G.'s
Johnny Cash
The Isley Brothers
**The Jimi Hendrix
Experience**
Sam & Dave
The Yardbirds

1993
Ruth Brown
Cream
**Creedence Clearwater
Revival**
The Doors
Frankie Lymon & The
Teenagers
Etta James
Van Morrison
Sly & The Family
Stone

1994
The Animals
The Band
Duane Eddy
Grateful Dead
Elton John
John Lennon
Bob Marley
Rod Stewart

1995
**The Allman Brothers
Band**
Al Green
Janis Joplin
Led Zeppelin
Martha and The
Vandellas
Neil Young
Frank Zappa

1996
David Bowie
Gladys Knight & The
Pips
Jefferson Airplane
Little Willie John
Pink Floyd
The Shirelles
**The Velvet
Underground**

1997
The Bee Gees
Buffalo Springfield
Crosby, Stills & Nash
The Jackson 5
Joni Mitchell
Parliament/Funkadelic
The Rascals

1998
Eagles
Fleetwood Mac
The Mamas & The
Papas
Lloyd Price
Santana
Gene Vincent

1999
Billy Joel
Curtis Mayfield
Paul McCartney
Del Shannon
Dusty Springfield
Bruce Springsteen
The Staple Singers

2000
Eric Clapton
Earth, Wind & Fire
The Lovin' Spoonful
The Moonglows
Bonnie Raitt
James Taylor

2001
Aerosmith
Solomon Burke
The Flamingos
Michael Jackson
Queen
Paul Simon
Steely Dan
Ritchie Valens

2002
Isaac Hayes
Brenda Lee
**Tom Petty & The
Heartbreakers**
Gene Pitney
Ramones
Talking Heads

2003
AC/DC
The Clash
**Elvis Costello & The
Attractions**
The Police
The Righteous
Brothers

2004
Jackson Browne
The Dells
George Harrison
Prince
Bob Seger
Traffic
ZZ Top

2005
Buddy Guy
The O'Jays
Pretenders
Percy Sledge
U2

2006
Black Sabbath
Blondie
Miles Davis
Lynyrd Skynyrd
Sex Pistols

2007
Grandmaster Flash and
The Furious Five
R.E.M.
The Ronettes
Patti Smith
Van Halen

2008
The Dave Clark Five
Leonard Cohen
Madonna
John Mellencamp
The Ventures

2009
Jeff Beck
Little Anthony and
The Imperials
Metallica
Run-D.M.C.
Bobby Womack

2010
ABBA
Genesis
Jimmy Cliff
The Hollies
The Stooges

2011
Alice Cooper
Neil Diamond
Dr. John
Darlene Love
Tom Waits

2012
The Beastie Boys
The Blue Caps
The Comets
The Crickets
Donovan
The Famous Flames
Guns N' Roses
The Midnighters
The Miracles
Laura Nyro
**Red Hot Chili
Peppers**
Small Faces/The Faces

2013
Heart
Albert King
Randy Newman
Public Enemy
Rush
Donna Summer

2014
Peter Gabriel
Hall & Oates
Kiss
Nirvana
Linda Ronstadt
Cat Stevens

2015
The Paul Butterfield Blues
Band
Green Day
Joan Jett & the
Blackhearts
Lou Reed
Stevie Ray Vaughan &
Double Trouble
Bill Withers
The "5" Royales
Ringo Starr

bibliography

Dimery, Robert (ed.)
1001 Albums You Must Hear Before You Die
(Universe Publishing/Cassell Illustrated, 2005)

Dimery, Robert (ed.)
1001 Songs You Must Hear Before You Die
(Universe Publishing/Cassell Illustrated, 2010)

Du Noyer, Paul (ed.)
The Story of Rock 'n' Roll (Virgin, 1995)

Frame, Pete
The Complete Rock Family Trees (Omnibus, 1993)

Goddard, Simon
Mozipedia—The Encyclopedia of Morrissey and The Smiths (Ebury Press, 2009)

Harris, John
Hail! Hail! Rock 'n' Roll (Sphere, 2009)

Heatley, Michael (ed.)
Rock & Pop—The Complete Story (Flame Tree, 2006)

Heatley, Michael; Lester, Paul; Roberts, Chris
The Encyclopedia of Albums (Dempsey Parr., 1998)

Hillmore, Peter
Live Aid—The Concert (Sidgwick & Jackson, 1985)

Hoskyns, Barney
Hotel California (John Wiley & Sons, 2007)

Hounsome, Terry
Rock Record 6 (Record Researcher Publications, 1994)

Jeffries, Neil (ed.)
The Kerrang! Direktory of Heavy Metal (Virgin, 1993)

Larkin, Colin (ed.)
The Guinness Encyclopedia of Popular Music (Guinness, 1992)

MacDonald, Bruno
Rock Connections (Collins Design/Omnibus Illustrated, 2010)

Makower, Joel
Woodstock: The Oral History (Doubleday, 1989)

Maycock, Stephen
Rock & Pop Memorabilia (Miller's Publications, 1994)

Miller, Jim (ed.)
The Rolling Stone Illustrated History of Rock & Roll (Plexus, 1992)

Palmer, Tony
All You Need Is Love (Futura, 1976)

Rees, Dafydd; Crampton, Luke
Q Rock Stars Encyclopedia (Dorling Kindersley, 1999)

Roberts, David (ed.)
The Guinness Book of British Hit Singles & Albums (Guinness, 2006)

Roberts, David
Rock Atlas (Clarksdale, 2011)

Roberts, David (ed.)
Rockopedia (Guinness, 1998)

Rosen, Craig
The Billboard Book of Number One Albums (Billboard, 1996)

Smith, Steve
Rock Day-By-Day (Guinness, 1987)

Strong, Martin C.
The Great Rock Discography (Canongate, 2004)

Southall, Brian
Brits 25—The Official Story of Britain's Biggest Music Show (British Phonographic Industry Ltd, 2004)

Wenner, Jann S. (ed.)
The 100 Greatest Artists of All Time (Rolling Stone, 2011)

Whitburn, Joel
The Billboard Book of Top 40 Albums (Billboard, 1995)

Whitburn, Joel
The Billboard Book of Top Pop Singles (Billboard, 1993)

websites

www.allmusic.com

www.archive.classicrockmagazine.com

www.billboard.com

www.bpi.co.uk

www.britishmusicexperience.com

www.contactmusic.com

www.discogs.com

www.grammy.com

www.ifpi.org

www.members.ozemail.com.au/~cruekiss

www.mojo4music.com

www.rockhall.com

www.rockonthenet.com

www.rocksbackpages.com

www.rollingstone.com

www.thejamuk.org

www.theofficialcharts.com

www.riaa.com

label abbreviations

amp	Ampex
asy	Asylum
at	Atlantic
bar	Barclay
bb	Bureau B
bro	Bronze
bru	Brunswick
c	Caroline
che	Cheapskate
cor	Coral
de	Destiny
eas	Eastworld
fli	Flicknife
fo&d	Fuck Off & Di
fon	Fontana
fp	Flipside
gd	Grateful Dead
gf	Geffen
hm	Hear Music
hy	Hydra
imm	Immediate
itm	Inedit Music
ja	Janus
kkp	Kirin Kid Productions
la	Liberty Artists
lib	Liberty
mf	Music Factory
mir	Miramar
onl	One Little Indian
par	Parlophone
pmk	Potamak
pol	Polydor
ps	Private Stock
rea	Reaction
rnr	Roadrunner
rrp	Reprise
rt	Rough Trade
rz	Regal Zonophone
san	Sanctuary
ta	Takoma
tel	Telstar
ua	United Artists
uni	Universal
v	Virgin
ver	Vertigo
we	WEA
wtr	Water
zap	Zapple
zip	Zippo
zk	Zick Zack

contributors

Chris Bryans (CB) has written about television, sport, and music for twenty years, with his work sneaking into *Radio Times, The Observer, Boxing Monthly, Record Collector,* and *Time Out* (Singapore). He was a contributing editor on *1001 Albums You Must Hear Before You Die* and a contributor on *1001 Songs You Must Hear Before You Die.* As he gets older and his mind turns to such things, he has decided he would like Mogwai played at his funeral.

Terry Burrows (TB) is a university lecturer who has written books on guitar (including 2011's *Guitar Family Trees: The History of the World's Most Iconic Guitars*) and musical instruction. As a musician, he has recorded more than forty albums in a variety of styles and under numerous pseudonyms. He has also taught music and technology courses at university level.

Bruno Ceriotti (BC) is a rock historian who writes artist biographies for music magazines and websites. He also worked as music consultant to a Hollywood film company and for a couple of record labels. In 2011 he published *My Little Red Book,* an annotated day-by-day chronology of the U.S. West Coast band Love.

Mick Dillingham (MD) Music writer, graphic artist, you name it and he hasn't done any of it except for the two mentioned above. Truly, if there ever were a renaissance man for the twenty-first century, then he would be the guy five places behind him in the line for fries.

Robert Dimery (RD) is a freelance writer and the general editor of *1001 Albums You Must Hear Before You Die* and *1001 Songs You Must Hear Before You Die.* He has contributed to *Time Out* (London) and *Guinness World Records,* will admit if pressed to copy-editing *Spice Girls: Live Spice!,* and is currently studying composing music for television and film. Robert lives in London with his lovely wife and a small collection of ukuleles.

Jim Harrington (JiH) is the longtime music critic for the *Oakland Tribune, San Jose Mercury News,* and the Bay Area Newspapers Group, and

was a contributor to *1001 Songs You Must Hear Before You Die.* He spends way too much time listening to Roxy Music and watching the Chicago Blackhawks. His world is filled with Grace—which happens to be the name of his daughter.

James Harrison (JaH) is a writer on popular culture who has contributed to *1001 Songs You Must Hear Before You Die, 1001 Paintings You Must See Before You Die, 1001 Books… 1001 Historic Sites…* (you get the drift). In the seventies he would spin twelve-inch disco singles in awe of Studio 54. He currently listens to Jonquil, Chad Valley, and Bronz—none of whom were selected for the current edition of this book, but who knows what the future might bring?

Drew Heatley (DH) is a journalist whose writings cover music, sport, and technology. He assisted on the *Times'* best-selling title, *Michael Jackson: Life of a Legend* and is the co-author of *Kings of Leon: Sex on Fire,* as well as a range of sporting titles, including *European Football Stadiums* and *Lost League Football Grounds.*

Michael Heatley (MHe) is the author of more than one hundred music-based biographies, as well as factual books on music, sport, and television. His biography of the late DJ John Peel sold more than 100,000 copies, while *Michael Jackson: Life of a Legend* topped the *Times'* best-seller list and has been widely translated.

Mike Hobbs (MiH) is a freelance journalist from London. He has contributed to many music magazines, starting with *Zigzag* in the seventies while still at school (his subject was Genesis). He has had more than twenty books published, ranging from music biographies through ghostwritten "autobiographies" to works of history.

Matthew Horton (MaH) is a freelance music journalist. He is a regular contributor and nostalgic list guru at www.nme.com, occasional columnist for the *Guardian Guide,* and an album reviewer for the BBC and Virgin Media. Matthew contributed to *1001 Songs You Must Hear Before You Die* and blogs at jukeboxjunior.com.

Jeff Hudson (JeH) has written or ghostwritten more than twenty books and has interviewed some of the greatest names in the music industry. He is the proud owner of the Freddie Mercury inflatable that escaped from Queen's concert at Wembley Stadium on July 12, 1986.

Dave Jennings (DJ) worked for the British music paper *Melody Maker* for more than a decade, and has now almost fully recovered. His music-related writing has also appeared in the *Los Angeles Times*, *The Guardian*, and *NME*, and on the feminist music website thegirlsare.com. He lives in Bradford in northern England.

Rob Jones (RJ) is a journalist, editor, and content strategist, based in London. He has written and reported on subjects as diverse as music, sport, construction, energy, and the public sector. He once held the Guinness World Record for eating a Terry's Chocolate Orange in the fastest time.

Spencer Leigh (SL) broadcasts a weekly show on BBC Radio Merseyside. He contributes to magazines and authored *The Beatles in Hamburg*. He writes obituaries for U.K. newspaper *The Independent* and says, "Quite often I have interviewed someone for radio, then written a magazine feature, and finally used the interview when they've died for the obituary."

George Lewis (GL) is a global rock disciple who has seen and written about it all, from the last gigs of Hendrix and The Doors at the Isle of Wight festival, through Mark Knopfler's debut with Brewers Droop at the Nags Head in High Wycombe, to John Fogerty's latest Creedence incarnation, live in Tatarstan.

Bruno MacDonald (BM) co-edited *1001 Songs You Must Hear Before You Die* and *1001 Albums You Must Hear Before You Die*. He edited *Air Guitar: A User's Guide*, *Pink Floyd: Through the Eyes of the Band, Its Fans, Friends, and Foes*, and *Rock Connections*, co-wrote *Rock and Roll Heaven*, and contributed to *The Rough Guide to Rock* and *Guinness Hit Singles*. He lives in Hertfordshire, with high maintenance cats and a very patient wife.

Joel McIver (JM) has authored twenty books on rock music, including *Metallica: Justice for All*, *Machine Head: Inside the Machine*, *Glenn Hughes: The Autobiography*, and *To Live is to Die: The Life and Death of Metallica's Cliff Burton*. His forthcoming titles include the autobiography of Max Cavalera. He contributes to several magazines, is the editor of *Bass Guitar Magazine*, and regularly appears on radio and television.

Olivia McLearon (OM) is a freelance writer and sub-editor from London. Her early musical obsessions were Madonna and Kylie, but discovering Britpop in her teens led to a lifelong love of Blur. Among her claims to fame is that she came face-to-face with Damon Albarn in a club, but was too shy to talk to him. She contributed to *1001 Songs You Must Hear Before You Die* and *Rock Connections*, and has worked on magazines ranging from *Doctor Who Adventures* to *Grazia*.

David Roberts (DR) worked as editor on twenty music book projects at Guinness World Records, including *British Hit Singles* and *Rockopedia*. In 2006 he was appointed consultant, writer, and filmmaker to the British Music Experience visitor attraction at London's O2 venue. Recently he created *Rock Atlas*, a guidebook to the music locations of the United Kingdom and Ireland.

Brian Southall (BS) was a journalist with *Melody Maker* and *Disc* before joining A&M. He moved to EMI and served as a consultant to Warner and HMV. His books include *Abbey Road: The Story of the World's Most Famous Recording Studios*, *Northern Songs: The True Story of The Beatles' Publishing Empire*, *If You Don't Know Me by Now: The Official Story of Simply Red*, *Treasures of the Bee Gees*, and *The Rise and Fall of EMI Records*.

Matthew White (MW) is the world's biggest Chris de Burgh fan, and a freelance writer, editor, proofreader, and researcher whose credits include Guinness World Records' *British Hit Singles & Albums*, *The Virgin Book of British Hit Singles*, and projects for the Official Charts Company. "Matt the Music Man" is the newly appointed music consultant for Guinness World Records.

performer directory

Dave Matthews Band 311, **311**
Beck 56–57, **56**
Beck, Jeff
 The Yardbirds 533, **533**
Becker, Walter
 Steely Dan 482–83, **482**
Beckett, Barry
 Traffic 504–5, **505**
Beers, Garry "Gary"
 INXS 236–37, **236**
Bei Bei
 Cui Jian 140, **140**
Beland, John
 The Flying Burrito Brothers 194, **194**
Belew, Adrian
 David Bowie 84–87, **85**
 King Crimson 267, **267**
Bell, Andy
 Oasis 356–59, **357, 359**
Bell, Eric
 Thin Lizzy 502–3, **502**
Bell, Richard
 The Band 44–45, **45**
Belladonna, Joey
 Anthrax 32–33, **32**
Bellamy, Matt
 Muse 343, **343**
Bello, Frank
 Anthrax 32–33, **33**
Below, Fred
 Chuck Berry 62–63, **62**
Benante, Charlie
 Anthrax 32–33, **33**
Bender, Ariel
 Mott the Hoople 340–41, **341**
Bennington, Chester
 Linkin Park 293, **293**
Berckmans, Michel
 Univers Zéro 514, **514**
Bernardi, Louis
 Public Image Ltd 398–99, **399**
Berry, Bill
 R.E.M. 420–23, **420, 422**
Berry, Chuck 60–61, **60**
Berry, Robert
 Emerson Lake & Palmer 174–75, **174**
Berryman, Guy
 Coldplay 112–15, **112, 114, 115**
Bert, Bob
 Sonic Youth 472–73, **473**
Bertignac, Louis
 Téléphone 500, **500**
Berz, George
 Dinosaur Jr. 156, **156**
Best, Pete
 The Beatles 52–55, **52**
Bethânia, Maria
 Gilberto Gil 206–7, **206**
Bettencourt, Nuno
 Extreme 178–79, **178**
Betts, Dickey
 The Allman Brothers Band 28–29, **28**
Bevan, Bev

Black Sabbath 68–71, **69**
 Electric Light Orchestra 172–73, **172**
Biafra, Jello
 Dead Kennedys 147, **147**
Biazzi, Marco
 Lacuna Coil 280–81, **281**
Bilerman, Howard
 Arcade Fire 34–35, **35**
Bilogan, Victoria
 B-2 38, **38**
Binks, Les
 Judas Priest 264–65, **265**
Biondo, George
 Steppenwolf 484, **484**
Birch, Bob
 Elton John 254–57, **255**
Birmingham, Mark
 The Saints 432–33, **433**
Birt, Jill
 The Triffids 509, **509**
Birtwistle, Spencer
 The Fall 184–85, **185**
Bisschoff, Dirk
 Prime Circle 389, **389**
Bittan, Roy
 Bruce Springsteen 476–79, **476**
Black, Bill
 Elvis Presley 384–87, **384**
Black, Jet
 The Stranglers 488–89, **488**
Black, Jimmy Carl
 Frank Zappa 542–45, **542, 544**
Blackmore, Ritchie
 Deep Purple 148–51, **148, 150**
 Rainbow 411, **411**
Bladd, Stephen Jo
 J. Geils Band 201, **201**
Blair, Ron
 Tom Petty & The Heartbreakers 366–67, **366**
Blake, Tim
 Hawkwind 222–23, **223**
Bland, Michael
 Prince 390–93, **391**
Bliss, Atlanta
 Prince 390–93, **391**
Bloom, Eric
 Blue Öyster Cult 75, **75**
Bloomfield, Mike
 Bob Dylan 162–65, **162**
Bluestein, Michael
 Foreigner 198–99, **199**
Boals, Mark
 Yngwie Malmsteen 302–3, **302**
Bobby Z
 Prince 390–93, **390, 392**
Bogios, Jim
 Counting Crows 126–27, **127**
Boguslavsky, Alan
 Héroes del Silencio 229, **229**
Bolan, Marc
 T. Rex 508, **508**
Bolan, Rachel
 Skid Row 451, **451**
Bolder, Trevor
 David Bowie 84–87, **84**

Uriah Heep 515, **515**
Bolin, Tommy
 Deep Purple 148–51, **149, 151**
Bolton, Mick
 Mott the Hoople 340–41, **341**
Bon Jovi, Jon
 Bon Jovi 78–81, **78, 80, 81**
Bonfá, Marcelo
 Legião Urbana 286–87, **286**
Bonham, John
 Led Zeppelin 282–85, **282, 284, 285**
Bonnet, Graham
 Rainbow 411, **411**
 Yngwie Malmsteen 302–3, **302**
Bono **479**
 U2 510–13, **510, 512, 513**
Bordin, Mike "Puffy"
 Faith No More 182–83, **182**
Borland, Wes
 Limp Bizkit 292, **292**
Bortnik, Igor "Lyova"
 B-2 38, **38**
Bosio, Zeta
 Soda Stereo 468–69, **468**
Bostaph, Paul
 Slayer 453, **453**
Boston, Mark
 Captain Beefheart and the Magic Band 96–97, **97**
Bottum, Roddy
 Faith No More 182–83, **182**
Bouchard, Albert
 Blue Öyster Cult 75, **75**
Bouchard, Joe
 Blue Öyster Cult 75, **75**
Bourdon, Rob
 Linkin Park 293, **293**
Bourguignon, David
 Mano Negra/Manu Chao 306–7, **307**
Bowen, Mark
 Faith No More 182–83, **183**
Bowie, David
 David Bowie 84–87, **84, 86, 87**
 Iggy Pop/The Stooges 378–81, **379, 380**
Bowman, Steve
 Counting Crows 126–27, **126**
Bown, Andy
 Status Quo 480–81, **481**
Box, Mick
 Uriah Heep 515, **515**
Bozzio, Terry
 Frank Zappa 542–45, **543**
Bradfield, James Dean
 Manic Street Preachers 304–5, **304**
Bradley, Liam
 Van Morrison 332–33, **333**
Bradshaw, Kym
 The Saints 432–33, **432**
Brainard, Josh
 Slipknot 454–57, **454**
Bramah, Martin
 The Fall 184–85, **184**
Bramblett, Randall
 Traffic 504–5, **505**

Bramlett, Bekka
 Fleetwood Mac 190–93, **191**
Brant, Jon
 Cheap Trick 104, **104**
Braunn, Erik
 Iron Butterfly 238–39, **238**
Braunstein, Les
 Blue Öyster Cult 75, **75**
Brecker, Randy
 Blood, Sweat & Tears 74, **74**
Breit, Gary
 Bryan Adams 20–21, **21**
Breytenbach, Neil
 Prime Circle 389, **389**
Britz, Corey
 Bush 89, **89**
Brock, Dave
 Hawkwind 222–23, **222**
Brock, Napoleon Murphy
 Frank Zappa 542–45, **543**
Broderick, Chris
 Megadeth 320, **320**
Brody, Bruce
 Patti Smith 464–65, **464**
Brookes, Steve
 The Jam 244–47, **244**
Broscoe, Myles
 Arcade Fire 34–35, **34**
Brown, David
 Santana 434–35, **434**
Brown, Ian
 The Stone Roses 486, **486**
Brown, Rex
 Pantera 362, **362**
Bruce, Jack
 Cream/Eric Clapton 128–31, **128, 130**
 John Mayall's Bluesbreakers 312, **312**
Bruce, Michael
 Alice Cooper 116–19, **116, 118**
Bruford, Bill
 Genesis 202–5, **203, 204**
 King Crimson 267, **267**
 Yes 534–37, **534, 536, 537**
Bruhn, Andreas
 Sisters of Mercy 450, **450**
Bruni, Jebin
 Public Image Ltd 398–99, **399**
Brunning, Bob
 Fleetwood Mac 190–93, **190**
Bryan, David
 Bon Jovi 78–81, **78, 80, 81**
Bryan, Mark
 Hootie & the Blowfish 233, **233**
Bryson, David
 Counting Crows 126–27, **126**
Buchholz, Francis
 Scorpions 436–39, **436, 438, 439**
Buck, Peter
 R.E.M. 420–23, **420, 422**
Buckethead
 Guns N' Roses 216–19, **217**
Buckingham, Lindsey
 Fleetwood Mac 190–93, **191, 192, 193**

The Prodigy 394–97, **394, 396**
Hubbard, Neil
  Joe Cocker 110, **110**
Hucknall, Mick
  Small Faces/The Faces
  458–61, **459**
Hudson, Garth
  The Band 44–45, **44**
  Bob Dylan 162–65, **162**
Hudson, Jon
  Faith No More 182–83, **182**
Huffman, Doug
  Boston 82–83, **82**
Hughes, Glenn
  Black Sabbath 68–71, **69**
  Deep Purple 148–51, **148, 151**
Hunt, Darryl
  The Pogues 373, **373**
Hunt, Peter
  Extreme 178–79, **179**
Hunter, Ian
  Mott the Hoople 340–41, **340**
Hunter, Steve
  Alice Cooper 116–19, **116**
Hurley, Andy
  Fall Out Boy 186, **186**
Hussey, Wayne
  Sisters of Mercy 450, **450**
Hutchence, Michael
  INXS 236–37, **236**
Hutchings, Ashley
  Fairport Convention 180–81,
  180
Hütter, Ralf
  Kraftwerk 278–79, **278**
Hynde, Chrissie
  The Pretenders 388, **388**
Hyslop, Kenny
  Simple Minds 446–47, **446**

I

Ian, Scott
  Anthrax 32–33, **32**
Ibold, Mark
  Pavement 363, **363**
  Sonic Youth 472–73, **473**
Iggy Pop see Pop, Iggy
Iha, James
  The Smashing Pumpkins
  462–63, **462**
Illsey, John
  Dire Straits 157, **157**
Immerglück, David
  Counting Crows 126–27, **127**
Inez, Mike
  Alice in Chains 27, **27**
Infante, Frank
  Blondie 73, **73**
Ingber, Elliot
  Captain Beefheart and the
  Magic Band 96–97, **97**
Ingle, Doug
  Iron Butterfly 238–39, **238**
Iommi, Tony 403
  Black Sabbath 68–71, **68,
  70, 71**
Irmler, Hans Joachim
  Faust 187, **187**
Irons, Jack
  Pearl Jam 364–65, **365**
  Red Hot Chili Peppers 416–
  19, **416, 418**
Ishizuka, Tomoaki see "Pata"
Ivins, Michael
  The Flaming Lips 188–89, **188**

J

J, David
  Bauhaus 46–47, **46**
Jabs, Matthias
  Scorpions 436–39, **436, 438,
  439**
Jackson, Eddie
  Queensrÿche 405, **405**
Jacob, Marcel
  Yngwie Malmsteen 302–3,
  302
Jacobs, Jeff
  Foreigner 198–99, **199**
Jacobs, Paul
  Meat Loaf 318–19, **318**
Jagger, Mick
  The Rolling Stones 424–27,
  424, 426, 427
James, Alex
  Blur 76–77, **76**
James, Andrew
  Midnight Oil 326, **326**
James, Brian
  The Damned 146, **146**
James, Tony
  Sisters of Mercy 450, **450**
Jamet, Daniel
  Mano Negra/Manu Chao
  306–7, **307**
Jardine, Al
  The Beach Boys 48–51, **48,
  50, 51**
Jelliman, Brian
  Marillion 308–9, **308**
Jenkins, Barry
  The Animals 30–31, **31**
Jenkins, Karl
  Soft Machine 470–71, **471**
Jobson, Eddie
  Frank Zappa 542–45, **543**
Johansen, David
  The New York Dolls 347, **347**
Johanson, Jai Johanny
  "Jaimoe"
  The Allman Brothers Band
  28–29, **28**
Johansson, Jens
  Yngwie Malmsteen 302–3,
  302
John, Elton **291, 530, 531**
  Elton John 254–57, **254, 256,
  257**
Johnson, Brian
  AC/DC 16–19, **17, 19**
Johnson, Damon
  Alice Cooper 116–19, **117**
  Thin Lizzy 502–3, **503**
Johnson, Gerald
  Steve Miller 327, **327**
Johnson, Johnnie
  Chuck Berry 62–63, **62**
Johnson, Mike
  Dinosaur Jr. 156, **156**
Johnston, Bruce
  The Beach Boys 48–51, **49,
  50, 51**
Johnston, James
  Nick Cave & The Bad Seeds
  100–3, **101**
Johnston, Tom
  The Doobie Brothers 158–59,
  158
Johnstone, Davey
  Elton John 254–57, **254, 256**
Jolliffe, Steve

Tangerine Dream 498–99,
  498
Jones, Anthony "Sooty"
  Humble Pie 234, **234**
Jones, Brian
  The Rolling Stones 424–27,
  424, 426
Jones, Craig
  Slipknot 454–57, **455**
Jones, Darryl
  The Rolling Stones 424–27,
  425
Jones, Gloria
  T. Rex 508, **508**
Jones, Glyn
  Arctic Monkeys 36, **36**
Jones, John Paul
  Led Zeppelin 282–85, **282,
  284, 285**
Jones, Kelly
  Stereophonics 485, **485**
Jones, Kenney
  Small Faces/The Faces
  458–61, **458, 460, 461**
  The Who 528–31, **528, 531**
Jones, Mick
  The Clash 106–9, **106, 108,
  109**
Jones, Mick
  Foreigner 198–99, **198**
Jones, Percy
  Soft Machine 470–71, **471**
Jones, Pete
  Public Image Ltd 398–99, **399**
Jones, Richard
  Stereophonics 485, **485**
Jones, Ronald
  The Flaming Lips 188–89, **188**
Jones, Royce
  Steely Dan 482–83, **483**
Jones, Simon
  The Verve 522–23, **522**
Jones, Steve
  Iggy Pop/The Stooges
  378–81, **379**
  Sex Pistols 444–45, **444**
Jordison, Joey
  Slipknot 454–57, **454, 457**
Jorgenson, John
  Elton John 254–57, **255**
Joyce, Mike
  Buzzcocks 90–91, **90**
  The Smiths 466–67, **466**
Jugg, Roman
  The Damned 146, **146**
Junstrom, Larry
  Lynyrd Skynyrd 298–99, **298**
Justman, Seth
  J. Geils Band 201, **201**

K

Kaczmarek, Les
  Cold Chisel 111, **111**
Kakulas, Phil
  The Triffids 509, **509**
Kaminski, Mik
  Electric Light Orchestra
  172–73, **173**
Kane, Arthur "Killer"
  The New York Dolls 347, **347**
Kannberg, Scott
  Pavement 363, **363**
Kantner, Paul
  Jefferson Airplane/Starship
  250–51, **250**

Karoli, Michael
  Can 94, **94**
Karrer, Chris
  Popol Vuh 382–83, **383**
Kath, Terry
  Chicago 105, **105**
Katz, Steve
  Blood, Sweat & Tears 74, **74**
Kaukonen, Jorma
  Jefferson Airplane/Starship
  250–51, **250**
Kay, John
  Steppenwolf 484, **484**
Kaye, Lenny
  Patti Smith 464–65, **464**
Kaye, Tony
  Yes 534–37, **534, 536**
Kaylan, Howard "Eddie"
  Frank Zappa 542–45, **542**
Keel, Ron
  Yngwie Malmsteen 302–3,
  302
Keith, Ben
  Neil Young 538–41, **538**
Kelley, Kevin
  The Byrds 92–93, **92**
Kelli, Keri
  Alice Cooper 116–19, **117**
Kelly, Mark
  Marillion 308–9, **308**
Keltner, Jim
  George Harrison 220–21, **220**
  John Lennon 288–91, **288**
  The Traveling Wilburys 506–7,
  506
Kemper, David
  Focus 195, **195**
Kerr, Jim
  Simple Minds 446–47, **446**
Kerr, Mark
  Simple Minds 446–47, **447**
Kerslake, Lee
  Uriah Heep 515, **515**
Keuning, Dave
  The Killers 266, **266**
Keys, Peter
  Lynyrd Skynyrd 298–99, **299**
Khachaturian, Ontronik
  "Andy"
  System of a Down 494–95,
  494
Khoroshev, Igor
  Yes 534–37, **535**
Kiedis, Anthony
  Red Hot Chili Peppers 4
  16–19, **416, 418, 419**
Kilmister, Ian "Lemmy"
  Hawkwind 222–23, **223**
Kimball, Stu
  Bob Dylan 162–65, **163**
King, Ed
  Lynyrd Skynyrd 298–99, **298**
King, John (King Gizmo of Dust
  Brothers)
  Beck 56–57, **56**
King, Kerry
  Slayer 453, **453**
King, Simon
  Hawkwind 222–23, **222**
Kingsbury, Tim
  Arcade Fire 34–35, **35**
Kinkade, David
  Soulfly 474, **474**
Kinney, Sean
  Alice in Chains 27, **27**

picture credits

KEY
Band member images: numbered, left to right (1), (2), (3), (4), (5), (6), (7), (8)
Image-only pages: top = t / bottom = b / left = l / right = r / center = c / top left = tl / top center = tc / top right = tr / center top = ct / center bottom = cb / center left = cl / center right = cr / center left top = clt / center left bottom = clb / center right top = crt / center right bottom = crb / bottom left = bl / bottom center = bc / bottom right = br

2 Annamaria DiSanto/WireImage 6–7 Rob Verhorst/Redferns 9 Michael Putland/Getty Images 14–15 Donald Miralle/Getty Images 16 (1) Chris Walter/WireImage (2) Fin Costello/Redferns (3) © Jazzbacks at en.wikipedia (4) Anthony Reginato/Newspix/Rex Features (5) Michael Ochs Archives/Getty Images (6) Fin Costello/Redferns 17 (1) Bob King/Redferns (2) Denis O'Regan/Getty Images (3) Michael Ochs Archives/Getty Images (4) Mick Hutson/Redferns (5) Bob King/Redferns 18 tl Michael Ochs Archives/Getty Images tr Michael Ochs Archives/Getty Images cl Bob King/Redferns cr Richard McCaffrey/Getty Images b © Martyn Goddard/Corbis 19 t Fin Costello/Redferns cl © Martyn Goddard/Corbis crt Bob King/Redferns crb Bob King/Redferns bl Michael Putland/Getty Images br Mick Hutson/Redferns 20 (1) Time Life Pictures/DMI/Time Life Pictures/Getty Images (2) Dan Miller/Rex Features (3) © Bob Leafe (4) Mick Hutson/Redferns (5) Graham Wiltshire/Redferns (6) Michel Linssen/Redferns 21 (1) © Nicola Wright 22 (1) Paul Bergen/Redferns (2) Mick Hutson/Redferns (3) Marcel Thomas/FilmMagic (4) Jordi Vidal/Redferns (5) Fin Costello/Redferns (6) Michael Putland/Getty Images 23 (1) Richard E. Aaron f Redferns (2) Bob Berg/Getty Images 24 tl Richard McCaffrey/Getty Images tr Richard E. Aaron/Redferns c Gems/Redferns bl Fin Costello/Redferns br Richard E. Aaron/Redferns 25 tl Ellen Poppinga - K & K/Redferns tr Jim Steinfeldt/Michael Ochs Archives/Getty Images cl Jeff Kravitz/FilmMagic cr KMazur/WireImage b Kmazur/WireImage 26 (1) Stuart Mostyn/Redferns (2) Martin Bernetti/AFP/Getty Images (3) Mick Hutson/Redferns 27 (1) Classic Rock Magazine/Getty Images (2) Eddie Malluk/WireImage (3) Jeff Kravitz/FilmMagic (4) Eddie Malluk/WireImage (5) Christie Goodwin/Getty Images (6) Bernd Mueller/Redferns 28 (1) Michael Ochs Archives/Getty Images (2) Scott Gries/Getty Images (3) Gems/Redferns (4) Michael Ochs Archives/Getty Images (5) C Flanigan/FilmMagic (6) C Flanigan/FilmMagic (7) Boston Globe/Boston Globe via Getty Images (8) © Neal Preston/CORBIS 29 (1) Larry Hulst/Getty Images (2) © Carl Lender (3) Steve Eichner/WireImage (4) Angela Weiss/Getty Images (5) Charles Eshelman/FilmMagic (6) Rick Diamond/Getty Images (7) Larry Hulst/Getty Images 30 (1) Michael Ochs Archives/Getty Images (2) Popperfoto/Popperfoto/Getty Images (3) Gijsbert Hanekroot/Redferns (4) Hulton Archive/Getty Images (5) Sylvia Pitcher/Redferns (6) Petra Niemeier - K & K/Redferns 31 (1) Dick Barnatt/Redferns (2) Val Wilmer/Redferns 32 (1) Ethan Miller/Getty Images (2) © David Tyler (3) Michael Ochs Archives/Getty Images (4) © Neilturbin.com (6) Paul Hawthorne/Getty Images (7) Mick Hutson/Redferns (8) Metal Hammer Magazine/Future Publishing 33 (1) Paul Hawthorne/Getty Images (2) © Paul Crook (3) Kevin Winter/Getty Images (4) Larry Marano/Getty Images (5) Mick Hutson/Redferns 34 (1) Mick Hutson/Redferns (2) Mick Hutson/Redferns (3) © Myles Broscoe (4) © Greg Hefner (5) John Shearer/WireImage (6) Mick Hutson/Redferns 35 (1) Maury Phillips/WireImage (2) © Laura Vanags/Banff Indie Band Residencey, courtesy the Banff Centre (3) Mick Hutson/Redferns (4) Mick Hutson/Redferns (5) Mick Hutson/Redferns (6) Tiffany Rose/WireImage 36 (1) Dave M. Benett/Getty Images (2) Dave M. Benett/Getty Images (3) Dave Hogan/Getty Images (4) Dave M. Benett/Getty Images (5) Dave Hogan/Getty Images 37 (1) Michael Putland/Getty Images (2) Michael Putland/Getty Images (3) Michael Putland/Getty Images (4) Donna Santisi/Redferns (5) Robert Knight Archive/Redferns (6) Keystone/Getty Images (8) Robert Knight Archive/Redferns 38 (1) b-2 (2) b-2 (3) b-2 (6) b-2 (7) b-2 (8) b-2 39 (1) © Lynn Goldsmith/Corbis (2) Larry Hulst/Getty Images (3) Peter Noble/Redferns (4) Peter Noble/Redferns (5) Peter Noble/Redferns (6) Rex Features (7) Chris McKay/WireImage 40 (1) Jorgen Angel/Redferns (2) Michael Ochs Archives/Getty Images (3) Jorgen Angel/Redferns (4) Jorgen Angel/Redferns (5) William Greenblatt Photography (6) Jorgen Angel/Redferns 41 (2) Michael Ochs Archives/Getty Images (3) © Courtesy of AIM Inc. 42 (1) Michael Putland/Getty Images (2) Fin Costello/Redferns (3) Fin Costello/Redferns (4) Fin Costello/Redferns (5) © Katy Winn/Corbis (6) © Roger Ressmeyer/CORBIS (7) © Pat Cooley 43 (1) © Paul Cullen (3) J. Shearer/WireImage (4) Ron Galella/WireImage (5) © John Atashian/CORBIS (6) © 2004 allrightnow.com (7) © Lynn Sorensen (8) Neil Lupin/Redferns 44 (1) Michael Ochs Archives/Getty Images (2) Jan Persson/Redferns (3) Frank Driggs Collection/Getty Images (4) Frank Driggs Collection/Getty Images (5) Gijsbert Hanekroot/Redferns (6) Brigitte Engl/Redferns 45 (1) Jerritt Clark/WireImage (4) © Chris Vitarello 46 (1) Fin Costello/Redferns (2) Fin Costello/Redferns (3) Fin Costello/Redferns (4) Fin Costello/Redferns 48 (1) Hulton Archive/Getty Images (2) Hulton Archive/Getty Images (3) Hulton Archive/Getty Images (4) Hulton Archive/Getty Images (5) Hulton Archive/Getty Images 49 (1) Michael Ochs Archives/Getty Images (2) Central Press/Getty Images (3) RB/Redferns (4) Michael Ochs Archives/Getty Images (5) Michael Ochs Archives/Getty Images 50 tl Michael Ochs Archives/Getty Images tr Michael Ochs Archives/Getty Images c Michael Ochs Archives/Redferns b Michael Ochs Archives/Getty Images 51 tl Gijsbert Hanekroot/Redferns tc Michael Ochs Archives/Getty Images tr RB/Redferns ct Terry Lott/Sony Music Archive/Getty Images cb ABC Photo Archives/ABC via Getty Images b Lionel Flusin/Gamma-Rapho via Getty Images 52 (1) David Farrell/Redferns (2) Fiona Adams/Redferns (3) Michael Ochs Archives/Getty Images (4) Keystone/Getty Images (5) Mark and Colleen Hayward/Redferns (6) Juergen Vollmer/Redferns 54 tl Michael Webb/Getty Images tr Max Scheler - K & K/Redferns cl Bob Thomas/Bob Thomas/Getty Images cr Terry O'Neill/Getty Images bl Hulton Archive/Getty Images br Express/Getty Images 55 tl Robert Whitaker/Getty Images tr BIPS/Getty Images c Hulton Archive/Getty Images b Tom Hanley/Redferns 56 (1) Victor Malafronte/Getty Images (2) © Bureau L.A. Collection/Sygma/Corbis (3) © Mr Bonzai (4) © Mr Bonzai (5) Steven Dewall/Redferns (6) Lester Cohen/WireImage 58 (1) Ian Tyas/Getty Images (2) Michael Putland/Getty Images (3) Keystone/Getty Images (4) Keystone/Getty Images (5) GAB Archive/Redferns 60 t GAB Archive/Redferns cl K & K Ulf Kruger OHG/Redferns cr Waring Abbott/Getty Images bl Waring Abbott/Getty Images br Bobby Bank/WireImage 61 t Michael Putland/Getty Images cl Michael Putland/Getty Images cr Dave Hogan/Getty Images bl © Trinity Mirror/Mirrorpix/Alamy br Chris Walter/WireImage 62 (1) David Redfern/Redferns (2) Ebet Roberts/Redferns (3) Paul Natkin/WireImage (4) © Courtesy Illinois Slim (5) Jan Persson/Redferns (6) David Redfern/Redferns 64 (1) Clayton Call/Redferns (2) Clayton Call/Redferns (3) Clayton Call/Redferns (4) Clayton Call/Redferns (5) Clayton Call/Redferns (6) © Howling Diablo (8) Ray Tamarra/Getty Images 65 (1) Harmony Gerber/Shutterstock.com (2) Ebet Roberts/Redferns (3) Erika Goldring/Getty Images (4) © Greg Rzab (5) © Scott D. Smith/Retna/Retna Ltd./Corbis (6) © Julia Allison (7) © Paul Stacey (8) Ethan Miller/Getty Images 66 (1) Alastair Indge/Photoshot/Getty Images (2) © Alison S. Braun/CORBIS (3) L. Cohen/WireImage (5) Alastair Indge/Photoshot/Getty Images (7) Frank Mullen/WireImage (8) © Copyright 2008 The Autograph Guys, LLC 67 (1) © bbs.sina.com.cn (2) © 12baobao.cn (3) © 12baobao.cn (6) © Yule.sohu.com (8) © Xinhua/Guo Cheng 68 (1) Harry Goodwin/Rex Features (2) Harry Goodwin/Rex Features (3) Harry Goodwin/Rex Features (4) Harry Goodwin/Rex Features (5) Chris Walter/WireImage (6) Chris Walter/WireImage 69 (1) Robert Knight Archive/Redferns (2) Jorgen Angel/Redferns (4) © 2002-2012 Encyclopaedia Metallum (6) Fin Costello/Redferns 70 tl Ellen Poppinga - K & K/Redferns tr Chris Walter/WireImage cl Gijsbert Hanekroot/Redferns cr Colin Fuller/Redferns b Jorgen Angel/Redferns 71 tl Denis O'Regan/Getty Images tr Peter Still/Redferns ct Chris Walter/WireImage cb Mick Hutson/Redferns bl Ebet Roberts/Redferns br DMI/Time Life Pictures/Getty Images 72 (1) Jim Steinfeldt/Getty Images (2) Jim Steinfeldt/Getty Images (3) Kristian Dowling/Getty Images (4) Jim Steinfeldt/Getty Images 73 (1) Brian Cooke/Redferns (2) Roberta Bayley/Redferns (3) Maureen Donaldson/Getty Images (4) Maureen Donaldson/Getty Images (5) Michael Ochs Archives/Getty Images (6) Chris Gabrin/Redferns 74 (1) Gems/Redferns (2) Michael Ochs Archives/Getty Images (3) Michael Ochs Archives/Getty Images (4) Michael Ochs Archives/Getty Images (5) Michael Ochs Archives/Getty Images (6) Michael Ochs Archives/Getty Images (7) Michael Ochs Archives/Getty Images (8) Michael Ochs Archives/Getty Images 75 (1) Jorgen Angel/Redferns (2) Jorgen Angel/Redferns (3) Tom Sheehan/Sony Music Archive/Getty Images (4) © LesVegas.com (5) Pete Cronin/Redferns (6) Jorgen Angel/Redferns (7) Pete Cronin/Redferns 76 (1) CARL DE SOUZA/AFP/Getty Images (2) Tony Buckingham/Redferns (3) Alastair Indge/Photoshot/Getty Images (4) Chris Jackson/Getty Images 78 (1) Ebet Roberts/Redferns (2) Steve Jennings/CORBIS (3) Paul Natkin/Getty Images (4) © Neal Preston/CORBIS (5) Paul Natkin/Getty Images (6) Steve Snowden/Getty Images 79 (1) Mick Hutson/Redferns 80 t Ebet Roberts/Redferns cl Chris Walter/WireImage bl Rob Verhorst/Redferns br Rob Verhorst/Redferns 81 tl Clayton Call/Redferns tr © Jurgen Frank/Corbis ct Ke.Mazur/WireImage cb TORSTEN SILZ/AFP/Getty Images bl JEFF KOWALSKY/AFP/Getty Images br © JEFFREY ARGUEDAS/epa/Corbis 82 (1) Tim Mosenfelder/Getty Images

(2) Ed Peristein/Redferns (3) Richard E. Aaron/Redferns (4) Ed Peristein/Redferns (5) Michael Putland/Getty Images (6) Boston Globe/Boston Globe via Getty Images (7) © David Sikes 83 (1) Tim Mosenfelder/Getty Images (2) © Curly Smith (3) © Troy K Bartlett (4) Mary Schwalm/Getty Images (5) Tim Mosenfelder/Getty Images (6) Jeffrey Mayer/Getty Images (7) © Sayre Berman/Corbis (8) © Sayre Berman/Corbis 84 (1) Michael Putland/Getty Images (2) Terry O'Neill/Getty Images (4) Fin Costello/Redferns (5) Ipo Musto/Rex Features (6) John M. Heller/Getty Images 85 (1) Michael Putland/Getty Images (2) Brian Cooke/Redferns (3) Clayton Call/Redferns (4) © John Soares, courtesy of Reeves Gabrels (5) Ilpo Musto/Rex Features 86 tl Popperfoto/Getty Images tr Michael Ochs Archives/Getty Images c Michael Ochs Archives/Getty Images b Justin de Villeneuve/Getty Images 87 tl Gijsbert Hanekroot/Redferns tr Tim Boxer/Getty Images cl Ron Galella/WireImage cr Simon Ritter/Redferns bl Phil Dent/Redferns br Jeffrey Mayer/WireImage 88 (1) Michael Ochs Archives/Getty Images (2) Michael Ochs Archives/Getty Images (3) Michael Ochs Archives/Getty Images (4) Michael Ochs Archives/Getty Images (5) Michael Ochs Archives/Getty Images (6) GAB Archive/Redferns 89 (1) Mick Hutson/Redferns (2) Mick Hutson/Redferns (3) Mick Hutson/Redferns (4) Mick Hutson/Redferns (5) Ethan Miller/Getty Images (6) Kevin Winter/NBCUniversal/Getty Images 90 (1) Fin Costello/Redferns (2) Chris Gabrin/Redferns (3) Peter Noble/Redferns (4) Chris Gabrin/Redferns (5) Chris Gabrin/Redferns (6) Rex Features 91 (2) Simon Horswell/FilmMagic (3) Graham Jepson/WireImage (4) Jo Hale/Getty Images (5) © Gifferette Gonad 92 (1) Ebet Roberts/Redferns (2) Jorgen Angel/Redferns (3) Michael Ochs Archives/Getty Images (4) Michael Putland/Getty Images (5) Gems/Redferns (6) GAB Archive/Redferns 93 (1) Ginny Win/Getty Images (2) Gems/Redferns (3) © 2012 Sarah Morrison Photography (4) Gems/Redferns (5) Gijsbert Hanekroot/Redferns 94 (1) /Michael Putland/Getty Images (4) Leon Morris/Redferns (5) © James Tworow (6) Chris Mills/Redferns (7) Richard E. Aaron/Redferns (8) Brian Cooke/Redferns 95 (1) Petra Niemeier - K & K/Redferns (2) Petra Niemeier - K & K/Redferns (4) Petra Niemeier - K & K/Redferns (5) Petra Niemeier - K & K/Redferns (6) Steve Snowden/Getty Images (7) Steve Snowden/Getty Images (8) Bobby Bank/Getty Images 96 (1) Doug McKenzie/Getty Images (2) Michael Putland/Getty Images (3) Michael Ochs Archives/Getty Images (4) Gems/Redferns (5) Michael Ochs Archives/Getty Images 97 (1) Gijsbert Hanekroot/Redferns (3) Michael Ochs Archives/Getty Images (4) Fin Costello/Redferns (6) Petra Niemeier - K & K/Redferns 98 (1) Ebet Roberts/Redferns (2) Ebet Roberts/Redferns (3) Ebet Roberts/Redferns (4) Ebet Roberts/Redferns (5) Ebet Roberts/Redferns 100 (1) Martin Philbey/Redferns (2) Gary Clark/FilmMagic (3) Michael Putland/Getty Images (4) James Emmett/Redferns (7) © Robert Carrithers (8) Jordi Vidal/Redferns 101 (1) © Roland Wolf (2) Jim Dyson/Getty Images (3) Michael Burnell/Redferns (4) Dave Hogan/Getty Images (5) Gary Wolstenholme /Redferns (6) Jim Donnelly/Getty Images (7) Mark Metcalfe/Getty Images (8) GAB Archive/Redferns 102 t Frans Schellekens/Redferns cl Frans Schellekens/Redferns cr Steven Richards/© Photoshot/Retna bl © Gavin Evans/Corbis br Ebet Roberts/Redferns 103 tl Patrick Ford/Redferns tr © Trevor O'Shana/Corbis cl Patrick Ford/Redferns cr Paul Bergen/Redferns b Meghan Sinclair/NBC/NBCU Photo Bank via Getty Images 104 (1) Michael Putland/Getty Images (2) Michael Putland/Getty Images (3) Michael Putland/Getty Images (4) Michael Putland/Getty Images (5) © Neal Preston/CORBIS (6) Chris Walter/WireImage 105 (1) Scott Kirkland/FilmMagic (2) Richard E. Aaron/Redferns (3) David Redfern/Redferns (4) G. Gershoff/WireImage (5) Chris Walter/WireImage (6) Scott Kirkland/FilmMagic (7) Julian Wasser/Time & Life Pictures/Getty Images (8) Larry Marano/Getty Images 106 (1) Ebet Roberts/Redferns (2) Ebet Roberts/Redferns (3) Michael Putland/Getty Images (4) Ebet Roberts/Redferns (5) Peter Noble/Redferns (6) Ray Stevenson/Rex Features 107 (1) Michael Putland/Getty Images (2) Gerry Images/Getty Images (3) Peter Still/Redferns (4) Peter Still/Redferns 108 t David Montgomery/Getty Images c Kevin Cummins/Getty Images bl Ebet Roberts/Redferns br Virginia Turbett/Redferns 109 t /Fraser Gray/Rex Features c Larry Hulst/Getty Images bl Ebet Roberts/Redferns br © Mike Laye/CORBIS 110 (1) Jack Robinson/Getty Images (3) Rob Verhorst/Redferns (4) Michael Putland/Getty Images (5) Jorgen Angel/Redferns (6) Estate Of Keith Morris/Redferns (7) Gems/Redferns 111 (1) Patrick Riviere/Getty Images (2) © Bob King/Corbis (3) Paul McConnell/Getty Images (4) © Bob King/Corbis (7) © Bob King/Corbis 112 (1) Dave Hogan/Getty Images (2) Dave Hogan/Getty Images (3) Dave Hogan/Getty Images (4) Dave Hogan/Getty Images 114 t Mick Hutson/Redferns c Jeff Kravitz/FilmMagic b Nigel Crane/Redferns 115 t Business Wire/Getty Images cl Mick Hutson/Redferns cr Peter Wafzig/Getty Images b Mark Metcalfe/Stringer 116 (1) Michael Putland/Getty Images (2) Michael Putland/Getty Images (3) Michael Putland/Getty Images (4) Bobby Bank/WireImage (5) Michael Putland/Getty Images (6) Jorgen Angel/Redferns (7) Jordi Vidal/Redferns (8) Jeff Kravitz/FilmMagic 117 (2) Gary Wolstenholme /Redferns (3) Ebet Roberts/Redferns (4) Bob King/Redferns (5) Tim Mosenfelder/Getty Images (6) Ethan Miller/Getty Images (7) Tabatha Fireman/Redferns (8) Jemal Countess/Getty Images 118 tl Jorgen Angel/Redferns tr Jorgen Angel/Redferns c Terry O'Neill/Getty Images bl © Bettmann/CORBIS br © Trinity Mirror/Mirrorpix/Alamy 119 t Fin Costello/Redferns cl © Lynn Goldsmith/Corbis cr Stefan M. Prager/Redferns bl Michel Linssen/Redferns br Chris McKay/WireImage 120 (1) Fin Costello/Redferns (2) © 2011 The Wild Swans (3) © Mick Finkler (4) Harry Goodwin/Rex Features (5) Harry Goodwin/Rex Features (7) Harry Goodwin/Rex Features 121 (1) Ebet Roberts/Redferns (2) © David Fowler/123rf (3) © 2008 Ted Emmett (4) Ebet Roberts/Redferns (5) © Nick Barber/Getty Images 122 (1) Randy Miramontez/Shutterstock.com (2) Randy Miramontez/Shutterstock.com (3) Estate Of Keith Morris/Redferns (4) Randy Miramontez/Shutterstock.com (5) Randy Miramontez/Shutterstock.com 124 tl Kevin Cummins/Getty Images tr Estate Of Keith Morris/Redferns c Roberto Bayley/Redferns bl Michael Grecco/Getty Images 125 br Michael Putland/Getty Images t Rob Verhorst/Redferns cl Estate Of Keith Morris/Redferns cr David Redfern/Redferns bl Michael Caulfield Archive/WireImage br Kevin Mazur/WireImage 126 (1) Jemal Countess/Getty Images (2) David Tonge/Getty Images (3) David Tonge/Getty Images (4) David Tonge/Getty Images (5) David Tonge/Getty Images (6) © Pam Bogert 127 (1) David Tonge/Getty Images (2) C Flanigan/FilmMagic (3) Joe Scarnici/FilmMagic (4) © Contographer/Corbis 128 (1) David Redfern/Redferns (2) Jan Persson/Redferns (3) Petra Niemeier - K & K/Redferns (4) Sylvia Pitcher/Redferns (5) David Redfern/Redferns (6) Steve Thorne/Redferns 129 (1) Mick Hutson/Redferns (2) Steve Thorne/Redferns 130 tl Paul Popper/Popperfoto/Popperfoto/Getty Images tr Chris Walter/WireImage cl Michael Ochs Archives/Getty Images cr The Estate of David Gahr/Getty Images bl Michael Ochs Archives/Getty Images br Terry O'Neill/Getty Images 131 t Time & Life Pictures/Getty Images c Peter Still/Redferns bl NBC/NBC via Getty Images br © Gustau Nacarino/Reuters/Corbis 132 (1) Michael Putland/Getty Images (2) Michael Putland/Getty Images (3) Michael Putland/Getty Images (4) Michael Putland/Getty Images 134 (1) Ebet Roberts/Redferns (2) Ebet Roberts/Redferns (3) Ebet Roberts/Redferns (4) Michael Ochs Archives/Getty Images (5) Jack Robinson/Getty Images (6) Jack Robinson/Getty Images (7) Michael Putland/Getty Images (8) Michael Putland/Getty Images 135 (1) Keith Baugh/Redferns (3) © Joseph Lala (5) Clayton Call/Redferns (6) Neville Elder/Redferns (7) Jeff Kravitz/FilmMagic 136 tl © Henry Diltz/CORBIS tr Julian Wasser/Time & Life Pictures/Getty Images c © Henry Diltz/CORBIS bl Terry O'Neill/Getty Images br Jon Sievert/Getty Images 137 tl © Henry Diltz/CORBIS tr © Neal Preston/CORBIS c © Neal Preston/CORBIS bl Steve Eichner/WireImage br Getty Images/Getty Images 138 (1) Tim Mosenfelder/Getty Images (2) Gareth Cattermole/Getty Images (3) Bob King/Redferns (4) Patti Ouderkirk/WireImage (5) Tabatha Fireman/Redferns (6) Kevin Mazur/WireImage 139 (1) Christie Goodwin/Redferns 140 (1) Forrest Anderson/Time & Life Pictures/Getty Images (3) © Nen.com.cn 141 (1) Erica Echenberg/Redferns (2) Erica Echenberg/Redferns (3) Erica Echenberg/Redferns (5) Erica Echenberg/Redferns (6) Linda Matlow/Rex Features (7) Jim Steinfeldt/Getty Images 142 (1) Michael Putland/Getty Images (2) Michael Putland/Getty Images (3) Michael Putland/Getty Images (4) Gabor Scott/Redferns (5) Michael Putland/Getty Images 143 (1) Fin Costello/Redferns (2) Fin Costello/Redferns (3) Michael Putland/Getty Images (5) Bob King/Redferns (6) Gustavo Caballero/Getty Images 144 tl Kevin Cummins/Getty Images tr Ebet Roberts/Redferns ct Ebet Roberts/Redferns cb Paul Natkin/WireImage b Rob Verhorst/Redferns 145 tl Michael Putland/Getty Images tr Paul Harris/Getty Images cl Paul Natkin/WireImage cr Liam Nicholls/Getty Images b Jo Hale/Getty Images 146 (1) Estate Of Keith Morris/Redferns (2) Estate Of Keith Morris/Redferns (3) Ian Dickson/Redferns (4) Estate Of Keith Morris/Redferns (5) Paul Natkin/WireImage (6) Marc Marnie/Redferns (7) C Brandon/Redferns (8) Steve Thorne/Redferns 147 (1) Peter Noble/Redferns (2) Peter Noble/Redferns (3) Peter Noble/Redferns (4) Peter Noble/Redferns 148 (1) Fin Costello/Redferns (2) Fin Costello/Redferns (3) Fin Costello/Redferns (4) Jorgen Angel/Redferns (5) Jorgen Angel/Redferns (6) Jorgen Angel/Redferns (7) Jorgen Angel/Redferns (8) Fin Costello/Redferns 149 (1) Fin Costello/Redferns (2) Michael Ochs Archives/Getty Images (3) Ian Dickson/Redferns (4) Ebet Roberts/Redferns (5) Michael Uhll/Redferns (6) David Redfern/Redferns 150 tl John Minihan/Getty Images tr Michael Ochs Archives/Getty Images cl Michael Putland/Getty Images cr Jan Persson/Redferns b Fin Costello/Redferns 151 tl Fin Costello/Redferns tr Peter Still/Redferns c Fin Costello/Redferns bl Mick Hutson/Redferns br Martin Philbey/Redferns 152 (1) Robert Knight Archive/Redferns (2) Robert Knight Archive/Redferns (3) Chris Walter/WireImage (4) Chris Walter/WireImage (5) Robert Knight Archive/Redferns (6) Robert Knight Archive/Redferns 153 (1) Robert Knight Archive/Redferns 154 tl Andre Csillag/Rex Features tr Chris Walter/WireImage c Michael Ochs Archives/Getty Images bl Dave Hogan/Getty Images br Michael Putland/Getty Images 155 tl Andre Csillag/Rex Features tr Harry Herd/Redferns c SGranitz/WireImage bl Jeff Kravitz/FilmMagic br Neil Lupin/Redferns 156 (1) Ebet Roberts/Redferns (2) Randall Michelson Archive/WireImage (3) © Dania Heller (4) © Walter Dietrich (5) © George Berz 157 (1) Gijsbert Hanekroot/Redferns (2) Gijsbert Hanekroot/Redferns (3) Rob Verhorst/Redferns (4) Gijsbert Hanekroot/Redferns (5) Rob Verhorst/Redferns (6) Mark Westwood/Redferns (7) Michael Putland/

tr Stuart Mostyn/Redferns **c** Brigitte Engl/Redferns **b** /Kevin Nixon/Classic Rock Magazine via Getty Images **244 (1)** Peter Noble/Redferns **(2)** Peter Noble/Redferns **(3)** Peter Noble/Redferns **246 tl** Ian Dickson/Redferns **tr** © Neal Preston/CORBIS **c** Steve Morley/Redferns **b** Ebet Roberts/Redferns **247 t** Ebet Roberts/Redferns **c** Victor Watts/Rex Features **bl** Gus Stewart/Redferns **br** ITV/Rex Features **248 (1)** Gregg DeGuire/WireImage **(2)** Nigel Crane/Redferns **(3)** Valerie Macon/Getty Images **(4)** Carley Margolis/FilmMagic **(5)** Barry King/WireImage **(6)** Jean Baptiste Lacroix/WireImage **249 (1)** Jeff Kravitz/FilmMagic **(2)** © Katy Winn/Corbis **250 (1)** Anthony Barboza/Getty Images **(2)** © Roger Ressmeyer/CORBIS **(3)** Ed Peristein/Redferns **(4)** © Lynn Goldsmith/Corbis **(5)** © Morton Beebe/CORBIS **(6)** Blank Archives/Getty Images **(7)** Clayton Call/Redferns **(8)** Central Press/Getty Images **251 (1)** Michael Ochs Archives/Getty Images **(2)** Michael Putland/Getty Images **(3)** Mike FANOUS/Gamma-Rapho via Getty Images **(4)** Michael Ochs Archives/Getty Images **(5)** Michael Putland/Getty Images **(6)** Michael Putland/Getty Images **(7)** Michael Putland/Getty Images **(8)** © Lynn Goldsmith/Corbis **252 (1)** Jorgen Angel/Redferns **(2)** Jan Persson/Redferns **(3)** Harry Goodwin/Rex Features **(4)** Harry Goodwin/Rex Features **(5)** Michael Putland/Getty Images **(6)** Michael Putland/Getty Images **(7)** Michael Putland/Getty Images **(8)** Michael Putland/Getty Images **253 (1)** Gems Redferns **(2)** Richard E. Aaron/Redferns **(3)** Ken Towner/Evening Standard /Rex Features **(4)** Jordi Vidal/Redferns **(5)** Pete Cronin/Redferns **(6)** © M Schurmann **(7)** Dana Nalbandian/WireImage **(8)** © Julian Hayr **254 (1)** Dave M. Benett/Getty Images **(2)** GAB Archive/Redferns **(4)** Harry Goodwin/Rex Features **(5)** Terry O'Neill/Hulton Archive/Getty Images **(6)** Michael Putland/Getty Images **(7)** Robert Knight Archive/Redferns **(8)** Amanda Edwards/Getty Images **255 (2)** The Elton John Archive **(3)** Jeff Fusco/Getty Images **(4)** Roberta Parkin/Redferns **(5)** © John Mahon **(6)** The Elton John Archive **256 tl** Jack Robinson/Hulton Archive/Getty Images **tr** Michael Putland/Getty Images **c** David Redfern/Redferns **bl** Richard Young/Rex Features **br** Richard E. Aaron/Redferns **257 tl** © David Lefranc/Kipa/Corbis **tr** Tim Mosenfelder/Getty Images **c** Anwar Hussein/WireImage **bl** Ida Mae Astute/ABC via Getty Images **br** KMazur/WireImage **258 (1)** Michael Putland/Getty Images **(2)** Michael Putland/Getty Images **(3)** Michael Putland/Getty Images **(4)** Scott Kirkland/FilmMagic **(5)** © Sayre Berman/Corbis **(6)** Michael Putland/Getty Images **(7)** Michael Putland/Getty Images **(8)** Jeffrey Mayer/WireImage **259 (1)** Michael Putland/Getty Images **(2)** Bobby Bank/WireImage **(3)** Tim Mosenfelder/Getty Images **(4)** David Pomponio/FilmMagic **(5)** Bobby Bank/WireImage **(6)** Jeffrey Mayer/WireImage **260 (1)** Rob Verhorst/Redferns **(2)** Lisa Haun/Getty Images **(3)** Lisa Haun/Getty Images **(4)** Lisa Haun/Getty Images **(5)** Lisa Haun/Getty Images **(6)** Jo Hale/Getty Images **261 (1)** Tony Woolliscroft/WireImage **262 tl** Martin O'Neill/Redferns **tr** Chris Mills/Redferns **clt** ITV/Rex Features **clb** Sheila Rock/Rex Features **cr** Kerstin Rodgers/Redferns **b** ITV/Rex Features **263 tl** Bob Berg/Getty Images **tr** Rex Features **c** Mark Allan/WireImage **bl** Jon Super/Redferns **br** Stuart Mostyn/Redferns **264 (2)** Paul Natkin/WireImage **(3)** Paul Natkin/WireImage **(4)** Chris Mills/WireImage **(5)** Chris Mills/WireImage **(6)** Neil Lupin/Redferns **(7)** Chelsea Lauren/WireImage **(8)** Chris Walter/WireImage **265 (1)** Fin Costello/Redferns **(4)** © Singerpictures.com **(5)** Fin Costello/Redferns **(6)** Naki/Redferns **266 (1)** George Pimentel/WireImage **(2)** Bryan Bedder/Getty Images **(6)** Lester Cohen/WireImage **(7)** Bryan Bedder/Getty Images **267 (1)** Paul Natkin/WireImage **(2)** Peter Sanders/Rex Features **(3)** Peter Sanders/Rex Features **(4)** Gems/Redferns **(5)** Michael Ochs Archives/Getty Images **(6)** Paul Natkin/WireImage **(7)** Paul Natkin/WireImage **(8)** Paul Natkin/WireImage **268 (1)** Frederick M. Brown/Getty Images **(2)** Dave Hogan/Getty Images **(3)** Jerod Harris/WireImage **(4)** Dave Hogan/Getty Images **270 (1)** Gijsbert Hanekroot/Redferns **(2)** Petra Niemeier - K & K/Redferns **(3)** DAVID MAGNUS/Rex Features **(4)** MARK SHARRATT/Rex Features **(5)** Harry Goodwin/Rex Features **(6)** Jorgen Angel/Redferns **271 (1)** Gijsbert Hanekroot/Redferns **(2)** Estate Of Keith Morris/Redferns **(3)** Harry Goodwin/Rex Features **272 (1)** © Lynn Goldsmith/Corbis **(2)** © Lynn Goldsmith/Corbis **(3)** © Lynn Goldsmith/Corbis **(4)** © Lynn Goldsmith/Corbis **(5)** Robert Knight Archive/Redferns **273 (1)** © Lynn Goldsmith/Corbis **(2)** Ebet Roberts/Redferns **(4)** © Neal Preston/CORBIS **(5)** Mike Coppola/FilmMagic **(6)** © Jay Blakesberg/Retna Ltd./Corbis **274 tl** Tom Hill/WireImage **tr** Chris Walter/WireImage **ct** Michael Putland/Getty Images **cb** Paul Natkin/Getty Images **b** Fin Costello/Redferns **275 tl** Michael Ochs Archives/Getty Images **tr** Paul Natkin/Getty Images **cl** Mick Hutson/Redferns **cr** KMazur/WireImage **b** Will Ireland/Class Rock Magazine via Getty Images **276 (1)** Paul Hawthorne/Getty Images **(2)** Annamaria DiSanto/WireImage **(3)** Bob Berg/Getty Images **(4)** Christina Radish/Redferns **(5)** SGranitz/WireImage **(6)** Jason Merritt/Getty Images **278 (1)** Ebet Roberts/Redferns **(2)** Ebet Roberts/Redferns **(3)** Michael Ochs Archives/Getty Images **(4)** Michael Ochs Archives/Getty Images **(5)** Bob King/Redferns **(6)** Bob King/Redferns **279 (1)** Bob King/Redferns **(3)** Marc Marnie/Redferns **280 (1)** Dave Etheridge-Barnes/Getty Images **(2)** Kevin Nixon/Classic Rock Magazine via Getty Images **(4)** © Claudio Leo **(6)** Steve Brown/Photoshot/Getty Images **281 (1)** Kevin Nixon/Classic Rock Magazine via Getty Images **(2)** Kevin Nixon/Classic Rock Magazine via Getty Images **(3)** Steve Thorne/Redferns **(4)** Gary Miller/Getty Images **282 (1)** Dick Barnatt/Redferns **(2)** Chris Walter/WireImage **(3)** Chris Walter/WireImage **(4)** Jorgen Angel/Redferns **284 t** Jorgen Angel/Redferns **cl** Charles Bonnay/Time & Life Pictures/Getty Images **cr** Michael Stroud/Getty Images **b** Michael Ochs Archives/Getty Images **285 tl** David Redfern/Redferns **tr** Richard E. Aaron/Redferns **c** Mick Gold/Redferns **b** Rob Verhorst/Redferns **286 (1)** © Ricardo Siqueira **(2)** Buda Mendes/LatinContent/Getty Images **(3)** Buda Mendes/LatinContent/Getty Images **288 (1)** Susan Wood/Getty Images **(2)** Susan Wood/Getty Images **(3)** K & K Ulf Kruger OHG/Redferns **(4)** Richard Upper/Redferns **(5)** Ebet Roberts/Redferns **(6)** Estate Of Keith Morris/Redferns **290 tl** John Reader/Time & Life Pictures/Getty Images **tr** Central Press/Getty Images **clt** Susan Wood/Getty Images **clb** Evening Standard/Getty Images **cr** Terry Disney/Getty Images **b** Tom Hanley/Redferns **291 tl** ABC Photo Archives/ABC via Getty Images **tr** Michael Ochs Archives/Getty Images **cl** Steve Morley/Redferns **cr** Michael Ochs Archives/Getty Images **b** Michael Ochs Archives/Getty Images **292 (1)** Mick Hutson/Redferns **(2)** Andy Sheppard/Redferns **(3)** © Markus Cuff/Corbis **(4)** Mick Hutson/Redferns **(5)** © Markus Cuff/Corbis **(6)** Evan Agostini/Getty Images **293 (1)** Amy Graves/WireImage **(2)** Victor Decolongon/Getty Images **(3)** Victor Decolongon/Getty Images **(4)** Jon Kopaloff/FilmMagic **(5)** Brian Ach/WireImage **(6)** Jim Smeal/WireImage **294 (1)** Michael Putland/Getty Images **(2)** Jim Shea/Getty Images **(3)** Michael Ochs Archives/Getty Images **(4)** Petra Niemeier - K & K/Redferns **(5)** Michael Ochs Archives/Getty Images **(6)** Michael Ochs Archives/Getty Images **295 (1)** Michael Ochs Archives/Getty Images **(2)** Michael Ochs Archives/Getty Images **(3)** Michael Ochs Archives/Getty Images **(4)** Tim Mosenfelder/Redferns **(5)** Anthony Pidgeon/Redferns**296 (1)** © Reuters/CORBIS **(2)** Ebet Roberts/Redferns **(3)** © Nelson Onofre **(4)** © 2002-2012 Encyclopaedia Metallum **297 (1)** Jan Persson/Redferns **(2)** Michael Ochs Archives/Getty Images **(3)** Michael Ochs Archives/Getty Images **(4)** Michael Ochs Archives/Getty Images **(5)** Gilles Petard/Redferns **(6)** Michael Ochs Archives/Getty Images **298 (1)** Tom Hill/WireImage **(2)** Richard E. Aaron/Redferns **(3)** Michael Ochs Archives/Getty Images **(4)** Gems/Redferns **(5)** Douglas Mason/Getty Images **(6)** Tim Mosenfelder/Getty Images **(7)** Michael Ochs Archives/Getty Images **(8)** Michael Ochs Archives/Getty Images **299 (1)** Tom Hill/WireImage **(2)** Getty Images **(3)** Michael Ochs Archives/Getty Images **(4)** Amy Graves/WireImage **(5)** Derek Storm/FilmMagic **(6)** Steve Thorne/Redferns **(7)** Tim Mosenfelder/Getty Images **(8)** © Jeff Moore/ZUMA/Corbis **300 (1)** MARTIN BUREAU/AFP/Getty Images **(2)** Michael Ochs Archives/Getty Images **(4)** Michael Ochs Archives/Getty Images **(6)** Michael Ochs Archives/Getty Images **301 (2)** Pascal Le Segretain/Getty Images **302 (1)** Chris Walter/WireImage **(2)** Ethan Miller/Getty Images **(3)** Catherine McGann/Getty Images **(4)** Michael Putland/Getty Images **(6)** Neil Lupin/Redferns **(7)** Fotex/Rex Features **(8)** © Göran Edman **303 (3)** © Patrik Hellström **(4)** Andre Csillag/Rex Features **(5)** Jordi Vidal/Redferns **(6)** Naki/Redferns **304 (1)** Denis O'Regan/Getty Images **(2)** Insight-Visual UK/Rex Features **(3)** Andre Csillag/Rex Features **(4)** Mick Hutson/Redferns **306 (1)** © Kim Kulish/Corbis **(2)** Foc Kan/WireImage **(3)** © Jacob Khrist **307 (1)** © Wilfried Rebré **(3)** Lyle A. Waisman/Getty Images **(4)** Lyle A. Waisman/Getty Images **(5)** Araya Diaz/WireImage **308 (1)** Joby Sessions/Classic Rock Magazine via Getty Images **(2)** © Mick Pointer **(4)** Barry Clack/FilmMagic **(6)** Joby Sessions/Classic Rock Magazine via Getty Images **(7)** Gary Clark/FilmMagic **309 (1)** Fin Costello/Redferns **(2)** © Jonathan Mover **(3)** Joby Sessions/Classic Rock Magazine via Getty Images **(4)** Gary Clark/FilmMagic **310 (1)** Stephen Shugerman/Getty Images **(2)** Kevin Winter/Getty Images **(3)** Arnold Turner/WireImage **(4)** John M. Heller/Getty Images **(5)** Michael Buckner/Getty Images **311 (1)** Tim Mosenfelder/Getty Images **(2)** Tim Mosenfelder/Getty Images **(3)** Jason Squires/WireImage **(4)** John Shearer/WireImage **(6)** Jeff Kravitz/FilmMagic **(7)** Tim Mosenfelder/Getty Images **312 (1)** Ivan Keeman/Redferns **(2)** Jeffrey Mayer/WireImage **(3)** Ivan Keeman/Redferns **(4)** Harry Goodwin/Rex Features **(5)** Michael Putland/Getty Images **(6)** Harry Goodwin/Rex Features **(7)** Bentley Archive/Popperfoto/Getty Images **(8)** © Roger Ressmeyer/CORBIS **313 (1)** Leni Sinclair/Getty Images **(2)** Leni Sinclair/Getty Images **(3)** Leni Sinclair/Getty Images **(4)** Leni Sinclair/Getty Images **(5)** Leni Sinclair/Getty Images **314 (1)** Michael Putland/Getty Images **(2)** Michael Putland/Getty Images **(3)** Estate Of Keith Morris/Redferns **(4)** Estate Of Keith Morris/Redferns **(5)** Gijsbert Hanekroot/Redferns **(6)** Richard Blanshard/Getty Images **315 (1)** Steve Catlin/Redferns **(2)** Jim Smeal/BEI/Rex Features **(3)** Araya Diaz/WireImage **(4)** Tiffany Rose/WireImage **(5)** Nick Harvey/WireImage **316 tl** Hulton Archive/Getty Images **tr** Anwar Hussein/Getty Images **cl** Evening Standard/Getty Images **cr** Alan Davidson/WireImage **bl** Keystone-France/Gamma-Keystone via Getty Images **br** Dave Hogan/Getty Images **317 tl** Time & Life Pictures/Getty Images **tr** Tom Hanley/Redferns **c** Denis O'Regan/Getty Images **b** Dave Hogan/Getty Images **318 (1)** Michael Ochs Archives/Getty Images **(2)** Michael Ochs Archives/Getty Images **(4)** Ron Galella/WireImage **(5)** Santi Visalli Inc./Getty Images **319 (2)** Jesse Grant/WireImage **(3)** Mark Weiss/WireImage **(4)** © 2005-2009 Meatloaf Tribute.net **(5)** Olivia Hemingway/Redferns **320 (1)** Chris Walter/WireImage **(2)** Mark Weiss/Getty Images **(3)** Kevin Winter/Getty Images **(4)** Jesse Wild/Rhythm Magazine via Getty Images **(5)** Mark Weiss/Getty Images **(6)** Mark Weiss/Getty Images **(7)** Chris Walter/WireImage **(8)** Mick Hutson/Redferns **321 (1)** Time & Life Pictures/Getty Images **(2)** Time & Life Pictures/Getty Images **(3)** Time & Life Pictures/Getty Images **(4)** Time & Life Pictures/Getty Images **(5)** Time & Life Pictures/Getty Images **322 (1)** Dave Allocca/Time & Life Pictures/Getty Images **(2)** Hulton Archive/Getty Images **(3)** Ron Galella Ltd./WireImage **(4)** Mick Hutson/Redferns **(5)** Krasner/Trebitz/Redferns **323 (1)** Krasner/Trebitz/Redferns **(2)** Patti Ouderkirk/WireImage **324 tl** Larry Hulst/Getty Images **tr** Fin Costello/Redferns **cl** Krasner/Trebitz/Redferns **cr** Ebet Roberts/Redferns **b** Mick Hutson/Redferns **325 t** Tim Mosenfelder/Getty Images **cl** George De Sota/Redferns **cr** Paul Bergen/Redferns **bl** Peter Pakvis/Redferns **br** Kevin Mazur/WireImage **326 (1)** Gaye Gerard/Getty Images **(3)** Serge Thomann/WireImage **(4)** Patrick Riviere/Getty Images **(5)** Gaye Gerard/Getty Images **(6)** © Tony Mott **(7)** Frazer Harrison/Getty Images **327 (1)** Gijsbert Hanekroot/Redferns **(4)** Jim Steinfeldt/Getty Images **(5)** © Ken Cooper **(7)** Ebet Roberts/Redferns **328 (1)** Gems/Redferns **(2)** Clayton Call/Redferns **(3)** Clayton

Call/Redferns (4) Richard McCaffrey/Getty Images (5) Michael Ochs Archives/Getty Images 330 (1) RB/Redferns (2) Gered Mankowitz/Redferns (3) Gered Mankowitz/Redferns (4) RB/Redferns (5) RB/Redferns (6) Gered Mankowitz/Redferns 331 (1) Michael Putland/Getty Images (2) Michael Ochs Archives/Getty Images 332 (1) Gijsbert Hanekroot/Redferns (2) Michael Putland/Getty Images (6) © Sanford Gossman Photography (7) Ebet Roberts/Redferns 333 (1) Samuel Dietz/Redferns (2) © John Allair/John Korty (3) Peter Noble/Redferns (4) © Ace Conference (7) Ollie Millington/Redferns 334 (1) Ron Galella, Ltd./WireImage (2) Ebet Roberts/Redferns (3) Robert Knight Archive/Redferns (4) Ebet Roberts/Redferns (5) Mick Hutson/Redferns (6) Paul Natkin/Getty Images 335(1) A. Nevader/WireImage 336 tl Chris Walter/WireImage tr Peter Still/Redferns clt Ron Galella/WireImage clb Ebet Roberts/Redferns cr Ebet Roberts/ Redferns bl Ron Galella, Ltd./WireImage br © Robb D. Cohen/Retna Ltd./Corbis 337 t Ron Galella/WireImage b Joey Foley/FilmMagic 338 (1) Fin Costello/ Redferns (2) Fin Costello/Redferns (3) ANAKA/Rex Features (4) Estate Of Keith Morris/Redferns (5) Ian Dickson/Rex Features (6) Fin Costello/Redferns 339 (1) Estate Of Keith Morris/Redferns (2) Fin Costello/Redferns (3) Gus Stewart/Redferns (4) Fin Costello/Redferns 340 (1) Gems/Redferns (2) Jacques Bernard/ Rex Features (3) Brian Cooke/Redferns (4) Brian Cooke/Redferns (5) Ian Tyas/Getty Images (6) Gems/Redferns 341 (1) © Mick Bolton (2) Michael Putland/Getty Images (3) Michael Putland/Getty Images (4) Ivan Keeman/Redferns (5) Fin Costello/Redferns 342 (1) Charles J. Peterson/Time & Life Pictures/Getty Images (2) Charles J. Peterson/Time & Life Pictures/Getty Images (3) Charles J. Peterson/Time & Life Pictures/Getty Images (4) Charles J. Peterson/Time & Life Pictures/ Getty Images (5) Steven Dewall/Redferns 343 (1) Benedict Johnson/Redferns (2) Mick Hutson/Redferns (3) Mick Hutson/Redferns 344 (1) Mauro Pimentel/ LatinContent/Getty Images (2) Rui M. Leal/Getty Images (3) © Lebrecht Music and Arts Photo Library/Alamy (4) © Mario Luiz Thompson/Arquivo 345 (1) Alastair Indge/Photoshot/Getty Images (2) Alastair Indge/Photoshot/Getty Images (3) Suzie Gibbons/Redferns (4) Photoshot/Getty Images (5) Photoshot/Getty Images 346 (4) © Bryan Spencer 347 (1) Peter Noble/Redferns (3) Erica Echenberg/Redferns (4) Michael Ochs Archives/Getty Images (5) Ron Galella/ WireImage (6) Michael Ochs Archives/Getty Images 348 (1) Peter Pakvis/Redferns (2) SGranitz/WireImage (3) Kevin Kane/WireImage (4) © My Eye & My Lens = My World Photography (5) SGranitz/WireImage (6) Rob Scott/Rhythm Magazine via Getty Images 350 (1) Kevin Mazur/WireImage (2) Dale Wilcox/WireImage (3) Jeffrey Mayer/WireImage (4) © Steve Jennings/CORBIS (6) Christina Radish/Redferns (7) Gary Miller/FilmMagic (8) Vince Bucci/Getty Images 351 (3) © Greg (4) Jesse Grant/WireImage (5) Annamaria DiSanto/WireImage (6) David Livingston/Getty Images (7) Astrid Stawiarz/Getty Images 352 (1) Jeff Kravitz/ FilmMagic (2) KMazur/WireImage (3) Jeff Kravitz/FilmMagic (4) © Gillian G. Gaar, 2012 (5) David Corio/Redferns 353 (1) J J Gonson/Redferns (2) J J Gonson/ Redferns (3) Charles J. Peterson/Time & Life Pictures/Getty Images (4) Jeff Kravitz/FilmMagic (5) Gary Wolstenholme/Redferns 354 tl J J Gonson/Redferns tr Michel Linssen/Redferns c J J Gonson/Redferns bl Michel Linssen/Redferns br Steve Pyke/Getty Images 355 t Jeff Kravitz/FilmMagic c Jeff Kravitz/FilmMagic b Frank Micelotta/Getty Images 356 (1) Dave Hogan/Getty Images (2) Dave Hogan/Getty Images (3) Jeff Kravitz/FilmMagic (4) Mick Hutson/Redferns (5) Rex Features (6) Mick Hutson/Redferns 357 (1) Yuji Ohsugi/WireImage (2) Tim Mosenfelder/Getty Images (3) Dave Hogan/Getty Images (4) Lyle A. Waisman/Getty Images 358 (1) Ian Dickson/Redferns (2) Peter Still/Redferns (3) Simon Ritter/Redferns (4) Dave Hogan/Getty Images 359 (1) Chris Pizzello/WireImage (2) Martin Philbey/Redferns (3) JOERG KOCH/AFP/Getty Images 360 (1) Mark Venema/Getty Images (2) Ralph Notaro/Getty Images (4) J. Shearer/WireImage (5) Ralph Notaro/Getty Images (6) John Sciulli/WireImage 361 (1) © Sayre Berman/Corbis 362 (1) Fred Duval/FilmMagic (2) Robert Knight Archive/Redferns (3) Annamaria DiSanto/WireImage (5) Ron Galella, Ltd./Getty Images (6) © Boss Tweed 363 (1) James Emmett/Redferns (2) Jill Douglas/Redferns (4) Tim Mosenfelder/Getty Images (5) Gary Wolstenholme/Redferns (6) Tim Mosenfelder/Getty Images 364 (1) Jeff Kravitz/FilmMagic (2) Peter Still/Redferns (3) Barry Brecheisen/ WireImage (4) KMazur/WireImage (5) Allen Berezovsky/Getty Images (6) © 1997 - 2012 Drummerworld.com 365 (1) Jeff Kravitz/FilmMagic (2) Jeff Kravitz/ FilmMagic (3) Barry Brecheisen/WireImage (4) Kevin Mazur/WireImage 366 (1) C Flanigan/Getty Images (2) C Flanigan/Getty Images (3) Michael Schwartz/ WireImage (4) C Flanigan/Getty Images (5) Jim Spellman/WireImage (6) Jim Spellman/WireImage 367 (1) Matt Stroshane/Getty Images (2) Isaac Brekken/ WireImage (3) Jeff Kravitz/FilmMagic 368 (1) HARRY GOODWIN/Rex Features (2) Harry Goodwin/Rex Features (3) CROLLALANZA/Rex Features (4) Harry Goodwin/Rex Features (6) Chris Walter/WireImage 370 t Andrew Whittuck/Redferns cl Michael Ochs Archives/Getty Images cr Gijsbert Hanekroot/Redferns bl David Redfern/Redferns br Richard E. Aaron/Redferns 371 t Ian Dickson/Redferns cl Peter Still/Redferns crt Moviestore Collection/Rex Features crb Rob Verhorst/Redferns b Denis O'Regan/Getty Images 372 (1) Matt Carmichael/Getty Images (2) Erik S. Lesser/Getty Images (3) J. Shearer/WireImage (4) Louise Wilson/Getty Images 373 (1) Matt Kent/Redferns (2) Mike Coppola/Getty Images (3) Neil Lupin/Redferns (4) D Dipasupil/FilmMagic (5) Philip Massey/FilmMagic (6) D Dipasupil/FilmMagic (7) Gary Wolstenholme/Redferns (8) D Dipasupil/FilmMagic 374 (1) Keystone/Getty Images (2) Fin Costello/Redferns (3) Ebet Roberts/ Redferns (4) Ian Dickson/Redferns 376 tl Janette Beckman/Getty Images tr Richard McCaffrey/Getty Images b Evening Standard/Getty Images 377 tl Denis O'Regan/Getty Images tr Janette Beckman/Getty Images cl © Lynn Goldsmith/Corbis cr © Catherine Bauknight/ZUMA/Corbis b © Ross Marino/Sygma/Co 378 (1) Leee Black Childers/Redferns (2) Leni Sinclair/Getty Images (3) Michael Ochs Archives/Getty Images (4) Michael Ochs Archives/Getty Images (5) Michael Ochs Archives/Getty Images (6) Michael Ochs Archives/Getty Images (7) © Scott Weiner/Retna/Retna Ltd./Corbis (8) Ebet Roberts/Redferns 379 (1) Ebet Roberts/Redferns (2) Ebet Roberts/Redferns (3) Phil Dent/Redferns (4) Denis O'Regan/Getty Images (5) Greg Williams/Rex Features (6) Kevin Winter/DMI/Time Life Pictures/Getty Images (7) Tim Mosenfelder/Getty Images (8) Samuel Dietz/WireImage 380 tl Leni Sinclair/Getty Images tr Tom Copi/ Getty Images ct Michael Ochs Archives/Getty Images cb Evening Standard/Getty Images bl Richard McCaffrey/Getty Images br L. Busacca/WireImage 381 t Time & Life Pictures/Getty Images c KMazur/WireImage bl Theo Wargo/WireImage br Frederic SOULOY/Gamma-Rapho via Getty Images 382 (1) GAB Archive/Redferns (3) Rose Hartman/WireImage (4) © Steffen Metzner (5) © Conny Veit (6) GAB Archive/Redferns (8) © Klaus Wiese 383 (4) © Peter Eising (5) © Bernd Wippich 384 (1) RB/Redferns (2) GAB Archive/Redferns (3) GAB Archive/Redferns (5) Michael Ochs Archives/Getty Images 386 tl Michael Ochs Archives/Getty Images tr Michael Ochs Archives/Getty Images cl ABC Photo Archives/ABC via Getty Images cr /Paramount Pictures/Courtesy of Getty Images b Michael Ochs Archives/Getty Images 387 tl Michael Ochs Archives/Getty Images tr Tom Wargacki/WireImage c Michael Ochs Archives/Getty Images bl Ron Galella/WireImage br Charlyn Zlotnik/Michael Ochs Archives/Getty Images 388 (1) Fin Costello/Redferns (2) © Lynn Goldsmith/Corbis (3) L. J. van Houten/Rex Features (4) © Lynn Goldsmith/Corbis (5) © Michael Ochs Archives/Corbis (6) © Michael Ochs Archives/Corbis (7) Sarah Kerver/ WireImage (8) © Tim Mosenfelder/Corbis 390 (1) Al Pereira/Michael Ochs Archives/Getty Images (2) Ebet Roberts/Redferns (4) Linda Matlow/Rex Features (5) Michael Ochs Archives/Getty Images (7) Ebet Roberts/Redferns 391 (1) Buckmaster © courtesy Eric Leeds (2) © Michael Porter (4) © 1997 - 2012 Drummerworld.com (5) CROLLALANZA/Rex Features (6) Steve Eichner/Getty Images (7) Michael Ochs Archives/Getty Images (8) Michel Linssen/Redferns 392 tl Waring Abbott/Getty Images tr Nancy Heyman/Getty Images c Michael Ochs Archives/Getty Images bl Frank Micelotta/Getty Images br Michael Putland/Getty Images 393 tl Ilpo Musto/Rex Features tr Andre Csillag/Rex Features cl Peter Still/Redferns cr L. Cohen/WireImage b Kristoffer Juel Poulsen/AFP/ Getty Images 394 (1) Michael Tullberg/Getty Images (2) Michael Tullberg/Getty Images (3) Dave M. Benett/Getty Images (4) Tim Roney/Getty Images 396 tl © Photoshot/Retna tr Mick Hutson/Redferns c Mick Hutson/Redferns bl Mick Hutson/Redferns br Neil Lupin/Redferns 397 t Pat Pope/Rex Features b Denis O'Regan/Getty Images 398 (1) Ollie Millington/Getty Images (2) Anthony Pidgeon/Redferns (3) Rex Features (4) Steve Thorne/Redferns (5) Peter Noble/ Redferns (6) Patrick Ford/Redferns 399 (1) © Maureen Baker (3) © William Sibick (5) Stefan M. Prager/Redferns (6) Ray Stevenson/Rex Features 400 (1) Michael Putland/Getty Images (2) Michael Putland/Getty Images (3) Michael Putland/Getty Images (4) Michael Putland/Getty Images (5) Dave Hogan/Getty Images 402 tl Andre Csillag/Rex Features tr Keystone Features/Getty Images ct David Redfern/Redferns cb Ian Dickson/Redferns bl Gus Stewart/Redferns br Ian Dickson/Redferns 403 tl Phil Dent/Redferns tr Michael Ochs Archives/Getty Images ct Popperfoto/Getty Images cb Denis O'Regan/Getty Images bl Michael Putland/Getty Images br Dave Hogan/Getty Images 404 (1) Neil Lupin/Redferns (2) Debbie Smyth/WireImage (3) Will Ireland/Classic Rock Magazine via Getty Images (4) Lyle A. Waisman/Getty Images (5) Jeff Kravitz/FilmMagic (6) Iris/WireImage (7) Theo Wargo/WireImage (8) Nigel Crane/ Redferns 405 (1) Larry Marano/Getty Images (2) Larry Marano/Getty Images (3) Larry Marano/Getty Images (4) Larry Marano/Getty Images (5) © Karen Mason Blair/CORBIS (6) Annamaria DiSanto/WireImage (7) David "Bagel" Ungar/FilmMagic (8) Larry Marano/Getty Images 406 (1) Peter Pakvis/Redferns (2) Peter Pakvis/Redferns (3) Nick Pickles/WireImage (4) Christina Radish/Redferns (5) Christina Radish/Redferns 408 tl Bob Berg/Getty Images tr Kevin Cummins/Getty Images cl Mick Hutson/Redferns cr Paul Bergen/Redferns b Larry Marano/Getty Images 409 t Kevin Westenberg/Contour by Getty Images c Mick Hutson/ Redferns b Kevin Mazur/WireImage 410 (1) J. Quinton/WireImage (2) Brian Rasic/Rex Features (3) Startraks Photo/Rex Features (4) Gary Miller/FilmMagic 411 (1) Fin Costello/Redferns (2) Fin Costello/Redferns (3) Fin Costello/Redferns (4) Fin Costello/Redferns (5) Gems/Redferns (6) IBL/Rex Features (7) © Sayre Berman/Corbis (8) © 2002-2012 Encyclopaedia Metallum 412 (1) Mick Hutson/Redferns (2) Mick Hutson/Redferns (3) Mick Hutson/Redferns (4) Mick Hutson/ Redferns (5) Mick Hutson/Redferns (6) Mick Hutson/Redferns 414 (1) Michael Ochs Archives/Getty Images (2) Michael Ochs Archives/Getty Images (3) Michael Ochs Archives/Getty Images (4) Michael Ochs Archives/Getty Images (5) Peter Noble/Redferns(6) Henry S. Dziekan III/Getty Images (7) Ebet Roberts/Redferns 416 (1) Dale Woltman/FilmMagic (2) Paul Bergen/Redferns (3) Michael Zito/WireImage (4) SGranitz/WireImage (5) Rolf Wolfson/WireImage (6) Ebet Roberts Redferns (8) Frank Micelotta/Getty Images 417 (1) Ebet Roberts/Redferns (2) Jim Steinfeldt/Getty Images (3) Paul Natkin/WireImage (4) © ToshiroKitty/Getty Images (6) © 4alanis.com 418 t L. Cohen/WireImage c Ebet Roberts/Redferns bl Michael Ochs Archives/Getty Images br Michel Linssen/Redferns 419 tl Steve Eichner/WireImage tr Tim Mosenfelder/Getty Images cl Ebet Roberts/Redferns crt Anthony Pidgeon/Redferns crb Peter Pakvis/Redferns bl Rick Diamond/ WireImage br Larry Marano/Getty Images 420 (1) SGranitz/WireImage (2) Jeff Kravitz/FilmMagic (3) Jeff Kravitz/FilmMagic (4) Rick Diamond/WireImage 422 tl Ebet Roberts/Redferns tr Paul Bergen/Redferns c Ebet Roberts/Redferns bl Michel Linssen/Redferns br Theo Wargo/WireImage 423 tl Dave Benett/Getty

Images tr Jeff Kravitz/FilmMagic ct Frank Micelotta/ImageDirect/Getty Images cb KMazur/WireImage b Scott Gries/Getty Images 424 (1) Richard Wolowicz/ Getty Images (2) Michael Ochs Archives/Getty Images (3) Michael Ochs Archives/Getty Images (4) Popperfoto/Getty Images (5) Terry O'Neill/Getty Images (6) © Ian Stewart @ The Musics Over (8) Alan Messer/Rex Features 425 (1) Michael Ochs Archives/Getty Images (2) Chris Walter/WireImage (3) © Baron Wolman (4) R. Diamond/WireImage (5) Paul Natkin/Getty Images 426 tl David Redfern/Redferns tr Keystone Features/Getty Images ct Jan Olofsson/Redferns cb Keystone-France/Gamma-Keystone via Getty Images bl David Montgomery/Getty Images br Denis O'Regan/Getty Images 427 tl James Garrett/NY Daily News via Getty Images tr Michael Putland/Getty Images cl Denis O'Regan/Getty Images cr Dove Shore/Getty Images b John W. McDonough/Sports Illustrated/Getty Images 428 (1) Brian Cooke/Redferns (2) Brian Cooke/Redferns (3) Brian Cooke/Redferns (5) Brian Cooke/Redferns (6) Brian Cooke/Redferns 429 (1) Time & Life Pictures/Time & Life Pictures/Getty Images (2) © Moody Klingman (5) Clayton Call/Redferns (6) Larry Hulst/Getty Images (7) Clayton Call/ Redferns 430 (1) Fin Costello/Redferns (2) © 2002-2012 Anthem Entertainment (3) Fin Costello/Redferns (4) Fin Costello/Redferns 432 (1) Paul McConnell/Getty Images (2) Mark Metcalfe/Getty Images (3) GAB Archive/Redferns (4) GAB Archive/Redferns (5) Denis O'Regan/Getty Images 434 (1) Robert Altman/Getty Images (2) Richard E. Aaron/Redferns (3) Larry Busacca/Getty Images (4) Michael Ochs Archives/Getty Images (5) Michael Ochs Archives/Getty Images (6) Michael Ochs Archives/Getty Images (7) Michael Ochs Archives/Getty Images (8) Michael Ochs Archives/Getty Images 435 (1) Michael Ochs Archives/ Getty Images (2) Alexander Sibaja/Getty Images (3) Larry Hulst/Getty Images (4) Michael Ochs Archives/Getty Images (5) Michael Caulfield Archive/ WireImage 436 (1) Frazer Harrison/Getty Images (2) Mark Mainz/Getty Images (3) Alexandra Beier/Getty Images (4) Jo Hale/Getty Images (5) Ethan Miller/ Getty Images (6) Krasner/Trebitz/Redferns (7) Krasner/Trebitz/Redferns (8) Steve Thorne/Redferns 437 (2) Jens Hartmann/Rex Features (3) © 2002-2012 Encyclopaedia Metallum (4) Neil Lupin/Redferns (6) © Achim Kirschning (8) Allen Berezovsky/Getty Images 438 t Michael Ochs Archives/Getty Images cl Gus Stewart/Redferns cr Larry Hulst/Getty Images b Michael Ochs Archives/Getty Images 439 tl Michael Ochs Archives/Getty Images tr Georges MERILLON/ Gamma-Rapho via Getty Images cl J. Shearer/WireImage crt Alain BENAINOUS/Gamma-Rapho via Getty Images crb Sipa Press/Rex Features bl Neil Lupin/ Redferns br David Wolff - Patrick/Getty Images 440 (1) Tim Mosenfelder/Getty Images (2) © Tim Mosenfelder/Corbis (3) Malcolm Clarke/Getty Images (4) © Segernet.com (5) Tom Hill/WireImage 441 (2) RB/Redferns (3) © John Atashian/CORBIS 442 (1) Mick Hutson/Redferns (2) Flavia Bechara/Getty Images (3) Mick Hutson/Redferns (4) SGranitz/WireImage (6) Naki/Redferns 443 (1) G. Gershoff/WireImage (2) © Sayre Berman/Corbis (3) © 2002-2012 Encyclopaedia Metallum 444 (1) Express/Getty Images (2) Popperfoto/Getty Images (3) Express/Getty Images (4) Express/Getty Images (5) Express/Getty Images 446 (1) Virginia Turbett/Redferns (2) Virginia Turbett/Redferns (3) Virginia Turbett/Redferns (4) Virginia Turbett/Redferns (5) Virginia Turbett/Redferns (6) Michael Putland/Getty Images (8) Fin Costello/Redferns 447 (1) Peter Still/Redferns (2) Martin McNeil/WireImage (3) Chiaki Nozu/Getty Images (4) Chiaki Nozu/Getty Images (5) Ebet Roberts/Redferns (6) Pete Cronin/Redferns (7) © Mike Peters Organisation/Getty Images 448 (1) CLIVE DIXON/Rex Features (2) Virginia Turbett/ Redferns (3) Fin Costello/Redferns (4) Ray Stevenson/Rex Features (5) Ray Stevenson/Rex Features (6) Gareth Davies/Getty Images 449 (1) Gabor Scott/ Redferns (2) Fin Costello/Redferns (4) Tim Mosenfelder/Getty Images (5) Mick Hutson/Redferns (6) © The Cliks 450 (1) Brian Rasic/Rex Features (2) © Tony Hobdern (3) © Ad v. Mierlo (5) Graham Tucker/Redferns (6) Brian Rasic/Rex Features (8) © Fabio Nosotti/CORBIS 451 (1) Steve Snowden/Getty Images (2) Steve Snowden/Getty Images (4) Annamaria DiSanto/WireImage (5) Astrid Stawiarz/Getty Images (6) Jeff Kravitz/FilmMagic (7) Steve Snowden/Getty Images 452 (1) Michael Putland/Getty Images (2) Michael Ochs Archives/Getty Images (3) Michael Putland/Getty Images (4) Michael Putland/Getty Images 453 (1) Mick Hutson/Redferns (2) Mick Hutson/Redferns (3) Mick Hutson/Redferns (4) Mick Hutson/Redferns (5) Mick Hutson/Redferns 454 (1) © Ravenscape.com (2) © 2002-2012 Encyclopaedia Metallum (3) Paul Archuleta/FilmMagic (4) Eddie Malluk/WireImage (5) Rex Features (6) © Dinho101 at en.wikipedia 455 (1) © Maggotland.net (3) Mick Hutson/Redferns (4) Steve Pope/Getty Images (5) Alexander Sibaja/Getty Images (6) Steve Pope/Getty Images 456 tl © MFKR1.com tr © Ashley Maile/Retna Pictures c © Gene Ambo/Retna Ltd./Corbis b Tim Mosenfelder/Getty Images 457 tl Tim Mosenfelder/Getty Images tr Mick Hutson/Redferns cl Rob Verhorst/Redferns cr Christie Goodwin/Redferns b Gary Miller/FilmMagic 458 (1) CA/Redferns (2) CA/Redferns (3) CA/Redferns (4) CA/Redferns (5) CA/Redferns (6) Courtesy Everett Collection/Rex Features 459 (1) Michael Putland/Getty Images (2) David Reed/Redferns (3) David Reed/ Redferns (4) Andreas Rentz/Getty Images (5) Mike Prior/Redferns 460 tl Jan Persson/Redferns tr Gilles Petard/Redferns c GAB Archive/Redferns bl Jorgen Angel/Redferns br Garry Clarke/Redferns 461 tl Michael Putland/Getty Images tr John Rodgers/Redferns c Michael Putland/Getty Images b Gems/Redferns 462 (1) Paul Redmond/WireImage (2) Mark Renders/Getty Images (3) Patrick Ford/Redferns (4) Valerie Macon/Getty Images (5) Tyrone Kerr/FilmMagic (6) Michael Loccisano/Getty Images 463 (1) Paul Bergen/Redferns (2) Vivien Killilea/WireImage (3) Amanda Edwards/Getty Images (4) Michael Loccisano/ Getty Images 464 (1) Richard E. Aaron/Redferns (2) Kevin Cummins/Getty Images (3) Jorgen Angel/Redferns (4) Michael Ochs Archives/Getty Images (5) Jorgen Angel/Redferns (6) Charlie Gillett Collection/Redferns 465 (1) Leni Sinclair/Getty Images (2) Astrid Stawiarz/Getty Images (3) © Bureau L.A. Collection/CORBIS (4) Sipa Press/Rex Features 466 (1) Kerstin Rodgers/Redferns (2) Ebet Roberts/Redferns (3) Andre Csillag/Rex Features (4) Andre Csillag/Rex Features (5) Andy Kropa/WireImage 468 (1) Michael Caulfield Archive/WireImage (2) Alexander Tamargo/Getty Images (3) JUAN MABROMATA/AFP/Getty Images 470 (1) Jan Persson/Redferns (2) Gijsbert Hanekroot/Redferns (3) Michael Putland/Getty Images (4) Steve Eichner/WireImage (5) Michael Ochs Archives/Getty Images (6) Michael Putland/Getty Images (8) Jeremy Fletcher/Redferns 471 (1) Tony Russell/Redferns (2) Gijsbert Hanekroot/Redferns (3) Tony Russell/Redferns (4) Paul Natkin/WireImage (5) © Howard Denner/Retna/Photoshot (6) Dave Peabody/Redferns (7) Andre Csillag/Rex Features 472 (1) Paul Hawthorne/WireImage (2) Lawrence Lucier/Getty Images (3) Tim Mosenfelder/Getty Images (4) J. Vespa/WireImage (6) Photoshot/Getty Images 473 (1) © Bob Bert (2) Stefan M. Prager/Redferns (3) Marc Andrew Deley/FilmMagic (4) Tim Mosenfelder/Getty Images 474 (1) Nigel Crane/Redferns (3) Mick Hutson/Redferns (4) Mick Hutson/Redferns (5) Alfredo Rocha/WireImage (6) Michael Burnell/Redferns (7) Raymond Boyd/Getty Images 475 (1) David "Bagel" Ungar/FilmMagic (2) Steve Eichner/WireImage (3) © Don Wallen (5) Ron Galella, Ltd./Getty Images (6) JJ Gonson/Redferns (7) Ron Galella, Ltd./Getty Images 476 (1) Theo Wargo/WireImage (2) Debra L Rothenberg/FilmMagic (3) Ed Peristein/Redferns (4) Debra L Rothenberg/FilmMagic (5) Debra L Rothenberg/Getty Images (6) Jeff Kravitz/FilmMagic (7) Scott Halleran/Getty Images 477 (1) ML Layton/Getty Images (2) Terry O'Neill/Getty Images (3) Michael Putland/Getty Images (4) Debra L Rothenberg/FilmMagic (5) Derek Storm/FilmMagic (6) Herry Scott/Redferns (7) Brian Rasic/Rex Features 478 tl David Gahr/Getty Images tr Richard E. Aaron/Redferns cl Larry Hulst/Getty Images cr Paul Natkin/WireImage b Mark Weiss/WireImage 479 tl Ron Galella/Getty Images tr DAN GROSHONG/AFP/Getty Images cl Rob Verhorst/Redferns cr Jeff Kravitz/FilmMagic b Kevin Mazur/WireImage 480 (1) Michael Putland/Getty Images (2) Fin Costello/Redferns (3) Terry O'Neill/Getty Images (4) Terry O'Neill/Getty Images (5) Chris Walter/WireImage (6) Gered Mankowitz/Redferns 481 (1) Mark Large/ Daily Mail /Rex Features (2) Christie Goodwin/Redferns (3) Christie Goodwin/Redferns (4) Christie Goodwin/Redferns 482 (1) SGranitz/WireImage (2) SGranitz/ WireImage (3) David Warner Ellis/Redferns (4) Michael Ochs Archives/Getty Images (5) David Warner Ellis/Redferns (6) Michael Ochs Archives/Getty Images 483 (1) Jim McCrary/Redferns (2) Michael Ochs Archives/Getty Images 484 (1) Larry Marano/Getty Images (2) © Henry Diltz/CORBIS (3) Michael Ochs Archives/ Getty Images (4) © Henry Diltz/CORBIS (5) © Henry Diltz/CORBIS (6) © Henry Diltz/CORBIS (7) Robin Little/Redferns 485 (1) Will Ireland/Classic Rock Magazine via Getty Images (2) Harry Herd/Redferns (3) Shirlaine Forrest/WireImage (4) Shirlaine Forrest/WireImage (5) Dan Kitwood/Getty Images 486 (1) Dave J Hogan/ Getty Images (2) Dave J Hogan/Getty Images (4) © Invisible girl music limited 2006 (5) Dave J Hogan/Getty Images (6) Dave J Hogan/Getty Images 487 (1) Jeffrey Mayer/WireImage (2) Joey Foley/FilmMagic (3) Joey Foley/FilmMagic (4) Neil Lupin/Redferns 488 (1) Mike Prior/Redferns (2) Mike Prior/Redferns (3) Mike Prior/Redferns (4) Ollie Millington/Redferns (5) Mike Prior/Redferns 489 (1) Regis Martin/Getty Images (2) © John Ellis 490 (3) Al Pereira/WireImage (4) Ross Gilmore/Redferns (5) Stephen Lovekin/WireImage (6) Evan Agostini/Getty Images (7) Evan Agostini/Getty Images 491 (1) Paul Warner/WireImage (2) Richard E. Aaron/Redferns (3) Rob Verhorst/Redferns (4) Michael Ochs Archives/Getty Images (5) Jeffrey Mayer/WireImage (6) David Livingston/Getty Images (7) Michael Schwartz/WireImage 492 (1) Rob Verhorst/Redferns (2) Hayley Madden/Redferns (3) Michael Putland/Getty Images (4) Michael Putland/Getty Images (5) Michael Putland/Getty Images (6) © Supertramp 493 (1) Gems/Redferns (2) The Image Gate/Getty Images (3) Hulton Archive/Getty Images (4) © Scott Hallock (5) Robert Marquardt/Getty Images (6) © 21st Century Greenstuff 494 (1) Michael Bezjian/WireImage (2) SGranitz/WireImage (3) Jean-Paul Aussenard/WireImage (5) Marsaili Mcgrath/Getty Images 496 (1) David Mcgough/DMI/Time Life Pictures/Getty Images (2) David Mcgough/DMI/Time Life Pictures/Getty Images (3) David Mcgough/DMI/Time Life Pictures/Getty Images (4) Larry Hulst/Getty Images 498 (1) Michael Putland/Getty Images (2) © Tamara Rafkin/Retna Ltd./Corbis (4) Michael Ochs Archives/Getty Images (5) Michael Putland/Getty Images 499 (1) Frederick M. Brown/Getty Images (4) Marc Broussely/Redferns (5) Brian Rasic/Rex Features 500 (1) Peter Noble/Redferns (2) Peter Noble/Redferns (3) Peter Noble/Redferns (4) Peter Noble/ Redferns 501 (1) Kerstin Rodgers/Redferns (2) Stephanie Chernikowski/Michael Ochs Archives/Getty Images (3) Roberta Bayley/Redferns (4) Roberta Bayley/ Redferns (5) Roberta Bayley/Redferns (6) © Jimmy Rip 502 (1) Fin Costello/Redferns (2) Michael Putland/Getty Images (3) Jorgen Angel/Redferns (4) Michael Putland/Getty Images (5) Fin Costello/Redferns (6) Fin Costello/Redferns (7) Jorgen Angel/Redferns (8) Peter Still/Redferns 503 (1) Daniel Boczarski/Redferns (2) Dimitrios Kambouris/Getty Images (3) Christie Goodwin/Getty Images (4) Stephen J. Cohen/Getty Images (5) Jadranka Krsteska/Redferns 504 (1) Sylvia Pitcher/Redferns (2) GAB Archive/Redferns (3) Michael Putland/Getty Images (4) Michael Putland/Getty Images (5) Richard Upper/Redferns (6) Michael Ochs Archives/Getty Images (7) Brian Cooke/Redferns 505 (1) David Redfern/Redferns (3) Richard E. Aaron/Redferns (4) Rick Diamond/Getty Images (5) © Marc Marot 506 (1) Time & Life Pictures/Getty Images (2) Bernd Mueller/Redferns (3) SGranitz/WireImage (4) Time & Life Pictures/Getty Images (5) Ebet Roberts/ Redferns (6) Robert Knight Archive/Redferns 508 (1) Gijsbert Hanekroot/Redferns (2) Ebet Roberts/Redferns (3) Estate of Keith Morris/Redferns (4) Estate of Keith

Morris/Redferns **(6)** Estate of Keith Morris/Redferns **509 (1)** Michel Linssen/ Redferns **(2)** © Thetriffids.com **(4)** Michel Linssen/Redferns **(5)** Michel Linssen/ Redferns **(7)** Michel Linssen/Redferns **(8)** Michel Linssen/Redferns **510 (1)** Peter Noble/Redferns **(2)** Peter Noble/Redferns **(3)** Peter Noble/Redferns **(4)** Peter Noble/Redferns **512 tl** Virginia Turbett/Redferns **tr** Erica Echenberg/Redferns **ct** Larry Ellis/Getty Images **cb** George Rose/Getty Images **b** © Roger Hutchings/In Pictures/Corbis **513 t** Mick Hutson/Redferns **cl** Paul Bergen/ Redferns **cr** KMazur/WireImage **cb** Peter Pakvis/Redferns **bl** © Jason DeCrow/ epa/Corbis **br** Mike Coppola/Getty Images **514 (1)** © Marie-Emmanuelle Brétel **(2)** © Univers-zero.com **(3)** © Marie-Emmanuelle Brétel **(4)** © Univers-zero.com **(5)** © Marie-Emmanuelle Brétel **515 (1)** Fin Costello/Redferns **(2)** Fin Costello/Redferns **(3)** Fin Costello/Redferns **(6)** Jorgen Angel/Getty Images **(7)** Fin Costello/Redferns **(8)** Fin Costello/Redferns **516 (1)** Richard E. Aaron/ Redferns **(2)** Fin Costello/Redferns **(3)** © Tina Fultz/ZUMA Press/Corbis **(4)** Richard E. Aaron/Redferns **(5)** Chris Walter/WireImage **(6)** Fin Costello/ Redferns **517 (1)** Tim Mosenfelder/Getty Images **518 tl** Fin Costello/Redferns **tr,** © Scott Weiner/Retna/Retna Ltd./Corbis **cl** Richard E. Aaron/Redferns **cr** Michael Ochs Archives/Getty Images **bl** Rob Verhorst/Redferns **br** Ron Galella/Getty Images **519 tl** Ann Summa/Getty Images **tr** Tim Mosenfelder/ Getty Images **c** Kevin Winter/Getty Images **b** Tim Mosenfelder/Getty Images **520 (1)** Michael Putland/Getty Images **(2)** Estate of Keith Morris/Redferns **(3)** Michael Ochs Archives/Getty Images **(5)** Michael Ochs Archives/Getty Images **(6)** Michael Ochs Archives/Getty Images **521 (1)** Michael Ochs Archives/Getty Images **522 (1)** Bob Berg/Getty Images **(2)** Bob Berg/Getty Images **(3)** Bob Berg/Getty Images **(4)** Bob Berg/Getty Images **(5)** Peter Pakvis/Redferns **524 (1)** CityFlies/WireImage **(2)** Annamaria DiSanto/ WireImage **(3)** Joey Foley/FilmMagic **(4)** Fin Costello/Redferns **(5)** Michael Putland/Getty Images **(6)** Fin Costello/Redferns **(7)** Fin Costello/Redferns **(8)** Fin Costello/Redferns **525 (1)** Fin Costello/Redferns **(3)** Fin Costello/ Redferns **(4)** Richard E. Aaron/Redferns **(5)** Mick Hutson/Redferns **(6)** George De Sota/Redferns **(7)** © Photoshot **(8)** Frans Schellekens/Redferns **526 tl** Fin Costello/Redferns **tr** Fin Costello/Redferns **cl** Peter Still/Redferns **cr** Fin Costello/Redferns **bl** Dave Hogan/Getty Images **br** George Rose/Getty Images **527 t** Jim Steinfeldt/Getty Images **cl** © Starstock/Photoshot **cr** Harry Herd/WireImage **b** Bob King/Redferns **528 (1)** Jan Persson/Redferns **(2)** Michael Putland/Getty Images **(3)** Jan Persson/Redferns **(5)** Chris Morphet/Redferns **(8)** John Rodgers/Redferns **529 (1)** Jon Furniss/WireImage **(2)** Dave Hogan/Getty Images **(3)** J. Vespa/WireImage **(4)** SGranitz/ WireImage **(5)** Paul Bergen/Redferns **530 tl** Jan Persson/Redferns **tr** Richard Young/Rex Features **c** David Montgomery/Getty Images **bl** Graham Lowe/ Redferns **br** Eamonn McCabe/Redferns **531 tl** Gijsbert Hanekroot/Redferns **tr** John Rodgers/Redferns **c** Michael Ochs Archives/Getty Images **bl** Graham Wiltshire/Rex Features **br** Tim Mosenfelder/Getty Images **532 (1)** David Wolff - Patrick/Getty Images **(2)** David Wolff - Patrick/Getty Images **(4)** Gary Miller/ Getty Images **(6)** Gary Miller/Getty Images **(7)** Jun Sato/WireImage **533 (1)** Michael Ochs Archives/Getty Images **(2)** Michael Ochs Archives/ Getty Images **(3)** Hulton Archive/Getty Images **(4)** Hulton Archive/Getty Images **(6)** Michael Ochs Archives/Getty Images **(7)** Hulton Archive/Getty Images **(8)** Michael Ochs Archives/Getty Images **534 (1)** Michael Putland/ Getty Images **(2)** Ebet Roberts/Redferns **(3)** Gilles Petard/Redferns **(4)** Ebet Roberts/Redferns **(5)** Michael Putland/Getty Images **(6)** Michael Putland/ Getty Images **(7)** Ian Dickson/Redferns **(8)** Michael Putland/Getty Images **535 (1)** Michael Putland/Getty Images **(2)** C Brandon/Redferns **(3)** Ebet Roberts/Redferns **(5)** Bob Berg/Getty Images **(6)** Morena Brengola/Getty Images **(7)** Startraks Photo/Rex Features **(8)** Ebet Roberts/Redferns **536 tl** Gilles Petard/Redferns **tr** Michael Putland/Getty Images **ct** Michael Putland/Getty Images **cb** Rob Verhorst/Redferns **bl** Michael Putland/Getty Images **br** Michael Putland/Getty Images **537 t** Rob Verhorst/Redferns **c** Rob Verhorst/Redferns **bl** Diana Scrimgeour/Redferns **br** David Livingston/ Getty Images **538 (1)** Hulton Archive/Getty Images **(2)** Ebet Roberts/Redferns **(3)** Ebet Roberts/Redferns **(4)** Michael Ochs Archives/Getty Images **(6)** Chris Walter/WireImage **(7)** Keith Baugh/Redferns **(8)** © Davis Deluxe **539 (1)** Ebet Roberts/Redferns **(2)** Michael Putland/Getty Images **(3)** Jorgen Angel/Redferns **(4)** Fred Duval/FilmMagic **(5)** Vince Bucci/Getty Images **540 tl** Robert Altman/Getty Images **tr** © Henry Diltz/CORBIS **c** Richard McCaffrey/Getty Images **bl** Michael Ochs Archives/Getty Images **br** Rob Verhorst/Redferns **541 tl** Paul Natkin/WireImage **tr** KMazur/WireImage **cl** Jeff Kravitz/FilmMagic **cr** Tim Mosenfelder/Getty Images **b** Steve Granitz/ WireImage **542 (1)** Michael Putland/Getty Images **(2)** © © PA/PA Archive/ Press Association Images **(3)** Petra Niemeier - K & K/Redferns **(4)** Petra Niemeier - K & K/Redferns **(5)** Petra Niemeier - K & K/Redferns **(6)** Jan Persson/ Redferns **(7)** Gijsbert Hanekroot/Redferns **(8)** Gijsbert Hanekroot/Redferns **543 (2)** © Mark R Friedman 2010 **(3)** Bob Rose/FilmMagic **(4)** Chris McKay/ WireImage **(5)** Ian Dickson/Rex Features **(6)** Bob Willoughby/Redferns **(7)** Jeff Kravitz/FilmMagic **(8)** Mick Hutson/Redferns **544 tl** Jan Persson/Redferns **tr** David Redfern/Redferns **c** Archive Photos/Getty Images **b** K & K Ulf Kruger OHG/Redferns **545 tl** Gijsbert Hanekroot/Redferns **tr** NBC/NBCU Photo Bank via Getty Images **cl** Michael Ochs Archives/Getty Images **cr** David McGough/Time & Life Pictures/Getty Images **bl** Ebet Roberts/Redferns **br** Frans Schellekens/Redferns **546 (1)** Gems/Redferns **(2)** Gems/Redferns **(3)** Gems/Redferns

acknowledgments

Quintessence Editions Ltd would like to thank:

Todd Hughes, producer of *Hit So Hard: The Life and Near-Death Story of Drummer Patty Schemel*

Mark Schaffer for his generous and invaluable Tangerine Dream rescue services

Andrew Greenaway, author of *Zappa the Hard Way*, for his much-appreciated assistance with the Frank Zappa and Captain Beefheart sections

Diane Chidrawi at www.totalexposure.co.za for her help with the Prime Circle section

Vinita at www.rocketgirl.co.uk for her help with the My Bloody Valentine section

Hartmut Fischer at www.neubaten.org

Andres Martinez at www.GreenDayAuthority.com

www.nickelbackgeeks.150m.com/index.html

Tristan de Lancey

The general editor would like to thank:

Martin Downham

Colin Hughes

Dave Whitaker